ACCIDENTAL GENIUS

ACCIDENTAL GENIUS

How John Cassavetes Invented
American Independent Film

By

MARSHALL FINE

miramax books

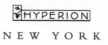

NEW YORK

For Kim

Contents

	INTRODUCTION	ix
ONE	A New York Street Kid	3
TWO	Through College	9
THREE	AADA	18
FOUR	Gena	25
FIVE	Post-AADA	30
SIX	Sam Shaw	37
SEVEN	"Paso Doble"	42
EIGHT	TV Star	48
NINE	Movie Star	54
TEN	The Next Level	61
ELEVEN	The Workshop	69
TWELVE	Origins of *Shadows*	74
THIRTEEN	*Shadows*	81
FOURTEEN	Shooting *Shadows*	89
FIFTEEN	Going Public	97
SIXTEEN	Beat, Square, and Cool	101
SEVENTEEN	*Johnny Staccato* and Back to the *Shadows*	112
EIGHTEEN	*Shadows*—A Postscript	125
NINETEEN	*Too Late Blues*	129
TWENTY	*A Child Is Waiting*	137
TWENTY-ONE	In Limbo	145
TWENTY-TWO	*Faces*	151
TWENTY-THREE	*Faces* 2	156
TWENTY-FOUR	*Dirty Dozen* and *Rosemary's Baby*	168
TWENTY-FIVE	*Faces* 3	176
TWENTY-SIX	Pre-*Husbands*	187

TWENTY-SEVEN   *HUSBANDS*   202
TWENTY-EIGHT   *HUSBANDS* 2   207
TWENTY-NINE   *HUSBANDS* 3   226
THIRTY   A LEG UP   243
THIRTY-ONE   *MINNIE AND MOSKOWITZ*   253
THIRTY-TWO   *MINNIE AND MOSKOWITZ* 2   262
THIRTY-THREE   *A WOMAN UNDER THE INFLUENCE*   274
THIRTY-FOUR   *A WOMAN UNDER THE INFLUENCE* 2   281
THIRTY-FIVE   *A WOMAN UNDER THE INFLUENCE* 3   285
THIRTY-SIX   *A WOMAN UNDER THE INFLUENCE* 4   297
THIRTY-SEVEN   JOHN AND GENA   308
THIRTY-EIGHT   MIKEY & NICKY   314
THIRTY-NINE   THE KILLING OF A *CHINESE BOOKIE*   319
FORTY   *BOOKIE* 2   329
FORTY-ONE   *OPENING NIGHT*   336
FORTY-TWO   *OPENING NIGHT* 2   345
FORTY-THREE   APPROACH OF THE '80S   351
FORTY-FOUR   *GLORIA*   359
FORTY-FIVE   RETROSPECTIVE TEMPEST   375
FORTY-SIX   *LOVE STREAMS* ON STAGE   384
FORTY-SEVEN   *LOVE STREAMS* ON SCREEN   397
FORTY-EIGHT   *BIG TROUBLE*   416
FORTY-NINE   VALEDICTORY   420

                FILMOGRAPHY   435
                NOTES   443

It's not so important that people like your films. It's only important that you make something that you like.

—JOHN CASSAVETES

Introduction

In 1989, the year John Cassavetes died, Hollywood's top-grossing films were *Batman, Indiana Jones and the Last Crusade,* and *Lethal Weapon 2.*

But it was also the year of films like *My Left Foot, Cinema Paradiso,* Kenneth Branagh's *Henry V, Do the Right Thing,* and, most significantly, *sex, lies, & videotape.* They were movies that reshaped and refocused attention on independent cinema in America—many of them made with the same resourcefulness and daring that characterized Cassavetes' work.

In the sixteen years since Cassavetes' death, independent film has gone through several incarnations, as studios attempted to co-opt the spirit and feel of these unruly films by establishing classics or specialty divisions. But even as companies like Sony Classics, Fox Searchlight, and others became part of the establishment, a new wave of insurgent independent companies have popped up like mushrooms. And every year, the Sundance Film Festival is inundated with tapes by filmmakers driven by a burning need to express something that could be fulfilled only by committing it to celluloid—or high-definition digital video, in the twenty-first century.

Such was the passion of John Cassavetes. And that independent film world—rambunctious, contentious, daring, outrageous—is his legacy.

Seymour Cassel, Cassavetes' long-time friend and sometime muse, said, "Independent film is film that has thought in it. There's no independent thought in studio films. It's collective thought. With independent film, they're forced to make a story that's important to them, a personal story that people can relate to, where you can see the love of the characters. That's true of the best films I've done—certainly Cassavetes' films."

Producer Guy McElwaine, a former studio head who was also Cassavetes' agent, said, "What truly separates a movie like *Adaptation* or *Auto-Focus* as an independent movie is that it was made because somebody wanted desperately to make it. It's not about the money; it's about getting the movie made."

I first remember seeing John Cassavetes in *Edge of the City*, probably on NBC's *Saturday Night at the Movies* when I was an adolescent. He registered again in *The Dirty Dozen* and *Rosemary's Baby*.

But it was *Faces*, which I saw as a freshman in college, that truly implanted him in my consciousness. This was a movie unlike anything I'd ever seen. At the age of eighteen, I knew too little about adult relationships to really understand what was going on—but I came away convinced, nonetheless, that I had seen something original and powerful.

When I undertook this book, my goal was to kindle the same kind of excitement and curiosity about Cassavetes' work in readers that his movies always sparked in me. Here was a cinematic artist whose work is still influencing young filmmakers in ways they aren't even aware of—and yet cinemaphiles of a certain age are unaware of who he was, what he did, or what his work meant, beyond the occasional reference to him in a review of a film that may echo his style.

As I did the research before commencing interviews for this book, my goal was a simple one: I wanted to write the book that I longed to read about Cassavetes, the one no one had written yet—the one that explained to a mainstream audience why they should know and care about the work of John Cassavetes.

When it comes to John Cassavetes scholarship, all roads lead to Ray Carney, who has been carrying the Cassavetes torch literally for decades. His monographs and books about Cassavetes and his films—including the expansive *Cassavetes on Cassavetes*—were an invaluable starting point in my research, and his enthusiasm for John's work is infectious. His encouragement on this project was always appreciated.

But as I told him when we first spoke, I planned to take a different approach than he does. Professor Carney tends to examine Cassavetes' work from a tradition of scholarly criticism. My approach has always been journalistic, piecing together a story—in this case, how Cassavetes' adventurous, inquisitive spirit propelled him to carve his own path as a filmmaker, a path that would be trampled into the super-highway known today as independent film.

But as any biographer discovers, pieces are all you ever get. Setting down a life in this way is like creating a mosaic; you collect as many fragments as you can, hold them up to the light, examine them—and then figure out where they fit in the larger picture. It is like doing a jigsaw puzzle with multiple thousands of pieces, knowing before you start that you will always be missing a couple of hundred at the end. Hopefully, you find enough of them that the picture you assemble is a clear one to your readers.

If you are going to write a book about John Cassavetes, you start with a letter to Gena Rowlands. My first one was written in 1993, and I received the same response most other such inquiries do from her:

> Dear Mr. Fine:
> . . . John didn't want a biography so I have just turned down any interest from authors . . .
>
> > Sincerely,
> > Gena Rowlands

Thankfully, when I inquired again ten years later, though I got essentially the same response, Ms. Rowlands graciously agreed to give the project her seal of approval. While she still felt she could not violate John's wishes and talk about him (and while she is intensely private about her own life), she said she would tell anyone who asked her that they should talk to me. With anyone truly in the Cassavetes inner circle (and the next few rings out, as well), the first question I received when I requested an interview to talk about John was, "Do you have Gena's approval?" It was invaluable to be able to say, "Yes, I do." I am deeply appreciative of her belief and trust and that of Nick, Xan, and Zoe Cassavetes.

Al Ruban and Seymour Cassel were particularly generous with their time and memories, as were Peter Falk and Ben Gazzara. So was Martin Scorsese. I also have to thank the members of Sam Shaw's family—Larry, Edie, Meta, and Jakob—who spoke to me at length about Sam and his relationship with John.

Tom Charity's book *John Cassavetes: Lifeworks* also provided insights and a different perspective. Tom was extremely generous in sharing his own research materials, and for that I am extremely appreciative. I am also indebted to Jack Mathews, who provided me with a taped interview with

Burton Lane about the Cassavetes–Lane Workshop that was made shortly before Lane's death.

For the gift of their time in talking about John Cassavetes, I want to thank Diahnne Abbott, Julie Allan, Joan Almond, Hollis Alpert, Robert Altman, Val Avery, John Badham, Bob Balaban, Ben Barenholtz, Martin Baum, Ned Beatty, Tom Berenger, Andrew Bergman, Joe Bologna, Helen Caldwell, Romeo Carey, Lynn Carlin, Randy Carter, Alan Caso, Matthew Cassel, Everett Chambers, Charles Champlin, Jay Cocks, Bill Conti, Mario Conti, Jackie Cooper, Bruce Davison, Ruby Dee, Wanda Dell, Caleb De-schanel, Kevin Donnelly, Richard Dreyfuss, Frederick Elmes, Richard Erdman, Michael Ferris, Robert Fieldsteel, John Finnegan, Geoffrey Gilmore, Carl Goldberg, Lelia Goldoni, Michael Haley, Pete Hamill, Bo Harwood, Molly Haskell, Michael Hausman, Buck Henry, Simon Hinkly, J. Hoberman, Tamar Hoffs, John Hough, Anne Jackson, Henry Jaglom, Laura Johnson, Elaine Kagan, Carol Kane, Richard Kaye, Victor Kemper, Erich Kollmar, Cloris Leachman, Jerry Lewis, Richard Libertini, Marvin Lichtner, Jeff Lipsky, Patti LuPone, Leonard Maltin, Abby Mann, A. Morgan Maree, Michael Margulies, Harry Mastrogeorge, Paul Mazursky, Guy McElwaine, Jonas Mekas, Holly Near, Tom Noonan, Gordon Parks, Hildy Parks, Nick Petras, Daniel Petrie, Johnnie Planco, Sidney Poitier, Stuart Poller, Tristram Powell, Bingham Ray, Bob and Adele Ringwald, Molly Ringwald, Alexandre Rockwell, John Roselius, Mark Rydell, Susan Sarandon, Andrew Sarris, John Sayles, Julian Schlossberg, Budd Schulberg, Fred Schuler, William Shatner, Carole Smith, David Sterritt, Andrew Stevens, Stella Stevens, Dan Talbot, Renee Taylor, Bob Thomas, Joyce van Patten, Michael Ventura, Harvey Weinstein, Barry Weissler, Haskell Wexler, James Whitmore, Max Wilk, Frank Yablans, and Stu Zakim.

Many thanks also to: Elizabeth Lawson, American Academy of Dramatic Arts; Jeanette Lollman, Colgate University; Milt Hoffman; Dave Henahan; Dan Sullivan; Philip Rinaldi; Mark Edlitz; Meg McCarthy; Leslee Dart; Nicholas Pasquariello; Gautam Dasgupta; Howard Lapides; Dr. Drew Pinsky; Paul Pflug; Ben Wolfinsohn; Ossining Public Library; White Plains Public Library; New York Public Library of the Performing Arts at Lincoln Center; Museum of Television and Radio in New York; British Film Institute; Academy of Motion Picture Arts and Sciences Library; Port Washington High School; and eBay and every weird Internet outlet and dealer who helped me track down hard-to-find Cassavetes titles.

My great appreciation to Bonnie Fuller, Joe Dolce, and *Star* magazine for letting me be their film critic.

Thanks also to my agent, Betsy Lerner, and my editor, Jillellyn Riley, whose name I finally learned to spell correctly.

A number of my friends and colleagues listened to me talk about this project and its various attendant crises for all or parts of a twenty-two-month period and I want to thank them: Georgette Gouveia, Barbara Nachman, Linda Lombroso, Heather Salerno, Keith Moyer, Larry Beaupre, Rebecca Baron, Flo Fox, Chris Kensler, Alex Panagakis, Stan Krome, Steve Rivkin, Ed Gubman, Mark Ryan, Jeff Lovich, Steve Illions, Buddy Cohen, Mark Levin, Bob Ashenmacher, Bonnie Jean Ritter, Chris O'Leary, Ken Rose, Gil and Patty Bassak, Joey Morris, and Larry Sutin.

I must thank my son, Jake, now off at college and greatly missed, who spent several weeks in the summer of 2003 learning the ins and outs of the periodical departments of several libraries in the greater New York area. It was his job to find me copies of every magazine article I had tracked down about Cassavetes, Gena Rowlands, Peter Falk, Ben Gazzara, and the underground and independent film movements, and all of the other research materials I didn't have time to collect for myself.

I also need to thank my son, Caleb, whose thoughtful gift of a large package of multi-colored Post-Its proved invaluable in color-coding my research material as I went through the writing process.

And, of course, I owe everything to my wife, Kim Jacobs, whose sacrifices are too numerous to mention. She is an amazing woman and I cherish her.

Part One

An artist is one on whom nothing is wasted.
—Henry James

I am a man; nothing human is alien to me.
—Terence

One

A New York Street Kid

On a chilly evening in early 1954, John Cassavetes and Mark Rydell—young actors who were working together on TV's *The Elgin Hour* in a juvenile-delinquent drama called "Crime in the Streets"—almost got a taste of the subject they were about to dramatize on live television.

The block on Manhattan's West Fifty-fourth Street was dark and deserted as they walked home, heading east from Seventh to Sixth Avenue. Suddenly they became aware that they were being followed by four thugs, who had materialized out of the shadows as Cassavetes and Rydell walked past.

Rydell, bright-eyed and energetic, was playing Lou Macklin, sidekick to Cassavetes' Frankie Dane, in the TV show. Frankie, the leader of a gang of small-time hoods, burned with resentment at the life he was born into in the Hell's Kitchen slum where he lived, using violence as a release for his anger. Lou was his rabbity lieutenant, a stone psychopath who worshiped Frankie and dug violence for the kicks it gave him.

In real life, however, the Bronx-bred Rydell was an actor, not a fighter. The approach of the quartet of street types had him contemplating an inevitable mugging and the surrender of his watch and wallet. There were four punks closing in on the two actors—and Rydell wasn't significantly taller than the equally wiry Cassavetes, who generously listed himself as 5-foot-9, though he was closer to 5-foot-7.

Then he heard John say under his breath, "Don't be frightened." Before Rydell could think about what John had muttered, John whirled on their would-be attackers and began to scream at the top of his lungs. Fists clenched, eyes bulging, voice rising, he was suddenly a madman having a full-blown psychotic episode—and the four thugs wanted no part of him. Spooked by his apparent frenzied rage, they turned and ran away.

John waited until they were out of earshot, then laughed delightedly and clapped Rydell on the back, as they continued walking home.

Cassavetes loved those moments when he could turn life upside down by doing the unexpected. To him, that's what acting was about: finding something unplanned and spontaneous, creating happy accidents that yielded surprising behavior and truthful emotions.

Or just a few laughs. There was more than a little of the prankster in Cassavetes, who, as a young man, delighted in stirring things up with impromptu gags. They were put-ons, a kind of extemporaneous acting that, decades later, would be claimed by some as performance art.

A friend from his brief tenure at Champlain College in Plattsburg, New York, recalled being fooled by one of John's routines during a casual evening away from their studies. Stuart Poller, who lived in the same dorm—Ticonderoga Hall—when they were freshmen, used to play cards and basketball with Cassavetes. One night, after a pick-up basketball game, he and John headed for Charley's, a bar just outside the main gate of the college, to have a few beers.

As they sat at the bar, John looked at Poller and, with a decisive air, said, "I think I'll try it," as though he'd just made a significant decision.

"Try what?" Poller said.

John fixed him with a serious look and said, "Water." Sensing Poller's skepticism, he continued. "I'm allergic to water. It's been so long since I've had pure water."

Poller laughed and said, "You're crazy," then watched as Cassavetes signaled the bartender and ordered a glass of water. When the water was placed before him, John looked at it for a couple of dramatic seconds, then picked it up and gingerly took a sip.

Almost instantly, John erupted. Clutching his throat, he fell to the floor, making loud noises and flailing about. He kicked his feet. He flung chairs about the room as though possessed by a demon.

Then he stopped and, surveying the wide eyes and gaping mouths of the patrons who were watching him, began to laugh uproariously at the reactions he'd gotten with his improvised joke.

Cassavetes loved to walk that tightrope as a young man: to act with people who didn't know he was acting, then to go with the moment and see what he could turn it into. The late Burton Lane remembered John living dangerously when they were scuffling as actors. He would seemingly pick fights with people, then talk his way out of them with dazzling alacrity.

One afternoon, sitting in the Horn & Hardart automat across the street from the American Academy of Dramatic Arts (located in Carnegie Hall at the time), Lane and Cassavetes were drinking coffee and talking, when a stranger who was obviously a bodybuilder sat down at a nearby table. To Lane's horror, John suddenly started speaking in a loud voice, denigrating the idea of spending time developing one's physique simply so you could admire yourself in the mirror, observing that only an idiot could pursue such a pastime. Without ever talking to the man, John made clear whom he meant, ridiculing the level of intelligence required to enjoy such a hobby.

The bodybuilder took offense and rose from his seat, approaching their table. He was significantly larger than Cassavetes, but John didn't flinch. Fixing him with that intense stare, John quietly said, "Go ahead—show how stupid you are. Employ violence." The man was stopped in his tracks—at which point, John said, "C'mon, Burt, let's go," and he and Lane casually walked out.

Afterward, however, Lane lit into his snickering friend: "What the hell are you doing?" he said. "I don't want to play that game."

But as Lane recalled shortly before his death, that was the fun to John: to emerge the victor from such an encounter, having used only words. He referred to these improvisations as life studies. He would assume a character and play it for real, provoking a response and then responding to it and manipulating it as truthfully as possible—without ever letting on to the other people that they were, in fact, acting in a scene of John's devising.

John Cassavetes loved to shake things up. He was happiest when people were off-stride, out of their comfort zones, in uncharted territory.

"I'm a New York street kid," he once said. "Not that I like to fight so much—it's just that I like to win."

As an actor, he loved the unexpected. That was the essence of his most basic acting tenet: being in the moment. When someone did something he wasn't prepared for, it forced him to react through instinct, rather than from a rehearsed, rote response.

As a writer and director, he lived for those moments of revelation when his actors did something unplanned, whether it was imbuing a line with a contradictory emotion or doing some physical action that they'd never done before. Sure, a piece of improvised blocking might throw the camera operator off-balance—skewing the focus or moving the player out of the lights. But what did that matter if this accident, this moment of invention, struck a spark or shone a light on a previously dark corner of the scene—or the soul?

As a filmmaker, Cassavetes thrived on upsetting an audience by confounding its expectations. He created films that made people uncomfortable for a variety of reasons, almost every one of them deliberate. The feelings he depicted cut to the quick, delving into a kind of emotional intimacy Hollywood had pointedly avoided for much of its first fifty or sixty years. His characters' lives didn't describe neatly configured plots; his films would never be confused with well-made plays or conventional Hollywood formulas.

His scripts had the feeling of overheard dialogue—and he spent an entire career alternately battling and encouraging the misconception that his movies were all improvised, as though he simply pointed the camera, said "Action!" and let the actors make it all up.

Yet the sense of his characters as real people came from those scripts, and from a repertory company of actors and a fairly constant crew—beginning with his wife, Gena Rowlands, and including Seymour Cassel, Peter Falk, Ben Gazzara, and such off-screen presences as Al Ruban, Sam Shaw, and several others—who understood Cassavetes' vision or believed in it or both.

He kept his camera trained on his actors, waiting patiently for their humanity to seep through whatever acting they might be doing. He wasn't afraid to let a take run for the entire ten minutes of a reel of film—which made for a mountain of celluloid in the editing room. There was always something more to discover, he believed, some way to get at an untapped layer of emotion—if he just did another take.

In some ways, Cassavetes' entire career was a series of happy accidents—of things that took him in an unforeseen direction and worked out more positively than could have been hoped. In a sense, John had a genius for accidents—of taking the thing that wasn't supposed to happen (but did) and transforming it into something better than he could have planned.

His love of spontaneity, his itch to see what would happen if you just tried things a little differently, meant that even the accidents weren't happenstance, strictly speaking. From almost the beginning—for example, a chance encounter with friends who were going to attend acting school as a way to meet girls—his life and career took sharp turns, which seemed to mirror the surprising twists of his father's life.

It was an accident that John became a filmmaker at all, an unintended offshoot of the acting workshop he created as a side project to channel some of his boundless energy, at the point when he was one of the hottest actors in television. And the film that came out of that workshop—*Shadows*—grabbed acclaim beyond anything Cassavetes could have imagined. In part, its influential impact derived from technical qualities that, while hailed by critics, were accidents of inexperience by a novice filmmaker who actually thought of them as mistakes he should have fixed.

The word "accident" implies that Cassavetes lucked into his subsequent career. That makes it sound as though it were undeserved, that it was somehow all a trick. Nothing could be further from the truth.

Cassavetes was a talented actor with the intensity of an acetylene torch, even in the most mundane of roles. And he was an artist as a filmmaker, uncompromising in the vision that created a body of work unique for its subject matter and approach. His films were unlike any others of their time or that had come before; to this day, they remain *sui generis*, because no one has ever had his particular passion for capturing the lives of exactly the kinds of people the movies most often ignore.

If accidents happened that propelled him forward, it was his sheer force of will—the magnetism generated by his optimistic enthusiasm, his fascination with ordinary people, and how their lives offered insight into all of the cosmic riddles—that propelled his career forward, once he started making movies of his own. Finding the money to make them was always a struggle. "Oh, John, not the house," Gena would moan when Cassavetes would admit that, in fact, he'd taken a second mortgage on their home in the Hollywood Hills near Laurel Canyon to fund his next production.

The fact that she still has the house is testament to his tenacity. The number of times he mortgaged it speaks to his unwillingness to let Hollywood dictate what films he could and couldn't make.

This, of course, was before the era of an independent movie scene fueled by film schools, maxed-out credit cards, or studio-financed "classics" arms. Before there was Miramax, before there was John Sayles, before there was anything that anyone even thought of in the aggregate as "independent film," there was John Cassavetes.

Cassavetes may not have been the first successful independent filmmaker, but he easily qualifies as the progenitor of the modern indie scene. He didn't just make the movies the way he wanted to. He did it with his own money—and on several occasions he also distributed them. He created the advertising campaigns and the posters and found the theaters to play the films in. He did it because he was forced to, at a time when making an "independent" film and trying to distribute it in the United States was seen as both madness and heresy (while bumping up against union politics, as well).

But then, Cassavetes rarely swam with the tide. Most often, he fought the current—whatever was in fashion, whatever pulled the popular culture along. Once in a while, the tide shifted and he found himself having a slightly easier time of it, buoyed by a moment of unexpected popular success, whether as an actor in hit movies (such as *Rosemary's Baby* and *The Dirty Dozen*) or the maker of a sleeper hit (*Faces* and *A Woman Under the Influence*).

Inevitably, he resisted that. He wanted people to see his films, but he wasn't willing to compromise by making those films audience-friendly. He fought the idea of happy endings and easily synopsized stories and cute-patter dialogue and lovable characters and even manageable running times. On at least one occasion, he took what seemed to be a finished film and recut it because it drew such a positive response. The audience had reacted so enthusiastically to a preview (with laughter and cheers) that he felt he'd let them off too easily. If they were enjoying his movie, then he knew the film wasn't as tough or upsetting as he believed it should be.

Life is full of accidents of all sorts, and Cassavetes wanted his films to celebrate the very human nature of the way strokes of fate, luck, and misfortune affected his characters—and his audience.

Two

Through College

olgate University figures prominently in the story of John Cassavetes' early life—or, perhaps more accurately, the mythology of that life. It is often cited as a school he attended before discovering the theater—specifically, before reading the plays of Robert E. Sherwood (who won Pulitzer Prizes for writing *Idiot's Delight, There Shall Be No Night,* and *Abe Lincoln in Illinois*).

"He studied at Champlain and Colgate universities, majoring in English because he was bent upon becoming a playwright and scenarist," says a 1955 Columbia Pictures studio biography for *The Night Holds Terror.*

A profile of him in the *New York Journal American* that same year observed, "John Cassavetes had been preparing his way on the ladder to the stars in as careful a fashion as possible. He'd studied, majored in English Lit at Colgate University, wanted to be a sports announcer until one day he wandered into the bookshelves wherein Robert Sherwood, Moss Hart and other playwrights were stored in book form—and went home stagestruck. He never could quite explain the fixation: 'I don't quite know. It seemed an exciting way to express myself.'"

Studio biographies, of course, are written by studio publicists, based on information furnished by the stars. So the story became more detailed for the bio that went with the release of the film version of *Crime in the Streets* in 1956:

"The field of fiction lost a writer when John Cassavetes, then a student of English literature at Colgate College and with an ambition to become an author, suddenly decided to make acting his career. One day, he recalls, he found himself in the college library reading plays and imagining himself in the roles of some of them. That did it. A short while thereafter, he left that college to enter the New York Academy of Dramatic Arts."

The following year, a *New York Herald Tribune* article described Cassavetes as "an olive-skinned black-haired man who was born in New York. . . went to Port Washington High and Colgate University for two and a half years."

The bio for the 1958 film, *Virgin Island*, doesn't mention Colgate but does note that Cassavetes "chose to become an actor out of several other potential careers. As a student, he was a great sportsman and could well have become a professional baseball player. At one time, he was going to devote his life to writing but became a medical student instead. It was then that he got the acting bug that took precedence over all his other ambitions."

But a good story dies hard, particularly when reporters go back to old clippings for their facts. So the article pegged to his film *Faces* in the *New York Times* in December 1968 said, "He majored in English at Colgate and had almost decided to become a sports announcer when he began reading plays by Robert Sherwood: 'That did it,' he said. 'I caught the acting bug.'"

And, of course, once it's been in the *New York Times*, it stands as fact. So, in the obituary that appeared in the *New York Times* on February 4, 1989, the day after John died, writer Albin Krebs noted, "Mr. Cassavetes majored in English at Mohawk College and at Colgate University. . . . After reading the plays of Robert E. Sherwood, he enrolled in the American Academy of Dramatic Arts in Manhattan."

Of all of these assertions about Cassavetes' path, only a fraction of the facts are true. He did attend Champlain College, if briefly. He did enroll at the American Academy of Dramatic Arts. He may well have read and been influenced by Sherwood's plays. He could easily have considered becoming a sportscaster, given his passion for sports, both as observer and participant.

But a phone call to Colgate's alumni affairs office shows that Cassavetes never graduated from Colgate University. A further check of their student records reveals that at no time was John Cassavetes—or anyone else with the unique surname Cassavetes—ever enrolled at Colgate, even for a single day.

It's not surprising that Cassavetes would adopt a school like Colgate as an imaginary touchstone in his early life. Academic achievement was a source of pride in his family, if not something John ever truly aspired to.

He was more comfortable with the idea of having people think he had been an academic achiever than in actually being one.

So if he couldn't please his parents by graduating from college (like his older brother, Nicholas, did), let alone from an Ivy League institution (as his father had), he could at least give the impression that he had. Colgate looked good on the resume, and it wasn't as if the entertainment reporters of the day (let alone an overworked studio publicist) were going to check up on him.

Education—particularly the hallowed name of Harvard—figured prominently in his father's life. When he was growing up on Long Island, John heard the story frequently of how his father, an immigrant from Greece, had worked his way into Harvard—indeed, had worked his way through college and used his intellect and his persuasive abilities to keep himself enrolled when his money ran short.

Born in 1897, Nicholas Cassavetes Sr. was all of eleven years old when he arrived at Ellis Island on the first day of 1908, with his younger brother, Arthur, in tow. He had been born in Larissa, Greece, but the poverty in the Epirus province in northwestern Greece was crushing—and young Nicholas had received a vision of something better from a traveling missionary a year or so earlier.

The United States was indeed the land of opportunity, the missionary told him. It was a land of brotherhood, a place where you could succeed— if you wanted to learn and were willing to work. Americans would automatically embrace any immigrant who met those requirements. The future was golden in America.

Astute for a lad who had not yet reached puberty, Nicholas decided that this golden future should belong to him. So he and Arthur and their sister traveled to Bulgaria, where the sister was left with relatives, while Nicholas and Arthur went on to Constantinople. There they took jobs to earn money for passage to America. Once they'd accumulated the fare for the boat to New York, Arthur and Nicholas bought their steerage tickets for the long passage, arriving in their new home on January 1, 1908.

The immigration officer at Ellis Island looked at the two small boys and asked who they knew in the United States who could vouch for them. Thinking quickly—and having heard of Providence, Rhode Island— Nicholas fabricated a story about a generous and wealthy benefactor from Providence who had personally invited the Cassavetes brothers to come and work for him in America. The skeptical official demanded some sort of written proof that the boys were expected; Nicholas nimbly replied that the man had been on the boat that arrived just before theirs and would not be back in Providence for a couple of days—but he definitely was expecting them to follow him.

Then, remembering what the missionary had said, Nicholas looked the officials squarely in the eye and said with convincing earnestness, "I want to work. And I want to learn."

It did the trick. Not only did the immigration officer let them into the country; he and his co-workers put together five dollars—a princely sum in 1908—which they gave the boys to help buy something to eat and pay for train fare to Rhode Island.

Not that they actually knew anyone in Providence. But Nicholas seemed to know the way the world worked: that, in a strange land, newly arrived countrymen tended to congregate, to seek their own kind to help make the transition to a new culture a little less daunting. So he and Arthur walked the streets of Providence, looking for people who looked like them—the dark hair, the olive skin. When they came across an enclave of Greek immigrants, they were taken in and given a place to live and jobs to pay their room and board.

Nicholas took and held many jobs, mostly in coffee shops, restaurants, and ice cream parlors between Providence and Boston, as he and Arthur saved enough money to pay their way, even as they enrolled in public schools. Nicholas learned English, to complement the Greek and French he already spoke. He convinced the Mount Hermon School near Boston to give him a scholarship, then completed all of the course work in six months.

He was a good enough student not only to be accepted at Harvard but to receive a partial scholarship. Even then, he went to school during the day, then worked from 6 P.M. until midnight to keep himself and his brother afloat—and to send some back to his parents in Epirus. As John would repeat the story he'd been told growing up, "Every time he'd run into money difficulties, he'd say to someone, 'I want to work and I want to learn.' And somehow he'd get the money he needed to continue his studies."

Studying both classics and chemistry at Harvard, Nicholas scrambled to keep his tuition paid from semester to semester, striking deals with the dean of the college to stay in school the next year. But eventually his luck ran out.

As Gena Rowlands remembers hearing the story, "In the middle of his schooling there, the kid brother got tuberculosis, so Father quit college and took a full-time job until the boy had recovered."

Nicholas left Harvard in 1915 to serve in the U.S. Army as an interpreter, then went to work doing whatever he could to make ends meet, taking low-level food service and janitorial positions. At the same time, he began his quest to help the people of Epirus, which had fallen under Albanian control after World War I. He wrote a book, published by Oxford University Press in 1919, arguing for the Americans to help the Epirote people—his people—gain governmental self-determination. He also conducted a letter-writing campaign to American officials on the issue.

Nicholas was a scholar but also a diplomat who loved meeting and engaging people. He met Katherine Demetri, American-born but of Greek descent, and married her in April 1926, though she was fifteen years younger than he was. He was an immigrant, living the American dream; she was a Park Avenue princess, full of brash opinions and obviously rebellious enough to marry someone her parents had to see as beneath her station.

Elaine Kagan, Cassavetes' secretary for several years, said, "John's mother was a spitfire. She had a lot of pizzazz." Seymour Cassel, who knew Cassavetes for more than thirty years, offered, "John's mother was like she was in *Minnie and Moskowitz*. She was a wonderful character. She always spoke her mind. John's father was one of the nicest, most intelligent men. He used to do taxes for dancers and actors who were out of work, for nothing."

"John's father was a philosopher," says cameraman Mike Ferris, who worked with Cassavetes *pere et fils* on *A Woman Under the Influence*. "And the way he looked at life, I know, had a huge effect on his son."

In December 1927, after a year and a half of marriage, Nicholas and Katherine had their first son—named Nicholas John. Almost two years later, on December 9, 1929, their second son was born at New York's Polyclinic Hospital and christened John Nicholas.

But the Depression arrived at the same time, plunging the Land of Opportunity into more than a decade of economic despair. Unable to support his new family with the meager living he was able to scrape together, Nicholas took his wife and his two small boys back to Greece, where they stayed for the next six years. When John Cassavetes left the United States, he was two years old. When he returned, he was eight—and spoke no English.

"I'm told that at school at the time I couldn't speak English, only Greek," Cassavetes said later. So he and his brother made a pact: "My brother and I wanted to be completely American, so we didn't speak foreign languages for years."

Back in the U.S.A., Nicholas still had to hustle to make ends meet, working a variety of jobs and moving the family frequently, sometimes a step ahead of the landlord he couldn't pay: Jackson Heights (in the New

York City borough of Queens), Forest Hills, Kew Gardens, and, eventually, Port Washington on Long Island.

John's long-time friend Sam Shaw recalled, "John's father went up and down economically, up and down. They moved a lot."

For young John and Nicholas Jr., the challenge was making new friends every time the family relocated. Each new school required John to reinvent himself to fit in with a new set of kids.

"I used to size up what different people wanted from me," Cassavetes recalled. "Once, when I couldn't break through to a really tough bunch of kids, I told them, 'Go ahead, try to break my hand by squeezing it.' Well, they didn't know it but I was double-jointed and nobody could break my hand that way. The trick worked and I was accepted. Otherwise, I'd work up routines. By doing all those things, I inadvertently trained myself to be an actor."

John and his brother had no sense of the family's financial situation. Nicholas and Katherine kept things upbeat, no matter what.

"We never knew what poverty was," Cassavetes said. "We never knew we were poor when we were poor. We never knew we were rich when we were rich.

"At one point during the Depression, I remember this Armenian trader of Turkish rugs came in, and he wanted to buy all kinds of tapestries and lace that my mother had. He offered my mother, for these Damascus tablecloths, twenty-five cents apiece. She sold everything we had in order for us to eat, and she never batted an eye. She made it seem very jolly and gay and happy so that we wouldn't be upset. My mother and father were never frightened of anything. They always felt that they should go through life happily and without fear and they did that. And it was a great boon to my brother and myself."

And as he told a newspaper reporter in 1957, at the point when his career as an actor was really beginning to take off, "I have had every advantage in life."

His memories of his childhood are of sunny days, of playing baseball and hanging out with his friends. Later in life, when asked how he first got interested in making movies, he recalled his fondness for the films of James Cagney, whom he described as "my childhood idol, the guy most responsible, I suppose, for getting me into films. I loved him. I love everything I've ever heard or seen about the man . . . He was almost like a savior to all the short guys in the world, of whom I am one. As a kid, I idolized him just because he was short—and tough."

That translated into an early fascination with the kind of films Cagney specialized in: "One of my favorite movies is *Angels with Dirty Faces*, Cassavetes said. "I remember seeing it as a kid and crying. It was a great, enigmatic movie. Cagney went to the electric chair and you never knew if he was a coward or a hero."

Cassavetes talked about early hands-on experience making movies with home-movie cameras with his friends—sometimes recalling it happening at the age of eight with a small Bolex, other times at ten or eleven. Often the memory is set at the beach—usually Coney Island—with children happily making believe amid the sand and the crowds on the boardwalk.

Still, John developed a reputation as an incipient juvenile delinquent, negatively influenced by being on the streets of the New York boroughs. So Nicholas Sr., who had started a business to help immigrants in the early 1940s, decided he was earning enough to move the family to a house on Long Island. The family moved to the Sand Points neighborhood of Port Washington, an upper-middle-class suburb on the north shore.

Yet despite the staid suburban quality of the town, "my family was a wild and wonderful place, with lots of friends and neighbors visiting and talking loud and eating loud and nobody telling the children to be quiet or putting them down," John said.

Nicholas Jr. was the serious student, the quiet, intense one, while the teen-age John was the class clown, playing baseball and chasing girls, once puberty hit. The later studio bios, which talk about his athletic skill, his sportscasting ambitions, and his dream of playing professional baseball were a true mirror of his personal agenda.

"I was a totally uninterested student in high school," he confessed later on.

"'Cassy' is always ready with a wisecrack," his high school senior yearbook says under a photo of a young, short-haired Cassavetes, flashing his wolfen smile, "but he does have a serious side. A 'sensational' personality. Drives his 'heap' all over."

A "sensational" personality: He needed it, to compensate for his stature, which, while never strapping, had failed to achieve even a very modest 5 feet in height by high school.

"When I was fourteen years old, I think I was just about five feet tall, which meant that I had enormous problems getting dates with girls," he said later on. "So you have to compensate for it; you become funnier, more outgoing. Being short is a great character builder, even though it sure as hell doesn't seem that way when you first start out."

So he became a show-off, quick with a quip, bounding around, doing standing flips that always drew a reaction. It could easily have been one of these stunts—a lunchtime dare at high school, perhaps—in which John chipped his front teeth. The story about his teeth was never terribly specific and changed over time. Early in his career, he said he'd chipped them in "an accident." Later in life, he claimed they'd been chipped in a fight.

The result was that lupine grin, which never, never exposed those imperfect teeth. Even years later, after he had his teeth fixed, Cassavetes couldn't break the habit of smiling with his mouth closed, a look that was equal parts humor and malice with its tight-jawed resemblance to a grimace.

As John finished high school, he had no plans for the future. When brother Nick, who had enlisted in the army straight out of high school (he just missed World War II), came home after a two-year hitch and headed off for college, John decided to follow him, though he had no particular academic ambitions.

"It was important to my family that I go to school and, when my brother got out of the Army, he enrolled at Mohawk College, a veterans' school in upstate New York," John later said. "I went along, I stayed there for a year and then Mohawk closed down and I went to Champlain, another New York state veterans' college. But I got kicked out of there pretty quickly, mainly because I didn't want to be there. Classes were held in huge assembly rooms seating more than 200 students. The teachers would shout into microphones and I wasn't getting anything out of it. College in the Fifties was just a way of getting a diploma, that ID card which would permit you to get a job after graduation."

Champlain College, in the upstate New York town of Plattsburgh, had been created on a former army base, with barracks serving as dorms. It was opened in response to the wave of returning servicemen, who took advantage of the G.I. Bill to further their education. The Associated Colleges of New York, which would later grow into the State University of New York (SUNY) system, created new schools to handle the overflow of new students, including Champlain, Mohawk, and Samson Colleges.

Carl Goldberg, who lived across the hall from Cassavetes in Ticonderoga Hall dormitory, recalled him as "a character." Nick Petras, another Champlain student at the time, remembered Cassavetes as "a wild guy. He wasn't a great student but he wasn't stupid. But I would say he took school very lightly. I was a studious guy. He was there to have fun."

Stuart Poller, who also lived in Ticonderoga Hall, recalled him mostly for his basketball play, saying John was "pretty good, for his size," playing for a dorm team in an intramural league. Goldberg remembered him as "very speedy on the basketball court. He ran like the wind."

He was also a speedster with the ladies. Goldberg recalled Cassavetes bragging about fooling around with one of the older cooks in the dorm cafeteria, after a snowstorm stranded the staff at the college.

Poller remembered John owing him money from a card game. When he couldn't come up with the cash, he honored the debt by giving Poller his record collection.

Cassavetes was merely marking time in college. In the fictitious voice of his character, Gus, in the "Husbands" novel, he wrote, "At college, all we did was cut classes, sleep late, go out with girls and gamble."

He had an idea about his future, but it was strictly pie-in-the-sky, with no real thought given to what was involved: He loved the attention when he showed off—so he would become an actor.

Midway through the school year, Cassavetes told Poller, "I'm going to Hollywood to become an actor," and disappeared from campus. To Goldberg, he said, "The next time you see me, I'll be a star in Hollywood."

And, in fact, the next time Poller saw Cassavetes—in 1956—it was on the big screen in *Crime in the Streets.*

Three

AADA

When he first met John Cassavetes at the American Academy of Dramatic Arts (AADA), Burton Lane recalled that John was hanging out in the locker room at the Academy, drawing attention to himself by banging his head against a locker.

The Academy, as alumni refer to AADA, had been the best thing that ever happened to John: It focused him, gave him a purpose and a new set of goals against which to pit his seemingly inexhaustible supply of energy. He was now an actor—that would be his career. But like many recent graduates, he was also out of work.

So like most young actors of the early 1950s in New York, he would spend his mornings making the rounds, popping in and out of the offices of agents and casting directors, hoping for at least an audition. Then, in the afternoons, when classes were winding down and the students still hanging out, John would head back to the Academy locker room, to gab with students he knew from his time there, or to find teachers and pump them about possible jobs they might have heard about.

It hadn't been a straight line for John from Champlain to the AADA. He'd failed out of Champlain after a single semester. He hitchhiked to Florida with only a vague goal in mind. Images of beach bunnies and tropical adventure gave way to the reality in St. Petersburg, where Cassavetes' last ride took him: mostly the flock of snowbirds, elderly people from the cold Northeast, who migrated annually in the winter or retired there permanently. Young, alone, broke, and aimless, he called his parents to rescue him. His father wired him the money to catch a bus home.

But back home John was both restless and feeling parental pressure. Brother Nick was still in college, pursuing a chemistry degree, while John, of whom similar things were expected, showed every sign of becoming a bum. It had been two years since high school, and he had nothing to show for his time except a lot of experience playing basketball and chasing girls.

That eye for girls ultimately set him on his life's path. When he decided to enroll at AADA, it wasn't out of some newfound passion for acting, his testimonials about the power of Robert E. Sherwood's plays to the contrary. It was because he ran into a group of friends who had decided to audition for the Academy, and they'd mentioned that the place was crawling with women.

When he announced to his parents that he wanted to be an actor and that he wanted to attend the Academy (and have them pay for it), his mother exploded, "An actor?"

But his father took a more philosophical approach. "At least it's something. Let him be something," Nicholas Sr. said. Looking at it in considerably more depth than his son did at the time, he added, "That's a very noble thing to do. Do you know what kind of responsibility that is? You are going to be representing the lives of human beings. You will speak for all the people who have no voice."

But John was there for the girls and for what he saw as the scam of it: "I went to the Academy to escape the conformity of entering into a business life," he said later—"a business life" being his euphemism for doing the 9-to-5 routine. "It was so heady. I didn't want to have anything to do with that world. Here, you just act nuts."

His father's proviso was that John earn his way: that he would pay for the first semester, but John had to pay for the second. Cassavetes spent several months at the beginning of 1949 working part-time jobs to save money for tuition. Once he had a sufficient sum, he asked his father to cover the rest, and his father agreed. Given John's rap sheet until then—no interest in academics, mischievous, woman-chasing—it stands as a true testament of fatherly faith.

"Up until then, all I'd ever done was play basketball and run around with girls," John later recalled. "I'd never studied or applied myself or been anything but completely lazy—and I'd never felt guilt about it. I couldn't wait for the next day to come so I could get involved with some new girl and promise to marry her and then stop seeing her. In those days, I promised to marry just about every girl I took out."

He auditioned for the AADA on February 8, 1949, using two pieces: "The Youngest," by Philip Barry, and a cutting from *The Merchant of Venice*. Among the comments he received: "Latin type," "short," "sensitive temperament," and "fine intelligent boy."

The Academy consisted of two six-month academic years, the first being the junior year and the second referred to as the senior year. The curriculum focused on acting, voice, and speech, with courses in movement, fencing, and dancing, as well as dramatic study and doing scenes. There was a class in radio acting; TV had not yet become popular.

When he was accepted, John enrolled for the school year that ran from April to September 1949, then for a senior year from September 1949 to April 1950.

Sensitive temperament; fine intelligent boy—it had obviously been an award-winning performance. As Cassavetes later admitted of his decision to audition for AADA, "I loved it because it was women—all kinds of girls—and showing off."

"John was always flirting with girls," recalled Harry Mastrogeorge, a classmate at AADA. "The school was pretty fair. What gave it the extra sense of magic was that it was in the Carnegie Hall building. The green room was always bustling."

Mastrogeorge, who was in the middle of his junior year when Cassavetes arrived, recalled that, upon his own enrollment at AADA, the pragmatic admissions secretary advised him that his lengthy Greek name would never fit on a theatrical marquee and suggested taking a different professional name. He agreed ("Like a scared rabbit, I said, 'OK'") and became Harry Masters.

But Mastrogeorge remembered Cassavetes being given the same speech, ending with the assertion that, if he didn't change his name, people would have trouble spelling it. To which John replied, "They'll learn."

Years later, John recalled, "They told me they couldn't put a name like that on the marquee. I told them the Greeks had a word for it—and the word is Cassavetes."

Mastrogeorge and Cassavetes—two Greeks—took to each other immediately and wound up living together. They were both middle class, but with less pretension than some of their classmates: "A lot of our classmates were phony baloneys, pseudo-intellectuals," Mastrogeorge said. "John and I were not like that. I hate to use the word normal, but we were the normal ones."

Gradually they developed their own cadre of friends "who didn't behave like actors," as Mastrogeorge puts it. The group also included Fred Draper (who would go on to appear in many Cassavetes films) and Anne Bancroft, a classmate who was still going by her birth name, Anne Italiano.

Cassavetes was the perpetual live wire: "He was an outgoing, fun, crazy kind of wonderful guy," Mastrogeorge remembered. "He was just nutty. He would act up in the subway station, crawling through the windows of the subway train."

Mastrogeorge recalled a spring evening when he, Cassavetes, and some friends were wandering down Broadway. They came upon a crowd watching the red-carpet arrivals for a premiere: the Sadler's-Wells Ballet at the former Warner Theater, at Forty-seventh and Broadway. The group bellied up to the police barrier to watch the swells roll up; they'd been standing there a couple of minutes when Mastrogeorge realized that Cassavetes had disappeared. Then, his attention on the red carpet, he watched in amazement as a large car rolled up—and out stepped John, in T-shirt and jeans, waving to the crowd as he sauntered into the theater.

"When they threw him out, the crowd cheered him," Mastrogeorge remembered.

Erich Kollmar, who would be the cinematographer on *Shadows*, started his junior year when Cassavetes was a senior and remembered him as "crazy. He jumped on tables. He was always in perpetual motion. I never thought he was a very good stage actor, but we were all learning."

Mastrogeorge recalled differently: "John was serious about the work at the Academy. I was watching a fellow actor. He had a healthy approach and was a good student. When we did plays in the Carnegie Hall Playhouse, I really had to work. John didn't have to work."

The chief arbiter of acting style at AADA at the time was Charles Jehlinger, who had been a student in the Academy's first class in 1884. Reared in Princeton, Illinois, Jehlinger had graduated from AADA to directing and acting in Broadway shows, then returned to AADA in 1896 to join the faculty. He took over the school in 1923 and taught until his death in 1952.

A natty little man who wore wire-rimmed spectacles, sported a boutonniere, and parted his hair in the middle, Jehlinger had a powerful voice that was belied by his mild-mannered "Mr. Peepers" appearance. His roster of students over the years included Lauren Bacall, Hume Cronyn, Robert Cummings, Cecil B. DeMille, Nina Foch, Ruth Gordon, Garson

Kanin, Grace Kelly, Agnes Moorhead, William Powell, Thelma Ritter, Edward G. Robinson, Rosalind Russell, and Spencer Tracy.

"He was the greatest teacher alive because he was so simple," is Cassavetes' description.

But Jehlinger would never be mistaken for Mr. Chips. He could be a cutting taskmaster who loudly disdained anything that remotely resembled acting. At his most complimentary, he might allow, "Crude, but there are possibilities." When he saw something he didn't like, he could verbally flay a student. "He'd make fun of us if we were dramatic—he was a tough, tough teacher," was Renee Taylor's memory.

Jehlinger's sharp wit kept actors off-balance. When an actor sneezed one time in rehearsal, Jehlinger whirled on him, fixed him with a steady gaze and said, "If you must sneeze, sneeze in character."

"Jehlinger was a little guy, very old, with a hearing aid," Mastrogeorge recalled. "He was tyrannical, hard, and harsh, but it was all to do with loyalty to the play. His approach to acting was very simple, very direct, no frou-frou. Jehlinger would say, 'Stop acting.' To be a successful actor, he said, you have to have the hide of a rhinoceros and the heart of a baby. That was the core of his teaching, the essence of what he taught: that you needed childlike innocence."

Jehlinger offered an endless string of aphorisms, each simple and to the point—almost like haiku about acting. As AADA alumnus Erich Kollmar recalled, "He said, 'Hearing is not listening.' " His philosophy made an impression on Cassavetes, who seemed to absorb the ideas as he worked with Jehlinger on senior productions and classroom scenes:

"Human impulse is the only thing that counts, not stage directions."

"You can feel your deepest emotion without moving a muscle."

"Don't think of acting; think of living."

"You must constantly see with fresh eyes, feel with a fresh heart."

"You cannot change reality. Hold the mirror up to nature."

"Life is the only true school of acting."

AADA's curriculum focused on stage work: on stagecraft, as opposed to acting methods. It was a more practical approach, with less of the pretense toward capital-A Art than, for example, the Actors Studio, which was in its heyday.

But the AADA students were well aware of the revolution in American acting—for stage and screen—that was being fomented a few blocks down Broadway at the Actors Studio and in off-shoots and rivals of the Actors Studio and in the classrooms of teachers such as Sanford Meisner and Stella Adler.

At that point, in 1949, two actors seemed to shine over everything—to blaze with an unusual new quality, blending emotional realism and vulnerability in an explosive combination that no one had offered previously: Montgomery Clift and Marlon Brando.

Clift had arrived first, working on Broadway for ten years before scoring with one of his first films, Howard Hawks' *Red River*, in 1948. Even more influential, however, Brando seemed to loom everywhere in the early 1950s.

By 1949 he had spent two years playing Stanley Kowalski for Elia Kazan in *A Streetcar Named Desire*. Acting students flocked to the Ethel Barrymore Theater to soak in Brando's dynamic performance, to vicariously gain the connection to "the Method."

"The Method," as it came to be known, was drawn from the teachings of Russian actor-director Constantin Stanislavsky, who told actors to draw upon their emotional memories in playing a character, to delve into the character's psychological motivation and find it within, rather than imposing a character on the writing by an external reading of the material.

Few actors, however, had the kind of finely tuned instincts of Brando or Clift; many saw only the externals—the seeming inarticulate grunts and primitive canniness with which Brando imbued Stanley, for example—and mimicked the most obvious aspects of his technique, without getting beneath the surface of their own characters.

Only a few of the young actors who came in Brando's wake—such as James Dean and Cassavetes—seemed to have the same intensity, intelligence, and courage. Dean was a product of teachers like Lee Strasberg, Martin Ritt, and Kazan. Cassavetes, however, had a certain sense of disdain for the Actors Studio. There was a class consciousness that rankled him, a sense of intellectual superiority that grated on his more egalitarian impulses.

After getting out of AADA, Cassavetes applied to the Actors Studio and was denied membership. He took classes with Lee Strasberg, according to Mastrogeorge, but quit after three weeks: "They were doing all this awful, crazy stuff and John dropped out."

In the late 1950s, after becoming a hot property in live television and movies, John was invited to join the Studio, which understood the value of being identified with the most popular actors of the period.

By that time, Cassavetes had started the Cassavetes–Lane Workshop, which he viewed as a direct competitor with the Actors Studio. Cassavetes, who often stated the belief that "Anyone can be an actor," had more of an open-door policy for his classes and perceived the judgmental selectivity of the Actors Studio as snobbery.

Even though he had been invited to join without an audition, he of-fered to prepare a piece anyway. He enlisted then-partner Burton Lane, and at his audition, he announced they would be doing a cutting from an original play called *Bill Bauer's Boys*. He and Lane then launched into a seemingly life-and-death encounter, acted with spontaneity and freshness. The Studio arbiters, a panel that probably included Strasberg, were effu-sive in their praise, both for the scene and for the acting—until Cassavetes laughed in their faces and told them he and Lane had improvised the scene on the spot just for the audition.

"Screw you," Cassavetes told them. "I don't want any part of you. I've got my own school and I'll drive yours out of town."

Four

Gena

The first time John Cassavetes saw Gena Rowlands, she was standing backstage at the Academy, after appearing in one of her senior acting projects, a production of J. B. Priestley's *Dangerous Corner.*

"I spotted this doll one day and pretended that I wanted to talk to her about a role," Cassavetes recalled a few years later. "And that was it."

He embellished the story in a later retelling, in which he was with actor John Ericson when he saw her. He turned to Ericson and said, "That's the girl I'm going to marry."

Rowlands saw him coming and didn't like what she saw. More precisely, she didn't like how what she saw made her feel.

"I was a woman with a plan," she later recalled. "The only thing that could really stop me from succeeding was to fall in love. In those days, if you got married, you had children and quit what you were doing. I wanted to be an actress bad enough that I would forego the comfort of love. I was going to be very careful.

"So I went in to lunch and put my books in my locker and I saw John Cassavetes. And I thought, Oh damn, not this. This is just exactly what I don't want."

All of her resolve—her conviction that she could avoid romantic entanglements in order to focus on becoming an actress and forging a career—went out the window.

"I brushed him off but he kept asking and, after a week, I started dating him. I couldn't get rid of him so I married him. And that was that. Up until then, I was not sure why I had left Wisconsin," she said.

In fact, she'd left Wisconsin, where she'd been attending the University of Wisconsin out of a sense of duty to her parents, to find herself as an actress in New York. She wasn't getting where she wanted or being who she thought she should be by attending classes in Madison.

Rowlands, who was born in 1930 (a year after Cassavetes), had grown up in Cambria, Wisconsin, known as "Little Wales." Cambria was settled by four Welsh families, including Rowlands' great-great-grandfather, and was filled with people of Welsh heritage who spoke Welsh until her grandfather's day. About an hour from the state capital in Madison, it was a small town of 700 that took its ethnic identity seriously, reveling in semi-annual ethnic musical gatherings. Welsh people from around the area would invade the town for group singing, which Rowlands remembered as lasting for days at a time.

Her father, E. M. Rowlands, had migrated upward through a series of increasingly well-paying and prestigious jobs, including vice president of the local bank, where his father was president. He'd been elected to the state assembly and the state senate and moved from there to positions in Washington, where the family lived from 1941 to 1948. There Gena indulged her interest in acting, being accepted in a program for students at the Jarvis Repertory Theater in Washington.

In fact, by the time she was sixteen, Gena had lived in Cambria, Madison, and Milwaukee in Wisconsin; Arlington, Virginia; and Houston, Texas (where her father was involved in the oil business). Gena wasn't outgoing, and the transitions were difficult; she was a sickly child who had spent a great deal of time in bed, reading or listening to the radio to pass the time. There may also have been an element of hypochondria, with time in bed meant to defuse the stress of new surroundings when it became too great.

Her mother, Mary Neal Rowlands, later known as Lady, regularly pursued artistic interests to occupy her between the chores of being housewife and mother to Gena and her brother, David. Lady acted, and she sang and painted, though her "hobbies" were only tolerated by her husband.

"My dad never forbade that," Rowlands would later recall. "He just never encouraged her."

"My mother is an artist and I would say that, looking back, she had the happiest, most complete home life I've ever seen," Rowlands said. "Yet she wasn't the momma in the kitchen. She was the momma who, when we came home at lunch time, would be making ceramics and her hands would be covered with clay up to her elbows and she'd look up and say, 'Oh, is it lunch time?' And we'd say, 'Oh, that's all right, we'll make a peanut butter sandwich for ourselves.'

"I was brought up in an unusual situation: My mother was a feminist and my father was a male chauvinist, but they got along marvelously."

As a girl, Rowlands absorbed feminist lessons from her mother, who was never overtly political but made statements in other ways. Lady Rowlands would look crossly at her daughter, for example, if she talked about being a nurse—instead of a doctor—and tried to pass along the notion that all choices were open to Gena. If her daughter had to be better than a boy to do it, so much the better.

"Everything I know is something my mother told me," she said. "She said, 'Don't skirt around life or be frightened to do things.' She told me it was important to put your arms into life, up to the elbows. Do it all—dig in."

But her parents didn't necessarily want her to do that digging very far from home. After his stint in Washington, E. M. Rowlands took the family back to live in Madison, as Gena closed in on her high-school graduation. Her parents began playing on the behavior they'd inculcated in her—to be a dutiful daughter—and convinced her to attend the University of Wisconsin, right there in Madison. She majored in English literature and tried out for college plays but wasn't cast. "I did a little in drama but I couldn't seem to get into it," she later recalled. "So I quit college and came home to tell my family I was going to New York to be an actress. I expected a stony attitude."

She later described her father as "an understanding man" who, when faced with her request about acting school, said, "Dear, do anything you want. Be an elephant trainer, even."

When she arrived at AADA, she wasn't quite the country mouse in the big city; she'd lived in and around Washington, D.C., in addition to her time in Wisconsin. But being in New York in the 1950s, she thought, was like being in the Golden Age of Greece. She was determined not to be found lacking by the sophisticated students in her class.

"I had no sense of humor," she remembered. "It took such an enormous effort to get out of Wisconsin. I was so afraid of being deflected from my goal. I just wanted to study."

It was apparent from the start that she had talent. Classmate Erich Kollmar recalled her as an actor with sensitivity and intelligence: "She would listen," he said.

"It's funny," Rowlands later said. "When I was a kid, I was clumsy and shy. As soon as I became an actress, among other actors, there was no problem."

She stayed at AADA long enough to attract Cassavetes' attention. He came backstage after her performance in *Dangerous Corner* and gushed, "You're such a great actress."

Confronted with the handsome young actor, she was helpless to say no when he asked her out on a date.

The relationship, however, could easily have ended on that first night out together. Cassavetes arrived to pick Rowlands up in his mother's car, a late-1940s bulge-mobile whose size only accentuated how small and young Cassavetes looked. Then he began driving around, obviously with no plan for the evening.

They drove for an hour, Cassavetes eventually driving them into New Jersey, seemingly unintentionally. Rowlands was convinced that her date was lost when he suddenly pulled into the parking lot of a roadside honkytonk and said, not very convincingly, "Here it is."

Once seated in a booth inside, however, all Cassavetes could talk about was his dog, a German shepherd named Henry. As she sat there smiling, mentally Rowlands was screaming, "Get me out of here."

When he got her to her door, Cassavetes tried to kiss Rowlands, who leveled him with a stare: "You've got to be kidding me," she said. When he seemed perplexed, she told him, "Look, we've got nothing to talk about. All you talked about was your dog."

"What do you want to talk about?" Cassavetes asked.

"Plays, literature, things like that," she said, terminating the date.

Undeterred, Cassavetes went home and asked his father's help: What should he read to impress this girl who wanted to talk about plays and literature? The senior Cassavetes, a scholar and intellectual, made a number of suggestions and gave John a stack of books. And Cassavetes went and read them, then called Rowlands for another date.

"I want to go out with you again," he announced. "I've read this book and this book and this book—and I want to talk about them with you."

So they met again, and Cassavetes dazzled her, not only with the fact that he actually had read the books in question, but because he was able to analyze and interpret them in an astute, original way. And Rowlands found herself falling in love with this electric young man, convinced almost instantly that he was a genius.

Five

Post-AADA

S hortly after graduating from AADA, Cassavetes, Mastrogeorge, and their roommate Bill Stafford all enlisted in the army to avoid the draft.

The draft had been reinstituted in 1948, and with war a probability in Korea, the army was making noises about calling up a wave of new recruits to provide enhanced troop strength. Having no interest in fighting a war, John found his loophole: a reserve unit for actors and musicians called the 306th Special Services Company. The three friends enlisted and found themselves detailed to monthly meetings of their reserve unit at the Algonquin Hotel and two weeks each summer of reserve training. Mastrogeorge remembered Cassavetes, with his military haircut, looking very much like he did in *The Dirty Dozen*.

John Cassavetes and Gena Rowlands both left the Academy to face the world as actors, but the world didn't stop for them—at least not for three or four years. Which didn't really matter because John had enough ambition and aggression to make it stop, or at least to try.

"I was a young guy, looking for adventure," John later said of the period.

It was an exciting time to be a young actor at large in Manhattan. As the 1950s unfolded, the country—and the city—seemed to shake off the last traces of World War II. The baby boom exploded, and a decade of peaceful

prosperity also begat the first television generation, as well as the first generation of television stars.

Brando's success on Broadway had energized the young actors in New
York; when *Streetcar* made it to the big screen and the rest of the country
saw what they'd only been reading about, the number of young actors who
longed to follow in Brando's footsteps seemed to grow exponentially—
studying with Adler and Strasberg, living in the Village, working in the burgeoning off-Broadway scene.

And they all became competition for John Cassavetes, who believed
not only in his own talent but in the idea that, given a fair audition, he
could win any part. It was all a new experience, being part of a community
of artists who not only took the work seriously but expected him to as well.
If it was an adventure, it was less a lark than a quest.

But that quest mostly meant the search for jobs, an enervating, de-
meaning process that involved "making the rounds": going door to door in
various office buildings that housed warrens of offices for agents and casting directors, dropping off head shots and resumes, and begging for work.

As the 1950s dawned, there was a lot more casting going on. It was no
longer just Broadway and stock, with the occasional film that was shot in
New York. Live television was mushrooming, and it was almost all based
in New York, because that's where the headquarters were for the radio networks that spawned the TV networks.

By the end of the decade, most TV shows would have shifted from live
broadcast to film, and like the Brooklyn Dodgers, most TV production
would have moved to Los Angeles. But for the first half of the 1950s, New
York was the home of live television, and the work was plentiful, even if it
didn't pay much.

It might take three or four days to rehearse and present a half-hour
drama. An hour-long live show might get a week's rehearsal. Bigger-budget
shows took longer.

But first you had to land a role. Which proved a challenge to Cassavetes: "Nobody would cast me because I was quote such an unusual type,"
he recalled.

What type? Call it Mediterranean: olive skin, darkly flashing eyes, black
hair, and a hawkish profile that was enhanced by the intensity of his stare.
He was handsome but threatening, an impression that was reinforced by the
forcefulness of his personality.

On the other hand, nothing daunted him. No one seemed to try harder
or make a wilder impression than John Cassavetes.

Erich Kollmar recalled, "When he first went to get agents, he would jump up on tables and shout, 'Listen to me, I'm the greatest actor around'—but he'd do it in a funny way."

He resented having to prove himself over and over again to people who didn't have the same passion that he was ready to bring to a role. "John hates subways because they remind him of his years of scratching for acting jobs on TV after he left AADA," playwright Meade Roberts recalled in a 1960 journal entry, quoted years later. "He once chained himself to a radiator at CBS to land a walk-on on *You Are There.*"

Cassavetes said, "I was young. And I felt that everybody had talent. And that for some reason they were being arbitrary and not employing that talent. Because I thought, Well, these people are the giants of an industry, they have a good brain and a good heart and ability. How come they don't use it? And Gena would say, 'Look, a lot of people just don't have the same drives, the same desire, the same gun that sparks them, as you do. You're acting like these people all understand you. Nobody understands you. I don't understand you. Who the hell can understand you? You're nuts.'"

Mastrogeorge recalled Cassavetes in an agent's waiting room, when a receptionist was rude to him, blasting her with nonsense German a la Sid Caesar. "Or, in the middle of the office, he would yell in pain and double over. We knew his antics. We would pick him up and carry him out. Then we laughed and ran away."

Still, his approach worked up to a point. He found acting jobs in Connecticut and Rhode Island, working winter and summer stock in low-paying (but paying, nonetheless) theater jobs. There was also the occasional extra work in TV and film. Not that that kept him from putting an optimistic spin on whatever he found. He even found an agent, Robert Lang.

At one point, he landed his first TV role (which he recalled variously as on *The Kraft Hour* and *The Lux Video Theater*). In it he played, essentially, a spear carrier with one line. But Cassavetes was sure he had arrived as a star.

"I thought I was brilliant when I finally got my first acting job," he later recalled. "When it was over, I raced from the TV studio to where all my friends had met to watch the show and I said, 'Did you see me?' They said they hadn't. I got indignant. 'You morons!' I shouted, 'I was the guy in the iron mask who ran on and said, "Halt!" And I was magnificent!'"

Cassavetes and Mastrogeorge roomed together at AADA and afterward, sharing apartments on West Seventieth Street near the Hudson River and, later, at Ninety-sixth and Riverside Drive. "We had a railroad flat at Ninth Avenue and Fifty-seventh Street," Mastrogeorge said. "We'd have all-night canasta games."

At one point, they were part of a group (estimated as anywhere from six to ten) sharing a small apartment. Cassavetes recalled living "with a bunch of guys in one large room. We survived by taking turns getting work to support us while the rest knocked on producers' doors. It was rough."

Mastrogeorge remembered: "I was asleep one morning and John came in. There was a woman bending over my bed and I thought I'd died and gone to heaven because she looked like an angel. And it was Gena. John said, 'I've met this great girl.'"

Mastrogeorge was quiet and serious, though he enjoyed John's unfettered sense of humor and his impulsive passion. Cassavetes, in turn, nicknamed Mastrogeorge "The Monk" because of his studied, straight-arrow approach to life: "I guess I was more moralistic," Mastrogeorge said now.

Mastrogeorge followed the rules, which always amused Cassavetes, the perpetual corner-cutter. The mercurial Cassavetes once told him, "It will take ten times longer for you to do something that I can do overnight." Which only added to Mastrogeorge's impression of John as someone guided by impulse which, to Mastrogeorge, was synonymous with recklessness.

After AADA, while they looked for acting jobs, Mastrogeorge paid the rent by working jobs as a waiter or busboy, between low-paying small roles on live TV. But John never seemed to have to work an outside job. Mastrogeorge remembered weekend trips to the Cassavetes house in Port Washington, a beautiful home where, according to John, gangster Frank Costello was a neighbor. Nicholas Sr.'s business was thriving: "They were well-off," Mastrogeorge said simply.

As TV began to take off—the popularity of live dramatic TV reached its zenith in the mid-1950s—actors in New York found themselves increasingly drawn to the mushrooming new medium.

"Live TV was so exciting," Mastrogeorge remembered. "The challenge was that, if you made a mistake, 20 million people are watching. It was very exciting: *Playhouse 90, Studio One.*"

As Cassavetes recalled, "Film was unknown to us because we did not expect we could get into it. We hated Hollywood and everything it stood for, mainly because we thought we had no chance of getting there. TV offered an enormous opportunity to express ourselves."

Rowlands also loved those days when "the really good writers were working fast and furious and there were all those wonderful big, dramatic shows. I could play a hussy in *The Great Gatsby* one day and a pregnant wife the next, then a career girl—even a scientist with huge horn-rimmed glasses.

It was a terribly exciting time, everybody writing, working, directing, creating as hard as they could."

Gena was finding work as well, though not always the job she was hired for. She talked her way into a job at the Provincetown Playhouse for summer stock, by touting her skills with a sewing machine. So she was made wardrobe mistress—and quickly found herself overmatched, assigned to costume three historical dramas.

"I couldn't even wind the bobbin of the machine," she said. "It sat in the corner while I sewed costumes by hand. I was a miserable flop so they made me resident ingénue." She played small roles with the company, then went back to New York.

Eventually, she was hired for a nightclub revue, *All About Love*, which played for a winter at the Versailles, a grand nightclub on West Fiftieth Street. The Versailles had annually booked singer Edith Piaf for a winter run. When Piaf decided not to play New York in the winter of 1953, the club hired writers Max Wilk and George Axelrod, whose revue *Small Wonder* had been a Broadway hit the year before, to create a two-act musical revue for the club, with songs by Irvin and Lillian Graham.

The Grahams had seen Gena in Provincetown and wanted her for *All About Love*—as a singer. But Rowlands' singing voice? "I don't sing at all," Rowlands admitted. So instead she became the narrator of the show and acted in sketches in the piece.

Wilk recalled that it was easy to write for Rowlands: "She knew how to play comedy," he said. "She knew how to do the jokes. She was this talented, brilliant, wonderful girl. She was superb, very funny."

Through Axelrod, Rowlands landed work in the road company of his hit *The Seven Year Itch*, playing a small role, eventually returning to New York to take over the role in the long-running Broadway production.

In an era where stars seemed to look more wholesome, Rowlands, at twenty-four, was almost exotic: a slim, glowing blonde, but with green, feline eyes, creamy skin, and a lively, bubbly intelligence.

"She was gorgeous," recalled Wilk, who said Rowlands would rehearse for *All About Love* in black tights. "That winter, George's and my wife were both pregnant. We'd go to rehearsal and see this extraordinary woman in black tights and we'd just moan. George and I were both madly in love with her."

Eventually, she did more stock, then landed a role opposite Melvyn Douglas in a touring company of *Time Out for Ginger* before returning to New York, where she picked up live TV work when she could.

John continued making a spectacle of himself in agents' offices across town. He burned with desire, but no one would give him the chance to show what he could do. For a long time, he took it in stride, hustling, working when he could, hanging with his friends. Live TV was a way to get work, get paid, and still hold your head up, even if the wages were meager.

"Before TV was unionized, I got $15 for playing a lead," Cassavetes recalled. "It seemed like not a lot and not a little."

"John handled the business aspect of it more healthily than other people," Mastrogeorge remembered. "He never let it get the upper hand. You see that in people who survive. The people who don't are the ones who succumb to the nastiness and harshness of the business. John was oblivious to that."

He may have been competitive, but he was also collegial. Director Paul Mazursky, then a struggling young actor from Brooklyn, remembered the day in 1953 when he and Mastrogeorge were working behind the counter of the Salad Bowl, one of New York's first health-food stores, and Cassavetes walked in. Though John and Mastrogeorge were friends, he and Mazursky had never met, so Mastrogeorge introduced them.

Cassavetes told the two countermen, "There's a guy at MGM who's looking for kids for this movie, *Blackboard Jungle*. You should go over."

When Mazursky and Mastrogeorge seemed uncertain, Cassavetes said, "C'mon, I'll take you over there," and took them to meet the casting director—and from that, Mazursky won his first movie role, as one of the hoodlums in the class that harasses teacher Glenn Ford, in Richard Brooks' classic picture about juvenile delinquency.

Cassavetes' own career was moving forward by fits and starts, impeded at times by the standards he tried to uphold. Cast in a soap opera, he would agonize over the corny dialogue he was given, feeling that it was beneath his dignity to have to utter such awful writing.

"We would laugh at the lines," he recalled. "I remember one I just wouldn't say: 'Strong I am and have helped in the building of houses.' But then Gena and I talked about it. We made fun of it; we played with it. When I went back the next day, they said, 'Maybe you're right, John—we'll cut that line.' And I wouldn't let them."

But it taught him a lesson: that even a bad show can be educational. No matter how bad the material, if you can make an audience believe it, you've succeeded as an actor. The key was in putting aside judgment of the material, and ignoring the fact that people are watching and judging you. Surrender to the moment; believe in it yourself and the audience will go with you.

Cassavetes talked his way into a walk-on in Henry Hathaway's *Fourteen Hours* in 1951. Then he endeavored to meet Gregory Ratoff when Ratoff was shooting a film called *Taxi*.

Ratoff, a Russian who had acted at the Moscow Art Theater and served in the czar's army before emigrating to the U.S., had built a career as actor (most memorably, he played producer Max Fabian opposite Bette Davis in *All About Eve*), director (*Intermezzo*, *The Corsican Brothers*), and producer, both in film and theater. He was a large, loud man with a thick accent. Ratoff also had a volcanic temper that would explode when the pressure got too great, which was almost daily. He would begin shouting that he was losing his mind, then yell, "The day that I am crazy, I give up fox hunting."

"After working with Ratoff," John once said, "nothing in the theater scares me."

Cassavetes supposedly heard that Ratoff liked Greeks and took to stationing himself near the Twentieth Century Fox office, where Ratoff was based. After passing him at the same spot for a week, Ratoff asked him about himself, and Cassavetes casually mentioned that his friends called him "the Greek." According to Cassavetes, that became Ratoff's nickname for him: "He couldn't pronounce my name so he called me 'the Greek.'" But Cassavetes also admitted at one point that he got the role because he refused to take "no" for an answer from Ratoff.

Ratoff gave him two lines in *Taxi*—and put him to work as a gofer on the film. He then hired Cassavetes as his assistant for a TV series, *Cradle of Stars*, and then as assistant stage manager for a Broadway play Ratoff was directing, *The Fifth Season*, which starred legendary Yiddish actor Menasha Skulnik. It was, at least, steady work, a job whose hours allowed Cassavetes to spend much of his day going on auditions.

(Later, Cassavetes tried to put a different spin on it: "After AADA, Cassavetes turned his hand to anything that would give him useful experience of the entertainment world . . . He proved his versatility by filling in a gap between acting assignments as stage manager of *The Fifth Season* on Broadway," is how he put it in a 1958 studio biography.)

It was while working on *The Fifth Season* at the Cort Theater one night that Cassavetes met the man who would change his career—and become a lifelong mentor, friend, collaborator, and sounding board.

"There was a fellow backstage one night who saw me do a flip and said, 'Gee, you'd be a terrific actor. You should write a script,'" John later recalled. "And that was Sam Shaw."

Six

Sam Shaw

Cassavetes always told the story of meeting Sam Shaw when he was a twenty-four-year-old struggling actor, working as an assistant stage manager for a play in which he got to go on as an understudy on rare occasions. He was bursting with energy, with ideas, with the kind of enthusiasm that created a spark with Sam Shaw.

As John recalled it, "He came up to me and said, 'What are you doing now?' I told him and he said, 'Well, I'll produce a feature picture if you write it.' It was just like that."

Shaw, a photographer for *Life* magazine, was a seasoned forty-year-old who had established himself as the premiere movie-set photographer in American journalism. He always had a camera or two around his neck and counted Marlon Brando, Marilyn Monroe, and Anthony Quinn among his closest friends.

But he spotted something in Cassavetes that interested him and subsequently tried to help his career. He and Cassavetes would form a bond that would last until John's death and beyond.

Shaw's son, Larry, remembered Cassavetes as "the most self-confident, assured person you ever met. He was physically coordinated and supremely confident." John became a regular presence at the Shaw home, taking the teenage Larry to see prizefights at Madison Square Garden, or to the Village to see blues and jazz singers.

"He was like an older brother to me at that point," Larry Shaw said. "To Sam, he was like a son, which is not easy for me to say."

It's not surprising that Shaw and Cassavetes would click. Both were consumed with the need to create, and both found ways to express that need and assemble a body of work in the process. In Cassavetes, Shaw found a student who became a partner. Eventually John would be the artist and Sam would provide support and backing. But early on, it was John, who had barely listened in high school and dropped out of college, who learned the most from the ongoing tutorial on art, jazz, film, wine, and food provided by the quietly ebullient Shaw, who taught without even meaning to.

Born on the Lower East Side at Hester and Mott Streets shortly before the United States entered World War I, Shaw and his family moved to Mulberry Street in Little Italy when Sam was ten, then moved to Ninety-ninth Street on the Upper West Side before his bar mitzvah.

The oldest of five sons of Russian immigrants, Sam was both enterprising and artistic. As a child, he made sculptures of animals out of blobs of tar he got off the street. By high school, he was such an accomplished painter that he was offered his choice: a scholarship to study art at Pratt Institute or a studio in which to work.

He chose the latter, sharing it with another scholarship winner, painter Romare Bearden, with whom he became lifelong friends. Shaw eventually turned to photography and concentrated on it, realizing, as daughter Edie put it, that, while he was a serious painter, "when you're raising a family, you have to make a living."

But he never stopped painting and never stopped loving art.

"We grew up going to the [Metropolitan Museum of Art] every Sunday," recalled his daughter, Meta Shaw Stevens. Edie Shaw said, "You may think that's stuffy for a child but it was exciting for me. He'd give us mini-lectures about the styles of painting."

To support himself, he painted signs, then began to find work as a political cartoonist and then as an art director for publications such as the *Brooklyn Eagle* and the *Daily Worker*. By the end of the 1930s, he had discovered photography as a medium with which to express himself and photojournalism as the style that seemed to suit him the best. He hung out with the photographers of the period, everyone from spot-news artist Arthur Fellig, better known as Weegee, to artist Man Ray.

Through most of the 1940s, he shot for the magazines *Fridays* and *Colliers*. At one point, *Colliers* teamed him with writer Harry Henderson; together, they crossed the country, documenting life during wartime in an award-winning series.

Quiet but astute, easygoing and likable, Shaw made friends everywhere he went, establishing connections that seemed to last a lifetime. Often one thing would lead to another: Introduced to agent-producer Charles Feldman, Shaw quickly made himself useful by becoming Feldman's adviser about which of the new painters in the suddenly hot modern-art market to add to his growing collection.

As a favor to Feldman, he took photographs on the set of one of his films, which proved useful in creating a poster for the film. Shaw, with his background in art and graphic arts, took pleasure in coming up with the image that could define an entire film (and, with Cassavetes, would often design the posters for his films).

At the same time, he found that the increasingly movie-hungry mainstream media were interested in behind-the-scenes exclusives from movie sets. Larry Shaw explained, "He'd go to a magazine and say, 'I can get on the set of these movies.' It was a whole new career. And the producers loved it because he was selling the movie. He did *Panic in the Streets,* on which he might have been one of the first special photographers selling a movie by getting stories in magazines."

The family lived on and off in Europe, where Shaw took photographs on the sets of Roberto Rossellini and Vittorio de Sica, among other directors. Back in the States, after working with Elia Kazan on *Panic in the Streets,* Shaw was hired for *A Streetcar Named Desire* and created the iconic image of Marlon Brando in a torn T-shirt that would define Brando to the public. While shooting Brando again on the set of *Viva Zapata!* Shaw was given another protégé of Kazan's as his driver to ferry him back and forth to the set: a young actress named Marilyn Monroe. They became fast friends, with Shaw offering career advice.

He photographed Monroe constantly and, eventually, took perhaps the most famous picture of her of all time: standing on a subway grate, skirt billowing, for the movie *The Seven Year Itch.* It had been a scene in the movie; hired to create the poster for the film, Shaw recreated the moment in front of the Trans-Lux Theater on Lexington Avenue, where there was a particularly gusty grate. Asked later about the iconic image, he said, "You have to give Marilyn credit, too. She was very inventive. She loved the camera."

Shaw's work kept him so busy that his time at home with his three children became precious. So when he was home between assignments, he played with them, entertained them—even rode the bus to school with them. And if a New York job came in, often he would scoop the kids up and take them along with him.

Edie Shaw Marcus remembers her father taking her along on an assignment that took them to a townhouse in Greenwich Village, without mentioning that it belonged to Paul Newman and Joanne Woodward: "In order to see us, he'd take us with him," she said. "I went with him to Frank Sinatra's home, to Duke Ellington's. I went to the All-Star Game with Joe DiMaggio. These are things I did as a kid and I thought they were a natural part of being a kid. His work and personal life—there was no division."

His friendships put him in the right place at the right time. Through his relationship with Charles Feldman, he was able to pair the producer with comedian Woody Allen, who wrote *What's New Pussycat?* and *Casino Royale* for Feldman.

Earlier Shaw had done a story for *Life* on a waterfront priest in New York who was battling organized crime among the labor unions. Through that story and his friendship with Budd Schulberg and Elia Kazan, he developed the script—only to have Kazan cut him out of the final deal when he made *On the Waterfront*. Shaw wound up suing; he won a monetary award, but his contribution to the film was never credited.

Shaw was a networker before anyone had thought of the term. He was a collector of people and had an eye for talent.

"He knew everyone in the entire world. If you wanted a message delivered, you gave it to Sam. He was welcome everywhere," recalled Al Ruban, who worked with Cassavetes from *Shadows* until the end of his life, including producing several of the Cassavetes films with Shaw.

On the day he ran into Cassavetes backstage at Ratoff's play, Sam Shaw had spent part of the day at the Actors Studio, watching actors trying to be spontaneous, to be real. Then, while chatting with Ratoff at *The Fifth Season*, he spotted the young assistant stage manager showing off before the play: declaiming Shakespeare and doing a standing backflip. This, Shaw felt, was real spontaneity.

So he approached Cassavetes with the idea of writing a script for himself, planting a seed that lasted the rest of Cassavetes' life. When Cassavetes said he had no idea what to write about, Shaw told him, "I know a great writer living in Duxbury, Mass. His name is Edward McSorley. If you drive up there and see him, he'll write it with you. But you've got to put an outline of all your ideas on paper and write about what you know."

Cassavetes began writing furiously, then went back to Shaw, who told him it was time to approach McSorley. He gave Cassavetes the address and said he'd already called McSorley to tell him to expect the would-be collaborator.

Cassavetes was relatively broke, making $85 a week as assistant stage manager. He borrowed a car from a friend but ran out of gas and had to "borrow money from a cop." When he finally arrived at the snowy cottage and knocked on the door, the man who answered was "a craggy-faced fifty-five-year-old short prune who looked like a writer's supposed to look."

McSorley, the author of a well-regarded novel about the Irish immigrant experience, *Our Own Kind*, sized up the diminutive young man on his doorstep, then said, "Hello. What do you want?"

Cassavetes introduced himself, began describing his manuscript and then noticed the quizzical look on McSorley's face and said, "You're expecting me, aren't you? Sam Shaw said he called you."

McSorley snorted and said, "I haven't seen Sam in ten years." But he invited Cassavetes in, and they eventually, over time, hammered out a script together. In fact, Shaw even managed to find a buyer for it, though it was never produced. But a lifelong partnership between Cassavetes and Shaw had begun.

Seven

"Paso Doble"

Then, in early 1954 John Cassavetes landed the role that changed his life forever.

If ever a single performance could be said to have launched a career, it was Cassavetes' role in Budd Schulberg's "Paso Doble" on NBC's *Omnibus* series, which aired on February 14, 1954, and quickly catapulted John into the ranks of the sought-after. It started him on a run of TV and movie work that made him one of the biggest stars of live TV and one of the hottest young actors in a period full of next big things. Even the roles he didn't get made news.

"John got into that Budd Schulberg thing and that was his springboard," Harry Mastrogeorge recalled. Yet Cassavetes nearly lost "Paso Doble" before he landed it because he couldn't keep his mouth shut.

John Cassavetes was never one to keep his opinion to himself. Having found a calling in acting, having been through the Academy, he knew what he needed as an actor from a director—and he wasn't shy about letting a director know it when he went in a different direction.

First of all, it had to be fun. That's what acting was about. Why do it if you couldn't enjoy yourself doing it? He claimed to have learned the lesson from actor Menasha Skulnik, a legend of the Yiddish theater, whom he encountered daily when Skulnik was starring in *The Fifth Season*. Skulnik at that point was in his sixties and had been performing onstage for almost a half-century. When Cassavetes expressed awe at the aging actor's energy and freshness, even in the long run of a play, Skulnik said, "If you can't have fun and be involved, there's no sense in being an actor."

Mostly John wanted to be allowed to discover the character for himself, unguided by a director's preconceived notions of how a role should be played. Who, he wondered, was the director to tell him—the actor playing the character—how to feel? It seemed to cut off so many options.

And so, in late 1953, when he became too enthusiastic (and, more likely, attention-getting) as a background player on an episode of *Omnibus* and said what he thought about the approach of director Burgess Meredith, Cassavetes was fired. The kid may have been a good actor, but he had a big mouth.

At roughly the same time, Cassavetes signed with a new agent, William McCaffrey. Less than a week after signing him, McCaffrey had Cassavetes auditioning for a role at *Omnibus*; needless to say, Cassavetes had not mentioned his being fired from the series to McCaffrey. If he did, he soft-pedaled it in a way that didn't raise red flags to the veteran agent.

And so when Cassavetes turned up for the audition, the same producer who had fired him previously took one look at him and ordered him out. When McCaffrey asked him what had happened, Cassavetes confessed that there was bad blood with *Omnibus*, but he told McCaffrey that he knew he could do a good job there if he was just given a chance.

Omnibus was a program funded by the Ford Foundation, as part of a two-pronged approach to making TV an outlet of culture and education. These were the early, idealistic days, when TV still held out hope of being something more than a medium for selling laundry soap. The Ford Foundation's idea for public television eventually turned into PBS. And its idea for a commercial educational program turned out to be *Omnibus*, a live weekly show that featured science, music, film, and theater, including plays by the more prominent writers of the period. Running from 1952 to 1959, it was part of the golden age of live television drama that helped start John Cassavetes' acting career.

Budd Schulberg, son of producer and studio boss B. P. Schulberg, had been writing for movies for decades. His novels *What Makes Sammy Run* and *The Harder They Fall* were considered insider masterpieces to two very different worlds: the movies and boxing, Schulberg's two passions. And he was about to have his hottest streak: the movie scripts for *A Face in the Crowd* and *On the Waterfront*, for which he won the Oscar.

Schulberg wrote "Paso Doble," he said, "based on my having lived in Mexico from time to time. I heard a story of a great bullfighter whose son didn't want to follow him into the ring. He wasn't like his father. The whole story inspired me. The boy eventually was wounded in the ring, but not killed. I took it all the way."

The late Daniel Petrie, interviewed a few months before his death, recalled reading Schulberg's script and being moved by it. But as the director of the piece, he was perplexed about how to cast it.

"Finding a bullfighter was a difficult task," he said. "I couldn't find anybody unless I went to Mexico. The population was not the same as today, with all the Latino actors. The pickings were slim."

The *Omnibus* casting director told Petrie he had the perfect actor for him, but that he probably couldn't cast him. "I don't dare mention his name," he told Petrie, then proceeded to tell him Cassavetes' history with the show. The show's producer, Petrie was told, couldn't help but remember Cassavetes' name and face. Petrie insisted on knowing who the actor was and was told that he was the assistant stage manager of a Broadway play. "But you didn't hear that from me," the casting director added. Intrigued, Petrie called Cassavetes in for an audition.

Cassavetes impressed Petrie, who was a hot young TV director at the time. Here was an actor who brought exactly the intensity of feeling to the role that Petrie was looking for. He was young, he was handsome, and he read the part with a feeling that was impassioned but not overheated. Cassavetes *was* the bullfighter, with all the tragic charisma that Schulberg had written into the role. So Petrie gave him the part.

Before the end of the day, the show's producer had heard the news and came storming into Petrie's office, saying, "How dare you cast this bum?"

"He'll be great," Petrie replied.

"I just laid him off," the apoplectic producer continued. "Get rid of him."

But Petrie refused. Voices rose. Petrie finally offered an ultimatum: "If I can't cast him, I'll walk away from the whole thing." The producer acquiesced—and Cassavetes got the part.

"And this is the way you get started," Cassavetes later said. "Somebody stands up for you. Dan Petrie stood up for me."

Cassavetes started rehearsals, but as he recalled, "I didn't know what the hell I was doing. I'd never done anything and here was this wonderful part and I'm playing opposite Kim Stanley. And this producer was saying, 'This guy stinks. I don't want him here.'"

But Stanley, a veteran TV actress who was starring in the hit play *Picnic* on Broadway at the time, stood up for the young actor.

"Let this guy alone," she'd snap at the producer. "He's fine. He doesn't need your shit." Then she'd turn to the stricken Cassavetes and say, "Forget about him. Just look at me. Just concentrate on what we're doing. Forget about what they're saying.'"

It was a live presentation, which meant a week or ten days of rehearsal before putting it in front of cameras: "On the appointed hour, with fingers crossed, with Hail Marys said, you plugged in," Petrie said.

"Paso Doble," which lasted less than forty-five minutes, opened the *Omnibus* broadcast; it was a drama, set in an upscale bar in Mexico City. A pair of American tourists, the Harpers, stop in for a drink amid their tourist wanderings. As they relax, several boisterous locals come in and start talking about the disgrace in the local bullring. When the Harpers ask the bartender what the commotion is about, he tells them that a matador has had a crisis of confidence in the ring. Worse, this matador is Pepe Contreras, the son of one of the three greatest bullfighters currently fighting.

"He lost his nerve in the bullring—he cannot keep his feet still," the proprietor explains. "He put the sword in the lung instead of the heart. Bottles and fruit were thrown. He lost control and ran and jumped behind the barrier. Pepe Contreras—the best bullfighter in Mexico, if you take away the bull."

Almost as if bidden, Pepe himself (played by Cassavetes) enters the bar and sits alone, all too aware of the insults and snide comments being made by the aficionados at the bar. So Mrs. Harper (Kim Stanley) invites him to join them at their table: "A gentleman can never refuse the request of a lady," he says, sitting with them but obviously downhearted.

He says simply, "The devil has stolen my luck." He knows what the other denizens of the bar are saying about him, but he remains humble, open, and honest with the tourist couple, talking ruefully about the way he has disappointed his father's expectations: "I do not know if I'm brave or unbrave. I only know that I thought too long. Is the brave man the one who overcomes his fear—or the one who has no fear to overcome? I'm not stupid enough to be brave the way my father is brave."

Pepe and Mrs. Harper rapidly forge an emotional bond; there is genuine longing in the performances of Stanley and Cassavetes, when she realizes that he means to go back into the ring against a particularly dangerous bull, though he could easily die. She tries to offer alternatives, choices he could make that would preserve his life, if not necessarily his honor. He is grateful but unreceptive: "You worry about someone who is almost a stranger to you," he says.

Later she hears the news: Pepe has been killed in the ring. But his death carries a whiff of disgrace because he flinched from the bull before the bull killed him. When Pepe's father comes in, bemoaning the son's lack of courage but not his death, Mrs. Harper explodes at him, "Have you no feeling?"

"No," he replies. "I'm a Mexican. We have no feelings."

The performance drew glowing reviews in the trades, which got noticed by casting directors—because Cassavetes and McCaffery and Sam Shaw made sure they saw them. As much as he had been chasing success as an actor, he couldn't quite believe the immediate impact the performance triggered.

"The day after the show," Cassavetes recalled, "Twentieth Century Fox called my agent and asked, 'Who was that Mexican guy? Does he speak any English? We have a part for him'."

Within days Cassavetes had been suggested to Twentieth Century Fox as the perfect replacement for the lead role in the big-budget period picture *The Egyptian*, which cost $5 million. The story of a peasant who rises to become physician to the pharaoh Aknahton, it was set to star Marlon Brando, but he had walked out at the last minute.

Director Michael Curtiz went in the opposite direction. Rather than the red-hot Brando, he decided to make a star out of an unknown. So in short order, John was on a plane to Hollywood for the screen test.

How had Curtiz found him? Cassavetes had made a point of cultivating Hollywood columnist Hedda Hopper, writing her letters and flattering her, while winningly promoting his own career. She was among those who sang his praises most loudly for "Paso Doble," bringing him to the attention of Fox producers: "I suggested John Cassavetes, a young actor I'd seen on TV," she later wrote. "I met him, when he came to Hollywood for a test."

"Hedda was real big," recalled Seymour Cassel. "She and Louella [Parsons] and Ed Sullivan and Walter Winchell. They all wanted news from actors who were accessible to them. Hedda Hopper liked him and Gena. And John knew the value of publicity. Hedda would call John, or Gena would talk to Hedda."

After giving "Paso Doble" a positive review, *Variety* profiled Cassavetes, proclaiming him the "find of the year." The article reported that John was ready to dump his stage-managing job "if he gets Twentieth Fox's affirmative decision on a screen test made last Saturday on the Coast. Cass was rushed out there as a potential replacement for Marlon Brando in the latter's ankling of the lead in *The Egyptian*. Meanwhile, Columbia Pictures wants him for a test and he's being yenned by NBC's Samuel Chotzinoff for an upcoming opera in web's television series."

Instead of Cassavetes, Curtiz cast Edmund Purdom in *The Egyptian*. But Cassavetes was able to turn the experience into a positive one. In his studio bio for MGM a few years later, it was noted that he had not taken the role in *The Egyptian* because "he decided the role was not right for him. He returned to New York and gradually began getting roles on television."

Eight

TV Star

John Cassavetes and Gena Rowlands were married March 19, 1954, at the "Little Church Around the Corner" (the Church of the Transfiguration), at Twenty-ninth Street and Fifth Avenue.

The fact that they were both unemployed did nothing to spoil their happiness on their wedding day.

Actress Joyce van Patten remembered sitting at a table at the Cromwell Drugstore in Rockefeller Plaza, a hangout for young actors, when John and Gena came walking in with proof sheets of photos of their wedding (shot by Sam Shaw): "She was this raving beauty," van Patten said. "John was so proud of the woman he'd married."

The combination of "Paso Doble" and the publicity about *The Egyptian* turned John into the new actor of the moment, suddenly in demand by casting directors at all the live dramatic shows. He appeared in twenty-six shows in 1954, including *Kraft Television Theater*, *Philco Television Playhouse*, and *Armstrong Circle Theater*. He did another twenty-three in 1955—more than ninety, ultimately, before live television faded away.

Everett Chambers, a casting director at NBC in this period, remembered, "He was a very good actor. He had great intensity inside. There was always a motor going behind his eyes. He knew so much about a lot of things: baseball, jazz, the environment. But he told me he'd been kicked out of every school he'd been in."

"I did thirty-nine live shows in one year," Cassavetes recalled, referring to one consecutive twelve-month period—more shows than he would have done as the star of a series.

"He was getting famous," Burton Lane remembered. "That 'Paso Doble' got noticed and then he got jobs on TV."

"Paso Doble" director Daniel Petrie recalled, "His acting was so personal, where the others guys were conventional."

His parts included roles as a teenager, roles as a young adult—even a role in the TV opera *John the Baptist.* Not a singer, Cassavetes mouthed the lyrics while a trained tenor sang offscreen.

John Finnegan, who was making rounds while studying at the Actors Studio, found that, even when you worked regularly in TV, you had to have another job to make ends meet: "You'd get $50, $75—$100 if you were lucky. That was a lot of money in those days."

"It was easy to get something on TV," said actress Renee Taylor, a classmate of John's at the Academy. "It was easier to get on TV than to get to Broadway."

John himself sang television's praises in a 1955 interview, when he was at peak productivity on the small screen. "We feel we're very lucky to have this new medium to express ourselves," he said. "We're serious about our work but won't let it throw us. It's great and it's money and I don't mean to be materialistic—you've got to have it. TV is a great showcase, a melting pot for young people to pour out their talents and dreams for producers, thousands of miles away, to sit there and see you and maybe give you the break. There's been nothing like it in the history of the drama, for training or breaks. And there's relatively little typecasting. You can play all sorts of parts once you've established yourself."

And he did, including as a poor boy in love with a rich girl in *Winter Dreams,* an F. Scott Fitzgerald adaptation, and as a contemporary Raskolnikov in a modernization of *Crime and Punishment,* earning strong reviews and words of praise from his co-stars.

"He's a firecracker and exceedingly funny," said Dana Wynter, his co-star in *Winter Dreams.* "It's true, though, that he becomes terribly serious when he works. His concentration is enormous, his application tremendous. I found that, unlike actors who simply project their own personalities, John delivers a real performance."

His Raskolnikov earned him several glowing reviews. The *New York Journal American* said, "John Cassavetes, one of the most important young actors playing the realistic boards, was . . . amazing. Full of depth and tense, coiled emotional wallop like a taut steel spring ready to twang off to emotional explosions at any given moment."

At that point TV still had the sheen of respectability. It wasn't uncommon for a well-received TV drama to be expanded from an hour show into a feature film.

More important for John, he was not only acting in TV shows that jumped to the big screen, but unlike many other actors, he was making the leap with them. Where Robert Cummings and Franchot Tone had played leads in the TV version of *12 Angry Men*, their roles went to Henry Fonda and Lee J. Cobb in the movie. Rod Steiger played the title role in Paddy Chayefsky's *Marty* on television, but Ernest Borgnine won the Oscar for playing him in the film.

When *Crime in the Streets* took the move from *The Elgin Hour* to the big screen, Cassavetes and Mark Rydell, playing the main antagonists, made the transition to the cinematic version, with John being given an "And Introducing John Cassavetes" credit, even though he'd starred the year before in *The Night Holds Terror*.

On the other hand, when John was cast in *Edge of the City*, he took over the role from Don Murray, who played the character of the insecure army deserter in the TV version, "A Man Is Ten Feet Tall." (Murray, in turn, would later take the role of Johnny Pope, originated on Broadway by Ben Gazzara, in the film of *A Hatful of Rain*.)

Cassavetes was finding a niche playing hoods, juvenile delinquents, and other troubled young men. "He has that rare animal magnetism of a young Humphrey Bogart, combined with the languid tilted pelvis school of acting, like Marlon Brando and the late Jimmy Dean," wrote the *Sunday Mirror* in early 1956. "Cassavetes is electrifying in his enactment and brought to mind several actors who forged to stardom with initial impact roles."

"Those who have seen him act liken him to the late James Dean," *TV Guide* wrote in late 1957. "Those who have seen him away from his work liken him to Dean Martin. Those who know Cassavetes best liken him to no one anywhere. To them, he's John Cassavetes, boy individualist."

Gena continued to chase jobs, working mostly in small television roles during the early years of their marriage. "I was playing all kinds of parts in television plays in New York," she recalled, "from dumb blondes to smart career women, when Josh Logan's casting agent brought me the script of *Middle of the Night*.

Her good fortune resulted, at least in part, from John's own advances.

As his stock was rising in TV, thanks to McCaffery, John found himself looking expectantly toward the film world. He finagled a meeting with a movie agent, Martin Baum, and rather dramatically confronted Baum with his desire to act in movies. After a few minutes of chitchat, Baum said, "John, let me ask you—can you act?"

Even with a growing list of TV credits and solid notices, John still had to sell himself to yet another skeptical agent. So Cassavetes jumped up, grabbed Baum by the front of his shirt, then latched on to his tie, which was attached to the shirt by a tiepin. He ripped the tie loose from the shirt, ripped the buttons off Baum's shirt and said, "Can I act? Can I act? I can act!"

Baum was unnerved—but also impressed by this prospective client's obvious passion. He got on the phone to the head of casting at Columbia Pictures and landed him an audition.

As Baum worked with John, he also got to know Gena and gained an appreciation for her talent, understanding also that by keeping the wife working, he kept his client happy. So when he read the script for *Middle of the Night*, the first Broadway play by noted TV and film writer Paddy Chayefsky, he thought of it as an opportunity for Gena.

But he knew it would be a struggle because, at that point, she was still unknown. On the other hand, he also knew the play's director, the legendary Joshua Logan, who by that time had such hits as *Mister Roberts*, *Charley's Aunt*, and *South Pacific* to his credit. Baum and Logan had been army buddies and remained friends, even as they became business associates.

When Gena was cast in Reginald Rose's "The Expendable House" for *Goodyear Television Playhouse* in a small role opposite John, Baum decided he had to make sure Logan saw her performance. So Baum and his wife made the trek to Connecticut the day the show was to air, because Logan was hosting a cocktail party at his home there.

The party started to break up at 5, but the broadcast wasn't until 9—and Baum knew better than to leave things to chance. So he began to tell old army stories with Logan, getting himself invited to stay for dinner. Eventually he maneuvered them to Logan's playroom, turning on the TV and telling Logan, "You've got to watch *Ed Sullivan*; it's hilarious."

As Baum recalled, "It was the worst show Sullivan ever did. Josh was ready to kill me. But then the other show came on and there was Gena—and she was superb. The following day, she was invited to Josh's apartment to read. And she had a lead in a Broadway play with Edward G. Robinson, written by Paddy Chayefsky."

It was a major break: a high-visibility role in a script by a hot writer—
and featuring the first Broadway appearance by movie star Edward G.
Robinson in more than twenty-five years, since he left for Hollywood and
found stardom with *Little Caesar.*

The play cast Robinson as a middle-aged businessman, a widower
who meets a young woman and, to the surprise of his daughter and the
rest of his family, decides to marry her. Chayefsky already had a reputation
for writing realistic, emotional dramas for TV and films. The idea of an
older man and a much younger woman was still considered shocking, and
Chayefsky explored the taboo as forthrightly as he could for the times.

The director, Joshua Logan, was known as a domineering, dynamic
producer-director who expected actors to follow his vision, rather than
bring their own interpretation. He was also a man of drastically shifting
moods because of what was, only years later, diagnosed as bipolar disorder.

Anne Jackson, who played Robinson's daughter in the play, was warned
about Logan by her colleagues at the Actors Studio: "Actors Studio people
were inclined to think that you should work only with a Stanislavsky-
trained director," she recalled; as she learned, Logan had traveled to Moscow
while in college to study with Stanislavsky himself. "He directed in his own
way. He'd give line readings—but they were right."

Rowlands arrived at rehearsals, young and beautiful and well aware
that she was working with legends. The relatively green Rowlands did exactly as she was told by Logan, who molded a performance that struck
many as shrill and overheated.

When the play tried out in Philadelphia before it went to Broadway,
the critics there compared it to *Death of a Salesman*, because of its strong
drama built around family conflict. Jackson and Martin Balsam, who was
also in the cast, could only shake their heads: "Not that we were being dis-
loyal to Paddy, but we didn't think it was even close to *Salesman*," Jackson
remembered. "That play was a learning process for Paddy."

When it reached New York, *Middle of the Night* drew mixed reviews,
though the play ran for fifteen months. Robinson got the best notices,
while Chayefsky's were respectable. But many of the critics had harsh words
for Gena Rowlands.

George Jean Nathan wrote in the *New York Journal American*, "The girl
is a recruit from television and the nightclubs who resembles the currently
favored voluptuous taffy blondes of the films, telescreens and Broadway
cheesecake farces about Hollywood. Her name is Gena Rowlands and she
is the kind who still often mistakes vocal volume for emotional."

The *Saturday Review* allowed that "Gena Rowlands makes a striking

Betty, although she works with interior emotions to such an extent that we do not always feel that the intensity of her performance is justified."

Not all the response was negative. The *Times'* Brooks Atkinson said, "Gena Rowlands is especially good as the blonde involved in a situation that she does not know how to handle."

Critic Richard Watts was one of the only critics who pointed out that Rowlands' performance didn't occur in a vacuum, particularly given Logan's notoriously domineering approach. "I'm not sure whether its chief flaw, the characterization of the girl, is the responsibility of actress Gena Rowlands or director Joshua Logan," Watts wrote in the *Post.* "But since Miss Rowlands is a newcomer, here playing her first major role, and Mr. Logan is a brilliant and authoritative director, I doubt if she would have conceived the part as she does without his approval."

The day after the reviews came out, Logan marched into the theater, called the actors together, and took the blame for Rowlands' notices: "It's all my fault," he said. Then he rehearsed the cast anew, offering Rowlands new ideas for how to re-size her performance.

"What I admired was her professionalism," Jackson said. "She was quite a young woman with the lead in a Broadway play. But she forged her way through. She started giving a good performance."

Nine

Movie Star

"John Cassavetes . . . turns out to be, seen in person, the antithesis of tough," begins a 1955 Columbia Pictures press kit bio. "He's a mild-mannered twenty-five-year-old on the inhibited side. His lively enthusiasms are equally divided between acting, writing and producing . . . His eventual goal is to write, produce and act in his own plays or film scenarios . . . Cassavetes, 5–10, weight 155, would seem to be a young actor—plus—a young actor with a high potential for becoming a triple threat in the entertainment world."

Cassavetes, 5-foot-7 on his tallest day, cashed in the capital he accrued as a TV actor to become a movie star. Even as he continued to rack up TV credits, he breezed through a handful of films between 1955 and 1957 that created his movie persona without confining him to a single type of role. The movie work also allowed him to slow the frantic pace of his TV work, to become more selective in the roles he chose.

"When you start out, you don't have ethics," he said. "You just have a hunger. I must have done 9,000 bad shows."

"He was one of a new breed," said Peter Bogdanovich. "He was thought of that way as an actor. He was a legend in New York in the Fifties."

Cassavetes seemed to get better with each film—and seemed to pick movies that were not just compelling properties to act in but that became audience hits. Films such as *Crime in the Streets* and *Edge of the City* provided a gritty, New York-flavored alternative to the safely suburban vision of Eisenhower's America that television was offering.

Coming off "Paso Doble" and several other TV shows, including the TV version of "Crime in the Streets," Cassavetes took on the role of the ringleader in a kidnap plot that drives the story of *The Night Holds Terror.* Martin Baum, the agent whom Cassavetes had assaulted to convince of his seriousness, was asked by the film's casting director whether his new client had the intensity to handle the role of this chilly psychopath. "Intensity?" Baum replied. "He tore my shirt off. That's pretty intense."

The Night Holds Terror was based on a true case of a trio of criminals who kidnapped a man and his family and forced him to come up with a ransom. The same case was also the basis of the play *The Desperate Hours,* which opened in February 1955 on Broadway. The film version of *The Desperate Hours,* which starred Humphrey Bogart and Frederic March, was released in October 1955, but *The Night Holds Terror,* the cheaper copy, hit theaters first in July.

The film was written and directed by Andrew Stone, a journeyman who had been directing since the late 1920s; his greatest claim to fame was 1943's *Stormy Weather,* with Lena Horne and every other prominent African-American performer of the period. A B-movie director who worked for several of the studios, by the 1950s he was directing films with titles like *Highway 301* and *Confidence Girls,* starring fading actors like Eddie Bracken and Joseph Cotten.

The Night Holds Terror was low-budget all the way. Made for $70,000, its biggest star was Jack Kelly, who had been working (if unremarkably) in films for a few years. Otherwise, it was a no-name cast: Cassavetes (who, at least, had a TV following), Vince Edwards, Hildy Parks, and David Cross.

In the film, Kelly played Gene Courtier, a California businessman who stops to pick up a hitchhiker and winds up kidnapped by a trio of criminals: Robert Batsford (Cassavetes) and his henchmen Victor Gosset (Edwards) and Luther Logan (Cross). They've grabbed Courtier at random and, before they are finished, have kidnapped his wife (Parks) and their two children as well.

Cassavetes, barely twenty-five, lean and piercing, was the mastermind, who had to control the swaggering Gosset and the weakling Logan. As Gosset, Edwards pushed the limits of the production code with his leering, suggestive approaches to Parks, as Courtier's wife. Cassavetes is forced to talk about just how cold-blooded he's prepared to be far too often to be believable. But with his laser-like stare and tensely coiled physicality, he seemed credible controlling the much-taller Edwards, even if John looked a little unlikely wandering the couple's house while wearing the business-man's silk dressing gown.

Cassavetes made Batsford chilly, reptilian—a quality that only softens to mildly sadistic glee, as he casually threatens to kill Courtier's wife. Direc-tor Peter Bogdanovich, who later became a friend of Cassavetes, saw the film as a teen-ager and thought the actor looked like "a psychotic Jerry Lewis."

The timing of the film's July 1955 release led *Time* magazine to write that it "may well cut the ground from under the Broadway hit *The Desper-ate Hours*. What emerges is a surprisingly good movie."

Variety observed that the cast, "while offering nothing for the mar-quees, plays assignments to the hilt." *Newsweek* singled out Cassavetes, saying, "The slender, sharp-featured newcomer Cassavetes plays the sadis-tic leader of the hitchhikers. He does his terrorizing with a cool sureness, exercising a commendable restraint but making the fiend show through."

Cassavetes became the key element in transferring *Crime in the Streets* from the version that aired on *The Elgin Hour* on February 8, 1955. The TV production, written by Reginald Rose, had been directed by a newcomer, Sidney Lumet, and, beside Cassavetes and Mark Rydell, starred Robert Pre-ston, as the social worker trying to stop a murderous street punk from killing a man and ruining his own life. But when it was expanded from sixty minutes to ninety minutes for the big screen, Lumet was replaced by veteran Don Siegel, who used James Whitmore (Robert Preston was work-ing on Broadway) but kept Cassavetes and Rydell, and added rising teen star Sal Mineo to the cast.

Juvenile delinquency was a hot-button issue of the period, repre-sented in films as diverse as *The Blackboard Jungle*, *The Wild One*, and *Rebel Without a Cause*. As always, the responses to the social problem ran to both sides of the spectrum: from the conservative notion that these trou-blesome kids should be punished until they straightened out, to the lib-eral idea that delinquency was a symptom of some other dysfunction that should be examined and treated.

Crime in the Streets, despite its lurid title, fell into the latter category. Cas-savetes played Frankie Dane, the leader of a gang of teen hoodlums on one Hell's Kitchen block, who rumble with another gang under the opening credits. Frankie lives with his mother and young brother but barely engages with them; instead he burns with anger at the world's unfairness and lashes out at it by having his gang (which includes Rydell as the twitchy, giggly Lou and Mineo as the aptly named Baby) terrorize everyone else on the block. When one of the street's residents, a middle-aged man, rats on one of the gang members, Frankie vows to kill the man and sets in motion a plot involving his gang. But the local social worker (Whitmore) gets wind of the plot and tries to reason with Frankie, to no avail. It is only at the final moment—when Frankie's young brother pleads with him not to commit the murder—that Frankie takes a step toward a different kind of life.

Filmmaker Martin Scorsese remembered seeing the film and recognizing the milieu—tough streets, dominated by gangs of hoodlums—as well as the Hollywood license that was taken: "He had a gang of guys wearing those satin jackets," Scorsese said. "Where I came from with organized crime, you didn't wear jackets. The idea was not to be noticed."

Newsweek said the film "delivers the artistic shock treatment of a brass-knuckled uppercut." *Time* magazine, on the other hand, called it "a fairly serious little sociological thriller that is flawed by a streak of what might be called sentenement-ality: the idea that every garbage can has a silver lining." Though the *New York Herald Tribune* said Cassavetes "plays the bitter youth with taut conviction," *Time* joked that his acting style made him look "as if his name were Marlon Sinatra."

But Mark Rydell remembered, "He was thrust into lead roles in the movies from the start. He could have been a really big movie star because he had a certain magic, a danger as a leading man. He was dangerous and unpredictable. That's an absolutely bankable quality, when you can feel somebody's danger. But that wasn't enough for him."

And Budd Schulberg said, "When you looked at Dean, you couldn't help but think of Brando. Brando put such a stamp on the time. But you wouldn't think that of Cassavetes. He had his own thing, which was special. You didn't compare him to anybody."

Cassavetes continued to pile up TV credits, even as his films began to hit theaters. His sudden visibility—combined with his friendship with Sam Shaw—got him an introduction to director Robert Rossen, only recently off Hollywood's blacklist. Rossen, in preproduction for his film *Alexander the Great*, screen-tested Cassavetes, but wound up casting Richard Burton instead.

Cassavetes found that some of his roles had already made a lasting impression, at least on other directors. "I've been looking for a play on Broadway," he said. "I want to do something that I can do well. But I've been typed. The only things I've been offered are little gangsters."

Not that Cassavetes accepted the idea that he was portraying anything in particular: "I'm not a torn-shirt actor," he said in 1957. "People have mistaken me for an intense, troubled specimen of modern American youth because during my first two years in television, I invariably had a knife in my hand. The fact is, I'm not a delinquent and I never have been."

A friend at the time told a reporter, "John has set very high standards for himself—and on these he won't compromise. He's turned down many lucrative offers because he felt it would be compromising to accept them, yet he gladly made *The Night Holds Terror*, which was budgeted at only $70,000—and that's a quickie by Hollywood standards—because he liked the script. Essentially, he is just a regular New York kid who's taken the usual hard knocks."

Edge of the City seemed at least a partial step in a new direction. Written by Robert Alan Aurthur, it had been produced as "A Man Is Ten Feet Tall" for *Philco Television Playhouse* in October 1955. A seeming knock-off of *On the Waterfront*, dealing with corruption and racism in the freight yards of New York, it was picked up for big-screen treatment, with newcomer Martin Ritt (until then a TV and theater director) at the helm. Sidney Poitier was the sole actor to transfer from the TV production; the producers were looking for someone other than Don Murray to play the film's central character, Alex North, a troubled Army deserter tormented by his relationship with his father and the accidental death of his brother, for which he blamed himself.

It wasn't a hoodlum role; it called for emotional availability but not the kind of laser-like sharpness that Cassavetes had shown in his first films. So director Ritt and producer David Susskind were dubious when agent Martin Baum suggested his client, Cassavetes, for the role. Ritt agreed to let Cassavetes read for the role opposite Poitier but wanted to see if the pair had real chemistry. So he told Baum, "I don't want them to rehearse first—I want the audition to be spontaneous."

"Don't worry," Baum replied. "We'll do it just the way you want."

Baum's first call was to Cassavetes; his second was to Poitier, who also happened to be his client. He introduced the two actors and, for the next two days, had them rehearse the scenes that Cassavetes would be reading at the audition.

At the reading, the two actors clicked instantly; they had a rapport that seemed spontaneous and unforced, a cohesion that couldn't be acted, and a grasp of the characters' relationship that seemed to go beyond the script.

"This is sensational," Ritt said, afraid to trust his luck that he'd found someone who could hold his own with Poitier in a cold read.

"And it's unrehearsed—guaranteed," Baum helpfully lied. And Cassavetes was offered the role.

Poitier recalled Cassavetes as "eccentric in every way, but most especially in the creative area. He was very gifted, very talented—but eccentric. But he came from a real place. He hit fewer false notes than most actors I worked with. That's my greatest compliment."

Cassavetes' paycheck for *Edge of the City* was $15,000, which was several times what he had earned annually only a couple of years earlier.

In the film, Cassavetes plays Axel North (née Nordmann), who arrives in Manhattan on the run, as it turns out, from the army, from which he has deserted. A friend has given him an 'in' at a local freightyard, where the corrupt boss Charlie Malik (Jack Warden) gives him a job in exchange for a percentage of his pay—a rake-off he takes from everyone he hires. But Axel angers Malik by befriending Tommy Tyler (Poitier), a sub-boss who is the subject of Malik's racist hatred.

Tommy helps draw Axel out of his shell, taking him home to meet his wife and fixing him up on a date. Axel eventually confesses that he was driving the car when his brother died in an accident and his father blames him for his brother's death—and that's why Axel ran away from home to join the army. Now he's deserted from the army; on the run, he hopes to make a new start working at the shipping yard.

The two become best friends, which further infuriates Malik. After a series of confrontations, Malik attacks Tommy; they fight with shipping hooks and Malik kills Tommy. Axel, at first intimidated into not speaking to the police, confronts Malik, beats him and goes to tell the police how Tommy died and, one assumes, to turn himself in to pay his debt to society.

Edge of the City drew inevitable comparisons to *On the Waterfront*, the seminal 1954 film about working men battling labor corruption, but got mixed-to-positive reviews, both for its story and for Cassavetes' performance: "John Cassavetes gives an excellent portrayal of a mixed-up guy," Dorothy Masters wrote in the *New York Daily News,* while Archer Winsten, who would become a friend and champion of Cassavetes' work, referred to Cassavetes' "sense of personal doom and fear" in observing that "both Poitier and Cassavetes bring assurance to the acting of their contrasting roles."

On the other hand, *Time* magazine wondered "why so engaging a Negro would waste time on so boringly primitive a white man." And Arthur Knight wrote in *Saturday Review* that, in Cassavetes' performance, "the image of Brando seems to hover over his every move and gesture and incoherent word."

The film was notable for its matter-of-fact treatment of the races. It was bold to depict overt racism in the mid-1950s, before the civil-rights movement really found its voice. It was even bolder to have an interracial pair of best friends without ever commenting upon it. It was rare to show a positive relationship between blacks and whites in a Hollywood film, unless the movie's theme specifically was brotherhood or interracial relationships.

Brendan Gill, writing in *The New Yorker*, called the film "a worthy attempt to demonstrate, in low-pitched dialogue laced with the shrilling of melodrama, that the color barrier is not insurmountable." Bosley Crowther, writing in the *Times*, compared it to *Casablanca* in that regard: "There have been few films from that far-off day to this that have treated friendship between Negroes and whites as naturally as [*Casablanca*] did. This may be why the little picture *Edge of the City* seems particularly forthright and unusual in handling such a friendship on the screen."

Having spent his adolescence in all-white Port Washington and at mostly white colleges in upstate New York, Cassavetes brought a natural curiosity to his friendship with Poitier. It's hard to say for certain whether his work with Poitier triggered or merely highlighted Cassavetes' fascination with race relations and his level-headed approach to the subject. But it's not hard to make a connection between his work with Poitier—on both *Edge of the City* and the subsequent *Virgin Island*—and the themes he would explore just a couple of years later in *Shadows*.

Ten

The Next Level

By the end of 1956 Gena was enjoying success on Broadway and a steady stream of movie scripts was rolling in for John. But the pickings seemed to be exceedingly slim in terms of substantial work to choose from.

Critics of the time lamented the doldrums into which Hollywood had fallen, bemoaning the promise that movies squandered by trying to reach an ever broader audience with the same watered-down melodramas.

"The bigger productions often look like a compendium of the worst filmic crimes of the past, achieving a really massive staleness," Pauline Kael wrote at the beginning of that year about the state of Hollywood films. "The wide screen and the rediscovery of Christianity have restored films to their second childhood. In the thirties, we thought Cecil B. De-Mille passé; the American film of 1955 represents his full triumph."

"There might have been good movies if there had been no movie industry," producer David O. Selznick told writer Ben Hecht. "Hollywood might have become the center of a new human expression if it hadn't been grabbed by a little group of bookkeepers and turned into a junk industry."

The movies Cassavetes was being offered were mostly insubstantial potboilers, nothing that would build upon *Edge of the City*, which was seen as an important film. The movie scripts were mundane or just silly; meanwhile, television was moving away from quality live dramatic offerings in favor of situation comedies, cop shows, and westerns, filmed series that were more easily packaged and marketed than the weekly omnibus theater form. It had been hoped that TV could be a true form of entertainment for the masses, with a little something for everyone. Instead, commercial interests transformed it into mass entertainment, with only those things that were thought to appeal to everyone.

By 1958 TV's brief golden age was virtually over: "Television drama, live television drama in the hour or longer form, is almost extinct today," producer David Susskind said on his show *Open End*, in a discussion with TV writers Tad Mosel, Robert Alan Aurthur, and Paddy Chayefsky. And as Aurthur put it on the same show, "We did not abandon television. Television left us."

But Cassavetes knew he had to keep working. For one thing, that was what an actor did; for another, he and Gena now had a penthouse apartment on East Seventy-fifth Street just off Fifth Avenue, with a small roof garden ("Maybe I could get a couple of tons of earth up on this roof and raise our own vegetables," he suggested to one reporter).

Though he talked about wanting to do Broadway, he couldn't resist the movie offers that came with increasingly substantial paychecks; his quote was $25,000 a picture. So he played a gigolo in *Affair in Havana*, opposite Raymond Burr and Sara Shane—and got a trip to Havana out of the bargain.

In the film, he plays Nick, a nightclub pianist who has been having an affair with Lorna (Shane), the wife of a rich man named Mallabee (Burr). (Cassavetes would lift the name Mallabee and use it for a female character at the end of *Husbands*.)

Mallabee, an international industrialist who lives in the countryside outside Havana, is a paraplegic, confined to a wheelchair. Unbeknownst to his wife, Mallabee knows who her lover is. So he makes sure he and his wife have dinner at the restaurant where Nick is playing, then invites the pianist to the table to compliment him (and watch his interaction with Nora). Mallabee invites Nick to come visit them on their plantation, plotting how he will trap his wife into confessing her infidelity. The plot takes a bizarre turn when one of the servants on the plantation turns out to have an obsessive crush on Lorna as well and winds up killing Mallabee himself. The servant's wife is so jealous that she stabs Lorna to death before anyone can stop her. And Nick, seemingly unfazed and unscathed, winds up back at the Havana nightclub, still playing his gig.

Once Cassavetes got to Cuba and saw what the script was—and recognized that he was the biggest star in the cast—he demanded revisions, then phoned an old AADA friend, Burton Lane, to come to Cuba and do the rewrites.

When Lane arrived, they were shooting scenes at the airport, where Mallabee returns from a trip to Florida: "Castro was coming, but I didn't know it," Lane recalled, referring to the metastasizing revolution that Fidel Castro was leading against Fulgencio Batista.

The film's original writer, Maurice Zimm, was still in Havana, apparently unaware that Lane had been brought in to rewrite him. So Zimm labored away on the script that wasn't being used (though he would receive the credit), which Lane rewrote in another hotel room, as the crew sat on location waiting to shoot.

One day Lane heard Cassavetes blow up while filming a scene. "This is no good," Cassavetes said angrily. "Let's move it to the beach." When someone protested that it couldn't be done, Cassavetes piped up, "I'll take responsibility."

So the flustered producer and director, a journeyman named Laszlo Benedek whose credits included *The Wild One* and *Death of a Salesman*, scrambled to shift the shot to a beach location. Meanwhile, Cassavetes shot Lane a smile, as if to say, "Can you believe they really think I'm angry?"

Later Cassavetes admitted that, as a movie, *Affair* "just didn't come off—but things there were agreeable. Making the movie is the important thing. What happens afterward is interesting but not stimulating: whether it gets good publicity and good press reception. Actually being creative in it is what counts most."

But his star was rising enough that MGM signed him to a three-picture deal. First up: a western, *Saddle the Wind*, that teamed Cassavetes with Robert Taylor, Julie London, and Donald Crisp. After a run of urban characters, Cassavetes, the most New York of actors, had to play a cowboy, a role for which he had to learn to handle a gun and ride a horse.

The film was written by Rod Serling, a veteran and much-respected TV writer who had written *Requiem for a Heavyweight* and would go on to make his mark with *The Twilight Zone*. The script centered on Steve Sinclair (Taylor), a former gunslinger who has put his past behind him and settled down as a rancher. But his life is disrupted by the appearance of his younger brother Tony, played by Cassavetes. Wild and impulsive, Tony returns home complete with a new bride, a former prostitute named Joan (London). Even as Steve tries to serve as enforcer for the area's biggest land owner, Deneen (Donald Crisp), and keep settlers from putting down stakes on their range land, Tony decides to take a run at Steve's reputation as a quick-gun killer—and kills a man, though arguably in self-defense, but in a fight he provoked. Tony runs afoul of Deneen and even shoots him, jeopardizing everything Steve has worked for. It leads to a final show-down between Steve and Tony, but before Steve can shoot him, Tony shoots himself.

In the film Cassavetes is loose and wild, a young man with poor im-pulse control who seems all jacked up on youthful hormones and blood-lust. His trigger-happy immaturity and outsized passion give the performance an energy that jolts the stolid western to life whenever Tony shows up to misbehave.

Richard Erdman, who played Tony's drunken sidekick, a saddle tramp named Dallas Hanson, remembered Cassavetes arriving in Colorado full of New York attitude about working in Hollywood.

"He was a terrific pain in the ass in the beginning," Erdman recalled. "He'd come out from New York. The director was Robert Parrish and John was pretty defiant, kind of paranoid about Hollywood. He was pretty dis-tant until about halfway through."

What set Cassavetes and Parrish at cross purposes was Tony's death scene, which was filmed early in the production. Parrish had his location picked out, but while driving to it, Cassavetes spotted a field of wildflow-ers and declared that this was where he wanted to do the scene. Parrish de-cided it would be impractical.

In retaliation, Erdman remembered, Cassavetes stretched out a track-ing shot on horseback to almost twenty takes by mumbling or otherwise refusing to play the scene. Eventually the scene was cut.

There were also disagreements about the fateful encounter between Tony and Deneen, in which Tony shot the older rancher in cold blood.

"Nobody can kill lovable old Donald Crisp in the movies," Cassavetes said later with a certain sarcasm. "I knew because I tried it. In *Saddle the Wind*, I ride up and blast him—but we did it over. When the original scene was shot, everyone thought it was too vicious and Crisp too sweet a guy to die. Director Robert Parrish agreed and we did it over so that Donald would recover from the wound."

The reviews were mixed, though Cassavetes drew his share of atten-tion, good and bad.

"One of the distinctions of *Saddle the Wind* is a spitfire, whirlwind per-formance by John Cassavetes," the *New York World Telegram and Sun* wrote. "He is bursting with ferocity and defiance, a raging and laughing scourge. This young actor certainly has soared rapidly from his small movie begin-nings only a couple of years ago." The *New York Herald Tribune* hailed his "excellent performance as the unpredictable, treacherous, ambitious young brother."

Newsweek, on the other hand, said that "Cassavetes, who talks and looks about as Western as a member of the switchblade set, turns out to be a roamer—a prairie delinquent perpetually on the prowl for a range rumble." *Time* followed a similar tack, referring to Cassavetes, as "a Stanislavsky-type buckaroo who looks sort of lost in all those wide-open spaces."

Cassavetes returned from Colorado and almost immediately packed up Gena and headed for the Virgin Islands, where he was to reunite with Sidney Poitier for a trifle called variously *Virgin Island* and *Our Virgin Island.*

Virgin Island was a mannered British comedy in which Cassavetes and newcomer Virginia Maskell play two young people who meet, fall in love, and marry in the space of a couple of days, then take off for a small uninhabited island, where they hope to charter a society of their own.

"A happy go lucky pick whose atmosphere compensates for a slim story," *Variety* said. "Two sparkling performances by John Cassavetes and Sidney Poitier will stimulate U.S. interest in this amiable entertainment."

It's hard to know how much more amiable it might have been. The script was written by Ian Hunter and Ring Lardner Jr., under a pseudonym. They'd done rewrites that had been shown to Cassavetes and Poitier to secure their participation. But by the time they all arrived in the Caribbean, there was a new "final shooting script" that had been considerably changed. Recalled Lardner, "It had the added defect of being, in our opinion, not nearly as good. Sidney Poitier told me later that he and John Cassavetes shared our disappointment in the new one."

The location shooting was mostly a vacation for Cassavetes, who had worked almost nonstop in films and TV for the better part of two straight years. But he didn't feel as though he was growing as an actor—or being allowed to grow—because the technical demands of movie-making seemed to render the actual acting an afterthought, or so Cassavetes felt. By the time an actor learned where his mark and his key light were, any spontaneity in the performance had drained out of it because the actor was so aware of having to meet the camera's demands.

While on location, co-star Ruby Dee would have late-night discussions with Cassavetes, in which he encouraged her to think about making films of her own. He was, he said, already caught up in a project that he was extremely excited about.

"He was always encouraging me to make a film," Dee remembered. "He gave me my first movie camera, a 16mm Bolex wind-up, with a light meter and books on the subject. John seemed to believe that I would have been a good filmmaker."

His encouragement meant a lot to the young black actress, who had been working with husband Ossie Davis at the American Negro Theater. Though she was critically acclaimed for her theater work, at that moment in Hollywood history her movie work was limited to servant roles—though she had played wife roles opposite Poitier in both *Edge of the City* and *Virgin Island*.

"Being black, you're trying not to buy into a system that excludes you," Dee explained. "When you sneak through a crack, you wear the scars of the scraping. That deep-down belief in my future—it didn't exist for me. But John was an encourager. He would praise me as a performer and he talked to me so much about my making my own films. 'Ruby, you can do it,' he'd tell me. He saw a capacity in me that I didn't see in myself."

As Cassavetes talked about his own ideas and plans, Dee could feel that this was more than just idle fantasizing, that Cassavetes was already operating on several levels at once. "I always felt he was a very aware human being, but not in obvious ways. He was a subtle man. You could see the thoughts bubble up before he laughed," Dee said. "He was a great member of what I call the human symphony, with the intangibles of triple-track thinking. He exemplified to me the complicated process of thinking, how as actors we walk on one track when we need to be dancing on three or four at the same time. The complexity and beauty and symphony of thought: so many things contribute to the moment. And Cassavetes epitomized that."

Part Two

Cameras do not make films; filmmakers make films. The most important part of your equipment is yourself: your mobile body, your imaginative mind and your freedom to use both.

—MAYA DEREN

The underground film is a medium of and for the individual, as explorer and artist.

—SHELDON RENAN

I'm a great believer in spontaneity because I think planning is the most destructive thing in the world.

—JOHN CASSAVETES

Eleven

The Workshop

As 1957 dawned, success had John Cassavetes bored and restless. He had climbed to the top of the TV ladder, then made the transition to movies seemingly effortlessly—and found that, once the initial excitement of landing the well-paying roles wore off, the work itself offered far less creative input from him, the actor, than he had hoped.

As much as he'd enjoyed working with Sidney Poitier and Martin Ritt on *Edge of the City*, he had bristled at the distractions for the actors: the makeup and costumes, the lighting and blocking, the total absence of room for a spontaneous creative moment.

Gena was still working in *Middle of the Night*, but Cassavetes was between pictures. He did a short tour of Connecticut with Tennessee Williams' *27 Wagons Full of Cotton*, but found that theater wasn't the answer, either. He'd felt, in fact, that theater was even more restrictive: the same blocking night after night, the same character, the tedium of repetition, the inflexibility toward sudden inspiration onstage. TV and movies were paying the rent, but John was looking for something more, though he wasn't quite sure what.

"I was working all the time in the early days of television," he recalled. "I had quite a good start. But my friends were miserable. I was making money for the first time and trying to get them jobs on the shows I was on."

The problem was that there was no place for his friends to showcase themselves, so that producers, agents, and casting directors might see them work. In the days before videotape, if you weren't performing, you weren't being seen. Cassavetes, after being egged on by friend Maurice McEndree, another would-be actor, thought he had a solution for that.

He would rent a big studio with a stage and create a performance space where actors could perform scenes and invite casting directors, writers, directors, and producers to see them.

The studio they found was on the main floor of the Variety Arts building, at 225 West Forty-sixth Street between Broadway and Eighth Avenue. The building was full of rehearsal studios, with actors and dancers trooping in and out of the building all day long.

"It was the greatest place in the world, all these floors of rehearsal halls," recalled Seymour Cassel. "Bob Fosse rehearsed there, so there were all these girls."

Except for one thing, Cassavetes said: "No one showed up. None of these friends came to work there." Cassavetes was desperate. He had the space on a year's lease at considerable rent. So he and McEndree decided just to open the doors and invite anybody who wanted to, to come in. Cassavetes took ads in *Show Business,* the *New York Times,* the *Daily News,* and the *Mirror,* saying that anybody who wanted to work as an actor could come to this studio.

"The next day, the studio was full of amateurs, people off the streets, pickpockets, lawyers, bankers, policemen, students who had come there to work," Cassavetes said. "All they had was a desire to be actors, and very few had any experience whatsoever, hadn't had a part as an extra or maybe not even seen a camera before. So we worked every evening there."

But having created his own workshop, Cassavetes found himself on the hook to actually conduct classes. McEndree was fine as a businessman and manager for the workshop, but he wasn't a teacher. Cassavetes himself didn't have the time to work with all the people who were interested. On the other hand, he was charging less than $10 a person—sometimes as little as $2 or $3, called "dues"—and still had a large monthly rent payment to meet, so he needed as many "dues" as he could collect.

As he and McEndree were trying to figure out how to make the workshop work, John ran into Burton Lane on the street—someone he hadn't spoken to in a couple of years after they'd fallen out over a script they had written together.

Lane had been a classmate of Gena Rowlands at AADA and had been friendly with both Rowlands and Cassavetes. After school, he had enlisted in the armed forces and had looked John and Gena up when he came back two years later. John, encouraged by his experience working with Edward McSorley, convinced Lane that the two of them should write a script together.

"We spent thirty weekends writing a script based on a book about Belmonte, the bullfighter," Cassavetes remembered. "But when we finished it, Burt and I disagreed about one scene and nothing—screaming fist fights, you name it—could get us to resolve the situation. So to show our manhood, we threw the script away. We both felt it would demonstrate that we had the confidence and ability to write again."

When Lane ran into Cassavetes on the street John treated him like a long-lost brother. When he found out that Lane was working in advertising, Cassavetes was shocked. How could Lane even consider working for an ad agency? He was too good an actor, Cassavetes insisted, too good a writer, too good a teacher not to be working with other actors and changing the face of theater in New York. And Cassavetes had just the right situation for him. "Why don't you teach?" Cassavetes said. "You know more about acting and writing than anybody in the world."

And so he sold Lane on the concept of them jointly running the workshop, with McEndree as administrator. Lane found himself swept into Cassavetes' enthusiastic vision by John's mixture of seduction and flattery.

"John had been doing this workshop," Lane recalled. "It was this old place, decrepit, but there was room for a theater and an office. We built it into the workshop, with a soundproof theater where only people we invited could come. People paid dues. It was really a theatrical environment. It was the Cassavetes–Lane Theater Workshop. He got top billing. At tops, we had twenty, forty, maybe sixty members. We had beginning, intermediate, and advanced acting classes. I was doing it like a school."

To John, the school would be philosophically contrary to everything he knew about the Actors Studio's approach. They would stress what he referred to as "the heroics of acting," he said. "Heroes have been forgotten—nowadays everyone wants to play the schmo. We don't allow negativism of any kind. A student doesn't attack another's work. Our school is not for psychoanalysis or airing personal problems. It's a time and place for work and creative happiness."

Though his was the box-office name that attracted the dozens of students and actors who signed up for the workshop, John didn't set himself up as the guru. He was, as always, just John—an inquiring mind with more questions and insights than anyone else.

"I could have gone every night and sat in on John's class," Meta Shaw

Stevens recalled. "I was crazy about him. He had energy like I never saw before. I remember going out on Eighth Avenue and doing scenes."

Once he got the workshop off the ground, Cassavetes had to face the realities of his career. Though he loved spending his evenings with other actors—analyzing scenes, acting them out, discussing how to attack the material—the fact was that he had signed on for two movies (*Saddle the Wind* and *Virgin Island*) and that when he wasn't away on location, he would probably be in a TV studio somewhere, rehearsing or performing.

"John was hardly ever there," Lane recalled. "He was always doing a project. He went away to do film and TV shows. He couldn't have an ongoing class in a regular way. Meanwhile, I was barely subsisting." Lane's students recall him with great fondness as a strong teacher who helped clarify the acting process through scene work and vocal and relaxation exercises.

In Lane's class, Meta Shaw Stevens recalled, "You would do a monologue or a scene with a partner. Sometimes Burt would tell you, 'I want you to do this and then talk about the pros and cons of what you did.' He was fabulous, an incredible teacher with terrific insight. He was so generous and kind to me. I was probably the youngest person in the class and I had no experience."

By contrast, she recalled, the classes would erupt when Cassavetes would make an appearance: "John would burst in and run up on the stage and scream or yell or do a flip and then go out," she said. "At first, I thought, This is a crazy man. He had a way of calling people's energy up and getting a performance. If he thought your energy level was down, he had a way of getting you back up again."

"I'm watching the actors in his class and thinking, 'They're not very good,'" recalled Lelia Goldoni, an eighteen-year-old from California on her own in New York. "They were doing scenes from various plays, where the psychology was clear. And I didn't think they were all that hot for New York actors."

Cassavetes, however, "was absolutely fascinating in class," Goldoni said. "He had this extraordinary energy. Some people would call it charisma but, when you know something about John, it was beyond charisma. He was like a gigantic energy machine."

In one acting class, Goldoni was doing a monologue from Oscar Wilde's *Salome*, in a scene that included Hugh Hurd and Ben Carruthers, who would be her eventual castmates in *Shadows*. At the end of the scene, Cassavetes, referring to John the Baptist, asked Goldoni, "What do you want? Why do you want his head?"

Goldoni thought about it, then said, "Because he wouldn't kiss me."

"Oh yeah?" Cassavetes challenged. "Well, try and kiss me."

The acting exercise quickly turned into a fight, with Goldoni and Cassavetes wrestling onstage, pulling hair, squealing and grunting with effort and pain in what seemed like a genuine struggle. Finally, Cassavetes, his alligator smile beaming, stopped the action and said to Goldoni, "Now, do the scene."

And the scene was completely different in a very substantial way, with Goldoni more clearly in touch with the physical anger of a woman scorned.

Twelve

Origins of *Shadows*

S eymour Cassel arrived in New York at the age of twenty-one, fresh out of the navy and convinced, after stabs at college and various kinds of manual labor, that he wanted to be an actor.

After kicking around for a month or so, he spotted an ad in *Backstage* offering scholarships for acting classes led by John Cassavetes. Cassel knew who Cassavetes was; he'd seen him on TV and in *Edge of the City* and *Crime in the Streets*. Scholarships meant free acting classes—with a big star. What was there to lose?

So he wandered into the Variety Arts, where he saw Cassavetes sitting by himself studying a script. Never shy, Cassel approached him and asked him about the scholarships. He didn't get the subsidy, but he wound up as a lifelong friend, collaborator, and alter ego of Cassavetes, one of the signature actors of Cassavetes' films from the beginning to the end of Cassavetes' career.

Show business, certainly, was in Cassel's blood. Born in Detroit in 1935 to a dancer on the Minsky burlesque circuit, young Seymour never knew his father. He lived with his mother, whose stage name was Ann Sullivan; they traveled by train as part of a troupe of sixty, moving from city to city, hotel to hotel. Seymour grew up backstage around the other dancers, the comedians, and the specialty acts. By the time he was six, he realized later, he'd seen more naked women than most men see in a lifetime.

Yet his mother believed that merely because her lifestyle was unconventional, she wasn't going to abdicate her parental responsibility. Though little Seymour hung around with the baggy-pants comics, learning their shtick and joking with them, he was extremely well-mannered around the performers, saying "please" and "thank you" and refusing unsolicited gifts from his mother's colleagues unless his mother first approved.

His idyllic life on the road screeched to a halt when, shortly before his seventh birthday, his mother parked him with her family in New York in order to start school: "I didn't want to go to school but once I was there, there was nothing I could do," he recalled.

His mother married Eugene Pitt, who took the newly constituted family to Panama City, Florida, where he had won a nightclub, the Palm Terrace, in a crap game. They also lived in Birmingham, Alabama, and elsewhere in Florida, before his mother divorced Pitt and sent fourteen-year-old Seymour to live with his godmother in Detroit.

In Detroit he finished high school but also drifted into juvenile delinquency. He had begun drinking, which fueled the anger inside. At seventeen, facing charges for a series of increasingly less petty crimes, he was given a choice—jail or military service—and opted to enlist in the navy: "It was a great thing because it saved me from a life of degenerate crime," he admitted later. He spent three years traveling the world for Uncle Sam before returning to Detroit, at decidedly loose ends.

He was hired to drive a car from Detroit to Miami and, thinking he might like to try college under the G.I. Bill, he enrolled at the University of Miami when he got there. But it only took about four days for him to realize that college meant studying and going to class, not just chasing girls. So he dropped out, working odd jobs around Fort Lauderdale and then signing on as a deckhand on deep-sea fishing boats; eventually he signed up to crew on a 100-foot schooner that was going around the world in September 1956.

But a couple of months before he shipped out, he headed back to Detroit to see old friends. One morning, he noticed an ad in the newspaper looking for apprentices at the Detroit Playhouse. The job description included acting lessons. Game for anything, Seymour stopped in—and won the apprenticeship. Almost immediately, he felt at home. "From the minute I started acting, I knew that was what I was meant for," he said.

Quickly realizing that there was a much larger theatrical world out there beyond the stages of Detroit, Seymour wrote a letter to the Actors Studio in New York, asking for an audition. Not that he had any idea how to prepare an audition or how to select an audition piece that would showcase his talents. So he selected a dense excerpt from Eugene O'Neill's *Mourning Becomes Electra*, because "I just liked how it sounded. I had no understanding of what it meant."

Invited to audition in New York, he put on his navy uniform because he knew service personnel traveled at reduced rates. But he was fraught with nerves as he made his way to New York, unsure whether it was a crime to impersonate a sailor and convinced he'd be spotted as a fraud by the Shore Patrol. Nobody questioned him.

The Actors Studio, however, turned him down. So Seymour Cassel, scheduled to crew on an around-the-world trip and also officially an apprentice of the Detroit Playhouse, cut all ties to his previous commitments. He got an apartment, signed up for acting classes with Stella Adler, and became a struggling actor, working as a waiter at the Stork Club and Jack Dempsey's by night while auditioning for theatrical and TV roles by day.

That's what he was doing when he spotted Cassavetes' ad looking for actors interested in working with the Cassavetes–Lane Workshop. He strolled over to the workshop on West Forty-sixth Street, walked in, and met John Cassavetes.

Cassavetes spent the next hour quizzing Cassel about himself and his life. Cassel was flattered and immediately seduced; here was this actor he'd seen in movies and on TV, and he was interested in a nobody former sailor who had decided to become an actor.

"We talked for a while and I immediately loved him because there was no bull about him," Cassel recalled.

Finally Cassavetes admitted that all of the scholarships had been given out. Noticing Cassel's interest in the increasing activity around them, he told him, "We're shooting a movie here tonight."

"Can I stay and watch?" Cassel asked, to which Cassavetes said, "Sure."

And so Cassel sat down and observed as the actors rehearsed a scene for what would become Cassavetes' first film as a director, *Shadows*, on a set they'd built in the Variety Arts workshop. No one knew on this day in 1957 just how groundbreaking or famous this project would become; they barely knew what they were doing at all.

As he watched, Seymour noticed that every time cinematographer Erich Kollmar changed the position of his camera, it required an elaborate and time-consuming series of steps: unscrewing the camera from the tripod, moving the tripod, refastening the camera, then retraining the lights before starting over again. So Cassel jumped up to help and wound up working on the movie all night long, until they quit at 6 A.M.

At breakfast with the cast and crew afterward, Cassavetes turned to the newcomer and said, "So what did you think?"

"Wow, I've never seen that done live before," young Seymour enthused.

"Well, that's the way *we* do it," Cassavetes chuckled.

"When are you going to do it again?" Cassel asked and was told that filming would resume that very night.

"Do you mind if I come back?" Seymour asked, not knowing that, by the time the movie was finished, he would be listed as its associate producer.

Shadows had begun as an offshoot of an improvisational exercise in one of Cassavetes' classes. It became the film that initially defined Cassavetes' career, providing a template that would help him create his best work.

As an actor, Cassavetes wanted more than anything to embody real human behavior. But at this point in his career, he felt that impulse was being stifled at every turn: by a director's ideas, by the writer's vision, by the demands of the camera.

What he hoped to recapture in the workshop was that sense of elation at that moment of accidental discovery, when the actor connects unexpectedly to the script in a way he hasn't before and acting moves from make-believe to real art. And he was getting that kind of excitement out of a group of young actors he was working with, particularly when they would put the text of a scene aside and begin to improvise in character.

Now he wanted to take it a step further and create the character and story. Cassavetes had continued to write since his early encounter with Edward McSorley. So it was nothing to doodle a sketch of a scene—a situation, characters written in broad strokes—and bring it in to class to have the actors fool around with.

At the same time, he had reconnected with Erich Kollmar, who had gone to work as a movie-sound technician at a production house in Manhattan after the Academy. Kollmar learned to do location sound on *The Joe Louis Story* when a union soundman got sick and eventually wound up directing and producing films for the company.

At one point in 1953, Kollmar's employer was hired to make a dramatization of the history of the White Sisters of Africa, a group of Catholic nuns who had taught the native Africans, while also providing health care. When the film's director fell ill, the company shipped Kollmar off to finish the film.

What he found was a production with an outline but no script and an amateur cast of the real locals, who had never acted before. So Kollmar would explain the scene through a translator—say, a mother bringing her sick child to the nuns—and let them improvise dialogue.

"I couldn't understand a word they were saying," Kollmar recalled. "But you could tell by their expressions and emotions. And when I showed that to John, he thought of *Shadows.*"

In describing his African experience, Kollmar caught Cassavetes' interest when he mentioned the relative cheapness of shooting in 16mm, as he had been doing—that, even with sound, 16mm cost a fraction of the 35mm used in feature films while looking just as professional.

The subject of the film may also have grown indirectly out of Kollmar's African experience: "I mentioned to John that I was totally astonished by the insecurity of black people about their identity in this country," Kollmar said. "The ones I met in Africa were sure of themselves and where they came from. But not the ones here. John took that and evolved it."

Cassavetes showed up at class one night in January 1957 with a new idea for an improvisation, but he kept it to himself. Rather than say anything, he sidled up to several members of the class during breaks and, quietly, invited them to come by on Sunday for a special session.

On Sunday, he picked out Lelia Goldoni and teamed her with Benito Carruthers, who appeared to be of mixed race (though he himself would never go into detail about his ethnic background), and Hugh Hurd, a black man.

"OK, you're his sister," he told Lelia, indicating Hugh, "and you're Ben's sister, too. You're all in the house." And then he had them start talking about it—creating a scene in which they talked about how they felt about being siblings and yet looking so different. Cassavetes would expand upon the discussion—did Lelia think about passing for white? Did she or Ben pass for white without thinking about it?—sending new actors into the scene with new assignments.

They worked on the characters over a period of several classes. The results were electrifying, with the kind of honesty about race and human relations that was virtually absent from popular culture in 1957. And the energy seemed to build the longer they worked.

Finally, at the end of one particularly energetic session, John called a halt, though he was obviously jazzed about what they'd been doing and what he'd been able to summon with just a group of actors and a couple of ideas.

"I dreamed up some characters that were close to the people in the class and then I kept changing the situations and ages of the characters until we all began to function as those characters at any given moment," he recalled. "During one class, I was so impressed by a particular improvisation that I said, 'Hey, that would make a terrific movie.' It was about a black girl who passes for white; she loses her white boyfriend when he meets her black brother."

Cassavetes sought out a *New York Times* reporter and promised him an exclusive: the story of a fiercely independent film about to be shot right in Times Square. In fact, Cassavetes hoped to use the newspaper story to attract potential investors. Already Cassavetes understood, at least on an instinctual level, that what he was doing was unusual enough to be newsworthy, and that his name could seal the deal. Newspaper attention could only encourage people with money to step forward as benefactors.

The *Times* referred to it as "a feature-film project dealing with Negro-white relationships" and to Cassavetes and company as "a dedicated group of young movie, TV and theater people, headed by John Cassavetes."

But no angels stepped forward to shower him with funding. So in early February, he decided to try again, during an appearance on the Jean Shepherd show, *Jean Shepherd's Night People*, on WOR-AM radio. Shepherd had publicized *Edge of the City*, and Cassavetes wanted to stop in and thank him on the air.

Airing from 1 A.M. to 5:45 A.M. weeknights, *Night People* blended free-flowing interviews with comedic bits and the hipster ramblings of Jean Shepherd, who talked comically about everything from his own beleaguered childhood to current events. Shepherd had a large and rabid following—and most of them apparently were listening the night that Cassavetes came on.

Sitting in Shepherd's studio, cackling at Shepherd's wisecracks and chain-smoking cigarettes, John found himself thinking about the class he'd just left and mentioned it to the host. Egged on by Shepherd, the always voluble Cassavetes described the scene they'd worked on, how it had approached the racial issue from a new angle, then said, "I think it could be a good film."

"Do you think you could raise money to make something like that?" Shepherd asked innocently.

Cassavetes went along with the gag: "You bet," he said.

"Well, how would you do it?" Shepherd said, playing straight man.

To which Cassavetes said, speaking directly to Shepherd's audience, "If people really wanted to see a movie about people, they should contribute money. Just a dollar each would do it, if enough of them contributed. I think there are thousands of men and women who would like to know they could help to have a movie made."

"Well, there you have it," Shepherd announced, even giving the address of the Variety Arts before thanking Cassavetes and ushering him out. And that, John assumed, was the end of that.

The next day, what appeared to be a flood of envelopes from Shepherd listeners began to pour in—both to the Cassavetes–Lane Workshop and to the WOR studios. By the end of the week, Cassavetes had received more than $2,000 in contributions, almost none in denominations larger than $5, most of them in the form of single dollar bills.

At class the following night, he got up and announced, "Jean Shepherd's people are sending me money to produce a movie called *Shadows*. And it's going to come from our improvisations."

As he noted later, "We didn't know the first thing about making a movie. It was an experiment. I never thought I'd be a director."

Thirteen

Shadows

I f you watched *Shadows* with contemporary eyes—with no context, other than the fact that it was a film from the late 1950s—you might be entertained, but you probably would otherwise be unimpressed. If you watched knowing only that it was a landmark—but not knowing why—you'd probably remain mystified, at least until the closing titles told you the film had been improvised.

Yet in it can be seen the skeleton of what would become the independent film movement in America: films made with the idea that a personal artistic expression could be achieved in movies, one that took chances and experimented with form but was still recognizable as a film, with characters you cared about and paid attention to. Plot wasn't necessarily optional, but it was definitely not the first concern.

And it was a film whose maker had, for the most part, paid for it himself. He'd taken a gamble on a vision—and eventually worked out his own distribution deal, getting an unknown film into theaters without the participation or interference of the movie establishment: the Hollywood studios. You can draw a straight line from *Shadows* to such independent landmarks as *Return of the Secaucus Seven*, *sex, lies, & videotape*, and *Clerks*.

Yet watching it today, it seems like such an unprepossessing little film in many ways, given what it has come to mean in the intervening decades.

Shadows opens on a raucous rock 'n' roll party, crowded, with people playing piano and guitar, clapping hands and dancing. The lone sourpuss in the crowd is Ben (played by Ben Carruthers; all of the characters had the actors' names, because that's how they had started out in the early improvisations), who skulks at the edge of the crowd, ostentatiously carrying a set of bongos and wearing sunglasses. But no one pays any attention to him, as he stands off to the side, watching with a studied lack of interest.

Walking down the street in the theater district, he meets his friends Tom (Tom Allen) and Dennis (Dennis Sallas), as well as a crewcut Seymour Cassel. "Hey Benny, you got the loot? The boys are waiting," Cassel says, sliding on the slick heels of his loafers across an expanse of sidewalk as though it were ice.

"Yeah, I got the money but you ain't coming," Ben responds. After some roughhousing between the four of them, they start to leave—and then Ben turns around and punches Cassel in the stomach, indicating that he shouldn't follow.

They wind up at a bar at night, where they find three girls and pair off in adjoining booths. Ben tells his girl that he's a musician, that he plays the trumpet, while Tom exchanges sexual innuendos with his girl, and Dennis tries the sincere approach with his. Each of them seems on the verge of getting lucky when the scene abruptly ends.

Ben is next seen strolling through Times Square in broad daylight. He stops in to a rehearsal hall (in fact, the Variety Arts workshop space), where his brother, Hugh (Hugh Hurd), and Hugh's manager, Rupert (Rupert Crosse), are arguing with a Philadelphia nightclub manager (Jack Ackerman), who is auditioning girls for his danceline. Hugh is a singer who wants to be treated as a singer; the club manager, however, just wants someone to introduce the girls. He'll let Hugh sing, but he's there mainly as an announcer, to bring on the dancing girls.

Even as Hugh wrestles with this question of compromising his artistic integrity, the jittery Ben interrupts to ask Hugh to lend him some money. But when the nightclub owner breaks in, demanding an answer from Hugh about the proposed deal, Ben takes the offered $20 from Hugh, then quickly leaves. Hugh, meanwhile, must swallow his pride and take the job, even though he has to pay his own way to Philadelphia.

The scene itself is an audio mishmash, with obviously unsynched dialogue, some of which was dubbed in, including the girls' singing "A Real Mad Chick," a last-minute composition that echoes "A Pretty Girl Is Like a Melody," for which the rights were too expensive. But the scene establishes the relationship between Hugh and Rupert, who are longtime friends, and between Hugh and Ben, who are brothers seemingly from different generations.

This scene obviously was meant to precede the earlier scene with Ben and his friends, in which he waves a $20 bill and announces, "I got the money." Money seems to be an issue; both scenes have a certain tension based on its availability. Reversing the scenes' order would have made logical sense, but would have gotten the movie off to a much slower start.

At the Port Authority Bus Station, Hugh and Rupert meet Hugh's sister, Lelia (Lelia Goldoni), who sees them off to Philadelphia. But Hugh is concerned about Lelia walking home on Forty-second Street, though she waves off his concern. Sure enough, even as Hugh and Rupert run to catch their bus, Lelia finds herself accosted by a strange man under the neon of Times Square. But a stranger (played by Cassavetes himself) intervenes, and Lelia gets away.

In Philadelphia, Hugh and Rupert get ready for the gig, but Hugh can't figure out what he can say onstage when he's not singing. Rupert tries to teach him a joke, but it's obvious Hugh isn't comfortable with the idea. It ultimately doesn't matter because the gig is a disaster. The audience ignores Hugh's crooning, and the club owner cuts him off in mid-song, telling him to introduce the girls. Hugh tries to tell the joke Rupert has taught him, but before he can even get a line out, he's interrupted by the band, playing the girls onto the stage.

Back in New York, Ben, Lelia, and several of their friends are sitting around a coffee shop, trying to come up with something to do. The most bored is David (David Pokitillow), who obviously is interested in Lelia and just as obviously is the square peg among these freer spirits. Still, when Lelia kids Ben that David is writing a novel about him, Ben snaps, "It better not be any of that Beat Generation jazz like the last one."

David chastises Ben and his friends for doing nothing with their lives, then invites them to a literary party. Lelia tries to discourage him but he won't be denied, though Ben and his friends Dennis and Tom are obviously snickering at him.

Those three take off, headed for the Museum of Modern Art. There they stroll through the sculpture garden, while Tom denounces it as a place for "a lot of sexless women without any love in their life, a lot of big deal professors, a lot of creeps trying to show off how much they know."

Dennis tells him that he has no respect for art—to which Tom replies that Dennis is an ignorant little slob, offering a rant that could easily be Cassavetes himself talking: "I went to college, Dennis, and all I ever got out of it was dissipation and a lot of early bells disturbing my sleep. And a lot of supercilious slob professors, shooting off their mouth about some-thing, trying to teach me about something they'd already failed at in life themselves."

Ben, meanwhile, crouches before a large, primitive head on a pedestal, then announces to Tom that he's going to put the face—"just a mask!"—on a Christmas card. "Don't send one to me, pal," Tom barks at him. When Ben tells him to cool it, Tom says, "I suppose you understand this stuff."

"It's not a question of understanding—if you feel it, you feel it," Ben snaps back at him, vocalizing one of Cassavetes' tenets.

At David's literary party, David is trying to apologize to Lelia for in-sulting a story she's written, apparently at his insistence. In another part of the room, Tony (Tony Ray) tries to work his way into an obviously written conversation in which two women are arguing about Sartre and "existen-tial psychoanalysis."

Tony finally gives up and moves over to Lelia and David; interested in Lelia, he gets David to introduce him. Lelia obviously reciprocates his in-terest: When David criticizes a scene in her story, in which a girl kisses a stranger on a street corner, Lelia says, "If I wanted to, I would," then stands up and gives Tony a passionate kiss, much to David's chagrin.

Tony then tries to take Lelia home; when David objects, Lelia says that neither of them will be doing that, as she has other plans. Tony tries to make a date for the next day; when David says he and Lelia had plans to go to the park, Tony invites himself along.

In Central Park, Lelia walks between the two young men. They run into a friend, Mo (Maurice McEndree), who distracts David long enough for Tony and Lelia to run away and leave him behind.

They walk and talk until they're standing in front of Tony's apartment. Tony invites Lelia up and winds up telling her he loves her, then making love to her. He only finds out afterward that she was a virgin, when she says, "I didn't know it could be so awful."

Tony tries to sweet-talk her until she asks about their future. When he thinks she means she wants to move in with him, he panics—and she takes her cue from that, saying no, she doesn't want to live with him. In fact, she wants to go home.

As she gets dressed, she says, "I thought being with you would be so important, mean so much, that afterward two people would be as close as it was possible to get. But instead we're just two strangers."

Tony insists on seeing her home and walks into the apartment, where Ben is playing cards with his friends. The three of them are all bruised and scuffed up—a continuity error that seems to indicate the fight they have at the end of the film originally was intended to be earlier in the story.

Ben and his friends call some girls to meet them at the drugstore and leave. Tony puts on some music, and he and Lelia start to dance, then start necking on the couch. But they're interrupted by the doorbell; by the time they've stood up and rearranged their clothes, Hugh and Rupert have let themselves into the apartment.

Lelia introduces Hugh to Tony as her brother, and the look on Tony's face provides the emotional fulcrum for the whole film. He tries to mask his surprise, then interrupts Lelia and Hugh's conversation to announce that he has an appointment and has to go.

His response is a mixture of shock, disbelief, and revulsion on an unthinking level—as though Tony, in realizing that Lelia is mixed race, is shocked at what that means about his own behavior. It's as if he had violated some personal taboo by sleeping with a woman who was at least partially African-American, even if he didn't know it. Lelia tries not to see it, but Hugh recognizes the look instantly. And so, while the subject of race never is mentioned, it is there quite plainly: Tony has encountered something within himself that is ugly and mean, but also something so deeply ingrained that he is shocked at his own response.

The scene is choppily edited, as though Cassavetes had to whittle it down for maximum impact; thus, when the camera angle shifts, looking in from outside the apartment door after Tony opens it to leave, the velocity and abruptness of both Lelia and Tony's movements make it seem as though some moment of potential violence had been cut out. There's a sudden frantic emotional quality to Lelia that also seems to arrive out of nowhere, as she fights tears at Tony's departure.

Similarly, when Hugh intervenes and confronts Tony, telling him to leave, the emotions are big but unjustified, given what we've observed. It's not hard to imagine a scene that simply couldn't be edited together, with Cassavetes trimming it down to its essence, giving the racial tension an increased power by leaving it unspoken.

It was that sequence, principally, that gave *Shadows* its impact. In the space of twenty minutes, Cassavetes presents, examines, and dramatizes the racial questions of his time: racial identity, racial prejudice, interracial romance. And he does it without ever having a character utter the words "race," "Negro," or "colored."

Which made the moment truly ground-breaking: Race had to be approached cautiously in Hollywood, lest anyone take offense at the suggestion that Americans weren't all racially color-blind. This, despite the fact that there were few roles for black actors and actresses in Hollywood films or on television—and that the American South still practiced legal racial segregation. That Cassavetes could so matter-of-factly deal with the issues, without making them the centerpiece message of his movie, put him far ahead of his time.

The next morning, Hugh, Lelia, and Ben battle over the bathroom as the day begins. Hugh tries to get Lelia to talk to him, but she won't; when Ben teases her, she explodes at him. Hugh won't explain the situation but says, "It's just a little problem with the races. Nothing you'd be interested in."

That night Hugh has a party at the apartment—"just some people," he tells Lelia. Lelia's friend Vicky (Victoria Vargas) introduces Lelia to Davey (David Jones), a polite and good-looking young black man whom Lelia tries to ignore. When David (Pokitillow) arrives and tells Lelia he needs to talk to her about Tony and that it's important, she blows him off as well.

The predominately black crowd is drinking and laughing—except for Ben, who sits by himself with a look of loathing (self-loathing?) at all these loud, demonstrative black people. Like Lelia, Ben seems to occupy some racial limbo, in which he is able to pass as white and seems to do so purposely. There are no racially identifying markers, but while Lelia seems simply not to be thinking about passing, Ben seems to be thinking about it quite consciously.

Thus, when a young black woman sits down next to him and tries to cajole him into joining the party, Ben puts on the pose of the moody, stand-offish outsider with her. When she puts her arm around his shoulder and tries to coax him to have a drink, he tells her not to touch him, then violently shrugs her arm away. The soundtrack erupts with a female screech, though it doesn't come from the woman with Ben. Instead, she throws her drink in his face. He backhands her—and then Hugh hurtles across the room to jump on Ben.

Almost instantly, the much-taller Rupert has grabbed Hugh and wrestled him away from Ben. Ben gives Rupert and Hugh a shove, then stalks out of the room, while Rupert tries to calm Hugh down and Lelia follows Ben to the door. She and Hugh wind up yelling at each other—as brother and sister will—in front of all the guests before stomping out of the room.

Ben takes off for a nightclub, which he enters after reciting "Mary had a little lamb" to himself while standing in the street. Meanwhile, back at the apartment, the party is over, and Rupert and Hugh sit with their dates, talking. But a mild disagreement turns into an all-out attack as Hugh lashes out at Rupert. You can hear the anger and frustration of the Philadelphia gig spill out, along with feelings from years of similar show business experiences as Hugh expresses how unhappy he is with the state of his career.

The next day Ben returns. He remains sullen and uncommunicative, despite Hugh's attempts to find out what's wrong and to reconcile with him.

When Davey shows up to take Lelia to a dance, she berates him for not bringing her flowers, then tells him to wait for her. "Will you be long?" he asks. "I'll be as long as I am," she replies.

As he waits, Rupert and Hugh are trying to work out the arrangement for a song. Davey butts into their conversation to tell them that he sings the same song in his act and begins to sing it, unaware that Hugh and Rupert are mocking him. Finally Lelia butts in, reprimanding Davey for bothering her family and telling him to sit down and be quiet until she is ready. But after waiting more than two hours, Davey complains, and Hugh takes his side.

Finally ready, Lelia and Davey get ready to leave, and as they do, the doorbell rings. It's Tony, who stands wordlessly as Lelia and Davey make their exit; he and Lelia exchange looks but not words. After she leaves, Tony insists on coming in and talking to Hugh, who is ready to fight with him. Ben intercedes; when Tony says he just wants to leave a message for Lelia, Ben agrees to transmit it: "Tell Lelia I realize now there's no difference between us. She'll always mean a great deal to me. Just tell her Tony said I'm sorry." Tony leaves. Hugh realizes he hasn't packed for his gig in Chicago and goes to get ready as Rupert leaves.

At the dance, Lelia is still feisty and full of attitude. When Davey tells her that the women where he comes from aren't so mouthy, she jokes that she obviously wouldn't fit in there. "Look, Davey, I am what I am and nobody tells me what to do," she says.

"I don't know who you think you're fighting," Davey tells her. "You know, I saw the way he looked at you back there—and I also saw the way he looked at me." Her face crumples; she melts into his shoulder as they dance to the soft music.

At Grand Central, Hugh shows up to find an angry Rupert; the club owner from Philadelphia has gotten a job they had booked in Cincinnati cancelled. While they still have a gig scheduled in a Chicago club, it almost doesn't pay to go. Rupert unloads all of the frustration he's been feeling and seems ready to quit. But Hugh gushes out his belief in Rupert as a manager and a friend and tells him they'll make it together.

The film circles back to Ben and his friends, who once again try to pick up some girls at a local coffee shop. This time, their boyfriends walk in; after some taunting back and forth, the men go outside to fight, and the boyfriends leave Ben and his pals battered and nearly unconscious, lying in an alley.

"No more of this jazz for me—I don't know why we do this," Ben says, as they nurse their bruises in a bar afterward. "If you want me to be corny and say it's taught me a lesson, well, it's taught me a lesson."

The three friends stand together near Times Square, say their good-byes and separate. Ben is once more left alone, standing on the street with his sunglasses on at night, finally walking off by himself into an uncertain future.

Watching this film as an NYU college student, Martin Scorsese recalled, changed everything for him: "All of a sudden, cinema could be made any-where," he said. "Cassavetes was very interesting as an actor and then to have him come out of that school and shooting on the streets of New York in 16mm—it was a breakthrough in the way of thinking."

Fourteen

Shooting *Shadows*

T he project had been christened *Shadows*, as Cassavetes later recalled, because one of the actors had been sketching the other cast
members with charcoal during rehearsal. He called the drawing
"Shadows," a name Cassavetes felt fit the story they were developing for
the film—about people who live in the shadows of society, daring to put
themselves into the spotlight.

As workshop members began building sets to make the Variety Arts
space look like, variously, the family apartment, a nightclub, and a rehearsal hall, Kollmar and McEndree began rounding up the film equipment they thought they would need to shoot the film (with some donated
by filmmaker Shirley Clarke). Cassavetes and the cast used the next two
weeks of evenings to work out the individual lives of the characters.

"I chose a basic melodramatic situation in which a young girl was seduced by a young man, who then realized that she was colored," Cassavetes
said. "We chose a situation like this so the actors would have something
definite and emotional to react to."

"The scenes were predicated on people having problems that were
overcome with other problems," he noted. "At the end of a scene, another
problem would come in and overlap. This carried forward and built up a
simple structure."

He ordered his actors to begin spending their time together outside of the workshop. They were also told to haunt the neighborhoods where their characters would hang out, to get the feel for them and to develop a rapport that was more sibling than collegial, so it would come across on film.

In the typewritten synopsis he circulated, Cassavetes wrote, "*Shadows* is the story of people in a city, not ten million, but just a few, a specific group, a picture of a family that lives just out of the bright lights of Broadway . . . They are shadows of youth in a neighborhood of dreams, and for those of us who stand directly beneath the lights, we cannot imagine the problems that face these people, for our dreams are too distant for them to reach."

Cassavetes' typewritten synopsis included descriptions of each of the family members, based on the improvisations and the actors themselves:

> "Hugh, the oldest brother, is a singer, at first beating out the crude chants of his African heritage, trying to make it a technique of singing that can be readily bought and sold . . . He is a second-rate entertainer with great ambition.
>
> "Ben is driven by the uncertainty of his color to be accepted in the white man's world. Unlike his brother, Hugh, or his sister, Lelia, he has no outlet for his emotions. His life is an aimless struggle to prove something abstract and so he moves with a casual insecurity among the poor, diligent followers of trends.
>
> "Lelia: the youngest member of the family, a girl with tremendous artistic impulses who reaches far out of her society, whose entire life has been colored by the great novelists, French impressionists, by the romantic poets of England and by the somber symphonies of Beethoven . . . Lelia is ready to be hurt."

As Cassavetes later recalled, "I gave them neighborhoods to go to and then we would shoot in those neighborhoods. They hung around Broadway and different places downtown. They would listen to jazz musicians or go out and have a beer and try to pick up girls. And when we finally started shooting, they had assimilated. They pretty much became the people they were playing. They had something to say and they took it seriously. We wrote life studies for each character and then we improvised."

Improvisation was a technique, not an end in itself. Whether Cassavetes' students were working on scenes from classic texts or trying to extrapolate a scene of their own from a suggestion, it was meant to push the actors into unfamiliar territory, to make them think about the scene or the character in a new way, which is how Cassavetes started using it in classes at the Variety Arts.

"First we improvised to get the feel of the characters," he explained.

"Then, as the actors become easy in the roles, we go back to the text. If it doesn't work out, then we go back and improvise some more and again return to the text. We keep working like this until we feel complete identification between actor and role."

The crew for the film consisted of members of the workshop, as well as new people who found their way to West Forty-sixth Street, drawn by what they had heard Cassavetes talk about on Jean Shepherd's show.

Seeing this outpouring of interest—the raw urge to do something new and creative for the sheer love of doing it—seemed to strip Cassavetes of any ideas of gaining personal glory from a filmmaking venture. Too many people suddenly believed too much in what he was doing.

It offered a chance to shake off the shackles of conventional movie acting, or so Cassavetes hoped: "The actor is expected to go through a dramatic scene, staying within a certain region where the lights are," Cassavetes said of film acting. "If he gets out of the light just half an inch, then they'll cut the take and do it over again. So then the actor begins to think about the light rather than about the person he is supposed to be making love to, or arguing with.

"I had worked in a lot of films and I couldn't adjust to the medium. I found that I wasn't as free as I could be on stage or in a live television show. So for me it was mainly to find out why I was not free. It was an experiment."

The experiment meant that, while Cassavetes was the director, he wasn't going to do the things normally associated with directing. He was part traffic cop, part mentor and spirit guide, or so he said.

"I didn't pick and choose what I wanted—things just happened," he later said. "And it was more natural because it was real. It didn't emanate from me and it didn't emanate from the camera. It emanated from the people that were creating, because in life you live and in entertainment of any sort, you have to create it. I think the important contribution that *Shadows* can make to film is that audiences go to the cinema to see people; they only empathize with people and not with technical virtuosity."

Kollmar was used to filming documentary-style footage, which allowed more flexibility in what Cassavetes hoped would be a production that allowed the actors' inspiration to lead the camera instead of vice versa. As Kollmar gathered the equipment, Cassavetes and his cast worked out scenes for the movie in the studio, and turned part of the workshop into a soundstage meant to look like the family's apartment.

"The cameraman had to light the scene generally, so that the actor could move when and wherever he pleased," Cassavetes said. "A strange and interesting thing happened, in that the camera, in following the people, followed them smoothly and beautifully simply because people have a natural rhythm."

It quickly became clear that this was something special—but it became equally apparent that, as willing as they all were to do it for free, it was still going to cost more than the $2,500 people had sent in. Cassavetes began putting the arm on people he knew, asking them to contribute anywhere from a couple of bucks to a hundred dollars for his acting/filmmaking exercise.

The *World-Telegram and Sun* reported that "actor John Cassavetes can be seen roaming the Broadway area these nights, trailing a camera and an entourage of young actors, writers, friends and curious policemen." Cassavetes referred to *Shadows* as "an off-Broadway movie" and talked about the fact that most of the contributions from the Jean Shepherd show came in envelopes without return addresses: "So I couldn't send back the money. In order to live with my conscience, all I could do was to go ahead and make the movie." The same article noted, "Mr. Cassavetes, who is one of our fastest rising young actors, emphatically denies that he has any directorial ambitions."

So he started asking the show-business people he knew or was meeting—many of them friends of Sam Shaw—to donate to his project. Cassavetes convinced everyone from Josh Logan to Hedda Hopper, from writer Reginald Rose to director Jose Quintero, to contribute, making up the rest of the initial $12,500 shooting budget himself.

But having the money and equipment was one thing; figuring out how to actually make a movie was something very different. Cassavetes had played featured roles in only four movies at that point, and had not paid much attention to the technical details. But that was more experience than most people in his group had; because he was a rising movie star, when he discussed making a movie, people assumed he knew what he was talking about.

In reality, the only one in their merry band with any actual filmmaking experience was Kollmar, but he happily deferred to the charismatic and increasingly famous Cassavetes, no matter how unusual his approach seemed to be. Cassavetes talked a great game and then seemed to make things happen, as though his sheer force of will could overcome the obstacles of inexperience and its fallout.

The crew, like Cassavetes, was learning by doing. The on-the-job-training, Seymour Cassel said, was invaluable. "On that picture, I learned everything on a film that I *didn't* want to do," Cassel said. "I didn't want to be a camera operator or a best boy or a boom guy or a mixer. But I learned how to do all that."

"I think we made all the mistakes that can be made," Cassavetes said. "But that's how we learned what moviemaking is all about. That's how it starts: people getting out there not knowing what they are doing and trying to do anything that pleases them."

The mistakes were myriad. In his work in movies, Cassavetes had never really noticed what the job of the script supervisor was. So he had never made note of the fact that, when the director shouted, "Cut! Print!" the script girl at his elbow was making note of which take it was.

So as they began filming, when John would grow excited about a take he'd happily bark, "Print take 3!"—never realizing that, because everyone else on his crew was a novice as well, no one was taking notes about which takes he liked. All of the film had to be printed to sort through what they had shot: "Not having a script girl set us back six months—these are the things that kill you," Cassavetes said later.

There was also the problem of the sound: "We filmed it with a 16mm camera and a handheld microphone, which often failed to pick up the talk," Cassavetes explained. "It was not intended to be technically proficient."

Erich Kollmar recalled Ben Carruthers mumbling, frustrating the microphones with his low tones. But it wasn't always his fault: "The sound department often looked at the recorder only to see no signal whatsoever," Cassavetes said.

There was also a problem with synchronizing the sound to the film; in the end, 250,000 feet of film was shot—much of it with the sound either nonexistent or out of synch. That alone would account for a large chunk of an editing process that eventually would stretch out over more than two years.

The first week's shooting, when seen in dailies, was virtually useless: bad sound, bad lighting, lack of inspiration. But it gave them a sense of how they should be doing things and a feel for the equipment.

They alternated between shooting on the set they had created at the workshop and on the streets. There were advantages and disadvantages to both. The workshop offered a safe, enclosed space, where lighting and the camera could be arranged in advance. On the other hand, the walls and ceilings were so thin that the pounding of Broadway dancers rehearsing on the floor above often intruded into the dialogue they were recording, such as it was. The streets offered the real New York, but also overwhelming street noise and ambient sound that often submerged the dialogue being captured by primitive recording equipment.

They carried out street-filming like guerrillas, with waiting taxis sitting with motors running so that, as the police approached, the cameraman, with camera, could jump in and speed away, even as the actors and the rest of the crew ran like hell. The cops' concern? In setting up his production, John had neglected to secure any of the necessary permits to work on the streets of New York.

Electricity was also a problem: "We'd just knock on people's doors and ask if we could plug our electric cable into their socket," recalled Al Ruban, who met Cassavetes playing baseball in Central Park and wound up on the crew of *Shadows*.

It was part of the fun, as far as Cassavetes was concerned. He and his crew and cast were bold adventurers in uncharted territory.

"It was really the height of ignorance in filmmaking," he later said. "But we just loved what we were doing—we thought we were the cat's nuts."

Once Cassavetes and crew got caught up in production, an evening's shooting would often stretch into the very late hours. John would get back to the apartment and fall into bed at 5 A.M., then be up at 7 to go back to work on it: "There seemed nothing else in the world more fun or more worth doing," he said.

Not that everything they did was golden. But Cassavetes tried to discipline himself against expressing any negative reactions to any of the actors' discoveries. The characters belonged to the actors; their dialogue and action would also have to spring from that source.

"I loved the relationship that I had with my actors and that they had with me," he said later. "If they felt they were in a hurry to do something, they said, 'Get out of the way, John, just leave us alone and we'll get it right'," he said. "I'd sit down and anxiously await something. I felt like screaming when they did something that wasn't any good but I didn't and they'd say, 'All right, all right, we didn't get it right. We'll try it again.'"

And always, resolutely, they worked without a script (and without anyone to keep a list of the scenes they'd shot): "It was totally impossible to keep track of anything because we went too fast," Kollmar remembered.

They would improvise scenes at the workshop, decide which parts worked, and incorporate all of the best elements into the finished scene when it went before the cameras. Sometimes Cassavetes would just suggest the situation—coming up with something new—and then turn the camera on and let the actors thrash their way through it until something worthwhile emerged, if it did.

"We began shooting without having the slightest idea of what had to be done or what the film would be like," he said. "We had no idea at all. We didn't know a thing about technique; all we did was begin shooting."

He resolutely avoided telling them what to do or how to do it; there were no camera directions. Rather, the actors would create their own blocking and staging and the camera would follow them. At times, improvised scenes would run through a full ten-minute film magazine. But Cassavetes, behind the camera, didn't tell the actors where to go physically or dramatically. Even a scene that seemed to be going nowhere would be allowed to play out, to let the actors fully explore the dead ends, rather than move in a direction dictated by Cassavetes.

Which could be frustrating at times. Not all of the actors were gifted at improvisation, which made for scenes that could go in circles, or nowhere at all.

But Cassavetes exercised great patience, inspired, perhaps, by his thrill in playing with this gadget, the camera: "What a way to tell a story," Cassavetes said. "I'm like a kid with a toy pistol with it. I just run around shooting everything."

They continued to film, on and off, over the course of forty-two days spread over ten weeks. Shooting schedules were dictated by the demands of John's schedule and, to a lesser degree, the schedules of the cast and crew.

Even then, not everyone who started the project was willing to be on call for Cassavetes. David Pokitillow was a violinist who attended the workshop. He'd been involved from the beginning, but after filming the party scene where he nearly loses Lelia to Tony, he simply stopped coming.

Cassavetes, however, had another scene in mind, one in which the three of them—David, Tony, and Lelia—go for a walk in Central Park. When a friend of David's stops them (actually, Maurice McEndree), Tony and Lelia go running off across the Sheep Meadow, leaving the pudgy, slow-moving David trailing far behind.

But Pokitillow didn't show up for shooting, and, when Cassavetes turned up at his door, Pokitillow was adamant that no one was going to film him running. Cassavetes had to promise—and then produce—a special chess set Pokitillow had been coveting before he could coax the musician out of his apartment and into Central Park.

Cassavetes had worked off and on throughout the *Shadows* production, mostly television shows. Between the time he started *Shadows* and the time he finished it and showed the final version in 1960, he had also acted in *Saddle the Wind, Affair in Havana,* and *Virgin Island.*

Even as he maintained a busy acting schedule, he also faced a monumental editing task: taking the mountain of footage he had shot and shaping it into a film. Yet he had already accomplished at least part of his goal, which was to prove that he could make a movie independently of the system that didn't cost a fortune and could stand on its own merits.

"*Shadows* from beginning to end was a creative accident," he said. "We got the things we did because we had nothing to begin with and had to create it, had to improvise it."

Fifteen

Going Public

H e had shot a quarter-million feet of 16mm film—"spaghetti," he
said despairingly at one point—but John Cassavetes had very little footage in which the sound was synchronized to the picture
once production ended on *Shadows*.

So in addition to trying to get editor Len Appelson to assemble a workable film out of the mountains of footage, he had to figure out what people
were saying and match it to tape—on a film where there was no script to use
as a guide.

"The editing took two years because we had no story, just a group of
shots," Cassavetes said. "What story came out was conceived entirely in
the cutting room."

It took literally months to put together a working print. Seymour Cassel
remembered working nine months—well into 1958—as a volunteer editor
on the film, so long that Cassavetes gave him the credit "associate producer."
It gave him a chance to spend time with Cassavetes in the cutting room,
where John was a regular presence when he could be.

To figure out what was being said in the footage so it could be matched
to the sound, Cassavetes finally took the film to a school for the deaf, where
they lip-read the dialogue aloud. It was taken down by a secretary and used
as a script to guide them in the editing.

Even as he was fine-tuning the editing, he put together a rough assemblage to show to jazz musician Charles Mingus. Cassavetes, who had been

introduced to Mingus by Sam Shaw, felt that what he was doing with *Shad-ows* was on the same wavelength as what Mingus was doing with jazz: mak-ing it up as he went along. A collaboration between the two seemed like a natural marriage. But Mingus, a Juilliard-trained musician, wanted to com-pose the score, not toss it off in a jam session. And he spent six months writ-ing the five minutes of music that wound up in the final film.

Mingus and Cassavetes got together for a three-hour session in which Mingus played what he'd written for Cassavetes, which amounted to a few minutes of music. When Cassavetes asked him to improvise in the studio as he watched the film, Mingus played and sang, got his combo to switch instruments and play, and came up with as much music as they could get on tape, which was still not enough.

Cassavetes was after spontaneous combustion; Mingus wanted to cre-ate something thoughtfully, not crank it out on the spur of the moment: "You can't write a score that quickly," he told Cassavetes. "It takes months."

Mingus' contribution found its way into the first cut of the film. When Cassavetes decided to reshoot and reedit the film, Mingus was nowhere to be found, so Cassavetes called up saxophonist Shafi Hadi and paid him $100 to spend a couple of hours improvising in the studio while watching the movie. In the film that was released, there was very little of Mingus' mu-sic: just an altered twelve-bar blues sequence in E flat called "Nostalgia in Times Square."

John had little better luck with the other music he intended to use. He had selected a version of Irving Berlin's "A Pretty Girl Is Like a Melody" for the nightclub scene in which Hugh sings and is forced to introduce the girlie line. There was also a Frank Sinatra recording that Cassavetes wanted to use as background. He put them in the first cut, then removed them before he finished the film because he didn't want to pay the stiff licensing fees.

Even as Cassavetes was editing, however, he was interrupted by movie roles he had committed to, which were paying the rent and, eventually, the expenses of *Shadows* that contributions didn't cover.

Ostensibly to ensure his own financial security, when he agreed to star in *Saddle the Wind* with Robert Taylor for MGM, he signed a three-picture deal with the studio. In mid-1957, when *Middle of the Night* closed, Gena Rowlands signed to make her movie debut opposite Oscar-winner Jose Fer-rer, in a comedy he was directing that would eventually be called *The High Cost of Loving*. Like John, she also signed a deal with MGM. But both would prove to be short-lived: She gave her contract up willingly after having her first child.

It took four months of sporadic shooting and eight months of editing to produce the first finished print of *Shadows*. Cassavetes arranged to show the film in three special midnight screenings at the Paris Theater, across from the Plaza Hotel in New York, hoping to get a sense of what the film looked like with an audience.

The audience, as the saying goes, voted with its feet. Within the first fifteen minutes each night, people began walking out. The ones who stayed for the whole film often were friends of John and the cast, who were sympathetic at a moment when they were supposed to be enthusiastic.

Al Ruban, a new acquaintance of Cassavetes at the time, remembered, "When I saw the first version, I didn't care for it that much. It had holes, or slugs saying, 'Scene Missing.' But it was what John had shot up to that point. He wanted a public reaction. He knew it wasn't finished. So he screened it for three nights and, at the conclusion, he knew he needed to do certain things."

"One friend of mine patted me on the back and said, 'That's OK, John, you're still a good actor,'" Cassavetes recalled. "There was one person in the theater who liked the picture and it wasn't me—it was my father, who thought it was 'pure.' No one tried to phony up their reaction to it."

Cassavetes didn't need to be told. Despite his best intentions, he'd made what he thought of as "a totally intellectual film"—though he would never have considered himself an intellectual.

But having seen the first version of *Shadows* on a screen with an audience, Cassavetes had ideas about how he could fix it. It would require a few thousand dollars and a couple more weeks of shooting. When investors couldn't be found, Cassavetes began to create accounts for the Variety Arts workshop and charge expenses—film, equipment, development—to Cassavetes-Lane.

"He ran up a $30,000 tab on the movie and billed it to the workshop," Lane recalled. "I went crazy. I said, 'Where am I going to get that kind of money?' But he paid every penny. He never stuck me for any money."

Cassavetes' contagious enthusiasm had been stoked by the response of a producer named Nikos Papatakis, who convinced John that he could have his cake and eat it, too: With a little more work, he told John, he could have a film that could be released in theaters—that he was looking at a potential goldmine of both artistic and financial success.

That, however would go against everything Cassavetes had been preaching. From the start, he'd called the film an experiment, a chance to try something new, unfettered by the commercial concerns of Hollywood. He'd gone so far as to tell reporters that, because the film was made by a nonunion crew that was unpaid, the film could not be shown commercially.

"When we made *Shadows,* we had no intention of offering it for commercial distribution," Cassavetes said later. "Nobody knows who owns it. We finished the picture and can't sell it because everybody worked for nothing and we can never trace all the people who sent in money to help make it."

For all John's feeling that more work was needed, there were those who got excited after seeing the first screenings of *Shadows.* One was a University of Pennsylvania student, a would-be actor named Henry Jaglom. A friend of Seymour Cassel's, he would hop the train to New York from Philadelphia, where he went to college, coming in on Thursday to attend acting classes and spend a night with Seymour before checking in with his parents on Friday afternoon. One weekend in November 1958, Cassel told him that he'd been working on a movie, and it was being screened that night. Cassel put Jaglom on the ticket list, and Jaglom turned up for the film.

"I was blown away by it," remembered Jaglom, to whom Cassavetes became a mentor. "I've known I wanted to be a moviemaker since then. I saw the possibilities of making movies in America, comparable to what I loved about the European movies of the time."

There was at least one other person who believed Cassavetes had created a masterpiece: "Everyone left," Cassavetes recalled, "except for one critic, who walked over to me and said, 'This was the most marvelous film I've seen in my life.'"

That critic was filmmaker and journalist Jonas Mekas, who had created *Film Culture* magazine a couple of years earlier. He was among those who turned up for the Paris screenings—and he was bowled over by what Cassavetes had done for $15,000. He felt he'd been witness to the birth of something altogether new, as though he'd been in the opening night crowd for Stravinsky's *Le Sacre du Printemps.*

"The film was very different from anything anyone had seen, in terms of the improvisational aspect," Mekas recalled. "It was very fresh, like suddenly some fresh wind had blown in. I had never been in on an occasion like that. It was excitement, electrifying. Everyone knew it was important, that something really happened, that we were seeing a new thing."

What he admired about that first version was the spontaneity and the fact that Cassavetes refused to let story dictate character: "The first version was like a collage of scenes, with no connection other than it was the same characters," Mekas said. "I liked it because it was a direction I was moving in. It was pure chance. On that first occasion, he struck gold."

Sixteen

Beat, Square, and Cool

Within a year of the first screening of *Shadows*, Jonas Mekas and most of the filmmakers at the forefront of New York's avant-garde film scene would have christened their movement the New American Cinema, though it was just as commonly referred to as "experimental" and "underground" cinema.

At that point, in late 1958, the splintering of popular culture and the explosion of a counterculture was still almost a decade away. But New York, where Cassavetes was working, was a hotbed of new ideas and burgeoning movements in almost all of the arts.

The visual arts, which had produced de Kooning and Pollock a few years earlier, were transforming themselves further into abstract expressionism and minimalism, before producing the pop artists of the 1960s. Bebop and cool jazz had shattered conventional notions of what improvised music could sound like—and rock 'n' roll still seemed threatening. Theater had spawned experimental work off-Broadway, and literature had introduced the Beats: Jack Kerouac, Allen Ginsberg, William Burroughs, and the rest.

Film, too, had spawned its own avant-garde in New York and elsewhere. By 1958 there was an expanding community of filmmakers—Stan Brakhage, Maya Deren, Lionel Rogosin, and others—who believed film could be more than simply a medium that fostered the mindless entertainment that Hollywood promoted. Film could be art that dealt in time, space, color, shape, shadow—and not just plot and character. It could be a way of reflecting and refracting life, rather than a mere vehicle for fantasy.

In France, critics such as Francois Truffaut, Claude Chabrol, and Jean-Luc Godard were trying to apply their vigorous appreciation of American movies to a new way of making French film. There was also a feeling of a new wave gathering in the United States, but one that rejected what it saw as the stale formulas of Hollywood film.

As Lewis Jacobs wrote in Mekas' *Film Culture*, "The motion picture, alone, or rather the theatrical motion picture has neglected to reach out for new aims and forms that can give it fresh vigor and keep it contemporary." He assailed Hollywood for sticking to "the same old tired theatrical concept of 'Famous Players in Famous Plays.' New motion pictures can only appear as a reaction against established standards. This is film away from the mainstream of theatrical exhibition, film which for most of its life has led an underground existence. It is film of fits and starts; of little cost and great devotion; of surreptitious screenings and small audiences; but above all, a film of bold images, new concepts, diverse issues and fresh techniques."

In 1958, when he saw *Shadows*, Jonas Mekas was a thirty-five-year-old part-time film critic and publisher, a Lithuanian immigrant who had been in the country for eight years. A publisher of underground resistance newspapers during the Nazi occupation of Lithuania, he and his brother Adolfas had ended the war in concentration camps, then spent five years in displaced-person camps, before arriving in New York in November 1949.

Huge fans of American movies, the Mekas brothers haunted the New York movie theaters, using films to improve their English. They also began attending the monthly screenings of Cinema 16, the avant-garde film society that served as a showcase for films outside the mainstream: experimental art films and documentaries, curated by Cinema 16 founder Amos Vogel, a Viennese émigré.

It wasn't until the early 1960s that university film societies sprang into being as a movement. While there was a movement of experimental cinema in the early 1950s, there were few places for experimental filmmakers to exhibit their films, few outlets for art films and other work outside the mainstream. There was also an issue of censorship; films that showed too much sex or even nudity—as a number of these films did—made the exhibitor liable under obscenity statutes in some jurisdictions, which turned the operators into artistic outlaws of a sort.

Still, there were places for these films to be seen. Raymond Rohauer operated the Coronet in Los Angeles, and Frank Stauffacher regularly showcased new work in his Art in Cinema course at the San Francisco Museum of Art. In New York, Amos Vogel had found a way around censorship by making Cinema 16 a subscription club.

Vogel, who had escaped Austria and the Nazis, started the film society almost as a hobbyist; he was someone interested in film who happened to have the right idea at the right time. He had seen filmmaker Maya Deren's success when she rented the Provincetown Playhouse in Greenwich Village to screen her films. So Vogel and his wife, Marcia, put together a program of films and rented the same theater. They started the screenings in 1947 and, before long, had a monthly schedule, with several showings of the same program to accommodate a membership list that expanded beyond 5,000.

"I wanted films that would disturb you in some way, would add to your knowledge and make you change," Vogel said. "The whole notion of change was very basic to Cinema 16. I always went by what interested me and what involved me, feeling that there had to be others who'd be interested."

The fervent, expanding audience included Jonas Mekas. "In 1958, for the avant-garde or experimental filmmaker, you had Cinema 16 film society, which projected a film every month," Mekas recalled. "If you wanted to see old Hollywood commercial films, there was the Theodore Huff Society, once a week, and a number of others. Actually, there were more places than today that would be willing to show a movie like *Shadows*."

Mekas became fascinated with these efforts at expanding and breaking the form—to the point that he and Adolfas pooled their meager resources to create a quarterly journal devoted to work from the fringes: *Film Culture*, which published its first issue in 1954. They saw it as a way to promote serious film criticism at a time when they found it in short supply in the United States.

"There was very little real film criticism in this country at that time," Mekas said. "In England, they had *Sight and Sound* and, in Paris, *Cahiers du Cinema*. But in the U.S. the only thing there was was *Film in Review*, which was a very conservative, low-level monthly. There was *Film Quarterly* at the University of California, which came out once a year or something; and the leftists had something that came out, *Film Sense*. That's why we felt we needed *Film Culture*. It was a way for young people to write and exchange ideas about film. We had a network of outlets in university bookshops that took *Film Culture* from the third issue. By the late sixties, we had 5,000 subscribers."

In 1958, after four years of self-publishing *Film Culture* (at a loss) while working at other jobs to pay the rent (and to finance the movies he and his brother were making themselves), Mekas had walked in off the street to confront *Village Voice* entertainment editor Jerry Tallmer about why the *Voice* didn't write about movies. Tallmer offered him a column, which made Mekas the one man in New York with a passion for new directions in cinema, and the megaphone with which to broadcast his enthusiasm. Two megaphones, in fact.

So when Mekas saw *Shadows*, his excitement was kindled: "The film was very different from anything anyone had seen, in terms of the improvisational aspect," Mekas recalled. Mekas immediately jumped into print with a column in the *Voice*, broadcasting his discovery of this amazing new filmmaking talent: John Cassavetes.

"We know Cassavetes as an actor," Mekas wrote. "In this film, he proves to be a most sensitive director. The film itself is almost plotless and was shot without a script. Through improvisation and outbursts of feeling, the film slowly builds up and grows, without any sense of imposed force and simultaneously an image of the city emerges with its downtown nights and its night people. . . . The film begins in the middle and ends in the middle; nothing much is changed or resolved. But this casual, fragmentary quality is precisely what seems so convincing, so spontaneous and so contemporary."

A dozen years later, Mekas would write, "The screening of John Cassavetes' *Shadows* . . . became an occasion from which the rise of the New American Cinema is usually dated. I still remember the excitement some of us felt that late night at the Paris Theater. We stood there, in the lobby, and we didn't want to leave. Independent film in America, known at that time as experimental film, had been going strong since 1943, but it was beginning to need a fresh impulse. The screening of *Shadows* and, a few months later, *Pull My Daisy* . . . started moving the strange forces which grew and spread and exploded into what eventually became known as underground cinema."

After the Paris showings and his review of them, Mekas arranged further screenings of this first version of *Shadows*. These attracted a larger audience, who had read Mekas' encomium in the *Voice*.

After the November screenings, Mekas used the cover of the January issue of *Film Culture* to announce that the magazine was creating the Independent Film Award "to point out original and unique American contributions to the cinema."

His first recipient? John Cassavetes and *Shadows*: "Cassavetes in *Shadows* was able to break out of conventional moulds and traps and retain original freshness. The improvisation, spontaneity and free inspiration which are almost entirely lost in most films from an excess of professionalism, are fully used in this film."

In the same issue, in an extended essay called "A Call for a New Generation of Film Makers," Mekas tried to make a case for Cassavetes and some of his contemporaries as the American answer to the French New Wave and an extension of the Beat movement. The disparate film movements shared certain characteristics, he wrote:

"Basically, they all: Mistrust and loathe the official cinema and its thematic formal stiffness; Are primarily preoccupied with the emotional and intellectual conditions of their own generation, as opposed to the neorealists' preoccupation with materiality; Seek to free themselves from the over-professionalism and over-technicality that usually handicaps the inspiration and spontaneity of the official cinema, guiding themselves more by intuition and improvisation than by discipline."

In fact, Cassavetes' awareness of the French *nouveau vague* was less acute than his appreciation for Italian neorealists like Rossellini and De Sica; indeed, none of the French New Wave films had emerged at the time when Cassavetes and crew were shooting *Shadows*. As for being a Beat (because of the timeframe and because *Shadows* is linked with Robert Frank's *Pull My Daisy*, which it inspired), Cassavetes was an unlikely candidate. While he may have been anti-authority in the actor-director relationship (at least when he was the actor), it had nothing to do with a political agenda and everything to do with his personal sense of entitlement to create the work that most pleased him.

While the Beats had their own sensibility that called for a rejection of materialism and establishment values, Cassavetes only accidentally fell into that category with his film, which flouted the conventional approach more out of ignorance than design. It was Cassavetes' personal interest in the conflict of human emotions that led him to focus on young people of the time dealing with racial issues, and not an effort to make a political statement.

"To tell the truth, I don't know what underground films are," Cassavetes later said. "In its time and in its own way, *Shadows* was a sort of underground film, a sort of new-wave film. In fact, all these filmmakers are people who are just trying to express themselves; the labels come afterward . . . When you make a film, you aren't a part of a movement. You want to make a film, this film, a personal and individual one, and you do, with the help of your friends."

Still, when Mekas offered him the chance to contribute a piece to the same issue of *Film Culture* in which the award was announced, Cassavetes wrote a lengthy essay about where Hollywood had gone wrong.

Artists, he wrote, are looked down upon, instead of being venerated, particularly in Hollywood, where the bottom line inevitably trumped any notion of artistic achievement. Art is too important to be trusted to financiers: It was a theme that would recur throughout his career.

"Hollywood is not failing. It has failed," he wrote.

"The fact is that filmmaking, although unquestionably predicated on profit and loss like any other industry, cannot survive without individual expression. Motion pictures cannot be made to please solely the producers' image of the public. For as has been proved, this pleasure results neither in economic nor artistic success . . .

"Without individual creative expression, we are left with a medium of irrelevant fantasies that can add nothing but slim diversion to an already diversified world. The answer cannot be left in the hands of money men . . . the answer must come from the artist himself. He must become aware that the fault is his own, that art and the respect due his vocation as an artist is his own responsibility . . . Only by allowing the artist full and free creative expression will the art and the business of motion pictures survive."

Yet at the same time he wasn't ready to concede the future to these artists, at least not if they didn't hang on to some of the values of the classic filmmakers. Pessimism and nihilism weren't his thing either.

"I think the old filmmakers had one thing the new filmmakers should take into consideration, and that is that they liked people," Cassavetes said. "They were interested in the epic quality of man, rather than the lessening of his ideals, showing how little morality and how little soul he had. The old filmmakers showed that everybody had a soul, even the most violent, evil people. Their soul was black, OK, but at least it was a definite thing. And I think people who go to the cinema don't want to say, 'Yes, we are confused, we are nothing.' It destroys all kinds of entertainment."

Mentioning *Shadows* and the works of Robert Frank, Morris Engel, and Jerome Hill, Mekas said their films "clearly point up a new spirit in American cinema: a spirit that is akin to that which guides the young British filmmakers centered around Free Cinema, a spirit which is being felt among the French film newcomers . . . We think such a movement is about to begin."

Of the films of that period, only *Shadows* remains as a recognizable part of the film canon. The Beat films, the underground films, the experimental films—all the efforts that comprised the New American Cinema of the early 1960s—eventually fell by the wayside, the province only of the more experimental art museums or organizations like Mekas' own Anthology Film Archives, which continues its mission to celebrate film from the fringe.

Cassavetes' film was an accident that got swept up on this brief wave, then moved on to create its own wave—and to eventually launch Cassavetes into a new phase of his career.

To celebrate the presentation of *Film Culture*'s first Independent Film Award, Mekas booked the ballroom at the Waldorf-Astoria for a banquet, at which the award would be presented to Cassavetes. There was only one problem: Cassavetes had gone to Los Angeles, to start work on a TV series, *Johnny Staccato*, and wouldn't be able to attend.

Oh, and one other small thing: He had reassembled the cast of *Shadows* and shot new footage, which would replace about two-thirds of the film that Mekas had championed.

"At the time the magazine came out announcing we had given him our award, he'd already done the new version," Mekas said. "We had to cancel the award ceremony. The controversy was already raging."

In fact, after *Shadows* screenings that Mekas promoted at the 92nd Street Y in early 1959, Cassavetes was unsure what to do. Chalk it up as an experiment and move on? He considered it: "Like all failures, you get a sense of humor about it," Cassavetes said later, "I thought, this was so bad, it couldn't be repaired."

As Gena Rowlands recalled, "The first time he showed *Shadows*, he said, 'No, that's not the picture I meant to make.' So he went back in and reshot and reedited it."

As he was considering those options, he was approached by Nikos Papatakis, who had read Mekas' column about the film in the *Voice* and made a point of seeing it when Mekas showed it at the Y. Papatakis was a producer, investor, and hustler on the international film scene: "I have to be blamed for Nikos," Mekas said. "He came to see it after reading my review. When he saw it, he decided to improve it."

Cassavetes had already thought about what needed to be done to make *Shadows* seem more coherent and of a piece, rather than a collection of loosely connected scenes. He obviously had to do something about the sound, but he also had to impose at least a hint of structure. He'd been so caught up in the immediacy of the spontaneous creation of drama—in the process itself—that he had neglected to attend to the result: the film.

And while the project had begun as an experiment in the freedom of improvisation, it began to take on the weight of other possibilities once he'd seen it with an audience. Sure, it had not been meant to be seen commercially—but what if it could? Papatakis only added fuel to the fire, assuring Cassavetes that he had created the skeleton of a theatrical feature; all he needed was to flesh it out a little.

"Papatakis thought the film could be released and commercially accepted if John would reshoot about a third of it, write some scenes, eliminate some others and make it more conventional," Mekas said. "He sold the idea to Cassavetes—and that was the second version."

Cassavetes sat down with writer Robert Alan Aurthur, who had written the TV and film versions of *Edge of the City*, and wrote several scenes that expanded upon part of the first version. The romance between Lelia and Tony took on greater importance, more clearly stating the themes and tension of the film. Ben and Hugh's connections to her were also strengthened, but with dialogue crafted by Cassavetes and Aurthur to match the artless feel of the improvised dialogue.

"The film you have just seen was an improvisation": The title card over the closing shot of *Shadows*, which comes after the credits for producer McEndree and director Cassavetes, caused a sensation when the film was shown. The idea of a completely improvised film created not only a mistaken impression of what improvisation meant (as though the actors had ad-libbed an entire film), but tagged Cassavetes with a reputation that he could never shake.

In the future, only small chunks of his films (and only a couple of them, at that) would be improvised in front of the camera; his scripts were notoriously complete and written almost word for word as spoken. Yet he was forever known as the director who let—nay, encouraged—his actors to improvise on camera, as though this meant he were some wild man with no discipline who happened to get lucky.

In reshooting *Shadows*, Cassavetes cast the improvisation experiment aside. About two-thirds of the finished version of the film consisted of these new scenes he and Aurthur had written, and the improvised scenes from the first version are most often the ones in which the dialogue is either badly synched or sounds dubbed.

To convince everyone to come back and give him another two weeks, Cassavetes promised the moon, which was not unusual for the ambitious, easily excited young man. Early on, Cassavetes took an end-justifies-the-means approach, which alarmed some of his friends.

Kollmar recalled Lane telling him, "If you read *What Makes Sammy Run*, that describes John Cassavetes."

To rekindle excitement about *Shadows* among the cast and crew, he spun a vision for them in which the finished film not only found a distributor and played in theaters—making them all famous stars—but one in which it earned them all thousands of dollars. If they would just donate their time and talent, they would all get a share when the film went into profit.

"He promised a lot of people," Kollmar recalled. "He promised Burt Lane a producer's credit. He promised me one, too. I was going to get a single-frame credit with my name as big as his. But that all disappeared."

The additional ten days of shooting and subsequent editing cost almost as much as they'd already spent on the film, most of which came out of Cassavetes' pocket. He arranged with Amos Vogel to screen the finished *Shadows* at Cinema 16 near the end of 1959.

Vogel programmed it under the banner "The Cinema of Improvisation," pairing it with Robert Frank's *Pull My Daisy*, a film narrated by Jack Kerouac and starring Allen Ginsberg, Gregory Corso, and Larry Rivers whose improvisational style had been inspired by the first showings of *Shadows*. Vogel rented Cooper High School on the Lower West Side of Manhattan for the Cinema 16 screenings. Seymour Cassel remembered seeing Allen Ginsberg in the crowd; Cassel went with Ben Carruthers, who brought along author Carson McCullers, who had her own fifth of gin, which the three of them sipped from while sitting in the back.

Most of the Cinema 16 audience responded positively, but Mekas was infuriated by what he saw. "At this fateful night, I realized what I have to say, if I have anything to say, I'll be able to say it only as an anarchist," he wrote in his diary on November 11, 1959. "My realization that I was betrayed by the second version of *Shadows* was the last stone. They didn't know what they had: a blind man's improvisation which depended on chance accidents."

"The difference was immense," Mekas later recalled. "With the second version, he moved toward what he would do later, controlling the action; more writing came in. The improvisation was more controlled and contrived. It was still very different from Hollywood. But I felt betrayed. I could not believe he could do this. I realized he did not understand what he had. He never wanted the first version."

So Mekas leapt back into print—now condemning the new *Shadows* as a sell-out, a fraud, a travesty of the film he had championed a year earlier.

The combination of his review—and a letter to Cassavetes from Amos Vogel, advising him to speak out before Mekas further muddied the waters about which was the "real" version of *Shadows*—led Cassavetes to write a letter to the editor that was published in the *Voice*:

"In a recent edition of the *Voice*, Mr. Jonas Mekas, who had for over a year been a staunch supporter of a 16mm film experiment called *Shadows*, blustered forth ridiculous accusations at the second version of the picture, implying that it was done as a commercial concession to would-be distributors . . . The truth of the matter is that the original version of *Shadows* was not accepted by the great majority of thinking people, who had been very much in favor of this kind of picture. The truth . . . was that the audience failed to empathize with the characters as depicted in the film, and the natural rhythms and style employed in the film, of which we were all so proud, stood surrounded by the thinness of the characters and the flaws of all-around design.

"It would have been easy to side with those few who refused to believe that the film was anything but marvelous, for it is one weakness that all human beings are prone to . . . It would be impossible for me personally to have people think I am ethical and pure and to know inside me that I am a fraud. It would make me live with the fear of time, the fear that I would waste the only life that I have. The second version of *Shadows* was attempted with this in mind."

But Mekas kept the controversy alive: "I have been praising and supporting *Shadows* from the very beginning," he wrote in the Voice, ". . . pulling everybody into it, making enemies because of it (including the director of the film himself)—and here I am, ridiculously betrayed by an improved version of that film, with the same title but different footage, different cutting, story, attitude, character, style, everything: a bad commercial film, with everything I was praising completely destroyed. So everybody says, What was that critic raving about? Is he blind or something? Therefore I repeat and repeat: It is the first version I was and am still talking about."

Cassavetes rejected Mekas' charges of commercialism: "This is very insulting, of course, because I think you'll discover when you see the film, it is not a commercial film in the usual sense. And I just did not think the first version was very good."

Mekas was fighting for a losing cause. For one thing, *Shadows*—at least for the moment—seemed like a moot point, since no one was rushing to offer Cassavetes distribution, at least not in America. And for another, Mekas was preaching to an audience that, for the most part, had no investment in what he was railing about.

"There were two groups: those who had seen the first version and those who had not," Mekas said. "If you hadn't seen the first version, you had no idea what was lost. And only about five hundred people had seen the first version."

What he didn't realize was that, with his early raves about *Shadows*, followed by the award in *Film Culture,* Mekas had provided a tipping point for *Shadows* and Cassavetes.

While Mekas reached a small audience, it was both influential and international. The film didn't fire the imaginations of American studios, but when Mekas trumpeted the trail-blazing quality of *Shadows,* he was heard in London, at the British Film Institute. It selected *Shadows* for its Beat, Square, and Cool Festival in 1960, at a point where Cassavetes had almost forgotten about the film.

Seventeen

Johnny Staccato and Back to the Shadows

By the beginning of 1959, Gena Rowlands was noticeably pregnant. She had finished shooting *The High Cost of Loving* with Jose Ferrer and had asked MGM to let her out of her contract.

She and Cassavetes were living in New York while John struggled to put *Shadows* into shape; he, also, was between jobs.

Having acted in a series of movies, he had immersed himself in *Shadows*, with the decision to reshoot and reedit. He had put what was then an alarming amount of their money into finishing the film, turning down work in the process. He was obsessed with the movie, and everything else paled in importance; little intruded on his steely concentration. He had been so caught up in *Shadows* that the imminent arrival of their first child had barely registered with him.

Which is where he was mentally when he got a call early in 1959 about the possibility of starring in a TV series. Though he had done almost 100 television shows by this time, including guest-starring appearances on other series, doing a series himself was something he had rejected out of hand as a compromise of artistic integrity.

"Since the investors had pulled out, I was responsible for [the *Shadows*] debts," he later recalled. "I had all kinds of bill collectors after me. Gena was pregnant at the time and I was so busy with the movie that not until the day I finished reshooting did I become aware that, within a week, she was going to give birth to our first child."

Cassavetes got a call from a producer at Universal. The season before, NBC had had a hit with *Peter Gunn*, a show about a cool West Coast private eye with as much of a jazz flavor as a mainstream television network could handle at that point. Now NBC was hoping to repeat its success with a variation on the same theme. It would be called *Johnny Staccato*, and Cassavetes would play the title role—a jazz pianist in Greenwich Village who solved crimes and captured criminals.

Cassavetes listened to the pitch, said, "Bullshit!" and hung up. But a hit TV series offered the potential to give him financial security for years to come. Even if the show didn't run more than a season, TV salaries were lavish enough to cover the bills that nagged from the still-unfinished *Shadows*.

Gena, who always worried much more than she let on about John's tightrope approach to life and finances, listened to his phone call, then said with a straight face, one hand on her middle, "You're absolutely right, John. You can't do that stuff."

Cassavetes looked at her pregnant belly and had a "Eureka!"-like flash. He picked up the phone, called the producer back, and stammered an excuse: That he thought the producer was actually a friend of his playing a prank and only realized his mistake after he hung up—and yes, he'd love to talk about *Johnny Staccato*.

(Supposedly, shortly after Nick was born, John had a meeting in New York. When he and Gena eventually reconnected after a couple of weeks, he was so preoccupied with *Shadows* and *Staccato* that he could only offer a perfunctory "I'm really glad to see you" to his wife. After talking a few minutes, she said impatiently, "Aren't you going to ask about the baby?" Without thinking, Cassavetes, said, "What baby?")

As he thought about it and discussed it with Sam Shaw, Cassavetes realized that the TV series presented an opportunity. John had enjoyed the filmmaking process enough with *Shadows* that he wanted to repeat it. But during the *Shadows* reshoots he'd also found that there was a way to blend his approach with written material. And he was canny enough to know that, if he was going to break into directing in Hollywood—which still seemed to be the only game around—he would have to learn to do it their way, at least on the surface.

What better place to learn from real professionals the technical things that had eluded him on *Shadows*? Where else could he get paid to develop his ideas about what film could capture? It would offer him the opportunity to hone himself as a writer, to try on different voices and play with the notions of what a plot could be, using a primetime drama as his laboratory.

Cassavetes knew that, to get anything done in a network setting, he needed a buffer—and a good one. He could help direct the creative aspects of the series if he had someone to insulate him from the network and the sponsors, which held great sway at that point.

So he turned to Burton Lane, who had been struggling to make ends meet while running the Variety Arts workshop in John's absence. There was money to be made producing a network series, but Burt said no, he didn't want to move to Los Angeles. And having been involved in one venture with John, he wasn't keen to take on a second.

"We never had a written agreement," Lane recalled. "There was nothing on paper. After he made the movie, we went to this bar, the Horse Tail Bar, and I said, 'You take the movie and I'll take the workshop.' People said he took the wheels and left me the chassis. He said, 'I've gotta go to Hollywood,' and left."

Cassavetes then called Everett Chambers, whom he'd known when Cassavetes was a scuffling actor. Chambers was working as casting director for the film of *Middle of the Night* (which starred Kim Novak and Frederic March in the roles played by Gena Rowlands and Edward G. Robinson on Broadway) when he got a call from Cassavetes, asking if Chambers wanted to be the producer on *Johnny Staccato*. When Chambers jumped at the opportunity, Cassavetes invited him to a meeting at his apartment with Jennings Lang, who headed Universal's Revue production company.

But Cassavetes had neglected to consult Lang about his decision to hire Chambers, and Lang balked, putting Chambers in an uncomfortable position. "No, I have a producer," Lang said, then turned to Chambers. "You'll be the associate producer."

Cassavetes almost exploded but contained his anger. He took the contract Lang had brought for him to sign and tore it into pieces, walked over to the apartment door and threw them into the hall. Then he took Lang by the arm and brusquely ejected him from the apartment as well.

Cassavetes turned to the stunned Chambers: "Let's play some chess," he said with a wolfish smile.

Within a couple of days, Lang called back: Chambers would be the producer, starting him on a TV career that would include a lengthy mid-1970s stint producing *Columbo*.

John, Gena, and baby Nick (born May 16, 1959) moved to Los Angeles to start the series. It was only the latest of several career moves back and forth between coasts in their five years of marriage, and Gena was tired of the turmoil. She was enjoying being a mother more than she ever imagined she would and had decided to take some time off.

She wanted a place of her own and a sense of permanence, a nest for what she hoped would be a brood of kids. After earning some of his *Staccato* salary and paying off his debts, including the costs of finishing *Shadows*—Cassavetes was able to afford a house on a hillside off Woodrow Wilson Drive near Laurel Canyon. Big enough for a family—and, as it later turned out, perfect as a movie set for several pictures.

Talking about *Johnny Staccato* before its first airing, he said, "I'm fighting to make this a good series, and each episode is going to be different. Just don't judge us by the first few scripts. We're working on better ones."

Still, he probably should have taken his cue from the network executive who told him early on, "Don't get any big ideas. All you have to remember is that you're just a twenty-four and a half minute fill-in between commercials."

The first episode, "The Naked Truth," aired at 8:30 P.M. on Thursday, September 10, 1959. It was touted as the hot new detective show of the season but, as Cassavetes explained it, calling *Johnny Staccato* a detective show missed the real point.

"First of all, I don't play a private eye," he said. "I'm a jazz pianist. That's a hell of a lot of difference, pal. True, I get mixed up in a little intrigue, but it's like a sideline with me."

The show opens with a nervous jazz piano figure, punctuated by the chatter of a cymbal, over images of Cassavetes running into and out of shadows, stopping to look and listen nervously, then racing off again. Eventually he runs up to a window and, from behind it, smashes it with a pistol he then thrusts through the broken glass and fires as the words *Johnny Staccato* blaze across the screen. Then an intent-looking Cassavetes stares into the camera from behind the jagged edges of the broken window; when the title "Starring John Cassavetes" pops up, it covers everything but his piercing eyes, still looking straight at the lens.

When the show debuted, the similarities to *Peter Gunn* did not go unnoticed. Critic Hal Humphrey wrote in the *Mirror News*, "Producers of the new *Staccato* series . . . prefer that it not be compared to *Peter Gunn*. I would like to oblige them but even the most myopic viewer is soon going to see that Johnny and Pete are kissing cousins."

The ratings started low and didn't shoot up in the first month. So when Cassavetes came to New York in early November 1959 to film some location shots to be inserted into the show (which was being shot on a Hollywood soundstage), he took the opportunity to talk the show up to the press, which he invited along to watch the filming at the now-deserted Polo Grounds and in tenement doorways in Harlem and the Lower East Side, even at a stop outside a Bowery mission. At one point, they filmed Cassavetes running back and forth against traffic on Fifth Avenue, dodging buses and cabs

The show order was for thirty-nine episodes, a full season's worth. They were farmed out to the studio's staff writers, though Cassavetes and Chambers wrote a couple together. And they rewrote almost all of the scripts before putting them in front of the cameras.

"We would shoot for three days and then rehearse and rewrite for two days," Chambers recalled. "There was a lot of rewriting. John wouldn't read the script until the weekend and then there'd be a knock on my door and we'd start rewriting."

Film critic Hollis Alpert recalled seeing an episode he co-wrote, "The Poet's Touch." A friend of his, Bob Hector, had gotten an assignment writing a *Staccato* script and asked Alpert to help him. So Alpert wrote with him and turned in a script that had both their names on it.

When the show aired, Alpert watched in disbelief: "I remember seeing the show and thinking, 'That isn't what I wrote,'" he recalled. "Cassavetes changed everything around. But I got paid. Unfortunately, I also got a credit. One *Variety* critic wrote, 'Here's a movie critic trying to be a TV writer—and look what he came up with!'"

Cassavetes himself directed five episodes: "I tried to do each one differently, hoping to develop some kind of style and technique," he said later. In one, Staccato was called in by a famed defense attorney (Elisha Cook Jr.) to solve the mystery of a pacifist (Cloris Leachman) charged with murdering her husband. But the episode itself featured only the three characters—almost like a play, a throwback to Cassavetes' beginnings— with the camera moving back and forth between close-ups of Cassavetes, as the interrogating Staccato, and Leachman, as the defendant charged with stabbing her husband nine times.

She denies and denies and denies—until Staccato, hoping to get a rise out of her, asks whether her husband ever struck her. Then he hauls off and slaps her fiercely across the face. As he turns his back on her to talk to Cook, she picks up the murder weapon (handily left unattended and within reach on the floor of the interrogation room) and attempts to stab Staccato—just as she had her husband when he hit her.

Cassavetes' excitement and enthusiasm included a continued penchant to roughhouse and show off. Chambers recalled a day when Jennings Lang, who was close to 6-foot-3, came into the production office for *Staccato* to complain about something Cassavetes had done. In a show of mock anger that was both physical and convincing, Cassavetes leapt up and grabbed Lang by the throat, shouting, "You son of a bitch, I'll shoot you in the balls!" before bursting out laughing.

(A decade earlier, Lang had been shot in the groin by producer Walter Wanger, when Wanger found that his wife, actress Joan Bennett, was having an affair with Lang, her then-agent. The attack was followed by a highly publicized trial, in which Wanger was charged with attempted murder.)

Everybody Cassavetes knew, it seemed, was hired to work on *Staccato*. Cassavetes found roles for Gena, Seymour Cassel, Rupert Crosse, Maurice McEndree, John Finnegan, Lelia Goldoni, and several other East Coast friends, including Harry Guardino, Val Avery, Martin Landau, and Cloris Leachman. He also used real jazz musicians—Shelly Manne, Pete Candoli, Red Norvo—to play at Waldo's, the Village *boite* where Staccato played piano and hung out with excitable owner Waldo, played by Italian actor Eduardo Ciannelli. Cassavetes sold them all on appearing with the idea that he was calling the artistic shots.

The actors may have embraced the show, but the network and the sponsors weren't getting the program they'd bargained for. For one thing, its ratings were unremarkable, up against the cornball comedy hit *The Real McCoys*, starring double-Oscar-winner Walter Brennan. For another, Cassavetes' idea of what a TV detective series should be didn't align with the network's vision. Venality and brutality may have been elements, but to Cassavetes they weren't the centerpiece. Staccato was just as likely to help out a friend suffering from mental illness as he was to chase down killers.

Cassavetes completed only twenty-seven of the thirty-nine *Johnny Staccato* episodes before he and the network parted ways. "They wanted a slick *Peter Gunn* kind of cop show and this one was a little esoteric," Chambers said. "So John had a very rough relationship with the network."

There were arguments almost from the start, beginning with the title of the show: Cassavetes preferred the whip-crack sound of the onomatopoetic mononym "Staccato," while the network and the advertising agency for the sponsor preferred the full name. *Johnny Staccato* it was, though eventually there were episodes that identified it just as *Staccato*.

Almost immediately, there were struggles over the subject matter Cassavetes wanted to deal with, including the pacifism episode and one he wanted to do about heroin addiction, called "The Wild Reed." That episode, in which Harry Guardino plays a jazz musician just recovered from a mental breakdown but now strung out on heroin, barely touched on the elements of addiction; but in 1959, the fact that it dealt with drug use at all made it a hot potato. It was shelved in November and was not shown until the end of the series. Meanwhile, the network scrambled to get a Christmas episode, scheduled for late December, on the air in late November.

"It is virtually impossible to get approval on a script that has substance, more so since the outbreak of the TV scandals," Cassavetes complained at the time. "There is no limit on violence; you can get approval on a story in which a woman is slaughtered, but an honest story about a dope addict is rejected because it would be injurious to the sponsor's product. In this case, the product is an underarm deodorant."

When Cassavetes flew to New York at the beginning of 1960 to meet with the sponsors and the network, he went to make as much trouble as he could. They thought he was coming in to discuss renewing the show for a second season, but Cassavetes, ever the provocateur, brought them a decidedly different message. He started by arguing about the censorship— and then he began insulting the sponsor, making cracks about being told what was and wasn't appropriate for television by the makers of "armpit juice." By the time he walked out, *Johnny Staccato* was dead.

As he was getting ready to quit *Johnny Staccato*, Cassavetes had a talk with Sam Shaw about the fact that he was going to be out of work and was concerned because he had no prospects—and an actor's strike loomed.

As it happened, Shaw was friends with the writer of a movie that was going into production in Ireland. So Sam recommended John for an audition, and he was cast in the low-budget British film *The Webster Boy* (also known as *Middle of Nowhere*).

The writer, Ted Allan, met Cassavetes for the first time when he arrived at the film's Irish location, accompanied by Seymour Cassel. Cassavetes put Allan on the defensive almost immediately, bombarding him with notes about the film's screenplay—only to confess later (after identifying himself as Sam Shaw's friend) that he had never read the script.

Cassavetes shot for eight weeks near Dublin, sharing his quarters with Cassel. Cassel would spend the days wandering Dublin, then meet Cassavetes back at their apartment and play a fantasy baseball game they'd made up, using a deck of cards and the names of players currently in the major leagues. Cassel, who had spent formative years in the Motor City, would be the Detroit Tigers; Cassavetes, who appreciated the number of Greek players on their roster, would be the Baltimore Orioles.

As Cassavetes was finishing the film, a review of *Shadows*, based on one of the Cinema 16 showings in late 1959, had turned up in the spring 1960 issue of *Film Quarterly*. Written by Albert Johnson, a programmer for the San Francisco Film Festival, it once more raised the banner for this ground-breaking American film—and British film programmers, their interest tweaked already by Jonas Mekas' early review, had taken notice.

Johnson called it a "celluloid diamond of neorealism," terming it "the best American film about racial relations yet made . . . Despite the crudities of lens and the occasionally discordant soundtrack, the truthfulness is inescapable, making *Shadows* a notably dynamic film gesture toward total reality."

As a result of that review, Cassavetes and Cassel were invited to a meeting at the British Film Institute's National Film Theater. The two headed for London the weekend after finishing *The Webster Boy*, in the spring of 1960—and their BFI meeting resulted in a verbal invitation for Cassavetes to screen *Shadows* at BFI's 1960 Beat, Square, and Cool festival in July.

Cassavetes and Cassel quickly agreed and, apparently, just as quickly forgot all about it (or assumed that the other would take care of the details). Cassavetes went back to California to look for work, while Cassel stayed on in Europe. One Friday in early July, Cassel got a call from the BFI. The screening of *Shadows* was scheduled for the coming Monday, but there was a problem about the print. Specifically, BFI didn't have one and wanted to know how to reach Cassavetes to try to find one.

Cassel called Cassavetes, who hurriedly packed up the print and shipped it to London in time for the showing. It screened to glowing reviews—and proved to be possibly the most significant moment in his career, the turning point from which all else flowed: from Cassavetes' own career to the direction of American independent film and filmmaking.

"It is a landmark in the American cinema," declared Derek Prouse in the London *Sunday Times*, referring to "a stratum of New York's society bared to the bone; the fringe society of beatniks and insecure intellectuals drinking, necking and talking the night through to a shifty dawn."

The *Observer* said, "To an art half-strangled by professionalism, it brings a breath of spontaneity. It's as though we were offered, instead of a column of glossy print, a smudgy penciled note telling us something we've been wanting to hear."

Cassavetes, still in L.A., received another collect call from Cassel in London: "Listen, John, *Shadows* was a great success at the festival and the critics are still going crazy over it. You've got to come over here and we've got to sell the movie to a distributor. It's now or never."

Cassavetes couldn't imagine how his film had become a phenomenon, but it had, catching the crest of the Angry Young Man movement that
would spawn the mods, the rockers, the Beatles, and the whole of Swinging London of the 1960s.

When Cassavetes reached London, there was interest from a distribu-
tor, British Lion, and an invitation for an August showing at the Venice Film
Festival, where it won the silver cup. Cassavetes signed a deal with British
Lion, which capitalized on the reviews from the BFI festival screenings in
July and opened *Shadows* at the Academy Cinema on Oxford Street, a Lon-
don art house, in October 1960, where it played to sold-out crowds.

Shadows set a house record in its first week at the Academy, grossing
more than £11,000 its first week—a bundle, given that it was a 500-seat
theater. Audiences were drawn by the buzz generated by the film's festival
success and the renewed rhapsodizing by the British critics at the film's
theatrical run.

"I like this film," C. A. Lejeune wrote in the *Observer* when *Shadows*
opened in October. "It makes me feel young again, partly because its
strain is human, partly because the new ideas it advances are so refresh-
ingly old. We were looking and hoping this way as far back as 1923. We
thought we could find a new world for the cinema by speaking simply
and speaking true. We failed. Now perhaps Cassavetes and his kind can
find it."

When the film caused a sensation in its theatrical run in London, the
mainstream American press picked up the scent. "As a work of art, *Shadows* is uneven and its improvisation sometimes shows," *Newsweek* wrote
on the London phenomenon, then added, "But when its peculiar, impromptu chemistry is really working, *Shadows* is both real and rousing—
sometimes humorously, sometimes tragically."

With the exception of a few hundred cognoscenti in New York, hardly
anyone had seen the finished *Shadows* in the United States. But virtually
everyone in Hollywood had seen the review in *Variety* from the festival in
London. It said *Shadows* was a "case where an unusual approach has paid off
with a pic that gives an incisive picture of human tensions and problems
without preaching or proselytizing. *Shadows* is new in its bite, drive and intensity and its insistence on content over form."

As a result of the reports of the London success of *Shadows*, two mistaken impressions were formed. One impression—held by the cast and
crew of *Shadows*—was that the movie was churning cash by the barrelful.
The other was that Cassavetes, the hot new director of the moment, should
immediately be funneled into the Hollywood studio system.

Word spread in the trades about this critically acclaimed American independent film made by the controversial actor who had just gone head to head with Universal over *Johnny Staccato*. Cassavetes suddenly found himself sought after by the same American studios that had ignored him.

One studio finally decided to hire him to direct a mainstream film. The offer from Paramount was generous: to write and direct a film of his choosing, with what was (for Cassavetes) a lavish budget of about $350,000, a full studio crew, and big-name actors. And it came to Cassavetes almost sight-unseen. All Paramount seemed to know was that Cassavetes had something and they wanted a piece of it, even if they didn't know what it was.

All of the attention being paid to Cassavetes in the trades and other newspapers fueled the belief among the *Shadows* crew that Cassavetes had forgotten them. They also assumed that the British success would translate into a lucrative distribution deal for *Shadows* in the United States.

But that hope ignored the reality that, in 1960, the United States was still a racially segregated country. In the American South, segregation was still state law in many places, which made showing a sympathetic film about black-white relationships unthinkable in a large swath of the country. That limited what was, realistically, a small potential audience for a movie that was already so far out of the mainstream. New York might have been ready for a movie about mixed-race characters confronting the racial divide, but Dixie wasn't.

The reality of how extensive an American release would be didn't seem to filter down to the cast and crew. All they could see were reviews and stories declaring *Shadows* the hit of London, headlines proclaiming Cassavetes' new directing deal with Paramount, and the glowing reviews when *Shadows* finally opened in New York. Cassavetes appeared to be riding high, while the rest of them—to whom he'd promised fame and fortune—were watching him from a distance.

"He never paid anyone for *Shadows* and so they all sued him," Burton Lane said.

The lawsuit found its way to New York State Supreme Court in April 1961, naming Cassavetes; British Lion, the distributor; producers Maurice McEndree and Seymour Cassel; and Cassavetes' Gena Productions as defendants. It was a $500,000 civil suit filed by David Pokitillow, an actor in the film; Ben Carruthers; Jay Crecco, a crew member; and Erich Kollmar, charging that they'd been deprived of their rights and profits in the movie.

Marvin Lichtner, a still photographer who had photographed some of the filming, recalled, "They thought he was getting the dough and some of them sued. I knew enough to know how it works and that there was no serious money. John was in debt. I refused to join the suit. They didn't understand how little money comes from something like that."

And Seymour Cassel said, "If John made money on *Shadows*, he deserved it. We all got something. Every couple of years, I get a check for $900 or $1,000 for *Shadows* or *Faces*. But you didn't have to pay me to do those films. And I don't know any company that's still paying forty years later. But the people who filed the lawsuit thought there was more money. They thought John was screwing them. But you couldn't find a more honest guy than John in this business."

"I didn't agree with the lawsuit," Lelia Goldoni said. "We had an agreement and we had to live by it."

But the suit had been filed in a New York state court, and Cassavetes had moved to California in the days before states had reciprocity on these kinds of cases.

British Lion couldn't scare up an American distributor, so it finally opened *Shadows* itself in New York City in March 1961, at the Embassy Theater, to reviews almost as effusive as the ones in England.

"There is much that is good about John Cassavetes' *Shadows* and also much that is bad, but what's good is good in the important sense, while what's bad is bad where it should count least," Paul V. Beckley wrote in the *Herald Tribune*. "At its height the film has a high sense of style and a psychologically acute insight into life while in technique it is often rough, sometimes to the point of endangering its substance. Story in the usual sense is the least important element of *Shadows*, which is bent rather on portraying the psychological crises of three people and the giddy and bewildering double world they live in."

The *New York Times'* Bosley Crowther grumbled disapprovingly about the improvisational nature of the film, then finally allowed, "*Shadows* is an unfinished picture in every sense of the word. Yet it is fitfully dynamic, endowed with a raw but vibrant strength, conveying an illusion of being a record of real people and it is incontestably sincere."

And *Variety*, reviewing the film again for the New York opening, said, "The technical quality of *Shadows* is crude. At times, the audiences can barely hear or even see what is going on, but one can always feel the impulse of excitement generated by the picture. Its very crudeness captures the spontaneity, the unpredictability, the raw unruly pattern of human behavior."

The foreign furor for the film didn't translate to interest among American viewers. The interested few saw it in New York, and a few more saw it during a July run in Los Angeles. Then *Shadows* wound up back on Cassavetes' shelf.

The saga of *Shadows* had also reached a young college student at New York University named Martin Scorsese, who harbored dreams of making films himself. Suddenly, Scorsese thought, here was someone—an actor, at that—who had found a way to make a feature film for very little money, telling the kind of story Hollywood films seldom tried to tell in a style that seemed excitingly fresh and new. "After James Dean was killed, when John started directing, it was as if James Dean had started to direct movies," Scorsese said. "You can't gauge the amount of hope that such an act created for young people. It was like a starting pistol for a race that still keeps going."

The myths spawned by *Shadows* grew and flourished. Foremost among them, of course, was the notion that the finished film as released was the total product of improvisation (thanks to the end-card saying it was), which many people equated with ad-libbing. Forever after, Cassavetes would fight the reputation that he was some glorified maker of home movies who made the films up as he went along.

There was also the notion that what wound up in the finished film of *Shadows* was put there by design: that the abrupt cuts, the scratchy sound that sometimes includes heavy doses of ambient traffic noise, was a deliberate stylistic choice, as were the selection of locations and camera angles.

As Cassavetes said, "When we opened *Shadows* in London, they said it had the truest sound they'd ever seen. At that time, all the pictures were looped, cleaned up, and made to be almost sterile. It was just voices, the dialogue was so clear. But we recorded most of *Shadows* in the dance studio with Bob Fosse dancers working overhead. We never considered the sound. We didn't even check it. Then we spent hours, days, weeks, months, years trying to clean it up. But it was impossible so we went with what we had. And they said it was an innovation."

"It was all accidents," Burton Lane later said. "Everything that was praised was all accidents. They did everything wrong. There were sharp cuts because there were no transition shots. A lot of shots didn't follow or match. A lot of things were wrong. But it looked like a personal film. He patched it up and it seemed to be part of the trend for auteur movies. It was 'John Cassavetes' *Shadows*.'"

At the time, however, it all seemed like a great idea that was a lot of fun to do, but whose moment had passed.

"All that tremendous hoopla stayed on the other side of the Atlantic,"

Cassavetes later said. "In America, we had what we started out with—a 16mm black and white grainy rule-breaking nonimportant film that got shown only when someone was willing to do us a favor."

He went even further at the time. With the Paramount offer in hand, Cassavetes said that he'd never make another movie that way again. "All this was terribly exciting, of course, but it is not something I am likely to do again," he said. "It's like doing summer stock; it's a good experience to have had. I couldn't do it again because, for one thing, I just wouldn't have the energy."

Little did he know that he had already established the model for doing the most important work of his career.

Eighteen

Shadows—A Postscript

"**A**ctually, there are two versions of *Shadows*: a first version and a second," John Cassavetes said in a 1961 interview. "That simply means that when we finished the first, we were dissatisfied with it and we reshot for ten days."

The lore of the first version lingered on, however. In the forty-plus years since the first screenings and eventual release of *Shadows*, the film itself has become regarded as a landmark of its time, the movie that lit the long-burning fuse on both Cassavetes' career and American independent film. But the story of *Shadows* and its making always included that first cut—the one that Cassavetes reshot and reedited into the *Shadows* that was released into theaters in London and America, the one that became a staple of revival houses and film-history classes.

But the first version still tantalized at least one Cassavetes scholar: Ray Carney, a Boston University professor, who wrote the first book on Cassavetes, *American Dreaming: The Films of John Cassavetes and the American Experience*, published in 1985. In subsequent years, he corresponded with Cassavetes and wrote several more books and monographs about him, including *Cassavetes on Cassavetes*, a kind of oral biography in which Carney collected every quote of Cassavetes' that he could find, arranged them chronologically, and linked them with his own transitional passages filling in facts and dates; and a 2001 volume for the British Film Institute on

Shadows, in which he used interior clues and interviews with the principals and people who had seen it to reconstruct what might have been in the first version of *Shadows*.

The entire time, Carney had also been searching for clues to the fate of that first version. When he had asked Cassavetes about it before the director's death in 1989, Cassavetes professed ignorance. He believed that he had given it to someone so film students could use it for editing practice. But he had no idea where it wound up—and the fact that there was only one spliced-together 16mm print of the film seemed to point toward its eventual disappearance and/or destruction.

Carney, however, was convinced that the print still existed, and he was determined to track it down. It became his Holy Grail: to find the film that not only started a revolution but was deemed inadequate and discarded by its maker. It represented a piece of film history too important for Carney to abandon his search.

"Given that the 1957–58 print of *Shadows*—and not the 1959 version—was really his first feature film, I set myself the task of determining once and for all if the earlier print survived," Carney wrote on his website. "What made the *Shadows* story especially interesting was that a number of critics and viewers who saw both versions were convinced that Cassavetes had made a grievous mistake."

Which is probably a generous reading, given the generally negative response to the first film in most reports. Nonetheless, Carney, an academic with bulldog tenacity, had his quest. Through a number of coincidences too elaborate to delineate here (but available in full on Carney's website), he found what he believed was the print of the first version in an attic in Florida.

In the interest of preserving the film—in spite of the fact that, by his own estimate, he had spent seventeen years and as much as $40,000 of his own money searching for it—Carney did not screen the print once he received it. Rather, he waited the additional ten days it took to transfer the print to video so as not to damage the original when he screened it.

When he watched it, he found that it was in near-perfect condition: "It's only run through a projector three to five times at most," he said. "It's better quality than any print you'll find in a theater."

Carney found that his hypothesis about what had been in the first version was very close to what was in the film. It's also a longer film than Carney expected, running seventy-eight minutes, compared to the finished version's eighty-one.

"It's a totally different film," he said. "The earlier version is more in the vein of *Husbands*. It's the story of three buddies carousing and carrying on and bonding on the streets of New York. Ben and Tom and Dennis are the central figures. Tony and his relationship with Lelia are significantly different. It's a different film."

Having come across the print in the second half of 2003, Carney excitedly began offering it to film festivals. The first one to accept his offer was the Rotterdam International Film Festival in January 2004, which began advertising its big catch and quickly sold out both of the screenings it had scheduled.

Word of the screenings eventually reached Al Ruban, who is partners with Gena Rowlands in Faces International, the distribution company that owns the rights to all of the Cassavetes films he financed himself, including *Shadows*.

But Ruban, who is the clearinghouse for all presentations of any of the Cassavetes-owned films, had never given permission or even been approached about screening any version of the film. So he called the films' London distributor to see whether anyone had sought permission to show the film. No one had.

Ruban informed Rowlands, who was outraged. She contacted Carney and told him that he had no right to show one of Cassavetes' films, no matter how important he thought it was, without her permission. As far as she was concerned, there was only one version of *Shadows* that was authorized for public presentation—and that was the finished version that had been released in 1959.

Ruban, meanwhile, was on the phone to the Rotterdam Film Festival, which was caught in an uncomfortable position: On the one hand, they had sold out all of their screenings of what was seen as an international film event. On the other hand, they had no legal right to show the film and could get in serious trouble if they did so.

Eventually they reached a compromise, distributing a flyer at the screenings that contained the same message that was posted on the festival website:

"Please note that the version of *Shadows* screened at the International Film Festival Rotterdam was unauthorized. It has been brought to our attention that authorization was never sought from the owner of all rights to *Shadows*, her company or its agents or representatives. Unfortunately, this was not known to the RIFF at the time and had we been aware of this, we would not have allowed the film to be screened here. It is not the policy of the RIFF to knowingly circumvent legal responsibility and our sincere apology is extended to those adversely affected.

"The ownership of the film *Shadows* in any form resides with Gena Rowlands Cassavetes and is managed by her company, Faces Distribution Cor-
poration, and their authorized representative, In-Motion Pictures Limited.
There is only one authorized version of *Shadows*, that which was released to
the public by its director, John Cassavetes, in 1959. Any prior screening was
a work in progress with an invited, nonpaying audience. Therefore, requests
for exploitation of anything other than the authorized version will not be
entertained."

Carney compares watching the first version of *Shadows* to "looking at
the sketchbooks that precede the final version of a painting, or the note-
books of a poet that eventuate in the final poem. It is a chance to peep into
the workshop of an artist and see Cassavetes' actual, unreleased first film,
the work that preceded the current print of *Shadows*."

When repeated requests that Carney surrender the print of *Shadows*
went unanswered, Rowlands and Ruban brought attorneys into the affair.
Carney still has the print and continues to show the video version in his
film class at Boston University, apparently protected by the tenets of academic freedom. On his website, he has cast himself as the lone voice of
reason against a tide of barbarians.

"Her goal was not merely to ignore the print but to suppress it and even
suppress knowledge of it," Carney wrote of Rowlands. "She told me that
she would suppress or even destroy the print if necessary to keep it out of
circulation. To protect the print, I have been forced to hire a lawyer and
spend money I do not have, but I am doing it to save it from suppression,
loss or destruction. I am doing it for posterity. I am doing it for John."

Al Ruban was angered by Carney's response: "I take exception when
he begins to speak for John. No one can speak for John, including myself
and Gena.

"The film was not finished," Ruban said. "When an author or a creator
lets people see a work to see whether he's on the right track, it's a work in
progress. That's not what's going to be released. It's an effort to get to the
point of finishing.

"I don't dispute that Ray Carney found a print of the first version of
Shadows. The problem is that what he has is material he's not entitled to
keep and the film is copyright protected. And he didn't even have the courtesy of telling us that he'd arranged two special screenings at Rotterdam."

Nineteen

Too Late Blues

It's tempting to assume that, out of the freeing experience of improvisation and making it up as he went along in *Shadows*, Cassavetes unleashed the spirit of a maverick independent, determined to work outside the system and make films his own way.

But, in fact, as Cassavetes himself repeatedly said, *Shadows* was an experiment. Cassavetes wasn't part of the film underground, though he had suddenly become its unwitting poster boy. He wasn't looking to expand the boundaries of cinema the way the directors of the French New Wave were—perhaps even inspired by *Shadows*.

That outsider instinct would eventually come to the fore. Cassavetes finally would come to understand that he simply couldn't work within the studio system. Though he occasionally would make subversive forays back into it—as an actor and, rarely, as a director—he said at the time, "I'll never make a film that way again."

In the wake of *Shadows* and even *Johnny Staccato*, however, Cassavetes had developed the taste for writing and directing. *Staccato*, despite the constant struggles about content, had taught him some of the technical things he needed to know about filmmaking.

Riding the London success of *Shadows*, before the film had even really been shown in the United States, Cassavetes jumped at the chance to develop a film of his own at Paramount. He was being advised by Martin

Baum, a young agent of the old school, who believed that rising within the system was the desired career track. As wild and unconventional as Cassavetes could be, Baum understood that John was having the kind of moment that needed to be capitalized upon. And Cassavetes himself assumed that the studio system was the preferred route, because there was no viable alternative at that point in history except the one he'd just taken, which he was not eager to repeat.

So when Martin Rackin, head of production at Paramount, called and asked Cassavetes if he had a script and could he bring it out for a meeting in Hollywood, Cassavetes said certainly—and then called Richard Carr, who had been the story editor on *Johnny Staccato*, and together they rewrote a script they'd written together during *Staccato* (though Cassavetes later claimed to have cranked it out with Carr in a single, hurried weekend).

After he gave the script to Rackin, Cassavetes got an almost immediate yes. Production, he was told, would begin in two weeks. So shortly after *Shadows* opened commercially in London, Cassavetes made his deal with Paramount, which was announced at the end of December 1960. He had earlier told the *New York Times* that he and Carr had written a script Cassavetes called "a jazz or blues type of drama, the theme of which is the idea that, despite any success we may achieve, society pushes us to the point of unhappiness."

He and Carr called the script *Too Late Blues*, though Paramount, in a fit of obviousness, wanted to retitle it "Dreams for Sale." Initially Cassavetes was convinced that the studio was sincere in its offer to allow him to make the movie his way (the studio's unstated hope being that they could bottle the same lightning Cassavetes had caught with *Shadows*). *Variety* declared that the studio "was going to take every conceivable chance on a new approach and concept."

"It's about time that artists stopped complaining about the impossibility of making good films through major studios and started exerting influence and accepting responsibility in the areas in which they are most qualified," Cassavetes said at the time. "I think it's about time the artist worried only about making a good picture and not about whether he's going to have a job with the next picture."

And, he added, "The fact that a major Hollywood studio thinks it can make money with an art film is a big step forward."

Paramount already had taken that plunge with actors as directors: The studio was about to release *One-Eyed Jacks*, which had gone wildly over schedule with Marlon Brando as director, and actor Edmond O'Brien was scheduled to produce and direct *Hell Is for Heroes* (though he was eventually replaced by Don Siegel). Still, Cassavetes recognized that the studio was taking a chance on him.

"The one picture I made was a $40,000, 16-millimeter experimental film. Paramount now insists that I produce as well as direct, so that no one would be sitting over my shoulder telling me what to do. That becomes a big risk when hundreds of thousands of dollars are at stake."

Almost immediately, he ran into problems: He had written the lead roles, John "Ghost" Wakefield and Jessica Polanski, with two actors in mind: Montgomery Clift and Gena Rowlands.

Gena hadn't acted much since Nick's birth. John thought the part would be perfect for her and would give them the chance to work together. And Clift had been a hero of Cassavetes since his acting-school days. Shortly after leaving AADA, John had seen *A Place in the Sun*, with Clift's incomparable performance for George Stevens, opposite Elizabeth Taylor, and it had made an indelible mark on him.

But Paramount said no to both casting choices. They didn't want Gena Rowlands because she was an unknown; she'd never followed up *The High Cost of Loving* with another picture, and her maternity leave had robbed her of whatever heat she'd had at that moment.

Clift was going through a rocky phase in his career. It was only three or four years earlier that he'd smashed his car—and his face—during the making of *Raintree County*. He was a lifelong sufferer from colitis, which had led to a dependence on painkillers and alcohol. His addictions were exacerbated by his own internal conflicts about his sexuality, and his problems were all well known within the industry, if not by the general public.

So Paramount vetoed him, for fear that a relatively inexperienced director would be unable to handle the temperamental star. In his place, they recommended Bobby Darin, a pop singer who had only just started acting. The studio's choice for the role of Jessica was Stella Stevens, who had just made another film for the studio—*Girls! Girls! Girls!*—opposite Elvis Presley.

Cassavetes, whose name was nearly synonymous with the word "improvisation" after *Shadows*, found himself answering the same questions over and over: How would he cope with directing actors performing a script, as opposed to an improv? Though he didn't say it in so many words, Cassavetes was laying the foundation for his idea that the true improvisation came from the actor's emotional connection to the material and the way he interpreted the script. That was the actor's and the actor's alone.

"I believe in my players having complete emotional rights because, after all, they're the only ones on the production who work from pure emotion," he said. "I may feel with them but I'm the director, an observer. My position on the picture is to help stimulate their emotions but not to tell them how to depict them. What do I seek to portray? The absolute emotional truth of people as they are."

Cassavetes lined up some of the same jazz names that had appeared on *Johnny Staccato* to play the music for the combo in the picture: pianist Jimmy Rowles, drummer Shelly Manne, bassist Red Mitchell, saxman Benny Carter, and trumpeter Uan Rasey.

He was able to give jobs to a number of friends in the film, since the leads had been dictated by the studio. He filled the band roles with friends such as Seymour Cassel (Red, the bass player); Cliff Carnell (Charley, the sax player); and his post-Academy roommate Bill Stafford (Shelly, the drummer). He gave roles to Rupert Crosse and Val Avery and to actor Mario Gallo, both of whom had done episodes of *Johnny Staccato*.

He also cast Vince Edwards, with whom he'd become friends after *The Night Holds Terror*, and his *Staccato* producer, Everett Chambers, who had done some acting in live TV before becoming a casting director.

Cassavetes' budget was $350,000; he had six weeks or thirty shooting days. And, of course, he had to have a script. Larry Shaw, who had followed in his father Sam Shaw's footsteps and become a set photographer, had been doing photos for *The Comancheros* at Fox. At Cassavetes' request, he went over to Paramount to shoot *Too Late Blues* for Cassavetes.

"That was a very organized set," Shaw said. "He was doing it on the strength of the success of *Shadows* and it was like being on the Fox set, which was being directed by Michael Curtiz. There was no difference. It was a studio production."

Even for 1961, *Too Late Blues* looks naive and square. The idea that these guys are hipster jazz musicians, representative of the time, is laughable, despite their efforts at speaking the lingo. And the music they play (written by David Raksin, who wrote *Laura*) has little or nothing to do with jazz, particularly as it was played in 1961.

The film centers on pianist John "Ghost" Wakefield (Bobby Darin) and his jazz quintet. First seen playing a gig at a school, they are guys who want to make it as musicians but feel they're going nowhere fast.

The guiding force in their career is sharklike agent Benny Flowers (Everett Chambers). Ghost runs into him at a party where Benny is squiring a singer named Jessica Polanski. But when he urges her to sing, she sings poorly—and Benny tells her as much, before turning his charm on Ghost, promising him a recording date.

Ghost, however, is interested in Jessica. He takes her home, though he rejects her advances when she tries to sleep with him. Instead, he invites her to sing with the band at the recording date Benny is arranging.

(At the same party where they meet, the party's host, a jazz musician named Baby Jackson [Rupert Crosse] upbraids Benny, who is also his agent. He orders Benny around, a scene of such concern for Paramount that the studio removed it before the film played in the South, so it didn't appear that the white agent worked for a black musician or that the black musician was berating the white agent.)

But after the recording session, when they all go to the pool hall to drink and unwind, Benny gets jealous of Jess's interest in Ghost. As the band celebrates, they attract the interest of two other pool players, Tommy (Vince Edwards) and Skipper (Alan Hopkins). The two strangers start drinking with the band, then start insulting them—and then Tommy instigates a fight.

In the film's best scene, the drunken Tommy baits the musicians with insults until Charlie knocks him to the floor. Helped to his feet, Tommy manages to knock out everyone in the band, then rounds on Ghost, who is caught flat-footed. When Ghost refuses to respond to Tommy's scurrilous taunts, Jess attacks Tommy and gets shoved aside as Tommy sneers at Ghost, "A girl's got more guts."

Tommy grabs Ghost in a headlock, chokes him, and throws him to the floor at Jess's feet. Humiliated, Ghost can only cower there—and then viciously snarls at Jess after the fight, as though she has caused his humiliation. He leaves, then goes to Jess's apartment, where she is being comforted by Charlie. She tells Ghost to leave. When he tries to explain his behavior—"I'm not a prize-fighter," he shrugs—she snarls, "I didn't want a prize-fighter."

In the film's most improbable twist, Ghost goes back to Benny, who lands him a gig as a gigolo, playing jazz piano in a supper club and servicing his "benefactor," the Countess (Marilyn Clark). But he quits after being told that his talent is nothing special and that Benny probably can't find him any other work.

The interval between Ghost's overture to Benny about the gigolo job and the scene in which he quits the same job consists of a momentary fade-out on the screen. One scene he's asking about work; the next scene he's quitting. Supposedly Cassavetes' original cut of the film included lengthy character-study sequences of Ghost that were trimmed for time, making this transition jarring, to say the least.

Having quit the Countess, Ghost goes looking for his old band and finds them playing shlock dance music in a nightclub. Charlie, however, is glad to see him—and even tells him where he can find Jess. He goes to a bar, where he finds her negotiating what is obviously a prostitute's fee with two men.

Seeking to redeem himself, Ghost attacks the two men, tossing them out of the bar, then apologizing to Jess and asking for a fresh start. She goes to the ladies' room and tries to slash her wrists, but Ghost stops her, then drags her back to the nightclub where the band is playing.

There, everyone in the band vents anger at Ghost, telling him to leave. Ghost just stands there and takes it—and suddenly Jess, who has come unwillingly to the club, begins singing the same song they were supposed to record together, a wordless croon of a piece that, again, has little or nothing to do with jazz.

The film feels flat and lifeless at times, because Darin was an inexperienced and not particularly expressive actor. He needs to seem sensitive but mostly seems smug and sarcastic. There are also large chunks of the story missing, excised in the name of moving the plot along.

In style, the movie seems to have little in common with *Shadows*, though its theme of an outsider trying to be true to his own beliefs and vision—like Hugh or even Ben in *Shadows*—seems to carry forward from the previous film, and would remain a constant in Cassavetes' work.

As he was filming, Cassavetes described the film as not being about anything "except hope. It's about people who like to dream. No one seems to dream anymore. It's a soft word, an outdated cliché . . . It's the most fantastic role ever given a woman. This film will make Stella the biggest money star in Hollywood."

But Cassavetes knew the script wasn't right going in. He claimed he and Carr had written the screenplay in a single weekend—and then the studio had OK'd it as it was and vaulted directly into production. He had never had a chance to rehearse and rewrite; the run-up to production was too short and the shooting schedule too tight to allow for any kind of overhaul on what was, in Cassavetes' view, a glorified first draft.

"The studio people liked and accepted the first thing I did," he said later. "I intended to change quite a few things, to add things, but I had no experience at all in the tactics to follow in Hollywood studios.

"Later, I realized that I had to fight the studio system, which I did. But that's why *Too Late Blues* is an incomplete film."

The studio system also meant dealing with a chain of command, which meant more hoops to be jumped through to get anything done: "It's a system based on departments and department heads," Cassavetes said. "I'm not very good at dealing with department heads, so I find that I really can't get anywhere that way, simply because I'm not concerned with their problems. I'm only concerned with mine. That might be a selfish attitude but there it is. All I want to talk about, all I want to think about, is getting my picture made."

That included focusing on such mundane subjects as the size of his budget (it seemed huge in comparison to what he'd had to work with on *Shadows*—particularly because none of the money was his own) and what his offices would look like.

"I intend to make it as cheaply as [*Shadows*] and I intend to make it as cheaply as possible so that I hope it will make money for them," he said.

Cassavetes, the artist, didn't recognize the symbolic weight such mercenary, materialistic concerns could carry with the studio bosses and dismissed them as irrelevant, to his own detriment. In working cheaply, he sent the wrong message.

"There is no such thing as a low-budget picture at a major studio," Cassavetes said later. "At least not from a director's point of view—once you say it's a low-budget picture, it's like being a man with no credit in a rich neighborhood."

Cassavetes had worn his low-budget status as a badge of honor, in the mistaken belief that his artistic integrity carried weight. So when the studio asked him whether he wanted to have offices at the studio, he said yes but asked for just four small rooms.

Almost immediately, Cassavetes found himself unable to get cooperation from any of the department heads he had to deal with. Offices were considered a status symbol; people assumed that the studio had assigned the office space to Cassavetes as an expression of its regard for him. "People were thinking I'll be fired because I had such small offices," Cassavetes said later. "My friend Don Siegel came over and said, 'No wonder you're a failure—you have small offices.' So I picked the largest office I could find—and I was now the biggest director on the lot because I had the biggest office."

Paramount decided to open *Too Late Blues* in Europe, beginning in Paris, prior to its American release in early 1962. Cassavetes liked the idea of the European release. He referred to Paramount as an "ahead" studio, saying this pattern made more sense than screening it in the United States and then opening here first. At advance screenings in the U.S., he reasoned, "nobody sees it except people who don't want to," meaning critics and industry people. But the European opening would be for the public, rather than critics.

When *Too Late Blues* did finally play for critics in the U.S. and England, they seemed to bend over backward to put a positive face on the film. Cassavetes had earned so much good will with *Shadows* that *Too Late Blues* got reviews that were respectfully hopeful and forgiving. When the criticism was harsh, it often had to do with the perception that an independent visionary had sold his soul to the studio.

"*Too Late Blues* is what happens when a filmmaker of mingled gifts tries to match his talent for screen improvisation with the rigid demands of the front office," wrote Philip Oakes in *Sight and Sound*. Philip Hartung, writing in *Commonweal*, said, "The finished picture is so diffuse that it seems more amateurish than *Shadows*."

Newsweek's review referred to *Too Late Blues* as "one of the most fascinating movies of recent years," but said that the film "often drags." Still, its nameless critic allowed that the film was "more enjoyable in failure than many movies are in success."

Time magazine was less charitable: "The dark-eyed darling of American cinema's avant-garde confidently picked up the directorial baton—and fell flat on his face," its critic wrote.

And Jonas Mekas weighed in, piling on with an I-told-you-so review in the *Village Voice*: "*Too Late Blues*, John Cassavetes' first Hollywood film, is as bad as I expected it to be. . . . It is clear by now that the first version of *Shadows* was a workshop project and that the contribution of Cassavetes consisted mainly of a proper coordination of the workshop. When Cassavetes, seduced by the success of the film, began improving upon the workshop project, *Shadows* became a second-rate Hollywood movie. . . . Whatever the case, *Too Late Blues* is a total disaster."

Twenty

A Child Is Waiting

Before Cassavetes even finished *Too Late Blues*, Paramount had made assumptions about his future value—big assumptions.

The studio signed him to a seven-year nonexclusive deal as a director, and Cassavetes began planning his next film. Paramount's nonexclusive contract called for two pictures a year. The contract was announced in May 1961.

Production on the next film would dovetail with the planned European release of *Too Late Blues* in the fall of 1961, placing Cassavetes on the continent to both direct his next film and publicize his last one. Cassavetes, who was struggling with finishing *Blues*, couldn't believe his luck.

"When *Too Late Blues* was over, I thought I would be over, too," Cassavetes said. "And then the studio, Paramount, asked me if I'd like to sign a contract. At that point, I realized that success and failure weren't necessarily success and failure. I had heard so much about people who fail and then get enormous contracts. I never could quite believe it, until it happened to me."

The first film in his contract would be "The Iron Men," a World War II drama that would reunite Cassavetes with Sidney Poitier; it would begin shooting in the fall of 1961. Poitier would play a member of an all-black unit in Italy who becomes involved with a young Italian resistance fighter driven to kill Nazis.

Working again with Richard Carr, Cassavetes put together the script and gave it to producer Martin Poll: "I wasn't going to play producer again," Cassavetes said. Having served as both producer and director on *Too Late Blues*, he found his attention divided, both in terms of time and in terms of being forced to make decisions about the movie on financial, rather than artistic, grounds. So he was happy to work with an experienced producer, at least until he turned in the script.

"He began going through it with a pencil and muttering, 'This is too long, far too long'," Cassavetes recalled. Having learned his lesson on *Too Late Blues*, Cassavetes went to Marty Rackin, the head of Paramount, and told him that he couldn't work in this way and that he was going to quit the picture. Rackin, however, pleaded with him to stay, and Cassavetes acquiesced.

Cassavetes met with Burt Lancaster, who was cast as a loud-mouthed war correspondent in the film. The two hit it off and talked about Lancaster's next picture, *A Child Is Waiting*, from a script by Abby Mann; it was produced by Stanley Kramer (the team that had just done *Judgment at Nuremberg* with Lancaster) at United Artists. Shortly afterward, with Cassavetes still in preproduction on "The Iron Men," he got a call from Kramer himself; the socially conscious producer of such films as *High Noon, The Defiant Ones,* and *On the Beach,* wanted to see if he could entice Cassavetes to drop "The Iron Men" and take over *A Child Is Waiting.* Almost as soon as Cassavetes demurred, "The Iron Men" fell apart, and Cassavetes signed to do Kramer's film.

Which was just as well because when *Too Late Blues* hit theaters, it bombed. Paramount quickly rethought its commitment to Cassavetes and his notions of studio-financed art films. "Mr. Cassavetes said he had learned that it was foolish to be honorable in dealing with a major studio," a *New York Times* story reported in early 1962.

An old-fashioned problem drama, *A Child Is Waiting* is set at a state hospital for the mentally retarded in rural New Jersey (though it was actually shot at Pacific State Hospital for the Retarded in Pomona, California), run by Dr. Clark (Burt Lancaster). It begins with a father, Ted Widdicombe (Stephen Hill), leaving his son, Reuben (Bruce Ritchey), with Dr. Clark, who entices Reuben out of his father's automobile by offering a toy car to ride in.

Sometime later, Jean Hansen (Judy Garland), a would-be teacher, arrives and walks into the main hall of the school just as classes break. She is immediately surrounded by the retarded students, who are moving from class to class. It's a baptism by fire, but she reacts with kindness, rather than fear.

In Dr. Clark's office, she admits she has no teaching experience but says, "All my life, I've tried to find something to give it meaning and so far, I've been unsuccessful." With no experience or teaching skills to speak of, she is immediately hired to create a music program.

But she finds herself beguiled by Reuben, a problem student who doesn't look retarded but is apparently developmentally disabled. She is shocked to learn that Reuben's mother hasn't been to visit in the two years that he's been at the institution and asks Dr. Clark for permission to write to her, but he refuses. When Jean's friendship with Reuben threatens the discipline in the cottage where they both reside, Dr. Clark moves her to another set of living quarters.

Convinced that Reuben needs to see his parents, Jean surreptitiously gets hold of Reuben's file and reads it. In flashback, we see Reuben's parents, Ted and Sophie (Gena Rowlands), as they slowly come to the realization that there is something wrong with Reuben—something they won't really admit to themselves until he is nearly eight.

Jean clandestinely contacts Sophie, telling her that Reuben is sick. So Sophie and her new husband, Douglas Benham (Lawrence Tierney), come to the school. Angered to discover that it has been a ruse, Sophie sends for Dr. Clark, then leaves without seeing Reuben, but Reuben spots her and is traumatized when she leaves without talking to him. The next night, Reuben gets up in the middle of the night and sneaks off the grounds and runs away.

Dr. Clark confronts Jean and tells her that she has hurt Reuben by coddling him—that retarded people needed to be challenged to be as self-sufficient as possible if they are ever to survive in the world. Rather than be warehoused, they need schooling or jobs that fit their skills in order to have lives with meaning.

Chastened, Jean teaches her music class and even reprimands Reuben for bad behavior. She begins to organize a Thanksgiving play with music.

Meanwhile, Ted Widdicombe has met with his ex-wife to discuss what to do for Reuben. They finally decide to take him out of the facility and find private care for him. But when Ted arrives at the school, he sees Reuben participating in the Thanksgiving play—an extraordinary leap forward—and decides to leave him there after all.

Even as the families disperse after the show, Dr. Clark finds Jean Hansen and asks for her help. A new boy has arrived at the school; would Jean help coax him out of the car and into the building? And so the circle begins again.

The film is conventional in most regards, except for one: It used actual retarded children in the scenes at the school (though Reuben is played by a normal actor, Bruce Ritchey, who seems to play Reuben as autistic, rather than retarded).

Lancaster, as the hard-driving Dr. Clark, brings great compassion to the role, but also toughness that's unexpected. Being Burt Lancaster, he seems to vibrate with energy, even in scenes when he's sitting still. Garland, looking pudgy and sleep-deprived, appears to be on the verge of tears in most scenes.

The dialogue has the earnestness of the period and the occasional dollop of preaching, as in a scene in which Dr. Clark must justify his funding to a pair of inspectors from the state. Lancaster spits facts and figures that Mann and Kramer obviously had included as part of the movie's message about society's treatment of the retarded: "It can happen to anybody," Clark barks at one point. "It happened to the sister of the president of the United States," referring to President John F. Kennedy.

Kramer had purposely chosen the treatment of the retarded as a topic. He had devoted much of his career to producing and, later, directing, films with a social conscience, at a time when Hollywood was running scared from controversy, in the wake of the Army–McCarthy hearings and the blacklist that made the whole industry timid.

Kramer, however, made films about racism (*Home of the Brave, The Defiant Ones*), nuclear proliferation (*On the Beach*), Nazi war crimes (*Judgment at Nuremberg*) and, later, interracial relationships (*Guess Who's Coming to Dinner*). With *A Child Is Waiting*, Kramer hoped to create a piece of mass entertainment that would open people's eyes to the problems of the retarded.

Writer Abby Mann, who would go on to create the *Kojak* TV series and write TV miniseries about Martin Luther King Jr., and Simon Wiesenthal, had written *A Child Is Waiting* for TV's *Studio One*, which produced it in 1957, with Pat Hingle playing Dr. Clark. But unlike other TV-to-cinema transfers (such as *Crime in the Streets* and *Edge of the City*), the material in *A Child Is Waiting* was not considered suitable for the film audience until Mann expanded it for Kramer.

Kramer was excited to hire Cassavetes, seeing him as a new voice to be encouraged, at least on the basis of *Shadows*.

"Cassavetes lets things happen in front of the camera, instead of plotting everything out," Kramer said at the time. "I'm giving him all the freedom he wants."

When he read the script, Cassavetes liked the idea and was excited about the prospect of working with Lancaster, one of the biggest stars in Hollywood at the time (and a pioneer in his own right in the area of independent production companies).

Lancaster had been recruited by Kramer, who had just directed him in *Nuremberg*, which had also starred Judy Garland. Mann convinced Kramer that he should also cast Garland, whose career had been in eclipse until she was nominated for an Oscar for *Nuremberg*.

As production began in January 1962, Garland was in a fragile state at a critical moment in her career. *Judgment at Nuremberg*, released in 1961, had been something of a comeback vehicle—her first film since *A Star Is Born* in 1954. Garland wanted to keep the momentum going but was also continuing a long-time struggle with drugs and alcohol that had given her a reputation for being erratic in her work habits.

Garland and Cassavetes clashed almost immediately, and Lancaster wasn't much happier with Cassavetes' willingness to devote long chunks of time to scenes with the retarded children who were part of the cast. But Cassavetes, focused only on the film, always direct and to the point, trampled on more than a few toes until Lancaster exploded to Mann, "That boy doesn't know what he's doing."

"I'm going to kill him," Garland added.

Garland, self-conscious about her weight, instructed her makeup person to put dark makeup on her neck, to disguise her double chin by making it look as though it was in shadow in the black-and-white cinematography. Instead, it just looked smudged, and Cassavetes forced her to stop the practice.

Cassavetes assigned Cassel to babysit Garland in her trailer: "She'd sit in her dressing room, watching *Amos 'n' Andy* reruns," he said. "We played gin and she beat me all the time. She had a thermos while we were playing and she'd occasionally pour herself a drink. When I asked her what it was, she said, 'Tea.' When I asked her if I could have a glass, she said, 'It's medicated tea.' So I told John, 'I think she's drinking.' John said, 'I don't care, as long as she's not drunk.'"

The children in the film only exacerbated Garland's mental state. According to one biographer, the days when she worked most closely with the retarded children "overwhelmed her; sometimes she was medicated and under the care of a new doctor, who had been brought in to help keep her on an even keel."

Mann would prowl the set, trying to discern whether the actors were speaking his words or improvising their own lines. As Cassavetes would try to ready the next shot, Mann would be standing next to him, flipping through the script, muttering, "Did Burt improvise that line? Where's this scene? Where are we?"

At one point during filming, when Cassavetes called "Cut!", Mann turned to Cassel and said, "Burt didn't say that line. Tell him to say it."

Cassel sidled up to Lancaster as the next shot was being set up and said quietly, "Abby wants you to say the line." Lancaster nodded.

After the next take, Mann turned to Cassel, indignant: "He didn't say the line again. Tell him to say it."

Cassel again quietly got next to Lancaster and delivered the message: "Abby said you didn't say the line."

Lancaster turned to him and, with a smile, said, "Tell Abby to go fuck himself."

At another point, Lancaster and Cassavetes clashed over the scene in which Dr. Clark reprimands Jean for going against his wishes with the Widdicombes.

"Cassavetes really wanted me to be angry, to rip into it, tear her to pieces, tell her she's a fucking idiot," Lancaster recalled. "I said, 'John, I can't do that. I'm playing a doctor, a man of enormous responsibility. Even if I felt that anger, I'd have to handle it.'"

Lancaster believed his character would have enough control that he wouldn't succumb to the anger and told Cassavetes as much, then agreed to try the scene Cassavetes' way, though he was furious while he was doing it.

The next day, Kramer came up to Lancaster and said, "I just saw the rushes. What were you doing in that scene? You look ridiculous." Lancaster shot a glance at Cassavetes, who immediately confessed.

"Burt didn't want to do it that way but I asked him to," he admitted to Kramer. They reshot the scene, but later Lancaster took Cassavetes aside and told him, "Johnny, you can't do that. You cannot take an actor, even if you're right, when he is so against something, and make him do it. You've got to find some other way of doing it that he can live with and make it right. He said, 'Yes, you're right.' And we became very good friends after that."

Yet the clashes on the set were mostly the kind of day-to-day friction that goes with any studio production, exacerbated by Cassavetes' lack of diplomacy and the kind of youthful exuberance that can be mistaken for arrogance. And, of course, Garland's particular brand of temperamental behavior.

When a film wraps, tensions supposedly evaporate as people acknowledge their shared experience and camaraderie. But Garland was having none of it. Her limo pulled up to her trailer. The rest of the cast and crew, hanging around having a final drink, gathered to say good-bye to the star. But she got wordlessly into the limo. Then she rolled the window down.

"Everybody expected her to say, 'I love you all,'" Al Ruban recalled. "Instead, she stuck her head out and said, 'Fuck you all,' and drove off."

When post-production began, the real rift between Kramer and Cassavetes developed, over how to use the footage of the retarded children in the film. Cassavetes had shot hundreds of feet of film of them in classes, interacting with each other and with the stars. He felt that it revealed their good nature and unflappable spirit, in the face of what seemed like insurmountable odds.

"I found the kids funny and human and sad," Cassavetes said. "But mainly funny—and real. But the picture wasn't geared that way at all. I wanted to make the kids funny, to show that they were human and warm, not cases but kids."

Kramer, however, thought humor involving the retarded would make audiences uncomfortable. It sent the wrong message for the film he wanted to make.

They went back and forth about it, but Kramer kept assuring Cassavetes that he would have the chance to show his version before a decision was made.

Recalled Al Ruban, "Stanley Kramer said this was a love story between Burt and Judy. He took it away from John. He had it recut without telling John."

Kramer invited Cassavetes to a screening room at Universal to look at the finished film, telling him it would just be the two of them. Cassavetes called Cassel and asked him to drive him over to the studio; moments after Cassel dropped him off and started to drive away, Cassavetes came running back out and pulled him out of the car and into the screening.

As it turned out, Kramer had eight or nine of his people there for the screening; Cassavetes brought Cassel along so he'd have at least one person to back him up. He watched mutely as Kramer ran the film—with all of the editing changes that Kramer had wanted, minus Cassavetes' touches.

"At the end of the screening, all of Kramer's guys are talking about how great it is and John stood up and said, 'Take my name off it,'" Cassel recalled.

Kramer said he would do no such thing.

"If you don't, I'm going to sue you," Cassavetes said.

As they walked out, Cassavetes rounded on Kramer, who wasn't much taller than Cassavetes. He pushed Kramer up against a wall, his elbow braced under Kramer's chin and told him off.

Cassel, watching all of this, was afraid he'd start laughing at Cassavetes' audacity. Finally, Cassavetes eased off of Kramer, turned to Cassel, and said, "Come on, let's get out of here."

As they got outside, Cassel turned to Cassavetes and said, "Why didn't you hit him?"

To which Cassavetes replied with a laugh, "How stupid do you think I am?"

Al Ruban said, "John never hit Stanley Kramer. But those stories get around and change. It depends on who's telling the story."

And the story was that Cassavetes had decked the Oscar-nominated producer-director. And then he went public with his complaints about what Kramer had done to his movie.

"Kramer had one kind of movie in mind and I had another," Cassavetes said. "Sure, we're enemies. But it was good for my self-respect to fight him every inch of the way. I lost but he'll think twice before hiring a young director again. If I'd been open enough with myself, I would have known he and I never could have dealt on the same level."

Years later, Kramer would take some of the blame for how A Child Is Waiting turned out: "When you attempt a subject as difficult and delicate as this, you had better be sure that what you're making will be just about the best picture of the year. This one wasn't, though I still think it was worth doing . . . At times I became perhaps unreasonably impatient with John Cassavetes . . . I've been quoted as saying that he didn't properly appreciate the story or do a good job managing the children we used . . . Looking back, I think I had to settle for something less than my dream because I didn't provide the script and cast it would have taken to end up with the kind of film I was hoping for . . . I thought I would let John Cassavetes (who represented a younger school of directors) express himself in a more modern vein in terms of approaching the subject. I don't think that the result is a great film; I think it is a good one."

Perhaps if the film had become a sleeper hit, Cassavetes might have been able to move on to another directing job; success trumps bad behavior every time. But most of the critics dismissed the film; the kind ones called it well-meaning while the harsher ones found the use of real retarded children to be offensive.

As it was, the film did nothing to mitigate his well-publicized run-in with Kramer.

"I knew that it would cost me," Cassavetes said. "In Hollywood, you don't go around publicly badmouthing colleagues, especially big producers like Stanley Kramer. It cost me two years of work; after the noise I made, I couldn't have gotten a job with Looney Tunes.

"I didn't make a film for six years before getting the role in The Dirty Dozen, he said. "The phone didn't ring for a while."

Or as he put it to playwright Meade Roberts one snowy day that winter in Manhattan, "I'm blackballed, baby."

Twenty-one

In Limbo

Young, impulsive, convinced that being right was an end in itself, Cassavetes had stood up for his artistic beliefs. His integrity earned him several years as a movie-industry outcast.

"He wasn't very tactful or diplomatic. He didn't make it easy," Mark Rydell observed. "He didn't lubricate his career—he carved it with an ax."

"After *A Child Is Waiting*, I was relegated to obscurity both as an actor and as a director," Cassavetes said of the period in the mid-1960s, when he suddenly found himself persona non grata at the movie studios. "When I get sore, I go all the way. I stayed home and took care of my first child, Nick, who was just a baby. I was a good mother.

"Gena became the breadwinner of the family and I learned to write," he noted. "Two years of it was just about perfect for both of us at that point. Gena worked a lot on television; she was happy and I was writing. I wrote for two solid years. And I played with my kids and enjoyed myself and reevaluated my life, or at least examined the shit out of it."

He spent time indulging in one of his passions: gardening. The hill behind the Cassavetes house was virtually barren when he and Gena purchased it. With nothing but time on his hands, he created gardens, planted trees, tended the flowers—creating a lush landscape of greenery and color.

Not that he didn't work at all. He found acting jobs in episodic television, making appearances on shows such as *Rawhide, Dr. Kildare,* and *Combat,* as well as four episodes of *Burke's Law,* in which he played four different characters, and a pair of *The Alfred Hitchcock Hour* shows.

In one of the *Hitchcock* outings, Cassavetes acted with Rowlands for the first time on film since they'd done a *Johnny Staccato* episode together a few years earlier.

"I'll never forget a scene we had together in a Hitchcock movie for TV," she recalled. "I was on the phone and John was sitting behind me. Not till I saw the show did I know that, instead of sitting quietly, John was pulling his ear, looking sharply right and left, looking at his watch. It was very entertaining, but it was my scene. When I told John I was shocked that he would do such a thing to his own wife, he said, 'Every man for himself.'"

As John's presence around the house suddenly became a full-time thing, Rowlands went back to work on TV and movie roles. She had acted for John in *A Child Is Waiting* and now landed a recurring role on *87th Precinct* as the deaf-mute wife of Detective Steve Carella, played by Robert Lansing.

She went into *Lonely Are the Brave,* with Kirk Douglas, and *The Spiral Road,* with Rock Hudson, as well as a steady stream of TV shows. And, in doing so, she rekindled her desire to act.

Cassavetes found work acting in a film—a TV film, initially—when his old friend Don Siegel, who had directed him in *Crime in the Streets,* approached him to play Johnny North in a new TV version of Ernest Hemingway's *The Killers.* It had been done as a film in 1946, but this new version would be set in the present and would recast several parts of the story. It was to be called "Johnny North," but the title eventually wound up as *Ernest Hemingway's The Killers,* despite only the most tenuous connection to Hemingway's work.

Johnny North is killed in the film's opening sequence, an unresisting victim to hired gunmen Lee Marvin and Clu Gulager. Then, as the killers try to figure out why a man would go so willingly to his death, Johnny pops up in flashbacks: a champion race-car driver who had participated in an armored car holdup as getaway driver and was then double-crossed by Sheila Farr (Angie Dickinson), the vamp who lured him into the scheme.

The role allowed Cassavetes to punch a future president in the face. Ronald Reagan, in his final acting role before starting his political career, played the villain, Jack Browning. In a critical scene in which Browning slaps Sheila Farr in front of North, her new lover, North socks Browning in the jaw (though Cassavetes had to reach up, because Reagan had almost eight inches in height on him).

Still, Cassavetes' own quirky enthusiasm for the people he liked nearly cost him the job before he got it. When Siegel showed up on Cassavetes' doorstep with the script for him to read, Cassavetes refused to take it from him, saying, "I don't have to read the script. If you want me, I'll do it."

Siegel, whom Cassavetes called his West Coast mother for the way he looked out for him, was equally stubborn: "You don't read the script, I don't want you. I not only insist on your reading the script immediately, but I need your input."

As Johnny North, Cassavetes was meant to be a driving ace, but Siegel quickly discovered that Cassavetes had no instinct for race driving; an erratic, inattentive driver at best in real life, Cassavetes didn't seem to recognize the need to drive differently on a racetrack than he did when guiding the family car around L.A.—little things like keeping both hands on the wheel.

The Killers, which had been produced for NBC as the first made-for-TV movie, ultimately was deemed too violent for primetime network television. So Universal put it into theaters, where it earned middling reviews for its hard-edged cynicism and tough-minded violence.

Shortly afterward, Cassavetes and Siegel met to discuss other possible projects; Cassavetes suggested he write a remake of Ben Hecht's 1934 film *Crime Without Passion,* which Siegel could produce and direct at Universal. He and Siegel screened the original film—about a brilliant attorney who kills his mistress in a lover's quarrel and must establish an alibi—and Siegel was convinced that Cassavetes could do a solid job of bringing it up to date. Cassavetes, in turn, was convinced that Siegel could smooth the way for his return to films at Universal, where he had burned a few bridges when he'd run *Johnny Staccato* off the rails.

But Universal's Lew Wasserman had a long memory, as was befitting someone who had gone from being an agent to running one of the most powerful agencies in Hollywood to heading Universal Pictures. And one of Wasserman's lieutenants was Jennings Lang, whom Cassavetes had abused when he was doing *Staccato.*

Yet despite Lang's misgivings, Wasserman gave Siegel the go-ahead to have Cassavetes write a first draft. Which Cassavetes did, quickly; Siegel had copies of the script—retitled "Champion of the Damned"—delivered to Wasserman and, three days later, was summoned to Wasserman's office.

Wasserman proceeded to upbraid Siegel, repeating over and over how much he hated the script. Though Siegel tried to get a reason from him, all he could say was that he hated it and that it was too violent for NBC, for whom they hoped to make it. Siegel pointed out that there were only two acts of violence and one of them happened offscreen. But Wasserman was hearing none of it. The script was dead, as far as he was concerned.

Siegel thought Wasserman was acting strangely and said so when he reported the news to Cassavetes. Cassavetes, convinced that he could talk anyone into anything, told Siegel he would go see Wasserman and either talk him into making the film or buy back the rights from him. Which he tried to do: Accompanied by business manager A. Morgan Maree, he met with Wasserman and offered him $30,000 for the script. Wasserman smiled and said he would have to discuss it with his associates and then would get back to them.

A day or so later, he came back to Cassavetes with a counteroffer. Cassavetes could buy back the script for $330,000. No negotiation—and far too rich for Cassavetes' blood. It was the final nail in the coffin. There was no way Wasserman was going to let Cassavetes make a film out of the script and risk having it be a hit. That could only reflect poorly on Wasserman for having turned it down. Better to price it out of existence.

The only directing work Cassavetes could find came through Everett Chambers, who hired him to direct a pair of episodes for *The Lloyd Bridges Show*, an anthology show with a repertory cast. Otherwise, he spent his time writing, playing with Nick, or working in the garden. One day, while taking a walk in Beverly Hills, he ran into Steve Blauner, a TV producer who had started as manager to singer Bobby Darin.

"Steve said that he thought it was time I got up off my ass and made some money," Cassavetes recalled. "He was working at Screen Gems and he asked me to come to work there. I went home and told Gena about it and she said that whatever I wanted to do would be OK with her as long as it was what I wanted to do. I got a hold of Mo McEndree and we began creating some TV shows, none of which got off the ground. I stayed there about six months."

Cassavetes worked in a suite of offices at Screen Gems that housed a number of other would-be writer-directors, including Frank Pierson and Robert Altman, working for Jackie Cooper, who was executive vice president.

At the end of the day, after working separately, the various Screen Gems employees would gather in one of their offices to drink and talk. Or they'd adjourn to a nearby bar, the Cock & Bull.

"His personality was totally consistent," Altman remembers. "He was an enthusiast, a little hyper. You see it in his performances. He had that intense stare. He challenged everybody he dealt with, but in a good way. Intellectually, he was fun."

Indeed, Cassavetes loved to argue—not out of anger but for the sheer sport of it. He would debate his side of a question and, if it seemed that he was winning the argument, he would casually switch sides.

"No matter what position you took, he was on the other side," Al Ruban recalled. "If you changed your position, so would he. He wouldn't allow you to join him because he enjoyed the conflict. If you joined him, the conversation was over."

If Altman was aiming toward a movie career and using Screen Gems as a launching pad (or, at least, a holding pen), so was Cassavetes. Even as he worked on ideas at Screen Gems, Cassavetes was getting the itch to do another movie. He and McEndree began looking at some of the things Cassavetes had written and shelved in the past couple of years

"Mo remembered a ten-page piece of dialogue I had written during my two-year exile, a thing about two men talking about the good old days. He suggested I develop it. So I got on a typewriter for a month and I wound up with 175 pages of script—which I thought was going to be a play. Val Avery and John Marley read it and liked it and both asked to be in it."

Finding a cast, of course, was never a problem. Fire a gun in any direction in Los Angeles and you're liable to hit someone who would be willing to act in a movie for nothing. But just because the actors came cheap didn't mean that film and equipment did.

"I had to pay for it myself," Cassavetes said. "To keep some kind of money coming in, I stayed on as long as I could at Screen Gems and after they kicked me out, I went over to Universal—my bank—and acted in two lousy TV pilots, which bought me a movie camera and film. I then had enough to start the picture and we shot for six and a half months. We wound up with an awful lot of footage."

He also got funding—enough to keep the family afloat—from Gena, who took a recurring role in *Peyton Place*, the breakthrough nighttime soap based on Grace Metalious' best-selling novel and subsequent hit movie.

With Gena earning and a minimum amount of money assembled, *Faces* began. Cassavetes rounded up a small but eager crew, including Seymour Cassel, John Finnegan, Fred Draper, Val Avery, and several other friends from their New York days and decided to make the movie at his house, with mother-in-law Lady Rowlands' house as the secondary set. Having sworn off self-financed, self-produced projects after *Shadows*, here he was back at the starting gate, digging into his own pocket. But he couldn't help himself.

"My wife and I have a high threshold for pain," Cassavetes said. "If you're enjoying yourself and you have a lot of friends and they're all suffering with you, you're fine. I'd hate to be the only one suffering."

Twenty-two

Faces

I f *Faces* is not John Cassavetes' masterpiece, it runs a close second to *A Woman Under the Influence*. At once intimate and raw, obviously of its period and yet startlingly of the moment, it offers a surprisingly sophisticated deconstruction of male and female role-playing—and the explosive quality of honest behavior when the roles are dropped.

The film starts with Richard Forst (played by John Marley) arriving at his office, where he is waited upon by his secretaries and staff as he prepares for a meeting. At the meeting, Forst is pitched a film: "We call it the *Dolce Vita* of the commercial field," says one flunky. Says another, "We came up with an impressionistic document that shocks." When Forst calls for them to roll the film, the lights go down and the credits for *Faces* come up. Or, more accurately, the single word "FACES," with white print on a black background.

Does this mean we're seeing a film within a film? Or is it merely a device—to pull us into the film by defying our expectations? There isn't much time to consider that idea because, as the word leaves the screen, Gena Rowlands' face appears—starkly beautiful, a vision in white light against a grainy black background—and the story begins. The film plunges directly into a scene at a bar, the Loser's Club, where Forst and Freddie (played by Fred Draper), who was part of the meeting in the opening scene, are apparently concluding a lost afternoon: finishing drinks and trying to talk a pair of call girls into leaving with them. Without much adieu, Freddie,

Forst, and one of the girls—Jeannie Rapp (Rowlands)—get into Freddie's car, share quick snorts off a flask, and head to her house.

Once there, Forst and Freddie perform for Jeannie, dredging up bits from their college days together (though Forst seems considerably older). It quickly becomes apparent that Freddie expects to share Jeannie with Forst. It just as quickly becomes clear that Jeannie prefers the more detached and dignified Forst, though it is Freddie who is making the play for her. In a beautifully subtle struggle for male domination—set to a syncopated, a cappella rendition of *I Dream of Jeannie with the Light Brown Hair*—Cassavetes clearly lays out the dynamics of male jealousy and competitiveness.

Both men dance with Jeannie, but while she does a few quick twirls with Freddie, she all but melts into Forst's arms as they slow to a shuffle that is more like an embrace. Angered at taking second place, Freddie attempts to insult her by asking her price, dragging what has become a romantic moment back to grimy reality. But Jeannie calmly puts him in his place and he leaves. Jeannie and Forst share a moment—then share a kiss, one that affects Forst more than he realizes as he heads for home.

When he gets home, late for dinner, his much-younger wife, Maria (Lynn Carlin), is talking to a friend, and Forst waits impatiently for her to get off the phone. They have a drink and banter about nothing; she asks him to take her to a movie, even suggesting the Bergman film that's in the neighborhood. "I don't feel like getting depressed tonight," Forst cracks.

Forst is searching the house desperately for a cigarette, though Maria keeps telling him they're out. There's obviously something else going on beneath the surface, nervous, angry energy channeled into the quest for a smoke. She eventually talks him into sitting down for dinner, warmed over in the oven. Their conversation turns to his friend Freddie, and Maria reports that Freddie's wife thinks he's cheating. The talk turns sexy, the vixenish Carlin squinting suggestively at Marley's Forst and laughing uproariously at jokes that seem gross and obvious—as though out of habit, rather than an actual reaction. Eventually the laughter stops as Forst's sarcasm takes a bitter turn, and the young Maria rolls her eyes with a "Here we go again" look.

In an instant, the real issue comes out: His sexual urges are at odds with hers. He maintains that she appeals to him, while she pushes him away with responses like, "I am not a sex machine. Don't be crude. The minute you get home, you want to jump into bed." She races upstairs—and he stalks off to play pool.

But with the next cut, she is in a nightie and he is in T-shirt and shorts—and they are in bed, laughing again at a series of stale riddles that are not particularly funny, though the two of them are in hysterics. They make an uneasy transition from jocularity to a sullen "Good night," after she implies that he's really not very funny. They roll over in opposite directions, each staring into space while pretending to sleep.

In the next shot, they are both up and dressed, though it is obviously late in the evening—perhaps even another evening, though there is nothing (other than logic) to suggest that. As Maria puts ice in glasses to make what appears to be a nightcap, Forst walks in and announces, "I want a divorce." He then dials Jeannie and asks her to meet him at the Loser's Club, stalking out and leaving a shocked Maria.

But while the bar is crowded, Forst finds no sign of Jeannie. At Jeannie's house, she and her friend Stella (Elizabeth Deering) are entertaining a pair of businessmen from out of town: McCarthy (Val Avery) and Jackson (Gene Darfler). But like Freddie before him, Jackson threatens to abort the evening by making a crude remark about hookers. McCarthy takes it further, following the disgusted Jeannie into her bedroom for a sensitive conversation— then coming back out, his hair mussed, his shirt untucked, as though Jeannie has just manhandled him in the bedroom.

Just as everyone calms down and things are reaching some equilibrium, Forst arrives. As before, when he and Freddie had become competitive, Forst and McCarthy are pitted together in a struggle of male hormones and the need for dominance. Forst, forced into a physical confrontation, knocks down the much-larger McCarthy, who then pleads that he has a bad knee. Again, Forst—with his blunt, honest demeanor—captures Jeannie's attention and ultimately gets the others to leave so they can get cozy, talking in a way he believes he no longer can with his wife.

Maria, meanwhile, has been taken in hand by a group of her friends, who shepherd her out for a night on the town to forget her problems. They land at the Whisky a Go-Go on Sunset Strip, where the music is loud and the dancing frenzied. They look obviously out of place in the crowded, noisy club and seem even more so when they are led to what appears to be the only open table in the room.

There, they sit primly, watching a roomful of people have the Baptist equivalent of sex: dancing uninhibitedly, doing the Frug, the Watusi, the Pony—whatever was of the moment in early 1965. The four women look like tourists or anthropologists studying the mating habits of the natives and finding themselves alternately attracted to and repulsed by what they see.

Then the spectators become part of the show when a self-assured young man, Chet (Seymour Cassel), casually dances up to their table and puts on a brief show for them, not unlike a mating dance. Flipping his blond hair as he displays just how in touch with his body he is, Chet puts ideas into the women's heads, particularly when he focuses on Maria, asking her to dance. She demurs but her friend Florence (Dorothy Gulliver), the oldest in the group, eagerly gets to her feet and enthusiastically begins to dance—and grind—with Chet.

The film then cuts to the Forst house, where Maria, her three friends, and Chet arrive. There is an unspoken vibe beneath the playful banter: that these women have picked up this young man but have no idea what to do with him. Or rather, two of the women have no interest in him; Florence, on the other hand, quickly makes it clear that she has one thing in mind—getting Chet to take her home and make love to her—and she isn't above begging him to do so.

Chet does take her home but then returns almost immediately for the woman he has had his eye on all along: Maria Forst. Maria, in turn, has been thinking about Chet and the combination of his return and the alcohol she's consumed allow her to drop her inhibitions and respond when he makes love to her.

The next morning, Forst and Jeannie face each other. Forst works hard to minimize the connection he and Jeannie have made, insulting her cooking and making a joke of everything else. But as they part, it's apparent that there has been a change in him and the way he thinks of himself.

The cold light of morning finds Chet in a panic: He discovers Maria passed out on the floor of her bathroom, having attempted suicide with an overdose of pills. This is more than the free-wheeling young hustler (the character is referred to variously in reviews of the time as either a surfer or a hippie, which said more about the critics than the character) had bargained for. He stands her up, walks her around, forces her to vomit, puts her under a shower, and retrieves her from the brink of death. Then he tries to cheer her up by telling her that she's not alone—that even he feels the loneliness and despair that she obviously succumbed to, but that giving in to it isn't the answer.

As they reach a moment of tender understanding, Forst pulls up outside. He is incongruously upbeat: singing, clicking his heels. Has his night with Jeannie revived his interest in his wife? Has he decided to go through with the divorce and try to make a go of it with Jeannie?

Again, there is no time to think about this because what he walks in on is the evidence of adultery: Maria, standing by the window of their bedroom, watching as Chet scrambles across the rooftop. As Forst sticks his head out the window, he sees the shirtless blond beach boy hop off the roof and race down the backyard hill to the street below.

Forst turns on Maria and the contrast is stark. Forst is showered, shaved, dressed in suit and tie. Maria's nightie is wet and torn; her hair is disheveled and her face is marked by rivulets of mascara down her cheeks. Though he's just spent the night with a call girl, Forst professes outrage at his wife's behavior.

"You get laid once and the whole problem is solved," Forst says. "You get all the soldiers in Vietnam laid and the whole Middle East problem is solved."

When she still doesn't say anything, Forst threatens her with violence, pushing her against a wall until she admits, "I hate my life. I just don't love you."

Forst walks down the stairs in silence, wanders into the kitchen, and takes a pack of cigarettes from a carton of Marlboros sitting on top of the refrigerator.

(This lends credence to the notion that the action of the film originally was spread out over more time and that, in the editing, Cassavetes decided to advance the idea that the action takes place all in one night. In a scene shortly before he had asked for a divorce, Forst had searched the house for cigarettes, while Maria trailed behind him, telling him, "There aren't any." It is supposedly only the next morning and no one has gone shopping. But, out of nowhere, here is a full carton of cigarettes in the kitchen.)

They sit on the steps, her near the top, him at the bottom and, when he lights a cigarette, she asks for one. She lights hers as well—and they both start to cough. And then both go upstairs, he to take off his suit coat, she to put on a robe. They pass once more on the steps, going in different directions both literally and figuratively. Their future together is uncertain: Either they will dissolve this loveless marriage or, worse, fall back into the deadening routine that has given it forward motion up to this point—an even more disturbing prospect.

Twenty-three

Faces 2

When John Cassavetes caught up with Al Ruban in New York in late 1964, Ruban had gone into the movie business as well, making exploitation films such as the one he showed Cassavetes in his New York office, called *The Sexploiters*.

"He laughed through everything I showed him," Ruban recalled of the movie he'd made, a relatively tame nudie film inspired by news stories of the time about a group of Long Island housewives who had started their own little prostitution ring to assuage their suburban boredom.

Then Cassavetes got to the point: He was going back to California to make another movie like *Shadows*. Did Ruban want to be involved?

"Sure," Ruban said. Cassavetes looked around the office of Ruban's production company and said, "What do we do?"

"I'll buy a second-hand camera and we'll go from there," Ruban said.

Still, Ruban thought it might just be Cassavetes spitballing, talking about what he'd like to do, as opposed to what he was going to do. So Ruban went back to work on his exploitation flick—until a check for $15,000 arrived from Cassavetes to buy equipment. At which point, Ruban went to his partners in exploitation and told them, "You can have the film."

No one could have been more surprised to find himself in the movie business than Al Ruban. His life had taken several turns since he'd graduated from Stuyvesant High School in Manhattan. Having grown up in the neighborhood of West Sixty-eighth and West End Avenue before it was bulldozed to make room for Lincoln Center, he had joined the army out of high school and was stationed at Fort Leonard Wood, Missouri. He liked the Midwest, and when he was discharged, he enrolled at the University of Missouri to study journalism.

But he also got started in minor-league baseball, playing infield for Joplin and Peekskill in the Sally League. When he dislocated a knee, he went home to New York to recuperate and consider future options. As he began to feel better, he started playing softball in Central Park for money, winning side bets while playing for teams in the Broadway Show League and elsewhere. In the Sally League, he was a semi-pro; in Central Park, he was a ringer.

As Ruban recalled, "A friend came to me and said he knew a group of actors who played baseball on Eighty-seventh Street. They kept playing against the same team and they couldn't win. So I went one day and asked to play. That was Cassavetes, Seymour, Mo McEndree. We still lost but not as often.

"Afterward we'd go to a beer joint on the East Side. Cassavetes came up to me one day and said he was directing a film and would I like to be part of the crew. I said, 'I don't know anything about that.' He said, 'I don't either so we'll all learn together.'"

Cassavetes needed help for the ten days he would be reshooting *Shadows*. Ruban had been to the Paris Theater screenings and knew the film needed work. So he did whatever Cassavetes required of him and, in the process, found a direction for his life.

He became so enamored of the film world—or the little bit that he saw working on *Shadows*—that, when the film was finished and Cassavetes went to California, Ruban and McEndree went to work for a company making exploitation films. Eventually they figured out how to do it themselves and opened their own business.

When Cassavetes offered them the chance to work on *Faces*, Ruban and McEndree headed west. Ruban packed up his wife and child and drove across the country, depositing his family at McEndree's brother's farm, in Iola, Kansas, before continuing on to California. Ruban had hitched his wagon to Cassavetes' vision, and would be a partner and collaborator for most of the next thirty years.

Faces began with the title "The Marriage" and, at one point, was called "The Dynosaurs" and "One Fa and Eight Las." The script had started as a play, inspired by what Cassavetes saw happening in America between married people.

At a time when independent films still tended toward the avant-garde—or focused on segments of society (such as African-Americans) whose stories weren't being told in Hollywood—Cassavetes decided that what would become known as the "silent majority" during the coming Nixon era had something to say for themselves. Until that point, suburbia was something to be made fun of, to spoof, whether benignly on TV sitcoms or with more teeth, as in the hollow lives depicted in the writing of John Cheever and John Updike. Cassavetes, however, wanted to do something different.

"It is a picture about the middle-aged, high-middle-income-bracket people that are made fun of in our society," he said. "This is the white American society that certain social groups talk about all the time. One day I woke up and realized that I'm part of that society and almost everyone I know is. There's no sense in pretending that I am back in New York in the early days looking for a job. I'm not. And I knew there was something to be said about these people and about their insular existence and about their place in a society that is frowned upon today."

Cassavetes started with a ten-page fragment of a script: a conversation between two old friends about the good old days. After a month of writing, he'd shaped it into 175 pages of dialogue. In it, a businessman named Richard Forst and his friend Freddie are performing together for a woman. The second act featured a pair of women performing for a man. And the combination of the two acts brought you to the same conclusion: that something has to give if marriage is to have a future as a viable institution.

Cassavetes worked on the script at Screen Gems and would invite friends in to read it out loud with him. One of them, actor John Marley, said, "Gee, what a heck of a good part. Can I play it?"

"Sure," Cassavetes replied. "We'll do it as a play."

But readings of the play convinced Cassavetes and McEndree that it should be a film, one they could make by themselves, as they did with *Shadows*. Having been through the studio grinder, raising the money to make a movie his own way seemed less and less onerous. He'd done it before; he could do it again.

As Cassavetes shaped *Faces*, the script began to focus on one of the men, Richard Forst, and one of the women: his wife, Maria. Eventually, it turned into one long dark night of the soul for both of them, in which Richard announces he wants a divorce and goes to spend the evening with a call girl he has met. In retaliation, Maria and several of her friends go on a bender and wind up back at Maria's house with a randy young guy, Chet, they've picked up along the way. From a four-page treatment scrawled during an airplane flight, Cassavetes had fleshed it into a mammoth screenplay; eventually he would jettison whole sections of the script that told the audience things they could figure out for themselves.

"The first part of the script was structured very carefully to set up a whole new pattern of thinking so that the audience could not get ahead of the film," he said. "Most people think, 'Oh yes, this is what's going to happen in the next moment.' What happens with *Faces,* though is that the first half of the film really bugs people because it doesn't fit an easy pattern of behavior.

"The whole film is just one day and a little bit of a morning in two people's lives. I don't think life has a beginning, a middle and an end. The form is in the content. We've taken the climax of a relationship, a changing point in a marriage, picked it up at the moment where it's accelerating."

For the cast, he began with Gena as Jeannie, the sympathetic hooker who becomes involved with Richard Forst. For Rowlands, the role was the best she'd been offered in years.

As Forst, Cassavetes cast Marley, a veteran actor who had worked for him in *A Child Is Waiting* and in the "A Pair of Boots" episode of *The Lloyd Bridges Show.* After a journeyman career as a little-noticed character actor, Marley had landed the best role of his life.

"That picture put John Marley on the map," said John Finnegan, an actor friend of Cassavetes from his New York days, who was cast in the opening scene of *Faces.*

Despite kidding with him about being too old for the part, Cassavetes had written the role of Chet for Seymour Cassel: "I was happy because it was the best and biggest part I'd ever had up to that point," Cassel said.

Cassel had followed Cassavetes to California, taking whatever bit parts came his way, working odd jobs when he needed to. He was exactly the kind of free spirit that Cassavetes described in the character of Chet. To Cassel, Cassavetes was like an older brother, a mentor who was as wildly, impulsively prone to grab large handfuls of life as Cassel.

Based on his appearance in *Too Late Blues* and his own hustling, Cassel came up with two or three roles in episodic television every year. Over time he amassed a list of credits that included nine episodes of *Twelve O'Clock High* and a reputation as a quick study, someone who could be called at 3 P.M. and be counted on to show up the next morning and learn eight or ten lines for a scene, earning $150. It was enough to keep himself afloat, and he wasn't afraid to take work parking cars at restaurants on Sunset Boulevard, if that's what it took to pay the rent.

Cassavetes had learned on *Shadows* and again on *A Child Is Waiting* that nonactors could be even more natural on screen than professionals.

So he mixed things up, with about half of Maria's friends played by women he knew, who weren't actors.

To play Maria Forst, he looked no further than the office down the hall at Screen Gems. Lynn Carlin was Robert Altman's secretary. She had never acted professionally, but Cassavetes saw something in her that convinced him to cast her. Carlin had no idea what she was getting into.

Carlin had been in advertising, as was her husband at the time. Out of work, she had landed a job as a secretary at ICM, the agency that handled Altman, eventually working for Altman's agent. Without inquiring about her secretarial skills, Altman had hired her away because "I liked the way she looked and talked. It seemed like good casting, so I hired her," Altman said.

But Carlin spent more and more time in Cassavetes' office. One afternoon when Altman was out of town, Cassavetes was reading actors for the play that would become *Faces* in his Screen Gems office. Short one player, he popped his head into Altman's office, where Carlin was working. "Could you help us out?" he asked and Carlin sat in.

Shortly before Cassavetes was to begin shooting, Carlin was fired by Altman, though why he let her go is a matter of contention. Carlin says Altman fired her because her involvement with Cassavetes meant she wasn't doing her work for Altman. According to Seymour Cassel, Altman caught her typing the *Faces* script for Cassavetes and terminated her.

"She was crying and when John asked her why she was crying and saying good-bye, she said Altman had fired her," Cassel said. "So John said, 'Well, play this part.' Altman went bananas. He said, 'She was a lousy secretary. What makes you think she can act?'"

But Altman tells a very different story: that Carlin, whose marriage was troubled, had attempted to commit suicide by slashing her wrists. Altman got a call at home and went to the hospital, where he talked to Carlin's husband, telling him, "She's got to show up at work tomorrow. If she confronts this immediately, she'll be able to go on. But in two weeks, she's fired because I can't have the responsibility of having her around when something's obviously bothering her."

According to Altman, Cassavetes was outraged when he'd heard about the way Altman had treated Carlin: "How can you fire this girl?" he demanded of Altman. "I'm not speaking to you. You did a terrible thing firing that girl."

Carlin denies Altman's story. But Al Ruban, who was working with Cassavetes at the time, remembers it the same way: "Lynn Carlin had gone through difficult times," Ruban said. "She had tried to end her life. That was one of the reasons Altman let her go. John struck up a friendship with her; he liked her for the part. He saw that character, that wife just entering middle age, faced with difficulties in getting along in love and with men."

Johnnie Planco, who later represented both Altman and Cassavetes as their agent, also heard the story from both of them: "Each blamed the other for Lynn Carlin," he said. "John said Bob was abusive. Bob said John was too close to her. The truth probably lies in the middle."

Having assembled a cast and earned enough through TV work to put together equipment and film, Cassavetes started shooting *Faces* at the beginning of January 1965.

While he tried to shoot in continuity, Cassavetes divided this particular production in half as much as possible, to finish Gena Rowlands' scenes first. Gena was three months' pregnant with their daughter, Alexandra, and needed to get her scenes shot before it became noticeable. As it turned out, Carlin was also pregnant—and two years later, when Cassavetes called her to reshoot a handful of scenes, she was pregnant again, exactly as far along in her pregnancy as she had been the first time.

They shot the scene where Forst meets Jeannie at the Losers Club for a week, then moved to the home of Lady Rowlands, which would double as Jeannie Rapp's house, where she brought Richard Forst and the other men in his scenes. Once those scenes were finished, they moved on to Cassavetes' house, which served as the home of Richard and Maria Forst, where Maria and her friends brought Chet after their foray to the Whisky a Go-Go.

For his crew, Cassavetes brought together Al Ruban, Mo McEndree, and camera operator George Sims. Cassavetes' cousin, Phedon Papamichael, would do production design.

"On *Faces*, we shot for six months—and for the first three months, I was on the crew," recalled Seymour Cassel, whose scenes weren't shot until after Gena's were finished.

"That way of making a film was so much fun. No unions to deal with, no time schedule. We shot it in continuity, which John did with every film after that. For an actor, that's ideal. You build the characters as you go along, like with a play."

Because of the small crew and the reality of being self-financed, Cassavetes kept things lean. Still, he was willing to experiment as he went.

"We were using different film stock on every scene," Cassavetes said. "For instance, where they all come into Jeannie's apartment, the lighting man said, 'Look, it's 5 o'clock in the afternoon and it's always grainy to me. Do you mind if I shoot it that way?' So he lit it purposely that way to get the grainy feeling of that time in the afternoon, when you've got a few drinks in you. The morning after should be crisp and kind of light and beautiful, so he used a different stock."

Cinematographer Haskell Wexler, who had met Cassavetes in the early 1960s, was invited to watch shooting and to bring the 16mm Éclair he owned. Wexler would get phone calls from Cassavetes, saying, "Haskell— what are you doing on Thursday?" Wexler, who was friends with John Marley, would stop in and take a turn behind the camera on occasion. He found Cassavetes exciting to be around because of the sense that he was doing more than simply moving actors around a set.

"It was like working on a film with a living sketch pad," Wexler said, "when the artist has a sense of what the film should be, but he doesn't know whether to use a pen or make this part longer. He would try not to impose his view and hope that the actors could improve and expand upon it with improvisation, without letting them know what he had in mind. They would try and please him and he would hope it would turn out better than he imagined."

Cassavetes took an egalitarian approach, which finally pushed Ruban to say something about what was quickly turning into chaos in the first weeks of production.

"John was letting everyone shoot," Ruban recalled. "I would shoot the first shot and then John would say, 'OK, George, you shoot the next one, and Seymour, do you want to shoot the next one?' He was giving everyone in the crew a chance to use the camera. John's thought was that everyone should be involved and share the experience. What was happening at that moment was what was important. He gave no thought to the finished product. What was going on was more important."

But it also meant that the quality of the imagery and what the different cameramen chose to shoot varied wildly—and it showed during dailies. Finally, McKendree convinced Ruban to say something to Cassavetes.

"If you continue this, I'm going home," Ruban told the director. "Doing it that way, there's no way to know where you are. You have to have one guy shoot the camera and have faith in him. I'll do the lighting."

Cassavetes couldn't help but agree, particularly because the first month of filming had yielded almost no usable footage.

Cassel referred to the film as "the first Communist film shot in America" because everyone worked for free with a promise of a share of the profits.

The film was shot almost exclusively at night, and the daily routine was always the same. People would arrive at 5:30 at the Cassavetes house, where they'd all have dinner together, often spaghetti. Then Cassavetes and the actors would go into a room and rehearse the scene that they were going to do that night, rewriting it if necessary, while Ruban, McEndree, and the rest set up lights to accommodate any eventuality in a given room. At which point, Cassavetes and the actors would run the scene for the crew and filming would begin.

The rehearsal period was crucial, Ruban recalled, to develop the scenes in ways the writing alone couldn't anticipate.

"The rehearsal is not just for the actors to get up on their parts, but to see the flaws in the script," Ruban said. "You can write something and write it rather well—but when a certain person is playing that part, it takes a slightly different turn. Unless you know that actor so well that you can build the nuances into his character, it will always change right before your eyes. So the rehearsal period is extremely important for that actor to mold the character into the type of person that he or she can play."

Cassavetes didn't want a cinematographer, with a grand visual scheme into which actors must be inserted. He wanted a camera operator, who could go with whatever was happening in the scene, who would keep the actor in the frame no matter what he did—someone for whom camera artistry was secondary to the actors' instincts. Which was at 180-degree odds with accepted filmmaking practice.

"In *Faces*, Al Ruban did the lighting and I had a great operator [George Sims] who worked the camera," Cassavetes said. "It wasn't decisively important how beautiful their photography was, except to them personally. The question was: What are we working for? And the obvious answer was that we were working for these people. It doesn't make any difference whether the wall behind them is white, dark, black. I don't think it means anything to anybody. It's what these people are thinking, what they're feeling. And that's the drama of the piece.

"The idea was, How do we get to these people the fastest, quietest, most expedient way before that little feeling that they have disappears? So sometimes we'd shoot when the lights weren't ready. We'd shoot whenever the actors were ready. We were slaves to them. All we were there to do was record what they were doing."

Cassavetes would rehearse each scene, but the rehearsals were meant to clue the technicians—the camera operator, the sound man—where the actors might be going during the scene, although it was also possible that they would do it differently when the camera rolled.

It was almost a decade since *Shadows*, but Cassavetes still bore the reputation of a director who improvised. He always pointed out that every subsequent film had had a detailed script that was followed closely, in terms of the dialogue. But he would muddy the issue by pointing out that he used improvisation as a tool to explore the characters during rehearsal. Often he would incorporate something the actors came up with into the script, where it was written down and inserted.

Yet there was an emotional improvisation that Cassavetes sought from his actors. The script was a framework on which the actors were layering their vision of their character. And whatever emotion they wanted to bring to a line or a scene was their choice, based on their knowledge and understanding of the character. Cassavetes couldn't tell them how to feel in a scene—and hoped fiercely that they would surprise him with what they discovered in the character.

"He'd drive everybody crazy insisting we shoot something again and again," Ruban remembered. "He kept looking for something else to happen in the scene. He always thought the actors would come up with something. There was no bigger thrill for him than having something happen spontaneously in a scene."

In shooting the various scenes at Jeannie's house, he kept asking actor Val Avery (who played a crass businessman customer of hers) to do repeated takes of a long, emotionally complex scene. This went on into the wee hours of the morning until, finally, Avery had had enough.

"Fuck you, John, I'm going home," the actor finally said. Cassavetes, who could turn on the high beams of his charm in an instant, engaged Avery, even as his eyes first found Seymour Cassel for a second. He pleaded with Avery to stick around, asking him to do just one more take. Avery would have none of it, though he stood and listened to Cassavetes' arguments before saying no and walking out the door—and found that Cassel had let the air out of his tires.

As Avery recalled, "I said, 'Come on outside, you sonuvabitch, I'm tired of your bullshit.' And he looks at me and says, 'Wait a minute—can you fight in the dark?' And I broke up laughing."

At another point, when Cassavetes wasn't getting the performance he wanted from Carlin, he came over to her and leaned over, as if to give her a note quietly and unobtrusively. But instead of saying anything, he slapped her face. Then he immediately walked away from her and said loudly, "Roll camera." As the camera started to roll, he looked at Carlin and said, "Don't you dare cry."

Carlin said Cassavetes inspired belief that everything he did was done for a purpose: "With John, you had such faith in him," she said. "You let it go. He would let you go. If you got too out of hand, he'd let you finish, then go back and do it again. He had such an ability to see honesty."

Al Ruban said, "John would never explain anything, which could drive you crazy. He didn't know what he was looking for but when he found it, he knew."

It wasn't just the hired actors who were frustrated with his sometimes inarticulate approach to a scene or his refusal to discuss their characters with them. Gena Rowlands also ran into unexpected flak from John. She found this to be the most trying collaboration of her career. She went to bed every night wondering whether their marriage could survive the stress of working together as they shot the film.

"Things didn't start out well—we had terrible battles," she said later. "My mistake was in thinking that since the director was also my lover, he would think everything I did was perfect. Once I began to regard John as a director, the problems straightened out quickly."

Rowlands was still adjusting to the idea that Cassavetes had decided to pursue filmmaking, rather than acting.

"My idea of the future was of us acting together, like the Lunts," she recalled. "It took me by surprise when he became interested in directing and writing, but once he had started, he didn't have the interest in acting he had had before. He looked at it simply as a way to make money so we could make our films."

Cassavetes used *Faces* to explore uncharted territory, such as the sexuality of older women. He put the full glare of the spotlight on it by having one of Maria's older women friends, Florence (Dorothy Gulliver), practically beg Chet to take her home and make love to her.

"That was just not seen at the time," Rowlands said. "It was considered embarrassing for an older woman to have anything to say about anything emotional."

Money was always an issue. Yet when Avery turned up for his scenes, Cassavetes said he wanted Avery in a tuxedo. Avery demurred: "Nobody wears a tux in L.A."

"Do you have a blue suit?" Cassavetes asked. Avery, who worked on both coasts, said, "Not out here."

Knowing that Cassavetes was strapped for cash, Avery was surprised when Cassavetes directed him to visit a certain haberdasher in Beverly Hills, where he was instructed to buy the works—shirt, tie, suit—and put it on Cassavetes' account there.

Again Avery demurred: "That's crazy," he said. "That will all cost more than $300. Let me go to the May Co. and get a cheap suit and nobody will know the difference."

No, Cassavetes replied, he had no money for that.

"Then how are you going to get me clothes from this haberdasher?" Avery said. To which Cassavetes replied, "I have a charge account there."

It took three months of shooting to get to the scenes with Maria and Chet, which comprised the bulk of Carlin's role.

During that period, Cassel was working on the crew and watching Cassavetes shoot the scenes with Rowlands, Marley, Draper, and Avery. He got progressively more eager to get in front of the camera himself.

But when he got there, he started, well, acting. He was an actor saying lines rather than a character behaving for the camera. In less than an hour, Cassavetes said, "That's a wrap."

The next day, the same thing. Cassel, tightly wound and desperately needing to do well for Cassavetes, again seemed to be acting. "I don't feel like working," Cassavetes said, trying to spare Cassel's feelings. "Let's shoot hoops. That's a wrap."

The problem, Cassel said, was that he was trying too hard. He'd been waiting his turn in front of the camera. Now that it had arrived, he said, "I felt, 'I've got to show how good I am.'"

By the third night, he had finally relaxed in the role of the laidback Chet. "We started shooting with a different attitude and never looked back," Cassel said.

The film became an obsession for Cassavetes and Rowlands: "*Faces* became more than a film," he said. "It became a way of life, a film against the authorities and the powers that prevent people from expressing themselves the way they want to, something that can't be done in America, that can't be done without money."

They shot for five months, filming almost every day. The work was concentrated, with a lot of footage being shot in the five- or six-hour window of energy the actors had.

As heavy as the subject matter was, Cassavetes was convinced that he was making an entertaining film.

"I think all these problems are very funny, really," he said. "I just make these films for fun. It's like a man I know who keeps following other people's wives home and seducing them. I don't know why he does it but I do know he's likely to get shot. That's pretty funny, eh?" (It was particularly funny because the man Cassavetes was describing was Cassel.)

Shooting in continuity meant that Marley had a long time to think about his final scene, when he comes home from his night with Jeannie to find Maria disheveled, the house a mess, and a strange man escaping out a window, across the roof, and down the hill behind his house.

Cassavetes' enthusiasm for what Marley finally came up with in that scene almost killed the shot. Cassavetes was notorious for talking to his actors during the scene ("almost like being in a movie audience," he described it), speaking audibly. At times, his directions would become a veritable alternate soundtrack, which is what happened as he watched the waves of realization wash over John Marley's Forst as he watched Chet— and, symbolically, his youth—hoof it across the roof of his house.

"Marley was standing there and I kept saying 'Don't look at her, don't look at her, don't look at her,'" Cassavetes recalled. "Finally Marley yells, 'For Chrissake, John, you blew the whole goddam thing. I can't think when you're talking constantly in a stream.' And I hadn't even been aware that I'd been talking all through the picture."

Ruban, the cameraman, was positioned on a corner of the roof so he could get the shot of Marley sticking his head out the window then swivel to follow Cassel as he ran across the roof and dropped thirteen feet to the ground below. Cassel then scampered and shoe-surfed down a gravelly dirt hillside before reaching the street below.

It wasn't a complicated shot, but when the still huffing-and-puffing Cassel walked back up the hill (after running nearly two blocks) and climbed the stairs to the second floor of the house, Cassavetes said, "Let's do it again."

So the always-enthusiastic Cassel did it again: scrambling across the roof, dropping to the ground, running down the hill to the street, and sprinting out of the frame. He walked back up the hill and climbed the stairs again.

"Can we do one more?" Cassavetes asked. Cassel, with a little less spring in his step, repeated the demanding shot one more time: roof to hill to street.

Cassel dragged himself back up the hill about a half-dozen times in all, eventually thinking to himself, "Jesus Christ, let's get this right."

He climbed the stairs once more—to find Ruban and Cassavetes shaking with laughter. They'd gotten the shot the second time and continued shooting it as a practical joke, to see how long Cassel would keep repeating it before he said something.

Twenty-four

Dirty Dozen and Rosemary's Baby

After five months of shooting *Faces*, Cassavetes had to go back to work. He had a new baby to support—Alexandra, or Xan, born September 21, 1965—so he took TV jobs and a film role in a Roger Corman motorcycle flick. Even as he acted, he was focused on editing the massive amount of footage he had accumulated shooting *Faces*.

"We've shot 250,000 feet of film," he said at one point (it translated into 115 hours). "Now we have to synch the sound and we're averaging two reels a day. Such is the price of not having money. Half the battle of making a good film is getting free film."

He had been doing television steadily, with appearances on shows like *The Virginian, Voyage to the Bottom of the Sea,* and *Bob Hope Presents the Chrysler Theater*. At one point, he took a role in a pilot, "Alexander the Great," which was not picked up as a series. Instead, the pilot played as a made-for-TV movie. But it came close to making the cut.

During waits between shots, Cassavetes and William Shatner, who played Alexander, shared their dreams of making their own films. Cassavetes talked about *Faces*, which was still in pieces. Shatner shared his own notions of making movies: "We were young actors who wanted to show the establishment how to do it," said Shatner, whose career would be forever changed when he was cast in *Star Trek* the following year. "He showed everybody how to do it on a shoestring. His films didn't fit the norm. I think I was too into the norm then to fully appreciate how iconoclastic they were."

Cassavetes incongruously hired himself out to make *Devil's Angels*, a half-hearted biker movie meant to draw the same audience that made 1967's *Wild Angels* one of the most successful exploitation films of that year.

Cassavetes plays Cody, the clean-cut leader of a scruffy biker gang that's just looking to have some fun and do its thing. But they are constantly being hassled by "the man," so Cody points them south to happier hunting grounds. On their way down the California coast, they stop in a small town, where they freak the residents out. Cody cools things out but the townsfolk nearly lynch the gang when a town girl, seeking a little adventure, gets drunk with the bikers and finds out how rough they can get. It's as lifeless a drama as you could imagine, with Cassavetes walking through the role, surrounded by a cast of unknowns that included Mo McEndree as Joel-the-Mole, a loyal member of Cody's gang.

Both *Devil's Angels* and *Machine Gun McCain*, a slightly better but equally mediocre movie, show that Cassavetes had an electric presence, even when he mentally seems to be barely in the scene.

Variety thrashed *Devil's Angels*, calling it a "hastily put together carbon of a successful film."

Cassavetes was seemingly indifferent to the film's fate: "I don't watch my acting career. It doesn't make any difference to me what part I play. I did a motorcycle picture just because I wanted to learn how to ride a motorcycle. It also afforded me a trip to Mexico, where I'd never been. And so I went and enjoyed myself tremendously."

But even when he was acting for money to finance *Faces*, Cassavetes was never willing to compromise a principle. Nor, it seemed, had he learned his lesson about clashing publicly with the studios that hired him. The week before NBC was going to air a *Bob Hope Presents the Chrysler Theater* production, called "Free of Charge," in which Cassavetes starred with Ben Gazzara and Diane Baker, Cassavetes spoke out about how Universal Television, which was producing the show, had forced script changes to make a semi-edgy drama more palatable to the public. It may have been a stand on principle—or a slap in the face of Lou Wasserman, with whom he still had issues.

But he had to work to pay for *Faces:* "At one point, they threatened to take the film away when we couldn't pay Pathe Labs $17,000 for processing," Cassavetes recalled. "That night, I literally dreamed 'Bank of America, Vice President, Beverly Hills Branch.' I had nothing to hock, not the first collateral. We called him up the next morning and the guy gave us the money. I still don't believe it."

To finish *Faces*—to edit it, synch the sound, and so forth—Cassavetes found more work in front of the camera. He said, "When *Faces* was done, it cost $225,000. I just about broke even."

Editing *Faces* turned into an ordeal not much less severe than the one Cassavetes had endured for *Shadows*. Once again, to save money, he had shot on 16mm film. As he and his editors tried to assemble it, the skinny strands of film, with their tiny, brittle sprockets, tore with maddening regularity, and Cassavetes would find himself doing minute repairs on splinters of celluloid. And once again, he had serious problems with the sound.

Even as he was struggling with editing *Faces*, Cassavetes was cast in one of the best film roles of his career: as the weaselly, homicidal but ultimately redeemable Victor Franko in Robert Aldrich's *The Dirty Dozen*. The role took him to London, where the film was shot from spring into fall of 1968.

Cassavetes appreciated Aldrich's no-nonsense approach and his willingness to work with actors as equals: "Bob Aldrich treats his actors like people, not with contempt. He makes you feel like you're the greatest actor in the world."

The cast—which included Lee Marvin, Robert Ryan, Ernest Borgnine, Telly Savalas, Charles Bronson, Richard Jaeckel, Clint Walker, Donald Sutherland, and Jim Brown—seemed to hit it off.

In a cast full of hungry supporting actors scrapping for screen time, the toughest job may have fallen to Marvin, who had recently won an Oscar after a journeyman acting career. He was forced to play the on-screen babysitter to this tribe of misfits, who took every opportunity to steal their scenes from him.

Yet even in London, Cassavetes was editing *Faces*. The editors would work all day and he'd come back from shooting and examine the results, then edit into the night.

There were those nights, however, when Cassavetes and a group of his *Dirty Dozen* costars—including Lee Marvin—would head out to the casinos of London.

"John could outdrink anyone," Larry Shaw said. "A guy like Lee Marvin drank as much as John, but you could tell he was drunk. With John, you never could."

As Cassel noted, "Lee Marvin was an incredible drinker, but John had a great capacity. He practiced for years. I had to learn to drink that way."

Playwright Meade Roberts visited Cassavetes in London during that period, and Cassavetes talked about the fact that, even as he was shooting

The Dirty Dozen and editing *Faces,* fellow American Stanley Kubrick was filming *2001: A Space Odyssey* on a nearby soundstage. Cassavetes had heard that Kubrick had turned down an elaborate and huge set of the moon that MGM had built for him. Kubrick wanted a different moon.

"When I want a moon," Cassavetes cracked to Roberts, "I go outside and shoot what's up there in the sky. But Stanley's a genius, while I'm a bum from Port Washington who grew up on the Long Island Railroad."

Even though he thought he was acting simply to earn enough to finish his own movie, Cassavetes was giving one of the best performances of his life—one that earned him his only Oscar nomination as an actor.

The film itself earned mixed reviews. Based on a best-selling novel by E. M. Nathanson, it was considered extremely violent for its time, in the days immediately before the introduction of the rating system.

The *New York Times'* Bosley Crowther called it "an astonishingly wanton war film" and said Cassavetes was "wormy and noxious, as a psychopath condemned to death." *Newsweek's* Paul D. Zimmerman, who praised Cassavetes' "nicely balanced cowardly swagger," criticized the film's use of graphic violence for entertainment value, calling it "no substitute for imagination. The film destroys itself with its own weapons."

Writing in *Life* magazine, Richard Schickel countered in a later review, "Flawed as it is, it seems to me one of the most interesting films about the brutalizing effects of war that we have had from American filmmakers in the last decade."

Cassavetes continued editing *Faces* when he returned to the U.S., but he was having a problem extracting the film he envisioned from the cutting-room sprawl of 16mm film. So he called Al Ruban in New York, almost exactly a year to the day after his departure. Cassavetes was unhappy with the film and wanted Ruban to come to California and look at what he had.

Ruban made the trip and watched the film—and thought it was awful. But he didn't want to say that directly so he came at it from another angle. Knowing that Cassavetes had almost complete recall of every frame of film he'd shot, Ruban began to ask him questions: What happened to this scene? What about that scene? Cassavetes said, yeah, those were good. When Ruban asked him how the film had come to be assembled in the way it was, he found Cassavetes had taken the same democratic approach to editing that he'd attempted with the cinematography. He'd given individual reels to different editors and each of them, working independently, had cut their reels with no thought given to how it would fit with the rest of the film.

Ruban went back to step one, reassembling the dailies and starting from scratch. He moved into Cassavetes' house and, for the next year, edited the film.

Ruban admitted that his family suffered from his extended absences in pursuit of his movie dreams: "I abused them terribly," he said. "I told my wife early on, 'I can go the straight life and attempt to be a 9-to-5 person. Or I can attempt to be in the film business where there's no real money but it's what I really want.' She said go do what you want. It's been like that my entire marriage. She's very supportive. It's a debt that's impossible to pay."

Even as Ruban worked, Cassavetes left again, to shoot *Rosemary's Baby* for director Roman Polanski. Ira Levin's novel had been one of the biggest best-sellers of 1967. The movie, which was to be directed by Polish wunderkind Polanski in his American debut, was one of the prestige studio productions of the year, and it caused even bigger news when Polanski cast twenty-two-year-old Mia Farrow, the young actress whose career had exploded with TV's *Peyton Place*. (Farrow had sparked headlines with her recent marriage to Frank Sinatra, thirty years her senior.)

There had been a frenzy about the casting of Rosemary Woodhouse's husband, Guy, a struggling actor whose career is jump-started by his willingness to make a bargain with Satan. Seemingly a sympathetic figure, he eventually is revealed to have betrayed his wife in order to get what he wants.

Polanski wanted Robert Redford for the role, but Redford was being sued by Paramount. When Paramount executive Robert Evans invited Redford to meet with Polanski unofficially, a Paramount attorney barged into the meeting and served Redford with a subpoena. Redford, furious, took himself out of the running.

Jack Nicholson wanted the role but was a relative unknown, still more than a year away from his breakthrough in *Easy Rider*. Warren Beatty was considered but, after Cassavetes suggested himself to the film's producer, William Castle, Polanski agreed to take a chance on him.

But the two found themselves at odds almost from the beginning. Part of it may have been that Polanski, in some ways, worked the same way as Cassavetes: He preferred long takes, which he was prepared to do thirty or forty times.

Cassavetes, however, used those long takes to allow the actors to explore the scene. Polanski, by contrast, had a predetermined notion of what he wanted out of the actors, and he was prepared to have them repeat it until they got it exactly as he wanted, right down to the line readings. That kind of control and precision was anathema to Cassavetes.

"John's approach could not have been more different," recalled co-star Mia Farrow in her memoir. "His films had a raw, improvised quality, while Roman, who had adapted the script from the book himself, expected the actors to utter every word precisely as written and, of course, to hold up through as many takes as he wanted to shoot. John felt that this killed all the life in a scene . . . I felt embarrassed and upset when the two men openly disagreed and grew apart."

There were reports of daily shouting matches between the two. Polanski was quoted in the press as saying that he had cast Cassavetes to play himself and, in doing so, hadn't been concerned about his acting ability.

"He isn't a director," Polanski said. "He made some films. Anyone can take a camera and make a film like he made *Shadows.*"

The film was one of the huge hits of 1968, a multiple Oscar-nominee that gave Cassavetes a visibility that could only help *Faces* when it reached critics and viewers later in the year.

"Even readers of the book who know how *Baby* comes out are in for a pleasant surprise," *Time* allowed, and *Variety* called it "an excellent film version of Ira Levin's diabolical chiller novel," praising Cassavetes' performance because "it's impossible to pinpoint him as a pure heavy and rightfully so."

But the same critics who had championed such Polanski films as *Knife in the Water* and *Repulsion* reviled this piece of Hollywood entertainment: "Why on earth does a major filmmaker feel seduced by a dumb piece of boo-in-the-night like this story?" Penelope Gilliatt asked in *The New Yorker.* Stanley Kauffman sniffed, "We realize that [Polanski] must no longer be burdened with the standards he set for himself with *Knife in the Water.*"

Most of the critics at the time gave Cassavetes short shrift: "John Cassavetes has little flavor," Stanley Kauffman wrote in the *New Republic.* And *Time* magazine called his work as Guy "much too blah a character to have done what the script says he did."

Cassavetes himself thought Polanski had sold out a promising artistic career as a filmmaker to create Grand Guignol for Hollywood.

"You could see [in his earlier films] a pulse that was meaningful and creative and intense," Cassavetes said. "You can't dispute the fact that he's an artist but yet you have to say that *Rosemary's Baby* is not art. I think *Dirty Dozen* in its way is more artistic, you know, because it's compulsively going forward, trying to make something out of the moment without preordaining the way the outcome is going to be."

The *Faces* script, which Cassavetes referred to at various points as being anywhere from 250 to 350 pages long when they started shooting, produced a six-hour first assemblage. Cassavetes and Ruban pared it down to four hours and, finally, to a three-plus-hour version, which they screened in Canada.

But despite the length, the screenings in Toronto and Montreal produced a rapturous response, despite the fact that the first of two Toronto screenings started at midnight. Ruban recalled the Canadian screenings as a watershed moment, at least for their confidence in the film. He remembered the film having a three-hour, forty-minute running time, though he said, "We knew it couldn't go out at that length."

So Cassavetes, McEndree, and Ruban began cutting again. They eliminated extended chunks of the film, scenes that established who the characters were and their relationships to each other. Ruban saw the different facets of Cassavetes' creative personality at the various stages of the filmmaking process.

"When he was the writer and it was his film, he did the best he could," Ruban said. "He was a terrific writer. But when it was going to be shot, then he became the director and got rid of the writer. The director took over. In post-production, then his editing sense took over. So you got three different versions of the picture. He was never satisfied with what the other guy did. He was always looking for something new, something different that would appeal to him."

After Forst tells Maria he wants the divorce and leaves, Cassavetes had filmed a long scene in which Maria's best friends answer her distress call. They descend on her house and chatter among themselves about what she should do, punctuating the conversation with revelations about their own marriages. Eventually they convince her to have a girls' night out and wind up at the Whisky a Go-Go on Sunset Strip. To move the film along and get to the point, Cassavetes cut everything before the women arrive at the Whisky. Maria is seen coping with Forst's abrupt departure, then is seen out on the town with her girlfriends.

"It just wasn't necessary to explain why all of a sudden we find this woman going out with a bunch of broads we've never seen before," Cassavetes said. "We just decided, We understand who these women are. They're friends. We don't need that other scene. It was a shock to us to make that discovery and see how idiotic we really are. We were able to shorten the film and, at the same time, make the audience do a little work, make the jump, the connection, themselves. We realized we originally had been talking down to the audience."

Then they went to work on the scene in the middle of the film, in which two businessmen have drinks with Jeannie and her friend at Jeannie's apartment—until Forst arrives, which pits him against one of the men, McCarthy, for Jeannie's attentions.

"The McCarthy scene was cut considerably," Cassavetes said. "It was originally an hour and twenty minutes long and that's a movie in itself."

But cutting the film took an emotional toll on the filmmakers, who made the amputations unwillingly, in the interest of helping the film be seen. Eventually, friction between McEndree and Cassavetes led to McEndree's departure—not just from the project but from the entire Cassavetes circle.

Every creative decision was shaped by economic forces: what they wanted to do versus what they could afford to do. Inevitably, the funding came out of Cassavetes' own pocket. "We started with $10,000 and it has cost well over $200,000—and that was on 16mm," Cassavetes said at the time. "I'm the sole financier but I'm not too sure of the final cost."

Cassavetes understood the downside of that. "*Faces* has got to be successful," he said. "My actors gotta get paid. They worked for nothing; if the picture makes it, they get a percentage. But since we all worked together for no money, there was always a great feeling of rapport and freedom among us. We were doing something we cared about; money didn't enter into it. It showed that people can go out with nothing and with their own will make something that didn't exist before."

As he noted later, "The wonderful thing about *Faces* is nobody expected anything for it. It started as a play and we couldn't get a theater, so we made it into a movie. What happens is, if you believe in an idea, you have to believe strongly enough to fight for it. If you're willing to give up everything for it, then you can retain it. Then no one can take it away from you."

Twenty-five

Faces 3

When Cassavetes started screening *Faces* in Los Angeles in early 1968, the initial response was less than enthusiastic. Even when he got it down to a little more than two hours, his stark vision of American married life was too blunt and unexpected for most tastes in Hollywood.

It was as simple as the difference between old Hollywood and new. Lelia Goldoni was sitting behind actor Dana Andrews and his wife at one screening of *Faces*. After a little while, Andrews stood and stage-whispered to his wife, "I'm going. If you want to stay and watch this shit, that's up to you."

Cassavetes staged a couple of midnight screenings and, in his words, "the picture bombed." Cassavetes had invited the whole cast and didn't want to face them afterward because he wasn't sure he could maintain an upbeat demeanor for their benefit. But even trying to stay unobtrusive in a restroom stall, he couldn't escape: "Jesus, John wasted four years of his life on that piece of shit," he overheard someone say.

That seemed to galvanize him. He headed back to the post-screening party and put on a happy face, shaking hands and acting as though the whole thing had been a triumph. Though the actors were depressed by the audience's lack of response, Cassavetes' positive attitude kept them from taking it too seriously.

Cassavetes was undeterred. After the successful Canadian screenings, he took *Faces* to London and screened it at the National Film Theater, as a kind of thank-you for the institution's importance to the success of *Shadows*. Then he entered it in the Venice Film Festival, where it was nominated for the Golden Lion and won the best-actor award for John Marley.

But Cassavetes had been through this drill before. European accolades were all well and good, but they didn't count for much if his film wasn't embraced in the United States. *Shadows* had been the buzz among a certain stratum of American film cognoscenti, but ultimately it had gone largely unseen in America. Cassavetes wanted to avoid that fate for *Faces* and even harbored the idea that he could use it to reach mainstream audiences. To do that, it needed a distributor, and to land a distribution deal, it needed exposure at a major American festival.

So he and Ruban sent the print to the New York Film Festival, which had been housed at New York's Lincoln Center since its inception in 1962, when it had been created by Amos Vogel and programmer Richard Roud. By 1968 it had established itself as the premier American showcase for films from Europe's New Wave, as well as for American directors working outside the mainstream. But the film had been rejected out of hand by the festival's directors. So Ruban called Andrew Sarris, who was on the selection committee but hadn't seen *Faces*.

When Sarris saw the film, he called Vogel and arranged a lunch with Vogel and Roud, a flamboyant and opinionated programmer who directed the festival to prominence. At the lunch, Roud made it clear that he felt strongly that *Faces* didn't belong in the New York Film Festival. Sarris countered that he firmly believed that it did. Vogel, who couldn't withstand Roud's browbeating, said nothing.

Sarris presented his final word: "I feel very strongly about this," he told them. "I'm not a fan of Cassavetes. I don't believe in improvisation and I'm certainly not into naturalism. But if we don't put this film in, I don't see a point in continuing on the committee. There wouldn't be hard feelings but that's how I feel."

Sarris knew there was an unspoken agreement on the selection committee: Each member was allowed to choose one or two titles, even if his colleagues opposed the films. Roud had to accede to Sarris, and *Faces* was launched with a bravura screening at the New York Film Festival.

Faces fulfilled the fantasies that Cassavetes' coterie of East Coast followers had been harboring. Martin Scorsese, who was teaching at New York University at that point, said, "From 1963 to 1968, we'd hear these stories about Cassavetes shooting a film in his house in Los Angeles. There was this hope that Cassavetes would come back. We were praying that his picture could turn everything upside down. And when I saw it at the press screening at the New York Film Festival, it was one of the great experiences. It was like a vindication of *Shadows*—and the promise was fulfilled.

"I was a kid and not experienced in those kinds of relationships. But what came through was this extraordinary love, the feeling of love, passion and anger because of the love on the screen. The characters were behaving badly but they were not being judged. The emotion was in the emulsion, the psychological complexity."

Time magazine film critic Jay Cocks, Scorsese's friend, was also excited about seeing *Faces* and was not disappointed when he saw it: "It sounded like a guy who not only blazed a trail through the wilderness, but found his way home to a better place," Cocks said. "It was a relentless, unsparing, unforgiving masterpiece."

Still, until the reviews were published, there were no takers among distributors. And the earliest reviews weren't favorable. In June 1968, before the film had been picked up by the New York Film Festival, *Variety* called it "an overblown opus" and denounced it as "not in the same class as *Shadows.*"

But early word from the New York Film Festival in late September was strong. Renata Adler reviewed it in the *New York Times*, calling it "incomparably better than John Cassavetes' first film, *Shadows*, and a really important movie about the American class, generation and marriage abyss. The movie is very blunt and relentless, sometimes redundant, at moments nearly unintelligible—but the entire effect is of a high-strung, very bright documentary about the way things are."

And Jonas Mekas, writing in the *Village Voice*, noted that he had seen *Faces* three months earlier at a midnight screening and had loved the film—but was hesitant to say that too loudly for fear that Cassavetes would do what he did with *Shadows* and reedit the film in a way that invalidated Mekas' opinion.

But Mekas called it "a very moving film, an original film, a difficult-to-make film. It's a merge between Warhol and Chekhov . . . His professional actors succeed in breaking through the usual Hollywood acting techniques and open to the camera a different, unfilmed-yet reality. The cinema of Cassavetes is the cinema of emotion."

Cassavetes wasn't even in New York for his triumph. As *Faces* was being cheered at Avery Fisher Hall at Lincoln Center, Cassavetes was on the other side of the country, shooting exteriors for *Machine Gun McCain* in San Francisco.

That's where Ruban found him by telephone after the festival showing. A representative of Cinema One on New York's East Side had tracked Ruban down and made an offer to play the film. But when Ruban called Cassavetes, Cassavetes said, "Aw, that guy's a crook. Besides, I already made a deal with the Walter Reade people."

The national chain took on *Faces*, opening it in New York at the Little Carnegie Theater beneath Carnegie Hall at Thanksgiving, where it stayed for almost five months.

The film opened to mostly glowing reviews. Cassavetes' approach appealed to the populist critics more than the intellectuals. Frances Herridge, in the *New York Post*, took issue with its length but noted that it was "a compelling and haunting work for those who have the patience to stay with it."

New York magazine's Judith Crist wrote, "It is a movie of substance, a substance that not only transcends its sins—of self-indulgence, of overstatement—but also transforms them into minor virtues—of ardor for theme, of unslickness. It is a personal and probing film concerned with the middle time of a childless marriage, when the routine of a relationship supersedes its passions and the nothingness obtrudes . . . Just as our patience is being tried, it is rewarded with a brilliant flash of illumination, a moment of silence that tells all . . . *Faces* is a fine achievement, with a style and statement of its own."

Life magazine's Richard Schickel said it was "a great courageous film in which Cassavetes has dared more than any American director in recent memory . . . Cassavetes is one of those remarkable artists who has learned to dissect us without at the same time learning to despise us." Andrew Sarris called *Faces* "the revelation of 1968, not the best movie to be sure, but certainly the most surprising." Claire Clouzot, writing in *Film Quarterly* in early 1969, said, "It may not be the best American film of the decade, but it is no doubt the most important."

But one critic in particular used the release of *Faces* to heap scorn on Cassavetes—past, present, and future. Pauline Kael would prove a critical nemesis for all of Cassavetes' career, someone who not only did not see the merit of his work and objected to him doing it, but had only disdain for anyone who was taken in by Cassavetes and his movies.

This was the Kael who, only a couple of months later, in her famous *Harper's* essay "Trash, Art and the Movies," would write, "The problem with a popular art form is that those who want something more are in a hopeless minority, compared with the millions who are always seeing it for the first time, or for the reassurance and gratification of seeing the conventions fulfilled again."

But for something as new and confrontational as *Faces*, Kael offered little understanding. She called the acting in Cassavetes' film "so bad it's embarrassing," noting that it "sometimes seems also to have revealed something, so we're forced to reconsider our notions of good and bad acting."

She compared *Faces* to Norman Mailer's homemade films *Wild 90* and *Beyond the Law*, referring to both men as the cinematic equivalent of primitive painters "who expect the movie to happen when the camera is on."

"There are scenes in *Faces* so dumb, so crudely conceived and so badly performed that the audience practically burns incense," Kael wrote. "I think embarrassment is not a quality of art but our reaction to failed art."

It didn't matter what Kael thought; the film was a hit. When it opened, Cassavetes stood outside the Little Carnegie, talking to the people who were going to see the film and trying to convince others to buy a ticket. After each show, he'd buttonhole audience members and ask them what they thought.

Walter Reade distributed the film nationally as well—and *Faces*, which cost less than $300,000, wound up taking in more than $8 million.

"I call the box office every night," Cassavetes said, "and see how *Faces* is doing. I love the profits. I mean, I go crazy. But the thrill I get, I don't care about the money—it's that all those people are going to see it."

The film's cast and crew, who took no salary but signed on for participation in any profits, still receive checks on a regular basis. Lynn Carlin remembered that her contract with Cassavetes had been written on a cocktail napkin: "But ten years afterward, a big check came one day because there had been an accounting report," she said. "He was an extremely honest man with great integrity."

When the film turned into the most talked-about movie of late 1968, the press came calling. Here was Cassavetes, the star of one of the most successful summer movies of the year (*Rosemary's Baby*), chatting with whoever would listen about his bold experiment in filmmaking: creating movies about and for adults and paying for it himself.

He seemed surprised when journalists and others would ask why the film took so long to finish. They seemed to think these things should happen more easily.

"How long have we been fighting the Vietnam War?" he said. "If it takes that long to do something that destructive, why can't we be allowed to take four years to do something constructive?"

Cassavetes would routinely test reporters, asking them what they had thought of the film. He had an ear for dissembling and wasn't afraid to argue with them if he disagreed with their opinions—and if they weren't crazy about his film, well, he obviously disagreed with that.

"John grew intent on finding out why I hadn't liked *Faces* and insisted that discussing this was far more meaningful than responding to the usual questions," wrote Phyllis Funke, a reporter for *Suffolk Sunday,* a Long Island publication. So she told him: "I found that when the film successfully conveyed the boredom of the characters in it, I grew bored with their boredom."

"But they are not bored," Cassavetes insisted. "They are really living life. If anything, their plight is exhausting . . . What I love about them is that they don't quit. They will make jackasses of themselves but they try to keep it going. It doesn't matter if you're wrong if you try."

That word—"boring"—bothered him in particular. "I didn't find *Faces* boring in any sense," he said. "As a matter of fact, I found it extremely fast-moving. Sometimes, when it slowed down from extreme speed, it was like stepping off a fast train."

By Christmas, the film was a genuine hit in New York and Los Angeles, and a larger rollout was being planned. Cassavetes continued talking to the press to stimulate awareness of the movie, even as he began to plan his next move.

He had a script he had written about three friends confronting death and middle age. And because of the heat surrounding the first weeks' grosses on *Faces,* he was able to generate interest from independent financiers to give him the money to make it. No more self-financing—someone else could pay the freight.

The success of *Faces* at the box office was gratifying. And when the film received three Oscar nominations—Carlin and Cassel in the supporting acting categories and Cassavetes for his script—it was icing on the cake.

The nominations were sweet for Cassavetes, who had almost given up on having his work accepted in the United States the way it was in Europe. "Surprise of surprises, I had an artistic and financial hit on my hands, this time in my own country," Cassavetes said, "proving to me that it was worth all the nonsense I went through. Proving to me that moviemakers don't have to spend their time doing garbage they hate.

"You know, I think I'm crazy. What's worse, I get other people involved in my craziness and then I'm obligated to do something about it. I have terrific ambition," he said, adding with a wheezy laugh, "My ambition is so pompous."

Faces had no hope of winning an Academy Award, it was believed, because, the nominations aside, it was a nonunion picture competing against big-budget, studio-driven, union-staffed movies such as *Oliver!, Funny Girl,* and *The Lion in Winter.* In fact, Cassavetes had to go before a Screen Actors

Guild tribunal over the fact that he had made the film with a nonunion crew and cast.

Facing a committee headed by Charlton Heston in New York, Cassavetes listened to the charges against him and the various disciplinary measures that could be applied. Finally, he said, "Go ahead and fine me. I think you should." Heston attempted to suggest a compromise, but Cassavetes was hearing none of it and walked out.

Ultimately, no fine was levied. As Heston himself wrote in his autobiography, "This is union heresy, but I think John Cassavetes deserved a little elbow room."

As it turned out, Carlin lost the Oscar to Ruth Gordon for *Rosemary's Baby*, while Cassel watched Jack Albertson win for *The Subject Was Roses*. The screenwriting Oscar went to Mel Brooks for *The Producers*, leaving empty-handed both Cassavetes and Stanley Kubrick (who'd been a conominee with Arthur C. Clarke for *2001: A Space Odyssey*).

But the recognition brought by the nominations, along with a boost in the already hearty box-office returns, was the final validation that the years of work had been about something that people valued.

"I'd been an actor for almost ten years when *Faces* came out," Cassel said. "Suddenly people are going, 'Hey, you're an actor—you're good.' It was because of John. He wrote that part with me in mind." Cassel was pleased to be noticed, but he was also well aware of who was doing the noticing: "It was the same people who never gave me the time of day before," he said. "I knew which ones were phonies. I knew I was great in the film because the audiences were telling me. I didn't need anybody else to tell me. I didn't do it for the Stanley Kramers. I did it for myself and for John."

Cassel had gotten a taste of just how deeply the film had penetrated public consciousness that Halloween. The film was still a month away from release but was burning up the screening circuit in Hollywood, following its success at the New York Film Festival. Cassel, still relatively unknown, was walking his children around the neighborhood just above Sunset Boulevard as they went trick-or-treating, when they knocked on one particular door— which was answered by Ozzie and Harriet Nelson. The couple, along with their sons, David and Ricky, had been a television staple with *The Adventures of Ozzie and Harriet*, which had gone off the air a couple of years earlier after a sixteen-year run.

Now here they were answering the door, and they recognized Cassel from the film.

"They'd seen the movie and they loved it," Cassel recalled. "They invited us in for coffee and were telling us how much they liked the movie.

I'm thinking, 'We're in Ozzie and Harriet's house.' I kept expecting the lights to go on and David and Ricky to come down the stairs and we'll be on the show. I kept thinking, 'I can't wait to tell John.'"

Box-office cachet, Oscar nominations: Suddenly Cassavetes' home movie was being seen as something else entirely—a shot across the bow of the major studios by a tiny independent movie filmed on a bare-bones budget. It startled the Hollywood establishment, which already was in something of a panic about being deserted by the youth audience. And it gave heart to other would-be filmmakers who saw how much Cassavetes had done with so little.

The inspirational aspect of the success of *Faces,* Martin Scorsese recalled, was that Cassavetes had been able to make the film at all—this deeply personal expression—and then to have it released into actual movie theaters.

"Independent films hardly ever were distributed," he recalled. "With *Faces,* he showed you could make a film in that style within modest means on an offbeat subject in grainy black and white."

But, again, the commercial success was a by-product of a communal experience that was uniquely gratifying.

"We always try to think about what was the very best time of our lives," Cassavetes said later. "Usually it's college or childhood or something like that. Making *Faces* was the very best time of my life—because of the people. I'd never met people like that and I'm talking about every single member of that company and cast, people who made my life really worth living. I never thought once during the whole time we were making that film that there was anything else in the world except those people. They were that devoted and pure."

Part Three

The most ordinary human dramas glow with the glare of ultimate things.

—Czeslaw Milosz

I've got to work out this problem. When I'm acting, I want to direct. And when I'm directing, I want to act.

—John Cassavetes

You think this is easy, realism?

—"D. J.," David Bowie

Twenty-six

Pre-Husbands

I
n the spring of 1967, as he worked on editing *Faces,* Cassavetes took an acting role in a crime thriller to be shot in Acapulco, Mexico. He never got a chance to make the film, but accepting it seemingly would haunt him the rest of his life. The film, called *Sol Madrid,* was about an undercover government agent, played by David McCallum, hot off his role as secret agent Illya Kuryakin on TV's spy hit *The Man from U.N.C.L.E.*

Cassavetes was cast as a vicious mobster, Dano Villanova, who, together with a drug kingpin played by Telly Savalas, was Madrid's target. Stella Stevens was to play a hooker, formerly Villanova's mistress, whom Madrid uses to infiltrate the criminal operation.

Everett Chambers, who knew Cassavetes needed acting work to finance *Faces,* had heard from producer Elliott Kastner, who was putting *Sol Madrid* together. Kastner wanted Cassavetes because he needed a star, and Kastner knew that Cassavetes was friends with Chambers.

Almost as soon as shooting began in early June, however, Cassavetes came down with a bad case of infectious hepatitis on location, probably from unclean water. He became so ill that he left the film and was flown back to Los Angeles to Beverly Hills Doctor's Hospital to recover.

Stevens had filmed a couple of scenes with Cassavetes when Cassavetes had to quit the production: "In the midst of shooting, everyone was told we had to have a gammaglobulin shot because John had come down with a certain type of hepatitis," she said. "So we had to reshoot his scenes."

Ruban, who was in Mexico with Cassavetes, remembered him being carried out on a stretcher: "He was very sick. We all had to get shots."

In early July, *Variety* announced that, after closing down production for three weeks, shooting would resume, with Rip Torn stepping in for Cassavetes as Villanova.

"I feel strangely responsible and guilty," Chambers said of the illness that would come back to haunt Cassavetes in his final years. Cassavetes returned to California in June to recuperate: two weeks in isolation, three more weeks at home.

Hepatitis is a disease of the liver; depending on the strain, it can be treated with gammaglobulin. But its effects can also be devastating, inflaming the liver and eventually impairing its function. The effects, in fact, are not unlike those that chronic alcoholism has on the liver. In Cassavetes, they became a ticking time bomb that eventually took the form of cirrhosis, the fatal liver disease.

But Cassavetes, feeling better after early treatment for hepatitis and with spare time on his hands, was restless at home and began to work again on editing *Faces*. Then in August he was cast in *Rosemary's Baby*, which meant a trip to New York for location work before moving on to the soundstage. So there was no real time to recuperate from the illness.

And despite doctors' admonitions that he needed to avoid alcohol for several months until he recovered completely from the hepatitis, Cassavetes began drinking again. He had always been a drinker and wasn't about to stop. For Cassavetes, no day was considered complete unless it included cocktails to end a day on the set or to fuel a marathon editing session. "Hepatitis and drinking don't go together, but John continued to indulge," Chambers said.

Seymour Cassel explained Cassavetes' thinking: "I'm thirty-eight and I can't drink? What does that mean? I can still play basketball, I can still smoke. Why can't I drink?" Cassel said. "It was a social thing. That's what you did."

Added Ruban, "He continued to drink and drink heavily."

Did that ultimately contribute to his death? According to medical experts, the long-term effects of infectious hepatitis (hepatitis A) don't often include cirrhosis. Only a serious, long-term drinking problem—or exposure to hepatitis C, which is contracted from intravenous drug use (or sex with an IV-drug user)—would produce the kind of life-threatening liver damage Cassavetes had sustained by the time he was diagnosed in 1983.

Not that any of his friends thought he had a drinking problem. It was part of who Cassavetes was—and at that point in the 1960s, alcohol was part of the social structure, the accepted social lubricant of choice. And Cassavetes never seemed to show the effects of the drinking.

"I never knew he was a heavy drinker," Chambers said. "John was so alive you wouldn't know that he was loaded."

Larry Shaw remembered going bar-hopping with Cassavetes on the East Side of New York: "I could not keep up with John," Shaw said. "He could drink so much you couldn't believe it and you couldn't tell."

John Finnegan, another actor friend, said, "Irish guys get Irish drunk. They're ready to fight the world. John was a Cadillac drinker. You never knew when he was bombed. The fucking guy could put it away."

Ruban said, "In all my years, I never saw him drunk, not to the extent that he was out of control. But he couldn't have a discussion or be on the phone without one or two cigarettes. He would have a drink in his hand, a full glass."

As the fall of 1968 approached, Cassavetes could feel the momentum swing his way with the advance reviews and film festival heat for *Faces*. Not wanting to miss an opportunity—and not wanting to go through the agonizing process of making another movie with his own money—he, Ruban, and Shaw began looking for backers for his next venture. He had an idea for a drama about a trio of male friends, and he knew who he wanted for the cast.

As he shaped the script that would become *Husbands*, Cassavetes tested several themes he was working with. But while the phrase would not come into popular usage for several more years, what Cassavetes was writing was a drama about male midlife crisis: What happens to a trio of friends in their early forties when their best friend—the most vital person they know—drops dead at the same age.

Cassavetes admitted a direct connection between the themes of the story he was crafting and his reaction to the death of his own brother, Nicholas, a decade earlier.

"It's not autobiographical, in the sense that it has nothing to do with real incidents," Cassavetes said. "Only the feelings in the film are related to my own life, just as Peter [Falk's] and Ben [Gazzara's] are. The truth is that the story of *Husbands* is very personal to me. My older brother died when he was thirty years old, so I know very well the effect of the death of a loved one."

Cassavetes had always looked up to his brother, following him to

Champlain College after his brother returned from the service. But Nicholas was the student; John was always the cut-up. Nicholas finished college and found a job on Wall Street (though there were family rumors for years that, in fact, the intense, chain-smoking Nicholas had been involved in secret operations at MIT for the CIA; one story had him designing spy planes).

It was undoubtedly a sibling relationship like that between most brothers separated by a couple of years and a mile of temperament. Younger brothers inevitably admire and resent their older brothers; older brothers routinely pick on or ignore younger brothers, even while harboring deep (if unspoken) feelings for them. Some of that seemed to come through in the novel of *Husbands* Cassavetes would write while the movie was being edited.

"My brother taught me how to swim," notes Gus, the character Cassavetes played in the film. "He and his buddy, Donny White, took me out to the middle of Manhasset Bay on a Comet—that's a sailboat—and they threw me in. That's the way I learned to swim."

But Cassavetes obviously looked up to his brother, even going so far as to mention him in his MGM bio for *Saddle the Wind*: "His older brother, Nicholas, is a successful Wall Street broker."

Nicholas died in October 1957, suddenly and unexpectedly. He may have died of a heart attack while skiing. It was unclear; during an interview with the *New York Daily News* shortly before Halloween 1957, Cassavetes and Rowland chatted about their recent films, with Cassavetes talking enthusiastically about *Saddle the Wind* and *Virgin Island*. When Cassavetes left the room, Rowlands said in an aside to the reporter, "I am so happy he was able to perk up by a discussion of the business. You see, his thirty-year-old brother died Friday. Skiing. He left a wife and twenty-one-month-old baby."

All of this was swirling around Cassavetes' consciousness as he sketched out a script about three guys coping with the death of a friend: With him went their youth and youthful dreams, or so it seemed.

"We found a subject that we like," he said in the fall of 1968. " 'Whatever Happened to Sentiment in the World Today?' So we're going to do a picture on sentiment. I think the idea's exciting."

He would later refine the pitch to something more tangible, though again, there was the sense that he was refining the idea even as he talked about it.

"*Husbands* has to do with three men whose best friend dies and we go out on a three-day wake without going to sleep," Cassavetes said. "Then one of us takes a shower. It's that simple. He goes home and changes his clothes. We get so angry with the son of a bitch for changing his clothes that we have to play a joke on him. And the result of the joke is what the picture is about.

"You could say it's about three married guys who want something for themselves. They don't know what they want but they get scared when their best friend dies. It's the story of three guys—they're not fags—who like each other better than they do their wives."

But *Husbands* was also about three actors, all roughly the same age, forming a bond of friendship and, together, addressing as characters the very issues they were struggling with as men.

"Falk, Gazzara and myself started with ourselves and a kind of simple idea of a guy dying: What it would mean to us if one of us, if one of our close friends, died," Cassavetes said. "How would we handle it? From the very beginning, we made a pact that we would try to find whatever truth was left in ourselves and talk about that. Sometimes, the scenes would reflect things that we didn't like to find out: how idiotic we were, or how little we had to do with ourselves, how uptight we were. We felt that it was important to find a way to have the courage to put that out on a line for whatever it was, even if the picture itself would not be exciting."

It would be the mid-1970s before Gail Sheehy would put a name on the transitional points in adult life in her book *Passages*, but Cassavetes already seemed to have a number of the same ideas worked out.

"There are phases in everyone's life that are extreme, when emotions are naturally heightened. This one week changes everything about them—their thoughts, feelings, their relationships to each other," he said. "Getting old doesn't bother us. It's still being young and not having done anything. We have to make a game out of everything. We enjoy the games, as part of our lives which has always given us comfort when we needed it. And then, when the games are over, we're tired and the thoughts and fears come back again.

"Men have a different relationship with men than they have with women—a different kind of honesty. Men look for friends with whom they don't have to put up a front. A man with whom you can be comfortable becomes your friend. You're not married to him, so you don't have to prove anything or carry the responsibility for that friendship outside of just being there."

Or as Gazzara put it, "At a certain age, every man fears his zest for life and youth is fast disappearing and it's scary. Nothing makes you feel this more than the death of a friend your age. When John first told us the idea, Peter and I were there with so many personal notions about it—and marriage, too.

"It's the first time," Gazzara said, almost as a pronouncement, "real male love has been shown on screen, male love for another male. Men are more comfortable around men. This is the first picture that admits it."

Cassavetes had written the parts with Gazzara and Falk in mind, though Val Avery later said, "During *Faces*, he said one day, 'I got a part for you.' He wrote the part in *Husbands* for me—and then turns around and decides he wants to play it himself."

Cassavetes didn't know either Falk or Gazzara very well. Falk was two years older than Cassavetes but had come to acting much later. Gazzara was a year younger and had had success on Broadway at roughly the same time Cassavetes was a star on TV.

They were all native New Yorkers, though Gazzara grew up in Manhattan, while Cassavetes roamed the boroughs with his family before settling on Long Island, and Falk had grown up in the Westchester County river town of Ossining. They were all of European extraction, though each of a different ethnicity: Cassavetes, Greek; Gazzara, Sicilian; Falk, Jewish by way of European ancestry.

Indeed, had anyone else been in charge of casting, Cassavetes noted later, there's no way the three of them would have been teamed: "For one thing, we all have dark hair," he said. As Gazzara observed, "Louis B. Mayer would have put a blond in the middle to break up the blackness."

And each was at roughly the same stage in his career: They had tasted stardom and had hit peaks early on, only to realize they had merely reached the top of a foothill en route to the pinnacle of stardom. Having reached a pinnacle that turned out to be a plateau, they each wanted something more from the work they were doing but were unsatisfied with what Hollywood had to offer.

So both Falk and Gazzara were willing to take a flyer with Cassavetes, whose enthusiasm won them over even when the script was in its most preliminary stages.

Falk had grown up in Ossining, about thirty miles north of New York City, where his parents, Michael and Madeline, had moved from Manhattan when Peter was six. His parents, a Russian father and Polish mother, ran a dry-goods store in Ossining.

The defining event of his childhood, it seemed, was the loss of his right eye to a tumor when he was three. In truth, however, it became a bigger deal to people he met than it ever was to him: "It's like having flat feet all your life," Falk said. "After a while, you don't give it a thought unless someone calls it to your attention.

"There's a time when you're young when you're very sensitive about things, like a false eye. Now, if somebody asks me which eye is the bad one, I have to stop and think about it."

Not that he was shy about using it to get a laugh: As a smart-mouthed preadolescent, Falk was playing in a Little League game and an umpire called him out sliding into base on a close play. Without missing a beat, Falk popped the glass eye out of its socket and offered it to the umpire, saying, "Here, you need this more than I do."

Falk played basketball and baseball in high school and was president of the Ossining High School class of 1945. Though he enrolled at Hamilton College in Clinton, New York, where he took a few drama classes, he lasted a month, then dropped out.

He tried to join the Marines and nearly faked his way through the eye exam, until someone noticed that he was covering the same eye twice (but with different hands) while reading the chart. Instead, he joined the Merchant Marine and spent a year and a half traveling the globe, before returning to finish college. He spent two years at Hamilton, then completed his degree in literature and social science at the New School for Social Research in Manhattan.

Still, Falk felt bootless, rootless, and at loose ends. He had felt stirrings about acting but from an early age had discarded it as something that would get him laughed at.

"In Ossining, when I was growing up, I would have been embarrassed to tell any of my friends that I had any idea of being an actor," he said. "My conception of being an actor was very naive and very romantic. I thought actors were some rare species. I thought they were artists and I thought artists were Europeans. I never saw any actors where I came from."

When Falk eventually did decide to commit to acting and told his parents, his father said, "You're going to paint your face and make an ass of yourself all your life." Then his father shook his hand and said, "Good luck to you."

Whatever he chose, Falk knew he had to make up his mind. As much fun as he'd had, he came to a realization: "Jesus Christ, I'm twenty-six years old. I'd better do something about earning a living."

Yet the act of making a choice was never a simple one. His first wife, Alyce Mayo, whom he married in 1960 after a courtship of several years, once referred to him as "a man of long indecisions." Falk himself said, "I'm not a daredevil. I don't jump in. I inch."

He enrolled at the University of Syracuse, where he earned a master's degree in public administration. That qualified him to take a job as an efficiency expert for the state of Connecticut, where he went to work in the budget bureau in Hartford.

With little else to do with his spare time, Falk finally indulged the urge to act, joining Hartford's Mark Twain Masquers and finding that he liked acting tremendously. He enjoyed it so much that when he heard about an acting workshop being given by Eva Le Gallienne at the White Barn Theater in Westport, Connecticut, two hours away, he signed up for it, despite the fact that it was a class for professionals. He talked his way into the class and began making weekly round trips from Hartford, just for the chance to be in the class.

But between his work schedule, the traffic, and his penchant for tardiness, Falk attracted Le Gallienne's wrath by repeatedly arriving late for the class. Finally, one night, the formidable grande dame stopped everything when Falk once more walked in after class had begun.

"Young man, why are you always late?" she asked.

"I have to drive down from Hartford;" Falk replied.

Le Gallienne gathered herself to glare at him down her nose and said, "What do you do in Hartford? There's no theater there. How do you make a living acting?"

Falk, a little embarrassed, said, "Well, I'm not a professional actor."

To which Le Gallienne responded irritably, "Well, you should be."

That was all the impetus the twenty-nine-year-old Falk needed. He quit his job in Hartford and moved to New York, using a recommendation from Le Gallienne to meet and secure representation at the William Morris Agency.

His new agent seemed hesitant to speak once he met Falk but finally said, "You know, son, you could never do television or the movies." It took Falk a minute to realize the agent was talking about his glass eye. Since Falk had no aspirations toward TV or movies, that didn't matter. He wanted to act on stage; he wanted to join the Actors Studio. He wanted to be an actor, not a star.

Almost immediately, he began working off-Broadway, landing a part in a production of Moliere's *Don Juan* (with another newcomer, George Segal) that required him to wear blue satin knickers and black shoes with silver buckles: "What the hell are we doing in these ridiculous outfits?" Falk muttered to Segal.

Another audition netted him the role of the bartender in the landmark 1956 Circle in the Square production of Eugene O'Neill's *The Iceman Cometh*, opposite Jason Robards. It wasn't the lead, but it might as well have been: Whereas Robards' Hickey came on for lengthy monologues at the end of each act, Falk's Harry Hope was on stage for the entire play.

"That play established me with producers and directors," Falk said. "I only stayed in the play for two months but it was worth four years of exposure."

More off-Broadway and TV work followed. Eventually movies beck-oned, but not eagerly at first. Falk was recommended to Harry Cohn, the notoriously boorish studio chief at Columbia Pictures. Falk arrived with encomiums hailing him as a young John Garfield.

But when Cohn met Falk in person, all he saw was the glass eye. Telling Falk he was concerned about Falk's "deficiency," he declared, "For the same money, I can get an actor with two eyes."

Still, Falk began getting movie work in 1958 and in 1960 landed the first of two Oscar nominations, playing Abe "Kid Twist" Reles, a vicious killer in the gangster film *Murder, Inc.* A year later he was nominated again, this time for playing a comic gangster in Frank Capra's *A Pocketful of Miracles.*

Two Oscar nominations—and the movie work was plentiful. Everyone wanted a taste of the Falk magic: the pugnacious, squinty little guy with the gravelly voice, great timing, and offbeat delivery. But the roles were mostly as second bananas and comic foils, in films such as *It's a Mad, Mad, Mad, Mad World, The Great Race,* and *Pressure Point.*

In 1965 he'd starred in his own TV series, *The Trials of O'Brien,* playing a battling attorney in New York. But the material was weak and the series was cancelled after a season.

By the time he ran into John Cassavetes at the Paramount commissary in 1967, Falk was feeling frustrated, because he felt he wasn't getting the kinds of parts he could really do something with. "I was proud of the stuff I did in the years from 1955 to 1962," Falk said. "But for the next seven years, I wasn't pleased with my work."

At that point, Falk had just shot *Prescription: Murder,* a made-for-TV movie that would serve as a pilot for the show that would make Falk's for-tune and become his annuity: *Columbo.* Falk had gotten the role only after Bing Crosby and Lee J. Cobb had turned it down. The pilot aired in Feb-ruary 1968.

According to Falk, the first time he ever spoke to Cassavetes was at an L.A. Lakers game. Falk got up to get a hot dog at halftime and ran into Cas-savetes coming in the opposite direction. Though they'd never met, they rec-ognized each other and started talking—long enough to discover that Cassavetes had gone to high school on Long Island with Falk's wife, Alyce.

In late 1967, as Cassavetes was shooting *Rosemary's Baby* and still strug-gling to finish *Faces,* Falk saw him at lunch at Paramount. Falk had a script by Elaine May, *Mikey & Nicky,* that he thought Cassavetes would be perfect for. After an initial misunderstanding—in which Cassavetes agreed to do the film without even hearing about it and Falk thought he was putting him on—they began to talk about *Faces,* which Cassavetes was still editing. Pausing from that discourse, Cassavetes told Falk, "What I really want to do is make a movie with you and Ben Gazzara."

He briefly described his initial idea for *Husbands,* but Falk took it all with a grain of salt: "I've heard that bull for so many years," Falk said later. "You know, you see a couple of guys you like and you say, 'Yeah, we should make a movie. Sure, we're going to make a picture.'"

Ben Gazzara had the same reaction when he ran into Cassavetes in early 1968. He had just finished the last episode of his latest TV series, *Run for Your Life.* As he was getting in his car, he saw Cassavetes across the parking lot. They'd run into each other as struggling actors in New York but weren't really friends, though they'd worked together briefly on a TV drama.

Now Cassavetes was waving and calling his name: "Did Marty call you?" Cassavetes wanted to know, referring to Martin Baum, their mutual agent.

"Not yet," Gazzara replied, to which Cassavetes said with a smile, "He will."

The encounter could not have come at a better time for Gazzara, who was tired and disillusioned after three years of a TV series playing a dying man who's been given one to two years to live.

At that point, Gazzara was already questioning where he was headed professionally. His career had lost much of the sense of possibility that it had had when he burst onto Broadway in 1953 at the age of twenty-two in *End as a Man*—the sense that good work would follow good work, that remaining true to his craft was the only credo he needed to follow to keep it coming.

Gazzara had grown up in an Italian neighborhood on New York's East Side, in the area then known as the Gashouse District—First and Second Avenue in the Twenties. His parents were Sicilian immigrants, working people with large extended families, all of whom seemed to live in the neighborhood.

He discovered acting at the age of twelve, joining a production at the neighborhood Boys Club. The head of the dramatics program, a former actor named Howard Sinclair, recognized something in young Biagio Gazzara and not only encouraged his talent but validated it.

"Coming to know him was like finding a new father from another world, a kind of world I had only dreamed about before," Gazzara said. "It was as though I had found a new home. I really began to live on the stage. By the time I was fifteen, I had definitely decided to become a professional actor. When I had doubts, I would tell Sinclair about them, and he would say he was sure that I would have a place in the theater."

Even at that age, Gazzara had a presence and a commitment onstage that stood out. According to Irving Harris, an alumnus of the Boys Club program who later became a TV producer, "Even then, Ben was great. At rehearsals, some of the other kids would start horsing around, but not him. He would immerse himself in the part."

Gazzara quit high school at one point, then finished and enrolled in City College of New York night school, with an eye toward studying engineering. By day, he held various menial jobs: as a silver replater, an elevator operator, making slipcovers for furniture.

One night, a neighborhood friend invited him to see a production by Erwin Piscator's Dramatic Workshop at the New School for Social Research. It was *The Flies*, by Jean-Paul Sartre. Gazzara was "stunned by the theatricality of what I saw. I decided to quit night school and try to join the Workshop."

He auditioned for a scholarship and received it, studying Piscator's epic style of theater avidly at first. But within a year or so, he began to hear rumblings from other actors about a new approach that was unsettling the acting world: the Actors Studio.

Gazzara went to see Tennessee Williams' first Broadway hit, *The Glass Menagerie*, shortly before it closed, then immediately went to see the new Williams sensation, *A Streetcar Named Desire*. Marlon Brando's performance "got me terribly wrought up," Gazzara recalled. "I reacted strongly to the raw emotion, the animal vitality in his acting."

Gazzara auditioned for the Actors Studio and was admitted on his first try. Actress Anne Jackson, who was studying there at the same time, remembered, "Ben was a very handsome young man with a lot of charisma. He seemed to have been typecast because he had an ethnic look."

"At the Actors Studio, you cared about being real, being honest, being there, being as good as you can be," Gazzara recalled.

After working there for a couple of years, he and a group of his fellow students put together a stage version of Calder Willingham's *End as a Man*, a taut, humorous tale of a power struggle among cadets at a military school. It began as an actors' exercise, but the production suddenly took on a life of its own: From a studio presentation at the Actors Studio, it transferred off-Broadway to the Theater de Lys. When gushing reviews greeted its opening, it moved to Broadway, where it played for four months. The cast included fellow Studio members Pat Hingle, Albert Salmi, and a young James Dean, who was replaced by Anthony Franciosa when it moved to Broadway.

At the beginning of 1955, Gazzara followed *End as a Man* by creating the role of Brick in Elia Kazan's premiere production of Tennessee Williams' *Cat on a Hot Tin Roof*, opposite Barbara Bel Geddes, as Maggie, and Burl Ives, as Big Daddy. Once again, he was the toast of Broadway.

Peter Bogdanovich, who saw that production as a young adolescent, remembered, "Nobody onstage ever conveyed such dynamism through silence. In that first act, he hardly says much. The way Kazan staged it, his character hardly moved. But you couldn't take your eyes off him. There was such a coiled violence there."

He followed that play with another Broadway debut: Michael V. Gazzo's *A Hatful of Rain*, in which he played a heroin addict named Johnny Pope. It was one of the first realistic treatments of drug addiction on Broadway, and Gazzara was hailed once again.

But he wasn't happy with the work he was doing, at least at first: "At that time, if I wasn't crying or hysterical onstage, I thought there was no drama to my role," he said. "Now I realize that simpler behavior can be more touching. When I rejoined *Hatful of Rain* on the road six months later, in Milwaukee, it came to me that even in a part as serious as this one, there was room for humor and that one must be less rigid and look for humanity."

His predecessors in the "hottest young actor" category—Marlon Brando and James Dean, among others—had quickly abandoned theater for films. But Gazzara wanted to remain a purist, working in theater rather than selling himself to Hollywood. So he waved off numerous offers that would have raised his profile, perhaps enough for him to win the roles he'd created on Broadway when the plays were turned into films.

As he later recognized, "I thought those wonderful parts in the theater would keep coming. I thought, Who needs movies?"

So he held off on accepting any film roles until *End as a Man* was filmed as *The Strange One* in 1957; the film was made outside of the studios and was barely released. By that time, it seemed, Gazzara had blown his opportunity. Suddenly Don Murray was playing Johnny Pope in the film of *A Hatful of Rain*, and Paul Newman was playing Brick opposite Elizabeth Taylor in *Cat on a Hot Tin Roof*.

"I never took advantage of my success because I never felt I was successful," Gazzara said. "I turned down motion pictures I should have done. That was a big mistake; I remained a struggling artist. I made a lot of mistakes in the beginning that hurt me in the middle."

Meanwhile, Gazzara's Broadway winning streak had come to an end. He appeared opposite Janice Rule in Gazzo's next play, *The Night Circus*, which closed in less than a week (though Gazzara's affair with the then-married Rule eventually led her to divorce her husband and marry him).

"I was made a star much too quickly," said Gazzara, with unusual insight for someone of his age in 1955. "Stardom should come after years of work. There's plenty of time to be a star after forty."

But certain kinds of show-business success have a brief shelf life, and by 1960 Gazzara was just another working actor, looking for parts and taking the best of what was offered. He played the brooding, volatile defendant in Otto Preminger's *Anatomy of a Murder*, knowing that it was Jimmy Stewart's film, then slid into a role as an idealistic physician in *The Young Doctors*.

"I had a rude awakening to say the least," Gazzara said. "The good roles didn't keep coming, and by the time I was ready to go to Hollywood, the motion picture people were not so enthusiastic."

By 1963, married to Rule and with children to support, he agreed to a TV series, *Arrest and Trial*. In it, he would play a cop who chased down criminals in the show's first half; in the second half, Chuck Connors (as a public defender) would get the criminals off.

It lasted one season, murdered in the ratings on Sunday nights by *Bonanza* and *The Ed Sullivan Show*. Both of the stars were grousing to the press before Christmas.

"I'm not satisfied—the show hasn't developed in terms of a character, the way I was led to expect it," said Connors, the former Brooklyn Dodger who had become a star in TV's *The Rifleman*.

Gazzara wasn't disillusioned enough by his *Arrest and Trial* experience to ignore the offer of another series when it came shortly afterward. In *Run for Your Life*, he would play Paul Bryan, an attorney who learns that he has an incurable disease and only a year or two to live. So he hits the road to experience life to the fullest. The weekly series dealt with his adventures with people he encountered in his travels. It went on the air in the fall of 1965 and drew enough of an audience to last for three seasons.

As the sole star, Gazzara was able to involve himself in the show more, to make his opinions felt in terms of the writing, to even direct a few episodes. But he found himself confronting the same kind of artistic issues that had bedeviled *Arrest and Trial*.

As *Run for Your Life* was finishing its run, Gazzara had his encounter with Cassavetes in the Universal parking lot. Within the month, Gazzara had a phone call from Cassavetes, asking to meet him at the Hamburger Hamlet on Sunset Boulevard for lunch: "I want to tell you the story of my movie," Cassavetes said.

Over lunch, Cassavetes laid it out for him: Gazzara, Cassavetes, and Peter Falk would play three guys whose best friend drops dead. The death unmoors them, in terms of how they look at their own lives. And the movie would be about what they do in response.

But, Cassavetes told him, he had no intention of financing the film himself this time. He had an Italian financier, Bino Cicogna, who had heard the buzz about *Faces* and was anxious to underwrite a new Cassavetes film.

Like Falk, Gazzara had heard these kinds of pitches before. He liked Cassavetes but barely knew him; he had no way of knowing whether Cassavetes was serious about any of this, although it all sounded good.

"What's the title?" Gazzara asked him.

"*Husbands,*" Cassavetes replied. "What do you think—like it?"

Gazzara, who was having marital problems at the time, said, "Being a husband or the title?"

"Take your choice," Cassavetes said.

"I hope my character has more fun than I'm having," Gazzara observed, to which Cassavetes countered, "That's up to you. You can take him anywhere you want to."

"You've got a deal, John," Gazzara said, meaning it but unsure whether anything would ever come of Cassavetes' idea.

As it turned out, even as Cassavetes was finishing the *Husbands* script in early 1968, he and Falk were cast in *Machine Gun McCain*, requiring them to spend a couple of months shooting in Rome, with additional location exteriors in San Francisco, where the story was set. Falk was in Belgrade, Yugoslavia, filming his part in Sydney Pollack's *Castle Keep*, when he got a call from Cassavetes in Rome, where Falk was headed next.

"Did you get the offer?" Cassavetes asked him.

"What offer?" Falk said, convinced that Cassavetes was out of his mind.

"You know, the picture we're making together—you, me, and Benny," Cassavetes said, as though it should have been the first thing to pop into Falk's head, despite the fact that it had been months since they had discussed the vague possibility.

"No," was all Falk could say. Cassavetes exploded into curses, then apologized to Falk and said, "I'll get back to you."

Two days later, Falk received a telegram: an offer to make *Husbands* with Gazzara and Cassavetes, including salary, production dates, and the like.

"I didn't even know what the picture was about," Falk said. "I knew it was Cassavetes and me and Gazzara and it was about three guys who take off. Well, that's pretty good.

"I thought it was silly at first. But then I saw how fertile John is and I began to realize that *Husbands* was a lot about me. So I agreed to do it with him."

Gazzara was in Prague in the late spring of 1968—the so-called Prague Spring, when Czech culture seemed on the verge of shaking off the shackles of Russian oppression. He was making a World War II film called *The Bridge at Remagen*, with George Segal and Robert Vaughn, when Russian tanks rolled into Prague.

Images of the heavy-handed act of repression were broadcast around the globe. Gazzara could see it all unfold from his hotel-room window. In Rome, Cassavetes and Falk were watching it on television, and Falk turned anxiously to Cassavetes.

"What happens if Ben gets killed?" Falk asked. "Do we do the picture if Benny gets killed?"

As Gazzara gazed at history unfolding beneath his hotel balcony, the phone rang in his room. It was Cassavetes.

"Ben, don't get killed," Cassavetes and Falk shouted over the line from Rome, as Cassavetes added, "I got the money for the movie."

As film historian Leonard Maltin noted, "Here were two guys who had been known for their mainstream work on stage, TV, movies. Both had starred in TV series. They might have been forever regarded as first-rate actors had they not come under the spell of Cassavetes, who cast them in these really daring and venturesome film projects. Those are lifetime credentials."

But as Al Ruban observed, it was a collaboration forged out of mutual dissatisfaction: "Ben and Peter had become actors for hire and they were unhappy," he said. "It was like they all needed to be involved in something they could devote themselves to."

Twenty-seven

Husbands

Perhaps John Cassavetes' most controversial film, *Husbands* was also one of his loosest and most adventurous: an extended exploration of the American male at midlife that didn't bother with niceties such as linear narrative, whether from start to finish, or from scene to scene.

According to all who saw it during the year that Cassavetes spent editing it, *Husbands* was markedly different from cut to cut. The earliest cut was reportedly extremely funny and audience-friendly. At various points, Cassavetes came up with versions that seemed to focus on each of the principal characters: Archie (Falk), Harry (Gazzara), and Gus (Cassavetes).

The version that was finally released in the United States in December 1970 was about 140 minutes, though there had been a 154-minute cut in October at the San Francisco Film Festival; Columbia forced Cassavetes to trim it to 140, then trimmed an additional eleven minutes once it was in release, which is the version that was released on VHS in 1999. Shorter, hacked-up versions began playing on television in the early 1970s, trimmed haphazardly by individual stations and networks to fit time slots and make room for commercials.

The film begins with a photo montage, accompanied by the sounds of a large backyard picnic. The images are of a group of male friends who appear to be in their late thirties or early forties, gathered around a pool at a barbecue, striking muscle-man poses with and without their shirts. It finally halts on an image of the four: young, vital, unquenchable, and unstoppable.

The scene shifts to a funeral. A taxi pulls up, then another—and out step Archie, Gus, and Harry, shepherding an elderly woman from the taxi to the gravesite. She is the grandmother of the fourth man, Stuart Jackson (played by Gena's brother, David Rowlands, in the photographs), who has dropped dead of a heart attack.

Stuart Jackson obviously was a beloved figure, to judge by the large crowd gathered at the gravesite; the minister, in fact, is heard giving his eulogy over a loudspeaker system as the three men help the grandmother work her way through the thicket of people to a chair by the grave. As the mourners disperse at the end of the service, Harry, Gus, and Archie find Stuart's widow, who dissolves in tears in Harry's arms when she sees them.

In a taxi, following the burial, the three can't quite process what they have just been through. Their only recourse: a refusal to go home and a vow to get drunk.

Which they do—not once, but twice. They are first seen loudly singing on a dark street; it is before dawn, and they've obviously closed down the bars. With nowhere else to go, they head for the subway, where they ride aimlessly until sun-up, smoking and talking, trying to make sense of Stuart's death. Gus holds forth on the various ages at which men are stripped of their illusions that they, too, could still become professional athletes—and what a psychological blow the final realization is.

They decide they need to do something physical and head for the gym, but it is closed when they get there. Still determined not to go home to the Long Island suburbs, they have a walking race on the sidewalk, while they wait for the gym to open. Once inside, they play basketball, then go for a swim. But they wind up at another bar, where they convince the denizens to engage in a singing contest, after buying them many pitchers of beer to unleash inhibitions.

The three of them are the judges as the locals take turns singing standards like "When Irish Eyes Are Smiling," "When It's Apple Blossom Time," and "Pack Up Your Troubles." They sing along, make harsh judgments and rude comments—but all in the name of searching for genuine feeling in the singer and what is being sung.

Eventually the three of them wind up in the men's room, where Gus and Archie vomit copiously and loudly. They both decide it is a physical manifestation of the grief and confusion they are experiencing because of Stuart's death. And they both regard the drunkenly overbearing Harry with a certain disdain: "You can't even vomit," Archie says, as though this were proof of his lack of sensitivity.

Offended when Archie calls him a phony, Harry eventually makes up with the two friends. He tells them, "Apart from sex, which my wife is very good at, I love you the best." He calls home and, when his wife doesn't respond the way he wants, Harry nearly demolishes the phone booth, then decides to go home, take a shower, and change clothes. But when he gets there, his presence provokes a scene with his wife (played by Sam Shaw's daughter, Meta). Harry, confused, grieving, looks for a human connection with his wife, pushing too hard on what obviously is already a badly strained relationship.

But she tells him he makes her uncomfortable, adding with unintended humor, "It's nothing personal." He races back upstairs and grabs his passport, then comes back downstairs and forces a kiss on her. The moment escalates when Harry's wife knees him in the groin, then grabs a knife and threatens him with it. Her mother disarms her and Harry chokes his mother-in-law, then slaps both wife and mother-in-law before Gus and Archie can break them up and get Harry out of the house.

Sitting on his own front lawn with his friends in that early morning hour, Harry decides he's leaving—and that's that. He's going in to work and then he's getting on a plane to London. When his friends don't respond enthusiastically, he angrily tells them they can join him or they can stay behind, but he's going.

On the train, he gets increasingly angry, even as Archie and Gus laugh among themselves, punchy from their bender and amused at Harry's sudden sobriety. Gus in particular makes Harry furious, playing with his cigarette like Jerry Lewis, allowing it to fall out of his fingers, and snorting with giggles every time the angry Harry says, "Just cut it out."

"Children," Harry spits derisively.

Archie follows Gus to work, where they debate what to do, even as Gus, who is a dentist, tries to attend to a patient. The pair decides they will, in fact, accompany Harry to London, if only long enough to "tuck him in at his hotel and then come home." They try to call Harry at work, where he's an art director, but he won't take their call. So they head over to his office and catch him coming out of his building. "We're going to London," Gus announces, then calls his wife to ask her to round up their passports.

In London they check into a hotel, take naps, order up tuxedoes, and hit the casinos. Their goal is to gamble, to drink, and to each find a woman. The least confident in that endeavor is Archie, who tries first to proposition an obviously upper-class woman and her grown daughter. Then, at a roulette table, he finds an elderly woman whose face practically melts in a smile when he makes a pass. Her response, in fact, is so eager that he recoils, though it takes some talking to get his hand away from her.

Eventually they wind up back at their hotel with three girls and order drinks in Harry's room. When Harry, lying on one of the beds, begins to weep, his date Pearl (Jenny Lee Wright) comforts him and guides him into another room, and Gus and his date, Mary (Jenny Runacre), leave as well. It's all done in one continuous eight-minute take that never calls attention to itself.

Gus, with the much-taller Mary, necks and wrestles and apparently makes love to her overnight. Archie's girl, Julie (Noelle Kao), is Asian and doesn't seem to speak English, but responds to his kissing so enthusiastically that she becomes aggressive and uses her tongue, causing Archie once more to recoil, the anxious adulterer unable to cross the line. Harry winds up impotent, talking to Pearl about his confusion about the future.

The next morning, Gus can't bring himself to make romantic small talk in the coffee shop with Mary, and she stalks off into a rainstorm. Meanwhile, Archie is trying to stop Julie, who also marches off into the storm in search of a taxi, spouting a language Archie can't name or speak.

The two men wind up wet and abashed, staring at each other in the hallway outside their hotel rooms, then go into their separate rooms without speaking. But Archie can't take it; he seeks out Gus and tells him they have to go home or they'll really be in trouble. So they knock on Harry's door—and find Harry entertaining three new women, whom he tries to pair off with Archie and Gus. But they tell him, no, they have to go back.

Once home, they both stop at the New York airport gift shop and burden themselves with bags full of ridiculous toys for their kids—barely an afterthought. They share a cab to their adjoining houses in Port Washington, Long Island, and as they part, Archie says aloud with great concern, "What's he going to do without us?"

Gus doesn't answer. He is met in his driveway by his very small daughter (three-year-old Xan Cassavetes) and by his son (played by Cassavetes' son, Nick). The daughter is crying, apparently because she has missed her father (in fact, just before Cassavetes called, "Action!", unbeknownst to his father, young Nick Cassavetes had snatched a toy away from Xan to induce tears for the scene). The son says loudly to Gus, "Boy, are you in trouble. Mom!" Gus stands and looks around, takes in the scene, and seems, for a moment, to have an appreciation he previously lacked.

As a film, *Husbands* is often disjointed and could easily be called indulgent, given Cassavetes' use of long takes, even when what is happening on screen does nothing to move things forward. He knows that, in fact, he is deepening his characters, looking further into their psyches than they could imagine and with an insight they could hardly muster. These unhappy, inarticulate men reveal themselves in their behavior and their interaction, in moments the camera seems to capture almost by accident.

Their responses are always surprising, their laughter spontaneous, their rapid shifts of mood believable without being predictable. The performances were, in some ways, the best each would give for some time. Gazzara covered a wide spectrum, all with vulnerability that was apparent behind Harry's bluff style, right up until he could conceal it no longer. Falk, who spent much of the production confused about what Cassavetes wanted from him, conveys Archie's inability to get fully into the swing when the adventurers turn to debauchery. And Gus is one of the warmest performances Cassavetes gave in his entire career.

Twenty-eight

Husbands 2

The *Husbands* package—Cassavetes, Gazzara, Falk—was attractive to a handful of studio executives, but they also wanted some sort of contractual creative rein on Cassavetes—something he was adamantly unwilling to grant.

So despite the growing drumbeat about *Faces*, he could find no one in Hollywood willing to give him the money for *Husbands* with no strings attached.

"The reason no one was all that eager to gamble on *Husbands* was simply business," Cassavetes said later. "*Faces* was just an experiment that made money. But not nearly as much as a mere commercial film like *The Sound of Music* would. That's the only kind of film most of these people will take a risk on."

Bino Cicogna—actually Count Bino Cicogna—was an Italian producer, the head of a company called Euro International, who had hired Cassavetes and Falk to star in *Machine Gun McCain*, which he was producing.

While talking on the set of *McCain*, Cassavetes brought up the possibility of Cicogna financing one of Cassavetes' films. When Cassavetes saw the glint of eagerness in Cicogna, he made a point of talking regularly to the producer during breaks on *McCain*, in that conspiratorial manner he had that pulled people in, as though he were literally grabbing them by the lapels and making love to them at the same time. Suddenly Cicogna felt like a Cassavetes confidante, with John telling him what a great film they could make together, flattering Cicogna as having the vision to know that, when he hired Cassavetes, he was hiring him for his artistic vision, something that a mere producer would never dream of tampering with. When *Faces* became the *cause célèbre* of late 1968, Cicogna committed funds to produce the new story Cassavetes was pitching him, *Husbands,* and wrote an artistic freedom clause into the contract.

But Cicogna, who also produced Sergio Leone's *Once Upon a Time in the West,* was—if not actually a shady operator—certainly a suspect customer. Tall and elegant, with a quiet manner, he seemed to always be one step ahead of creditors (eventually absconding to Brazil, where he was murdered in the early 1970s).

So the opportunity to produce what sounded like a prestige film with American stars, directed by a rising American filmmaker, looked like a foot in the door to Hollywood legitimacy. Cicogna was only too happy to commit his funding—to the tune of $1.5 million—and to cede all artistic control to Cassavetes. The contract Cassavetes had worked out with Cicogna, Al Ruban recalled, "was totally in our favor. Contractually, they had nothing to say."

Still, Cassavetes was aware of the risk he was taking: "I'm involved in a commercial project again, big budget, color, so the pressure is on, no getting away from it," he said. "It won't be as personal or free-wheeling as *Faces.* It just can't be the same."

As Cassavetes and Falk worked on *McCain* in Rome, Gazzara flew in to join them and to work on the *Husbands* script. Already the screenplay had expanded upon what Cassavetes had described, and Cassavetes himself was more passionate about the work than either actor had realized.

They would discuss the scenes, suggest other action and directions for the characters, improvise dialogue—and then Cassavetes would go away and write and rewrite the script.

"The script we first read was nothing like the movie we finally made," Gazzara said. "After each reading, we'd have intense discussions, throwing out ideas about character and story. I was breathing fresh air again. I had been away from this kind of work for too long."

They reconvened in San Francisco during the *McCain* location work there, further hammering out the script. They were hoping to begin shooting in early 1969, with a month of shooting in New York to be followed by another month in London.

Cassavetes had chosen Falk and Gazzara perhaps because he saw them as peers, as actors of similar taste and sensibility, perhaps even as doppelgangers—or perhaps because he intuitively sensed that their disparate approaches could create a chemistry that would catalyze all three of them. He knew the key to the film's success was for the trio to become the friends in real life that they portrayed in the film. They needed to bond, to become a unit that could translate off-screen trust into an on-screen friendship.

"We didn't know each other before *Husbands*—we started off absolutely clean and we became friends on that picture," Cassavetes said.

Cassavetes invited Gazzara and Falk out to dinner in New York to talk about the film and to begin to create the kind of relationship they needed on-camera. They went to Frankie and Johnny's, a theater district favorite for actors. When things suddenly dipped into quiet, they started talking about their characters' names. As written, the characters had the actors' names: Peter, John, Ben. But both Falk and Gazzara felt that was just laying themselves open to the critics, if they didn't like the film.

Cassavetes piped up, "Look, since we have to come up with names sooner or later, why don't we each think of some? Let's all choose the names for our characters—and whatever names we want, we'll have in the movie."

They thought for a moment before Falk piped up, "I like Archie."

Cassavetes gave him a look and said, almost immediately, "C'mon, Peter, you can't be an Archie."

Falk couldn't believe his ears: "Jesus Christ, John, first you tell us to choose our own names, then when we do it, you say we can't," he said. "This is freedom?"

Gazzara, lost in his own thoughts for a moment, suddenly said, "I'd like to be called Harold. Or we could call me Harry. Harold will know who I mean."

(Harold, according to Cassavetes, referred to Harold's Show Spot, a New York bar Gazzara used to frequent. Gazzara later claimed that, in fact, the name was a homage to Harry Ackerman, "the only Jewish boy in the neighborhood I grew up in. Antisemitism was alive and well on Twenty-ninth Street and I saw Harry fight his way home more than once.")

Cassavetes named himself Gus, a name that he'd particularly revered since being a fan of Gus Triandos, an all-star catcher of Greek heritage who played for the Baltimore Orioles from 1955 to 1962.

Cassavetes achieved his goal with that dinner and with Falk and Gazzara in general: "By the end of the evening, we were really able to talk to each other," he said. "When the picture began shooting, we were buddies. You need friends to function better but that was our problem with the picture. When *Husbands* was finished, we all had a terribly empty feeling. The main reason we did so much press stuff together afterward—talk shows and interviews—was that we didn't want to give it up."

They became such close companions during production that, while filming the scene where they play basketball, Falk slumped to the floor with his co-stars for the shot; when the camera was cut, he turned to Cassavetes and said, "Is my eye straight?"

Cassavetes and Gazzara both studied Falk for a moment and agreed that all the running and jumping had jarred his glass eye out of alignment. Falk would have to adjust it, which meant taking it out and repositioning it. Falk obviously was self-conscious about it because he said to both Gazzara and Cassavetes, "OK, turn around."

Neither budged.

Falk, almost to himself, said, "I never even did this in front of my wife."

"We love you more than she does," Gazzara joked. But the grain of truth was there as well. So Falk removed and reset the glass eye, smiled, and said, "OK, let's shoot."

Their individual personalities helped shape the characters they were creating: Gazzara, outgoing and unselfconscious—not a loudmouth but usually the loudest voice in a conversation; Falk, more reserved and hesitant, wary but, occasionally, impulsive and exuberant; Cassavetes, the needler, the facilitator, the conciliator, the conspirator.

"If that picture succeeded," Gazzara said, "it was because in playing those three characters, we ourselves came to trust and like and even love each other. We had become real friends through the process."

It was an odd trio that, like most such friendships, often degenerated into a two-against-one situation, usually with Falk and Cassavetes teaming against the taller Gazzara, just as Gus and Archie would team to ride herd on Harry.

"In *Husbands*, Gazzara's character was continually frozen out by me and Falk, and Benny was really getting personally paranoid about it," Cassavetes said later, "In a three-person relationship, there's always one guy on the outside and during the picture, Benny was usually it."

More often, however, the feeling among the three men was all for one and one for all—the stars against the crew, the producers, the world. There was strength in numbers.

"I didn't think it was possible to make new friendships at forty, but it is," Cassavetes observed.

Al Ruban was working on a TV documentary about Vince Lombardi, then the Super Bowl–winning coach of the Green Bay Packers. Cassavetes convinced him to wrap up early and head for New York, to produce *Husbands*.

Preproduction began at the end of 1968. Cassavetes had taken rooms in the now-demolished Piccadilly Hotel on West Forty-fifth Street in Manhattan's theater district, where they would meet daily, along with Ruban and Sam Shaw, to rehearse and rewrite the script. They hoped to shoot the New York scenes just after the start of 1969, before moving the production to London. The script, Gazzara found, had continued to evolve.

"Once we began to read the new script, I saw right away that my part was richer and funnier than it had been in Rome," he said. "So was John's and so was Peter's too. In fact, it was almost an entirely different script. Nothing was off limits, as far as John was concerned. His delight when one of us did something surprising gave me the feeling I could go in any direction with my character and it would be alright with him."

"There was a whole script and another script and a whole background written," Cassavetes recalled. "We rehearsed for two weeks where we did nothing but improvisation. When we got the scene absolutely polished, we threw it out and wrote the dialogue on the spot, right there. Then I would say, 'The camera goes here'; and we'd get in front of the camera and do what we had to do. I suppose we had the feeling of being extemporaneous."

Ruban remembered the rehearsals as being all-consuming. When Cassavetes, Falk, and Gazzara got into a groove together, there was little that could distract them. During one such rehearsal, they could barely hear themselves over the racket coming from outside the hotel. Cassavetes finally looked at Ruban and snapped, "What the hell is that?"

Ruban looked out the window and said, "It's a street-repair crew."

"Well, tell them to stop it," Cassavetes said impatiently and went back to rehearsing.

There was another presence as well, when they began rehearsing in New York: a documentary film crew from the BBC, led by director Tristram Powell. A staff producer for the British network, Powell had heard that Cassavetes was shooting a new film and, based on his own fascination with *Shadows* and *Faces*, had asked for permission to document it.

"It was the first film he was making with a full-size crew and not on a small scale," Powell explained. "He found it very frustrating that everything took so long to prepare, lining up shots. He was a little caught between the old style of making a film and this rather more rigid style of making one. He was trying to do a movie with Hollywood values, not shot so much on the hoof, as it were."

So here were Cassavetes, Falk, and Gazzara in the rehearsal room, trying to establish their working relationship, trying to establish their characters, working to forge a workable script from the rehearsal process itself—and allowing it to be captured on film at the same time.

"John liked the presence of the camera because it gave an edge of discipline to the rehearsal," Powell said. "It gave it extra energy, having to perform all the time. I think he was able to use that to his advantage."

As the start of principal photography loomed, the actors—meaning Falk and Gazzara—began to hear whispers. Most of them had to do with the fact that Cicogna hadn't sent the money necessary to underwrite preproduction.

"By John's behavior, Peter and I would never have known it," Gazzara said. "We showed up at rehearsal day after day, even though it looked like the movie would never be made. John was being advised by friend and foe alike to take a kill fee and walk away. No dice. He wasn't going to let this go."

Then, near the end of December, Cicogna and Ralph Serpe, his American representative, walked into the production office and told Ruban to shut it all down. Cicogna's money had fallen through; even though Cassavetes had already spent a large chunk of it getting ready to shoot and principal photography was scheduled to start in ten days, the money itself was not going to appear.

Ruban coolly walked over and locked the door from the inside and pocketed the key. Then, saying, "Let's talk about this," he got on the phone to Cassavetes and Gazzara. Within the hour, they had arrived, along with Jay Julien, Gazzara's manager, and David Begelman, agent for all three actors. The conversations went on all afternoon, with Cassavetes focusing his attention on Serpe, who had been Dino de Laurentiis' right-hand man.

"There was a lot of pacing, arguing and intense but quiet conversations that afternoon," Gazzara recalled.

"They went round and round," Ruban recalled. "We had to change how we got the money. They'd bring money in every few weeks in a suitcase."

After several hours, hostilities cooled and conciliation seemed a possibility. Cassavetes pulled Gazzara aside.

"I think we got a deal," Cassavetes told him. "But we've got to take a gamble. It'll make it easier on Bino if we only take expenses, no salaries, until the picture's sold. We'll sell it and when we do, we'll get a much better payday."

"We're gambling on our own talent," Gazzara said later. "I feel young again."

It amounted to almost $1 million between the three of them, a considerable risk, but they were buying the right to make the movie their way. And they were convinced that it would be a hit.

As Falk later observed, "I worked for nothing—but because I had a one-third share in the picture, I received the largest paycheck I'd yet received."

Almost as soon as shooting started in New York, Cassavetes realized he'd made a mistake in choosing a director of photography. Coming off *Faces,* he was used to working with a crew—a minuscule crew, at that—that was malleable to his wishes, capable of shifting direction in a heartbeat to suit his inspiration. But with someone else's money, Cassavetes could hire a full crew, and he picked Aldo Tonti, a cinematographer he'd worked with on *Bandits in Rome*.

Tonti was a legendary figure of Italian cinema who had shot everything from Fellini's *Nights of Cabiria* to Nicholas Ray's *Savage Innocents* to John Huston's *Reflections in a Golden Eye*. But by the time Cassavetes hired him, he was sixty and set in his ways, not the kind of artist who could or would easily adapt to a seat-of-the-pants approach to working.

Because Tonti was a foreigner, the New York local of the American Society of Cinematographers decreed that Cassavetes had to hire a standby cameraman. The union called Victor Kemper, who had gotten his first camera-operator credit on Arthur Penn's *Alice's Restaurant*. But Kemper couldn't see any point in taking a standby job when he was hoping to actually work as a camera operator.

"Why would I take a standby job? Get somebody who needs the work," he told the union representative who called him with the job offer.

But the union rep was insistent: "Cassavetes likes running multiple cameras. You'll be busy."

Kemper, who lived in New Jersey, hit it off with Tonti during that first week, because the aging Italian reminded him of his grandfather. By midweek, he had invited Tonti to come out to his lake house in New Jersey on the weekend after shooting wrapped for the week, and Tonti accepted.

Kemper didn't realize that Cassavetes was having problems with Tonti. Tonti worked slowly and traditionally; he also apparently was intimidated by Cicogna and the Italian financiers, hinting that they had organized-crime ties—or their money did. But Cassavetes was unhappy with the d.p.'s productivity and was convinced that Tonti was, in fact, a spy for Cicogna, phoning back reports despite the contractual agreement not to interfere.

He finally went to Al Ruban and said, "Al, get rid of him," because he always had the sympathetic, straight-shooting Ruban do the tougher tasks. He would even tell people, "If you want somebody fired, let Al do it."

On Friday, after Kemper got home to New Jersey, he got a call from Ruban, asking whether Kemper could come back into the city on Saturday because Cassavetes wanted to talk to him. So Kemper drove in on Saturday morning and arrived at the office a few minutes early, just in time to see Aldo Tonti (whose next destination was Kemper's lake house) come out of Cassavetes' office dejectedly and leave without a word.

Summoned into the office, Kemper didn't even get a hello from Cassavetes: "How would you like to shoot the film?" Cassavetes asked.

Kemper was stunned. Cassavetes explained that he had met Tonti in

Rome and the two of them had hit it off. But things were different when they tried to collaborate in New York.

"I was stupid," Cassavetes admitted. "In Italy, I had an interpreter. But here, I can't understand a word he says."

"You fired him?" Kemper asked.

"I fired him," Cassavetes said simply.

It was Kemper's first credit as a director of photography on a feature. And, in the end, his weekend with Aldo Tonti involved no hard feelings: "It turned out to be delightful and I went in and shot for John on Monday," Kemper recalled.

Cassavetes said later, "When I saw Vic's first work, I could just feel by the way he was moving the camera and the confidence he had that I wouldn't have to tell him anything. I didn't have to tell him anything on the close-ups in the bar. He just shot everything by himself."

As it turned out, the first thing Kemper was asked to shoot was the vomiting scene. The location they were using was a claustrophobic men's room, made even less hospitable to filming because the stalls were painted black. And the three characters were wearing black suits.

"The only thing that was white were the fixtures," Kemper remembered. "I said, 'John, this is one hell of a deal. How do you expect to light this?' He said, 'You're the cinematographer. You figure it out.'"

So Kemper flooded the space with as much backlight as he could, in such a way that the light caught the actors' faces wherever they went. He even held a small light under the lens.

"It was a gamble but it worked—no one ever said anything negative about the scene," he said. "That was something I learned from my mentor, Arthur Ornitz. I used to watch him work and he always seemed to shoot off the top of his head. But what I learned was that when things turn sour, you don't look at the negative. You say, 'OK, there's a way to do this and I've got to figure out what it is.'"

The controversial vomit scene followed the almost equally controversial singing contest, perhaps the film's most tenuous and uneven sequence. Originally Cassavetes had scripted a long barroom scene in which Harry, Gus, and Archie sit around together in a deserted bar and talk seriously about life, death, politics, women, and everything else that scares them. But as they rehearsed it, they all reached the same conclusion: It felt written, it felt stilted—it lacked the crucial sense of reality they were seeking. After all, these were not supposed to be articulate men.

When it came time to shoot, they used an empty bar, and the three of them sat drinking and singing their favorite songs. When they watched it at dailies the next day, Cassavetes was roaring with laughter, which concerned Gazzara, who thought the sequence was frightfully flat. But then, between guffaws, Cassavetes moaned, "This is the worst piece of shit I've ever seen."

So Cassavetes found a new bar and filled it with extras, who thought they would simply be background for a barroom scene. Instead, Cassavetes ordered up pitchers of real beer and shots of whisky (actually, iced tea), then announced an impromptu singing contest for the camera: Each extra would sing his or her favorite song and the three principals would judge them based on the amount of feeling they believed the singer was putting into it.

To shoot it, he had Kemper set up dolly tracks on both sides of the table and ran two cameras, one on each side.

"We were shooting toward each other, so we had to give each other hand signals so we could pan off and not shoot each other," Kemper said. "We'd literally see each other in the shot. It was funny in the dailies—and difficult in the editing."

One singer, John "Red" Kullers, nearly stole the show with his a cappella version of "Brother, Can You Spare a Dime." The camera stops moving to watch his deeply felt performance, sung in a quavering but self-assured tenor and ending with actual tears streaking down Kullers' cheek as he sings the final lines.

Cassavetes, Falk, and Gazzara gave the hardest time to a former stripper named Leola Harlow, middle-aged and primly dressed in a wool plaid jumper; every time she started a frail little tune called "It Was Just a Little Love Affair," one of the stars was right in her face, telling her they didn't believe her, that they wanted it sung with more feeling. By the end of the scene, Gazzara was wearing her red plaid tam and Falk had stripped to his shorts to get a reaction from her. To her credit, Harlow hung in with them, though she had tears in her eyes at several moments.

"John badgered her until she cried," Kemper said. "That wasn't acting. He knew he could get what he needed if he treated her like that."

Powell remembered, "To me, there was an element of bullying about it that was kind of disagreeable. Or perhaps that was what Cassavetes wanted you to think."

"A lot of that scene is improvised," Ruban said. "They were smashed, particularly Ben. They were enormous drinkers."

The vomiting scene became the touchstone for the film: the one that winnowed the weaklings from the crowd. As former *Los Angeles Times* film critic Charles Champlin said, "I can't think of anyone else who could do a great vomiting scene."

Gazzara remembered it as a meaningful sequence that seemed to take on gravity the longer they did it. "I thought we were making a very simple point throughout that scene," he said. "These guys are broken up at their pal's death. They feel bad that they don't feel more remorse. So they get drunk to get more angry. They berate the woman in a way that they'd really like to berate each other, which is what they eventually do in the toilet."

"I bet we spent a week in that bar on Ninety-first Street on *Husbands*," recalled Larry Shaw, who was photographing the production for his father and Cassavetes. "How much were they drinking? Every day? On every take? And forget shooting ratios of 6:1. John shot 10:1, 20:1."

The scene would prove controversial, provoking scores of viewers to head for the exit, particularly when Gus and Archie start vomiting and retching loudly. It was a shocking moment, something that was never seen in a mainstream film of the time, but audiences that simply saw it as shock value missed what Cassavetes was trying to get at.

"The characters weren't vomiting because they happened to be drunk," Cassavetes said later. "They got drunk so they could vomit—vomit for their dead friend. Some people may find that disgusting, but that's their problem. When somebody dies, I want to feel something. I want to be so upset that I could cry, throw up, feel the loss deeply."

As always, a great deal was done with handheld cameras, despite the larger budget. The handheld changed the way the actors related to the camera—if anything, creating a more intimate relationship.

"It's not really interesting to me to set up a camera angle," Cassavetes said. "At some point in the filming, you really want to take the camera and break it for no reason except that it's just an interference and you don't know what to do with it."

Well, that wasn't strictly true, particularly in the singing scene: "I liked the camera low because we were dealing with three short guys," he said with a laugh. "We had the camera low so we wouldn't look like total dwarves."

"John's attitude toward shooting was not to give us instructions," Kemper said. "After a while, you could almost anticipate what the actors would do. I always had a camera where I was reasonably sure they would wind up. But it was always an educated guess."

Cassavetes had never directed himself in a film before, though he'd put in small cameo appearances in *Shadows* and *A Child Is Waiting*. He initially didn't want anyone to take the role of director, but Cicogna drew the line there. So Cassavetes assumed the title but conferred constantly with Gazzara and Falk.

They took the production out to Port Washington, John's old stomping grounds, to film the funeral scene and to shoot the sequence of Harry's confrontation with his wife, which triggers the exodus to London.

But Cassavetes had yet to cast the wife. Edie Shaw, who was helping her father, Sam, design the ads and the posters for the film, was riding down in an elevator from the production office as the day to shoot the scene approached. Cassavetes was stewing because the role was still unfilled. Edie turned to him and suggested her sister: "Ever thought of Meta?"

Cassavetes grinned. "Gee, you know, I never did. Let's get her."

Meta Shaw, who was married and living in New Jersey, was stunned. Though she had taken classes at the Variety Arts as a teen and had known Cassavetes almost her entire life, she hadn't done any acting in years.

Because there was no costume designer as such, Edie and Sam Shaw went to a department store to pick out a nightgown and robe for Meta to wear. They also took things from Edie's and Meta's house—things that indicated that the house was inhabited by children as well as adults—to dress the set and make it look lived in.

"She was nervous—all these men standing around and she was going to be in a nightgown," Edie Shaw Marcus recalled.

For Meta Shaw Stevens, it was a surreal experience: "I'm a young housewife in a New Jersey suburb with two children and I get a delivery of a script from John with a note to read it and be ready to shoot," she said. "I was twenty-seven—and I was playing Ben Gazzara's wife."

The scene between Harry and his wife was needed structurally, Cassavetes realized, because, before and after, none of the wives was seen. At a moment of political ferment in the country, when the women's liberation movement was prominently in the news, Cassavetes knew a movie about disaffected middle-aged married men would set off alarm bells and wanted at least a little ammunition of his own.

"We knew that people would say, 'Gee, you never saw one wife,'" Cassavetes said. "That just kept ringing in my mind. We decided to show the one wife. To do that, we had to come up with some kind of relationship that would be meaningful for the other two guys. We wrote a very quick scene. I knew that it would pay off once he choked the mother-in-law."

Gazzara figured out what Cassavetes was looking for almost from the start: "John is more interested in behavior than he is in structure," Gazzara later said. "He searches for that moment of revealing behavior, for the surprising thing. And it often seems like he comes across it by accident. But that's not true."

It wasn't until they reached London that Peter Falk found a comfort zone working with Cassavetes. While Gazzara loved the freedom that Cassavetes gave him to discover every moment for himself, Falk was looking for direction from Cassavetes, while Cassavetes wanted Falk to find the answers to his questions himself.

"Peter was upset at first because he needs the kind of professionalism where at least you have a few beats," Cassavetes noted. "I prefer to work with no beats at all. I believe that if an actor creates a character, he should do with that character what he wants. With people like Ben and Peter, you don't give directions. You give freedom and ideas."

"Peter was a little hesitant at the beginning," Gena Rowlands said. "Peter used to say, 'I dunno, I don't know what he's talking about.' It takes a while to get used to freedom."

As Cassavetes once noted, "With Peter, on take 32, he's just warming up."

But Falk's frustration was genuine. For one thing, he found Cassavetes' antic streak could be distracting: "On *Husbands,* he'd run in front of the camera, put a banana up your behind—he'd do anything."

Cassavetes, in turn, found it difficult to read Falk at times: "When you write something for Ben that he likes, he smiles, he gets excited, or he kisses you or something," Cassavetes said. "With Peter, it's always the same. I say, 'What do you think, Peter?' He says, 'Uhh . . . uhhh . . . ehhh.' Whether he likes it or he doesn't like it, whether it's expressing anything that he wants to say is very hard to determine."

Through much of the New York shooting, Falk felt ill at ease, not quite sure who the character was. And he was getting no help on that score from Cassavetes, who didn't want to even hint at the approach he wanted; he wanted Falk to discover it himself.

So if he gave instructions, they had to do with tempo and pace, rather than character or tone: "Don't rush, Pete, don't rush," he said at one point. "Don't let it take you. You gotta control it. If you don't control it, it becomes a jungle."

Cassavetes would respond when Falk asked him a question—but he would ramble for five or ten minutes, barely touching upon what Falk had asked about. Finally, in frustration at one point, Falk turned to Gazzara and asked, "Do you understand what this man is saying?"

"Yeah, he wants you to go over there," Gazzara replied with a laugh.

"If he wants me to go over there," Falk rasped, "why doesn't he say, 'Go over there'?"

"In some ways, he deliberately tried to keep you off-balance, so you wouldn't bring out old-fashioned technique and old ideas," Falk said.

"But it was impossible. I didn't understand him. I wanted to strangle him. I had no idea what *Husbands* was about. After it, I told him, 'I'll work with you as an actor, but not as a director.'"

What Cassavetes recognized in Falk was a reliance on the audience for approval: He was gearing his performance for the response he hoped to get. Cassavetes kept nudging him off that track.

"Peter couldn't take [the audience] and push them anywhere," Cassavetes said. "The three of us really like to grab a scene and do something with it. But we had to work more like amateurs. We had to be really involved with each moment, without ever allowing anybody to grab onto that moment and make it their own."

Cassavetes believed in his actors and didn't want to rush them. The discovery was as important as the performance because it would inform the performance.

"As director, I went under the assumption that sooner or later, Peter would know what he was doing and sooner or later Ben would know what he was doing and we'd wait it out until we did know what we were doing," he said. "Then that would be close to what the characters would want to express, for whatever reasons. I was shocked by Peter's choices. It really surprised me that he would go off in a certain direction."

Falk later admitted that he found fulfillment once he stopped resisting and went with Cassavetes' instincts. "It's very hard to just start a scene and see what will happen, what will come out of it without imposing on it some idea that you have," Falk said. "That's hard to do and in *Husbands*, I didn't do it. I did it sometimes. But I didn't trust him. I'm used to seeing the whole part laid out, so I know where I am going.

"I think as the film went on, I did it more but in the beginning, I was hanging on to an old way. I was just angry and confused because I was working without a part. There was no character. There was me."

By the time they moved the production to London in spring of 1969, *Husbands* was almost out of money again.

Cicogna was complaining about how long it had taken in New York, and he wasn't sure that they needed all of those expensive scenes Cassavetes had written for London. But the actors knew that even when a scene ultimately wound up not being in the picture, the experience of creating it, of playing it—of making it part of the character—came through in the subsequent scenes. The longer the production went on, the more lived-in the characters felt, both to the actors and, they believed, the audience.

None of that meant much to Cicogna. All he knew was that they'd only shot half the movie but had already used almost all the money. While he loved the idea of producing a John Cassavetes film, he had no idea what the film would become and, based on the footage, had doubts that sense could be made of it in editing.

"The money ran out and Bino wouldn't send any more, not even our expense money," Gazzara recalled. "He'd seen the dailies and had gotten cold feet. I don't think he understood what the hell was going on in this movie anyway. But what did John do? He kept shooting. Bino would either have to give us the money or lose the movie. We would then own it and he would never be able to get the film back."

Cassavetes instructed Ruban to rent the Round House, a mammoth nightclub in Chalk Farm just outside London that had been a railroad roundhouse, and trick it out with runways and stages and a mammoth bar. He wanted it filled with 500 extras and the ceiling covered with nets holding balloons that could be dropped at a key moment. Oh, and trapezes with scantily clad girls riding them. Ruban stared at Cassavetes in disbelief.

"John, I've got $65,000 left and we're only halfway through the film," he pointed out.

"Don't worry," Cassavetes said with one of his conspiratorial grins. "I've been busy."

In fact, having squeezed what he thought was the last money he could out of Cicogna, Cassavetes had called representatives at MGM, Paramount, and Columbia and invited them to come to the set and watch them film the Round House scene, with an eye to purchasing the rights to the film.

"That scene lasts all of fifteen seconds in the film," Ruban said. "But when they came to the set, and saw the dailies, they couldn't resist. They bought the picture. And they not only bought it, but they were bidding against each other."

As Gazzara later noted, "John had no intention of putting that scene in the movie. But his scheme worked. Both United Artists and Columbia wanted the picture. The film was sold to Columbia and Bino received his investment plus some and we three had ourselves a very good payday. We'd made an independent movie and I thought we'd be lucky if we got some small distribution company to handle it but now it was going mainstream."

They set up the production office in Kensington, and most days would begin the same way: The crew and cast would arrive at eight and Cassavetes, Falk, and Gazzara would proceed to go over the scene they were going to shoot, rewriting it. Then they'd run the scene, and the script supervisor would have it typed up and distributed, and that would be the script they were shooting for that day.

"They would build a scene from nothing," recalled Simon Hinkly, Cassavetes' first assistant director in London. "John loved that, pulling stuff out of the air and writing it into the dialogue. Peter and Ben seemed comfortable working like that."

Powell remembered, "John had incredible hypnotic powers and high, high energy, a way of making it all feel more alive than ordinary life. There were long periods sitting around the table where they improvised, trying to dig something out of the scene. He would sit there and sort of stir the pot emotionally. Then he'd cackle with laughter at the absurdity of the venture."

The casino sequences were shot at the Sportsman's Club in London, and one scene, in which Falk approaches a pair of women who rebuff him, required both champagne and caviar. Despite their limited budget, Ruban recalled, Cassavetes insisted on the real thing.

After several hours of shooting, the prop man sidled up to Ruban and said, "I don't have any more champagne. We've gone through a case and a half. Should I send out for more?"

Thinking frugally, Ruban said, "No, put the cork back in the bottle and give them 7-Up."

On the next take, Gazzara took a swig from his champagne glass, then spit the soft drink out: "No fucking way," he said. So Ruban had to send for more champagne.

They would shoot all day at the Sportsman's, and then the crew would pack up and go home. But, Hinkly said, Cassavetes and Gazzara would stay and gamble.

"The next morning when we came in, they were still there," Hinkly said. "We'd lived a life in that night and they were still there. That told me about his stamina. He was living on coffee and cigarettes and whatever else. I just marveled at how he worked."

Cassavetes loved plucking people out of the crowd of extras and giving them lines, based on some hunch or vibe he had.

"John pulled in people off the street who were not actors—he had an a.d. recruiting passersby, asking if they wanted to be in a movie," Kemper said.

The practice, Hinkly recalled, would drive the costumer crazy.

"John would literally see people in the street, people in the office, and say, 'Come on, let's do a little scene.' It would come as a surprise and the costumer would throw up her hands. John would say, 'Don't worry, she's fine the way she is.'"

At one point, he cast an actual cashier at the Sportsman's Club for a scene in which the three principals come to his cage to get chips: "The guy behind the till had two lines and John was pulling teeth to get a relaxed reading," Hinkly said. "But he'd never give up. He'd be with that person, making them laugh, trying to get them relaxed to get that magic moment."

For the girls with whom the three friends get involved, Cassavetes found three relative unknowns with little experience between them. Jenny Lee Wright, who would play Harry's girl, Pearl, was barely twenty-one, but had acted on two British TV shows, including *The Benny Hill Show:* "She was cute and easy to work with," Simon Hinkly said.

Noelle Kao, who played Archie's girl, Julie, was a biochemistry student from Vietnam. Jenny Runacre, who was twenty-five and cast as Mary Tynan, Gus's girl, was a former model from South Africa who had moved to London. Of them, Runacre, who had done some theater acting, seemed to have the hardest time with Cassavetes' direction.

"I think she didn't know how relaxed she could be," Simon Hinkly said. "It took her quite a while to relax and realize that John wanted to have fun. Jenny found it a difficult way to work. She was an English actor: 'Could we see a script? Have some lines?' That would have been anathema to John."

She was also bothered by the presence of the documentary film crew, which Cassavetes allowed to film the rehearsals in New York and London.

Powell recalled, "He used the tension of our documentary to bring that tension to the rehearsal. He loved to be recording on the wing. Jenny had a hard time."

Runacre said, "The *Omnibus* thing was the most harrowing thing of all, because we hadn't done any of the movie yet, and to show your total inability in front of all those cameras had us all in a terrible state."

Runacre had just finished drama school and was looking for work when a friend mentioned that he'd heard that Cassavetes would be casting in London. The rumor was that he was driving around London in a taxi, jumping out whenever he saw a girl he thought might be right for the film, that he was hitting the nightclub circuit inviting women to audition for his movie. So when Runacre read about the cattle-call audition for *Husbands* at the Savoy Hotel, she turned up.

The audition consisted of improvising with Cassavetes; Runacre had to phone a bellboy and ask for some food to be sent up. Based on that, she was called back a few days later for an all-day improvisation session. At the end of the day, Cassavetes told her, "Look, I'm going back to the States. But I'll let you know."

Six months later, Runacre had all but forgotten the audition when she got the call: *Husbands* was headed for London; rehearsals would start soon and filming shortly after that, in the spring of 1969.

If she didn't actually battle with Cassavetes over the role, Runacre did have a hard time getting into the groove he sought: because she was young and inexperienced, and because she was a woman working with a trio of men pumping high-octane testosterone who also happened to be Hollywood movie stars.

"I thought they were all mad," Runacre said. "It was my first film, virtually my first acting and I thought it was all too much. I remember going on holiday and thinking, God, if that's what filmmaking is all about, I'm not sure that I want to do it."

"John was quite challenged by Jenny Runacre," Hinkly recalled. "She was a smart girl, a bit of an English rose. She wouldn't take any shit and he was quite challenged by that. Jenny was more of a rebel, more self-confident. That was beautifully borne out by her meeting onscreen with John. This cool English girl; she's a sexual fortress and he's running around trying to see the way in."

Cassavetes saw a quality in Runacre—a high-strung coltishiness—that took on an even more intriguing dimension when she was provoked by an aggressively predatory man who was obviously much shorter than she was.

"Go all the way all the time," he told her during rehearsals. "Don't give up or pull back. If you pull back for one second, you'll start to disappoint yourself. You have to hit it hard every time."

"That neurosis—he wanted it and he worked to achieve it," she said. "They were so bonded and macho, worked very well together. In real life on the set, they were like they were in the film. Little in-jokes between them. I got incredibly paranoid. I'm sure that's what he wanted me to feel."

They shot a lot of material that didn't make it into the final cut of the film: at a ballroom, at the Round House. Cassavetes' approach—not exactly making it up as he went along, but close—meant long hours, longer than a union crew in London was used to putting in. Cassavetes knew he was on a financial tightrope: He had to get to the other side before the money could be taken away again, but he didn't want to hurry in a way that would compromise the movie he was trying to make.

There was also reaction to Cassavetes' tendency to shoot full-magazine loads that used all 1,000 feet (about ten minutes) of film in the camera for a single take. Cassavetes essentially was creating a series of master shots, refusing to go back to do coverage: shots of the same scene from a variety of angles, including close-ups, that can be edited into the scene.

"John was against that," Hinkly said. "He didn't want the flow interrupted by editing. Ten-minute takes heighten things and all other reality fades. It's very much about concentration, particularly to do that for half a morning. You invest all that effort and rehearse and rehearse and rehearse. By four in the afternoon, you do the first take. Then you do six to ten takes—and it's two hours later and you go home. After three or four takes, people knew this was something very serious, even life-threatening. The actors were challenged but secretly pleased to get a chance to do that with their performance. We used an awful lot of film stock."

When they shot the emotional conclusion of the film—the scene in which Archie and Gus tell Harry it's time for them to go back to New York—the actors surprised themselves with the feelings that overwhelmed them, particularly Gazzara. The experience of making the film—and of actually forming the friendship with peers like Cassavetes and Falk—all came out in Gazzara's performance as they shot the encounter in Harry's hotel room.

When Gus and Archie go to tell Harry they're going home, Harry breaks down and begins crying, then tries to recover by singing "Dancing in the Dark" and getting his friends to dance with the new women he has gathered in his suite. Gazzara's performance was so affecting—with tears and heartfelt emotion—that, for once, Falk and Cassavetes didn't know how to react.

"I was terrific and they just sat there," Gazzara recalled. "Then they saw the scene and saw that I was really going great guns and they said, 'We're in the toilet,' so we had to do it again the next day. I had to get it up again, while they started inventing screentime, but that was OK because I discovered some new things."

As he starts singing "Dancing in the Dark," Harry introduces one of the women as Diana Mallaby. Harry sings, but Archie starts riffing on the name, rhyming "Mallaby" with "wallaby" and digressing from there.

"It was right in the middle of Ben's big singing scene," Cassavetes said later. "Ben had a fit when he saw Peter. 'What's he doing? What's he doing?' he said. Because he knew I'd like it and keep it in." And he did.

The final scene—in which Gus and Archie return to Port Washington, arms filled with gifts bought at the JFK gift shop—featured both tiny Xan Cassavetes, not quite four at the time, and Nick Cassavetes, nearly ten. Nick got to tell his father that he was in trouble, then go running in the house, yelling, "Mooooom!"

Which was not unlike what life had been like at home. Here was Gus coming back from London, even as John was coming back from making *Husbands*. And Gena was at home, having barely worked since Xan's birth. By the time *Husbands* came out, daughter Zoe would have been born. Rowlands wouldn't work again until she made *Minnie and Moskowitz* (1971).

Twenty-nine

Husbands 3

John Badham was a young television director, working on *The Bold Ones* at Universal TV, when he found himself trailing behind John Cassavetes and Don Siegel as they walked between offices in early 1970. Cassavetes was talking about editing *Husbands* and Badham heard Siegel say, "What do you mean, they want to cut it?"

"Well, people tell me it's too long," Cassavetes said with a smirk and a shrug.

"Listen, John," Siegel told him, "people who like John Cassavetes films will like it at this length. And people who don't like John Cassavetes films won't like it at any length. So leave it alone."

As he returned to California from London in July 1969 to begin editing the 280 hours of *Husbands* footage, Cassavetes was feeling the effects of the two-year push he'd been through since he'd contracted hepatitis. He'd acted in *Rosemary's Baby* and *Machine Gun McCain*, even as he edited and opened *Faces*; at the same time, he had been gathering the financing for, supervising preproduction of, and then shooting *Husbands*.

Remembering the ordeal that editing *Faces* had become, Cassavetes turned to Al Ruban and said, not quite facetiously, "Al, I never want to go into the cutting room again. You take over."

Cassavetes hired editor Peter Tanner, and together he and Ruban began assembling *Husbands* from the miles of footage Cassavetes had shot over the course of more than six months.

For Tanner, who came into the process late, the task was daunting. Watching the first rushes was a frightening experience because he couldn't detect the relationship between the scenes or even between individual shots. There was also the quantity of film being printed; on an average movie, the daily rushes—footage shot the day before—usually lasted a half-hour. But on *Husbands,* watching dailies often took two hours or more.

Still, the longer he worked with Cassavetes, Tanner said, the more he understood what the film was about. "I began to understand what he was getting at," Tanner said. "The seemingly unrelated sequences could, I found, be cut together very well. I discovered he knew exactly what he was doing."

Still, working with Cassavetes had its harrowing moments. When Tanner and Cassavetes would leave the editing room, John would be so caught up in their conversation that he would stop at the curb for a green light, engrossed in what he was saying. When the light changed from green to red, still talking quickly and with total concentration on what he was saying, he would step off the curb and charge into the street, heedless of the blare of horns and speeding traffic around him.

Cassavetes had shot the film with an eye toward a late 1969 release. Sam Shaw pulled strings at *Life* magazine and got the magazine to do a story about the making of the movie. In fact, the story—by writer Ann Guerin, who spent time at the Piccadilly Hotel in New York with the actors for the piece—was put on *Life*'s cover on May 29, 1969.

"When they were on the cover of *Life,* there was a lot of talk about the film," Ruban recalled. But the talk was premature: It would be December 1970 before *Husbands* hit theaters.

The rough cut was four hours and Gazzara recalled it as "*Husbands* at its best," despite its length. Tanner and Ruban brought it down to something more manageable, not quite three hours. When that cut was finished, a screening was set up at Universal, where Cassavetes had found offices just off the lot. In his enthusiasm to see it with an audience, Cassavetes had overbooked the two showings. So many invitees turned up that they filled two screening rooms in different buildings on the lot; reels of the print were bicycled from one projection room to the other.

The response was electrifying. Columbia, which had just finalized a distribution deal that gave Cassavetes, Gazzara, and Falk a terrific percentage after Columbia recouped its investment, was convinced it had a hit.

"Everybody loved the film," Ruban said, "It was light, it was comedic, and it had Ben as the central figure. Only one person hated it: John. My one mistake was I put it together the way he shot it. So he spent another seven or eight months recutting it and changed it 180 degrees. It became a serious piece."

The first cut of the film, Cassavetes later told Ruban, was too entertaining. "I'm not here to please the palate of the audience," he said.

He also felt the story arc was too simple: the last grasp at youth while confronting mortality for the first time. These characters, he believed, were desperate to hold their lives together, even as their assumptions about themselves were turning to ashes. Cassavetes wanted to show how the crisis affected their friendship with each other, something they treasured in a way that was different from their relationship with their wives or any woman. And now that friendship would never be the same.

Sam Shaw disagreed and told Cassavetes as much: "He thought it was more important that you could laugh," daughter Edie recalled. "The rough cut of *Husbands* was the most incredible thing—incredible laughs. But John reedited it. I think the laughs made John nervous. He said, 'It's a serious story.' When I saw the final cut, it was not as good a movie. Dad disagreed with the cut."

Cassavetes spent the end of 1969 and most of 1970 reediting *Husbands*. At various points, there was a version in which Harry was the focus, one that spotlighted Gus, and one that concentrated on Archie. Carole Smith, Falk's assistant at the time, remembered watching one cut and saying aloud afterward how much she liked it.

"Of course, she likes it," boomed Gazzara. "It's Peter's version."

Cassavetes went back and forth, seeking the balance, trying to find the film in the editing room that matched his vision. He had agreed to keep the length under two and a half hours, and when he finally brought it in, there were large chunks of everyone's performance on the cutting room floor.

"He cut *Husbands* and had so many screenings," recalled Elaine Kagan, his secretary at the time. "I don't know if any movie had as many versions. He had so much film and it was all so wonderful. It was a work in progress; it was like rewriting, only he was recutting."

Gazzara took it the worst. At one point, after seeing what was almost a final cut, he stormed into Cassavetes' office and told him loudly that he was ruining the film by obsessively reediting it. Cassavetes, never one to shy away from an argument, came back at Gazzara fiercely—to the point that Ruban and Falk, who were also in the room, nearly had to separate them physically. Instead Gazzara stalked out, slamming the door behind him.

Falk ran after him and caught him at his car: "Ben, it's all gonna work out," Falk said. "He's not finished yet." Gazzara subsequently apologized to Cassavetes for the outburst.

As he worked with the editors on the film, Cassavetes, whose daughter, Zoe, was born June 29, 1970, during the protracted editing of *Husbands*, found himself inundated with questions from the editors about how it was supposed to go together, about what the emotional or linear connection was between seemingly disjointed scenes, about how much the audience was supposed to know about the characters. So Cassavetes came up with a way to explain it that would also serve his need to further digest the material as he worked on it.

He began to write a novel of *Husbands* that would then serve as a guide to the editors. He would tell the story as dictation, the same way he wrote his scripts: dictating to a secretary, who would then type up the new pages and, frequently, would help him act them out.

Elaine Kagan, who was Cassavetes' secretary at the time, recalled, "During the year he cut *Husbands*, he wrote a novel of *Husbands*, which he dictated in all three voices. When he was dictating Archie, he did Peter. When he was doing Harry, he'd be Benny. And when he was Gus, he'd be John."

Ruban recalled, "He'd write the novel during lunch. He'd speak seemingly spontaneously, extemporaneously, while he was eating a sandwich and Elaine would take it down. John was always figuring out beforehand what he wanted and how to get it. He had a great capacity to work things out in his head. He could work a story for God knows how long in his head before committing it to paper. When he wrote, it never seemed to take too long."

But while movie novelizations were only just becoming popular at that point, Cassavetes was after something other than a literary rehash of the screen story. Instead, the manuscript, close to 400 typewritten pages with handwritten editing notes, alternated chapters between the three characters and was told in their voices. About 80 percent was interior monologue by the characters; most of that seemed like free association or stream of consciousness, with only about 20 percent of their time spent recalling or describing the events that took place in the movie.

Cassavetes wrote a novel that, while taking off from the same place, looked at the moments in the lives of all three men that weren't shown in the film, including flashbacks to their childhoods and college days. It allowed Cassavetes a chance to examine the relationship between the three characters and their dead friend, Stuart Jackson, in ways that would have been too explicit or expositive for his taste in a film.

At one point in the book, for example, Gus observes that Harry "has

this melodramatic way about him of making everything even more significant than it is."

Harry thinks to himself about Gus and Archie, "They're really two stupid son-of-a-bitches who would be very boring if they weren't my friends.
They have that dry Americanized emotionless way of avoiding anything
that might cause them feeling."

And Archie, feeling excluded by Harry and Gus, wonders, "What am I—
some outsider that doesn't have the same problems and the same needs that
these two guys have?"

As they finish their first night of carousing, Gus notes, "We wanted
three of us to be as good as four. And we were sorry that this night had
passed so quickly without event, without philosophical exchange, without
emotion. All I could think was—'I'm a dentist.' I felt very bad about that."

Harry decides, "If I were with my wife, I'd be thinking time is money.
When I'm with Gus and Archie, I think time is life." Later, Harry wonders,
"What's so charming about logic? And what's so true about truth?"

Indeed, reading the unpublished novel, it's hard not to hear Cassavetes himself speaking through the three characters. There are moments
when, in letting these characters examine their own thoughts, it feels as
though Cassavetes is using them to do the same thing.

"Beyond your control—that should be the title of life," Harry muses. At
another moment, with Cassavetes-like ruefulness, he decides, "One thing
leads to another and pretty soon you learn how to be a whore and do what
they tell you. But anything good you do comes out of love."

Cassavetes, an inveterate gambler, can be heard when Archie says,
"Gambling, to a man, is a test of courage because all our lives we say money
is not important." He's also audible in Archie's observation: "Why do men
work? Men work so they don't have to go home and face themselves. Because the nest that they created is fraught with absolutes."

His approach is evident when Archie says, talking about the fear of
failure, "It gives you a very high mark when you can overcome that." He
also says about trying something risky and falling short: "Be happy for failure because not everyone has the courage to do it."

But Cassavetes can most clearly be heard, naturally, in the writing
about his own character, Gus: "You know how you show off?" Gus asks at
one point. "Sometimes if you make a jerk of yourself, you gain energy.
Sometimes if you fight, it's because it's just what you need. A good time
can't be manufactured. But people can be moved if you allow them to
share with you, if you remember their names, if you catch their eyes."

Gus' discussion of his height also seems to have clear autobiographical elements: "I never was very tall. But I always liked tall girls. I get a big charge out of having girls taller than me. Tall women should take a chance with short guys, too."

And Gus seems to be stating Cassavetes' cinematic credo, when he says, "It always shocks me that people deceive themselves and do away with their own mystery. I find my own flaws endlessly fascinating and more important than the stance of manhood, my work or being a husband."

When he read it in Cassavetes' office, Falk was stunned by the novel, which offered the kind of insights into the role of Archie that would have been helpful during filming—and exactly the sort of thing Cassavetes would never offer to an actor.

"Why didn't you tell me this when we were making the picture?" the bewildered Falk wondered aloud.

Cassavetes was invited to show *Husbands* as part of a mini-retrospective at the San Francisco Film Festival in October 1970, at which they also screened *Shadows* and *Faces.* But where those earlier films drew avid audiences, the 154-minute version of *Husbands* seemed to agitate the packed house, which turned hostile when Cassavetes, Falk, and Gazzara took the stage after the screening.

"They were booing and they were going crazy," Cassavetes recalled. "They got hostile, eighteen hundred people really booing."

And that was before the credits finished and the lights came up, revealing a trio of chairs and microphones on the stage. Cassavetes, Gazzara, and Falk hurried up to the stage to a subdued rumble from the audience.

Audience members actually shouted, "Fascist!" at the bemused actors as they settled into their seats on stage and lit cigarettes. They could tell by looking at the largely college-age audience that these were middle-class kids—yet as the questions quickly revealed, they were angry at Cassavetes and his colleagues for making a film that examined middle-class life without either making fun of or passing judgment on it.

Not knowing what else to say, Cassavetes blurted, "How did you like the film?"—a question that drew stony silence from the audience.

Finally an audience member stood up and said, "I thought the whole point of *Husbands* was to show how offensive these three characters were. Typical, crude middle-class jocks. But if they're really you, then I don't know."

"It is us," Cassavetes said simply. "It's us." Falk nodded assent, saying, "That's right. That's right."

The epithet "Middle class!" was also hurled at the film by the audience. As Cassavetes recalled, "At that time, to be middle class or to make a film about the middle class was so abhorrent to people. I was looking down at the audience, at the faces of these college students and they were all middle class, which made me laugh."

"If this picture were trying to prove a point against the middle class that would be a different story," one viewer said. "But are you trying to say in this picture that these people were you?"

"Yeah," Cassavetes said. "These people are me. That's the way it is, yea, middle-class, mundane, not very well-thought-out, living in the past and in childhood, in the times when things were happy, yes, that's exactly what the picture was."

"Will you talk about your technique of intense close-ups?" one audience member asked. Cassavetes laughed: "I don't know what you're talking about. I just have the camera follow the people and the action the best it can."

The questions grew ruder: "Don't you think in all art forms that, if you don't have discipline," said one questioner, "you end up with a company of Portnoys?", referring to the popular Philip Roth novel about an inveterate masturbator. "I don't know," came the response.

The verbal abuse grew noisy and steady; the executives from Columbia who had flown up from Los Angeles for the screening shrank in their seats at the verbal torrent.

"We thought we were going to be killed," Cassavetes said later. "It was getting terrific. The only friends we had were Gena and Seymour, who were in the audience in the back. Anytime anybody said something, Gena would shout, 'Sit down!' A guy would get up and yell, and Seymour would say, 'Bullshit.'"

Still, the review in *Variety* by Rick Setlowe was positive, calling it "a memorably touching, human and very funny film." While Setlowe said the film was "self-indulgent to the point of boredom and too long by at least a half hour," he added that disciplined editing "should produce a major work of cinematic and dramatic art whose box office appeal should be considerably broader than *Faces*. Unlike *Faces*, *Husbands* is a work of love, compassion and humor . . . Cassavetes cannot be classed with other American directors, even those who write or develop their own original screenplays. He is more like a novelist creating or recreating his own slice of the work with typewriter, camera and formidable dramatic talent. However, he is not his own best editor."

The audience response in San Francisco only confirmed what Columbia already felt: The film was unconventional, confrontational—hardly the crowd-pleaser they'd screened a year earlier.

Cassavetes whittled and tinkered with the editing, eventually coming up with a cut that met the running time limit and still felt like his film. But Columbia was unhappy with the barroom scenes: the singing and the vomiting seemed to go on, well, ad nauseum. After meeting with studio executives, Ruban attempted to explain to Cassavetes how they could restructure the sequence slightly—just enough to convince the suits that they'd done what they'd been asked, without really changing the film.

"I think I could change it in some ways," Ruban told him. "And if you don't like it, you can put it back to the way it was."

"No, I don't want you to touch it," Cassavetes said dismissively, as though Ruban were a traitor for suggesting any form of capitulation. The two of them argued so fiercely that Ruban walked out and stopped speaking to him.

So the studio, unhappy with the film Cassavetes had given them, started dragging its feet on when *Husbands* would be released: "The studio says they know what people like," Cassavetes said. "They are full of shit. They don't know any more than I do. I don't even know what *I* like."

Cassavetes and his co-stars began papering Manhattan with the *Husbands* posters Sam and Edie Shaw had created. There reportedly was an exchange of angry letters between Cassavetes and Columbia.

The studio even tried a screening of its own—hoping to prove the film didn't work?—at an East Side theater. On what *Time* magazine referred to as a day of "bone-chilling rain," the screening sold out two hours ahead of time. Cassavetes reportedly was turned away by an usher, eventually proving his identity (perhaps by pointing to himself on the film's poster), then watched from the balcony.

The audience response was an active one, as Cassavetes later reported. He loved to provoke a reaction, to nudge the audience out of complacency—and the chance to experience it first-hand was irresistible.

"I love that stuff," he said. "When Peter Falk has that scene with the Chinese girl and he treats her so badly—well, people boo and I love to hear it. Afterward, they accuse me of being a racist. Of course I tell them that I am.

"Sitting in front of me were these two fags. During the scene where the two guys get sick in the bar and throw up, one fag turned to the other and said, 'I know what those critics are going to say. They'll say it was incisive.' That was just about the time another guy sitting down front went running up the aisle getting sick to his stomach. Terrific. I really loved it."

Columbia relented and released *Husbands* in New York on December

8, 1970, a year later than planned. "*Husbands:* A comedy about life, death and freedom," the opening credits announced. But Cassavetes may have been using the term "comedy" loosely or, perhaps, ironically.

The critics broke about the same as in the past, falling on far sides of the dividing line between declaring it a work of genius and calling it an exercise in self-indulgence.

Time's Jay Cocks, who had befriended Cassavetes, had been invited to rough-cut screenings and had seen a long version of *Husbands*: "I thought it was a masterpiece," Cocks said. "It was so good I broke my own law of conscience and reviewed it. I shouldn't do it but I did. The movie needed as much help as it could get."

"There are a few things that come first and easily to mind about *Husbands*," Cocks wrote in his review. "That it gives us a better picture of a kind of lingering desperation than has ever been shown before; that it is John Cassavetes' finest work; and that it is an important and a great film . . . *Husbands* may be one of the best movies anyone will ever see. It is certainly the best movie anyone will ever live through."

Archer Winsten called it "a work of startling originality" and "a considerable film achievement for John Cassavetes, larger, harder, more impressive than *Faces* and more consistent, too." Hollis Alpert said the film "towers above [*Shadows* and *Faces*] and amounts to a triumphant demonstration of the validity of his methods . . . Very often funny, even hilarious, there is not a single moment of farce; the humor arises from recognition of human fault and frailty and each laugh could just as easily be a tear."

Richard Schickel said the film "confirms what *Faces* indicated, that Cassavetes is a truly singular director, a man who puts an unmistakable stamp on his movies . . . One is constantly surprised by the choices the actors make, the directions they dart off in." Gene Shalit's blurb of a review called it "a true zinging film. *Husbands*. I love it."

But Andrew Sarris was less convinced, saying that the film confirmed that Cassavetes was a major American filmmaker "and one of the most tortured and turgid as well." He complimented Cassavetes left-handedly, saying the film was "conceived and executed by an artist who seems to keep stumbling onto ever higher ground in his quest for forms to contain his feelings."

Vincent Canby called the film "personal, almost private" and said it "puts one's tolerance of simulated *cinema verité* to the test." Noting that most of the scenes go on too long, Canby compared watching the film to "being at a party after the liquor and wit have run out and when nobody can quite bring himself to leave."

Rex Reed was not only upset by the film; he was outraged at the audience: "I find it offensive when an audience roars at a lot of dialogue about the painful intricacies of vomiting," he wrote, dismissing the film as "a laborious, humorless, banal and downright deadly little bore that is going around the country these days passing itself off as a movie."

Judith Crist, who had been a champion of *Faces*, also seemed personally betrayed by *Husbands*: "We speak in sorrow as well as anger at the sight of wasted talents and the realization that a sophisticated professional has fallen into the trap of personal moviemaking," she wrote.

Pauline Kael took an even more active dislike to *Husbands*.

"No matter how dispassionately you analyze what's wrong with *Husbands*—which is just about everything," began Kael, who was just clearing her throat before announcing: "If I were cutting it, I don't think there would be much left . . . Maybe twenty minutes in all, and that's stretching it."

The dialogue ("written to sound unwritten," she noted) "is deliberately banal," Kael said. The film didn't just compound the sins of *Faces*, which Kael had panned: "One might even say that *Husbands* takes those faults into a new dimension."

Kael branded Cassavetes a bully for his treatment of people on camera: "In the past, Cassavetes has given some erratic evidence of being a compassionate director," she concluded. "I think he forfeits all claims to compassion in *Husbands*."

It was the continuation of a contentious relationship between the director, who loved to argue with people who didn't like his films, and Kael, the shrewish *grande dame* of movie critics, who rarely met a filmmaker whose work she didn't feel she could improve.

Seymour Cassel recalled, "Pauline Kael had her own pets, if you read her. But John never catered to her."

Indeed, though he socialized with her a couple of times, it wasn't to butter her up. Cassel recalled a taxi ride to a bar after a screening that he had been to with Cassavetes and Kael. Kael was talking about the film they'd just seen and Cassavetes looked at her with a suspicious grin.

"Pauline, you don't know what you're saying," he said. Before she knew what was happening, he reached down and snatched the shoes off her feet. Even as she squawked in protest, Cassavetes hurled the shoes out the taxi window—then laughed heartily with Cassel because "he was a clown. He had that craziness. I loved that about him," Cassel recalled.

Once they arrived at the bar, Cassavetes and Cassel chivalrously offered to carry the diminutive Kael into the bar. She walked in her stocking feet instead.

Gena Rowlands said, "It was a personal thing between her and John. She didn't like him, didn't like the work. We were both at a party once and she sent someone over but I didn't want to meet her. I mean, I knew I'd just say something very bad, so what was the point?"

Cassavetes even tried to bar her from a press screening of *Husbands*. Only Gazzara's diplomacy led to her admission. Kael later wrote, "John Cassavetes, on the opening day of one of his psychodramas, grabbed me as I came out of the theater and hoisted me, and as I hung there helpless in his grip, my tootsies dangling at least three feet from the sidewalk, his companions, Ben Gazzara and Peter Falk, were chuckling. Cassavetes was saying, 'Love ya Pauline, just love ya'; and I felt that he wanted to crush every bone in my body."

As Cassavetes later told cinematographer Frederick Elmes, "The way I figure, if Pauline Kael ever liked one of my movies, I'd give up."

The critics were mixed about *Husbands*; it did have its share of staunch advocates, who saw it as the ultimate statement on what it meant to be a man at that split second in history.

Cocks remembered, "The first time I saw *Husbands*, I was floored. The power of that ending, the very ordinary, pedestrian line, 'Oh boy, Dad, are you in trouble.' The power of that ending is unusual in the idea of taking something ordinary and making it extraordinary."

Harvey Weinstein, who would go on to alter the face of independent film in the 1990s with his company, Miramax, remembered seeing *Husbands* while he was in college: "The metaphor was freedom," Weinstein said. "Here were these guys who probably inspired more road trips in the middle of the semester than any other movie ever."

And while women seemed to have a particularly hard time enjoying *Husbands*, no less a personage than feminist Betty Friedan, author of *The Feminine Mystique* and a founding voice of the women's liberation movement of the period, wrote, "*Husbands* zeroes in on the real state of love and sex in our time. It shows the actuality of the crisis between men and women in America today . . . Strangely enough, *Husbands*, a movie made by men about men's love for other men, is the strongest statement of the case for women's liberation I have yet seen on stage or screen."

Others couldn't decide what Cassavetes was trying to say about these men: Was he admiring? Was he disdainful? Was it satire or realism?

Cassavetes wanted none of it: "If I wrote it down literally and said exactly what I mean, I might as well have a narrator," he said disdainfully.

When the film was released, it was the vomit scene that got all the notice. Cassavetes was regularly fielding phone calls from Columbia, pleading with him: shorten the film. Take the vomit scene out—or at least make it much, much shorter.

"Many people walked out of *Husbands*—I'm aware of that," he said. "Well, *Husbands* is an extremely entertaining film in spots, just as I think life is extremely entertaining in spots. Like life, it's also very slow and depressing in areas. I won't make shorthand films because I don't want to manipulate audiences into assuming quick manufactured truths."

After toiling in the art house fringe for so long, Cassavetes had the surprising experience of having his film become a mainstream cultural touchstone, a punchline—if not necessarily for the reasons he would have liked.

"I was watching television one night and the news came on and it said 500 people in Cleveland got up and left the theater en masse and the name of the picture was *Husbands*," Cassavetes recalled. "I could only laugh at that because I thought, Jesus, what did that contain that could affect them so? I'm such an optimist, I think, isn't that marvelous that you could make a picture that can scare 500 people out of the theater without having a moment of violence, a moment of anything that would be any way near controversial? Just the idea that people behaving in a way that is not acceptable can take 500 people and throw them out of the theater. Now I've been bored with pictures and if it's a boring picture, I just sit there and, at a certain point, I say, 'Let's go.' But I won't get up and leave with 500 other people because it's boring, so it must be doing something else to an audience."

It didn't help his relationship with Columbia—or any other studio, for that matter—that Cassavetes continued blasting the studio ("I don't edit what I say for anybody, but not all studio executives are dumb," he noted) and the studio system in interviews about the film and in an essay of his own.

It appeared in a *Variety* anniversary edition in October 1970, two months before *Husbands'* release and was titled "Maybe There Really Wasn't an America—Maybe It Was Only Frank Capra." "The question was asked: What's wrong with our industry? The answer to this question is what it has always been. It has always been dependent on what kind of people are in our industry. What are they made of? And do they have anything to say that they themselves would listen to?"

As *Husbands* was playing out in secondary markets, Cassavetes spoke up again: "No head of any major studio today has ever made a film himself, has ever sweated through the ordeal a moviemaker has to go through to get a picture filmed," he said. Executives, he noted, "don't have anything to do with the making of a picture. They just say go ahead or don't go ahead. You have the money to make a film or you can't have the money. If they were to tell the truth, studio executives would say, 'We panic when they spend too much and we feel elated when movie makers finish a picture on time and don't spend a lot of our money on it. We really don't know if the public will like it or not and we get worried because there's a lot of money at stake.' And that's the truth about those people."

As the release finally approached, the three actors turned up everywhere to publicize the film. They were more than happy to try to explain the themes, to celebrate Cassavetes—and to sell the film, because, of course, they all had an equal financial stake in how it did.

"It's a film about male love and about how men express their feelings," Gazzara told one reporter. "But there are homosexual overtones. The three guys in the film don't know how to conform but they don't know how not to. They're never self-pitying. They want to have their cake and eat it too. Marriage is a tough adjust; I think it is with every man."

To another journalist, he said, "I had people tell me that watching *Husbands* was like looking at other people through a keyhole. What's wrong with that? People find that upsetting, because they're used to most films keeping them outside the door, so to speak."

Falk told one reporter that the reason the film was touching a chord with audiences was that "people are more interested in their own lives or lives they can identify with. It means more to them than killings, rapes, drugs, or riots."

They showed up on *The Mike Douglas Show*, where the host introduced them by saying, "My next three guests all starred in TV detective shows"— not the first thing that would come to mind when thinking of this particular trio, but true, nonetheless.

They sat down with David Frost on his syndicated show, where Cassavetes pitched over backward on his chair at least twice to make a point about spontaneity.

Falk objected at one point when Cassavetes described the film to Frost as being about "three ignorant men." "I could never explain this as being a movie about three men," Falk said. "It's really about three women who don't appear."

Gazzara did nothing to make the water less murky, when he said, "To get serious for a moment, the film is very funny. You could call it a comedy. On the other hand, it can break your heart. You couldn't call it a comedy that's hysterically funny. It's dramatic. It's very sad."

While they joked around and traded verbal japes with Frost, they were relatively respectful and, to all appearances, sober.

Such did not appear to be the case during their legendary appearance on *The Dick Cavett Show* in September 1970. Cavett was considered the thinking man's late-night talk-show host of the period, where he competed with Johnny Carson's dominant *Tonight Show* and *The Merv Griffin Show.* Cavett's show, though it attracted guests like Jimi Hendrix, Groucho Marx, and Orson Welles, also earned only minuscule ratings.

Cavett opened the show by announcing that, rather than his usual ninety-minute running time, his Monday night programs would be only forty-five minutes long during the coming fall season because of the debut of *NFL Monday Night Football* that very evening, which was expected to cut into his airtime. So, Cavett said, he would be devoting the Monday night edition of his show to special guests, who would be given the whole show, something Cavett couldn't normally afford to do with his multiple-guest format. (In fact, Cavett's show was taped three days earlier than it was broadcast.)

But it was obvious that something was up as soon as he introduced Cassavetes, Falk, and Gazzara. Though Gazzara was the only one carrying a drink, they all appeared to have been drinking before they went on (though Gazzara claims that they were all sober). Gazzara and Cassavetes both brandished cigars, while Falk smoked a cigarette.

Cassavetes opened by saying, "Can I say hello to my mother?" After doing so, he, Gazzara, and Falk sat and listened to Cavett explain a little about *Husbands,* before he asked innocuously what the film was about.

Cassavetes answered with non sequiturs then went silent. Allowing a beat or two of silence, Falk piped up, "Are you speaking to me, Dick?"

Attempting to make a joke, Cavett quipped, "Is the bar open backstage?" He was met with stony looks.

Cavett began talking again nervously, trying to make light of the discomfort he obviously was feeling, surrounded by three actors whose combined presence was powerful, even in silence. Finally, Gazzara offered a semblance of a straight answer to one of Cavett's questions and Cassavetes shouted, "Coward! We weren't going to talk to him!"

"That's not cowardice—it's sensitivity," Gazzara barked in reply.

In fact, just before the three of them went on, Cassavetes had turned to Gazzara and Falk and said, "Let's not say anything when he talks to us."

As Cavett threw it to a commercial, Cassavetes appeared to rise, then pitched forward onto the floor, as though he'd been shot. He repeated the move several times during the show, until Cavett joked, "Stop—you're going to be sued by Jerry Lewis."

It went like that for twenty minutes, with Cavett the continual butt of the unspoken joke between the three actors: "This is the reason I didn't join a fraternity," Cavett said, obviously steaming behind his professional smile. At one point, all three of them did pratfalls onto the floor, creating a pile of giggling movie stars. Cavett, furious, walked off the stage, then returned as the audience chanted, "We want Dick!"

"Are you guys all smashed?" Cavett finally asked.

"On what?" Cassavetes replied.

"John never drinks," Gazzara announced. "Peter drinks very little. I do drink."

As they cut to commercials, Cavett's orchestra broke into a chorus of "If I Could Talk to the Animals."

About twenty minutes into the show, Falk, who spent the entire program looking at the audience rather than at Cavett, said, "What did you want to ask us?"

An annoyed Cavett tried once more, sounding a little school-marmish when he said, "What's the film about, fellas?"

Cassavetes laughed sympathetically and said, "You're a terrific sport. We were clowning around."

That seemed to mollify Cavett somewhat and the final twenty minutes, while still not overwhelmingly serious, at least offered the three actors actually talking about the film. Falk admitted that the film helped him find out "I was more alive than I thought." Gazzara revealed that, when his wife, Janice Rule, saw the film, as soon as he uttered the line "Apart from sex—which my wife is very good at—I love you guys best," Rule had whirled on him in the screening room and hissed, "You wrote that line! I know you did!"

The three of them were more serious when they went on *The Tonight Show*, though Gazzara recalled another moment of silliness that typified Cassavetes.

"I was heading downstage to say something to the audience and I felt something on my back," Gazzara said. "It was John. He had jumped up on my back. John was not a fan of pontificating about his films. He loved to make a fool of himself."

Even as *Husbands* hit theaters, Columbia was still importuning Cassavetes to trim the film. As he told a seminar at the American Film Institute in January 1971, shortly after *Husbands* hit theaters, "I got a wire the other day and a letter from Columbia, saying, 'Would you please cut *Husbands* because we are really losing the audience, especially in the singing scene. They can't take that and the vomiting scene. Thirty to fifty people a night go up and ask for their money back during that sequence.' My answer to them at that time was, 'Buy me out of the film and I'll be happy to cut ten minutes out of the film for you. Just give me a lot of money and I'll cut it out.'"

Columbia took another route: It waited until the film was a few weeks into the run; just before going into wider release, they cut eleven minutes from the film in existing and subsequent prints, mostly from the vomit scene and the drinking scene. But Cassavetes lacked the funds or energy to pursue it into court; by the time the case was settled, the film would long since have been out of theaters.

Meanwhile, the film had drawn its share of vitriol from female critics for what they saw as a movie glorifying overgrown adolescents. Counterintuitively, Cassavetes assumed that women would be interested in a movie that depicted men as they were: struggling, insecure, still boys inside. "This is absolutely a man's story," he said. "I think that the interest a woman could have in a picture like this would only be in seeing the relationship between men done on a real level.

"I think the three men in the picture have more in common than, let's say, their wives would have in common or they would have with their wives. Although it's about three men, the picture is basically for women."

In fact, Cassavetes found that, in general, women hated the film: "They absolutely loathed the picture, with such a passion that it was unbelievable," he said. "Many audiences didn't like *Husbands* because it didn't coincide with what they expected an independent filmmaker to be making at the time. They needed someone to be making a picture that would go along and fight a cause for them. At the time that *Husbands* came out, I was considered a conservative."

As he finished *Husbands,* Cassavetes started planning his next picture. He announced that he was taking a three-month vacation (he didn't) and said, "I have a great idea for my next film. My wife, Gena Rowlands, and Seymour Cassel from *Faces* will be in it. I haven't written it yet but I think I'll take my typewriter along on vacation."

When Cassavetes took *Husbands* to New York to screen the final version for Columbia executives, he took Cassel along for company. The two friends would talk from time to time about chucking it all and moving to Brazil. And on this trip, they fell into the same old fantasy.

Cassavetes turned to Cassel, reached into his pocket, and pulled out a check made out to Cassavetes for $975,000. Showing it to Cassel, Cassavetes said, "Let's go to Brazil. We'll cash this and run away from it all."

Without missing a beat, Cassel said, "Great—let's go!"

Cassavetes smiled and sipped his drink, as if considering what that would be like: to simply let go and disappear. Then he said, "I can't. A third of this money is Benny's and a third of it is Peter's."

Cassel shrugged; easy come, easy go.

Then Cassavetes turned to him and said, "Sey, let your hair grow. I'm going to write a movie for you and Gena."

"What kind of movie?" Cassel asked.

Cassavetes thought about it: "I don't know. A romantic comedy."

"A love story?"

"Yeah," Cassavetes said.

Cassel considered further: "Do I get to kiss Gena?"

Cassavetes laughed. "Of course, stupid. It's a love story."

Thirty

A Leg Up

Martin Scorsese was an instructor in the film school at New York University, a would-be filmmaker who scrounged money and film to put together his first feature, *Who's That Knocking at My Door*, over the course of a couple of years beginning when he was in graduate school. The film starred a young Harvey Keitel and probed some of the same themes Scorsese would explore with more vigor and self-assurance a few years later in *Mean Streets*.

But like most independent filmmakers of that period, Scorsese was stymied. The film had played in New York but hardly anywhere else. Scorsese had gone back to teaching at NYU, and had gotten involved working for director Michael Wadleigh shooting and editing *Woodstock*, the documentary about the rock festival where, reportedly, Scorsese was the only person wearing a coat and tie.

Scorsese was also friendly with *Time* magazine film critic Jay Cocks and would regularly accompany Cocks to screenings. They were both serious Cassavetes fans, so Scorsese was thrilled when Cocks arranged for him to meet the filmmaker—and more than a little nervous when Cocks told him that, having heard Cocks talk about it, Cassavetes had agreed to watch Scorsese's film.

"It was at a time when student filmmakers were a rare breed, an exotic animal," Cocks recalled. "The idea of being a film student was humorous to most people, but I told John about Marty and he wanted to see his film."

As Scorsese remembered it, "We had dinner at my parents' house on Elizabeth Street and everybody in the building came down. But I was nervous about showing it to John."

They repaired to the Time-Life Building, where they were met by Sam Shaw. Cocks had commandeered a screening room and put the film on. Everyone settled in to watch—except the agitated young director, who paced outside the screening room as the film ran.

"I wouldn't sit and watch," Scorsese said. "I was mortified. It was three or four years of work and striving for something. I was embarrassed because of its limitations, the emotional content, the story of the film. It was too personal. It was hard enough to show it in a theater with people."

Scorsese was still suffering the effects of a comment by Richard Roud of the New York Film Festival, who had told him, "You're living aesthetically beyond your means." Scorsese had taken it to heart: "That hurt but it was true," Scorsese said. "I couldn't express everything I felt. I didn't have the technique. I wasn't able to express it in dialogue, camera placement, structure or story."

But when Cassavetes emerged from the screening, he grabbed Scorsese and gave him a big kiss. "It's great!" he enthused. "I think this is the best movie I've seen since *Citizen Kane*. No, you know what? It's better than *Citizen Kane!*"

As Scorsese remembered it, "He kept saying that it had a certain kind of passion, that it dealt with something genuine. He said, 'It's genuine, it's real, it's a beauty! You have a certain core, something authentic and genuine. You should stick with that.'"

It was exactly the kind of approbation that the insecure, self-doubting Scorsese needed: Here was one of his heroes, a genuine artist, an independent filmmaker who made movies his own way, favorably comparing Scorsese's film to what many regarded as the greatest film ever made.

That wasn't the last time Cassavetes would serve as a mentor or benefactor for Scorsese. Cassavetes was nothing if not encouraging of other people's talents and dreams. Even as he struggled to get his films made, he helped other people get a leg up, launching them into careers they might never otherwise have been given a shot at—or even have considered trying.

Jeremy Kagan, who had started his TV directing career in 1969, met Cassavetes a couple of years later, when he started dating Cassavetes' secretary, Elaine (whom he would eventually marry). He was in awe of the older director, but Cassavetes brushed the adoration aside: "I felt, I'm a novice and he's a master," Kagan recalled. "But he never made me feel that way. He was an incredibly inclusive guy. There was a continuous flow of humanity that he was embracing and including. But he was smart enough to know that the mythic stuff was good for publicity."

Henry Jaglom had met Cassavetes in New York around the time of *Shadows* through Seymour Cassel. When Jaglom told Cassavetes he wanted to write and direct his own films, Cassavetes told him to just do it: "Don't let anybody stand in your way or stop you or tell you what you can't do. It's what they can't do, not you."

Jaglom was able to get work as a writer during the last days of the studio system, moving to California in 1964. Cassel took him to see Cassavetes, who said, "Hey, how's it going, kid? Did you get to make your movie yet?" When Jaglom told him he had written a script, Cassavetes said, "Let me take a look at it."

"That was unheard of," Jaglom said. "He was already a very prominent actor."

Not only did Cassavetes read the script for *A Safe Place*, which would become Jaglom's much-maligned first film, he gave Jaglom extensive notes to help him solve his problems on the script.

"He didn't talk in terms of it not working," Jaglom said. "He had a hundred questions. How would you do this? He was trying to tell me all the different ways to do what I had written, not to change it and make it more commercial. And that became the basis of my first film. He gave me the courage to resist when everybody else said, 'Do it this way.'"

Cassavetes also befriended Peter Bogdanovich, the former film scholar and critic who became part of the vanguard of a new Hollywood with his 1971 film *The Last Picture Show*. When Bogdanovich finished the very different *What's Up, Doc?* in early 1972, he asked Cassavetes to one of the first screenings in New York.

Bogdanovich had much at stake with the film. Hailed as a wunderkind for the John Ford-like *Picture Show*, the classicist Bogdanovich now had chosen another role model: the fast-talking screwball comedy of Howard Hawks a la *Bringing Up Baby* and *His Girl Friday*. But his version starred Barbra Streisand and Ryan O'Neal.

The screening gathered about 300 tastemakers, including Cassavetes. Bogdanovich remembered the audience response as OK, not great: "A little reserved." But, about ten minutes into the film, Cassavetes said loudly, "I can't believe he's doing this" and burst out laughing. It broke the ice with the audience, which also succumbed to laughter.

"From then on it played great," Bogdanovich said. "He understood it and everybody else got it then, too."

Photographer Gordon Parks, the first African-American on the staff of *Life* magazine, had published his semi-autobiographical novel *The Learning Tree*, in 1963, detailing a boyhood as a young black man in the Kansas of the 1920s. While Parks was a colleague of Sam Shaw, he barely knew John Cassavetes—and so was surprised to get a call from him in 1967.

Cassavetes told Parks he'd just finished reading *The Learning Tree*: "I think it should be made into a movie," Cassavetes told him. "And I think you should direct it."

Parks thanked him for the thought but pointed out that none of the major studios had ever hired a black man to direct a feature film.

"I know," Cassavetes said, "but I still think you should direct it."

"I'd love to, if I could," Parks countered. But inside he had no hope that it would ever happen. Cassavetes had other ideas.

"Can you get to Hollywood the day after tomorrow?" he asked Parks. When Parks said that was possible, Cassavetes said, "Do it. Come to Warner Brothers/Seven Arts and I'll be at Ken Hyman's office. Ken and I are on the outs, but I'll be in his office." Kenneth Hyman was the head of Seven Arts at Warner Bros. and the producer of such films as *Whatever Happened to Baby Jane?* and *The Dirty Dozen.*

So Parks decided to take a chance and flew from his home in New York to Los Angeles. When he got to Hyman's office, Cassavetes led Parks into Hyman's office, said hello to Hyman, and introduced the two men—then said, "See you later," and walked out, leaving Hyman and Parks to talk.

Hyman, gesturing to the volume of *The Learning Tree* on his desk, said, "John forced me to read this. He thinks you should direct a movie of it. How do you feel about that?"

"I'm with John," Parks said.

"Who would you like to write the screenplay?" Hyman asked. When Parks admitted that he didn't know any writers in Hollywood, Hyman said, "Well, why don't you write it?" Parks quickly agreed.

Thinking a moment, Hyman said, "Cassavetes told me you're a composer. Would you like to compose the music for it?"

Again, the increasingly amused Parks assented.

Finally, Hyman said, "Since this would be the first major studio film with a black director, I think you should produce it as well."

"Why not?" Parks replied. At this point, he was convinced that this was an elaborate practical joke or a put-on of some sort: "I didn't believe one word of it," Parks said. "At least not until I saw it in the newspaper."

The Learning Tree, released in 1969, marked Parks' debut as a director and opened the door for every other African-American filmmaker who has come since.

"To that time, no black person had directed at a major studio in Hollywood," Parks recalled. "John was the guy who brought it all about and he didn't ask anything for it. John said, 'All I could do was lay it out for [Hyman]. I said, 'Read this, it would be a great film.' And Ken listened to Cassavetes. His innate belief in the project and the whole system backed him up to let a black director in. All black directors should be thankful. He became like a brother to me."

As he was editing *Husbands* in California, Cassavetes met a young, long-haired musician who was working in an editing bay down the hall from where Cassavetes was cutting his film. Cassavetes befriended Bo Harwood and put him to work initially composing music for *Minnie and Moskowitz*. And when it came time to shoot *A Woman Under the Influence* and to put together a young, fast-moving crew that could work with the same passion and intensity as Cassavetes, he turned to Harwood and decided that Harwood should be the sound recordist for the film, despite the fact that Harwood had no experience at all.

Today Harwood is a veteran sound engineer and mixer who works regularly in television, where his credits run the gamut from *Pee-wee's Playhouse* to *My So-called Life* to *Six Feet Under*. But when he met Cassavetes, Harwood was, in his words, a flower child who had been in a rock band in Haight-Ashbury during the Summer of Love. When the band broke up because some members needed to flee their draft notices, Harwood and a friend came down to Hollywood to make a short film. The film screened at Universal, where *Husbands* was being edited, and Cassavetes saw it and took a liking to the long-haired, barefoot Harwood and his music from the film.

So he asked him to write music for *Minnie and Moskowitz* and took him into the editing room with him. When that film was finished, Cassavetes asked him to compose a score for *A Woman Under the Influence*—but wanted him to create the score on piano rather than guitar.

"I don't play piano," Harwood told him.

"That's OK—we'll rent one," Cassavetes assured him.

When it turned out that the sound man for *Woman* was not going to work out, Cassavetes turned once again to Harwood.

"One tape recorder is like another, isn't it?" Cassavetes asked him.

"I guess so," Harwood shrugged.

"Good. I want you to do sound for the movie," Cassavetes said. "You've got three weeks to learn."

Harwood got a Nagra tape recorder with a handheld microphone and ran around town, quizzing sound engineers about how best to record sound for a movie, while practicing using the machine.

"John loved putting people in unfamiliar territory and watching them squirm and get creative and make things work," Harwood recalled. "He was a mentor, an older man who looked down and said, 'You're wonderful.' I was completely winging it. And he let everybody know that they were free to make mistakes."

When Harwood met Cassavetes, along with Falk and Gazzara, "I thought they were a bunch of square businessmen. It didn't take me long to figure out I was the conventional one and John was the rebel. For whatever reason, he'd asked me to be part of an extraordinary team. We were the gang that went against everybody."

In the mid-1970s, Cassavetes was part of a group of actors who made themselves available to act in a special series sponsored by PBS, in which young filmmakers were hired to direct one-hour adaptations of American short stories. A young director named Bill Kelley chose Richard Connell's "The Most Dangerous Game," about shipwrecked people who wash ashore on an island whose owner, the mysterious Count Zaroff, is a big-game hunter who hunts humans to amuse himself. Cassavetes, still strapped from producing and releasing *A Woman Under the Influence*, had been cast as Zaroff, a role he took mostly for the paycheck.

"I'm sure John thought the whole enterprise was pathetic, but he never questioned my direction, never belittled me or suggested my inexperience might be a handicap," Kelley recalled. "Three times, he even smiled approvingly after I outlined a scene to him."

Even Cassavetes had his limit, however. When the young director suggested that his nostrils should be flaring in anger during the climactic scene, Cassavetes smiled, called the young director aside and said, "You know, I'm not Vincent Price—or Mr. Ed, either."

Around the same time, Cassavetes received a letter from an expatriate American who had left high school to move to Paris, where he worked at odd jobs and forged the life of a starving young artist. The American, Alexandre Rockwell, wrote about stumbling into a screening of *A Woman Under the Influence* in Paris and how, at the age of nineteen, it had changed his life—and how ironic he found it that he had to leave his country to discover this film.

To Rockwell's surprise, Cassavetes responded with a letter, saying, "Hey, kid, your letter was great. Keep writing."

Cassavetes wound up corresponding with Rockwell and talking to him on the phone regularly over the course of ten years, as Rockwell began his own career as a writer-director. In the late 1980s, Rockwell even wrote a role for Cassavetes in a film called *Sons*, which Rockwell told Cassavetes that he'd written as a reflection of *Husbands*. Cassavetes read the script and called Rockwell at home.

"I loved it," Cassavetes told him. "But unfortunately, I'm not going to be able to do it. I want to be home with my family."

Rockwell read between the lines: Cassavetes was dying. But Cassavetes suggested that Rockwell ask his neighbor, director Sam Fuller, to do the role—and Rockwell ended up making the film with Fuller, Stephane Audran, William Hickey, and Elizabeth Bracco in 1989. Rockwell later paid homage to Cassavetes in 1992 with his film *In the Soup*, in which he gave Seymour Cassel his best role since *Minnie and Moskowitz*.

Cassavetes was also encouraging to Tom Noonan, a young actor who landed a small part as one of the gangsters who kills Buck Henry and his family at the beginning of *Gloria*. Having bluffed his way into an audition and been offered a role, Noonan had the chutzpah to say he would take the part only if Cassavetes would come and see the play he was doing at the time.

Noonan would go on to win directing and writing awards at the Sundance Film Festival in 1994 for his uniquely personal *What Happened Was . . . .* During one of his early discussions with Cassavetes, Noonan observed that he understood how to make a movie, but he didn't know how to sell it once he made it.

"If you're worrying about that," Cassavetes replied, "don't make the movie. You should only make the movie because you want to make the movie."

Tamar Simon Hoffs was a fledgling filmmaker in 1981, making a midlife career move by attending the American Film Institute. For one of her student films, she had written a script based on an experience she had had in an old-fashioned barbershop in downtown Los Angeles. As she thought about casting, Cassavetes came to mind, though she had never met him.

But she knew Ben Gazzara. Her daughter, Susanna Hoffs (who would become the lead singer of the Bangles, a popular mid-'80s pop group), was friends with Gazzara's daughter, Liz, herself a novice film editor. Hoffs showed her the script for *The Haircut* and mentioned that she thought John would be perfect for the main role. Liz Gazzara read the script and agreed with her, and passed the script along to Cassevetes. Within a couple of days, Hoffs received a call from Cassavetes, who said he would happily act in her film.

"I'm doing a movie at the moment," he said, referring to *Tempest*. "But if you can figure out a way to do it, I'll be in it."

Hoffs recalled, "People said to me, 'How could you have the guts to ask him to be in your movie?' But he was such a nice guy on the phone."

Hoffs came up with a schedule that worked for Cassavetes, though it meant giving up his weekend. Cassavetes did have a few ground rules.

"I want the other actors thoroughly rehearsed," he said. "And then I'll come in and you'll tell me what to do and I'll just react to what they're do-ing. I want everyone there so I can be reacting to them. And I want to shoot chronologically."

The Haircut is a short film, in which Cassavetes plays a record company executive on his way to an important meeting. But he stops in the barber-shop for a haircut and is rapidly seduced by the loving attention of the shop's staff of barber (Nicholas Colasanto), manicurist (Joyce Bulifant), and shoeshine man (Meshach Taylor). Though he is in a hurry, he melts into a sybaritic puddle, regressing to infancy as they pamper him, then send him on his way.

"He was there to be part of the movie," Hoffs said. "He wasn't the big star coming to anoint the movie with his presence. He walked into a thoroughly rehearsed trio and the quality of the guy was so amazing. He was absolutely there, with hardly any direction. He was able to give it all up and just be a baby and react to the people who were ministering to him."

As they worked, he told her, "What you need to do as a director is be 100 percent prepared. Also, you have to be open to what the actor is going to do. You have to be trustworthy. When I work with a wonderful actor, his job is to act and mine is to be well-prepared so they can do what they need to know they can trust you."

And then there was Seymour Cassel.

Minnie and Moskowitz was Cassavetes' gift to both Rowlands and Cassel—but particularly Cassel, to whom it was also a kind of homage. As Cassel noted, "Moskowitz was the last hippie," and, in some ways, so was Cassel. In the free-wheeling young actor, Cassavetes had found a partner in crime, someone as ready for fun and trouble as Cassavetes had always been.

"I'm kind of weird—I don't want what other people want out of life," Cassel said at the time. "I'm happy with the few clothes I have. I don't want any more. I like my old car. I don't care about making a lot of money. There are so few movies I want to do. I don't like the idea of working just to be working. If I'm going to be making movies, they've got to be about real people, they've got to be saying things about the world."

The character of Seymour Moskowitz drew on Cassel's own experiences and stories he'd told Cassavetes about working as a parking-lot attendant between acting jobs. Cassavetes wanted to celebrate the unfettered quality of Cassel—a quality he used to see in himself but no longer indulged nearly as much.

Both *Too Late Blues* and *A Child Is Waiting* had been bitter disappointments. His sense of fun had been further tempered by what he saw as a kind of exile from filmmaking and then during the struggle to get *Faces* made and seen. But Cassel could still bring out that mischievous side of John.

"Together, John and my dad were trouble," Matthew Cassel remembered fondly. "They were crazy. They had a great relationship. They'd tease and joke; everything was a competition. They'd pitch quarters, play ball—they were guy's guys."

What kept it interesting for Cassel was the daily question, nay, the eternal question: What would happen next?

"I like the mystery of the way things happen," Cassel said. "You couldn't live if you had an answer for everything you do. I'd be bored. I surprise myself. I'm the most enjoyable person I know. That's why I like people too. I love the unpredictability. I love to nudge them, to make them show that to me and to themselves. To not be so damned protective. To open up, make mistakes, look silly, and not have it held against them."

Even with an Oscar nomination for *Faces,* marriage, children, and a suddenly burgeoning career, Cassel's playful approach to life hadn't altered—and Cassavetes encouraged that spirit in him.

"Seymour was John's alter ego," Al Ruban said. "In his youth, John was a wild guy. But John stopped being crazy when he had his difficulties on *Too Late Blues* and *A Child Is Waiting.* I saw a change in him then. Before that, at the drop of a hat, he'd do anything. It didn't matter the obstacle, he could overcome it. After that, he was still an energetic and gregarious character, but his life wasn't quite what he thought. John was no longer the crazy guy—Seymour was. John lived through him."

The character of Seymour Moskowitz, Cassel admitted at the time, "coincides with my own thing, which is why I like him. It was a chance to play a guy that I probably was a lot more like in the past than I am now. A guy with no responsibility except to himself. The idea that a job, car, house, are the measures of what you are is wrong. If anybody really wants to know about me, they have to make an investment."

Thirty-one

Minnie and Moskowitz

Despite Cassavetes' experience with Columbia on *Husbands,* he was relieved not to have to put his own money on the line to make a movie. So he was willing to take a chance on Universal and executive Ned Tanen with *Minnie and Moskowitz.*

It was going to be a less costly picture—which, at least to Cassavetes' thinking, meant there would be less studio interference: "*Husbands* is the last time I'm going to make an expensive picture," he said. "There are too many considerations when you're playing in that league. I can't really work for a living. It makes me sick to my stomach."

And, said Al Ruban, Cassavetes felt he had something to prove: that he could make a movie within the studio system and still do it *his* way.

"We decided John had written the script, we'd get it into the system, Universal would do it for $680,000, and we'd have a schedule," recalled Ruban, schedule being a relative concept on Cassavetes' other films. "We were committed to coming in on time and on budget and not changing the way we worked."

Still, Cassavetes couldn't shake the notion that he'd made a deal with the devil. All of his meetings, it seemed, dealt with how to sell the film instead of how to make it. If only, he thought, there was a way to eliminate the sales aspect—to keep profit and loss from being part of the decision-making equation so that it could be a purely artistic endeavor.

Cassavetes wrote *Minnie and Moskowitz* as a kind of mirror image of screwball comedies like *Bringing Up Baby* and *The Lady Eve*, where the strait-laced, naive male is overwhelmed by the unlikely attention of a fast-talking, impulsive female. The pairings are comically unsuitable: con woman Barbara Stanwyck and herpetologist Henry Fonda in *The Lady Eve*, flighty heiress Katharine Hepburn and paleontologist Cary Grant in *Bringing Up Baby*. Why not reverse the equation and see what happened?

The reason why not to is obvious: Men love the idea of gorgeous women chasing them, as happens to Fonda and Grant. That's a fantasy and unthreatening; it just doesn't happen to most men and so it's funny. Flip the script, however, and you have a situation that too many women are too familiar with: the unwanted attentions of a completely unsuitable man.

But Cassavetes hoped to push past that initial instant of revulsion and recognition to ask: But what if he really isn't that unsuitable? What if that kind of impulsive, consuming love *is* enough to create a lasting relationship? Then it would be kind of funny, right?

Cassavetes wrote it quickly, he said, "because the idea had been around in my head for a while: how and why people get married. Women have a tendency, when they get married, to say, 'All right, I will now set my life in order.' And like any guy, Seymour's instinct is to just go with the marriage thing. If you love a woman, you don't think marriage will change the relationship. The shock is that it does. When a woman gets married, she insists on a new maturity, while still holding on to the fun. A man doesn't usually know how to balance the combination very well, so either he tries to keep the fun or he gets terribly serious about being mature; he's usually unable to do both things."

The film was sponsored by Ned Tanen, who had established a new division at Universal at the behest of boss Lew Wasserman. Tanen's charge was to tap into the burgeoning pool of young filmmakers who seemed to have the vision that attracted the rapidly expanding youth demographic, suddenly a major part of the audience. This audience was rejecting the big-budget commercial fare produced by the studios and embracing smaller, character-driven films that featured antiheroes and youthful consciousness: *The Graduate, Easy Rider, Five Easy Pieces, M*A*S*H*.

"The initiative," Tanen told *Newsweek* in 1970, "has passed from the business people to the creative people."

Tanen's slate of films was budgeted to cost less than $1 million each. The first filmmakers he signed were Czech refugee/émigré Milos Forman, who cast Lynn Carlin in *Taking Off*, and Frank Perry, whose *Diary of a Mad Housewife* became the leading edge of the first wave of films about the blossoming feminist consciousness in America. Both had critical admirers; *Housewife* made momentary stars out of Frank Langella and Carrie Snodgress.

Before he was done at Universal, Tanen had also funded Peter Fonda's *The Hired Hand*, Dennis Hopper's *The Last Movie*, Monte Hellman's *Two-Lane Blacktop*, and Douglas Trumbull's *Silent Running*. None of them made much money, but Tanen more than recouped the cost of all of them when he gave George Lucas the funds to make *American Graffiti*, one of the biggest-grossing films of 1973.

Tanen's program included giving Cassavetes the money to make *Minnie and Moskowitz*. By the time the film came out, they were not on speaking terms.

Cassavetes, perhaps being playful with interviewers, routinely dismissed the idea that his films were depressing. He believed that all of his stories in some way offered hopefulness for the future of his characters, even when they wound up in a silent standoff as they did in *Faces*. If anything, he felt a bond with Frank Capra, whom he regularly cited as his favorite filmmaker.

It's not exactly Capra-esque, but *Minnie and Moskowitz* is Cassavetes' most obviously optimistic film. It's also the Cassavetes effort that flows closest to the mainstream (with the possible exception of the genre-based *Gloria*). It is a love story that ends happily—or at least more happily than *Faces*, *Husbands*, or *A Woman Under the Influence*.

But even that positioned Cassavetes against the tide yet again. In trying to do something that went counter to what Hollywood was offering, he also was moving in a direction different from other personal films of the time, which often focused on a character shucking off the bonds of commitment or obligation to the establishment to set out on his own personal journey. Here was Seymour, a seeming hippie, willingly—even eagerly—pursuing those most conventional of all family values: monogamy and marriage.

"In this particular society, in this day and age, when people don't marry and don't wish to, it can take its toll on them," Rowlands observed. "The film is about freedoms, freedoms which have a somewhat questionable value attached to them. In part, it's an answer to all those 'I want my freedom and won't commit myself to anything or anybody' pictures which seem to be the vogue these days. We're deeper than that, all of us. The greatest, most important thing is committing yourself to someone. And when you don't, you're really outsmarting yourself. Both characters have gotten to the point where they want to make a bigger commitment. But they're fighting it, too."

Yet the film is stubbornly offbeat, a romantic comedy without a shred of cuteness, in which Cassavetes uses every opportunity to go against the grain of the genre. Yes, boy meets girl, loses girl, and gets girl—but he also gets beat up several times, alternately alienates and endears himself to the girl, and nearly has his marriage sabotaged by his own mother. The reason for the attraction between the two is never obvious, but it is still a realistic portrayal of the ways that powerful feelings can take over a person's life and obliterate rational thought.

Cassel plays Seymour Moskowitz, who is first seen parking cars at a garage in New York. With his shoulder-length, taffy-blonde hair, a flowing walrus mustache, and a puppy-dog physicality, Seymour seems like a natural man, one who follows his instincts rather than societal dictates. He is an unregenerate hippie who has a job he enjoys; it doesn't demand a lot of him and it pays the rent. Otherwise, he is unconcerned with material things or status, happily doing what he wants without demands from anyone other than the people whose cars he parks.

But his after-work activities suggest loneliness. He goes to a greasy spoon, where he gets into a conversation—nearly an argument—with a raving fellow diner named Morgan Morgan (the ineffable Timothy Carey). At one point, they compare their movie heroes: Seymour favors Humphrey Bogart, while Morgan stumps for Wallace Beery. But Morgan is merely a late-night ranter, happy to have someone to engage with, if only to blow off a little steam.

Seemingly as a form of self-amusement, Seymour makes the round of bars, trying to engage strange—and better-dressed—women with the opening gambit, "Don't you remember me?" as though anyone could forget his shaggy, gangling presence. He almost starts a fight in one bar (narrowly escaping after challenging a large black man), then is physically tossed out of a second tavern moments after making his come-on to a woman sitting at the counter (played by future folk-singing star Holly Near). Even as he is lying on the ground outside, she follows him out and goes home with him.

It's hard to tell if it is this particular night's adventures, the cold weather, or a simple case of wanderlust, but in the next scene, Seymour turns up at his mother's house for dinner, carrying an enormous bouquet of roses. His mother (played by John's mother, Katherine Cassavetes) kvells over him, offers him dinner, then asks why he looks troubled.

"I'm going to California," he tells her.

The scene cuts to the airplane. Seymour has the window seat in a row with a mother and her little girl. The mother is berating the child for not eating her carrots, and Seymour comes to the rescue, picking up the carrot and doing a Bugs Bunny impression to rescue the child from her harridan of a parent. In Los Angeles he rents an apartment on what appears to be a freeway frontage road and we see him footloose on the Los Angeles streets, still alone but now in a climate where he can at least hang out in a T-shirt.

The story then shifts to Minnie Moore (Gena Rowlands), who is first seen riding a Los Angeles city bus. Single, closing in on forty, she is enjoying a girls' night out with a work colleague, Florence (Elsie Ames, Cassel's mother-in-law). They sit through a showing of *Casablanca*, then go to Florence's apartment, where they discover that Florence doesn't really have anything to eat or drink, other than wine.

As they drink, they discuss sex and the movies. Minnie wonders whether the desire for sex, for intimacy, diminishes with age—but the much-older Florence says, no, it doesn't. Minnie then begins to talk about how movies make suckers out of the audience by depicting romance as the norm in life, rather than a happy accident: "The movies are a conspiracy," she decides. You only find that kind of romance in the movies.

Slightly tipsy, Minnie stumbles down the stairs to a taxi, then ambles into her apartment, where she is startled to find that she is not alone. It is her married lover, Jim (played by Cassavetes, in an uncredited role). When she tells him to get out, that she doesn't want to see him, he hauls off and slaps her—four times. To calm down, he walks into the other room and mixes drinks, bringing her one. But she attacks him, slapping and then punching him. He lets her, as she cries and tells him she hates him. But by the time he leaves, she has been appeased.

Jim goes home; it is morning, and he has obviously been out all night. His wife sits angrily at the kitchen table, drinking and smoking a cigarette despite the early hour. When, in trying to make innocuous small talk, he compliments her on her bathrobe and asks whether it's new, she hisses, "No," and stalks out, as their kids wander in and start to make breakfast. As Jim chats with the kids about the game the night before, one of the boys comes rushing in to tell him, "Dad, it's Mom—she's on the bathroom floor and she's crying."

Florence, meanwhile, has called a friend to take Minnie to lunch, which angers Minnie, but there's nothing she can do because her date is there. The man who comes to pick her up at the art museum where she works is Zelmo Swift (Val Avery), who immediately puts her off by telling her how charming she is. She finally says, "Let's go to lunch," and he drives her to a restaurant, where Seymour Moskowitz parks their car.

Once inside, Zelmo starts by trying to be polite: "So, Minnie, tell me about yourself," he says.

Minnie, still wearing a massive pair of sunglasses as though they were protective goggles shielding her from Zelmo's aura, replies, "I can't." So Zelmo tries to guess about her background, which only makes her edgy. The small talk continues uneasily until he tells her again that she's a very lovely person and says, "Let's drink to something. What should we drink to?"

Minnie says, "Let's drink to happiness. Let's drink to your happiness."

He begins a torrent of babble about why he doesn't go out much ("I'm actually scared of women," he says with a note of hostility), how easy it is for him to make money, and how little regard he has for it. He explains his various insecurities to her, though she remains unresponsive.

Then, ignoring her mood, he tells her what a good listener she is: "You're very easy to talk to," he says. "You look like you care about me."

She still doesn't respond, and he takes that lack of response for interest. Finally, he blurts, "You know what my trouble is? I've got hair down my back and down my chest and on my arms. But not on my legs—my legs are smooth."

She puts her sunglasses back on and tells him she's going to order the veal piccata. He all but shouts, "I don't know why I can't get the feeling across to you. I can't get you to feel what I'm feeling. It's very hard."

She finally says, "Zelmo, I just want you to know that I have absolutely no personal interest in you. I really just wanted to have lunch."

"What is it with you blondes?" Zelmo explodes, "You all have some Swedish suicide impulse?"

They get up to leave, and Zelmo continues to berate Minnie as Seymour brings the car. Zelmo stalks to the car and drives away without her. Seymour offers to get her a cab, only to be interrupted by Zelmo, who comes back to abuse Minnie some more, calling her a whore. Seymour springs to her defense, wrestling and fighting with Zelmo in the parking lot, then grabbing Minnie and making a getaway in Seymour's pickup truck.

They drive to Pink's hot dog stand, an L.A. landmark, where Seymour licks his wounds, celebrates his triumphs, and buys Minnie lunch. But Minnie is too much in shock, both from the assault on her dignity by Zelmo and from her rescue by this unlikely Lancelot.

She finally gets up and walks off, leaving an angry Seymour nursing her hot dog as well as his. He follows her, first on foot, then in the truck, looking for a thank you. He even drives up on the sidewalk to chase her, pulling her into his truck and arguing with her before he drops her at the museum.

Minnie's day goes from bad to worse: Late getting back to the museum, she hears from Florence that her boss was looking for her. And then Florence adds, "Also, Jim is here."

Out in the museum gallery, Minnie encounters Jim, who introduces her to what appears to be a ten-year-old boy: his son. Jim tells her his wife has attempted suicide; to prove that he is serious about ending his affair, he has brought his son to meet the woman that he is giving up. Infuriated, she slaps Jim, who can only mutter, "I keep remembering the laughs we had."

She arrives home to find Seymour waiting for her. They go out for a bite to eat but leave the restaurant when he argues with the waitress. He takes her to a drive-in, offering opinions on everything that crosses his path.

Minnie tells him she likes the fact that he speaks about practical things—money, food, cars—and he tells her, "I talk about everything except what I want to talk about." But he flies off the handle, telling her how crazy she makes him, how beautiful she is, and how he dislikes her superior attitude. He angrily drops her at home, drives away, and then goes and picks up another girl (Elizabeth Deering, Cassel's wife), for what he realizes afterward is a meaningless one-nighter, given his growing feelings for the icy Minnie.

The next day he goes back to Minnie's, and she finally opens up to him, telling him, "I'm having trouble being myself." Even as she begins to list reasons why they are unsuited for each other, they start kissing, and he carries her to the bedroom. Later, after they've made love, she dresses quietly and sneaks out to a nearby ice cream parlor, where she calls him. He shows up, angry at having been walked out on, unsure whether to take her gesture as rudeness or rejection. But he is won over when the hot fudge sundae she preordered arrives at the table shortly after he sits down.

They drive around Los Angeles in his truck (to the soundtrack accompaniment of "The Blue Danube Waltz," perhaps an ironic comment on Stanley Kubrick's use of it in 2001). But then she tells him that she can't imagine their future and that she might be too old for a relationship. Seymour tells her to stop thinking so much and just feel.

He drives her to the Palomino, a country-western club, where Seymour wants to dance. She refuses, fearing she'll make a fool of herself. So he switches on the car radio, finds a station playing big-band music, and dances with her in the parking lot. They dip—and kiss tenderly.

It is a sweet moment, one that is spoiled when, walking to the club, they run into a pair of friends of Minnie's from work, who are there slumming. She talks to them but doesn't introduce Seymour—the obvious misfit of the group—then apologizes to him afterward, making the excuse that she couldn't remember their names. The angry Seymour stalks off, leaving Minnie to get a ride home from her friends.

But Seymour is waiting at her front door and gets into a punch-up with Minnie's businessman escort (played by Jack Danskin), who is much

larger and gives Seymour a thorough drubbing. What's worse, as the inde-
fatigable Seymour rises to fight once more, he accidentally punches Minnie in the jaw, knocking her out.

The two of them wind up in Minnie's apartment, nursing their wounds
and arguing about their future. He is desperate for her to see how right they
are together; she wants to hear none of it. Finally, in a last-ditch attempt to
prove his love to her, Seymour grabs a scissors and, threatening to kill himself, accidentally snips off a large chunk of his massive mustache. Momentarily in shock, he plunges forward and snips off the rest of it. When he
threatens to clip off his ponytail as well—a different kind of suicide—she
stops him and begins kissing him.

They call their mothers and, in the next scene, take them to dinner to
meet for the first time. Minnie's mother (played by Gena's mother, Lady
Rowlands) is reserved but friendly; Seymour's mother, however, is loud
and pushy, sizing Minnie up verbally ("Oh, Seymour," she says with audible surprise, "she's got a good body and a good face"), then expressing
shock when Minnie admits they've known each other only four days.

After an uncomfortable silence, Minnie's mother tells a story about
how much Minnie resembled Shirley Temple as a girl, then asks Seymour
what he does for a living—and looks surprised when he rhapsodizes
about parking cars. Finally Seymour's mother comes right out and asks:
Why would a woman like Minnie ever want to marry a loser like her son?
"She could do very well marrying some normal man," she observes. But
the wedding goes on—though the minister (played by Gena's brother,
David Rowlands) can't remember Minnie's name and has to pause in the
middle of the vows to check a cheat sheet in his pocket. Which sets both
the bride and groom to giggling uncontrollably. (Supposedly, something
similar happened during John and Gena's wedding.)

The scene then jumps forward a couple of years to a backyard birthday
party: Seymour wearing a kid's Indian headdress and with his mustache
fully regrown, and Minnie and their mothers rollicking in the backyard with
a group of young children, at least a couple of which appear to be theirs.
And as a good-timey song by Bo Harwood floats across the soundtrack, the
dialogue-free party scene ends as the credits come up.

Like all of Cassavetes' films, scenes begin and end in what would be
the middle of the scene in a more conventional film. There are a number
of scenes filmed at night, in which visibility is spotty, but Cassavetes didn't
care, as long as the feeling of the scene came across.

The film lives and dies, of course, with Seymour Cassel and Gena Rowlands. Rowlands has the more nuanced role, though her Minnie goes

through as many rounds of fisticuffs and violence as Seymour does. She is slapped by her lover several times and becomes the aggressor, physically attacking Jim, Seymour, and even the businessman who comes to her rescue after the Palomino. It's apparent that violence is something new, or at least out of the ordinary, for Minnie, yet being surprised by it doesn't keep her from fighting back.

Seymour Moskowitz was a direct reflection of Seymour Cassel, but just as much a gloss on Cassavetes' own personality and his whirlwind courtship of Rowlands. It had been nearly as sudden, their personalities almost as disparate as Seymour and Minnie, his overwhelming feeling overcoming her reticence.

Then there was Seymour's wardrobe. He favored T-shirts, jeans, and sneakers, a uniform that advertised a lack of seriousness. Yet Cassavetes himself had been transformed by California; where he once favored suits, ties, and sport coats, he now threw on whatever happened to be handy. He could dress up for an occasion; otherwise, he didn't give much thought to the way he looked.

Cassavetes drew on Cassel's past and his personality in writing the character: Rather than creating a laid-back long-hair, Moskowitz is a high-intensity hippie who tends to be volatile and spikes big energy surges. He is not afraid to denounce a phony to his face, another trait of Cassel's. It is a full-throttle performance, played with an excitable energy in almost every scene. Moskowitz goes off half-cocked all of the time, and Cassel's performance makes him someone whose intensity can't help but grate on people.

Minnie and Moskowitz has unusual rhythms and tones that slip like mercury from pathos to comedy to emotionally intense confrontations. Though Cassavetes brings the film to its eventual happy ending, he shows all the cul-de-sacs down which this relationship might have vanished had these two headstrong lovers not grabbed hold of the situation and hung on. He shows all the reasons they are wrong for each other, then decides that the heart can trump the brain.

Thirty-two

Minnie and Moskowitz 2

T imothy Agoglia Carey was a formidable actor in every way. Standing 6-foot-5, he had a hulking presence and a booming voice, even as a young man. Sweet if eccentric in private, he was a fearlessly scene-stealing actor, with large, dark-rimmed eyes that could flare with hints of madness until he looked like a spooked horse.

Though given to extra weight in later life, he was just plain burly in his thirties and forties, when he did his most memorable acting work. His elongated face gave his broad grin a demonic quality; if Carey was in a scene, no matter how little he was doing, you would be looking at him. He lived perpetually, inventively in the moment, which made him an ideal Cassavetes actor.

Carey had broken into movies as an extra on *Ace in the Hole*, eventually talking his way into a couple of lines after confronting director Billy Wilder. That was 1951. By 1953, Carey was playing heavies in Hollywood, in films such as *White Witch Doctor*, *The Wild One*, *East of Eden*, and Stanley Kubrick's *The Killing*.

But he also developed a reputation for unusual acting choices on screen, often to the surprise of the actors he was working with. At one point, while filming a scene with Marlon Brando on *The Wild One*, Carey shook up a bottle of beer before he popped the top and the foam squirted Brando in the face. Brando was not amused.

"I've been fired from several shows," Carey said. "I'm not proud of it but I do hold the all-time record. I wasn't trying to upstage anyone. I just wanted to do it for the good of the show. Sometimes I'd overdo it maybe. Sometimes I didn't do exactly what the director wanted. I try so hard, you know. To me, it's like the last film I'm gonna make and I want it to be the best."

Kubrick remembered Carey's towering presence (in *The Killing*, Carey snarled as he shot at horses with a sniper's rifle) and cast him as the ill-fated Private Maurice Ferol, a scapegoat who faced the firing squad for something he didn't do, in *Paths of Glory*. Early on, the operatic Carey decided that Ferol would be a sniveler and played him to the hilt; Kubrick obviously approved because Carey gave a "Wow—who is *that* guy?" performance and Kubrick used much of it. But Carey's methods upset his co-stars, including Kirk Douglas, the star of the film.

"Make this a good one," Kubrick muttered to Carey before one take, "because Kirk doesn't like it."

But Carey was bored playing villains. True, he had a large family to support and a mortgage on a home in El Monte. He even had a side business, training German shepherds for the police and military. He needed some other outlet for creative expression, as an actor and beyond. "I was tired of seeing movies that were supposedly controversial," he said. "I wanted to do something that really was controversial."

So he decided to make a movie of his own: *The World's Greatest Sinner*, in which he is an insurance salesman turned messianic politician, playing rock 'n' roll in a gold lamé suit a la Elvis. It was absurdist, overheated, and extremely weird for its time: Shooting began in 1958, but Carey couldn't get it finished and released for four years. The *Hollywood Reporter* called it "an apparent waste of time and money with very limited commercial appeal." Even the film's composer—an unknown named Frank Zappa—went on *The Steve Allen* show and referred to it as "the world's worst film."

John Cassavetes caught a screening of *Sinner* in 1962, even as he despaired of ever getting a chance to make another film of his own. He was excited by Carey's raw emotion, by his grandiose style, and his fearless over-the-top quality. After the screening, he approached the much-larger Carey, who stood nearly a foot taller than Cassavetes, and told him how much he liked the film: "It has the brilliance of Eisenstein," John enthused. A friendship was born that lasted to the end of Cassavetes' life.

"John told me about the time he brought Tim to meet a studio person," Martin Scorsese recalled. "He was going to help Tim get a job. Tim put a tie on and John said, 'Tim, don't overdo it. Just say yes and no and we'll get you the job.' It was a ground-floor office—and Tim scared the executive so much that he leapt out the window."

Over the years, Cassavetes lent Carey equipment and money. Perpetually in precarious financial straits because of his devotion to his own films, Carey knew Cassavetes as a benefactor who could be called upon for help. Richard Kaye, Cassavetes' assistant at the time, recalled the time Carey came into the office and said, "I need $6,000 or they're going to take my house."

Cassavetes was in Europe, filming *Brass Target*, but Kaye managed to track him down by phone. "Tell Andy Maree to give him the money," Cassavetes said, referring to his accountant.

Early on, Cassavetes learned a lesson about visiting Carey at his home. On one such trip, Carey had insisted that Cassavetes don the large, padded suit worn by attack dog trainers. Then he set one of his dogs on Cassavetes, offering the encouraging words, "It's not you—he just hates that suit," as the snarling beast assaulted the director.

Eventually John created a pair of acting roles for Carey, something not many directors were willing to do at that point. "It's amazing how people get so afraid and weak," Carey said. "I was up for a big part in *Bonnie and Clyde* but Arthur Penn took one look at me and almost fainted in my arms. He'd heard that I'd gotten into a punch-out with Elia Kazan on *East of Eden*. Which wasn't true."

As Cassavetes wrote *Minnie and Moskowitz*, he immediately thought of Carey to play Morgan Morgan, the coffee-shop Jeremiah who gets into a highly theatrical argument with Seymour Moskowitz. He wrote the role with Carey's bravura tendencies in mind, to give his innate theatricality some pathos by making him a down-on-his-luck character.

When he was working, Carey had a certain grandiosity about himself as well, perhaps as a defensive shield. It was often mistaken for arrogance or abrasiveness, but Cassavetes never had that problem with Carey.

Aware that Carey could be a handful, Cassavetes said to Ruban one day, "Want to know how to cure the guy?"

"Yeah, I'd rather do that than fight," Ruban replied.

"Get him a small trailer so he has someplace to go," Cassavetes recommended.

Which Ruban did—and Carey became a pussycat to work with. Ruban said, "He was so insecure, he was always on."

As they shot Carey's scenes, Cassavetes encouraged Carey to improvise—and he let loose. He was like a Beat poet spitting stream-of-consciousness verse, which Cassavetes filmed for hours.

When he finished shooting the scene, the diminutive director ran up to the grizzly-size Carey, wrapped his arms around him and said, "You made the film, Tim."

Al Ruban, meanwhile, had agreed to produce *Minnie and Moskowitz*, but only after a direct appeal from Ned Tanen. Ruban had not spoken to Cassavetes since their blow-up over the editing of *Husbands*.

For his meeting with Universal to pitch the film, Cassavetes took an unusual step: He called Universal executives Tanen and Daniel Selznick and invited them over to his office, in a refurbished motel across the street from the Universal lot. Then he had them sit down while his secretary, Elaine Kagan, read the entire script aloud to them. "Can you imagine anyone doing that today?" Kagan said. "We all sat there and I read it."

Once he had struck his deal with Universal, Cassavetes called Ruban, asking him to produce the film. But Ruban was still angry, so he put him off with a plea of needing time to think about it. The next thing he knew, Ruban was on the receiving end of a phone call from Tanen himself, asking if Ruban wouldn't reconsider.

"John is here and he gave us the script and he's going to do the picture," Tanen told him. "But I'd be much more comfortable if you were on it, too."

It was flattery, calculated to play on Ruban's ego and vanity and it worked. But the reasoning was solid in hiring him: Ruban knew how Cassavetes worked and functioned well in keeping him focused and moving forward. Ruban was the one who made the trains run on time.

"Al was the voice of reason," Elaine Kagan said. "Al was the only person who could ever say no to John."

Matthew Cassel, Seymour's son who grew up on Cassavetes' sets and wound up working on his *Love Streams* crew, said, "Al took care of everything so John didn't have to worry about it."

But there was a certain friction between Ruban and Sam Shaw, a tension that Ruban now admits was probably generated by his own insecurities.

"I had a lot of trouble with Sam, but it was because of me," he said. "I felt like he was encroaching on my territory, foolishly. Everybody liked Sam. He could gain entrée to any place. He was this very good friend of John who was knowledgeable about the business. But I resented him. You had to talk to him for ten minutes before he would reveal himself or the depth of his intelligence."

Ruban was the "get-it-done" guy, skilled at organizing the nuts and bolts of the physical and fiscal part of making the movie. Having been there from the start, having shot large chunks of *Faces* himself, Ruban was well schooled in Cassavetes' whims and sudden desires, capable of saying, "John, that will cost too much," if necessary, to keep a production on track.

By the time he finished shooting *Minnie and Moskowitz*, Cassavetes was on his third cinematographer, having fired the first two.

Cassavetes turned to Ruban, begging him to shoot the film. But this was a union picture and Ruban was not a member of the cinematographers' union. Nor was he likely to become one.

After shooting *Faces* as a nonunion project, Ruban had been recruited to join the union, the American Society of Cinematographers, but only if he would apologize for doing the nonunion work on *Faces*.

Ruban thought to himself, "Screw it—I can't take back what I've done. I'm proud of what I've done." So he refused—and still wasn't union. But this Universal production most definitely was.

So they turned to Michael Margulies, a staff camera operator at Universal who was one of the younger men on the staff at the age of thirty-five. Where Arthur Ornitz and Alric Edens, the first two cinematographers, had been of the old school, Margulies was new enough to bring the kind of flexibility to the job that Cassavetes craved.

"I had long hair and a beard," Margulies recalled, so the Universal brass assumed he was a free-thinker, which was how they viewed Cassavetes.

The standard approach to the job of director of photography, or cinematographer, involved a decided division of labor: The d.p. would light the scene, using the lighting to create a mood or underscore a dramatic point. The camera operator worked with d.p. and the director to plot out the camera's lenses, movements, and the like.

But in independent films, often the camera operator does both jobs—setting the lights and handling the camera. That was particularly true with Cassavetes' crew: "It's loosey-goosey and the cameraman was often an operator," Margulies said. "You cross the line back and forth in the indies, with electricians and grips helping to move things."

Having taken a guerrilla approach to his early films, Cassavetes still wanted someone with Ruban's understanding that the actor was the most important thing in any given scene—not the camera. What Cassavetes wanted was an operator, not a d.p.—someone who could keep the actors in frame, rather than forcing them to hit marks and key lights. That's what he found in Margulies—and what he was always looking for on his films.

The third camera operator on the film, Margulies had been hired about halfway through production. He admitted that when he saw the finished film, "I could tell in a couple of scenes the difference in photography. But all in all, I think it worked, even with having three d.p.s."

In what would become a regular habit, Cassavetes cast family members and friends in small roles.

"Everyone came in prepared," recalled Kevin Donnelly, the first a.d. "They all knew their stuff. They were all either family or friends of John. That makes it easy to work for him. Nobody would give him trouble or argue about the direction of a scene or take. He'd tell them to do something and they'd do it."

Cassavetes waited until the day that Rowlands was to shoot Minnie's first scene with Jim, her married lover—the scene in which he slaps her several times—before springing it on Rowlands: He would be playing Jim himself (though he didn't take an acting credit for the role).

Once they were on the set in Minnie's apartment, they began rehearsing the slap. Cassavetes hauled back and let fly, swinging his open hand hard enough that it seemed as though he had really connected with Rowlands' face when she crumpled to the floor.

"The secret is that the person who's doing the hitting is in the foreground and he pulls his hand back to the camera," Rowlands said. "It's not the forward motion of the slap you see. His hand doesn't touch you but, as it looks like he's hitting you, you have to snap your head back. At the same time, what I did was an old stage trick of clapping my hands loudly. You don't need that on film because you can always put the sound in. But it's just fun to do.

"So we did it and the crew threw down the lights and anything else they were holding and rushed and grabbed John by both arms. That's how realistic it looked to them."

"He got a good stunt slap," Margulies remembered. "It looked realistic."

Cassavetes was laughing and struggling against the crew members who held him while others helped Rowlands to her feet. Rowlands, keeping her smile to herself, milked the moment for suspense, moving slowly and unsteadily as though she'd just suffered a serious blow.

Cassavetes said, "Gena didn't get up off the floor after the take. She just lay there. The crew gave me the worst looks after that scene."

As Rowlands later joked, "If we ever get divorced, I'm taking that scene to court."

Donnelly, the assistant director, recalled, "I'm not sure he hit her hard but it made noise. It wasn't just one take; it was several takes. They were very good working together."

Indeed, Rowlands said later that, from *Faces*, she'd learned how to work with her husband as actor and director, putting the personal aside during the shooting day.

"I learned to keep the intimate relationship separate from the professional one, except in one respect," she said. "If you know someone loves you, then you trust him not to sell you out. You take risks for him you might not take with someone else."

But Cassavetes wasn't above pitting actors against each other to give their scenes a new dynamic. As they were shooting some of the early scenes between Seymour and Minnie, Cassavetes took Cassel aside and whispered, "Don't do anything for her. Don't open a car door—nothing. Believe me, she will kill you. Don't do anything for her."

Then he walked over to Rowlands, who was going through her own preparations for the scene, and challenged her: "You know, Seymour is stealing every scene from you. What are you doing?" And suddenly Minnie became an even more active character than she'd previously been.

Shooting mostly in sequence meant that, at the end of the picture, Seymour Cassel—who had been growing his mustache almost since he finished shooting *Faces* a half dozen years earlier—would have to cut off his beloved facial hair.

When it came time to shoot the wedding, Cassavetes brought in his old friend John Finnegan, who played Moskowitz's best man in the scene. The sequence was meant to be comic, with Seymour's obvious nervousness undermined when the minister forgot the bride's name and had to peek at a card in his pocket. The bride and groom start giggling uncontrollably on camera, which didn't involve much acting, Finnegan said.

As Cassavetes was shooting scenes at Minnie's place on location at the Villa Elaine apartments on Vine Street in a bad part of Hollywood, he got a call from Martin Scorsese. Scorsese was in Los Angeles, supervising the editing of a rock concert tour movie called *Medicine Ball Caravan*. He was lonely and sickly, plagued by asthma.

He'd spent time with Cassavetes since arriving in L.A. but this call was different. An earthquake had shaken Scorsese's faith in the apartment where he was living, he told Cassavetes, asking if the filmmaker had any suggestions.

"Well, do you know the Villa Elaine Apartments?" Cassavetes asked him. "We're shooting there. You can go sleep there."

"We hired him to sleep on the set that was Gena's apartment," Elaine Kagan recalled. "He was like our security guard."

As Scorsese later recalled, "It was the most scary experience of my life.

I don't know what all was going on around me. But John would take care of me. If I had a personal problem, I'd call him."

When the editing job on *Medicine Ball Caravan* ended, Scorsese was out of work. Harvey Keitel, who had acted in *Who's That Knocking at My Door*, had moved out to L.A. to try his luck as an actor and was living with Scorsese. Scorsese was too busy looking for work to pay attention to the script he'd been working on, an expansion of *Who's That Knocking's* themes called *Season of the Witch* after the Donovan song.

"So John said, 'Come work as the sound-effects editor on *Minnie and Moskowitz*,'" Scorsese said. "I was basically hanging around, following him. He would be dictating letters, cutting the sound effects at night. I remember, in one scene, he needed the sound of punches. So he was punching himself and I put the mike on him. It was like he was the master."

Cassavetes wasn't just encouraging; he actively engaged in the role of mentor: "The tolerance he had for young people," said Scorsese, who was not yet thirty, of Cassavetes, who was in his early forties. "He corrected you, guided you, cajoled you."

At one point, as Scorsese was watching Cassavetes edit a scene of *Minnie and Moskowitz*, the acolyte grew impatient and said, "Come on, John— get to the point of the scene."

Cassavetes fixed him with one of those piercing smiles—the kind where he seemed to be looking into your very soul—and said, "Never!"

Early on in Scorsese's nine-month tenure on *Medicine Ball*, he had been introduced to Roger Corman, the king of the exploitation films, who gave a start to everyone from Jack Nicholson and Peter Fonda to Jonathan Demme and James Cameron. They had hit it off, and Corman told Scorsese about a sequel he wanted to make to his film *Bloody Mama*, a gangster film about Depression-era fugitive Ma Barker (Shelley Winters) that featured a young Robert De Niro as one of her Oedipal sons.

Scorsese believed Corman was expressing an interest in having him direct—and then didn't hear anything further about it in the subsequent year: "I figured I'd never hear from him again," Scorsese said.

Almost a year later, Scorsese was working in Cassavetes' office when the phone rang and Elaine Kagan answered. It was Scorsese's agent: "We have a picture for Scorsese," he told her. Kagan, who was used to Scorsese as someone who hung around the office and was a glorified gofer, laughed and said, "Yeah, sure," and hung up.

The movie was *Boxcar Bertha*, starring David Carradine and Barbara Hershey, and Corman wanted Scorsese to film it in twenty-four shooting days, essentially four six-day weeks, at scale. The easily flustered Scorsese went to Cassavetes' house for a pep talk before he left for the location shoot in Arkansas. But Arkansas might as well have been Uranus to the New York-centric Scorsese, who said, "John gave me confidence, just being around him for a couple of hours. And I went and shot the picture."

When Scorsese finished the film, he set up screenings around Hollywood for friends, including Jay Cocks and his wife, actress Verna Bloom, when they came to town: "They were mortified by it," Scorsese recalled.

Other friends trashed the film to him as well. But Scorsese tried to rally his own confidence, telling himself that this wasn't going to be his signature film—that it was one step on the path to making the movies he wanted to do, which he figured would happen eventually. Then he showed it to Cassavetes, who told him eventually wasn't soon enough.

After the screening, Cassavetes took Scorsese back to his office at Universal. He smiled, then started laughing and affectionately embraced Scorsese. The laughter subsided as he disengaged and held Scorsese by the shoulders at arm's length and looked him in the eye.

"You just spent a year of your life making a piece of shit," Cassavetes told him as gently as one can say such a thing. "You shouldn't be making films like that. You should be making a film like *Who's That Knocking*. You got something you want to do? You've gotta do it. It needs to be rewritten? Rewrite the goddam thing."

In fact, Scorsese was set to direct another exploitation film, *I Escaped from Devil's Island*, starring Jim Brown. Instead he turned his attention to finding the money to make *Mean Streets*.

Though he mostly let Cassavetes make his film the way he wanted to, Ned Tanen still represented the oppressor, the studio, to Cassavetes. Perhaps it was Universal's early attempt to convince Cassavetes that he should cast Jack Nicholson as Seymour Moskowitz, rather than the still relatively unknown Cassel. Whatever triggered it, Tanen and Cassavetes had developed a poisonous relationship by the end of the production.

"It was Tanen's project and he was supportive in the beginning," Ruban remembered. "But then it was handed off to another guy because he and John got into it over something."

Cassavetes clashed with Tanen and Universal over the film's posters and ads. Universal's design featured Cassel and Rowlands, with the screen split between their faces: Rowlands, on the bottom, was right-side up, but Seymour, the top of his head blending into the top of hers because of their similar hair color, was upside down.

The studio dug in its heels; Cassavetes wound up printing up posters with his own money, featuring a photo by Sam Shaw of Cassel, Rowlands, and John Finnegan standing at the altar. He also paid for a two-page ad in the *New York Times*.

"Nobody tells John what to do," John Finnegan recalled. "He had a run-in with Universal about the poster, so he made a bunch of them and we went around nailing them up. We'd go into Hamburger Hamlet and put them in the ladies' room."

Ruban knew they would need a friend in high places if the film was going to succeed. He felt that it paid to mend fences with Tanen. Even though they'd finished shooting a week early and turned in the finished film three months ahead of schedule, Universal wasn't crazy about it.

The studio planned to dump *Minnie and Moskowitz* into theaters at Christmas with minimal advertising support. Instead, it would devote the bulk of its marketing budget to its Oscar hopeful, *Mary, Queen of Scots*, starring Vanessa Redgrave and Glenda Jackson, which was going to be its big holiday movie.

Hoping to spark a reconciliation with Tanen, who could potentially salvage the film before it was abandoned, Ruban convinced Cassavetes to let him invite Tanen to the office to smooth things over. Tanen came to their offices and was sitting with Ruban when Cassavetes came in. Almost immediately, Cassavetes tore into Tanen, accusing him of trying to sabotage the film: "He jumped right up his ass," Ruban said. "I was in shock. I faulted myself later because I never stood up to John on that. I should have said, 'That's enough of that.' I didn't take a stand and it still bothers me."

So much for studio support of the film.

If the point hadn't already been made, it was driven home shortly afterward, after a preview screening of the film in San Jose, attended by Lew Wasserman and the Universal brass. After the film, Wasserman remarked to Cassavetes, "It's a wonderful movie. Too bad you don't have stars in it." Translation: No stars = no marketing support.

When the film opened on December 22, 1971, at Cinema 2 on New York's Upper East Side, Cassavetes and Ruban walked over to the theater to see what kind of business they were doing. To their delight, there was a line around the block. But the line turned out to be for people waiting to see Stanley Kubrick's new film *A Clockwork Orange*, which was playing in the theater next door. There were twenty-two people in the 150-seat auditorium where *Minnie and Moskowitz* was playing.

Still, Seymour Cassel was ecstatic with the film: "If I never made another picture I'd still be proud of myself as an actor because of *Faces* and *Minnie and Moskowitz*," he said at the time. "By the time this movie is over, people not only like my character but they admire his independence. Guys with a lot more money and influence than this parking lot attendant Moskowitz grudgingly admit, I think, that he's got a great sense of freedom and the ability to enjoy life."

"*Faces, Husbands* and *Minnie and Moskowitz* form one of the most original trilogies in the contemporary American cinema," Jonas Mekas enthused in the *Village Voice*. "All three films explore a rarely touched area of the middle-aged man and woman. Cassavetes documents their emotions, their thoughts, their relationships. A unique chronicle of the contemporary average American middle-class man and woman emerges."

The film had other critical admirers, including Jay Cocks, who called it Cassavetes' "lightest, most accessible film and one of the few movies in recent times that could be called joyous." Wanda Hale in the *Daily News*, called it "a sonnet to his wife, Gena Rowlands," and said that it "converted a sad subject, loneliness, into a human, very funny comedy." Still, her compliments seemed more back-handed once she referred to it as "the funniest home movie ever made."

But the same critics who had dismissed *Husbands* were even more merciless regarding *Minnie and Moskowitz*. Stanley Kauffmann called it "by far John Cassavetes' worst film," going so far as to say, "I simply can't share Cassavetes' estimate of Gena Rowlands (his wife) as actress and star." *Variety* referred to it as "an oppressive and irritating film in which a shrill and numbing hysteria of acting and direction soon kills any empathy for the loneliness of the main characters."

And Vincent Canby lamented, "I wish I liked *Minnie and Moskowitz* more than I do. It's as open and vulnerable as someone who tells an elaborate ethnic joke, in an accent that isn't very authentic with a point that isn't very funny . . . I never laughed very much and only felt slight, distant tremors of the joy that, I assume, rocked everyone connected with the movie during its production."

As he did press interviews for the film, Cassavetes looked at his own pre-marriage days: "Before I met Gena, I was a bachelor going out and torturing people. When I saw her, that was it. One of the great things about America is that when two people fall in love, it erases all that's gone before. Love's the great eraser."

The film touched a nerve with its portrayal of a single woman at a time of growing awareness of the feminist movement—not as sharply as *A Woman Under the Influence* would three years later, but enough to cause further discussion of movies that explored women's issues as a serious subject.

Coming out of an early screening, Rowlands was approached by a young woman in her early twenties—"marriageable age," as Rowlands put it.

"Oh, I loved the picture," the young woman told her.

"Great, glad you did," Rowlands replied.

"But you should never have left the first guy," the young woman offered.

Rowlands looked at her, then asked, "You mean the married guy that beat me up and betrayed me and brought his son to the place where I worked and humiliated him and me and his wife and everybody else in sight?"

"Oh yeah," the young woman said, dismissing the behavior, "but he was so attractive."

As Rowlands later recalled, "My blood ran cold. That was an unusual reaction, but it was not the only time I'd heard it. When this picture came out, there hadn't been a long tradition of single women—it was just beginning to present itself as an idea and a lifestyle."

A couple of years after Cassavetes' 1989 death, twenty years after its release, *Minnie and Moskowitz* was revived at the Utopia Theater, a Paris movie house that played it for a solid year to large audiences. In the middle of its run, Seymour Cassel happened to be in Paris and slipped into the Utopia one day after the lights went down, to watch the audience watch the film. As the credits rolled at the end, the audience applauded. Cassel stood there at the side of the theater, and all attention focused on him when the lights came up. Could it be? The real Seymour Moskowitz, there in the flesh?

"You really like the movie?" he asked—and the audience clapped again, even more passionately.

"They must have been shocked to see this guy standing there," he said later. "I thought, 'John would have loved this.'"

Thirty-three

A Woman Under the Influence

As 1972 began, John Cassavetes had released three films in four years—three films created under a variety of circumstances that he'd still managed to make his own way, mostly. With them, he had achieved a unified vision, focusing on the unexpected possibilities within us all, even in the supposedly sterile setting of middle-class suburbia.

But in the industry *Faces* was still seen as a fluke—at best, an art-house hit. For all the publicity it had garnered, *Husbands* hadn't earned its money back. And *Minnie and Moskowitz* had been abandoned by Universal. No studio was clamoring for the chance to make Cassavetes' next film, and Cassavetes had just about had it with the studios.

"You can do well in Hollywood as long as you don't kid yourself that they want creative ventures—and I kidded myself," Cassavetes said. "You cannot work for a studio and make a personal film."

It would be three years between *Minnie* and *A Woman Under the Influence*. Initially Cassavetes thought he would make a different film after *Minnie and Moskowitz*, announcing "Two Days in Rochester" shortly before the release of *Minnie*. The film would star Ben Gazzara and Seymour Cassel and was meant as a follow-up to *Husbands*. But the funds never materialized, despite a number of readings. So Cassavetes decided he had to make *A Woman Under the Influence* and do it independently. Cassavetes would have to put his own—and Peter Falk's—money on the line to get it made.

Cassavetes' American Academy of Dramatic Arts portrait, 1950. Among the comments when he auditioned were "Latin type," "Short," "Sensitive temperament" and "fine intelligent boy."
Courtesy of AADA

When Cassavetes spotted Rowlands for the first time at AADA, he supposedly commented, "That's the girl I'm going to marry." Sam Shaw photographed them at their wedding on April 9, 1954 in New York. *Photo by Sam Shaw, Shaw Family Archives, Ltd. ©*

"And it's unrehearsed—guaranteed!" Agent Martin Baum got his clients Cassavetes and Sidney Poitier together to rehearse an audition scene for *Edge of the City*, but told director Martin Ritt that the actors had never met prior to reading for him. Amazed at their instant chemistry, Ritt cast Cassavetes in his biggest movie role to that time. *Sam Shaw, Shaw Family Archives©*

Cassavetes befriended *Life* magazine photographer Sam Shaw, who became his mentor—and photographed him extensively throughout his career, here capturing the intensity of the handsome young actor. *Sam Shaw, Shaw Family Archives, Ltd.* ©

Shadows: Seymour Cassel (left) was a former sailor and would-be actor who showed up at Cassavetes' theater workshop and stayed to work on the crew of *Shadows*. Cameraman Erich Kollmar (center) knew Cassavetes (right) from AADA—and was the only one with any experience operating a camera. *Larry Shaw, Shaw Family Archives, Ltd.* ©

Too Late Blues: Cassavetes hoped his film about a jazz musician would star Montgomery Clift and Gena. Instead, Paramount gave him Bobby Darin and Stella Stevens (who agreed to make the Elvis movie *Girls! Girls! Girls!* because Paramount promised her she would follow it with a film co-starring Clift). *Courtesy of Photofest*

A Child is Waiting: Given the tense relationship between Cassavetes and stars Burt Lancaster and Judy Garland, this light-hearted moment was probably more staged for the camera. *Courtesy of Photofest*

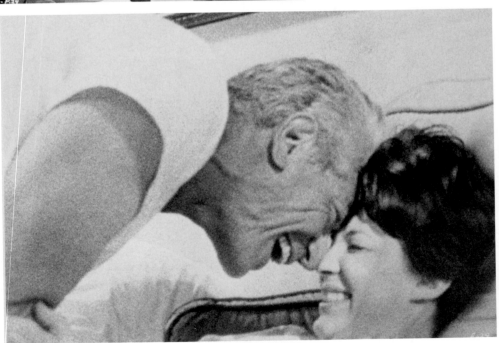

Faces: John Marley was a journeyman character actor whose career was ignited by his participation in *Faces*. Lynn Carlin had been Robert Altman's secretary when Altman and Cassavetes were both working on TV projects at Screen Gems in the mid-1960s—when Cassavetes decided to cast her in *Faces*. *Courtesy of Photofest*

The Dirty Dozen: Cassavetes always listed Robert Aldrich as his favorite among the directors he acted for. Though he was just one of more than a dozen in the ensemble, his performance earned Cassavetes an Oscar nomination as best supporting actor. *Courtesy of Photofest*

Cassavetes shares a quiet moment with young son Nick on location for *The Dirty Dozen*.
Sam Shaw, Shaw Family Archives, Ltd. ©

Rosemary's Baby: Robert Redford and Jack Nicholson were both considered for the duplicitous Guy Woodhouse role opposite Mia Farrow, but Cassavetes won it— and fought with director Roman Polanski on a regular basis. *Courtesy of Photofest*

Cassavetes (with Gena and son Nick in the background) made "Faces" with money from his own pocket because no one in Hollywood would touch him as a director. *Sam Shaw, Shaw Family Archives, Ltd.* ©

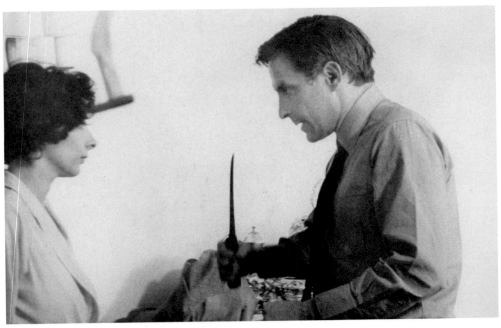

Husbands: Meta Shaw (left) gets a lesson in knife-wielding from Cassavetes before filming her scene as Ben Gazzara's wife. Cassavetes included the one wife because he knew he'd take flak if he never showed any of the spouses. *Sam Shaw, Shaw Family Archives, Ltd.* ©

Husbands: Sam Shaw captured this series of Gazzara, Cassavetes and Falk mugging during preproduction in New York. The trio developed an off-screen friendship during the film that lasted the rest of Cassavetes' life. *Sam Shaw, Shaw Family Archives, Ltd.* ©

Talking about *Husbands* later in his life, Cassavetes said, "I love men. We're so stupid." *Sam Shaw, Shaw Family Archives, Ltd.* ©

Ben Gazzara (right) had a auspicious start on Broadway in *End as a Man*, *Cat on a Hot Tin Roof*, and *Hat Full of Rain*, but like Peter Falk, felt that his career had stalled. *Husbands* rejuvenated his career and his passion for acting. *Larry Shaw, Shaw Family Archives, Ltd.* ©

Midway through filming *Husbands*, Peter Falk (right) was so frustrated with Cassavetes' refusal to explain anything that he told Cassavetes that he would never work with him as a director again. *Sam Shaw, Shaw Family Archives, Ltd.* ©

After screening Martin Scorsese's *Who's That Knocking at My Door*, Cassavetes told Scorsese that he thought it was better than *Citizen Kane* and became a mentor to the young filmmaker. L to R: *Time* magazine critic Jay Cocks; Scorsese; Cassavetes; actress Verna Bloom (Cocks' wife); and Sam Shaw. *Photo by David Gahr, courtesy of Martin Scorsese*

Individuality was at the core of Cassavetes' work. His films explored what diverse characters had in common as human beings, while celebrating the odd, entertaining and sometimes grating differences that make each of us unique.
Sam Shaw, Shaw Family Archives, Ltd. ©

Minnie & Moskowitz: Seymour Moskowitz was Cassavetes' gift to Seymour Cassel, who had become one of Cassavetes' best friends over the preceding decade and a half. The character of Moskowitz was an homage, incorporating parts of Cassel's personality and personal history. *Sam Shaw, Shaw Family Archives, Ltd.* ©

Actor Timothy Carey made a career of playing heavies and psychos, but found a patron in Cassavetes, who cast him in two films and offered artistic and financial support over the years for Carey's own film projects. *Sam Shaw, Shaw Family Archives, Ltd.* ©

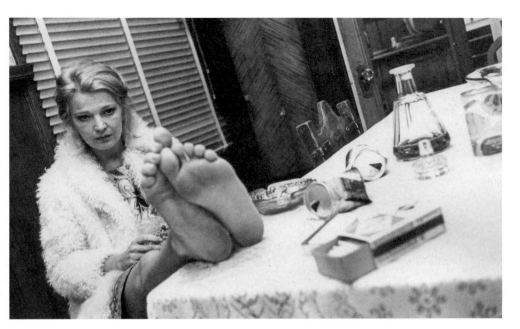

A Woman Under the Influence: Cassavetes originally wrote the script as a stage play for Rowlands. But when she read it, she told him the emotional toll of doing the play would be devastating: "I couldn't last two nights playing that and in a week I'd have to be hospitalized," she told him. *Sam Shaw, Shaw Family Archives, Ltd.* ©

A Woman Under the Influence: Cinematographer Mike Ferris (center, with Cassavetes and Falk) was still a rookie with a movie camera when Cassavetes fired Caleb Deschanel, director of photography on *Woman*, and replaced him with Ferris, one of Deschanel's assistants. Cassavetes launched Ferris into a career as a camera operator and d.p. which continues to this day. *Sam Shaw, Shaw Family Archives, Ltd.* ©

The Killing of a Chinese Bookie: Mike Ferris adjusts the camera for a shot during *Bookie*, as Cassavetes and producer Sam Shaw look on. Shaw argued with Cassavetes about the nudity and violence in the film; though it was set in a strip club, Cassavetes resisted because the nudity made him uncomfortable. *Richard Upper, Shaw Family Archives, Ltd.* ©

Opening Night: The film barely got a release; its only New York screenings were at the Museum of Modern Art (as part of retrospective) and at the 1988 New York Film Festival. (L to R: Zohra Lampert, Ben Gazzara, Paul Stewart and Gena Rowlands.) *Courtesy of Photofest*

Katherine and Nicholas Cassavetes, John's parents, both acted in John's films with his mother taking major supporting roles in *Minnie & Moskowitz* and *A Woman Under the Influence*. Sam Shaw, Shaw Family Archives, Ltd. ©

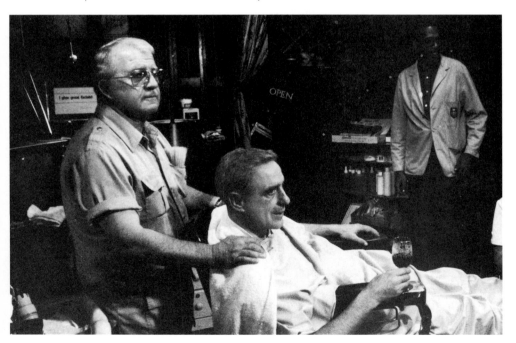

While he was finishing *Tempest* for Paul Mazursky, Cassavetes agreed to appear in *The Haircut*, a student film by AFI fellow Tamar Simon Hoffs. The short film was shot in a weekend and costarred Nicholas Colasanto (left) who shortly afterward became on of the stars of *Cheers*. *Photo courtesy of Tamar Simon Hoffs*

Gloria: Actor Juan (later John) Adames (left), then six, asked Cassavetes, "How many words will I learn?" when offered the juvenile lead in *Gloria*. When Cassavetes said, "Three-hundred," Adames took the role. *Larry Shaw, Shaw Family Archives, Ltd.* ©

By the time *Gloria* was finished, Cassavetes' health had started to worsen. By 1983, he had been diagnosed with cirrhosis of the liver, and was given less than a year, though he'd live until 1989. *Larry Shaw, Shaw Family Archives, Ltd.* ©

Jon Voight (left) played the male lead opposite Gena when Cassavetes mounted *Love Streams* by Ted Allan (right) on stage. When Voight said he would rather direct than act in the film version, Cassavetes said no and played Voight's role, as Rowlands' brother himself. *Sam Shaw, Shaw Family Archives, Ltd.* ©

Love Streams: John Finnegan (right), a friend of Cassavetes who pops up in many of his films, played the long-suffering cab driver who must chauffeur a menagerie of animals for Sarah Lawson (Gena Rowlands, left). Rowlands led the animals through the Cassavetes house for the camera: "We had a lot of poop in the place," she recalled. *Larry Shaw, Shaw Family Archives, Ltd.* ©

Big Trouble: When Andrew Bergman dropped out as director of the semi-sequel to *The In-Laws*, co-star Falk and studio chief Guy McElwaine offered the job to an ailing Cassavetes. Cassavetes finished the film with Alan Arkin (center), but said later, "God, I don't want this to be my last picture so I'll be known for this piece of shit." *Courtesy of Photofest*

John and Gena in the 1970s: She was devastated by his death in 1989. "Doctors are always saying, 'Now you must prepare yourself,' she said later. 'Yeah, how do you do that?'" *Larry Shaw, Shaw Family Archives, Ltd.* ©

Falk was flush with his earnings from *Columbo*, which had become a major hit and made Falk a TV star. Cassavetes even guest-starred in a 1972 episode, "Etude in Black," playing an orchestra conductor who murders his demanding mistress (Anjanette Comer) and is outsmarted by Falk's Lieutenant Columbo. The episode was directed by Nicholas Colasanto, who would become famous playing Coach on the early years of the TV hit *Cheers*.

The *Columbo* episode was his first exposure to the wave of the future: video playback, in which a video camera captures the same image as the film camera, so the director can see immediately whether the shot worked. Originally created by Jerry Lewis, it would become a staple of film production: "I don't want it on my film," Cassavetes said. "It would make me nervous."

Falk, meanwhile, had finally decided, after the *Husbands* publicity tour was completed, that he was willing to put himself through the Cassavetes wringer one more time. "I would like to do a film like *Husbands* again," Falk said. "I would be curious to know whether or not, if I did it again, I could be better."

For Cassavetes, *Woman* was about being caught in a marriage that doesn't fulfill the needs a woman thought marriage would satisfy: "She's a good woman fulfilling her end of the promise and not getting any reward for it," he said. "I think the way our world is structured, there is no room for women to have an education, an emotional education. I'm not saying that I would know how to give a woman an emotional education. But it is true that women do have problems being housewives, being married. And that is what interested me and everyone else who worked on the film. It was an exploration of the problems of women without really knowing what the answers are."

A Woman Under the Influence would be the start of a wave of films focusing on the lives of women and the roles society had carved out for them. Cassavetes' politics were all emotional, rather than social, but the film, along with its doppelganger by Martin Scorsese, *Alice Doesn't Live Here Anymore*, had an unexpected impact and audience appeal in 1974, at a point when the first feminist generation of baby boomers had left college and were confronting the realities of life.

Not that Cassavetes was courting that audience—just the opposite was true. "One of the reasons I made *Woman Under the Influence* is because I hate separatism in anything," he said. "Women's movements only spread distrust between people and move people further away from each other than they should be. I don't like people to be separate from me. I really like people to be accessible—not films so much, but people."

Woman still plays with as much raw intensity today as it did thirty years ago. It is bold and embarrassing and gripping, with a timelessly honest quality that compels you to watch and forces you to empathize.

The film opens with a quick blast of opera on the soundtrack and the sight of men in work clothes, hip deep in a watery trench, trudging home at the end of a day. The opera gives way to a hollow-sounding piano as the men change clothes and meet at a diner for beers. But their leader, Nick Longhetti (Peter Falk), the crew chief of this group of sewer workers, is already on the phone, fending off the efforts of his boss to bring his crew back to work to deal with a broken water main. Nick tells him he has an unbreakable date with his wife. He yells that there is no way he and his men are going to come back and work another shift and slams the phone down, to applause from his men. But the look on his face says that the choice already has been made for them.

At home, his wife Mabel (Gena Rowlands) is getting her three kids ready to spend a night with her mother (Lady Rowlands). But Mabel is frantic with worry, convinced something bad will happen while her kids are apart from her.

"I shouldn't let them go," she mutters to herself as her mother drives them away and she goes back into the house to wait for Nick. As the day fades into night, she changes clothes, smokes cigarettes, and listens to opera, in anticipation of her night with her husband.

Nick and his crew, however, are in raincoats, coping with a water gusher. One of his men asks him if he called his wife to tell her he wouldn't be home, and the frustrated Nick says, "How am I gonna call her?" When his colleague tries to tell him that Mabel "is a delicate, sensitive woman," Nick explodes: "Mabel is not crazy!"

By the time Nick calls to say he won't be home, Mabel has broken out the liquor and is sitting and drinking by herself. With no kids and now no husband, she walks to the neighborhood bars, finds one she likes and sits down next to a friendly-looking man at the counter.

As he buys her a drink, she says, "Do you know Nick stood me up?" More drinks eventually lead them to Mabel's front door. When she nearly collapses from drunkenness, he grabs her and starts dancing with her. But when he tries to kiss her, she pushes him away.

She awakens early the next morning to find this man—his name is Garson Cross (played by O. G. Dunn)—dressed and wandering around her home. "Nick?" she calls—and it all comes rushing back to her.

"Who's Nick?" the amiable Garson asks and Mabel, whether in denial or a momentary break with reality, snaps, "I'm not in the mood for games,

Nick. You're Nick Longhetti. I'm Mabel Longhetti." It's enough to freak out Garson, who makes a break for it. But Mabel, slipping further from reality for a moment, starts to panic: Where are her children, she cries as she races around the house.

Nick and his crew have been working all night, so Nick brings the men home for breakfast. He gets Mabel up from bed, and she gamely whips up spaghetti and sauce for a dozen people, then must sit around and make conversation with these men, when what she really wants—what she needs—is some time alone with her husband.

One of the men, Willie Johnson (Hugh Hurd), sings an opera aria and, to be friendly, Mabel tries to encourage one of the other men, Billy Tidrow (played by professional baseball player Leon "Daddy Wags" Wagner), to sing as well. When he demurs and she insists, Nick explodes at her, telling her to "get her ass down" and quit bugging the men.

Eventually the crew leaves and Mabel and Nick have a moment together, only to be interrupted by their kids and Mabel's mother returning home. So Mabel can't get the quiet time she needs to tell Nick what's bothering her.

Instead, she gets the kids out the door to school just in time for Nick to go to sleep and then go to work.

Later she waits at the bus stop to meet the children after school, stopping strangers on the street to ask the time and getting agitated when they ignore her request. When the bus arrives, she and the kids race home. But the kids have invited friends, who arrive accompanied by their father, the sour-looking Mr. Jensen (Mario Gallo). He looks unsure when Mabel puts *Swan Lake* on the record player and encourages the children to pretend to be ballerinas—and is even more upset when he sees the kids have trashed one of the rooms in the house, changing into costumes Mabel has given them. One little girl is running around the house naked.

As Jensen tries to round up his kids to go home, Nick returns (accompanied by his harpie of a mother, played by Katherine Cassavetes) and explodes: Who is this guy and what is he doing in his house? Why are the kids half-naked? When Mabel tries to explain, Nick slaps her and knocks her down, then chases Jensen and his children out of the house.

Egged on by his mother, Nick calls the family doctor, even as he tells Mabel, "I don't know who you are." When Dr. Zepp (played by Eddie Shaw, Sam Shaw's brother) arrives and starts talking about committing Mabel, Mabel rebels, calling the doctor a vampire and fighting the idea of a sedative injection. "This woman can't stay here!" Nick's mother shrieks. "This woman is crazy."

Like someone clinging desperately to life itself, Mabel stands up in front of everyone and starts to list the five points she has that prove that her life with Nick is good and their marriage works. But she collapses, rousing only enough to fight off Zepp's attempts to inject her: "Please let me stay in my house. I'll be content!" Mabel screams.

But it is too late. All we see is the unsettled Nick at work the next day, aware that people are talking about what happened the night before: "I don't want anyone discussing my affairs," he barks, even as everyone asks after Mabel's well-being. Nick's guilt is manifested in his snappish behavior; eventually he picks a fight with a member of his crew, causing him to fall down a long hillside and be badly hurt.

In a panic at how his life is going, Nick leaves work and, with one of his crew in tow, goes to the school to pick up his children, though it is the middle of the morning: "It comes to mind I don't know my kids," Nick says, taking them to the beach on a chilly day and forcing them to have fun. On the ride home in the back of the truck, he sits with a small black cloud of anger and confusion hanging over his head as he tells the kids, "I'm sorry I had to send your mother away. I'm sorry for everything."

It is six months later, the title card says. Everyone is racing around in high spirits, getting ready for a party. Nick and his crew change on the truck, going from work clothes to coats and ties. At Nick's place, he shepherds at least twenty people into the house.

Mabel is coming home, and Nick has put together a party to welcome her. But when Nick's parents arrive, his mother looks aghast: "Are you crazy? Have you gone out of your mind?" Nick needs to clear the house, his mother says; Mabel can't take this big crowd of people on her first day out.

So, in the rain, the guests head out—and run into Mabel as she arrives. They all wish her well awkwardly and leave her with Nick, both sets of parents, and Nick's siblings. Nick's mother is the first to greet her: "Mabel, you look fine, rested. I'm so happy to see you, darling."

Dr. Zepp has stopped by, but Nick's mother quickly shushes him: "Don't talk about the past, doctor."

Finally Mabel speaks: "Can I see the children now?"

As the rest of the family gathers around the dining room table, Nick pulls Mabel aside and tells her, "Just be yourself. There's nothing you can do wrong. Just be yourself."

Once at the table, however, he hits her with a tactless question: "What was it like—terrible? Good, bad—what?"

After more small talk, Mabel shocks everyone by telling them she'd like them to leave because "Nick and I want to go to bed."

But no one leaves, and eventually Nick explodes again when the conversation turns sour. Mabel finally breaks down and turns to her father (played by Cassavetes stalwart Fred Draper) and says, "Daddy, won't you stand up for me?" But he foolishly takes her literally and gets to his feet. Mabel cries, then flees to the next room, where she stands on the couch and begins humming *Swan Lake* and dancing to it.

In a frenzy, Nick chases everyone out of the house. Then, after being swarmed by his three angry kids, he pulls Mabel off the couch and slaps her, trying to get her to connect with reality. As he tries to bring her around, the kids jump him once more. As he struggles with them, she runs into the kitchen, grabs a knife, and tries to cut her wrists, but Nick wrestles it away from her.

He hauls the kids off to their rooms, but they escape, scrambling back down the steps to Mabel—not once but twice. By the second time, Mabel has come to her senses and things calm down. She and Nick put the kids to bed, as though nothing had happened. "You know—I think I *am* crazy," Mabel remarks to Nick as they head downstairs to make up their own bed, as Bo Harwood's mournful piano music plays over the closing credits.

A Woman Under the Influence is a film filled with sudden and rapid transitions, both in the plot and in the emotions within a scene. When the film was released, Mabel was embraced as a victim of society—the society that dictated that a woman's place was in the home, that women should be subordinate to their men, that the wife was a helpmeet to the husband with the job of caring for the kids, cleaning the house, preparing the meals, and catering to the husband's whims.

If anything, Mabel is less a victim of male domination than of the insecurities of one man: Nick. She is not under society's influence; she is in thrall to Nick. And Nick is threatened by her sense of personal freedom, which runs counter to what was obviously an upbringing that allowed for little display of emotion (except for anger).

Ultimately, Mabel isn't crazy; if anyone is a candidate for commitment, it's Nick, who does his mother's bidding without thought, even if it means betraying his wife. He has trouble controlling his temper, and his fuse is forever being lit by frustration over situations he can't control. So he focuses his anger on the one thing he seems able to dominate: Mabel.

Yet the film ends on an upbeat note: It's as if they've been put through some trial by fire and, having survived, are better equipped to go on with their lives together.

It is an uncompromising film that refuses to go where the audience would like. It has the untidiness and illogic of real life, with people acting against their own best interests, hurting the ones they love and immediately regretting it.

"People have said that my films are very difficult to watch, that they're experiences you are put through, rather than ones you enjoy—and it's true," Cassavetes said. "I remember when we made *Shadows*, some guy from my hometown said, 'John, what kind of movie is that? It's about me. Who the hell's interested in me?'"

Thirty-four

A Woman Under
the Influence 2

"Am I anti-Hollywood?" Cassavetes said. "No, but I'm unable to work in the big system. There's nothing wrong with them and something wrong with me. I'm spoiled. It's a fetish. I do what I want to do."

Still, he wasn't afraid to call things what they were: "I feel that I'm one of the few filmmakers in America who is truly independent in the sense that I've gone beyond my first film," Cassavetes said. "I've already beat the system. It's not practical to make films the way we make them.

During the years 1972–1974, the period when Cassavetes was writing, raising money for, making, and releasing *Woman*, Hollywood was going through a renaissance that many now look back upon as a kind of golden age when the young film-school generation and the outsiders were suddenly embraced by Hollywood and allowed to make the films that spoke to the baby-boom generation. Films like *The Conversation*, *The Candidate*, *The Last Detail*, and *Serpico* were being made by studios that were also producing more traditional fare, such as *The Way We Were* and *Murder on the Orient Express*, and disaster films like *The Towering Inferno* and *Earthquake*.

Martin Baum, Cassavetes' former agent who had become president of the short-lived ABC Pictures, said at the time, "This is a golden age for creative people because, with far lower budgets, we can gamble with new ideas and new talent." Producer David Wolper added, "This is the best of times for independents. With the big studios in trouble, even the top stars can be had for very little front money."

As director Frank Perry (*Diary of a Mad Housewife*) told *Newsweek* in a 1970 article called "The New Hollywood," "What you're seeing now is the flowering of personal cinema in America. It's a revolution that can't be reversed."

Or so he thought. Four years later, in another story headlined "The New Hollywood," *Newsweek* proclaimed the end of the independent spirit, just as Cassavetes was about to release *Woman*. The article quoted then-producer Peter Bart as saying, "The New Hollywood is the New Orthodoxy. People are scared that a failure will put them out of business. There's less venturesome spirit around here than I've seen in the ten years I've been around."

Cassavetes, who lived and breathed the concept of independent film, admitted, "It's hard to explain what independence means—but to those who have it, film is still a mystery, not a way out. To still do what you want after ten years, twenty years, is something. Somehow if you fight the system, you're going to lose to it. In my mind, if you fight the system, it only means you want to join it. So it is very important that you do something you like that you're involved in enough to hold your interest no matter how long it takes."

Charles Champlin, long-time film editor and critic for the *Los Angeles Times*, said, "Hollywood is a merciless town. There's so much cruelty built into the system. It's a tough place to be an individual—and a very lonely place to be unsuccessful."

The miracle of the 1970s was not that Hollywood suddenly got smart enough to let filmmakers like Hal Ashby and Bob Rafelson make personal films; it was that the independent-spirited filmmakers had the tenacity and guile to get those movies made before the studios' blockbuster mentality reasserted itself at the middle of that decade.

As Cassavetes observed at the time, "The main thing with Hollywood is that the top level has lost sight of the fact that there are talented people here who have the need to express themselves, personally, who regard their main job as expressing their version of what life is and what people are feeling. There's a group of us—Altman, Elaine May, Paul Mazursky, Mel Brooks, Woody Allen, Francis Ford Coppola, some actors like Peter and Gena and Ben and George C. Scott and others—who are attempting to maintain their independence in a milieu gone crazy from the desire for huge profits and the power that comes from those profits."

Al Ruban noted, "There's no relationship between John and Hollywood. What he makes is totally from the Cassavetes point of view." But that was not the same as being anti-Hollywood. As Ruban observed, "John never hated Hollywood. They make the best pictures in the world. John just wanted to be personal and, in Hollywood, that's not allowed. He managed to keep a foot in each world and did pretty well."

Cassavetes was philosophical, but he was also realistic: "Everyone is not going to be enamored of your particular art and I don't think that's an unhealthy thing," he said. "But American society says, 'Wait a minute— if that happens to you, then you won't get to make another film.' Therefore, you must make your films more accessible to people so that they will like it.

"I don't say I've been a saint in my life but I couldn't sell my soul out for things I just don't believe in. And if that means I'll never make a film again, then I'll never make another film again."

Certainly, Hollywood didn't embrace Cassavetes, even as he created perhaps his most disciplined effort, *Minnie and Moskowitz*, on time and on budget. Cassavetes was still considered a risky investment. But that didn't stop him from trying to give dramatic shape to some of the ideas he'd been mulling.

"I only knew one thing about *Woman* when we started: that it was a difficult time for today's woman to be left alone while somebody goes out and lives," he said. "I know when I was not working and Gena was working for me—because I was really in trouble in this business—I stayed home and took care of the baby and I was a pretty good housewife and all that. But I didn't have really the same reactions as a woman would have, mainly because I didn't have to think into the future of when I'd get older or when my attractiveness would fade or when the kids would grow up or when the baby would cease to cling to you. All those things are more interesting than what they're making movies out of."

Woman began when Rowlands mentioned in passing that she wished she could do a play, something she hadn't done in ages. Cassavetes asked her what kind of play she wanted and she told him vaguely that she was interested in something that dealt with what women were going through at that moment in history, but something that also had been a struggle for women in the past. Cassavetes took it as a challenge and a distraction.

One day he handed Rowlands a play he had written and said, "See what you think."

Rowlands recalled, "I couldn't believe John wrote it. I don't mean to be sexist because I don't really believe that women can't write for men and vice versa. But I really couldn't believe that a man would understand this particular problem.

"You can spend an evening with John among friends and think he hasn't noticed anything that's going on or heard anything anyone has said. And then later you discover this amazing understanding in his writing. He understands women of all ages."

But Rowlands was also daunted. The role Cassavetes had written was large, emotionally challenging and consuming—a thoroughly draining experience were she asked to act it for eight shows a week onstage. She felt like a whiner making the complaint to Cassavetes but knew she had to say something.

So she told him how much she loved it but said, "I couldn't last two nights playing that and in a week I'd have to be hospitalized." Cassavetes took it well, telling her he understood and mentioning that he had another idea.

The other idea, as it turned out, was two more full-length plays, featuring the same characters: a kind of emotional triptych that would be played in repertory onstage. Individually, the plays stood on their own. Together, they created a sweeping picture of a family suffering from its own repressed emotions, which find their release in the character of Mabel.

Rowlands was stunned—not only at the output or the breadth of Cassavetes' vision, but at the mountain Cassavetes had created for her to climb.

"I don't think you really understood what I meant," she told him gently. "Doing three plays is not going to be easier than doing one play."

But Cassavetes was convinced he was on to something. He refracted the material once more, distilling the three plays into a single screenplay: *A Woman Under the Influence.*

"It was hard to cut down and the finished film is long," Cassavetes said later. "As I get older, I guess I have a tendency to make longer pictures. But the subjects are almost more difficult. I don't think audiences are satisfied any longer with just touching the surface of people's lives. I think they really want to get into a subject."

Thirty-five

A Woman Under
the Influence 3

W hen Cassavetes sent *A Woman Under the Influence* to the supposedly hipper new studio suits of the early 1970s, they all
turned it down flat. "Nobody wants to see a crazy middle-aged
dame," one studio executive famously told him.

The studios' antipathy was a minor setback, though one Cassavetes acknowledged as a persistent annoyance. He drew the only conclusion he
could: He'd have to pay for the movie himself. "Working in television
taught me to do without money even when I'm making it," he said. "I
learned never to confuse making money with what you really want to do.

"There isn't too much respect shown to anyone who isn't a success. It's
too bad. People are stupid. If you get put down and find a way to fight it,
that's the main thing. You are an artist if you want to be. You've got to keep
that image of yourself in your own mind's eye."

As Rowlands said, "We didn't have the money to do it, but we had a
lot of friends, all actors and interested in the project. So they all helped us.
And we just did it."

At the top of the list: Peter Falk. When he played the role of Nick
Longhetti at a reading with Cassavetes and Elaine May, "I laughed out loud,"
Falk said. "He's funny, though not too aware of what's going on. A dope—
not a bad man, but a dope. He's in over his head. He's very much in love
with [Mabel] and excited by her—he can have fun with her. But he doesn't

quite know how to handle her. She makes demands on him that he can't handle."

Cassavetes said he was going to make the movie, and Falk immediately told Cassavetes that he wanted to do the part. But three days later Falk was offered a role in the film *The Day of the Dolphin*, by Mike Nichols, whose previous film had been the controversial *Carnal Knowledge*. It was toward the end of 1972, and Nichols wanted Falk within the month.

"And you don't have any money," Falk pointed out, as he explained his decision to accept the *Dolphin* role to Cassavetes.

"You can't do it," Cassavetes replied. And Falk dropped the role.

Instead, Falk invested himself in the part of Nick Longhetti, both figuratively and literally—putting up a half million of his own dollars to fund Cassavetes' vision of the script: "If we just had a million-two," Cassavetes would say to Elaine Kagan as they tried to raise money to make the film. As Kagan recalled, "That was always the dream number."

It was not surprising to anyone who knew him that Cassavetes would cover his half of the film's budget by mortgaging his house. That was the Cassavetes passion in action. Cassavetes believed in himself, and he believed in the film. Even if the film didn't do business, he could always take acting work that would cover the debt.

Which didn't mean it wasn't an outrageously bold move. The first rule of Hollywood: Never invest your own money. Cassavetes broke it with regularity.

"'John was in the trenches before there were sources of funding for independent films," said filmmaker Paul Mazursky, who first met Cassavetes in New York in the 1950s. "There was no Fox Searchlight, no Miramax. You put your fucking house up."

Cassavetes admitted, "My filmmaking is an expensive personal madness. If I didn't have a friend like Peter and a wife like Gena, it would be impossible for me. It might be too difficult a battle. I rely on their good graces. I'm in debt to all of them."

Still, it flabbergasted most of the people who knew him when Falk agreed to put up the other half of the film's budget, particularly the ones who were personally acquainted with Falk's tight-fisted approach to money.

"Peter would sit on a dime until it melted," Seymour Cassel said. "And John got him to put up the money for *Woman*. John said, 'I've got to shut down to get some money.' Peter said, 'No, we can't stop. I'll give you the money.'"

Bo Harwood, who had been conscripted to do sound as well as music for the film, recalled, "In those days, it was not cool to be nonunion. John's credit was cut off at the labs for using nonunion crews. Two days prior to the start of shooting on *Woman*, we had no film and no money. We were having a meeting at the house and someone said, 'What if we don't get the money?' John said, 'I don't think in those terms. Come November 1, we're going to be in this house and I'm going to be behind the camera whether we have film or not.' The night before we started, John found 10,000 feet of film."

Sacrifices would be required. Cassavetes, the actors, the crew—they would all be gambling on the film itself, using time they could otherwise spend earning money on other films. Cassavetes and Rowlands were betting the Cassavetes house to cover half the production cost. On the other hand, making it themselves would allow them both to work and still be home with the family, not a small matter to Rowlands.

"I've been very lucky—my husband makes his own movies and I've been able to keep my word about putting family first and still act occasionally," she said. "I've never had to leave my family, even for a day."

Cassavetes saw it as "one way of controlling our lives. Why not work with friends and family? We're comfortable, we're happy. Why not work together? It's a fantastic way to stay together."

And there was one more bonus, Rowlands said—the sheer thrill of the unknown that marked every part Cassavetes wrote for her. "With John's scripts, it's like being an astronaut on the moon for the first time," she said. "The air is very light, you have to wear heavy boots, you have to push yourself out into areas that are very frightening. I suppose I push further for John than for any other director, not because he's my husband. It's because he happens to be the kind of artist and director that he is. I know that other actors feel the same way—and they're not even married to him."

To get *Woman* made, they would have to work quickly, conserve money and find deals wherever they could. "I got a lot of people together, because I knew we wouldn't have any money to make the picture," Cassavetes said. "In *Woman*, the crew worked for a small fee and it was agreed without a contract that we would share any profits. That's what happened. I work with friends, people I like very much, and we agree because we have the same aims: to find a way to express sentiments, emotions."

Cassavetes started by expanding the duties of the office staff. His secretary, Elaine Kagan, would get the job of script supervisor—keeping track of what had been shot, which takes Cassavetes liked, and so on. Carole Smith, Falk's assistant, would serve as the production's coordinator; together, the two of them were the den mothers, seeing to Cassavetes', Rowlands', and Falk's needs—as well as those of everyone else.

Part of Smith's daily regimen was warming up the room Rowlands used as her dressing room, as well as warming up Rowlands' hair rollers. Rowlands did her own hair and makeup for the film. There was also only one copy of each of Mabel's outfits, so Smith and Kagan had to run the costume to the dry-cleaners for overnight service on an almost daily basis.

Cassavetes convinced Kagan that she could handle the script supervisor chores, in addition to everything else, even though she'd never done it before. She quickly decided it was not a job that appealed to her. "I was always afraid that, a month later, somebody would say, 'Was I holding this in my right hand or my left hand?'" Kagan said. "I hated the details. But I was so lucky; I learned how to do everything with John. He even put an Arriflex in my arms and said, 'Shoot this scene.'"

Kagan was a nice Jewish girl from Kansas City who had moved to Los Angeles and gotten a job as a secretary to an agent, Jack Gilardi, who represented Cassavetes at one point. Cassavetes hired her away to work for him when he came back to Los Angeles to edit *Husbands*.

A regular part of Kagan's job was to take dictation from Cassavetes, who always seemed to be working on a new script. Early in her tenure, she recalled, he would spend time in the editing room, cutting *Husbands*, then would race upstairs to the office, to dictate more dialogue for the script he was writing. When he dictated, he assumed the voice or demeanor of the character he was playing. He may have worked and reworked it in his head prior to speaking it aloud, but once he started talking out a script, it didn't take very long.

"Everything he wrote, he dictated and I took down shorthand," Kagan said. "Then he would invite anyone to listen. The guy in the hall, the guy delivering water: 'Hey, you got a minute? Sit down for a minute and listen to something.'"

To fill out his crew for *Woman*, Cassavetes hit upon an ingenious money-saving idea: He affiliated himself with the fledgling American Film Institute, which had established a conservatory on Mulholland Drive in 1969.

Cassavetes offered his services as the AFI's first filmmaker-in-residence in its Center for Advanced Film Studies. The AFI's press release tipped Cassavetes' hand: "Cassavetes' association with the center began October 9 (1972) when AFI Fellows aided the filmmaker with preproduction chores on *A Woman Under the Influence*. Actual shooting begins November 1."

It was student labor—but students who had been selected for their aptitude and who were eager to learn at the elbow of a legendarily independent filmmaker. And at student wages, no less.

"Cassavetes will meet with Fellows periodically to discuss his work," the press release noted, continuing, "On a rotating basis, Fellows will assume functional learning roles in the production and will have access to screenings of daily rushes. Fellows will not at any time replace regular crew members on the films."

The latter was either not conveyed to Cassavetes or, more likely, was simply ignored by him. He wanted go-getters who were willing to work cheaply on a nonunion, self-financed production—students or not.

Long after they'd finished shooting, Cassavetes was still in the AFI's editing room, trying to put his film together. "John wouldn't leave," Bo Harwood said. "He said, 'My movie's not done.' We were there for two years. It was like a bunch of bank robbers had taken over this eighteen-acre estate."

Cherry-picking from the advanced class for his crew, he designated AFI Fellow Caleb Deschanel as his cinematographer. Deschanel, who had gone to the University of Southern California film school, would go on to multiple Oscar nominations as a director of photography on films such as *The Right Stuff* and *The Natural*, but his painstaking, painterly approach to capturing images on film almost immediately ran counter to Cassavetes' purposes.

"I'd just come off an internship with Gordon Willis, who worked in a very formal way," Deschanel recalled of the meticulous cinematographer who shot *The Godfather* and *Manhattan*, among many notable works. "My impression of doing features was that you rehearse, do the blocking, figure out how to shoot the scene. John didn't work that way. He would rehearse with the actors, but he wanted the freedom to have people leave the frame. He wanted you to adapt to what was happening without it being totally rehearsed or everybody moving and hitting marks."

Cinematographer Haskell Wexler had recommended Deschanel to Cassavetes, but almost as soon as shooting began, Wexler had a call from Deschanel. They had been filming in a bar and Deschanel, toting a handheld 35mm camera, had braced himself to steady the image. As he was shooting, Cassavetes would push him, to make the camera jiggle.

In a snit, the very precise Deschanel called Wexler to ask, "What kind of nut is this?" The kind of nut who sees acting and storytelling as the two key components of cinema, with cinematography placing a distant third: "John was very scornful of the mechanics of the process called photography," Wexler recalled. "To him, it got in the way."

"I feel there is no such thing as setting up a shot that is right for the scene," Cassavetes said. "So I'm left just shooting the action and the selections are those of the operator. If the operator is free to think in those terms, he can simply photograph what's happening without constricting the actors. Usually the actors don't know what's being shot. They never know when the camera's going to swing on to them, so everyone has to play every moment. The fluidity of the camera really keeps it alive and allows the operator to make his selections emotionally."

The camera crew included another AFI recruit, Frederick Elmes, and Michael Ferris, a relatively raw camera assistant who had come to California from the East Coast, after college and a stint in the Air Force. Ferris had talked his way into jobs on low-budget films, learning as he worked cheaply, including a stint on Orson Welles' unfinished "The Other Side of the World."

Ferris had connected with Cassavetes one day, after running into Seymour Cassel on a Hollywood street. Ferris was in his car, Cassel on a motorcycle. A huge fan of *Minnie and Moskowitz*, Ferris impulsively introduced himself to Cassel, told him how much he admired the Cassavetes films, and wondered aloud how someone could get a job working for the director. Cassel told him Cassavetes was in the midst of preparing a film and that he should call him. Cassel even gave him the number.

Ferris rushed home and called the number—and almost immediately got Cassavetes on the line. Blurting out the story of meeting Seymour, Ferris offered his whole biography: "John just listened, he didn't stop me," Ferris recalled. "When I finally ran out of breath, he asked me what I was doing Friday and gave me an appointment."

When Ferris showed up, Cassavetes handed him the script for *Woman* and talked with him about it for more than an hour. At the end of the meeting, Cassavetes hired Ferris, who spent the next month working on preparing the house on Taft Avenue that would serve as the Longhetti home.

The Longhetti house had to be perfect because so much of the film was shot within its claustrophobic confines. It had to be big enough for a couple and their three kids, yet believable as a structure that would be affordable to a working-class family in which only the husband worked.

"We looked at maybe 150 houses in Los Angeles," Cassavetes recalled. "But it was really hard to find something in the right price range that would make you feel you were in a real house and also depict the kind of blue-collar existence we had in mind."

Beside looking at houses, Cassavetes looked at how people lived— and found that it was too mundane for what he hoped to achieve: "I knew what I was going to find and I knew I wouldn't like it," he said. "Plastic-covered furniture, a nice kitchen, a nice car, a clean façade, but nothing much inside, a general apathy to art and little interest in music. And a night out would be a family trip to McDonalds at the weekend for a hamburger. I am an artist and I cannot live in this way. So I had to transform all this in terms which were acceptable to me and at the same time to the people I was talking about."

The solution: a large house that the characters had inherited. That would account for its undue size (in fact, Cassavetes shot in only two or three rooms of the whole house), given the family's income: "We decided we needed a hand-me-down house, one that had been given to the Nick character and still had all the old furniture and old woodwork," Cassavetes said.

They found what they were looking for on Taft Avenue, near downtown Hollywood: "It was our standing set," Elaine Kagan recalled. "We shot there. We cut there. We ate there."

After a couple weeks of production, it was obvious Cassavetes and Deschanel were not clicking. John Finnegan recalled a day when Cassavetes asked Deschanel what the delay was. Deschanel told Cassavetes, "I'm waiting for the sun." At which Cassavetes exploded, "Fuck that—we'll make sun."

Cassavetes kept pushing Deschanel to loosen up and stop regarding the camera as the center of the film's universe. It wasn't—the actors were.

"John used to say he could sense me staring at him," Deschanel recalled. "I wanted to give it some visual style and he did not like my point of view. I didn't feel like I was given a chance to do decent work."

Finnegan remembered seeing Cassavetes throw an arm around Deschanel's shoulder and walk him up the street: "I said, 'That's the end of that guy,'" Finnegan recalled. Deschanel remembered Cassavetes sending Phedon Papamichael, his cousin and art director, to break the news: "That's the way John is," was all Papamichael would say. Deschanel left and so did his assistant, Elmes, mostly out of loyalty to Deschanel.

Cassavetes called in Ferris the next morning and told him, "Mike, you and I are finishing the picture."

Ferris could only say, "Wh-what?"

"Anybody can shoot," Cassavetes told him. "You care. You and I are doing the rest of this and that's it."

As Ferris recalled, "It was just follow John's lead and do the best you can."

Cassavetes turned to longtime pals to act in the film, casting Fred Draper as Mabel's father and salting Nick's work gang with actor-friends like John Finnegan, Cliff Carnell, and Hugh Hurd from *Shadows*.

Cassavetes had long since decided that amateurs brought an element of spontaneity to their acting that rubbed off on the professionals in the cast. So he cast former baseball player Leon Wagner as one of Nick's workers. Seymour's wife, Elizabeth Deering, and her mother, Elsie Ames, had roles. He cast Sam Shaw's brother, Eddie, a publicist for Frank Sinatra, as Dr. Zepp, the family doctor. And Cassavetes once again turned to his mother, Katherine, and Gena's mother, Lady, casting them as in-laws in the film. They were significant roles, not cameos, but Cassavetes was extremely comfortable entrusting them to his family.

"I really believe almost anyone can act," he said. "How well they can act depends on how free they are and whether the circumstances are such that they can reveal what they feel. If I have any special way of working, it's just to set up an atmosphere where what the actors are doing is really important, fun and nothing takes precedence over it."

Cassavetes cast Seymour Cassel's son, Matthew, who was not yet ten, to play the oldest Longhetti child, the largest of the children's roles.

To Matthew, Cassavetes was just John, a friend of his father's who was also Matthew's godfather. So Matthew didn't think anything of it when John called to take them out for ice cream. In the car, on the way to the ice cream parlor, Cassavetes turned to Matthew and said, "Oh, I wrote a part for you—will you be in my movie?"

Matthew, who had never really considered acting, said, "OK."

Though Falk had learned how to work with Cassavetes on *Husbands,* he still was capable of being thrown by the unpredictable director, who preferred his actors off-balance, rather than working on solid ground.

On the first day of *Woman,* Falk was in a pickup truck, feeling the normal nerves of the start of a big film. Just as "Action!" was called, he heard, "Wait, wait, hold it." Cassavates came running over to him, reached in through the window and put a floppy denim hat on Falk's head.

The hat worked: It gave Falk a new color, a different shade to the character. Then Cassavetes turned away from the window and said, "OK, action!" And Falk was suddenly in a different place as an actor: "Whatever plan I had was gone," he said. "Whatever I thought at that moment was incredibly spontaneous, even if it was, How do I look in this hat?"

Principal photography lasted thirteen weeks, shot largely in continuity: "The emotional strain was so great that we never went out socially for thirteen weeks," Cassavetes said. "No movies, no parties, no home entertaining, nothing. At night we'd collapse, make coffee, then start talking about the work. Yesterday's work, last week's work, last month's, next week's, next month's. We'd wake up in the night and talk some more. It was that kind of total commitment. One time, I remember, we lived it all so completely that I suddenly became Nick to Gena's Mabel. She looked at me with those big, glaring, beautiful eyes of hers and said to Peter, 'Will you hold him while I hit him?'"

Shooting the spaghetti scene took a week, though time was given to rehearsal for the carefully scripted sequence: "It's mainly Gena and those actors that were able to do that," Cassavetes said. "It's hard to say why it works so well."

Rehearsals were used to find out which sections of dialogue worked and which didn't. When an actor was struggling, Cassavetes believed, it was probably the writer's fault—his trust in his actors' ability was that complete.

"If you have a good actor and at one stage he can no longer act, it's the script that's bad," he said. "Either the dialogue is unworkable or the meaning isn't clear."

Finnegan caught on early in shooting the spaghetti scene that they were going to be there for a while. But Cassavetes expected them to be gobbling pasta in every shot, with enthusiasm, something that got harder the longer they went on.

Finnegan recalled, "They kept making big plates of it for Peter. I'd say, 'Just a little sauce on the bread, that's all,' and then Gena would pile it on Peter's plate. The first couple of days, the sauce was great; but by the end of the week, it wasn't spaghetti sauce—it was ketchup. I didn't eat spaghetti for a month after that."

Rowlands had been right when she had turned down Mabel as a stage role. The character invaded her being in ways that lingered after shooting wrapped. "You change your energy and allow another person to haunt your house, so to speak," Rowlands said. "It's like being a medium. It left me exhausted and depressed-feeling. Some of the time, when you're walking out there where the air is thin, you just hope you can walk back again."

Yet she felt an obligation to the character, an empathy that went beyond identification: "I loved Mabel so much that I wanted to do right by her. That's why, above all, I pleaded with John: Please, let's not romanticize her martyrdom."

As she submerged herself in the character, she brought out a series of tics and mannerisms that might almost be seen as a kind of Tourette's syndrome. Mabel would make the raspberry sound, or Bronx cheer, with her tongue, as she used her thumb to signal, "You're out of here," like a baseball umpire, or perhaps, "Take a hike, bub." It was not a planned gesture but something that bubbled up as Rowlands confronted the frustrations the character was struggling with but lacked the words for.

"All I know is that this woman couldn't speak, she could not express herself," Rowlands said. "And when you can't speak, when you're playing that kind of part and becoming involved in it, then things will start happening with your body. The human spirit will not take it silently. If you cannot express something verbally, it will come out in some way, and in her it came out in bizarre physical gestures. But I didn't plan it."

Cassavetes observed, "Gena put so much of herself into that as the picture went along, the problems became more and more hers. By the time the picture was over, she had so thoroughly understood the investigation that she had made, that she had become like Mabel, in a sense."

Playing the role "almost made me as wacko as the woman I played," she said. Cassavetes was seeing magic emanating from the woman he loved: "I find it difficult in terms of work to look at any other woman and see what I see in this woman," he said. "She's an incredible instrument. She has incredible excitement and she's exposed and she has all the attributes of being a great actress."

Elaine Kagan recalled, "He was tough on Gena, but she could take it. He'd put her up to the edge and then over the edge—and she'd deliver. I don't know if he could speak to other actresses the way he did to her. There was an intimacy."

As Falk approached the day they'd shoot Mabel's mad scene, he was concerned because he and Rowlands couldn't even talk about it before they played it in front of the camera. It was a Cassavetes rule. "He never allowed an actor to talk to another actor about their role," Rowlands said. "You could talk about anything else, but John felt that your character belonged to you."

Still, when Falk arrived at the house on Taft to begin shooting Mabel's breakdown and commitment, he assumed they would at least rehearse the scene before Cassavetes started filming. Wrong.

"I remember going there and John mumbled something about where we should stand, then suddenly the camera was going," Falk said. "I remember saying my lines but I don't remember having the feeling of acting. It was like I was watching somebody in life. I was riveted. Her descent into madness is the most extraordinary twelve minutes of sustained acting I have ever seen on film."

Mike Ferris was thinking the same thing, as he kept his camera on Rowlands: "I'm watching Gena, thinking, 'This is what Academy Awards are meant for,'" he recalled. "I was watching what I instinctively knew was the most brilliant thing I'd ever seen unfold in front of me."

Cassavetes shot it several times, spooling through the whole ten-minute film load on long, excruciating takes of Rowlands listing off Mabel's five points that prove they should be together, desperately making a last grasp at being allowed to go on with her life, rather than being ripped away from her children and committed. He claimed, "I'm not bright enough and I don't think anyone is really to get everything all at once. If there are emotions and revelations taking place a mile a minute, how can we separate all these things with our camera and then go into an editing room and try to make a selection?"

For Mabel's mad scene, Cassavetes used a long lens, knowing that, in trying to follow the action, the camera—the operator and the focus puller—would occasionally have to adjust focus, which would give the film the immediacy of a documentary. It would also create a less-than-perfect look, something still far outside the norm of conventional movies. But Cassavetes had dispensed with convention long ago.

"I have to get a take that plays," he said. "If we don't see Peter for a moment, or if we don't see Gena for a moment, it's not that important. I knew it would be technically impossible to do it all in focus because there's no way of knowing where the actors would be at any moment."

"The focus puller," Rowlands said, "was the biggest hero on our set."

Conventional cameramen—studio cameramen—learn an acronym, BLRS, to help consistency: block it, light it, rehearse it, shoot it. But on *Woman*, Cassavetes would simply turn to Ferris in a moment of inspiration and say, "Mike, turn your camera on."

Mabel's breakdown, Rowlands always believed, stemmed from Nick letting Mabel know that, for however brief a period, he was embarrassed by her and that he didn't love her. "That, in my opinion, is what makers her wacko, as he calls her—pushing her off the deep end," Rowlands said. "Sensing that love's gone, sensing betrayal, precipitates her breakdown. Because until this time, she is OK—a little flaky, perhaps, but a lot closer to the normal state of women than most people would like to admit."

For Cassavetes, while the scene was crucial to Mabel, it was even more revealing of Nick, who stands by while his mother bullies him and Dr. Zepp into signing commitment papers for Mabel. So he let the scene play out over the length of a full, agonizing reel.

"It's a very difficult thing for someone to double-cross somebody," Cassavetes said. "Unless you actually see them do that, unless you actually see the continuity of that, the actual idea that he would do this and carry it through could have been weakened. It was very important that he actually decide to commit this woman so that it would become a memory for him."

Cassavetes never would express an opinion about what any actor should do—never tried to point the actor in the direction that Cassavetes himself would like to have taken, but he did have his own ideas of what a scene should be like.

Sometimes he expressed them. Rowlands said of the mad scene, "John told me to go all out in my playing, because Mabel is someone without inhibitions. She's freer than normal people."

But at other times he would withhold his thoughts. As they were gearing up to shoot the scene where Mabel comes home from the hospital, Ferris overheard Rowlands take Cassavetes aside and say, "What would Mabel do here?"

Cassavetes just looked at her, then said, "You know the answer to that. Don't ask me again."

Rowlands erupted in anger: "If I had a knife, I'd put it through your heart right now," she hissed. Then she turned around and concentrated fiercely on the scene.

A couple of years after *Woman* was released, while promoting *Opening Night* on *The Tomorrow Show,* Cassavetes had to listen as overbearing talk-show host Tom Snyder said with unctuous gravity to Rowlands, "Did you think *Woman Under the Influence* was as depressing a picture as I thought it was?"

"To me, it was moving," Rowlands responded evenly, allowing that there might be people who the film would depress. "I don't get depressed if I see a picture about some emotional quality someone has. I know some people avoid that but I like to be wrung out."

Thirty-six

A Woman Under
the Influence 4

S elf-distribution: It was the ultimate act of independence in the movie business.

   For ages, self-distribution meant four-walling: renting a theater by the week, while assuming advertising and operating costs, in exchange for the revenue. It had largely been the province of makers of either exploitation films or family fare, those willing to personally work the circuit and roam the country, trying to make their money back a few theaters at a time. Actor-director Tom Laughlin had initially had success with the technique with his film *Billy Jack*, before Warner Bros. saw what a goldmine the independent film was and distributed it broadly in 1971, then rereleased it in 1973.

   But for a serious filmmaker like Cassavetes to consider mounting a distribution campaign for his own film—a film he had already mortgaged his house to make—seemed quixotic, at best.

   Yet Cassavetes thought nothing of throwing down the gauntlet early and often. "Everyone who makes a movie is at the major distributors' mercy," he said. "We're distributing *Woman* ourselves because the studios have had no interest in it. And if they did come to us, we wouldn't sell it cheaply because we've taken our risks and expect to be paid well for it. After all, who the hell are they? Unless they finance the production, they're a bunch of agents who go out and book theaters. That's what it really boils down to."

"It was the first time in the history of motion pictures that an independent film was distributed without the use of a nationwide system of
sub-distributors," said Jeff Lipsky, whom Cassavetes hired as a college student to work on distributing *Woman*.

"More than anything," said Al Ruban, who wound up running Cassavetes' distribution operation, "he showed people it could be done."

Though he released *A Woman Under the Influence* at almost two and a half
hours, Cassavetes initially was screening a longer cut.

"I remember seeing a four-hour version of *Woman Under the Influence*
that he showed at AFI. I was overwhelmed," recalled Peter Bogdanovich.
"It was one of the great films I'd seen. I liked it long."

Ruban, who had gone on from *Minnie and Moskowitz* to produce a
film with Gazzara that fell apart the day before production was to start, accepted Cassavetes' invitation to screen the long version and was devastated by it, calling it the toughest thing he'd ever seen ("much harder than
what was released; it would have made you crazy").

"Don't change a thing," he told Cassavetes, who just shook his head.

"It's too tough," Cassavetes said. "I've got to change it. I've got to
ease off."

Rowlands recalled, "When we finished *Woman Under the Influence*, I
looked at it and said, 'John, maybe twenty-six people are going to see this.'
I never dreamed it would be financially successful."

For one thing, the film looked at unremarkable, working-class people
whose stories Hollywood was not usually interested in telling.

"There is a belief that the public is only interested in rich people and
that the working class would not want to see itself on the screen," Cassavetes said. "Perhaps it's true but that's not my concern in this film."

As Rowlands observed, "Our pictures made people feel very uncomfortable much of the time. The characters were very emotionally exposed and
people weren't used to it. Everything was not spelled out. The old tradition
was that you prepared the audience, but with our films, you had to just sit
there and hold on to your seats. Some people like that and some don't."

The film's official launching pad was the New York Film Festival, which
had proved so crucial to *Faces*. It was part of a festival lineup that also introduced Louis Malle's *Lacombe Lucien*, Robert Bresson's *Lancelot du Lac*, and
Alain Resnais' *Stavisky*. *Woman* was hailed at the festival, though reporters
couldn't get over the documentary feel, which raised an old question: "Was
any of it improvised?" asked one writer during the press conference that followed the film's press screening at the festival.

"When someone walks across the room, that was improvised," Cassavetes replied. "Otherwise, there's not an improvised moment in the movie."

Cassavetes called Falk up after *Woman* screened at the New York Film Festival to tell him that, when Falk's name appeared in the film's end credits, women in the audience booed.

"A lot of guys looked at me like they just didn't know what to say," Falk said of Nick and the reaction to the character. "Neither did I. That's what made it fun to play. I didn't know what the motivation was. John loved the ambiguity because people are ambiguous. John was interested in a mixture that was in most people you know. He was not interested in evil as much as weakness."

Rowlands, on the other hand, was celebrated at the New York screening. As the film finished at Alice Tully Hall, cheers greeted the closing credits. The spotlight swept to where Rowlands and Cassavetes were seated for them to take a bow. Rowlands stood to a thunderous ovation and bowed to the applauding audience.

"To hear 1,800 people clapping their hands in unison is glorious," she said. "I was so thrilled that I turned around to John—but he wasn't there. And I knew what he had done. He wanted it to be my moment. My moment entirely."

"We were fully prepared for people not to like it," she said. "But they went crazy. That was so unexpected."

After the festival screening, *Newsday*'s Joseph Gelmis called the film "an emotional blockbuster that should touch a nerve in every family that shelters an adult who's never grown up." *Variety* said, "It has all the earmarks of a critical success," though it found its commercial prospects shaky.

Nora Sayre, writing in the *New York Times,* criticized the film as being too long, comparing it unfavorably to Ingmar Bergman's *Scenes from a Marriage,* a six-hour series made for Norwegian TV in 1973 that was cut down to feature-film length and released in American theaters in 1974. Yet she concluded by noting that "the most frightening scenes are extremely compelling and this is a thoughtful film that does prompt serious discussion."

Despite the ovation at Lincoln Center, "depressing" was the pejorative thrown at the film. So was "art house." The film was offered to the existing distributors—both studio and independent—and none could see a market for the movie.

"John, how are we going to get this into theaters?" Rowlands asked him as the situation became clear.

"Let's go down to the all-night newsstand," Cassavetes replied. "We'll get papers from Chicago and San Francisco, wherever we want to play. And

we'll look in the theater section and see where the movies we like are playing. And then we'll call them up and they'll take the call, if only to say, 'I
told John Cassavetes to take a flying leap.'"

He started by calling Al Ruban to ask him to spearhead the distribution
of *Woman*. To hedge his bets, Cassavetes also hired Moe Rothman, the former head of distribution for Columbia Pictures, to whom Sam Shaw had introduced him. But in less than two weeks, Rothman had had enough.

"This guy keeps calling me every ten minutes and I have to tell him to
screw off," Rothman complained to Ruban about Cassavetes. "I don't have
to put up with this. I've lived my life."

When Ruban conveyed Rothman's message, Cassavetes said, "Al, will
you please take it over?"

"I will," Ruban replied, "until you get somebody to replace me," something Cassavetes, of course, never did.

Fortunately for Ruban, with or without Rothman, Cassavetes already
had firm plans about how to proceed. He booked both screens of a first-
run twin theater in New York—the Columbia, on Second Avenue at Sixty-
fourth—and the Fox Wilshire in Beverly Hills. Then, riding the building
wave of critical word of mouth from the New York festival, he opened it
himself in the two cities on November 18, 1974.

When the film opened a month after the New York Film Festival showings, Cassavetes' critical admirers practically wrote in advertising blurbs.

"[Cassavetes' films] reach for a kind of truth that is closer to life as we
know it, not as we usually find it in our movies," Kathleen Carroll wrote
in the *New York Daily News*. "The film does finally what Cassavetes hoped.
It touches an exposed nerve in its audience."

Rex Reed, also writing in the *Daily News*, called the film "searing, scald-
ing." He compared Mabel Longhetti to Tennessee Williams' Blanche DuBois
in her epic suffering and called the film "shatteringly profound and disturbing in ways movies seldom affect their audiences. This film is a triumph because it bridges the gap between soap opera and real life." He called
Rowlands' performance "the most moving and artful acting achievement I
have seen on the screen this year."

David Sterritt wrote in the *Christian Science Monitor* that, while there
were problems with the film, "I do persist in calling *Woman* a masterpiece—and I have been no great Cassavetes fan before now . . . A film so
emotionally right, so gloriously emotionally right, makes most traditional
considerations seem paltry."

And in *Newsweek*, Paul D. Zimmerman wrote, "Cassavetes creates the
raw stuff of life as though it flowed straight from his camera. His problem

is that, like Eugene O'Neill and Thomas Wolfe, Cassavetes sacrifices structure and brevity for impact."

But Cassavetes' old critical foes had little good to say about his newest film—or anyone else who had anything good to say about it. Stanley Kauffmann grumped in the *New Republic* that "the film isn't really about anything. Cassavetes knew that if he ran this grimy film two and three-quarters hours, sentimental critics would be sure to find it deep and even those who might fault the film one way or another would have to admit that it really Faced Life. To me, this film is utterly without interest or merit."

Pauline Kael attributed Cassavetes' view of madness to an overly literal reading of R. D. Laing's writings on insanity—or just simplistic storytelling by Cassavetes.

"His writing and directing are grueling and he swathes his popular ideas in so many wet blankets that he is taken seriously—and flops," she wrote. "Once again he has made a murky ragmop movie. He doesn't know how to dramatize and one can try to make a virtue of this for only so long . . . Though some in the audience will once again accept what is going on as raw, anguishing truth, most people will—rightly, I think—take their embarrassment as evidence of Cassavetes' self-righteous ineptitude." She called Rowlands' performance "exhausting," noting that "nothing she does is memorable because she does so much. It's the most transient big performance I've ever seen."

But Cassavetes was irrepressible in the face of disapproval. At one point, accompanying Jay Cocks to a screening, he spotted critic John Simon, who rarely had a kind word to say about anything Cassavetes did. Though they had never met, Cassavetes walked up to him, smiled, put out his hand, and said, "I'm John Cassavetes. Jay Cocks tells me you think I don't have a brain in my head." Simon, flabbergasted, could only shake his hand and demur.

The positive reviews carried the day, helping turn the film into a word-of-mouth hit and a consistent sell-out in both New York and Los Angeles. Cassavetes took an office overlooking the Fox Wilshire in Beverly Hills and would count heads as people lined up for the film. One day, Rowlands was in the office, and she and John stood looking down at the people waiting patiently in line to buy a ticket to their film.

"You know, a lot of these people are tourists," John said.

"How do you know that?" she asked.

"I went down and asked them where they came from," he said, as if it were the most logical thing in the world for the filmmaker to shmooze the people in line to see his movie.

When the response proved so strong in the film's initial run, Cassavetes' first instinct was to find a distributor to take on the expense of striking prints, buying advertising, and keeping track of the grosses at theaters around the country. None, however, could satisfy him that they would give the film the kind of attention and care that Cassavetes thought the film needed. So he decided to distribute it himself.

Cassavetes said the studios were consumed by "the new art of American life, the only all-consuming art: the art of business," he said. "So that supposing you don't want to be in that art, you want to be in another art, of self-expression, then there's no outlet. That's why we're taking the picture on our shoulders."

"Cassavetes," *Variety* reported, "was 'a little amazed' by b.o. results in LA, NY and other early situations (as was the entire film trade) and now plans to handle the pic indefinitely through his Faces International Films. 'Being a maverick means keeping on when the major companies tell you to go to hell,' Cassavetes said."

As Jonas Mekas recalled, "There were no minor distributors for him to go with. In the 1970s, you didn't have much choice. Either it was the big ones or very small ones."

So Cassavetes, in essence, told them all to get lost: He'd do it himself. "He was hand-making and hand-showing them—he was like the old street singers who would paint a picture and tell a story," Martin Scorsese said. "John was the example of the pure independent filmmaker with no attachments to anybody."

Jeff Lipsky would become a minor force in American independent film as a distributor, working at Skouras and Samuel Goldwyn before co-founding October Films and, later, Lot 49 films. But when Cassavetes offered him a job in his distribution company, Lipsky was just a college student who was assistant manager of a Long Island movie theater, though one who'd been reading *Variety* since he was ten.

A fan of *Minnie and Moskowitz*, Lipsky had bought a ticket to see *Woman* at the New York Film Festival. Lipsky was so excited by the film that he called Cassavetes and offered to show *Woman* at the theater where he worked. Cassavetes invited him over to talk, then offered Lipsky a job with the impromptu distribution company he was setting up to get *Woman* into theaters. Lipsky was one of about a dozen people who would work for Ruban on the project.

"None of us knew anything about distribution," Lipsky said. "We were all kids."

In terms of movie distribution, the country had for decades been divided by the studios into thirty-one sales territories. Over the years, former studio distribution men in each territory went off on their own, creating subdistributors to cater to the much smaller network of theaters that played foreign-language films, B-movies, and exploitation fare on a regional basis.

The most prominent of the art house subdistributors were the Cinema 5 group, which dealt in foreign films, and the Walter Reade group. If you had a film outside of the studios, you either went through them or someone even smaller.

"There was a network of theaters and art houses, revival houses," Ben Barenholtz recalled. "You could get thirty to seventy play dates on a film without having to go to a chain. If you wanted to self-distribute on that level, you had to get on the phone."

In 1974 there was no ready access to box-office information on films released across the country; grosses were a deep, dark secret. This was before the days of the 3,000-screen nationwide release; you didn't find the weekend's box office in the *New York Times* or hear it announced on *The Today Show*. There were no faxes or personal computers. Even a big movie might have a first-run release in only a dozen or fifteen cities, playing at a couple of theaters in each city. While *Variety* reported the grosses at key theaters, it was several days after the weekend before the figures were available.

Which meant that, while studios made the movies and controlled distribution, the exhibitors controlled the money. Even the studios had to put pressure on the various theater chains to pay up in a timely fashion; the smaller distributors were squeezed even harder. And they lacked the resources to apply pressure in return.

A studio could threaten to withhold sought-after titles unless the chains turned over grosses more quickly on smaller films: "Pay up for *My Big Fat Greek Wedding* or you won't get *Star Wars: Episode II*," for example.

The independent distributors had no such carrot or stick to threaten them with. If you're an independent filmmaker and your next movie won't be out for another year, it's hard to apply pressure to get paid. So the filmmakers needed the distribution companies to keep the exhibitors honest.

But the success of his film in New York and Los Angeles, along with word of mouth and reviews, had created a demand for Cassavetes' film.

The sell-out crowds in New York and Los Angeles were big news in the trades; Cassavetes made sure of that. Suddenly instead of cold-calling theater owners out of the Motion Picture Almanac—the directory of theater owners and operators around the country—about playing an unknown film, Ruban found himself fielding phone calls from theater chains and owners all over the country, seeking to book Cassavetes' movie.

Ruban and Cassavetes took a page from the studios' book and would commit the film only if the theater would pay a guarantee upfront. Theoretically, that would be applied to the percentage of the grosses to which Cassavetes was entitled after the film paid back the guarantee. But Ruban knew that you needed to get the money upfront, because, as he put it, "The theaters all felt that, after the first week, the contract was open to renegotiation."

He and Ruban spent the next eighteen months booking *A Woman Under the Influence* around the country, in a long play-off that eventually earned the film between $8 and $10 million, depending on who you ask (on an initial investment of $1 million).

Remarkably, virtually all of those bookings were at mainstream theaters. While there is an art house circuit around the country today to service independent films, the only ones that would play an independent film in 1974 were the revival houses, and they weren't about to give anyone an open-ended run or meet the terms of someone like Cassavetes.

So Cassavetes and his crew created a circuit of their own: "I had 300 prints and, for most of the time, I had a half-dozen people working for me," Ruban said. "Every waking moment was spent talking about money. It made me crazy. But we had to be in business for real."

Lipsky discovered the rigidity of the world they were trying to break into. One theater chain in Iowa would only call the Faces International office collect. A Georgia chain refused to book the film unless Cassavetes opened an office in Atlanta.

But Cassavetes loved hustling, meeting the buyers and the bookers. This film was a personal mission, and John went on the road to sell it. He also found that college film societies would pay him more for his film than theaters, so he and Falk took the film around to show it and make appearances on campuses.

Cassavetes was convinced the film had a blue-collar audience, a constituency that he worried was having a hard time finding the movie. So he convinced Lipsky to book it at a drive-in theater in his hometown of Huntingon, Long Island. It played as a double feature with *Machine Gun McCain* and grossed $11,000, a surprisingly large sum for the time.

Cassavetes also believed the film would speak to black audiences and asked that *Woman* be booked into the Apollo Theater, the black entertainment mecca on 125th Street in Harlem. It opened there on a Wednesday and closed the same day.

"I think they sold two tickets to the first show—and one of those walked out," Lipsky recalled. "By the second show, the film buyer had called us and begged us to take it off the screen. But it played the Apollo."

Rowlands would watch audiences from the window of the office Cassavetes had taken above the Fox Wilshire, where *Woman* was playing: "At a certain point, there would be this mass exodus from the theater," Rowlands recalled. "The first night I was thinking, 'Oh my God, we haven't even gotten to the hard part.'

"Inevitably, several people would come out and they would be very upset. But most of the time they'd stand outside and have a cigarette, then turn around and go back in. We knew what we must be putting people through to get them to act like that."

Even the people who liked *Woman* had a hard time describing it in terms that would make a viewer rush out to see it. Actor Richard Dreyfuss was appearing on *The Mike Douglas Show* in Philadelphia, during a week when Peter Falk was Douglas' co-host to promote *Woman*. As they chatted on camera, Douglas asked Dreyfuss if he had seen *A Woman Under the Influence*.

Rather than simply say, "Yes and I thought it was great," the voluble actor launched into a description of the film: "It was the most incredible, disturbing, scary, brilliant, dark, sad, depressing movie. I went crazy. I went home and vomited."

At which point Falk piped up, "It's also funny. It's a funny movie."

As Dreyfuss said later, "I had committed this show business faux pas. I was not savvy about media stuff."

When the show went to commercial, Falk picked up a nearby phone and called Cassavetes: "This kid, he's telling everyone how terribly dark and scary the movie is," Falk said. And on the other end of the phone, Dreyfuss heard Cassavetes laughing, telling Falk, "He can say what he wants."

In fact, it worked to the film's advantage. Suddenly everyone wanted to see the film that made Richard Dreyfuss sick, to see if it would happen to them, too.

Though they'd made the film far outside the system—indeed, had taken on the system by distributing the film themselves—*Woman* was not ignored by the Academy Awards. It collected only two nominations, but they were two major ones: for Cassavetes as best director and for Rowlands as best actress.

Getting any nominations at all was a miracle, Mike Ferris believed: "Nonunion pictures didn't get nominations," he said. "But the picture was so strong—there was no way they could have resisted it."

The movie itself was squeezed out of a crowded field of best-picture contenders, its slot going to a big-budget disaster film, *The Towering Inferno*, while the other nominations went to *Lenny*, *The Conversation*, *Chinatown*, and *The Godfather, Part II*, the year's juggernaut.

Cassavetes was part of an elite group of directors nominated that year: Francois Truffaut (*Day for Night*), Francis Ford Coppola (*Godfather II*), Roman Polanski (*Chinatown*), and Bob Fosse (*Lenny*).

The nomination also put Cassavetes into an exclusive group of film artists: those nominated for Oscars as actors, screenwriters, and directors in the course of their career. Beside Cassavetes, only Orson Welles and Kenneth Branagh fit that particular profile.

Rowlands was a solid favorite in one of the few categories where *Godfather II* wasn't a factor, up against Valerie Perrine for *Lenny*, Diahann Carroll for *Claudine*, Faye Dunaway for *Chinatown*, and Ellen Burstyn for *Alice Doesn't Live Here Anymore*, directed by Cassavetes' friend and protégé Martin Scorsese.

"We all thought Gena was going to win the Oscar," Elaine Kagan said. Added John Finnegan, "When Gena lost to Ellen Burstyn, man, that was a fucking downer."

Still, they tried not to let the fact that Gena had not won dampen the post-Oscars party they had planned at Chasen's. After all, she'd won the best-actress awards from the National Board of Review and the Golden Globes.

So they drank and laughed—and stood and watched as Tim Carey got up "in a tux he'd taken off a dead man," according to Finnegan, toting a loving cup with dented sides. Carey loudly declaimed a speech hailing Cassavetes as a great man and berating the Academy as a fraud and a travesty, before making a dramatic exit. At which point Finnegan turned to an equally dumbstruck Ben Gazzara and said, "You told me Mussolini died."

One other celebrant turned up: Martin Scorsese. "He cried about the fact that Gena didn't win," Carole Smith recalled. "It hurt him so much that he had made the movie that beat her."

The success of *Woman* and *Alice Doesn't Live Here Anymore* touched something in women's lives that movies had avoided in the past. It exposed a part of life that the movies never focused on: the hard parts, the tragedy, the inability to cope or to comfort.

As Molly Haskell, who wrote *From Reverence to Rape: The Treatment of Women in the Movies*, said, "They were very influential for women, those films. They stretched boundaries. And remember—it was basically men looking at this. There weren't any women directors doing this in commercial cinema. These stories were prepolitical. They described a world with no self-help. It was Betty Friedan and Simone de Beauvoir. That was their world, the awakening of the housewife. *Woman* was Gena and John taking on the craziness of domesticity. It's not an issues film. His film was spontaneous and empty of criticism of domestic inequity."

Rowlands said at the time, "There are vast areas of the female experience that haven't begun to be tapped and which won't be except when women begin to write about them. For a long time, women were immensely unpopular in this country. However, the receipts from the film indicate a revival of interest in the women's picture, which might create a market."

The film wound up making Cassavetes money: "Everybody got back their investment on *Woman*," Ruban said.

But to hear Cassavetes talk at the time, nothing could dull the pain of making and distributing a film with his own funds.

"I don't think I could ever make another film like this again. It's too difficult. Right now, all I can hope is that the picture is extremely successful. And if it isn't, I won't make another one—that's all. Which in itself is no great tragedy."

As he told playwright Meade Roberts, "I'm an artist, not a frigging salesman."

Thirty-seven

John and Gena

The success of *A Woman Under the Influence* brought new attention to Rowlands' work and new recognition to a career that some thought had been spent in the shadow of her husband—under his influence, as so many clever headline writers would have it—even though she was starring in his films. But Rowlands felt blessed to be able to mix work and family in the way that Cassavetes' films allowed. Plus she was muse to a writer who kept handing her plum parts.

Filmmaker Paul Mazursky said, "Gena was his Giulietta Massina. I can't imagine them without each other."

Guy McElwaine, Cassavetes' agent before running Columbia Pictures, said, "She was not unlike Anne Bancroft in that she never was interested in being a movie star. It was always about the craft, the work, and the kind of people they worked with. Gena had the career she wanted."

Rowlands echoed that sentiment: "I've always thought of my whole life as my career and acting is just part of it," she said. "I didn't quit acting. I could never do that. Let's just say I put acting on simmer for a while. I decided to turn down any part that would take me away from my kids while they were growing up. When they're grown, I'll probably get back into it more. And I think being a mother can only add to my abilities as an actress. You can't learn much about life if you never leave a soundstage."

With the success of *Woman*, Cassavetes found himself forced into a role he'd never sought: a spokesman for a political viewpoint. Though he voted Democrat and supported Bobby Kennedy for president in 1968, Cassavetes didn't have much time for overt political demonstration. Not that he didn't see the issues. He just wasn't sure demonstrations would solve the problems.

Now, suddenly, he was expected to offer opinions about the struggle between the genders that his film seemed to illuminate. Cassavetes would forever deny having a political motive with his picture, but ultimately was trying to raise consciousness about women's lives, a subject on which he had no shortage of opinions.

Still, he admitted, "There's so much hostility between men and women now. That's what prompted us to make the film. We took a view in favor of marriage, because nobody else was for it. Let's face it; no one likes marriage at this stage of our lives. So the picture fluctuates between being a romantic picture and a realistic one."

Rowlands seemed more comfortable with speaking on the issues: "I do think that I can in some way represent women in America at this time," she said. "I'm a feminist in that I've been a self-supporting woman since I was eighteen years old. I am a wife to a husband; I'm a mother to three children. I am not a cupcake actress—though I have nothing against them and I don't mean that to sound condescending. My emphasis in life is deeply split between these two things—to be an actress and to be a mother. It's a great conflict in my life."

Inevitably Cassavetes and Rowlands found their own relationship under scrutiny by the media: What was he saying about the state of his marriage in movies like *Faces* and *Woman*? What had Cassavetes learned about his marriage from making the movie? Were there elements of Nick and Mabel in John and Gena?

"Gena and I have a normal marriage," he said. "It's not all roses, but there is a genuine love here that carries us through any kind of time, any kind of hardships. We're more than willing to make sacrifices for each other. Yet it comes to mind that marriage, like any partnership, is a rather difficult thing. And it has been taken rather lightly in the movies."

Usually, Cassavetes would speak generally about marriage and allow the listener to draw his own conclusions about what he was really discussing. Was he talking about himself and the obstacles he faced in being part of a marriage for what had become twenty years?

"It's easy to be in love with somebody for five minutes, but you put it over a twenty-year period of marriage—you get tired of a wife," Cassavetes said. "You like them, you love them, you get excited by them, but you also know all their stories, you know all their jokes and your tastes begin to splinter and go in different directions. Those are feelings that anybody that's been married any length of time or has lived for a while realizes is a true fact. It's not just make-believe."

Men, he argued, were by nature adventurous: "It makes for unhappiness in marriage when women don't understand the basic differences between them and that men do need adventure," he said. "Indiscretions are a small part of all life. If it's an indiscretion, it's not really important. Women must realize that men need adventure."

He came closest to admitting that his record of fidelity might not have been spotless when he said, "For years, I claimed the artist's right not to be headed down by anything or anybody. I made films, got drunk, stayed away from home. I destroyed my wife, yet she stood by me through child after child. So I made *Woman* as a tribute to Gena, for all the lousy things I'd done to her."

As he observed, he always wound up going home; he and Rowlands had been married almost thirty-five years when he died.

Seymour Cassel observed, "The greatest love affair I ever observed was Gena and John. There were ups and downs but the compassion those two people had for each other was remarkable. They were opposites, in a way. Gena is the most well-read person I've ever known and has such dignity. John was just a guy. We'd go shoot basketball at midnight."

Cassavetes was in general adamant about keeping his private life private. He would seldom talk about Rowlands as a wife, preferring to talk about their work together, rather than their life: "When Gena and I are home together, we're husband and wife," he said. "On the set, we're deadly combatants. We have great respect for each other, like enemies do. We're working to one end: her putting her view across and me setting an atmosphere for her to come out. There can't be any interest in anything else."

They were obviously a case of opposites attracting: the dark, outgoing, energetic, passionate Cassavetes; the blonde, thoughtful, proper, reticent Rowlands.

Observed Jay Cocks, "Together, John and Gena were like a bebop version of Tracy and Hepburn. They would play off each other, finish each other's sentences, look at each other and know where the other was going. They'd tease and say fondly dismissive things. He was a wild character and she was the adoring, occasionally impatient older sister. They were nuts about each other."

A Woman Under the Influence had been a film built around the fragile mystery of women, and it examined how little men ever really know about the women they live with. It recalled Cassavetes' own relationship with Rowlands early in their marriage and the perception that she was quiet and retiring in a group, at least next to her more forceful and voluble husband. She eventually learned to hold her own and to make herself heard.

An anecdote repeated at the time of Cassavetes' death related that, several years after they were married, Cassavetes had come home unexpectedly one day to find Rowlands playing the piano brilliantly, despite never previously expressing an interest in music or playing the piano in his presence. Cassavetes reportedly was furious that this secret had been kept from him, and Rowlands was infuriated that he knew her so little.

Their marriage grew to involve much more communication over the years. But it was privileged information; Rowlands was always reticent to talk about life with Cassavetes.

Ask her to talk about herself and her roles, and she could, easily: "Unlike Mabel, I know how to cope with my emotionalism, how to go off to the Actors Studio for a workout where, with a group of other actors, I can do it—act it out, perform it and discharge it," she said. "If it weren't for acting, I think that I would be a lot crazier than Mabel."

She was also more than willing to discuss her working relationship with Cassavetes: "A lot of problems are built into the situation of married people working together," Rowlands said. "Subsequent to *Faces*—that was bloody murder to go through—those have been resolved. I wasn't accustomed to John's professional scrutiny. I was used to him seeing me through the eyes of love. Since then, I've learned to disregard the fact that we're married at all. I really don't think of it."

Or she would turn questions about Cassavetes into a question about Cassavetes as writer and director.

"We talk about scripts all the time," Rowlands said. "I'd say maybe 80 percent of our life together—the other 20 percent we talk about the children. But about 80 percent of the time we talk about scripts and ideas and why people do things and what we saw and the irony of how much more dramatic people are in real life than they are on film."

She was capable of admitting that, like Mabel, "there are many times when I'm home and feel all those heavy emotions—anger, frustration, all of them. The kids are in a bad temper or the day hasn't gone right and I think, wow, wouldn't it be nice to be on a stage somewhere playing Blanche DuBois. But then, just as easily, I can be in a theater watching someone play Blanche and I'll think, 'Boy, I sure am glad I'm not up there on that stage.'"

She did allow herself to ruminate publicly, "How can you be married to the same person for twenty years? You can't. You keep changing and you either fall in love with the changed person or you don't. Maybe acting has been good exercise for our marriage, because it keeps us so exposed all the time. You get used to making an idiot of yourself early on."

But when interviewers would try to delve into the marriage itself, Rowlands would throw up a wall, politely but firmly, with an answer that became a kind of rote response: "So much of our relationship was lived publicly that I cherish the private parts," she said in a 2000 interview, almost eleven years after Cassavetes' death. "I want to keep that for myself."

Even in a recorded conversation with a long-time friend, playwright Ted Allan, Rowlands drew a line. When he asked her how she divided her thinking between Cassavetes as her husband and her director, she said, "I think of John as my husband, I think of him as the father of my children, I think of him as my lover—but also think of him as a director, as an artist."

Questions about her marriage produced superstitious responses: Rowlands said she and Cassavetes had made a vow never to say anything good about their marriage "because it just puts the evil eye on it."

But when Allan asked her if Cassavetes was as great a husband as he was a director, Rowlands said, "I consider that gossip. That's my own personal thing and it's none of your business or anyone else's. Don't you understand that three-quarters of my life is laid bare in front of ten million people? Is there nothing for me? Is there nothing private for me? If that's true or false, you'll never know. Nobody will ever know. It's mine and nobody will know."

Eventually, she refined her thoughts into a stock answer that was inviolate. As she would say in print on a number of occasions, "I've always made a rule: I never discuss my private life with the press. Call it superstition or whatever, it always seems to me that, when two people talk about their happy marriage, they wind up in divorce court six months later. I see no reason to tempt the fates."

Still, in the fall of 1975, there were whispers that Cassavetes and Rowlands had separated, en route to divorce. Gossip columnist Marilyn Beck reported in August that there were rumors about the marriage—that Rowlands was leaving Cassavetes for Falk. The tabloid press ran with the story, and as Beck noted, the gossip was fueled by the fact that Cassavetes was spending his time in a bachelor apartment in Beverly Hills, away from the couple's Laurel Canyon house. In fact, Beck reported, Rowlands had rented the apartment and decorated it herself, as a place for Cassavetes to get some writing done. But the couple had, until that point, refused to discuss it.

"John believes in the superstition that talking about something good in one's life will cause it to turn bad," Beck reported. "When I contacted them about the current rumor raging around town that Gena walked out, they both assured me everything was fine and that, as Gena put it, 'We haven't even had an argument in months—and I wish these silly lies about us would stop.'"

Speaking to a small weekly paper in the San Fernando Valley, Rowlands continued to deny the stories, saying, "I just can't understand the rumors. Our marriage is no different now than it was a year ago, five years ago or ten years ago. I don't know where the story originated."

Thirty-eight

Mikey & Nicky

I t made perfect sense that John Cassavetes would become friends with Elaine May. Both of them had percolating, fertile imaginations and aggressive, subversive senses of humor. And both of them had become famous for using improvisation in the 1950s: Cassavetes for *Shadows*, May for her work with the Compass Players and Second City. She teamed with Mike Nichols to become Nichols and May, the most influential comedy team of the mid-twentieth century, culminating with the nine-month run on Broadway, beginning in October 1960, of *An Evening with Mike Nichols and Elaine May*.

When Nichols and May split up in 1962, Nichols moved into directing theater, winning a string of Tony Awards for directing the plays of Neil Simon, then an Oscar for his second film, *The Graduate*.

May had turned to theater, writing and directing plays, doing a little acting in films, and, eventually, writing and directing her film *A New Leaf* (1971) and directing *The Heartbreak Kid* (1972).

She had harbored *Mikey & Nicky* as a personal project for more than a decade, beginning with a play she was writing when she joined the Compass Players in 1954. Falk had heard about it while acting with her in *Luv*, the failed film version of Murray Schisgal's hit Broadway comedy that they starred in together in 1967.

"In the course of one night, Elaine told me about this story," Falk recalled. "It was based on real people in a real neighborhood, people that were close to her, whom she had known when she was a child. She remembered it very vividly and it caused in her a need to write it. I thought it was a helluva story."

Cassavetes encountered her script while trying to convince Falk to do *Husbands* and jumped at the chance to work with the two of them: "He explained that if Elaine is directing and I was in it, he knew it would make a good picture," Falk recalled.

But other projects interfered with all of their schedules, so May had gone on to make *A New Leaf* and *Heartbreak Kid* before she could scare up the money for *Mikey & Nicky*.

In the meantime, she had befriended Cassavetes, whose maverick spirit and sense of cinematic adventure she shared, though she matched his tenacity with her own neurotic perfectionism. As she worked on her own films and doctored scripts for friends, she became a part of Cassavetes' circle and would show up to do readings of new scripts.

When *Heartbreak Kid* was a hit, May was able to secure financing to do *Mikey & Nicky,* a film about two small-time hoods in the Philadelphia mob. Mikey (played by Falk) is summoned to a hotel by his long-time friend Nicky (Cassavetes). Nicky has stolen money from their boss, who has now hired a killer to eliminate Nicky. Nicky wants Mikey to help get him safely out of town.

Instead, they spend a long night together, bouncing around Philadelphia, as Nicky says one last good-bye to people and places that mean something to him. At the same time, Mikey tries to make contact with the hired assassin (Ned Beatty), for whom he is trying to finger Nicky. Mikey harbors a blind rage at Nicky over slights and insults of the past and so, even as Nicky depends upon him to help, Mikey is in the process of betraying his friend.

Cassavetes took the role to work with Falk and May. It was also a means to a paycheck (and a welcome distraction) during the late 1973 and early 1974 editing on *A Woman Under the Influence,* and the gearing up to distribute it.

Around the same time, Cassavetes took two other roles for their paycheck, rather than their artistic challenge: *Capone,* in which he appeared as a favor to Gazzara, and the disaster film *Two-Minute Warning,* in which he played "a SWAT chief so hard-boiled he makes Charlton Heston's police captain look like a gutless peacenik," according to Janet Maslin in *Newsweek.*

Cassavetes, Falk, and May worked together on May's script, which shares a skewed noir sensibility with *The Killing of a Chinese Bookie,* also in process at the time. Though May received the "written and directed by" credit, Frank Yablans, the Paramount chief who left the studio before the film was finished, said, "I'm sure John had input to the script. John and Elaine were very close."

Al Ruban, who would produce *Bookie,* recalled, "John came to me and said that Elaine wanted me to produce *Mikey & Nicky.* But John said, 'You tell Ed Scherick [who had produced May's *Heartbreak Kid* and was now a Paramount exec] that we don't want him to come to the set.' I said, 'Do you want to draw the lines that quickly?' And he said yes. So I go to a meeting with Ed and he said, 'That's the first time anybody has said that to me. OK, I accept.' Elaine says, 'That's great.' A week later, I'm off the picture and Michael Hausman is on."

Hausman had been May's production manager and associate producer on *Heartbreak Kid.* That, however, was an entirely different experience because May had not written the script; Neil Simon had.

"Elaine couldn't change one word of Neil Simon's script unless she asked him," Hausman said. "On *Mikey & Nicky,* it was a different story. She had written it. She was always in consultation with Peter and John. It was a lot of collective effort, a lot of time spent discussing stuff."

Though it was definitely May's film, Hausman said, Cassavetes was a strong influence on it: "For them, it was like a personal, private movie," he said. "She admired Cassavetes as a filmmaker and they had a lot of discussions of how to shoot it."

The problem, Hausman said, was that May had wanted to make the film for so long that it became hard to commit to one idea: "She'd seen it so many ways in her head," Hausman said. "Certain people shouldn't be put in that kind of box."

When they went off to shoot the film in Philadelphia in the summer of 1973, May insisted on night-shooting all over the City of Brotherly Love. The film was shot in sequence, for sixty days in Philadelphia and then an additional fifty days in Los Angeles. Notoriously detailed-oriented, May never quite said what she wanted or what she thought, then would express vague approval or disapproval as the mood struck her.

Given that much of it consists of two-person scenes, the filming on *Mikey & Nicky* took an inordinate amount of time. Actress Joyce van Patten, who played Nicky's wife in one scene toward the end of the film, recalled it taking a week, filming with three cameras, for May to get the sequence in the can.

At one point in filming their scene, Cassavetes expressed concern to

May, because he had to strike van Patten, and multiple takes meant he was hitting her again and again, and he was concerned about hurting her.

"How hard are you hitting her?" May asked. "Show me."

So Cassavetes slapped her, knocking May back on her heels. May righted herself, then said, "Maybe go a little easier."

After weeks of shooting in Philadelphia, May had to stop production for a month while Falk started the new season of *Columbo*. After reviewing the footage—May ended up shooting more than a million and a half feet of film (by comparison, only about 450,000 feet were shot for *Gone with the Wind*)—Paramount had agreed to let her finish the film, but only if May shot the rest of it in Los Angeles, rather than Philadelphia, to save money.

"I'd guess we were two-thirds done when they pulled the plug," Ned Beatty recalled. "A month goes by and I get a call: We're going to finish in downtown L.A., on the equivalent of the Bowery. I'd just gotten my hair cut short so I had to go get a wig."

To make up time in Los Angeles, May and Hausman asked Cassavetes to head up the second unit, to get the material that May didn't have time to shoot herself. Beatty was the recipient of most of Cassavetes' attention. Cassavetes sat in the front seat with an Arriflex, filming Beatty's character driving around in search of Mikey.

Sensing something close to him, Beatty turned his head and almost bumped into the camera. "John, what are you doing?" Beatty asked.

"This is great, man," Cassavetes enthused, checking the camera. "You won't believe what this looks like."

Cassavetes claimed he'd won a macro lens in a poker game and this was his first chance to try it out: "He must have been shooting nosehairs," said Beatty, who found some of Cassavetes' other techniques off-putting. "John would do things to startle you," he said. "I never liked it when a director tries to fool actors into a performance. I never felt threatened by it with John, but it was not one of my favorite things, either."

May began cutting the film at Paramount, then shifted her base of operations to an editing suite she set up at the Sunset Marquis, spending more than a year on it before eventually surrendering the film to Paramount.

Editing was a laborious process made more difficult by May's indecisiveness. By the end of the process, even Cassavetes had lost patience with May's dithering over the editing. Jay Cocks said, "The film was too nuts even for John, and that's saying something."

At one point, with Paramount breathing down her neck for the finished film, two reels of the cut negative disappeared from the editing room.

Paramount brought law enforcement into the matter, but May denied any involvement.

According to one account, however, May had inveigled her psychoanalyst into taking the reels and hiding them in a garage in Connecticut. Paramount subsequently cobbled together a film out of what was left and dumped it into theaters at the end of 1976.

"It was not a film you open at Christmas," said Julian Schlossberg, who was vice president of worldwide acquisitions at Paramount at the time. Joyce van Patten recalled seeing a screening of the film with the rest of the cast. Afterward, Walter Matthau, whose wife, Carol, played Nicky's girlfriend, sidled up to her and muttered, "This would be a good movie, if you were on a train from Vladivostok to Moscow."

Some of the reviews were favorable, in a cautionary way. Stanley Kauffmann summed it up by referring to the project as "an odd, biting, grinning, sideways-scuttling rodent of a picture . . . a little furry film that first interests, then amuses, then bites you, then scurries away again, leaving you a bit sickened. But authentically sickened."

Then there were pronouncements like Judith Crist's: "Both characters are so obnoxious that the climactic dramatic moment of ultimate betrayal does little but relieve the tedium they've created." Frank Rich wrote that it was "a film that should not be reviewed so much as quietly buried and forgotten."

A year or so later, May was able to get her reedited version into circulation. That version was released in 2004 on a special edition DVD; the film's supporters remain a small but vocal minority.

Thirty-nine

The Killing of a
Chinese Bookie

"I can't take the fight anymore," Cassavetes declared when he had finished *A Woman Under the Influence*—the shooting, the editing, the distribution. "I run out of breath too fast. I think they ought to kill all the old directors over thirty."

But of course Cassavetes—who was forty-five at the time—didn't believe what he was saying. He had beaten the system with *Woman*, not only making the movie his way with his own money, but turning it into the most successful independent feature of its time. The experience only confirmed his already overwhelming belief in himself and his methods, and audiences seemed to agree with him.

But now he was impatient: *Woman* had taken more than four years by the time they collected the last receipts. There seemed to be a ripe market just waiting for another John Cassavetes film. Why couldn't lightning strike twice?

All of that time spent focusing on the distribution operation, moreover, put Cassavetes a little too closely in touch with what he euphemistically referred to as "a business life." It bred a certain panic in him, leading to only one possible conclusion: He had to start another film, in spite of the fact that he was exhausted from *Woman*.

"So I got everybody together," Cassavetes recalled, "and said, 'Anyone like to make a movie? We start shooting in two weeks. I'll write it as we go.'"

Jeff Lipsky, who was working in the distribution of *Woman*, said, "*Minnie and Moskowitz* was '71—and then it was three years where Hollywood gave up on him. It was three years between the previous two and he didn't want that to happen again. He didn't want to wait for Hollywood to offer a job."

What he came up with was *The Killing of a Chinese Bookie*, about a man whose world is falling apart and whose choices in a moment of crisis—choices true to his dreams—ultimately lead to his destruction.

Ostensibly a gangster movie, it is the story of a nightclub owner whose gambling debts threaten to ruin his life. It could easily be taken as a metaphor for John Cassavetes' career, a connection Ben Gazzara made while filming with John.

Gazzara and Cassavetes were in the back of a limo, where Cassavetes had been shooting handheld footage himself. On the ride back, Cassavetes began talking about the value of dreams—of the dreams of Gazzara's character and of people in general—and how the dreamers were at odds with the dream-killers, the kind of people whose only purpose is to offer obstacles and distractions to those pursuing dreams. And as he talked, Cassavetes eyes welled with tears.

"It was then that I understood," noted Gazzara. "The picture could have been a metaphor for John's life: a man with a dream having to battle people without vision."

The original cut of *The Killing of a Chinese Bookie* played in theaters for only a week and then disappeared. Cassavetes, on his own initiative, ultimately reedited the film, making it shorter and more plot-driven; it had an abortive release two years later.

The longer version has the feel of a Cassavetes shaggy-dog story, a plot he might spin out off the top of his head over drinks after work. "So you've got this guy . . ." But it also meanders and dawdles, digresses and goes off on tangents. The shorter version lops off some of the early character exploration and becomes more identifiable as a straight-ahead noir, though it still veers wide of that mark.

It is an oddly conceived film, one built around a strip club that features what appears to be an amateur-night host, slowly singing standards like "After the Ball Is Over" while the strippers casually gyrate. It is a deconstruction of the milieu, almost a takeoff on a gangster movie because the emphases are so strangely placed. Wherever a real gangster movie would have had a car chase or a shootout, Cassavetes substituted an act at the strip club.

From a distance of thirty years, the film feels more like an arty '70s experiment—a European take on an American genre—than like Cassavetes trying to solve a dramatic problem through a film. Maybe it's the picture's inorganic nature; it feels as though it was constructed by Cassavetes, rather than pulled from within him, giving it a disconnected feel. Or maybe it's just a film that doesn't work very well, in whatever form—an honorable failure.

The longer original version begins with Cosmo Vitelli (Ben Gazzara) arriving at a sidewalk cafe in Los Angeles to meet Marty Reitz (Al Ruban). There's an obvious air of distrust as Cosmo hands him a massive wad of cash, held together by a rubber band, in a crumpled brown paper bag. It is Cosmo's final payment on what apparently has been a sizable gambling debt, for which Marty is the collector.

Cosmo takes a taxi to the Crazy Horse West, his nightclub on Sunset Strip, a strip joint whose exterior is decorated lavishly with cartoonish paintings of nude women. He is, as he observes, finally working for himself again. And the satisfaction—the sense of a man at peace in his natural environment (however tawdry that environment might be)—is palpable as he goes about his routine at the club.

He observes the crowd, goes backstage to chat with the dancers, speaks to the audience through a backstage microphone to announce the next act, then goes outside to pace in front of the club and greet customers as they come in. "It'll pick up," he says knowingly to his bouncer/doorman Vince (Vincent Barbi).

(In the shortened version, Cassavetes starts with a slow night at the Crazy Horse West, with Cosmo saying encouragingly, "It'll pick up." He then goes to make his payment to Marty, which is broken up by a sequence backstage at the Crazy Horse, with Cosmo announcing the acts on a backstage microphone as the girls race up and down the stairs for a costume change. Then he meets Marty again, this time seemingly in the daytime; though at least a day has passed since their first meeting, Gazzara wears the same clothes from the beginning of the movie through this scene—and Al Ruban is wearing the same checked shirt as in the earlier scene. After making the final pay-off—"Paid in full"—Cosmo takes a cab to a bar where no one knows him, drinks, and celebrates.)

On this evening, Mort Weil (Seymour Cassel) shows up at Cosmo's club with three carloads of people, asking for Mr. Sophistication: "This is the best joint this side of Vegas," Mort announces to his friends, to Cosmo's delight. Mort identifies himself to Cosmo as a fellow club-owner and tells him that, at his club in Santa Monica, he features an honest, high-stakes poker game, if Cosmo is interested.

So Cosmo rents a stretch limo and invites his current girlfriend, Rachel

(Azizi Johari), and two of the other strippers, Sherry and Margo (Alice Fred-lund and Donna Gordon) out on a group date. It begins romantically, with Cosmo picking each up with a corsage in hand (though he makes his chauffeur, played by David Rowlands, pin the flowers on the girls) and of-fering champagne in the car. He is the picture of a high roller riding high, surrounded by a harem of adoring women.

(In the shorter version, Cassavetes eliminates most of the scene of Cosmo at both Sherry's and Rachel's houses. At Sherry's, Cassavetes' son Nick, at that point a strapping 6-foot-4 sixteen-year-old, is part of a family group at a dining room table that includes both of his grandmothers, Lady Rowlands and Katherine Cassavetes. They are glimpsed only in the short version, shown barely long enough for them to register even with people who might recognize them. In the longer version, Cassavetes included an extended scene of small talk between Cosmo and the family; at one point Nick walks past Cosmo, towering over Gazzara. The longer version also fea-tures a conversation in the limo between Cosmo and Sherry, about the rel-ative merits of champagne and vodka, which is not in the shorter version.)

Things are bubbly in the limo, but all has changed by the next scene, which finds Cosmo's women impatiently finishing cigarettes and fixing their makeup in the ladies' room, while grousing about the evening and the place Cosmo has brought them. As they leave the ladies room and re-turn to Cosmo, we see the reason: They've done nothing all evening but sit around and watch Cosmo play cards. They're bored, but they're also dis-gusted, because Cosmo has just dug himself into a sizable hole at the poker table and shows no signs of stopping.

He has lost so much money that the Commodore, the floor manager of the nautically themed Ship Ahoy club, has to tell Cosmo he's run out of credit, while Cosmo is in the middle of trying to raise a bet on a losing hand. The Commodore finally agrees to take a check if Cosmo can back it up with credit cards.

But after the game, Cosmo and the girls must go to the office to settle Cosmo's debt. Cosmo, who has always repaid his debts over a period of time, with interest, finds himself confronted by Mort and his colleagues Eddie-Red (Red Kullers, who sang "Buddy Can You Spare a Dime" in *Hus-bands*), Flo (Timothy Carey), Phil (Robert Phillips), and the boss, John (Morgan Woodward), who tell him they expect the money—$23,000— immediately. Cosmo had offered a gold credit card as collateral earlier in the evening, but this turns out to be a worthless gasoline credit card. Nor does Cosmo have enough in any bank account to cover a check.

(In the shorter version, Cassavetes included a scene of Cosmo and the girls in a waiting room with other losing customers. Cosmo and the girls are forced to listen as these other debtors receive the strong-arm treatment from the club's collectors.)

"Everything I make goes back into the club," Cosmo tells them, assuring them that he has paid off other gambling debts over time in the past without missing a payment and that he will get them the money as soon as he can. They make him sign some paperwork, a more corporate version of an I.O.U., except he's signing his club—his life—away.

"Twenty-three thousand dollars is a lot of money," Flo says ominously.

Cosmo drops the girls off; Rachel is last and she invites him in. He declines, saying, "I think the thing to do is to get some cash and go back down there," as though this is an option. Instead, he heads for the club, then walks up Sunset to The Source restaurant, a popular health-food eatery of the era, and sits at one of its outdoor tables, thinking about what to do.

Obviously he's a regular, because the waitress (Trisha Pelham) interrupts his mood to chat with him. "All dressed up with no place to go?" she says, referring to his tuxedo. Tall and well-built, she suggestively asks, "Are you gonna let me audition for you?" as though the subject has come up before.

"You don't wanna do that," Cosmo says, then eyes her appraisingly as she fetches his coffee. "You've got a good body," he tells her. "And I can dance," she tells him. "Want me to audition?"

(In the shorter version, this scene is briefer and much more ambiguous. The implication is that this is a game they play. Perhaps she regularly asks him and he turns her down to spare her entering into a tough life; or perhaps they've been fooling around for a while and this is the code they use to begin a tryst. Or perhaps he's had his eye on her all along but never acted on it until now, seeing the audition as a way to begin an affair that will distract him from his current predicament.)

Whatever the reason, he says yes, and she follows him back to the Crazy Horse. There she changes into a gauzy, sheer outfit; Cosmo, as usual, selects the most unlikely music for a stripper. All of Bo Harwood's music for the film reflects his folk-rock roots and sounds out of place in a strip joint of any era.

The waitress begins to do ballet-like leaps across the stage to the music. "You don't have to jump anymore, sweetheart, just walk up and down," Cosmo tells her. But before she can, they are interrupted by Rachel, Cosmo's stripper girlfriend, who walks in on this "audition" and physically attacks the girl.

Or so it seems: The camera is pushed away in the scuffle and never quite focuses on the action. There is the impression of motion and sound effects of punches and scuffling, before the waitress breaks away and runs into the dressing room, while Cosmo restrains Rachel. The girl, now in her jeans but still topless, runs out of the club carrying her shirt.

Cosmo tries to make amends to Rachel, but the best he can come up with is, "Look, I'm a club owner," as though this excuses and explains his behavior.

It is another night at the Crazy Horse West, where the crowd is large and vocal as a stripper in pasties and top hat comes out and recites Edward Lear's "The Owl and the Pussycat." She introduces Mr. Sophistication (though she calls him Mr. Fascination). He is played by Cassavetes' friend, playwright Meade Roberts: paunchy, overweight, balding. He has an oily manner and wears a top hat and a cape over an aged tuxedo; his face has an elaborate Snidely Whiplash mustache drawn on, as well as exaggerated eyebrows.

He tells the audience he is going to take them to Paris, the city of lights, then starts singing "I Can't Give You Anything But Love" a capella. As he warbles his enervated ditty, strippers in costumes—a gendarme, a Paris street walker, a French maid—come out and move with similar listlessness to the music.

(The Crazy Horse stage shows are the film's central flaw. They're amateurish, pretentious, even campy—like an Andy Warhol travesty. It's hard to imagine the Crazy Horse actually remaining in business as a going concern, given the kind of shows Cosmo presents.)

Cosmo's normal evening of work is interrupted by the arrival of Mort and the rest of the casino bosses, who have come to see him. They take him to a coffee shop, where they pull Cosmo into an uncomfortable discussion: Does he have the money he owes? When can he get it? Flo is particularly threatening, continually interrupting the discussion by saying darkly, "He owes the money, let him pay."

It quickly becomes apparent that Cosmo doesn't have the money or any way of getting it quickly. So the hoods offer to erase his debt if he'll do them a favor: There's a bookie in Chinatown, an older guy, who has overstepped his bounds and needs to be taught a lesson. Cosmo will eliminate his debt if he will rub the guy out.

Cosmo is mortified. "I'm a club owner," he offers again, as though it were a badge of honor this time.

When the hoods ask if he served in the war, he tells them he was in Korea. Did he ever kill anyone? they ask. He replies angrily, "That was in a war, that was different."

Instead Cosmo suggests they give him something smaller to do to reduce the debt, rather than eliminate it. Fine, they tell him: Take some of
his girls and go down to Chinatown and attract the bookie's attention. He
likes pretty girls; have the Crazy Horse girls be nice to him and invite him
to the club, where some of Mort's associates will take care of the rest.

But Cosmo's trip to Chinatown with his trio of strippers is a bust.
They see no sign of the bookie, then go to a martial-arts movie that makes
them late getting to the Crazy Horse for that night's show. As the show
goes on, Cosmo is approached by Mort, who takes Cosmo outside, where
Flo is waiting. When Cosmo tells them he's decided not to reduce the debt
and to just pay the money he owes over time, Flo takes Cosmo across the
street and into an alley, where he works him over. Then he shoves him into
the front seat of a car and squeezes in next to him; Mort and his boss are
in the back seat.

Now they're not asking but telling: Here's the gun. Here's where the
Chinaman will be. There are dogs, bodyguards, alarm systems to be care-
ful of. And there's a hot-wired car parked right behind us for you to use.
Now go kill the Chinaman and your debt is paid.

But the car they've given him breaks down almost immediately on the
freeway. Cosmo has to run for his life across several lanes of traffic in the
dark, then call a taxi to take him to the killing. As he waits for the taxi at
the phone booth, he makes another call, this one to the Crazy Horse: He
is checking up on how the show is going in his absence. But he grows frustrated with the bartender, who can't seem to tell him which production
number is going on at that moment. "Is it the Paris number? Are there letters on the curtain: P-A-R . . ." Cosmo practically shouts while standing in
the phone booth, as though he has no other more pressing concern in the
world.

Once at the Chinaman's house in the Hollywood Hills above Sunset,
Cosmo is as silent and undetectable as a ghost, despite having no apparent commando training. Rather, he is the beneficiary in a lengthy string of
happy coincidences: seemingly dozens of henchmen are distracted or look
the other way just as he walks past a doorway or the end of a hall, render-
ing him invisible.

He wanders through the house, then stands in the shadows as the
Chinaman and a beautiful young girl get out of a large indoor spa and
the Chinaman walks down the hall to an indoor pool. As the bookie blinks
unbelievingly, Cosmo steps out of the darkness and shoots him, then shoots
the first henchman to respond. Even as a swarm of bodyguards deploy to the
pool, Cosmo somehow finds a safe route out the back way, though he falters

momentarily when a shot rings out behind him. Then he's running—down the driveway, down the street, down a hill to flag a passing bus, which he boards for his getaway.

He gets off the bus and catches a cab and directs it to drop him at the Pussycat Theater on Sunset, then changes his mind and gets back in the cab. When the taxi drops him off on a residential street, Cosmo staggers and doubles over with pain. His hand goes to his right side and comes away bloody. He finds his way to Rachel's house, where Rachel's mother, Betty (Virginia Carrington), gets him to lie down. She opens his shirt, revealing a bloody gunshot wound in his right side. But Cosmo insists that she call him a cab, saying, "I have to get to the club."

The scene shifts to a different restaurant, where Mort Weil and a date (Elizabeth Deering, Cassel's wife) are eating with a friend (played by Val Avery), when Marty Reitz comes in to tell them of a shoot-out in Chinatown. The Chinaman has been killed, among others. Mort excuses himself and goes to another booth, where Flo is eating, wearing white gloves and with a red napkin tied around his neck like a bib. Mort tells Flo that the Chinaman is dead—and now Flo must kill Cosmo Vitelli.

Cosmo arrives at the Crazy Horse, goes behind the bar, and pours himself a drink. As he watches the show, he sees Flo come in. Flo tells Cosmo that he's meeting some guys at 11 and he needs Cosmo to come with him. They drive to an abandoned parking structure and go to its basement—but despite honking the horn and shouting, they find no one there. It's obvious to Cosmo that Flo means to kill him, but it's not so obvious that he actually will. And, in fact, Flo washes his hands of the task and drives away, leaving Cosmo standing in the dark.

But Mort and his henchman Phil are waiting for Flo, and when Flo tells Mort to do it himself ("That's my friend in there—take care of him," Flo tells Mort. "He's your problem"), Mort drives into the garage. Mort talks to Cosmo as Phil tiptoes through the shadows to sneak up on him. Mort apologizes to Cosmo, tells him he likes him personally but the situation is unavoidable.

Mort explains that Cosmo has been set up. The Chinaman, it turns out, is not some small-time bookie but "one of the heaviest cats on the West Coast." Cosmo has accomplished something that Mort and his colleagues couldn't have, because they're too well-known. But now Mort's friends are concerned: They don't know how much is known about Cosmo, whether he can be identified in the shooting or be traced to them. So, Mort lies, Cosmo will have to lay low. They'll help him hide out and take care of his club while he's gone.

It is only when Mort says to Cosmo, "I know you could kill me right now if you wanted," that there is any indication to the audience that Cosmo is armed. The way the scene is staged, the viewer never sees the gun in Cosmo's hand. But it must be there because, when he hears Mort's accomplice in the next room, Cosmo shoots and kills Mort—or seems to, although there's no identifiable sound of a gun going off. Cosmo flees into the shadows and Phil comes looking for him, playing cat and mouse through several floors of this abandoned structure without ever actually spotting him. Cosmo escapes out a back way. It is a needlessly long and suspenseless scene, yet one that plays the same length in both versions.

Cosmo turns up at Rachel's house, where he offers a rose to Betty. But then he asks what Rachel is doing at home when she should be working at the club. "Are you serious?" Betty says. "She may be my girlfriend but she also works for me," Cosmo says pragmatically. "There are people struggling to keep the show alive."

Betty regards him coldly and walks out of the room while Rachel, fresh out of a shower, asks what's going on. Cosmo says it's all a misunderstanding and goes to talk to Betty. He tells her he's not feeling well, then adds, "I didn't expect the double-cross."

He starts rambling about his parents, his mother, his father—but Betty mutters, "I don't give a shit about your mother," then "I don't give a damn about your father."

"Well, he was a moron," Cosmo allows, to which Betty says, "I don't care."

"Well, I care!" Cosmo explodes.

"Well, I don't!" Betty responds in kind, going nose to nose with Cosmo, who backs off.

But Betty is having none of his charm. She's heard the news reports about the Chinaman and seen Cosmo's wounds. She knows he's in deep. And she wants him gone: "I don't want you in my house no more," she says, "because I'm not strong enough for you." When Rachel refuses to even talk to him, he leaves for the club.

At the club, however, there is no show on, though it is showtime because the house is full of people clapping with rhythmic "We want the show!" impatience. Cosmo goes up to the dressing room, where there's obviously been some sort of rebellion by the performers about working conditions and employee grievances. Cosmo asks what's wrong and Mr. Sophistication airs his complaints; so do the girls. Cosmo launches into a rambling pep talk, telling them that he's learned the secret of being happy:

"You have to work hard to be comfortable," he says. "The only people who are happy are the people who are comfortable.

"Look at me. I'm only happy when I'm angry, when I'm sad, when I can play the fool, when I can be what people want me to be, rather than be myself," he tells them. "And that takes work."

Having rallied them back to work, Cosmo goes down to the stage to start the show, in an apparent valedictory. "I'm Cosmo Vitelli and I own this joint," he says, talking up the stage show and introducing all the waitresses in the room to applause for each (in the shorter version, he introduces only two of the help). Then he climbs down off the stage and walks out through the club, silhouetted in the follow spotlight that Mr. Sophistication has called for.

Cosmo walks out the front door and stands in front of the club, still wearing the same blue suit and hideous aquamarine shirt that he's worn for much of the film's final hour. His hand goes to his side, then he distractedly wipes it on his suit; for the first time, we can see that the blood has soaked through and is visible near the right-hand jacket pocket. Cosmo looks at the blood on his fingers, then gazes out into traffic. Cassavetes offers no indication of whether Cosmo will live or die, though it seems clear that, at a minimum, his way of life is about to disappear.

But the film doesn't end there—though it would have been a perfectly '70s kind of conclusion. Instead, Cassavetes takes the camera back inside to watch Mr. Sophistication and the girls, as he sings "I Can't Give You Anything But Love." All of the facial hair that had been so carefully drawn on when he came onstage is now gone; in his hair are traces of the shaving-cream pie-in-the-face he apparently received while the camera was elsewhere. As he sings and exits, the message is clear: The show must go on.

Forty

Bookie 2

After shooting *Mean Streets* at the beginning of 1973, Martin Scorsese reached a point in the editing where the film was nearly done, but input from friends for whom he screened the film was confusing the easily upset Scorsese about what to do with a particular scene.

It was the funny, revealing encounter between Harvey Keitel and Robert De Niro, in which the pair had improvised an argument about why De Niro's irresponsible Johnny Boy couldn't get the money he owed. Scorsese cut and recut the scene; he tried the film with and without the entire sequence and still couldn't decide.

When he screened the movie for Cassavetes—who, after all, had put him on the path to make the film—Scorsese decided to put the scene back in. Cassavetes' response: "Don't touch a frame," he told an elated Scorsese.

"And that was the turning point," Scorsese recalled. "A number of people who were very successful at the time—the picture was at two hours and they said, 'You've got to cut it to ninety minutes.' After that, I thought, it won't change the movie. No matter how much I take out, they're not going to like it in Waco."

In fact, Scorsese had bandied the notion of a gangster film with Cassavetes a year or so earlier. The two were sitting in Cassavetes' office one afternoon in 1972, and Cassavetes began spinning a story for Scorsese, which he had Elaine Kagan take down as dictation.

"He wrote a project for me one afternoon called 'I've Got a Yen for You'," Scorsese said. "And that became *Killing of a Chinese Bookie*."

The story treatment, which Scorsese still has in his files, is actually called "I.O.U. (I've Got a Yen For You)." Instead of Cosmo Vitelli, the central character has the unlikely (though less symbolic) name of Basil Rosen. But the plot is quite similar: Basil, a small-time club owner, loses big money gambling at a mobster's club. The mobster tells him he must kill a Chinese bookie to settle the debt.

In this version, Basil tracks the bookie, Mr. Loo, to his house, then shoots him in the shower. He eventually shoots Mr. Loo's wife, mother, and children before fleeing. But as it turns out, he only winged Mr. Loo. When the mobsters take Basil to the hospital to finish the job, Basil points the gun at Mr. Loo, then changes his mind and runs out, telling the mobsters, "I can't shoot a Chinaman."

Impatient at not having made a film of his own in more than two years, Cassavetes plunged ahead with the idea of making another film while there still seemed to be a demand for his work. So he pulled out the treatment and expanded it into a full-blown script.

"I was in New York with *Woman*, doing secondary and other runs," Al Ruban recalled. "John called and said, 'I've got to make another movie. I'm going to do this gangster thing.' Since the company was going really strong at the time, he took a lot of money from *Woman* and put it into *Chinese Bookie*."

Cassavetes said later, "We did *Bookie* just as an effort to get out of the distribution business. Years ago, Martin Scorsese and I were talking and in one night made up this gangster story. I didn't know what to make so I thought we'll do that story about this nightclub owner who owes a lot of money and is talked into killing someone."

The script for *Bookie* grew less out of an interest in gangsters than out of Cassavetes' own curiosity about the strip joints he saw on Sunset Boulevard as he drove to work each day. So he finally stopped one afternoon at one of them, went in, introduced himself, and talked to the owner.

"He told me he did his own acts: He structured them, wrote them," Cassavetes recalled. "He took enormous pride in them. I walked in and saw a world that was part of the American world. And I kind of liked the man. He was a very conventional man. But everything in the place was more ornate than most restaurants or cafes."

It was June 1975, as playwright Meade Roberts recalled in his journal from the period: "John is going to start dictating the screenplay this afternoon and hopes to have it finished in ten days, giving him a whole week for preproduction."

Before Cassavetes even wrote the script, he had pictured Ben Gazzara in the central role. He visited Gazzara in New York, where the actor was appearing in the title role of a well-reviewed but short-lived revival of Eugene O'Neill's *Hughie.* Cassavetes went backstage, and the two went out to dinner, though it was apparent to Cassavetes that Gazzara was unhappy because closing notices for the show had been posted, after only a month. But still Gazzara said he found stage work more fulfilling than making most movies.

As the meal progressed, Cassavetes told him that they would start a new picture together soon. "I figured he was just trying to cheer me up because he knew I was pretty upset about my show closing, so I didn't take him seriously," Gazzara recalled. "In fact, I forgot about it."

But shortly after Gazzara returned to Los Angeles, he got a call from Cassavetes, telling him they would begin shooting *The Killing of a Chinese Bookie* in two weeks. Two weeks later, Gazzara was on the set playing Cosmo.

Jeremy Kagan, who visited him on the set, recalled, "He was always revved up, working full bore. It would be way late in the night and he'd be totally energized."

Bo Harwood, who was once again handling sound and writing the music, said, "On *Bookie,* it felt like we were living in the street for months. There was still that string of love and camaraderie that John carried with him, inherent in all the characters."

As always, actor Timothy Carey brought the element of the unexpected to every scene he shot. He was playing Flo, the most threatening of the mobsters, who works Cosmo over at one point, then ultimately spares his life. It was a significant supporting role, and Carey made the most of it, rubbing Seymour Cassel the wrong way in the process.

It was the scene in which Cassel's character, Mort Weil, interrupts Flo's dinner at a restaurant to tell him that Cosmo has killed the Chinaman and now Flo must kill Cosmo. As they shot the scene, Carey, whose flamboyant shirt was accessorized with a bright red bib and a pair of incongruous white gloves, kept eating while Cassel was talking. And not just eating, but slurping up large mouthfuls of spaghetti. It wasn't the first time Carey had upstaged Cassel.

"As we're doing the scene, he's eating spaghetti, so I put my hand over his mouth to keep him from eating," Cassel recalled. "He was furious, but it was hilarious."

As the scene went on, Cassel grew increasingly frustrated, finally grabbing Carey by the neck to keep him from moving around and stealing focus. Carey asked Cassel not to squeeze so hard but, when Cassel did it
again on the next take, Carey went to Cassavetes and complained. To which
Cassavetes said, "Well, hit him over the head or punch him in the nose."

Although it was a film partially set in a strip club and a film with the
word "killing" in the title, Cassavetes resisted attempts to have it include the
kind of nudity and graphic violence that had become the norm by 1975.

Cassavetes hated sensationalism and was enough of a puritan to be uncomfortable with using nudity on the screen. There is nudity in the first version, but it was trimmed significantly when Cassavetes cut the film down.
Even then, the nudity is rarely the highlight of the shot, often happening in
the shadows while emcee Mr. Sophistication takes center stage.

"Dad felt it was a strip club—you should see nudity," Edie Shaw Marcus
recalled of her father, Sam Shaw. "John would not use nudity. My father took
a lot of pictures of the girls and they were nude. But that wasn't in the film."

The daily reworking of the script may have reached its apotheosis the
night they were supposed to shoot the title sequence. As the crew set up
the house for filming, Cassavetes and Gazzara had dinner in an Italian
restaurant on Sunset. In the middle of dinner, Cassavetes turned to Gazzara and, with dead earnestness, said, "Do you think we should kill him?"

"Who?" Gazzara ventured.

"The bookie," Cassavetes said.

Suddenly it was a real idea: They wouldn't kill the bookie. How could
they work their way out of that one? Mike Ferris said, "Half a night went by
with him pacing on the set, trying to be convinced that he's got to do this."

In the end, it was Ruban who got things moving again: "John, the picture is called *The Killing of a Chinese Bookie*," Ruban pointed out. "How can
you not kill him?"

With a distribution system already in place from *Woman*, Cassavetes
set a release date for *Bookie*, then had to hurry to finish the editing to meet
it. The film was released in seventeen cities in mid-February 1976, with
other theaters booked for later dates. Cassavetes had been able to demand
advance guarantees, based on his name and the performance of *Woman*,
without having to show exhibitors a finished version of *Bookie*.

"It's the only film I've ever made for reasons that were not altogether
pure," Cassavetes admitted. "I made this film as an intellectual experiment,
not because I am in love with it. It is a film that has little to do with me and
with how I feel about life."

As it was opening, a *Variety* article hailed the decision to self-distribute
as a viable financial trend for filmmakers. The story paired *Bookie* with the

Maysles brothers' *Grey Gardens,* a documentary they were distributing them-selves, in a story obviously written before the *Bookie* reviews were in.

But it was a little like comparing apples and oranges, given that documentary makers—including Emile D'Antonio and the Maysles—had been self-distributing their films to a limited audience for years. Cassavetes, how-ever, was unique among feature-film makers in his efforts to get his work into a much wider arena than the documentarians could ever hope for.

"Cassavetes is obviously hoping to repeat the killing he made last year with his self-distribution of *Woman,*" the *Variety* article noted.

As they readied the film for release, Ruban was convinced they had a winner: "I thought it would make our fortune, that this would do great box office," he said. But the response to an early screening was disheartening: "They threw popcorn at the screen," Mike Ferris recalled. "They razzed it."

The *Los Angeles Times* reported that the film drew boos and hisses at the advance screening in Westwood. Word of mouth was so immediately poisonous that a parking-lot attendant near the theater where the film was screened asked the *Times* reporter, "Was it really as bad as everyone says?"

John Finnegan apparently dealt with the same attendant: "I was stand-ing there and the kid came out and said, 'Did you see that?' And I said, 'Yeah, but I had a pass.' And he said, 'Yeah, but you had to pay for parking.'"

The critics—in New York and elsewhere—didn't help things. Cassavetes had purposely antagonized them by not press-screening the film before it opened—and then opening it on a Sunday. The film was staggered by re-views that could only be described as brutal.

"People went en masse the first day—and then we got killed by the crit-ics," Cassavetes said. "I think it became a sad film for most people."

Cassavetes' usual critical nemeses gleefully dismissed the film as further proof of what they'd been saying all along: that Cassavetes was a charlatan masquerading as an artist. To them, this was irrefutable proof that the em-peror had no clothes.

Vincent Canby wrote, "Watching the film is like listening to someone using a lot of impressive words, the meanings of which are just wrong enough to keep you in a state of total confusion. What is he trying to say? It takes a little while to realize that maybe the speaker not only doesn't know but doesn't even care to think things out."

Frank Rich, reviewing in the *New York Post,* said, "John Cassavetes' new film is such an outright disaster that by the time it's over, even its exotic title has lost its sting. Why he's gone so far out of his way to destroy himself is only one of several dozen questions that Cassavetes doesn't presume to an-swer." And John Simon, writing in *New York* magazine, said, "If Cassavetes is telling the truth and he really writes this trash that postures as plot, characterization and dialogue, he would be an even bigger simpleton than I take him to be."

The film had its defenders, including Jack Kroll, who wrote that, while the movie's jaggedness would put many people off, "this is a rewarding film that asks only that you stay alert and use your senses. Cassavetes' feel for this sleazy world is rich, rueful, totally human."

Yet even his supporters were shaking their heads, managing mostly ambivalent reviews that offered the most cautious of recommendations. David Sterritt, who had been a champion of *Woman*, tried to defend the new film's extravagances, calling the picture murky and flawed but allowing that "it bears the unmistakable stamp of this impetuously talented writer-director and manages to do things that we have never seen onscreen before." Jay Cocks, a friend of Cassavetes, had to admit, "*Bookie* shows much of what is exasperating about Cassavetes. The film is unfocused, loony, indulgent." However, he would ultimately say, "It is very much worth indulging— a brash, tense, mysterious night piece unlike anything Cassavetes has attempted before."

The intensity of the negative reaction shocked those involved in the film.

"I couldn't understand why the response was so vehement," Mike Ferris said. "I was remembering what we shot and thinking, 'Geez, it will be incredible.' But it was like no gangster picture anyone had ever seen."

Ruban said, "I was stunned when we had to pull it after six days in New York. The best way to convince people to see a movie like that is word of mouth. But people hated it. It was such a visceral reaction. People would leave the movie and yell at people in line not to go in."

The problem, as Cassavetes later acknowledged, was that he had hurried a film to which he did not have a personal connection. He had rushed the editing, rather than honing the film to the form he wanted, and the result didn't work.

Cassavetes had been convinced that he could repeat *Woman*'s performance at the box office and that he would reap the same benefits by distributing it himself. But he had only his own experience to guide him. While it had been a surprisingly good one, it was also unrepresentative of the average self-distribution situation.

Cassavetes began running into problems with the distribution almost immediately after the reviews appeared.

To some extent, he had covered himself with the guarantees he had demanded. Lipsky recalled that United Artists Theaters had put up a $150,000 guarantee, sight unseen, for the exclusive right to show *Bookie* in three cities.

But Cassavetes found that theaters which had agreed to take the film were now balking at the hefty advances Cassavetes and Ruban were demanding.

"It was presold—and they pulled it," John Finnegan recalled.

Variety reported in mid-April 1976, that, like a number of theaters, the Gopher Theater, a small first-run house in Minneapolis, had booked the film, then canceled the booking, based on the reviews and the fact that Faces International was asking for a $15,000 advance and a $10,000 guarantee.

"We offered to play the picture without the guarantee, but they wouldn't go for it," *Variety* quoted the theater's owner. When no other local theaters would bid on the film, Cassavetes had to settle for three nights at the U Film Society at the University of Minnesota, which screened *Bookie* in the lecture hall that served as its theater.

Not that the problems affected Cassavetes' opinion of the film. Lipsky attended a meeting with the United Artists executives, a few weeks after the film had closed in its initial booking, to see whether there was a way to play it off in their other theaters around the country. One of the UA people made the mistake of speculating how far the $150,000 they'd given Cassavetes for the initial three cities would go toward achieving that goal.

But Cassavetes quickly nipped that kind of thinking: "To show it in other cities would require additional film rental fees," he explained.

Lipsky said, "Now this film was dead. And he's asking for more money. After the meeting, halfway back to the office, he got this Cheshire Cat smile and said, half to me, half to himself, 'I've got balls down to here.'"

Cassavetes continued to brood about *Bookie* and, a year later, reedited the film to make it shorter, then gave it a brief re-release, to scant notice. As he said in an interview around the time of the re-release, "I'd like to make that film about four or five more times because it had interesting characters, interesting people."

Forty-one

Opening Night

J ohn Cassavetes was a human script factory. From the time of *A Child Is Waiting* until the end of his life, he was always working on something: a screenplay, a play, a novel—something was always underway when he wasn't making a movie, and often while he was.

"He wrote in excess of twenty screenplays he's never done," Al Ruban said. "He probably wrote a good dozen stage plays. He was constantly working on one thing or another. He had to occupy his mind all the time."

Outside of the circle of friends who participated in readings, those works have never been seen. Most of them had been through the same development process that would serve and amuse Cassavetes to the end of his life: a reading at his home.

"That was John's idea of a great Friday night, to sit around a table and read a script with his friends" recalled Guy McElwaine, who was called upon to read if he was there. All of the participants were expected to throw themselves into the roles fully; there were no halfway measures for Cassavetes. And anyone who was in the house—kids, in-laws, friends—was expected to pick up a script and pitch in. "No one was walking through this. These guys would assassinate you if you mumbled the words. You had to perform," McElwaine said.

Cassavetes would gather a group of friends at his home, break out the cigarettes and liquor, and read the play aloud. Observed John Finnegan,

"He'd call Pete and Elaine and read. And John would sit and listen. When you hear somebody read your stuff and inject something more in to it, that embellished it for the writer."

"Readings at his house were a party," recalled actor Joseph Bologna, who said his film *Made for Each Other* was influenced by *Husbands.* Cassavetes, in turn, admitted that, with *Made for Each Other,* Bologna had made the movie Cassavetes wanted to make with *Minnie and Moskowitz.*

Said Bologna, "It was just fun, people who loved theater. Everybody thought: This is what it's all about. Success has got to do with the world outside; but creativity is an expression of self. That's what this was."

To Cassavetes and Rowlands, this was the Hollywood social life they always dreamed of. Not the parties and premieres and red carpets—but an evening at home with friends, doing what they did, acting and working over a script with people they admired and enjoyed.

But even as Cassavetes worked through one script's problems, he was already thinking about the next one. Though a couple of the plays he wrote were eventually produced, most of the scripts simply went on the shelf, reminders of something that had once caught Cassavetes' fancy long enough for him to get it down on paper. Usually he had no interest in going back to dust off an old script when the opportunity came to make a film.

Which makes *Opening Night* something of an anomaly: a script he had worked on years earlier, then took up later and produced. It had been in his mind at least since the late 1960s; in discussing *Faces* with a *New York Times* reporter in 1968, Cassavetes mentioned the film in passing, saying he had plans to shoot it. "Gena and I are going to do a movie exploring a woman's fantasies called *Opening Night,*" he said, "which I'll direct after *Husbands.*"

It was late 1976, however, before he got back to *Opening Night,* by which point it had become something more than an exploration of a woman's fantasies. By the time the film was ever-so-briefly released at the end of 1977, it had been transformed into a theatrical tale, an examination of a woman coming to terms with aging, an account of an artist's journey, and a ghost story, all in one.

Opening Night begins backstage at a play, *The Second Woman,* in which movie star Myrtle Gordon (Rowlands) is starring in an out-of-town tryout. She adjusts her costume, and lets herself be sprayed with water by the prop man, Bobby (John Finnegan), before she makes her entrance from a fictional rainstorm.

The scene teams her with another actor, Maurice Adams (Cassavetes), her former lover, who is playing her current husband in the play. The dialogue is innocuous and unremarkable; when they finish the scene, the curtain drops and the audience applauds.

Outside the stage door, a vigorous mob of autograph hounds awaits Myrtle's walk from the door to her limo, though rain is falling in sheets. She signs autographs and finds herself confronted with a hysterical young woman in matching royal-blue rain slicker and floppy hat, who can only gush, "I love you, I love you," as Myrtle signs her book. Myrtle tries to calm her down and tells her to come see her the next day.

But when Myrtle gets in the limo with Maurice, director Manny Victor (Ben Gazzara), playwright Sarah Goode (Joan Blondell), and producer David Samuel (Paul Stewart), the young woman in blue rushes to the car and pounds on the window, despite the pouring rain. All Myrtle can do is wave. When her limousine pulls away, the girl, whose name is Nancy Stein (Laura Johnson), steps off the curb into the street to watch the limousine drive away—and doesn't see another car, which slams into her, killing her instantly.

Witnessing this as she drives away, Myrtle is frantic. What happened to the girl? Back at the hotel, she asks Maurice to accompany her to her room in the penthouse and the first words out of his mouth are, "I'm not staying." When she sheds her coat, pours a drink, then kisses him, he barely responds, saying, "You're not a woman to me. You're a professional. You don't care about anything."

She needs company after witnessing the accident—and because she is having problems with her role in this play. But Maurice leaves her standing alone in the sprawling, sparsely furnished room at Pasadena's Green Hotel (unconvincingly transformed into a New Haven hotel's penthouse suite by production designer Bryan Ryman). She begins to drink.

In another part of the hotel, Manny Victor is having an argument with his wife, Dorothy (Zohra Lampert), complaining that he needs more support from her, that she must befriend Myrtle and help her with the role. Manny himself feels in a rut: "My life is getting boring," he says. "There's no humor anymore and glamour's dead." But they seem to be finding a common ground, approaching intimacy when—

The phone rings—it is 4:30 A.M.—and Manny answers. It is a drunken Myrtle, upset over a scene in the play in which Maurice slaps her. Even as Dorothy tries to get Manny to get off the phone, Manny ignores her—even telling her to knock it off—while he sweet-talks Myrtle to bolster her confidence and keep her on track with the role: "There's no one in the world I love more at this moment than you," he tells Myrtle as his wife listens.

But at rehearsals the next day, Myrtle is intransigent and uncooperative. As they rehearse a scene in which Maurice must slap her, Myrtle first explodes and takes after Maurice after the slap; Manny must restrain her. The next time, she shrieks as his hand nears her cheek and drops to the floor, where she lies unresponsively, despite efforts by Manny and producer David Samuel to coax her back to her feet. Finally, she rises, but she hits the deck again when he slaps her, this time disrupting the rehearsal because her uncontrollable laughter prevents her from delivering her lines.

Myrtle flees to her dressing room, where she dismisses her Thelma Ritter–like dresser, Kelly (Louise Fitch), and then has a drink alone. But as she looks at herself in the mirror, she recognizes another presence: It is Nancy Stein, the fan who was killed by the car. She is dressed the same as Myrtle and sits next to her in front of the mirror, a reflection of the lost youth Myrtle will never regain.

The vision disappears, however, at a knock on the door. It is David, who lets Sarah into the room. The playwright, whose work Myrtle had derided from the rehearsal stage after the slapping incident, wants to get Myrtle to focus on the play, instead of fighting it so hard. "Let's be friends," she says.

"Oh," Myrtle says sweetly, "I don't think we'll ever be friends."

Myrtle had complained that the play lacked hope, something Sarah grudgingly agrees might be true: "At least you're not completely stupid," Sarah offers. But the conversation ends inconclusively, because Sarah doesn't see her play as being about a woman's aging—but Myrtle believes that it is, and is uncomfortable with the topic because she can't deal with the idea that she is aging herself.

Back at the hotel, Manny invites Myrtle to go for a drink, but Myrtle declines. In the newspaper, she sees the obituary for Nancy Stein and, on an impulse, goes to the family's shiva (at-home mourning period) at their apartment. (Only Cassavetes would have thought to cast a blue-eyed blonde named Johnson as a young Jewish woman.) But her parents, played by Meade Roberts and Eleanor Zee, make it clear that Myrtle is unwelcome there, as people tearfully grieve all around her. Shaken, Myrtle goes to a nearby tavern for a drink and winds up signing an autograph for a fan at the bar.

In her dressing room before the performance that night, Manny tries a "tough love" approach, telling Myrtle that she is no longer funny—that her rehearsal tantrums and behavior, things that used to amuse him, are becoming a distraction. Kelly tries to stand up for Myrtle, telling Manny he'll upset her before the performance. Manny, however, justifies his right to say these things by noting, "You're the most exciting woman that I've ever known—and the greatest actress."

Myrtle finally speaks for herself: "I'm not funny because I can't take myself seriously anymore," she says, adding that the play is too cruel. As she starts to walk to the backstage spot where she makes her entrance, she walks back and, on impulse, kisses Manny deeply before she goes on. It is a kiss that hints strongly at the affair they undoubtedly had in the past.

Myrtle, in agony playing a role she hates, takes out her unhappiness on the play itself. In the scene in which Maurice slaps her, she falls to the floor and remains there, whimpering. Maurice tries to continue delivering his lines, but she doesn't respond. He ad libs an exit line and walks off stage to ask, what now? Vamping, he comes back onstage and, to his relief, Myrtle rejoins the scene.

But now she breaks character, breaks the fourth wall entirely, by taking a pause and then saying, "We must never forget, Maurice, that this is only a play." Maurice can only laugh.

Manny, however, is not laughing. Backstage, he bawls her out in front of the playwright, the producer, and her co-star. She counters that she doesn't like the character, can't identify with or sympathize with her dilemma. "What is it you feel about her?" Manny demands. "Nothing," Myrtle replies.

Sarah sarcastically notes that, if Myrtle simply says the lines with a degree of feeling, the character will appear. When Myrtle begins to cry, Manny expresses disgust ("Now, the goddam tears"), but Sarah asks to speak with Myrtle alone.

She tries to talk to Myrtle about age, but Myrtle is so defensive she won't even tell Sarah how old she is. "If you can't say your age, you can't accept my play," Sarah says.

But Myrtle worries this play will now typecast her as an older woman. When Sarah asks her if she's going to quit the play, Myrtle narrows her eyes and says, "No. I'm looking for a way to play this part where age doesn't make any difference."

The problem, however, is that Myrtle's instrument isn't as finely honed as it once was: "When I was eighteen, I could do anything," Myrtle says. "My emotions were so close to the surface I could feel everything, easily."

But she may be able to be that in touch with her feelings again, she tells Sarah, because she has this dead girl, who reminds her of that youthful part of herself.

Sarah, however, looks alarmed: What now? "You say you have this dead girl—what do you mean by 'have'? Is she here now in this room?" Sarah asks. Myrtle, realizing she probably sounds crazy, abruptly says good night and leaves.

Back at Myrtle's hotel room, the producer, David, sits on the steps, waiting to buy Myrtle a drink. Instead, Myrtle invites him in, but as they enter the phone rings. It is obviously Maurice. Myrtle says, "I don't want to see you now—I'm with someone."

Does she mean to sleep with David? It seems so; when he says, "I'm very concerned," she kisses him and he seems ready to respond, until they hear footsteps and Manny walks in. David makes an awkward exit; Myrtle, however, picks up the bottle of scotch and heads for the other room, drinking straight from the bottle as Manny chases her yelling, "What the hell are you trying to prove? You're acting like some grade-school theatrical kid, for Chrissake. Everybody loves you."

They agree that the character is hard to decipher as written. Myrtle finally says, "Who gives a damn how old she is? Does she win or does she lose, that's what I want to know. Is that such a lousy question? I'm beginning to feel guilty for asking."

Manny goes out to the bar, pours himself a stiff drink, and downs it. In the bathroom, Myrtle sits on the edge of the tub—and watches Nancy Stein wash her face.

Nancy starts talking about what her youth was like, how easy it was to pick up boys—and Myrtle says, "I don't want to hear about your sex life." When Manny walks in, both women turn to look at him, but Manny sees only Myrtle sitting, talking to herself. She finally accuses Manny of being concerned only for himself, that he is only worried Myrtle's behavior will undermine his career if the play flops. When he denies it, she throws herself into his arms and kisses him again.

In the next shot, the two of them emerge from the limo at the theater the next day. When they ford the river of autograph seekers and get inside the stage door, Manny's wife, Dorothy, is waiting, and the look on Manny's face tells the whole story. Yes, he slept with Myrtle (again), but he had to do it for the good of the show.

Onstage for a performance, Myrtle is out of control. Just before an entrance, she had reminded the prop man to make sure she had matches or a lighter onstage for her cigarette. But when the moment comes to light the cigarette in the scene, the matches aren't there, and Myrtle begins an exaggeratedly comic search for them. She makes funny faces, ignores a ringing phone that provides a cue, and even exits when she's not supposed to. Finally, Manny runs backstage and demands that Leo, the stage manager, (played by Cassavetes' long-time friend Fred Draper) bring down the curtain to stop this travesty.

But when the curtain drops, Myrtle yelps and loudly demands that the curtain go back up, and Manny acquiesces. She finishes the scene but also talks to the audience and generally disrupts the show.

Afterward Sarah is concerned: Was it the dead girl? Did Myrtle see her? Is this why Myrtle is acting so strangely?

Myrtle insists that Sarah misunderstood about the girl: that it's just an actor's device, something she purposely imagined to help her in her role. "I can make her appear and disappear at will," she says. But Sarah insists on taking Myrtle down to New York to see the spiritualist she consults.

The spiritualist is played by Katherine Cassavetes in a flowing red-orange caftan and an imperious manner: "I feel she's very near to us now," she tells Myrtle. But before she can get the hands-holding séance started, Myrtle flips on the lights and calls a halt. There's no ghost, she claims: "It's like when you're a child and you have an imaginary friend."

Back at her hotel room in New Haven, she looks around expectantly for the girl: "Where are you?" she calls. But when Nancy appears, she attacks Myrtle physically. Myrtle knocks her to the floor, then escapes to the hallway.

She inveigles a hotel maid to let her into Sarah's room. A surprised Sarah, in bed, awakens to the sight of a groggy Myrtle, acting possessed—banging her face into the door frame until her sunglasses are broken and her face is bleeding.

"I'm a little shook," is all she can say to Sarah before asking to use her bathroom to clean her face.

The next day, Sarah brings Myrtle to rehearsal two hours late. As Myrtle sits in the limo, Sarah confronts Manny on the sidewalk: "She's crazy—she's got to be replaced," Sarah maintains. Manny looks at her in amazement: "One day before New York? Thanks very much."

Manny gets into the limo with Myrtle and tells Leo to have everyone take a break while he takes Myrtle out to give her a pep talk. At a coffee shop, he tells her she shouldn't worry about embarrassing herself onstage; that's what he was there to prevent. He recounts a story of an affair he'd had a couple of years earlier, in which he left his wife and children for a much younger woman and then had to grovel to be taken back after his lover dropped him.

He wants Myrtle to believe in herself, but he's alarmed when she takes off her sunglasses and he sees the scratches and bruises around her eyes. "I'm in trouble, Manny—I'm not acting," she says.

As if to prove it, she disrupts rehearsal to drag Sarah down to New York once more. She insists that Sarah find another spiritualist—that the first one she saw somehow provoked Nancy and now Myrtle needs to be rid of her: "I'm out of control," she says.

So Sarah takes her to another medium—this one played by Lady Rowlands—and leaves Myrtle with her. They adjourn to the spiritualist's room, and when the spiritualist says, "Now—Nancy is her name?" a loud piano chord sounds and Nancy appears, as if summoned (for some reason opening and closing the door as she enters, rather than simply materializing).

Nancy tells Myrtle she's not afraid of her and attacks her. Myrtle, however, fights back, landing several haymakers until Nancy is down on the floor, apparently slain. Myrtle breaks several glass objects over her inert form, and when the camera pulls back to capture the spiritualist's view of this encounter, all that can be seen is Myrtle standing over a pile of broken glass.

Myrtle resists a bellman's attempt to get her to calm down, catching a cab to Maurice's apartment. She shares familiarities with the doorman but is rebuffed by Maurice when she gets to his door.

"Let's take this play and dump it upside down," she pleads, but he says, "They don't pay me enough to make an ass of myself."

On opening night in New York, Myrtle is nowhere to be found. Manny, Sarah, and David sit backstage. "I can't say I'm not depressed, but it's not the end of my life," Sarah sighs. When David suggests excuses for Myrtle's absence in cancelling the show, Sarah says, "We'll just have to wait."

(Even though shot in 1976 and 1977—and filmed in Pasadena, rather than New Haven and New York—the film creates a kind of fantasy Broadway, one in which plays open the day after completing their out-of-town tryout, rather than scheduling a week or more of previews to fine-tune the production to the new theater. It's also apparently a world in which there are no understudies, since Myrtle's absence threatens to cancel the play's opening.)

The audience is filling the auditorium, many of the people in tuxedoes and formal wear. Peter Falk can be glimpsed having a cigarette outside, as though he's Mr. First Nighter.

Then the word spreads backstage: Myrtle has arrived. But she is falling-down drunk. She has to be helped to her dressing room and helped into her costume; when she tries to put on lipstick, she smears it all over her mouth. But Manny yells at Leo not to help her walk, even when she collapses every few steps; if she's going to do this, she's going to do it herself.

Again, it seems improbable that an understudy wouldn't literally be jumping into Myrtle's costume and readying to go on in her place. Myrtle is too drunk to walk, let alone remember lines and blocking. Yet Manny speculates that, if she's drunk enough, "I bet the audience is going to love her."

Myrtle collapses backstage just before going on. But they get her to her feet in time to make her entrance. Manny, however, can't handle the suspense. He leaves the theater and goes across the street to have a drink.

Suddenly, apparently exorcised of the girl, Myrtle's in the moment. She's so busy trying to focus on just remembering her lines and fighting through the alcohol that she can't think about what the play means or why she has problems with it.

She is standing a little more steadily backstage awaiting the start of the second act when Maurice comes ambling in, whistling happily (thus defying a major backstage superstition against whistling). "I'm gonna bury that bastard," Myrtle vows to Kelly under her breath.

Bobby, the prop man, helps her get ready for her entrance then says admiringly, "Miss Gordon, can I tell you something? I've seen a lot of drunks in my day, but I've never seen anyone as drunk as you and still be able to walk. You're fantastic."

As she and Maurice act their scene, they are more playful, more comic, finding new facets to the writing, which engages the audience and makes them laugh. Apparently Maurice has reconsidered her offer to turn the play upside down.

Suddenly Myrtle has found the life in this play and is riding it for all it is worth. She and Maurice play it out to a new ending that they improvise, one that ends with a slapstick vaudeville turn involving missed handshakes. The curtain comes down and the audience cheers. Though Manny, Sarah, and David all look as though they're en route to a wake as they head backstage, the audience is on its feet with applause.

Afterward, the audience comes backstage to congratulate the participants. Falk, Seymour Cassel, and Peter Bogdanovich can be seen in the crowd, as though they had been part of the audience. Even Manny's wife hugs Myrtle, and the frame freezes as the final credits roll.

Forty-two

Opening Night 2

Despite the fact that *Chinese Bookie* had died a quick death at the box office, Cassavetes was not discouraged. After all, his distribution company was still taking in money from *A Woman Under the Influence*.

"Filmmaking is a craft I want to keep learning," he said. "I'm in love with it and I would make films for nothing and do, and pay for them myself or with the help of my friends. I never mind if Gena thinks I am stupid or outspoken, ruining things for our everyday life. But I would hate it if she thought I was a coward or that I would back down on something to which we had devoted our lives."

He believed he'd figured out how to play the game. Here he was, after all, doing what he had worked so hard to be able to do: making movies his way, then releasing them to the public the way he wanted. One stumble didn't put him out of the game. *Bookie* had been a disappointment, to be sure, but it had also been an experiment, an effort to see if he could work as much with form as with content.

Opening Night, on the other hand, was playing to Cassavetes' strengths. A backstage story about theater, one that dealt with women and aging. And the ghost? Well, that was just a touch of the unexpected and certainly had precedent going back at least as far as Shakespeare, if not farther.

To fund the film, he took $500,000 he'd received in presales of *Bookie* in

Europe, added in his fee from *Two-Minute Warning* and another couple hundred thousand from the still-flowing receipts from *Woman*. Then he rounded up a cast that included Gena in the central role. He went to New York, where Ben Gazzara was acting in *Who's Afraid of Virginia Woolf*, to ask him to play Manny.

To play Nancy Stein, the young fan whose death triggers Myrtle's crisis, Cassavetes literally picked a girl off the street. While still finishing *Woman* at the American Film Institute, he spotted a pretty young blonde wandering around the AFI campus. "Hello—you, young lady—do you want to be an actress?" Cassavetes said, approaching the girl, whose name was Laura Johnson.

Johnson was a sixteen-year-old Valley girl, though one with an academic bent. She and a girlfriend had driven to the AFI, to apply for jobs filing in the Samuel Goldwyn Library. Suddenly here was this older man—probably the same age as her father—asking her if she wanted to be in a movie.

Johnson was convinced that it was a gag and said, "Yeah, sure."

But Cassavetes, who had Sam Shaw with him, said, "No, really," adding as Shaw took some photos of the girl, "You remind me so much of Gena."

"I had no idea who he was or who Gena was," Johnson recalled.

Cassavetes took her phone number and promised to call her when the photos were ready. But by the time she got home to Woodland Hills, Cassavetes was on the phone to her mother, telling her he'd like to pay for Laura to have acting lessons. Johnson's mother didn't know who Cassavetes was, either; it was only after talking to a family friend, a movie art director, that they realized he was legitimate.

Cassavetes got his AADA classmate Harry Mastrogeorge to take Johnson into one of the classes he taught. It was a year between the time he met Johnson and when shooting would begin. When production drew closer, Cassavetes arranged for her and Mastrogeorge to come to his office, then drove them to lunch to talk about the film.

Johnson wasn't sure she did, in fact, have the part. But one thing she did know: Cassavetes was a terrible driver. He would stop at a light and turn to her and start talking—and not notice when the light turned green because he was talking so avidly. Or he would be driving down the street and get so caught up in what he was saying that he would bring the car to a halt in the middle of traffic so he could focus on talking.

Finally, movie director or no movie director, Johnson spoke up: "Pull over," she told Cassavetes. "I'm going to drive."

Cassavetes thought that was marvelous: that this composed young woman was not intimidated by him, to the point that she was willing to tell him he was a bad driver. He gleefully switched places and continued on to lunch. In fact, Johnson recalled, "He was such a large personality that, during lunch, it was all I could do to swallow."

To play the play's producer, Cassavetes chose Paul Stewart, a member of Orson Welles' Mercury Theater, who had acted for Cassavetes in *A Child Is Waiting*. His original choice to play playwright Sarah Goode, Bette Davis, was unavailable, so he cast Joan Blondell, another still-active member of talking pictures' earliest generation of stars. For Blondell, the Cassavetes milieu was a foreign one.

The handheld camera made her nervous; although she'd been making movies since 1930, she never knew when she was being photographed on this one. "I hope he doesn't follow me to the bathroom," she muttered at one point to Gazzara.

Cassavetes had wanted Seymour Cassel to play Maurice, Myrtle's co-star and former lover. But Cassel was filming Ken Russell's *Valentino* in Europe, and it had run over schedule. So Cassavetes, who had planned to play Manny Victor, the director, got Ben Gazzara to play Manny and decided to play Maurice himself.

Cassavetes shot with a nonunion crew, using Al Ruban, the film's producer, as its cinematographer, with Mike Ferris and Fred Elmes as his camera operators.

Going nonunion wasn't a political statement; it was simply an economic fact of life. To get an independent film made, people had to work for wages far below the union minimums, and each had to do more than the single job a union position allowed. But it gave those productions an outlaw feel. As Bo Harwood observed, "Thirty years from now, I can say I rode with Billy the Kid."

"The only union workers on *Opening Night* were by a special arrangement with the theatrical workers union," Al Ruban recalled. "We had some straight talk and hit it off. Because we were working on a stage in a theater, we needed stagehands and we got them. They were terrific for us and we had no problems."

But Ruban became an object of dispute with International Photographers Local 659 of the International Alliance of Theatrical and Stage Employees. As Cassavetes finished shooting in Pasadena in January 1977, the local promised nationwide picketing at any theater that dared to show the film.

Then Cassavetes angered the Screen Extras Guild by recruiting an audience of local people as extras to fill the theaters where the plays were supposedly being performed. He ran a radio ad and an ad in a local newspaper asking for people who owned dress clothes to show up in costume and spend a few days making the film.

The Screen Extras Guild complained that its members were losing work to amateurs who were willing to work for nothing: "But we were doing this with our own money," Rowlands noted. "We couldn't afford to hire screen extras."

For all the cost-cutting measures, Cassavetes ran out of funds about six weeks into production. It took close to a month for Cassavetes to get a bank to give him a loan—yet another mortgage on the house—to finish his movie, but finally he did, based on the financial statements for *Woman*.

For the onstage scenes, they shot at Lindy Opera House on Wilshire (which was slated to be demolished) and at the Pasadena Civic Auditorium, with these California theaters doubling for New Haven and New York, which was beyond Cassavetes' budgetary reach.

Though John would perform for the audience between shots, the large crowd of extras would grow restive with the tedious filming process. And the actors, particularly the first-timers in the smaller roles, sometimes lost focus. Cassavetes, relying on their patience and good will, couldn't really yell at them, but he found other ways to make them pay attention.

At one point, while filming a scene from the play in which six actors were on stage, Cassavetes was unhappy with what the actors were doing. But most of them were amateurs, and Cassavetes felt that teeing off on them wouldn't solve the problem. Instead, he homed in on Bo Harwood, who was reloading the tape recorder for the next scene.

"We need to go now," Cassavetes said loudly to Harwood, who kept his head down and kept working. "How can you do this to us?" He grew more heated, purple in the face, as he loudly questioned Harwood's commitment to the show.

After calming down from the explosion of temper, he turned quietly to the actors, who had stood watching this from the stage, and said, "I'm sorry. Have you got one more in you?"

The outburst had its desired effect; the actors suddenly were totally focused, giving the scene everything they had. Then, as he walked past Harwood on his way back to the camera, John winked at him.

Laura Johnson recalled Cassavetes' favorite saying on the set: "Come on, let's face it," he would say. "We're all just a bunch of middle-class people trying to be artists."

Cassavetes began screening a cut of the film and playwright Ted Allan, a close friend of Cassavetes, recalled, "I saw a version where the audience went wild. They cheered and stood up. But John looked pale and disturbed. The next time I saw it, he had changed the last thirty minutes. You could say he doesn't want to be successful or he's frightened by enthusiasm or he didn't want them to like it the way they liked it. But first and foremost he has to satisfy himself."

Once the film was finished, Cassavetes and Ruban opened it in Los Angeles on Christmas Day 1977. Later they would also play it in Portland, Oregon, and Washington, D.C.

But having gotten that far, *Opening Night* was tapped out. There was no money available to market the film.

And they couldn't find a distributor willing to take on the film at a figure that made sense: "After it first played, I called people I know in Manhattan to see if they'd book it because it had good notices," Cassavetes said. "But nobody wanted it." The film played less than two weeks.

"Now there are people who said they'd take the picture but you have to realize that this is an extremely costly effort, to sell a picture," Rowlands said. "We had no distribution offers that would include the cost of promotion. And that is not an uncommon position for the independent filmmaker to find himself in."

Cassavetes said later, "It's just been a terrible experience. The financial conditions were impossible."

Jeff Lipsky, who was still working for Faces International, recalled, "By the time *Opening Night* came out, the cost of releasing had gone up and he didn't have the money to go out to more theaters with it. He was hoping to come up with money in advances but the jig was up for all the nascent independent film companies. There was a transition going on."

It wasn't a total debacle. The film opened around Europe to glowing reviews and made money in its bookings on the continent.

"I've sold it in England, Italy, Germany, Finland, Sweden and Norway," Cassavetes said. "But I'm not distributing it in the United States. That's too expensive. It costs $250,000 for advertising and promotion to open properly in New York. Gena and I spent $1.5 million to make *Opening Night*. The bank loves us."

So Cassavetes put it on the shelf, deciding that, rather than bankrupting himself chasing American bookings, he would hold on to the film, counting on its future value. Indeed, he made it a policy to refuse most commercial bookings, particularly in New York. It was a financial decision, but also a personal one.

Critic David Sterritt of the *Christian Science Monitor* remembered lunching with Cassavetes and Rowlands for an interview about *Gloria*, around the time of its release in 1980. Sterritt mentioned having seen *Opening Night* and how much he admired it.

"Those fucking distributors—they lost their chance," Cassavetes said. "If any library or university wants a print, I'll give it to them. But those fucking distributors can come up with all the money they want—they lost their chance."

Cassavetes allowed it to be shown during the retrospective of his career staged by the Museum of Modern Art in July 1980: "We're going to make it a collector's item at museums and festivals," he said.

With that MoMA showing finally came the kind of reviews the film had needed three years earlier for its abortive opening.

"It is demanding, overwhelming, sometimes exasperating free-form drama," William Wolf wrote in *Cue*. "The luminous Gena Rowlands brings remarkable complexity and pathos to the character, another in the series of bravura roles her husband has created for her."

And Judith Thurman, who had been championing the film in *Ms.* magazine, said, "Rowlands constantly dazzles you with her delicacy, her stamina, her flexibility, her resourcefulness, her courage. She is so good she can simultaneously dramatize and deflate the same convention."

A few months before Cassavetes' death, the film finally got the kind of broad media attention it had never received before, when it was selected for the 1988 New York Film Festival. The festival had asked for it earlier, around the time of the MoMA retrospective, but it wanted to include it in its "Lost Film" section, "which I resented," Cassavetes said. "How could it be lost if we have it? It's been breaking records in Italy, France and all through Europe."

Sterritt, who was on the selection committee for the 1988 New York Film Festival, suggested a Cassavetes retrospective, at which they could show *Opening Night*. They called Cassavetes, who said, "Sure, you can show it, but not as a retrospective. Show it as a new movie."

So the film played as one of the festival's selections of the most intriguing new films of the year, despite the fact that it was more than ten years old. Still, there was some trepidation about presenting such a challenging film in that kind of showcase setting, where it could easily draw a negative response from the cadre of critics with whom Cassavetes had always been at odds. It was known that Cassavetes was terminally ill, nearing the end of his losing battle with cirrhosis. Some worried that if *Opening Night* received negative press, it would end Cassavetes' life on a sour note.

Instead, the film drew an ovation from the packed audience at Alice Tully Hall.

Forty-three

Approach of the '80s

By 1977 *Newsweek* was announcing the end of the 1970s. And for John Cassavetes, the decade was almost over as well, at least as a filmmaker.

Finances had reached a sticky point. Between the cost of producing and distributing both *The Killing of a Chinese Bookie* and *Opening Night*, Cassavetes had dug himself into a financial hole that would take him several years to get out of.

The gamble of mortgaging his house had paid off handsomely with *A Woman Under the Influence*. But he'd put the Laurel Canyon hillside home on the line again to finance *Opening Night*. Though there was still a trickle of revenue from *Woman*, the last two films, which had failed at least partially because Cassavetes lacked the funds to market them properly, had put a serious crimp in the Cassavetes' household finances.

Rowlands took a movie role playing Peter Falk's wife in William Friedkin's *The Brinks Job*, and also won a pair of landmark TV roles. In 1978's *A Question of Love*, she played an aging lesbian who must fight a legal battle to keep custody of her children. And in *Strangers: The Story of a Mother and Daughter*, she played a woman who, learning she has a terminal illness, decides to reconcile with the aging mother (played by Bette Davis) from whom she'd been estranged for twenty years. Both earned her glittering reviews and marked the beginning of Rowlands' string of important social-issue-oriented TV movies, including *Face of a Stranger* and *An Early Frost*, TV's first dramatic feature about AIDS (in which she co-starred with Ben Gazzara). Most of them earned her Emmy nominations, if not Emmy awards.

In quick succession over the course of 1977 and into 1978, Cassavetes acted in two films and a TV miniseries: *The Fury, Brass Target,* and *Flesh and Blood.*

The Fury was the most sinister role he'd had since *Rosemary's Baby.* A horror film by the then-rising shockmeister Brian De Palma, an Alfred Hitchcock acolyte, it cast Cassavetes as the head of a dangerously anonymous government group that trains young people with psychic powers to work for their country as weapons (using the facade of a school for the gifted). Cassavetes' character, Ben Childress, kidnaps the telekinetically gifted Robin Sandza (Andrew Stevens) from his father, Peter (Kirk Douglas), who is Childress' friend and colleague. Even as Peter tries to track Robin to Childress's suburban Chicago mansion, he becomes involved with Gillian (Amy Irving), another teen with paranormal powers and a target of Childress' program.

In the film's hyperbolic finale, with everyone else dead, the seemingly victorious Childress talks to Gillian, who is now his ward, trying to apologize and cajole her into cooperation. But Gillian takes revenge for all of Childress' wrongs by focusing her mental powers on him, until his whole body begins to vibrate and he explodes in a shockwave of blood and flesh—one of the most over-the-top exits in film history.

For a change, Cassavetes had done something that perpetual crabapple Pauline Kael actually approved of: "Cassavetes is an ideal villain . . . He's so right for Childress that one regrets that there wasn't a real writer around to provide dialogue that would match his gloomy, viscous nastiness . . . only his end is worthy of him. This finale is the greatest finish for any villain ever."

If Cassavetes spotted *The Fury* for the silly escapism it was, he was more taken with *Brass Target*: "This is a good part," he said. "I'm no expert on the topic, but there appears to be some substance to the suspicion of a conspiracy to kill Patton."

"He thought the actual script was great," recalled Robert Fieldsteel, who was his assistant for several years. "He was disappointed in the movie."

If Cassavetes believed in the script, said co-star Bruce Davison, he was one of the only ones who did. "It was a big-budget Hollywood movie and everyone, it felt like, was there for the money," Davison recalled. And it did provide a substantial payday. Cassavetes reportedly received $350,000 to star in the film.

Cassavetes flew to Munich, where he would be part of a large international ensemble in an action-thriller about the death of General George S. Patton. Cassavetes was cast as the iconoclastic army investigator brought in to look into the car accident that killed Patton; eventually he uncovers a murder plot that was meant to mask the theft of a shipment of Nazi gold. Cassavetes' love interest was Sophia Loren; his nemeses, Robert Vaughn, Patrick McGoohan, and Max von Sydow; and he had a young sidekick in Bruce Davison.

Davison was a former ingénue whose career had taken off with his first films: *Last Summer* (opposite Barbara Hershey and Richard Thomas), *The Strawberry Statement*, and *Willard*. Now here he was in a cast with such old pros as Cassavetes, George Kennedy, Robert Vaughn, Edward Herrmann, and Max von Sydow: "I was playing with the big boys on this one," Davison said, "and John went out of his way to make me feel accepted."

Indeed, on the first day of shooting with the rest of the cast, Davison was fidgeting nervously before the beginning of a take when Cassavetes came up to him, smiled, and said, "You're doing great. Don't worry. It's just a movie."

Cassavetes had problems with the constrictive nature of the script. He had several scenes with Davison in which he needed to run through lengthy chunks of dialogue that was pure exposition. But he didn't do it easily.

"We had this hallway scene where we walked along and he had to give the whole plot to Robert Vaughn," Davison said. "And John turned to me and said, 'I know all this plot shit is just crap. So don't look at me because I can see it in your eyes.'"

Cassavetes also had trouble melding his style with that of his co-star, international sex symbol and Oscar-winner Sophia Loren. Loren is "not just the mythical star, but a real flesh-and-blood wonderful person," Cassavetes said at the time. But Loren found Cassavetes exasperating in their dialogue scenes because of the difference in the way they worked.

"It was sort of a major problem," recalled director John Hough. "John was very improvisational, always. Sophia stuck strictly to the words of the script. She learned it perfectly. John would just get an idea of what he was supposed to say and then improvise and be spontaneous. When it came time to put them together, she was waiting for her cue, but he never said it. Sophia could never improvise; it was not her style to be spontaneous."

Finally Loren called Hough over and said, "I'm having difficulty. I don't know where to come in. I can't work this way. I've done the work and I can't change at this point."

When two stars struggle for control on a movie set, top billing almost always wins out. Loren was billed above Cassavetes, so Hough asked Cassavetes to please try to accommodate Loren by finding his way back to her cues as he delivered his lines.

"John could improvise up to a point and then had to say the final cue word so she could respond," Hough said. "Perspiration was pouring down John's face. He wasn't pretending or playing games. He had difficulty memorizing lines. It was a physical problem with learning scripted lines that were written down. He had to work out how he could come back to that final word."

When Cassavetes returned from three months of filming *Brass Target*, his office staff asked what it had been like: "It was great," Cassavetes replied, "if you like having your ass kissed."

The film came and went without causing much of a ripple in the United States; the *Newsweek* review was about par for the course. Though it said Cassavetes' was "the only relaxed, graceful performance in the movie," it also noted that the film "has less to do with filmmaking than with international marketing . . . Clearly, neither the all-star cast nor director John Hough felt any commitment to this project."

John Roselius was a former teamster from the San Francisco Bay Area who'd gotten a taste of the movies while working as a driver on Sam Peckinpah's *The Killer Elite* in the mid-1970s. He had moved to Los Angeles, hoping to break in as a stunt man, and had had a measure of success acting in commercials.

One day, after looking for work at Paramount, he walked into Oblath's, the popular watering hole just across from the studio's main gate. There he spotted Cassavetes, sitting in a booth by himself. Overcome, the big truck driver introduced himself, gushing that Cassavetes was his sister's favorite actor. Cassavetes smiled and said, "Well, if you want to talk to me, you've got to buy me a drink," which Roselius eagerly did.

Six months later, Roselius ran into Cassavetes at Oblath's again. Roselius had just been hired as technical adviser for a TV miniseries, *Flesh & Blood*, to train star Tom Berenger to play a boxer. When he told Cassavetes about the job, Cassavetes brightened: "I'm on it, too," he said.

The show, based on a novel by Pete Hamill, was a Depression-era boxing story with more than a little schmaltz and a late-1970s twist aimed to shock: the seemingly incestuous relationship between the rising young boxer, Bobby Fallon (played by Tom Berenger) and his predatory mother (Suzanne Pleshette). Cassavetes was to play Gus Caputo, Bobby's tough, loving trainer (loosely based on Cus D'Amato, the legendary New York boxing guru whose final champion was Mike Tyson).

Though only an actor for hire on the miniseries, Cassavetes none-theless always had a sharp eye for the spontaneous moment that took the material to another level, whether in his own role or the roles of others. In one fight scene, Roselius, playing a dirty boxer Berenger had to fight, got caught up in the moment. The fight was being shot in front of 700 extras in a VFW hall in Chicago. The scene involved Roselius and Berenger getting their instructions from the referee in the center of the ring.

"I was chewing gum," Roselius recalled, "and as we started to walk back to our corners, I turned to Tom and said, 'Hey.' When he turned around, I spit my gum at him and hit him right in the eye. Well, the whole place was up for grabs. It was a spontaneous thing that woke them up. I thought Tom was going to go for me."

Cassavetes, meanwhile, turned excitedly to director Jud Taylor and said, "Did you get the gum?"

Taylor looked at him blankly and said, "What gum?"

With that kind of directorial vision at work, it was no wonder that *Cue* magazine referred to the miniseries as "infuriatingly simple-minded."

By 1979 it seemed that Hollywood had passed Cassavetes by as a film-maker. The personal, provocative, idiosyncratic cinema that had flour-ished for the first half of the decade had been subsumed by the reemergence of the blockbuster mentality. Films such as *Jaws* and *Star Wars* showed the studios that, in fact, there was no limit to how many people they could lure into the theaters with the right big-budget movie and a massive marketing campaign.

Cassavetes could feel the wind shift but had no interest in shifting with it. It wasn't that he wasn't aware of the studios refocusing themselves, just that he didn't want to—was probably incapable of—selling himself in the same way.

He addressed the issue in *East West Game (Mood Indigo)*, a play he wrote about an idealistic young playwright who comes to Hollywood to adapt his play as a movie script, with every intention of selling out his artistic ideals for a pot of money:

"Star Wars made 200 million dollars," the hotel maid tells the play-wright, as she cleans his room. "I don't think that includes the toys. The director makes toys. Motion pictures are just a sideline."

In the spring of 1979, Cassavetes was trying to line up money to film a new script he'd written for Peter Falk, called *Knives*. It was about a comedian who is put on trial for the murder of his wife, even as it bounces back and forth in the rather unfunny comic's consciousness and memories. But the outcome of a meeting with potential money people gave him an indication of where things stood with the film industry in general.

Cassavetes had been wooing some financial people from San Francisco; they would come to Los Angeles to talk about projects and potential investment in a film. Cassavetes had been trying to sell them on *Knives* and, in describing and telling it, had them almost to the finish line; he was even converting some offices to an apartment set for the film.

Then Falk spoke up and made the fatal mistake: He referred to *Knives* as "an art picture." It was like a stake in the heart of the deal.

John Finnegan, who was also in the meeting, remembered one of the Canadians getting up to leave and saying, "Well, it's Rose Bowl time."

After he left, Cassavetes asked, "What did he mean?"

To which Finnegan replied: "Rose Bowl time? He meant Pasadena— they were going to pass."

Part Four

A poem should not mean / but be.

—*Ars Poetica,*
ARCHIBALD MACLEISH

*The truth of the matter is that everyone feels like saying,
"I had no idea what that was going to be. I had no idea
that's the way it was going to turn out."*

—JOHN CASSAVETES

Forty-four

Gloria

The story goes that, in the mid-1970s, after Barbra Streisand had taken over the long-gestating rock 'n' roll remake of *A Star Is Born*, she called John Cassavetes and asked him to direct the film.

He is reported to have replied, "What would I want to do that for?"

John Finnegan recalled, "He was offered a chance to direct a Barbra Streisand picture and turned it down. He said, 'I'd end up breaking her fucking nose.'"

There couldn't have been a potentially odder couple than Streisand and Cassavetes: Cassavetes, with his bristling, restless (and messy) approach to probing the emotion of a scene; Streisand, the legendary perfectionist and control freak who kept close track of where she was in relation to the lights and camera at all times.

Yet here came Streisand again later in the 1970s, part of a confluence of events that ultimately led Cassavetes and Gena Rowlands to make the unlikely *Gloria*. But the elements of the story are in conflict, both about Streisand's participation and about Cassavetes' (and, for that matter, about Buck Henry's).

After suffering the combined financial toll of *Chinese Bookie* and *Opening Night*, Cassavetes wrote *Gloria* because he needed the money. But it wasn't strictly a commercial venture; at the least, he might get a part for Gena out of the deal as well. Cassavetes said, "The film is an accident. One night, Gena said to me, 'You never write anything about children. I wish you'd write a story about kids.' She loves children; she has three of them."

According to Cassavetes, he got a call from an executive at MGM: "You don't happen to have a story about kids, do you? If you could come up with something for Ricky Schroder, I'd buy it immediately," he said, referring to the actor whose performance in the not-yet-released *The Champ*, opposite Jon Voight, had turned him into a sought-after young performer.

"So I wrote this story to sell, strictly to sell," Cassavetes said. "It was no great shakes but I liked it and Gena liked it. I sent it over to [the MGM executive]. 'Great,' he said, and the next day Ricky Schroder left Metro and signed with Disney."

Around the same time, Streisand, in something of a movie-career lull since 1976's *A Star Is Born*, was looking for material. But when she was shown *Gloria*, as Rowlands recalled, "Streisand said she didn't want to do it because it's a maternal kind of thing and she felt she was too young for that and that her audience didn't see her that way."

Not that Cassavetes had developed any more of a fever to work with Streisand. Richard Kaye, one of Cassavetes' assistants at the time, said, "I was shocked to hear John say, 'I'm not that interested in her.' It sounded like more money for the movie. I'd never seen someone turn down money because they didn't want to direct a star they weren't interested in."

Eventually Cassavetes gave the script to his agent, Guy McElwaine: "You don't want to direct it?" McElwaine asked.

"No, no, but I want Gena in it since she suggested it," Cassavetes said.

It was called "One Winter Night," a title that would morph to "One Summer Night" (when it became clear that it would be shot in the summer) and, eventually, to *Gloria*.

"I've got good news and bad news," McElwaine said when he called Cassavetes to follow up about the script. "Columbia loves the picture and they want Gena in it."

"What's the bad news?" Cassavetes asked.

"They want you to direct it," McElwaine said.

"Columbia insisted I direct it, which I really didn't want," Cassavetes said later. "Too commercial. But now I'm happy with Gena and the kid and some of the execution. It's a harmless and entertaining film."

But McElwaine himself disputed the idea that Cassavetes would turn up his nose at a directing job, and his argument carries the ring of truth: "I never knew John not to want to direct," McElwaine said.

And, frankly, maybe all it took was being asked again after so long.

While he didn't envision himself making the film as he wrote it, he could see it a little more clearly once a studio expressed interest.

"I never thought anybody in the major companies would want me to direct, because I'd had my run-ins and I thought it had all been over for a number of years," he said. "I'd like to feel that everybody's against me but it's not true. Not everyone."

Cassavetes admitted that he wasn't quite sure how to deal with the newest wave of young, business-oriented executives who were increasingly burrowing their way into the studio's executive infrastructure: "It's confusing to go and deal with studios because a creator and an executive don't talk the same language," he said. "An executive is answerable to a lot of people so his whole way of dealing is to compromise. I don't know how to go into a meeting and compromise, because I'm stubborn. I just don't know how. If I did, I'm sure I would."

Ultimately he couldn't pass up the money: reportedly $1 million for him and Gena together. Richard Kaye (who served as dialogue director on *Gloria*) recalled them in New York about to begin shooting, toasting the deal: "Hey, we're out of the hole."

Cassavetes began to rework the script with Sam Shaw, who would be the film's producer: "Sam kept pushing it toward a more truthful area and now we're all in love with it," Cassavetes said.

If *The Killing of a Chinese Bookie* was a European version of an American noir—and *Opening Night* was a nod to Strindberg (and *All About Eve*)—*Gloria* was the closest thing to a straight genre film Cassavetes ever directed. But, of course, Cassavetes never did anything in a straight line. "I have a way of taking a simple piece of material and complicating it and making it non-commercial—and having no guilt about it," Cassavetes said. "That's a tough problem for a studio or somebody trying to make money."

The film begins with Jeri Dawn (Julie Carmen), riding the bus past Yankee Stadium and hurrying to her apartment. There is a rather large man standing in the lobby as she hurries in. For some reason she has been grocery shopping—even though she is about to flee for her life.

At the apartment, her nervous husband Jack Dawn (Buck Henry) hurries her to pack so they can leave. Jack is a bookkeeper for the mob and has made several mistakes: He stole from his bosses, kept an extra set of books on their deals, and then let that information slip out. He's also been talking to the feds. Now the gangsters are coming to kill him. So he has to get his family out of town fast.

There's a knock on the door, but it is only Gloria Swanson (Rowlands), a slightly blowzy-looking blonde, the neighbor coming to borrow some coffee. Jeri and Jack beg her to take the children to her apartment to hide them. Gloria squints and says, "I hate kids, especially yours." But they convince her to take their youngest, little Phil (six-year-old John Adames); Jack kneels and gives Phil his accountant's ledger, telling him it will save his life. "Be a man," he tells him. "Always be tough. Don't trust anybody."

Gloria coaxes Phil down the hall to her place, even as a carload of goons with guns shows up in front of the building and begin coming up the steps. As Gloria introduces Phil to her cat in her apartment, the hoods break down the door of the Dawn apartment and slaughter Phil's whole family with shotguns. Once the shooting is done and the men leave, Gloria and Phil get out of the building and hop a bus, fleeing with only Gloria's suitcase and Phil's ledger.

They arrive at a nicely appointed apartment in a well-preserved neighborhood of Washington Heights, though it is never explained whose apartment it is or why Gloria has a key and free access to it. ("There was originally a line in the taxi where I said, 'Now get in there, we're going to my sister's apartment,'" Rowlands recalled. "John cut the line and I said, 'But then they're not going to know whose apartment that is.' He said, 'Who cares? It's an apartment—an apartment of a friend or a sister.' That's very much in John's way of thinking. Just to help the audience know where they are, that's not something that John considers enormously important.")

In the morning, she attempts to make breakfast for them but can't quite manage it; there is no air of domesticity to her as she burns the scrambled eggs and then tosses the entire mess—pan and all—into the garbage. Nor does she really seem to know how to talk to little Phil, who is angry and scared and wanting his parents. He resists her authority; when she goes for her morning shower and tells him to wait for her, he instead leaves the apartment and runs several blocks, then stops to look at a newspaper and sees his own picture and those of his family on the front page.

Back at the apartment, Gloria is out of her shower and dressed. The phone is ringing but she's not answering. Someone is obviously looking for her and she doesn't want to be found.

She finds Phil crying on the landing and walks him down some stairs, to sit and talk to him, trying to figure out what to do. Then she hears something—it is the gangsters, looking for her at the apartment. They are on the elevator, but some are also coming up the stairs. She and Phil are able to duck out of sight, then slip past them back down the stairs. They find a rear exit to the building and even spot a taxi, but the taxi doesn't stop and they are stranded on the street for the moment, losing precious time.

As Gloria anxiously glances about, Phil starts clinging to her legs, hampering her movement. Finally, she tries to push him away by telling him that she used to work for the people who killed his family, that she can't be seen with him and that he should run away. But he latches onto her even more tightly.

Even as she tries to pry him off her legs, the car full of gangsters comes sailing past going the opposite way down the street, hits its brakes with a screech and does a squealing U-turn to pull up at the curb next to Gloria and Phil.

"Gloria, we're not interested in you," one of them tells her. "All we want is the book and the kid. Do you understand?"

She smiles and nods, tries to jolly them out of taking the kid, and finally (and with obvious forethought) pulls out a pistol and starts shooting the men in the car. As the car frantically pulls away, she fires again and again; the car goes sailing through the air in a spectacular crash. She watches the overturned car skid to a halt, its occupants dead or dying—then whistles and yells, "Taxi!" without a backward glance.

When Phil tries to apologize in the taxi for being a brat, she snaps at him, then softens and says they'll go get her money and treat themselves right. But after emptying her safe-deposit box, she and Phil board a bus, where she encounters an old acquaintance, a mobster who tells her she has really messed up. Word is out about the shootings already and everyone is looking for her.

"You gotta be outa your mind," he tells her, as she and Phil get off the bus.

They are rebuffed at an Upper East Side hotel, which has no rooms, so Gloria decides it would be better to stay in a less-expensive neighborhood. They wind up sharing a bed at a flophouse, with flashing neon lights outside the windows. It is the easiest, most emotionally open, and even humorous that Gloria has been with the high-strung Phil.

Little John Adames seems to be constantly gritting his teeth through these scenes, as though he is unbearably tense, not about Phil's situation but about what he's supposed to be doing in the scene. He also appears to have no neck, as though his shoulders are frozen in a permanent shrug. Combined with his high-waistedness and spindly physique, he has a physical awkwardness—a strangely stiff posture and body language, particularly in the next scene.

Gloria tells Phil that they are going to Pittsburgh. But first Phil is going to go with her to a cemetery. She feels he should say good-bye to his family, and since they can't go to the actual family burial place, any cemetery will do, she feels. Once there, she sends him to find a grave to talk to and "say whatever comes into your heart." Adames stands by himself at a gravestone and reels off a speech he has obviously memorized, fidgeting nervously and making strange faces, as though struggling to remember his lines. It is uncomfortably amateurish, not a kid being a kid but a child out of his depth as an actor.

On the ride back into Manhattan, Phil says listlessly, "No one knows where I am." He reels off a list of things he wants: "I want to play stickball. I want to go to school. I want to go home." It is the first moment that he seems like a vulnerable six-year-old child whose entire world has suddenly been upended.

"Don't be stupid—you got no home," Gloria responds. "You got me."

They arrive at Penn Station and buy tickets to Pittsburgh. But while sitting in the café waiting for the train, they encounter the gangsters who are looking for them. Gloria gets the drop on them and disarms them all. She and Phil escape through the restaurant's kitchen and check into yet another hotel.

The hoods in the café have confirmed her fear. This whole affair has been the work of mob boss Tony Tanzini, with whom Gloria obviously has extensive past history, judging by her response.

As she ponders what to do, Phil starts to get lippy again. She is no relation to him and so he is leaving, he tells her, standing on a corner on upper Broadway. He is going to find a new family and new friends. She glares at him, then tells him she is going into the bar across the street and he can join her if and when he wants. But he doesn't follow and, after sitting there long enough to order a beer and light a cigarette, she leaves and goes looking for him.

Riding in a taxi searching for Phil, she finds him sitting on a stoop with new friends. He runs from her and before she can reach him, the gangsters pull up in their car and grab him up and take him up into an apartment.

Gloria follows, killing one of the gangsters and holding the other two at gunpoint, then shutting them in a bathroom. Then she takes Phil and the book and flees again, with the gangsters hot on her trail. She faces them down at gunpoint in the street, then escapes in a taxi and then down into the subway. But she loses Phil when she gets off the train, and he is trapped on the train when the doors close. She yells at him to wait at the next station; then Gloria gets on the next train and finds herself confronted by the two gangsters she just escaped from.

She hauls off and slaps one of them, who slaps her back, knocking her to the floor. The other passengers grab the two hoods and restrain them as she gets to her feet and pulls her gun, pointing it at them as the train comes into the next station. Phil waves at her from the platform as the train slows: "Come on, I'd love it," she taunts the hoods from the platform, as the subway doors close them in the train. "You sissies. You let a woman beat you."

She and Phil catch a train to Newark, then try to get a train to Pittsburgh. But the depot makes Gloria nervous; they check into a hotel and resolve to start fresh after some sleep.

They have had discussions in the past about their relationship, with Phil firmly averring that Gloria is nothing to him. Though he doesn't quite say, "You're not the boss of me," that's what he's been telling her. But now, having seen her risk her life to save him on at least two separate occasions, he tells her, "You're my mother, you're my father, you're my whole family. You're even my friend, Gloria. You're my girlfriend, too."

When he falls asleep, she goes out to get some food but is stopped coming out of the coffee shop by Sill (Val Avery), another mob associate. Sill forces her into a cab and tells her that the game is up and bringing her in will be worth a lot of money to him. Gloria launches herself at him and starts hollering as though she is being attacked. When the cabbie tries to intervene, Sill tells him to mind his own business, then tells him he looks like an ape. The driver stops the cab and, when he gets out, he turns out to be a 7-foot-tall black man. He forces Sill out of the cab and is threatening to beat him when both notice Gloria has vanished.

Back at the hotel room, she calls Tanzini. She hopes he'll listen to reason since he used to be her boyfriend. Perhaps a simple sit-down will solve matters. Tanzini seems receptive. So she leaves Phil with a handful of $100 bills, along with instructions about what to do—where she'll meet him in Pittsburgh and how he should get there—if she doesn't come back to the hotel room in the next few hours.

At Tanzini's, she is told to wait, and then Tanzini himself sits down with her and tells her that she needs to turn over the boy. It quickly becomes clear that, in fact, her time is almost up. Still, she plays her string out to the end. She puts the ledger on the table between them, lighting a cigarette (as if before a firing squad?) and telling Tanzini, "I'm going to get up and walk out of here and if you want to shoot me, you can." She stands, saunters to the door—and is out the door and on to the elevator as Tanzini says, "She's leaving," to his henchmen. Caught unaware, they chase after her; as her elevator descends, they break the window in the door and shoot down the shaft into the roof of the elevator car, almost a dozen times.

Phil wakes up alone the next morning and, following Gloria's instructions, gets on a train to Pittsburgh. Once there, he takes a cab to a cemetery and performs the same ritual he did with his family: He has a conversation with Gloria, who he assumes is dead, to tell her good-bye. But even as he finishes talking, a limousine pulls up and an elderly woman gets out. Then she stops and fixes Phil with a stare and says, "Aren't you going to kiss your grandmother?"

It is Gloria, dressed in widow's weeds, a gray wig and pillbox hat. Phil runs to her and they embrace, the happy recipients of an incredibly unlikely coincidence that reunites them as the credits roll. Cassavetes often talked about *Gloria* as a fable, which is the only way to explain its ending.

"It's one of life's little miracles," Cassavetes said with a shrug and a smile. "Life is full of them. You can't explain them."

To shoot *Gloria* for Columbia, Cassavetes had to make certain compromises. For one thing, he couldn't bring his usual gang from California to shoot it with him. As Mike Ferris recalled, "After *Opening Night*, he took me on a walk and said, 'Gena's tired of me putting up the house every time I want to make a movie. The next show will be a union show in New York."

Because it was a studio film requiring a union crew, he couldn't ask Al Ruban to shoot it, either. So, as he had done with Ferris and Fred Elmes (and Ruban, for that matter), Cassavetes hired a camera operator with career ambitions (but no credits as a cinematographer) and gave him his break as director of photography: Fred Schuler, who had worked as a camera operator on such films as *Jaws, Taxi Driver, Annie Hall, Dog Day Afternoon, Manhattan,* and *The Deer Hunter.*

Schuler's phone rang one evening and a voice said, "This is John Cassavetes. You're Fred Schuler and I'd like you to do my movie."

"Would you like to know more about me or to meet?" Schuler asked.

"No," Cassavetes said, "I want you to shoot it."

"Well, I'm an operator, not a d.p.," Schuler felt compelled to point out.

"That's OK," Cassavetes said.

But after the conversation, Schuler heard nothing for almost a month. So when he was offered another job—as a camera operator on Paul Mazursky's *Willie & Phil*—he took it. Shooting hadn't started on Mazursky's film when Schuler got a call from Cassavetes, asking him to come to a meeting at the Wyndham Hotel on West Fifty-eighth Street in New York.

When Schuler walked into the hotel suite, he found a production meeting with Cassavetes and almost two dozen other people in full swing. Seeing his look of shock, Cassavetes invited Schuler to go for a walk and started to explain the film to him. But Schuler interrupted, and said, "I'm on a job already and I can't get out of it. I'm an operator for Sven Nykvist and Paul Mazursky. I'm committed to another film."

"I'm going to call Paul right now," Cassavetes announced. Schuler stopped him and said he would speak to Mazursky. When he did, Mazursky offered only encouragement and told him to take the job.

Gloria would be his first credit as a d.p. in a career that continues to the present day. Schuler remembered it as "a real oddball operation right from the beginning. It was not a conventional film in any sense."

Despite creating it with Ricky Schroder as a possibility for the role, Cassavetes had written the character of the child in *Gloria* as a Latino: "Why? Because it just felt better that way," McElwaine said. "That was one of the first questions [Columbia head David] Begelman asked: Why is this kid not Ricky Schroder? And John said, Because that's not how I want him."

Young Juan Adames (whose name was changed to John for the film's credits) was chosen out of an open casting call that drew "ten trillion kids," according to Rowlands. Cassavetes never asked actors to read for him; rather, he sat down and talked to them and did the same with the children who showed up to audition.

"The ones he remembered would mean something," Rowlands said. "And he picked this one out in about three days. He was only six and he was so macho."

Mike Haley, the first assistant director, remembered Adames having "something very natural about him," Haley said. "In no way was he a child actor. He was just a kid, with his mother, a sweet kid."

Cassavetes wanted to be sure that the lad knew what he was getting into.

"Look, Johnny, do you really want to do this part?" Cassavetes asked him.

"Yeah, I want to do it," Adames said.

But Cassavetes pressed him. It was summer, Cassavetes noted, a time when Adames could just as easily be playing with his friends or going swimming. Instead, he would be on the movie set, which could be tedious for a child.

"If you're doing it because someone else thinks you should but you don't really think it's such a great idea, it's not worth it," Cassavetes told him. "So take a couple days and think it over."

Instead, young Adames thought about it a few seconds then said, "Let me ask you this: How many words will I learn on this movie?"

Without missing a beat, Cassavetes said, "Oh, three hundred, easy."

Adames was impressed: "I'd go back to school and I'd know three hundred more words than everybody in my class," he said enthusiastically, and that sealed the deal.

"He was a unique little thinker," Rowlands said.

Buck Henry was a curious choice to play Jack Dawn, the mob accountant whose actions put his family's lives on the line. It was not hard to believe the deceptively nebbishy Henry, one of the preeminent comedy writers of his time, playing an accountant. But one who had married into a Puerto Rican family and lived in what looked like a tenement across from Yankee Stadium in the South Bronx? Debatable.

The story that was told for years was that Henry, who (like Cassavetes) had Guy McElwaine as his agent, expressed an interest to the agent in working with Cassavetes to see how he handled actors. Gena Rowlands at one point told the story: "John's agent is Buck's agent and Buck said to his agent, 'I'd love to be in Cassavetes' new film—I'd love to see how he works.'" Cassavetes response was that, while he had a part for which Henry would be perfect, it was too small for Cassavetes to consider asking him to do it. But Henry read the script and convinced Cassavetes to let him play the part: "He thought this role was not like anything he'd ever done before and that it would be a good acting experience for him," Rowlands recalled.

But Henry tells it differently: "It would never have occurred to me to make an approach like that," he said. As he recalled it, Cassavetes had asked someone else to do the role but had been turned down.

"So Guy said, 'Why not use Buck?'" Henry said.

Gloria's look was designed by Emanuel Ungaro: a series of bold, mostly monochromatic suits with shoulder pads and a sleek, no-nonsense cut. Rowlands herself owned several outfits by Ungaro; when Cassavetes suggested that they look at his new collection to see if there was anything that might be right for the film, they went to his showroom, where, Rowlands said, "There were Gloria's ideal clothes. Remember, not only does Gloria have money but she's highly individual. I think she saw the dresses in a window and said, I don't care what those cost—they're mine."

As she thought about the character and what her background might be, Rowlands shied away from the obvious. Gloria tells young Phil that the people who killed her family are her friends and that she's been in jail. But Rowlands didn't want the character's past to be a tawdry one.

"I tried very hard not to make her appear to be a hooker, even though from what we've seen of tough women like that all of our lives, we've been conditioned to think they are prostitutes," Rowlands said. Instead, Rowlands imagined Gloria as a figure not unlike Virginia Hill, mistress to real-life mobster Bugsy Siegel: not a prostitute but a bag woman, making money pickups and deliveries for the mob.

"Maybe she was a chorus girl when she was young and because night-clubs are hangouts for gangsters, the chorus girls can make these alliances with mobsters," Rowlands said. "They fall in love with one of them and suddenly find themselves in a new line of work."

Rowlands wanted to find something physically distinctive about the character, beyond the clothing, to build upon. Though she normally worked from the inside out as an actor, letting the physicality flow from the emotions, she decided that Gloria had adopted a defensive approach to life in her milieu: "When I read the script, I knew I wanted a walk for her," Rowlands said. "I wanted something that, from the minute you saw me, you would know I could handle myself on the streets of New York. So I started thinking about when I lived in New York, how different I walked down the street when there was nobody but me. It was a walk that said, They'd better watch out."

They started shooting in late summer 1979 at the Concourse Plaza Hotel, near Yankee Stadium. A former gangster hangout, the deserted hotel once served as a mob gathering place after Yankee games. Babe Ruth himself once kept a suite there. But it had fallen into serious disrepair. "There must have been six thousand cats in the lobby when we first got there," Rowlands recalled.

It was a particularly steamy summer in New York: "It was boiling hot," Henry said, "just this nasty, hot, summer week. What was interesting was that, in this weather, how John confined himself to these small spaces. The camera was governed by what was there; there were no moving walls or anything."

It got so hot that, at one point, Rowlands fainted. John Finnegan recalled, "I got on the walkie-talkie and said, 'The actress is down. The actress is down.' After they took her away, I said to John, 'Is that a wrap?' He said, 'Wrap, my ass. We'll continue.'"

They moved around New York, shooting scenes in Harlem, Times Square, the Upper East Side, Corona, and Flushing: "I've lived in New York on and off my whole life and I saw sections of the city that I never even knew existed," Rowlands said.

For Cassavetes, the union crew with its myriad work rules meant a tighter way of working than he was used to. For one thing, he couldn't rewrite on a daily basis, as he was wont to do. "We would work it out up-front," Schuler said. "So there was nothing unexpected. He wasn't going to change things 180 degrees. I gave him plenty of time upfront to work it out. We always had a rehearsal and the scene worked out. It was scripted. It was more like a regular film."

Rowlands noted, "I don't know how to describe what this is. It's not farce. It is satirical but I thought it was necessary to play very realistically against the actual written style of it. Much of it has a fairy tale quality and it's like an old Bogart movie or something."

Rowlands had never handled a handgun, though she had to look as though it was second nature: "At first the gun was heavy—amazingly heavy," she said. "But after a while, it begins to feel good in your hands, very good. So I understand the temptation to use it."

Because he was only six, Adames didn't yet know how to read. When Rowlands inquired how he would learn his lines, Cassavetes replied, "You'll just go over and over them with him—until he's comfortable."

So, though it was not her preferred way of working, Rowlands sat with Adames and ran lines with him to help him memorize his part. During one run-through, thinking about other things, she simply read the lines without acting them, and Adames called her on it.

"Wait a minute—you're not going to say that like that, are you?" he demanded.

Rowlands, caught off-balance, asked him to repeat himself. The six-year-old not only repeated the question but gave her a line reading that she should imitate.

"Hey, let's get this straight," Rowlands told him. "You learn your lines and I'll learn mine and we'll work with each other from that point on."

As she noted later, "Remember that this child had been acting for four days. I didn't want it to get out of hand on the fourth day of rehearsal."

Cassavetes was always diplomatic about young Adames' work, reveling in the kid-ness of the performance: "He's neither sympathetic nor nonsympathetic. He's just a kid. He reminds me of me, constantly in shock, reacting to this unfathomable environment."

Cassavetes saw no need to soften the character of Gloria—or her attitude toward little Phil—to appeal to an audience. Gloria was a tough, hard-shelled woman forced into an untenable situation and acting by her own code of honor and a previously untapped maternal instinct.

"I was stunned by Gloria because it's so far from anything I'd played," Rowlands said. "I can't even get my own children to clean up their rooms. How could I possibly play the authority over this child, that Gloria comes by so naturally? I'm not nearly that strong."

Though they'd been working together on films for almost two decades at that point, Cassavetes and Rowlands still had their moments of conflict. Schuler recalled a day in Harlem, when the two of them started arguing loudly about how to do a scene. In the middle of it all, Cassavetes said, "Roll the camera," so they were screaming at each other back and forth while the camera was rolling.

Finally Rowlands stormed off the set, casting one last insult over her shoulder as she departed: "There are only two people I'd rather work for than you—Otto Preminger and Adolf Hitler," she told him, then marched back to her dressing room. As Cassavetes came walking out, the script supervisor said, "Do you know that we're rolling?"

To which Cassavetes replied, "Yeah, print it so Columbia knows how hard we're working."

There were battles with the studio, recalled Mike Haley, the first assistant director, though Cassavetes' arguments were usually with the late Stephen Kesten, the associate producer and production manager, who was the buffer between Cassavetes and Columbia.

Haley recalled, "He and Steve had huge conflicts over how the whole thing was to be run. Underneath everything, there were problems signing off on the budget."

But Haley said, "Steve was probably the best production manager New York had ever known. It was his way or the highway. He and John were like two opposite electrons banging heads, plus fighting with the studio."

If Cassavetes had a problem with the production, it was the organization and structure that was required to film a studio picture on budget and on schedule. Cassavetes was used to discovering his film as he went along—reworking the script each day and shooting the new version. But he didn't have that luxury on this film because of studio oversight.

To help him, Schuler let Cassavetes shoot the handheld camera himself. That gave him a context in which to think about what Schuler was telling him needed to be shot.

Cassavetes was particularly suggestible when it came to camera movements, Schuler observed: "If a grip happened to park a dolly with the camera on it, John thought it was a great place to do the shot," Schuler said. "I finally told my crew, 'Don't take the camera and dolly out until we know what we're doing.'"

Most of Cassavetes' complaints about making the film had to do with the union crew, which he felt didn't care about the movie, perhaps because they lacked the kind of passion and intensity of the true believers who normally signed on for one of his ventures.

Used to the stripped-down, fast-moving crew of his self-financed films, he saw only waste and redundancy in the much-larger, union-mandated crew on *Gloria.*

At the time, Peter Bogdanovich was getting ready to shoot *They All*

Laughed in New York. He and Cassavetes got together one evening when Cassavetes, in a studio-provided car, had his driver bring Bogdanovich out of a restaurant to chat in the limo for a few minutes. "Mainly, he complained viciously about his lousy crew, called them all the names in the book, cursed them a number of times and then laughed his most diabolical Cassavetes laugh and said, 'Fuck 'em—I'll prevail over the bastards,'" Bogdanovich recalled.

The film's first editor, assigned to Cassavetes by the studio, was gone almost before he started. At one point, during the first week of shooting, the editor asked Schuler about a shot in which an actor was in shadow and Cassavetes fired him on the spot: "You're a spy—you're not with me," Cassavetes charged.

His conflicts with production manager Steve Kesten were usually about the amount of time a scene would take to shoot. Haley recalled Kesten as astute and forthright, a no-bullshit guy who angered the studio almost as much as he bugged Cassavetes because of his habit of saying exactly what he thought.

Kesten was working for the studio but, Schuler said, saw himself as standing on the director's side of the line, backing him up against studio interference. But Kesten also had deadlines and budgets to meet and had to keep Cassavetes on schedule as well.

Recalled Buck Henry, "John would change things at the last minute. I remember seeing the script girl with her eyes rolling."

"When we were shooting in Jersey, he and Steve almost had a fistfight," Haley said. "I think they fought constantly."

At one point, shooting Phil in a hotel bathtub, Cassavetes didn't like the angle of the camera, so he got a sledgehammer and knocked a hole in the wall so the camera could poke through.

"John was meeting the schedule but he would change his mind about certain things," Schuler said. "As a producer, you line up certain things and if you don't follow up, it costs money. But if you'd talk about money, well, that was exactly what John didn't want to hear. Toward the end, it got tense."

What bothered Cassavetes, he told Schuler, was that he was committed to doing a movie on someone else's terms.

"I need twenty-four weeks and all I've got is twelve," Cassavetes would mutter. "I wish they would fire me."

But they didn't. In fact, Columbia was pleased enough with the outcome that the studio entered the film in the Venice Film Festival, where it shared the Golden Lion with Louis Malle's *Atlantic City,* another film about women and gangsters.

Gloria was released in October 1980, and the critics were divided, though most found it a pleasantly unusual choice for Cassavetes and a further revelation of Rowlands' range as an actress. Nothing she'd done for Cassavetes before had suggested the coiled power she radiated as a woman with deeply ingrained street smarts and innate toughness.

As David Denby noted in *New York* magazine, "Playing a fearless, harsh-talking broad, a female Lee Marvin, Rowlands discovers things she's never done for Cassavetes in the past: a flair for blunt comedy, a stiff-shouldered walk, a way of dropping acid remarks from the corner of her mouth."

Richard Corliss said, "The movie's achievement is that it manages to be almost as effective as it is predictable. Its failure is in pretending to a naturalism it cannot maintain whenever movie actress and movie crew go slumming through the Big Apple and bystanders gawk into the lens, auditioning for stardom in some future Cassavetes film."

David Ansen called the film "Cassavetes' loopy version of an action movie, laced with hard-bitten sentimentality and wild, poker-faced humor. You don't have to believe *Gloria* for a minute to enjoy it. *Gloria* is pure, unembarrassed jive—a hipster's lark of a movie."

Still, Ansen made the same observation as most critics: Though the character of Phil was written with a sense of humor, it was not particularly well acted by the stiff, inexperienced John Adames: "His oh-so-cute tough-guy dialogue is so palpably written that he sounds like a ventriloquist's dummy."

Rowlands enjoyed her best reviews since *Woman* and earned an Oscar nomination, to boot. She was quick to credit her husband.

"If I've emerged as an important actress, it's entirely because of him," she said. "He pushes me harder than any other director. I take more chances for him. He knows my limits. I mouth off to him more than I would to a total stranger."

"There are lots of actresses in Hollywood who resent my working for John," Gena admitted. "I'd be happy to work for other directors if they made films with good parts for women. I like a hard part, a part in which I can work something out, find out things about myself."

Gloria was made at a moment of transition in the movie industry. It wasn't just the groupthink of the blockbuster mentality. There was a seismic shift of attention to a kind of movie that could be increasingly merchandised and marketed beyond the multiplex. Special effects and action or broad, adolescent comedy—movies that played to the suddenly coveted 12-to-24 demographic—were the order of the day. The studios had no interest in movies about human beings and their problems. They didn't want *A Woman Under the Influence;* they wanted *Gloria,* and they barely wanted that if it strayed too far from the formulaic path.

"If you watch television, if you read the newspapers, if you go to a movie, the first thing somebody asks is, 'How many people were there? Was it crowded?'" Cassavetes said. "That's the nature of the success of a film in this country."

Forty-five

Retrospective Tempest

"In my later life, I've become more successful with other people because I don't give a damn about personal ambition," Cassavetes said after finishing *Gloria*. "At my age, that's fruitless. I don't want recognition. Recognition is a pain in the ass. Making something indelible is what I want. Something concrete."

Still, Cassavetes wasn't having much luck drawing attention—or money—to any of the scripts he was having readings of at his house. So when he received not one but two offers for retrospectives of his films—one from the Los Angeles International Film Exposition (otherwise known as Filmex) for March 1980, the other from the Museum of Modern Art in New York for July of the same year—he agreed, liking the attention and hoping it would lead to something concrete, like another film.

The fact that he had just turned fifty also played into his decision: "By the age of fifty, I would like to know that I'm not dead—that there's some continuity to my life," he said.

At one point, shortly before Filmex's five-hour tribute program of film clips and an in-person interview, Cassavetes reportedly cancelled the event, though it eventually went on. There apparently had been some confusion about the scheduling of certain titles—seven features were to be shown, and Cassavetes, annoyed at last-minute changes, said, "I don't want to have anything to do with them. I don't want my films shown. The tribute is off."

But Filmex director Gary Essert told the *Los Angeles Times* that Cassavetes had made the same pronouncement six times already that week and changed his mind each time: "I think it's his method of operation," Essert said. "He'll probably cancel at least two more times before Sunday."

Cassavetes was more gracious when MoMA hosted a retrospective of his work. It was nice to be hailed as a pioneer, as an artist—as something other than a director Hollywood didn't want to deal with.

"I'm so honored because a scene from my first film was shot in the museum. I've always had a very soft spot for the place," he admitted. "You really do want a voluntary acknowledgement that you're an artist."

Cassavetes had *Gloria* set for release in a couple of months and whatever he thought of it, he was aware that it offered him a chance to, perhaps, get back in the game on his own terms once more. So he happily stumped for the upcoming *Gloria* even as he talked with the press for the retrospective.

"Ordinarily, I don't care about retrospectives," he said. "They make you feel awful. Are you dead? What's the point of going on if they've already given you a retrospective? But for the first time in my life I feel honored—the enthusiasm, the care, the passion of the people at the Modern has been marvelous. I couldn't be in nicer company."

The retrospective included the first-ever New York screening of *Opening Night*. Robert Fieldsteel, his assistant at the time, said, "What pleased him most about the MoMA retrospective was that there was a fight in the lobby to see *Opening Night*. It was a rediscovery. Everyone was very respectful. MoMA did it with respect and class."

Still, Cassavetes refused to make nice about critical response to some of his films, just because he was the center of attention. He felt conspicuously different, an artist pursuing personal visions at a moment when sequels, special effects, and increasingly bigger budgets were the renewed focus of a blockbuster-centric Hollywood culture.

"I'm interested in shaking people up, not making them happy by soothing them," he said. "The types of films we do are different. Commercial movies have no feeling, no sensitivity. Most people tell me that people won't understand films with feeling. But everyone can feel."

He talked up his next project, a script he'd written called "She's De-Lovely," for Gena: "The next picture we make will be a deep personal statement," he said. "I don't know if anyone will finance it."

Even as he came to New York in the summer of 1980 to be honored at MoMA, he was on his way to act in a low-budget Canadian horror film, *The Incubus*, in Toronto. It was a bizarre choice, one that made sense only because it was directed by John Hough, who had directed Cassavetes in *Brass Target*.

"I take some roles because I'm broke," Cassavetes admitted. "Like anybody else, I need money. And if someone's willing to pay that money, I'll go and do it and do the best I can.

"People have these ideas actors should be monks and they're not. They're good-time people who work extremely hard."

In the film, Cassavetes plays a doctor, Sam Cordell, who has moved to a small town with his teen-age daughter, Jenny (Erin Flannery). The town medical examiner, Sam becomes involved in investigating a series of hideous rapes and killings that point to occult possession. Cassavetes is as natural as possible but spends most of the film looking pained and serious, trying desperately to believe in the blandly outlandish material.

Hough found that Cassavetes was a supportive, cooperative actor. At one point, Hough mentioned to Cassavetes that he had never had a problem directing other directors as actors. Cassavetes smiled and said, "I'm so pleased to come on and just act. It's such a pleasure. I don't have to worry. I'm happy to concentrate on what I'm doing."

The film got an exploitation release in late August 1982. Vincent Canby dismissed it in the *New York Times*, noting, "Movies like this aren't totally worthless. They provide employment for a number of people."

For most of *Incubus*, Cassavetes looks like a relatively healthy fifty-year-old man. He seems vital and present, though middle age has inflicted signs of wear. There are lines of age around his eyes, the character-instilling pouches beneath the eyes that spoke of too much intensity, too many cigarettes and drinks, and not enough sleep.

But the gathering effects of cirrhosis started to take a toll, as Cassavetes went directly from *Incubus* in Toronto to *Whose Life Is It Anyway?* locations in Boston for a week, before finishing that film on soundstages in Los Angeles.

Though Cassavetes was cast in the role prior to the start of production, director John Badham did not meet him until the night before Cassavetes was to shoot his first scene. Badham had staged the play with Richard Dreyfuss and the rest of the main cast at the Williamstown Theater Festival in the Berkshires as a rehearsal for the film. But Cassavetes didn't participate.

"He was stuck in Canada doing a film," Badham recalled. "The night before we started shooting, I met him in the lobby of the Copley Plaza and we sat down for a drink. He was exhausted. He was worn out—and he had to do a scene the next morning. Coming from one film right into the other, with the next day shooting—it was not a good idea. He just wasn't with it. As time went on, he quickly adjusted. The more comfortable he got, the stronger he got."

The film was based on a play that had been a hit in London and then on Broadway, with Tom Conti in the central role as a sculptor who has been left paralyzed after an accident. But when he demands the right to be taken off life support and die, he must battle the hospital administration in court.

Dreyfuss, who had won an Oscar a couple of years earlier for *The Good-bye Girl*, was the film's star as the sculptor, Ken Harrison, while Cassavetes played the hospital's chief administrator. Christine Lahti was cast as Drey-fuss' doctor, who eventually takes his side in the argument, while Bob Bala-ban played Dreyfuss' attorney, who argued for his right to die.

For the second film in a row, Cassavetes played a physician, one sup-posedly comfortable with both medical esoterica and administrative jar-gon. Both modes seemed deliberately obscure to Cassavetes, whose first impulse was always to cut through the bullshit and get to the point.

Shooting a scene in the hospital cafeteria with Lahti, Cassavetes was supposed to pause in the conversation to make a call on the hospital tele-phone: "Prepare 10 milligrams for Mr. Harrison."

After one take, Cassavetes turned to Badham: "Why do I have to say this?" he asked.

"Because," Badham said, "that's what he wants."

"Well, why don't I say, 'Just give the asshole a shot?'" Cassavetes continued.

"Because doctors have to be precise," Badham explained. "They have to give precise instructions. Otherwise people will screw up and kill some-one. So he has to say exactly what he needs. He can't be vague."

As Badham recalled, "That was a whole new concept to John. His whole life was lived on the vague side."

At one point, Cassavetes, who was playing a physician, was supposed to exit on the line, "Well, I have to go now—I have a hospital board meeting to teach a bunch of retards the reality of the budget." But Cassavetes balked at the scripted dialogue: "I can't say that," he protested. "I worked with dis-abled children on a film. I feel as though I would be insulting them with that remark. I don't want to say that."

Knowing Cassavetes' reputation for spontaneously generating dia-logue for his own films, Badham offered him the chance to rework the line to satisfy himself. As the cameraman and his crew spent an hour setting the lights, actor and director sat and tossed ideas back and forth about what the character should say.

"Now I figure I'm talking to a guy who has written a bunch of movies, who has a reputation as a great improviser," Badham said. "We kept throwing ideas out and nothing worked for this guy. Finally, John looks up with this Eureka! look in his eyes and says, 'Tight-ass tick-tocks.' We'd tried 'penny-pincher,' 'bean-counters'—but that's what he came up with. By that point, I would have let him say the Gettysburg Address."

When they started to shoot the scene, however, Cassavetes couldn't summon his own phrase: "Every take, we'd get to that phrase and he'd get stuck—through twenty-three takes," Badham said. "It was just a half-page scene, all in one shot. He only has to remember four words. He made them up. It's his phrase! I thought, This is nuts."

Yet Cassavetes was the least of Badham's problems. Dreyfuss, in the throes of an addiction problem from which he would eventually recover, "was very sick," Badham said. "He had not gotten control of his drug problem so, if he caught a cold, it knocked him out and kept him down. We were more focused on Richard and when he would be able to work. There were many days where we only had him for two hours."

The longer the film went on, the stronger Cassavetes got in the role: "If he had the words straight, he was right there," Badham said. "He didn't have to go and go for take after take. He was somebody who could nail a scene time after time after time. In the editing, I got to see that intensity, that strange intensity. He was not forcing it, not trying to be an official head doctor of the hospital. It just came out of his being. It was a natural kind of strength, that intimidating quality."

In the play, the administrator, Dr. Emerson, was a one-dimensional villain, a heartless bureaucrat caught up in legal niceties. But as the role was expanded for the film, and played by Cassavetes, the character became a kind of medical zealot, a true believer in medicine's ability to heal and help mankind and to find solutions to even the most horrendous problems. To him, death is the enemy; even thinking of giving in to death is treason.

"By the end of the movie, in the courtroom scene, John had a hammerlock on the character," Badham said. "He was a guy you could believe was a doctor, rattling the complicated terms off."

The film also gave Cassavetes a new taste of the perks offered to a Hollywood star, a world he only occasionally dipped his toes in: "He never took being a star for granted," Robert Fieldsteel said. "Part of him was tickled pink by that. He had this big trailer on *Whose Life* and, when I went in, he said, 'Not a bad way to make a living, eh?'"

Cassavetes wasn't Paul Mazursky's first choice to play architect Phillip Dimitrius in *Tempest,* his modernized take (co-written with Leon Capetanos) on

Shakespeare's *The Tempest*, which had been a summing up of the Bard's career in a play about betrayal, forgiveness, and the magic within us all.

Mazursky's script transposed the story to contemporary times, making Prospero into a modern architect who believes he's sold out his own talent by designing casinos in Atlantic City for a mob-connected tycoon named Alonzo (Vittorio Gassman). When he finds that his wife is having an affair with his boss, the architect takes his daughter Miranda (Molly Ringwald) and absconds to a remote Greek outpost, picking up a footloose American singer named Aretha (Susan Sarandon) in Athens, en route to their island hideaway. Eventually his wife and her lover and a yachtload of sycophants are shipwrecked on the coast of the architect's Mediterranean retreat, with a concluding series of encounters that roughly parallels Shakespeare's plotting.

Mazursky's first idea was to cast Paul Newman as his modern Prospero. But when Mazursky gave him the script, Newman's response was, "I don't get it." As Mazursky said later, "It would have made it a different movie. But I never chase."

Then Mazursky was struck by inspiration: Why not get John Cassavetes and make the character Greek-American? "He was a real actor," Mazursky said, "a gutsy guy. I knew he wouldn't be thrown by this material."

It was shortly after Cassavetes had finished *Gloria*, and Mazursky was tantalized by the possibility of casting both Cassavetes and Rowlands as Phillip and his wife, Antonia. The couple rarely acted together outside of Cassavetes' films and Mazursky viewed it as coup when he was able to attract the two of them.

Cassavetes claimed that, like Newman, he didn't quite follow Mazursky's adaptation when he read it: "I didn't fully understand the script but that's a great sign," he said. "If a screenplay reads like a novel, it won't translate visually."

Tempest had a relatively large budget for the time and for Mazursky: about $13 million. That budget included six weeks in New York and Atlantic City, both for rehearsal and for shooting; then two months in Greece and Italy, including a week in Athens, and a month at Cinecitta Studios in Rome.

The rehearsals initially proved traumatic for young Molly Ringwald, then only thirteen and making her film debut. For starters, Cassavetes expressed alarm at her inexperience when he was introduced to her.

At their first meeting, he asked her what she'd done before and she mentioned a role in a children's theater production of *Alice in Wonderland*. (In fact, she'd been in a professional stage version of *Annie*.) Ringwald's mother, Adele, saw Cassavetes shoot Mazursky a look, as if to say, "Are you crazy?"

But Mazursky, who had had Ringwald read four times before casting her, said, "Trust me."

And, in fact, Cassavetes and Ringwald hit it off. Ringwald was midway in age between Cassavetes' daughters, Xan, who was sixteen, and Zoe, who was eleven. She was professional, she learned her lines, and she had a positive attitude. Plus she was giving a convincing performance.

"John made me feel immediately friendly—the first thing he did was he took me on a date to Rumpelmayer's, where we had ice cream sodas at the bar," Ringwald recalled. "When we were shooting in New York, he whisked me off to some hotel restaurant for caviar and champagne. I'd never had either of them. He was fun. He'd bet you he could beat you in a walking race. He was very charming."

"He treated Molly nicely, professionally—he didn't treat her like a kid," recalled her father, Bob Ringwald. "He treated her like a fellow professional. It was a terrific experience for her first film."

But Cassavetes scared her in an early rehearsal when, while exploring his own character in a scene with Ringwald, he began improvising some lines. Ringwald had no idea what he was doing; all she knew was that she apparently had learned the wrong scene or that she somehow had screwed up in some way, because she was so completely lost.

"Nothing he was saying was in my script—I panicked," Ringwald said. "So I put my script down and said, 'Excuse me, I have to go.' And I left. It took them about fifteen minutes to figure out what had happened, that I hadn't just gone to the bathroom. I had found my dad and climbed into his lap and burst into tears. I thought I'd done something wrong and that I was going to be fired. I didn't know what improvisation was."

Eventually, the rest of the cast figured out what had happened and tracked Ringwald down.

"You just have to wait," Gena Rowlands explained to her. "Eventually he'll come back to the words that are the cue and you have to jump in."

Cassavetes and Ringwald established a father-daughter connection off-screen that translated to their moments onscreen: "We'd go from talking and hanging out and having discussions about music—it would be like play time and then we'd go into a scene," Ringwald said. "It helped a lot. I felt my character was supposed to be a daddy's girl. So we established a natural bond. I was crazy about him and I think that comes through on the screen. The acting seemed effortless."

One point of contention with Mazursky was the relationship between

Phillip and Aretha, the stand-in for Shakespeare's sprite, Ariel; Susan
Sarandon was playing Aretha. Phillip and Aretha became lovers, but did
she actually love him? Or was she just a good-time girl along for the ride?
Sarandon believed the character had real feelings for the architect, but
Mazursky argued otherwise. Finally Cassavetes called Sarandon aside and
said quietly, "It doesn't matter what words we're saying. We'll play it the
other way."

And the chemistry between them is palpable, particularly their initial
encounters, when the newly liberated Phillip finds himself falling under
the spell of the free-spirited Aretha.

Cassavetes had begun to physically show the effects of cirrhosis; his
stomach was slightly distended with a build-up of fluid because his liver
function was so low. At one point, looking at the steep, rocky landscape
that Mazursky expected him to scale with energy and agility, he said irritably to the director, "What the fuck is this? I'm not climbing rocks."

Molly Ringwald remembered him having a pronounced belly, though
she said, "The rest of him looked pretty good. I didn't know what that was
about. He was a two- or three-pack-a-day smoker so he was wheezing. But
he always beat me in the races."

"He was the kind of guy who had a buzz on all the time—and not
from drinking," Mazursky said. "He was just charged with life and energy.
He and Gena may have had vodkas at night, but he'd be there bright and
early, ready to go, shooting all day."

"It seemed like there was a moon hanging over us, creating a glow," Cassavetes recalled. "We were going crazy with nothing to do at night, so on Sat-
urdays, we had these mad variety shows, where all the wives and children
performed."

Ultimately, for Mazursky, whose career had been launched—at least
in part—by a chance encounter with John Cassavetes in the early 1950s,
directing Cassavetes was an enjoyable experience. "People think I might
have had a hard time directing him but, in the end, it was an easy time,"
Mazursky said. "He never questioned my choices. Directors are easier to
direct."

The critics, however, savaged Mazursky for having the temerity to
turn Shakespeare's meditation on art and age into a contemporary dis-
sertation on midlife crisis. Cassavetes earned his lumps, but most critics
gave him the benefit of the doubt, attributing acting misfires on the director and the script.

Jack Kroll may have been the kindest when he wrote, "*Tempest* is too long and often rambles when it should scintillate, but it has wit and heart and some of its Shakespearean switcheroos have a touching charm."

But Vincent Canby wrote in the *New York Times*, "Experiencing it is like watching a ten-ton canary as it attempts to become airborne. It lumbers up and down the runway tirelessly, but never once succeeds in getting both feet off the ground at the same time."

"Mazursky presses a buzzer marked mid-life crisis and that's supposed to take care of why the hero is sour on everything and does all the nutty arbitrary things he does," Penelope Gilliatt wrote in *The New Yorker*. "Cassavetes isn't a bad actor and he has become handsomer with the years; with his hair gray and close-cropped, he looks remarkably noble. But he's one of the most alienating of actors. He has a dour, angry presence and even when he's smiling, there's something unreachable underneath—and ominous . . . The only genius he demonstrates is as a party pooper."

Cassavetes later referred to *Tempest* as "wonderfully imperfect." John Badham ran into him at a preview for the film and complimented him on his performance. Cassavetes said, "It's not that good. It's sort of a mess."

Later Cassavetes would say, "I think, from my standpoint, that Paul was Phillip and so was I. But so was he. Not only was he, but then he insisted that the whole crew make magic. And if the weather turned and it was all gray, then he'd go into the water and actually be doing these chants. So it was a delight."

Forty-six

Love Streams on Stage

T hough they were neighbors in the Laurel Canyon area of Los Angeles, Richard Dreyfuss didn't really know John Cassavetes before they shot *Whose Life Is It Anyway?* together in 1981. They'd met and would occasionally run into each other at the studio where Dreyfuss' production company had offices near Peter Falk's.

But that didn't stop Cassavetes from making a call to Dreyfuss—in New York, no less—in 1979. Dreyfuss told the story at Cassavetes' memorial service and continues to tell it to this day, doing a spotless impression of Cassavetes' wise-guy diction.

Dreyfuss was subletting an apartment in Manhattan and arrived home late one night. The call, he said in a 2004 interview, came out of the blue, a familiar yet surprising voice on Dreyfuss' answering machine:

"Richard, this is John Cassavetes. Call me back."

So Dreyfuss phoned Cassavetes on the West Coast. When Cassavetes answered, Dreyfuss thought, it seemed as though it took a moment for him to remember why he had called Dreyfuss. But he finally said, "Oh, uh, do you wanna do a thing?"

"A thing?" Dreyfuss said, unaware that "thing" was a catch-all word for Cassavetes, applied to whatever he happened to be talking about at the moment.

"Yeah," Cassavetes said, again sounding unsure, "I got this thing. You wanna read it? Why don't you come over on Saturday and we'll read it?"

Dreyfuss said sure and hung up, thinking, "That's weird." The next morning, he called Cassavetes back, as Dreyfuss put it, "to confirm that we were on the same planet."

"Did you call me last night about a reading on Saturday?" Dreyfuss asked him

"What? Saturday?" Cassavetes said, seeming uncertain, then said, "No, make it Sunday."

Dreyfuss returned to Los Angeles for the weekend and presented himself at the Cassavetes home on Woodrow Wilson Drive at the appointed hour on Sunday. Gena answered the door, greeted Dreyfuss, and told him that John was in the back and would be out in a minute. So she offered him a soft drink and led him into a room where a group of actors was mingling.

Within a few minutes, Cassavetes appeared, passed out a script, and organized a reading of a play called "Mood Indigo." The story dealt with a cab driver who has written a play that's an immediate hit. As the play begins, his Broadway smash has been purchased by Hollywood, and he is arriving in Hollywood to make a deal and write the screenplay. He is assigned a studio secretary, a jaded but idealistic type who views him as a lamb before the slaughter and tries to advise him, even as the cabbie decides that he wants to sell out for big bucks.

Dreyfuss read the role of the playwright and Gena read the secretary: "It was a cold reading, which I'm very good at," Dreyfuss recalled. "We're having a ball. But the minute it's over, I can see the other actors snickering behind their hands, suppressing giggles."

Dreyfuss turned to Cassavetes and asked, "What's going on?" Cassavetes smiled, put an arm around Dreyfuss' shoulders and walked him into the other room to explain.

The week before, Cassavetes had had a call from director Blake Edwards. Edwards was about to go into production on a new comedy, 10, in which he'd cast George Segal as the lead. But Segal had quit the film at the last minute. So Edwards called Cassavetes to see whether he knew Richard Dreyfuss, who he also thought would be right for the role.

Cassavetes didn't really know Dreyfuss. Nonetheless, he told Edwards, it would not be a problem for Cassavetes to call Dreyfuss and put him in touch with Edwards. But between the time he left the message for Dreyfuss and when Dreyfuss called him back, Edwards had called to tell him that, in fact, he'd cast Dudley Moore in *10* and wouldn't need Richard Dreyfuss after all.

When Dreyfuss called Cassavetes, however, Cassavetes was embarrassed to have to tell Dreyfuss that he'd called him about a movie role that Dreyfuss knew nothing about and that had now been filled. In a moment of panic, John had invited Dreyfuss to come to a reading instead of telling him the truth.

When Dreyfuss called back the next day to confirm the reading, Cassavetes had forgotten the conversation of the night before. Now he was doubly embarrassed, so he postponed from Saturday to Sunday, to give himself time to come up with a script.

Never mind that he probably had a stack of unproduced scripts on his shelf that would have been new to Dreyfuss. Cassavetes now felt compelled to write a new script specifically for the reading. So he dictated "Mood Indigo" between Wednesday and Sunday. When Dreyfuss arrived at Cassavetes' house, Cassavetes was in the back, finishing the play, which was the reason for the delay.

Eventually Cassavetes would rework the play and retitle it *East West Game (Mood Indigo)*, for a small theater production in October 1980 at the Callboard Theater on Melrose, in which his son, Nick, would play the cab driver. And that would rekindle an interest in theater that would start a new, if brief chapter, in Cassavetes' career.

Three Plays of Love and Hate grew out of Cassavetes' multiple career frustrations. He had been writing scripts and had a few—"She's De-Lovely," "Two Nights in Rochester," "Knives"—that he was convinced would make solid films.

But he couldn't find anyone to agree with him who had the financial wherewithal to do anything about it. And he wasn't about to invest his own money again, having finally dug himself and Gena out of the debt they'd incurred from *Chinese Bookie* and *Opening Night.*

Gloria had come and gone. Between that payday and his acting fees for *Whose Life* and *Incubus,* Cassavetes had some money, but knew that in 1981 making a movie on his own would be a multi-million-dollar gamble. That was something he simply didn't want to risk at this stage of his life, given the atmosphere of dumbed-down spectacle that seemed to be overtaking movie-makers and audiences alike.

But to get the money elsewhere meant going to the corporations that increasingly ran the studios.

"If I had to spend my life sitting down with people in corporations, I

don't think I'd stay in the business," Cassavetes said. "The people themselves individually are OK, but when you go to present a film idea, you're
dealing with the corporate policy, which has nothing to do with the film
or you or them. It has to do with some sort of corporate policy I don't
want to devote my life to understanding."

"He wasn't interested in charming the people he was getting money
from," Al Ruban said. "He realized that, if they wanted to get involved, it
was because of him. They wanted to exploit John Cassavetes. It wasn't necessarily the merits of the material but what his potential was. If that could
be marketed, he said, then I want these controls. All deals were structured
in the sense that the producers could only go so far. And it was tough for
the money people to do that, to give up that kind of control to him."

Theater, on the other hand, could still be produced on a shoestring,
comparatively speaking. Risking a million dollars on a movie seemed
foolish; risking $100,000 on a theatrical venture, on the other hand,
seemed quixotically attractive. It was a chance to get back to his theatrical
roots and to work with a large group of people on a project in which the
script and the acting could once again be the focus.

Indeed, it seemed to carry the same seat-of-his-pants sense that Cassavetes so cherished. When you made things up as you went along, the
chances for happy accidents—for the surprise outburst of genius—always
seemed high.

The idea came, in part, from his experience with *East West Game*, in
which Cassavetes' assistant, Robert Fieldsteel, had been involved, along
with Cassavetes' son, Nick.

"He was having trouble setting up a film," Fieldsteel said. "Making a
film on his own with his own money was just too hard. And, when we did
East West Game, he saw that the young people around him, Nick and me,
were interested in theater."

Bo Harwood recalled, "The plays were something to do that he could
do in a few months, rather than a movie, that takes a couple of years."

Carole Smith, Peter Falk's assistant, recalled, "Peter was acting in *All the
Marbles* and John was next door acting in *Whose Life*. And while they were
doing their respective movies, Cassavetes decides he wants to do these
plays. His idea was that we take this little theater and fix it up, do the plays
and we don't charge for them."

Cassavetes had been working with Ted Allan, trying to write a film version of Allan's play *My Sister's Keeper* (which had been performed in London
with Sean Connery as *I've Seen You Cut Lemons*). The new title was *Love
Streams*, and the collaboration had been fruitful for both men.

Cassavetes complained to Allan that the original play of *Love Streams* had the brother sitting, doing nothing, listening as his sister raved at him. As they worked on a screenplay version, the play had opened up to include the brother's story, as well as other characters who had been mentioned but not seen in the original version. Inspired, Allan rewrote it as the play *Love Streams* that Cassavetes mounted in L.A. in the spring of 1981.

Allan had another play that Cassavetes liked, a companion piece called *The Third Day Comes* that had not been produced. The play, a memory drama, examined the effect on two children when their family implodes in a maelstrom of alcoholism, abuse, and economic depression. Allan was interested in seeing what it looked like on its feet, and Cassavetes was inspired to do it, as well as *Love Streams*.

"But he thought it put too much heat on the play to just do it so we did a trilogy and that would put less pressure on any of them," Fieldsteel recalled. "Ted had a trilogy, but John didn't like the middle one. So he did *Knives*."

The theater was rented for six months. Cassavetes went into his own pocket for more than $100,000 to rebuild the theater's interior, giving it new seats (it only held sixty-two, plus however many more could be shoehorned in), and stage equipment.

"It was a rundown little theater that John put his own money into fixing up," Julie Allan recalled. "It was an Equity waiver house and a labor of love. It was filled every night."

"He spent a lot more than he was supposed to," recalled Bo Harwood, who took a leave from a job in Montreal, where he was living, to do sound for the shows (and lived with Cassavetes for the six months that it took).

The project would involve mounting three full-length plays at the same time and running them in repertory for five or six weeks, at which point Cassavetes and Rowlands had to leave to shoot *Tempest*. By the time it was finished, as many as 200 people had been involved in some way.

"I had never directed a play before, so I figured you might as well go down with three as one," Cassavetes said. "My own personal view of theater and film is it's experimental. Mostly the plays were staged according to the impulse of the actor."

"Most of the work was done by actors and volunteers," recalled Richard Kaye, who also acted in *Knives*. "There were three casts in rotating roles. John made himself accessible to everybody who wanted to get involved. He had plenty of help."

The point was to explore the work and, perhaps, to help shape at least one of the scripts into Cassavetes' next film. The two Allan plays would star

Gena, with Jon Voight appearing opposite her in *Love Streams*, playing her brother. *Knives* would star Peter Falk.

Casting Voight in *Love Streams* was Cassavetes' inspiration. When he mentioned that he envisioned Voight in the role in a conversation with Falk and Falk's assistant, Carole Smith, he also said he had no idea how to get hold of Voight. Smith, who had worked for Voight, said she could. When she called Voight, he was stunned: "John Cassavetes wants to talk to me?"

For *Love Streams*, Cassavetes cast Gena and Voight as Sarah Lawson and Robert Harmon, the siblings at the center of the story. To play a night-club singer named Susan, with whom Robert becomes involved, he called Diahnne Abbott, who he'd met several years earlier when she was married to actor Robert De Niro.

At rehearsals, Cassavetes encouraged the actors to improvise, then would use pieces of what they came up with to rewrite the scene: "The basic play remained the same," Abbott said. "But he would add little things. He was constantly rewriting."

Cassavetes seemed to be working around the clock, with all three casts shuttling in and out of the rehearsal hall and, eventually, the theater space, for lengthy rehearsals of material that was emotionally intense and, in the case of *Knives*, occasionally opaque.

Knives shifted back and forth in time in the consciousness of a comedian (played by Falk) accused of murdering his wife. None of his comedy is particularly funny and the dialogue can seem purposely obscure. Or at least that had been the response at some of its earliest readings, recalled John Finnegan, who had been to readings of the script at Cassavetes' house when John was still pursuing funds to do it as a movie.

"We're all sitting around a table reading *Knives*," Finnegan recalled. "Tim Carey, Elaine May, Ron Rifkin—reading the play. And Norman Lear is there. When John says, 'Take a break,' Norman Lear looks at me and says, 'What is this play about?'"

As the director of all three plays, Cassavetes juggled rehearsal schedules with production meetings for the three different casts and three different crews. His assistants had to keep pace with him and keep track of the details.

"We never slept," said Fieldsteel, who acted in all three plays. "I remember one night feeling grateful that I had four hours to sleep. But John would finish rehearsal at 1 A.M. and then we'd go to work, planning the next day, building stuff or rewriting."

Cassavetes' devotion to the production didn't stop there. Peter Falk recalled one evening after a performance. It was nearly 1 A.M.; the play was long, and a crowd of friends had gathered to talk backstage after the show. But when Falk finally got to his car, he realized he'd left his wallet in his dressing room.

"I went back and I heard a noise in one of the toilets," Falk said. "There was John, fixing a toilet with a wrench."

The plays, which would open in early May 1981, at the newly rechristened California Center for Performing Arts, were announced in the trades in early February. The three plays would be done in repertory, with both a matinee and an evening performance every day of the week.

Despite the heavy performance schedule, tickets were scarce because the theater was small. The cast and crew's families had first claim on seats. But Cassavetes wanted his theater to be accessible to the masses, so he put the rest on sale to the public, charging $4 for evening shows and $2 for matinees.

Cassavetes was adamant: No special favors for agents or studio executives. Anyone who wanted a ticket had to line up to get it. There was a daily lottery for the available tickets, and according to one report, hundreds of potential ticket-buyers were turned away.

Because of the casts—Voight, Rowlands, Falk—*Three Plays* became a much-coveted ticket and the audiences inevitably included famous faces.

"You couldn't buy a ticket," John Finnegan recalled. "Everybody in town came. The last night, name a name, they were there. Shirley MacLaine, Natalie Wood."

John Roselius, who had worked with Cassavetes on the TV miniseries *Flesh & Blood*, was cast in *Love Streams* as Sarah's husband, Jack. Roselius had never been in a play before: "I thought plays were for fairies," he said.

"I go onstage to say my first line and here's John Houseman in the front row, staring me in the puss, less than ten feet away," he said.

The reviews were mixed to negative. The theater itself earned top grades; the plays were another story.

"Cassavetes has taken over a hole-in-the-wall theater, gutted it and transformed it into a luxury playhouse with soft, first-cabin seats and state-of-the-art sound," Dan Sullivan wrote in the *Los Angeles Times*.

One criticism of the work itself—as on target as anything written about the plays—was that Cassavetes was merely using a theatrical setting to showcase scripts he obviously intended as screen projects. Though a *Variety* writer pointed out that *Shadows* had begun as a theatrical exercise, the article still took issue with presenting the scripts as stage dramas, if Cassavetes' intention was really to produce them as films: "If that's the case, he really shouldn't present them as theater," sniffed *Variety*.

"Is it possible for a play to be two hours and twenty minutes too long?" Jack Viertel wrote in the *Los Angeles Herald-Examiner* about *The Third Day Comes*, noting that, "for its first forty-five minutes, [the play] is a dense, sensitive portrait of a family collapsing under the pressure of the Depression . . . But things go badly awry and before long, *The Third Day Comes* turns from careful introspection to chaos."

The *Los Angeles Times* was hardly kinder: "For the aura of Hollywood noblesse oblige with which Cassavetes and company have deigned to face the public, the question comes up early, at least in this play: Who are they kidding?"

Writing about *Knives* in the *L.A. Times*, Dan Sullivan said, "An audience can put up with any amount of lights-down and lights-up if the story holds its interest. *Knives* doesn't. In fact, it's stretching it a bit to call it a story. Right now it is twenty-nine scenes in search of a backbone."

"Had these central roles been played by actors of less talent and stature than Rowlands and Voight," offered Sylvie Drake in the *L.A. Times*, "it is doubtful anyone would sit through *Love Streams* past intermission. As it is, sitting through it is no picnic . . . *Love Streams* is an unstitched and self-indulgent exercise in anguish that lacks real development."

Cassavetes had an offer to videotape the plays. Home video was in its infancy; cable, with its ravening maw clamoring for content, was just taking baby steps. Still, the financial incentive was serious enough that, as Bo Harwood recalled, "We all had dollar signs in our eyes."

But Cassavetes turned the offer down: "That's not what we're doing this for," he told them. "We're here to do the plays."

Similarly, when an offer came to move the rotating repertory to New York for a commercial run, Cassavetes rejected it as well.

"That's why I loved him," Harwood said. "He said, 'Look, we had a great time, it was a neat event—now let's move on.' He was that idealistic that he would act on that. Everyone had been working for free because we were young and starry-eyed. He felt money changed the intention of what we were doing."

It was a limited run—period. When it was over, Cassavetes went from *Three Plays of Love and Hate* to New York, Greece, and Rome to film *Tempest*.

As Cassavetes waited for *Tempest* to reach theaters, he was without an agent, because Guy McElwaine had been promoted to run Columbia Pictures. Not having been able to follow up on *Gloria*, he was discussing the issue with Sam Shaw one night in his room at New York's Wyndham Hotel in July 1982. Perhaps, Cassavetes said, an agent might be able to help him get a movie made. Shaw suggested Johnnie Planco, an agent at the William Morris Agency who represented Anthony Quinn, one of Shaw's close friends.

Planco was sitting in his office in the Morris suite at Fifty-fifth Street and Sixth Avenue when his phone rang. It was Shaw.

"I'm sitting here with John Cassavetes," Shaw began, "and John is perhaps looking for an agent—"

Planco heard the rustling sound of the phone changing hands and suddenly Cassavetes himself was on the phone, demanding, "Who is this? What do you want?"

"You're calling me," Planco pointed out.

"Well," Cassavetes said, thinking for a moment, "are you interested in representing me?"

"Absolutely," Planco said.

"Well, could you come right over?"

Planco immediately walked the three blocks up Sixth Avenue to the Wyndham, where Cassavetes handed him a pad and pencil, then began pacing the room, talking about one topic after another, never pausing to explain his segues—one minute discussing an omnibus movie about the end of the world, in which he would direct a segment and so would Martin Scorsese and Peter Bogdanovich, the next minute talking about why *Love Streams* would make a great film and the ideas he had to transpose it from stage to screen. A bottle of vodka made the rounds; Planco eventually staggered home at midnight and was deeply hung over when he arrived at his office the next morning.

At 10 A.M., his phone rang: "What have you done so far?" Cassavetes wanted to know, expecting Planco to have followed up on the various projects they'd discussed the night before.

"I've been doing this thirty-two years and this was the closest, most intense client relationship I've ever had," Planco recalled. "Everyday he was in town, he would suck me away from other work. He'd say, 'C'mon, we're going to meet this guy.' You couldn't resist, even if you wanted to. He was this animated, energetic guy who kind of took you over. You became part of his posse. I ended up representing Seymour and Ben as well."

One of Cassavetes' nicknames for Gazzara was Olivier—as in Sir Laurence. It was meant both out of respect for his talent and in mocking recognition of his occasional tendency to the grandiose. So Planco thought nothing of it some time later when Cassavetes called him up late one evening. Though it was pouring rain in New York, the Major League All-Star Game was on TV, being broadcast from fairer climes.

"I'm sitting here with Olivier," Cassavetes said to Planco, "watching the game. Why don't you come over?"

But it was late—and it was raining. When Planco begged off, Cassavetes insisted: "Come on, the three of us will hang out."

"No, it's late," Planco said. "I'm going to bed."

The next day, Cassavetes called Planco and said, "You've got guts."

"Why is that?" Planco said, playing along.

"Well," Cassavetes said, "I don't know anyone else in America who would not want to watch the All-Star game with Laurence Olivier."

As it turned out, Cassavetes had run into the venerable British actor at the Wyndham, where Olivier and many other British actors stay in New York. A big fan of American baseball, he had accepted Cassavetes' invitation to watch the game together.

Planco had first met Cassavetes when Planco was a kid and his mother owned Budd's Liquors at Seventy-fourth and Madison in the early 1960s. Though Planco was only twelve or thirteen and clearly underage, he made liquor deliveries to his mother's customers who, on the Upper East Side, included Basil Rathbone, Eleanor Roosevelt, and John Cassavetes.

"Usually you were delivering to the maid because these people don't answer the door themselves," Planco recalled. "But John would answer the door. I'd go in and he'd never have money to tip. So one time, he takes the bottle, pours me a shot of whisky and says, 'Here.' I was, like, thirteen. I took the shot."

Now, years later, here was Planco showing up at his hotel room, as his prospective agent. Cassavetes looked at him, cocked his head and said, "Didn't I used to give you a drink?"

As part of his new push for Cassavetes, Planco was able to arrange a meeting between Cassavetes and the late Joseph Papp, the off-Broadway impresario who had founded and ran the New York Shakespeare Festival at the Public Theater.

Papp had recently started thinking about expanding the performance spaces within the Public Theater's home on Astor Place in Greenwich Village. Cassavetes had an idea for a theater project that might work in one of those spaces.

"It was a great pitch," Planco recalled. "John said, 'Give me that theater and let me do plays where the working process is as important as the show itself.' His idea was you could buy day tickets and watch rehearsal."

The idea died, however, when Equity intervened. While *Three Plays of Love and Hate* had an Equity waiver, the Public Theater was another matter. If Cassavetes wanted to sell tickets to rehearsals, that was fine. But the Equity contract called for a maximum of eight shows a week, and the public rehearsals would count against that total, making the whole idea impractical.

Planco may have been his agent, but Cassavetes was the one who fielded the phone call from Wanda Dell, an Atlanta producer, with an offer of a role in a small independent film, *Marvin & Tige*, to be shot in Atlanta.

Dell was an independent producer who, with partner Eric Weston (who directed *Marvin & Tige*), had produced a couple of low-budget Tim Conway comedies that had turned a nice profit. A friend had offered her the script for *Marvin & Tige*—about an orphaned young African-American, Tige, who is befriended and taken care of by an alcoholic ragpicker, Marvin, whose own life is subsequently redeemed by the selfless act.

Robert Fieldsteel remembered, "He wanted to play that role. He liked that role."

Dell didn't have a lot of money to offer: $350,000, "including transportation and everything," Dell said. "He usually took more than that. But John loved the script."

When Cassavetes showed up in Atlanta, Dell recalled, "He seemed quite ill. He just didn't feel well; you could tell."

But he plunged in, and according to Dell, "He really directed the picture. He and Eric (who was the director) got along great, but John was the one who helped the child get through the picture."

The film's plot hinged on the fact that, after Tige's mother dies, it comes out that his biological father is actually a respected businessman (Billy Dee Williams), who has a wife and family in the suburbs. Marvin makes it his mission to get the father to adopt Tige so that he will have a real father.

Cassavetes and Williams hit it off after hours, becoming drinking buddies at various Atlanta watering holes. But on the set Cassavetes grew impatient with Williams' lackadaisical approach to the work.

"All of his scenes with Billy Dee were a problem," Dell said. "Billy Dee wasn't prepared and John was. No matter what, honest to goodness, I don't think John ever screwed up his lines. But Billy Dee always did. He would mess up and John would say, 'Keep the camera going, we'll do it again.' John would get a little ticked."

While it was apparent to Dell that Cassavetes was drinking, he was always ready when the cameras rolled. But he was obviously in pain, and Dell had a doctor look at him at one point.

"The doctor said, 'Don't make him stop drinking. That would be the worst thing you could do'," Dell said. "I think the drinking kept him from having pain."

Cirrhosis had already begun to distend Cassavetes' stomach. It had stretched the fabric of the kimono-like robe he wore in *Tempest*. And though the overcoat he wore through much of *Marvin &Tige* hid it for the most part, it was still apparent.

"I think John knew he drank too much but I don't think he considered himself an alcoholic," Dell said. "He was in total denial."

The film had been produced by a limited partnership, which had made a deal with Twentieth Century Fox to distribute the picture. But the partners had second thoughts about Fox and pulled the film before its release. When no other major distributor could be secured, they let a small independent company put it out and it quickly disappeared.

One other ultimately fruitless project occupied Cassavetes during this frustrating period of inactivity as a filmmaker. Called "Singles," it was a script he and Elaine May were co-writing that went through a prolonged development, with almost daily improvisations and writing sessions involving the two writers and a handful of actors.

The script was about a depressed hooker who calls a suicide hotline. It got an initial reading at Cassavetes' house, where actress Carol Kane had been invited for the first time, after meeting John at a party with Susan Sarandon.

"I thought I was there to watch," Kane recalled of the reading. "In fact, they wanted me to read the part of Elaine's roommate. We were hookers who were roommates; we were inept hookers. It was John and Elaine and me. John's character was a single bachelor of a certain age who lives alone and couldn't fit in. The characters were supposed to be misfits but they were perfect fits in the sense that they fit together with each other."

After finishing *Gloria*, Cassavetes had convinced Columbia to give him space to develop a new script and set up shop there working with May.

"He didn't have offices there, but there was this large room with bathrooms that he could play in," Robert Fieldsteel recalled. "We all had characters: Richard Kaye, Allen Garfield, Peter Falk, Elaine, Carol Kane."

Kane remembers working on *Singles* on and off for four months, mostly with the cast gathering every day to work over the script and improvise new scenes: "New characters would come in," Kane said, "so new actors came in to read them."

Cassavetes called John Roselius during this period to come in and listen to them read what they had: "He wanted to see what I thought," said Roselius, who added, "I laughed like hell."

But the ongoing process seemed not to have an end in sight. The longer Cassavetes and May worked, the more new ideas Cassavetes seemed to have for the project.

"The script kept getting bigger and bigger," Fieldsteel said. "Elaine was trying to rein it in. John started thinking of the possibilities of it as a film, of making it bigger. It was originally intended as a stage piece. At a certain point, we had five hundred pages of transcript of improvisation. Not a structured script: just this transcript of improvisation, sections of which had been shaped. But a large section was just transcript."

Actors came and went—everyone from Peter Falk to James Brooks—but Cassavetes was showing no urgency about ending the research-and-development part of the search and getting on with finishing the piece.

"From John, I got the impression that he was more here to play," Fieldsteel said. "But Elaine was more into shaping the piece. They were at cross purposes. John wanted it to be bigger and bigger and Elaine wanted to focus more. At a certain point, Elaine went to New York and didn't come back."

Cassavetes tried to take it in stride: "He was frustrated but not self-pitying," Fieldsteel said. "He was deeply disappointed. It was not just, 'Oh well,' and on to the next thing. He really invested himself personally in the work. I really admired that he was so resilient in creating stuff even when he was discouraged about whether he'd get to make films again."

More than a decade later, May resurrected the original piece and re-worked it as a one-act play called *Hotline*. It was produced as part of an off-Broadway triple bill called *Death-Defying Acts*, along with one-acts by Woody Allen and David Mamet.

Forty-seven

Love Streams on Screen

Having worked *Love Streams* over during its stage run in Los Angeles, John Cassavetes was now on the phone to his agent, Johnnie Planco, almost every day about the project, eager to get it made into a film. Cassavetes was convinced that he and Ted Allan had come up with a script that would fly. But he couldn't find anyone to fund him.

Planco had *Love Streams* on the brain as he sat in a staff meeting at William Morris. He perked up when it was announced that Menaham Golan and Yoram Globus had a group of films they were putting together to sell as a package. Golan and Globus were the Israeli shlockmeisters who had made Cannon Films synonymous in the early 1980s with cheap, factory-assembled genre crap. But they wanted one film of quality to lend a whiff of class to a lineup that included titles like *Death Wish II*, *Revenge of the Ninja*, and *Hospital Massacre*.

There were constraints: The movie had to be ready to shoot right away. It had to have names in it, it had to be set in Los Angeles, and it had to cost less than $3 million.

"The more he went on," Planco recalled, "the more I thought he was describing *Love Streams.*"

Planco called Cassavetes, whose response was, essentially, "Saddle up—let's roll." He arranged to pick up Planco and go see Menahem Golan to pitch *Love Streams*. Cassavetes didn't even bring the car to a complete stop for Planco, calling, "Jump in," from behind the wheel of his massive Cadillac convertible as he rolled by.

("John was the worst driver anyone has ever seen," Planco said. "He was very sensitive about it: 'Why does everybody say I'm a bad driver?' Well, one, you don't put your hands on the steering wheel. And, two, you never face forward.")

All the way to Golan's, Cassavetes raved to Planco about what a coincidence this was: that he'd gone to school with Golan, had been his roommate. "Let me do the talking," Cassavetes said. "He's a buddy of mine. I know how to pitch him. Don't open your mouth."

Golan kept the pair waiting for about twenty minutes, then ushered them in with an expansive air. Cassavetes looked stricken, turned to Planco and whispered, "It's the wrong guy." Cassavetes nudged Planco, who had to do all the talking, until the ice was broken with Golan.

Which it was very quickly, when Golan said, "I'll make the movie."

Cassavetes was set to direct, with the same cast he'd worked with onstage. They would have twelve weeks, from mid-May to mid-August, and it would cost $2.6 million. But there were quickly a couple of problems.

For one thing, even as preproduction for the film rumbled up to speed, Cassavetes began having problems with Jon Voight. Voight, an Oscar-winner for *Coming Home,* had teamed with Rowlands as the play's two central characters, who eventually are revealed to be siblings. The project had been sold to Cannon, in part, on the strength of Voight's involvement.

But Voight told Cassavetes, "I've already played this role. I don't need to play it again. How about if I direct the movie and you play the part?"

Cassavetes wasn't about to give up the reins on a project he'd been riding herd on for almost three years. So he let Voight go and decided that, beside directing, he would play the male lead, writer Robert Harmon, opposite Gena in the film.

"I was so angry with Jon when he decided not to do the movie," Cassavetes said. "We were two weeks away from shooting and there was no way I was going to let the whole production fall apart. So I did the role, reluctantly. I'm nowhere near Jon's disposition or personality. He and Gena look so much alike: they're both blond, they look like they could come from the same family."

As Rowlands noted later, "John said, 'Oh, hell, I'll do it.' I'm so glad he did, not that I don't love Jon Voight, but because that was our last picture together."

But that necessitated reworking the part to fit Cassavetes: "It was perfectly all right for Voight to be a ladies' man," Cassavetes noted, "but I'm not exactly James Bond."

In the stage version of *Love Streams*, Sarah's husband, Jack, was played by John Roselius. But when it came time to cast the film, Cassavetes went to Roselius with bad news. "Look, Seymour had a problem and I'm helping him out," Cassavetes told him. "So I'm giving him the part you had in the play. But I'll come up with something else for you."

Since receiving an Oscar nomination in 1968, Seymour Cassel had become one of Hollywood's premier party animals. A natural-born fun-lover who was already in his early thirties when fame hit, he got caught up in the celebrity that *Faces* had given him. It was the late sixties and Cassel definitely had the spirit.

A long-time grass-smoker, Cassel became part of the Hollywood wave that took avidly to cocaine in the 1970s. By the end of the decade, he was caught up in a scheme with director Sam Peckinpah (for whom he'd starred in 1978's *Convoy*) to make a film of Robert Sabbag's 1976 book *Snowblind*, which detailed life in the 1970s cocaine trade. They hoped such a project might afford them a way to smuggle a kilo or two of Colombia's finest to the U.S., something that never did happen.

Cassel described the period as a "wasted four or five years" during which his senses seemed finely honed to only one thing: "I could walk into any room and tell you who was holding," Cassel said. Though he found cocaine muted his desire to work, Cassel seemed otherwise to be handling his increasing use, "which was also a problem," he said. And if he wasn't working, well, he could always sell a little coke on the side; among other things, it meant he got his own supply of the drug more cheaply.

Which was fine until someone to whom he'd sold the odd gram was arrested and bartered Cassel's name for his own freedom. Arrested in 1982, Cassel was given a six-month sentence at the California state prison at Lompoc, where Watergate convicts John Ehrlichman and H. R. Haldeman had done their time. With good behavior, he was out in four months, then violated his probation and was given another seven months behind bars.

Cassavetes tried to help Cassel, writing a letter to the judge on his behalf. Robert Fieldsteel recalled Cassavetes being upset with Cassel, but also upset for him.

Even before his arrest, however, Cassel had kept his distance from Cassavetes, whose disapproval was practically palpable. It was the most important friendship in Cassel's life and he was unable to pursue it while he was caught up in the drug scene.

"Dad's problems were not good for their relationship," Matthew Cassel said of Seymour and John. "When he was doing that stuff, he couldn't hang with John. John told him, 'You've got to clean up your act.' Because of that, he lost years with a really good friend."

But now Cassel was out of prison. He was clean and sober, attending AA meetings regularly. And he needed a job. So Cassavetes cast him as Jack Lawson, the divorced husband of Gena's Sarah Lawson in the film.

"They made me swear to keep Seymour straight," recalled Larry Shaw, Sam Shaw's son, one of the film's still photographers who had been dealing with a cocaine problem of his own. "I guess prison is a real eye-opener."

"Seymour was back," recalled Robert Fieldsteel, Cassavetes' assistant. "It was weird when his parole officer would visit the set."

Love Streams begins with writer Robert Harmon (Cassavetes) at home (actually, the Cassavetes house), surrounded by what seems like a harem of women. It's his house, as it turns out, and they are his companions. He writes about women, he later says, and apparently does research by living among them.

"A beautiful woman has to offer a man her secrets," he tells one of his lovely roommates.

The scene shifts: Sarah Lawson (Rowlands) and her daughter, Debbie (Risa Blewitt), arrive at a divorce settlement hearing. Their attorney (played by Al Ruban) arrives, as do her husband Jack (Seymour Cassel) and his attorney. The judge awards Sarah custody of Debbie, despite Sarah's announced intention to take her to Chicago and New York, where her hobby appears to be attending funerals.

Robert, dressed in a tuxedo, is seen prowling a drag bar, seemingly entranced by the actual woman who is singing on the stage. Her name is Susan (Diahnne Abbott), and the drunken Robert talks her into letting him drive her home—in her car. But he is hopelessly drunk and hits a parked car as he pulls up to her house, then tumbles headfirst down the front steps after trying to walk her to her door. The exasperated Susan helps Robert, blood streaming down his face, into her house, and by the next morning, they've developed a rapport.

Sarah, meanwhile, is late for her next divorce hearing. But it doesn't matter: Her daughter announces that she doesn't want to live with Sarah anymore because she prefers her father. "I hate my life with you," she tells Sarah. Sarah walks out of the hearing room and faints.

Sarah is next seen with her psychiatrist (played by Rowlands' brother, David). She tells him that she believes love is "a stream. It's continuous. It does not stop." Which is why she rejects the contention that her ex-husband no longer loves her.

But the psychiatrist tells her, "Your love is too strong for your family." He advises her to take a trip to Europe. She arrives toting more luggage than three men could carry—but turns around and comes home almost as soon as she gets there.

Robert is at home with several women when a car pulls up in front and a woman and child get out. It is Robert's second ex-wife and his son, Albie (Jakob Shaw), whom he has never seen. She tells him she and her husband have an important business opportunity that will take them out of town. Will Robert take care of Albie for the weekend?

He agrees, but it starts badly, when Albie bolts from the house and Robert has to chase him down with the car. He brings him back and the next morning serves him a beer for breakfast. As they are talking, another cab pulls up: It is Sarah with a mountain of luggage, returned from Europe.

Robert seems happy to see her and introduces her to his son. And then he gives Sarah the keys to his car, calls a cab, and takes Albie to Las Vegas for an overnight. But once there, he abandons Albie in the hotel room and spends the evening drinking and whoring. He turns up the next morning, staggering drunk, to find a tearful Albie whining to go home.

When he drops Albie off at his parents' house, the distraught Albie bangs on the door to be let in, smashing his head against the door until it bleeds. His stepfather, seeing the blood, assumes that it is Robert's fault. He races out and begins pounding the stuffing out of Robert, while Albie tries to stop him. As the battered Robert rides away in the cab, a confused Albie calls, "I love you, Dad."

At home, Robert finds Sarah; they talk and then dance together. It is at this point, more than an hour into the film that it is explained casually that Robert and Sarah are brother and sister. It comes in a conversation between the two of them when one asks the other if they remember something about their father.

Robert leaves to go see Susan and her mother, who took care of him after he fell down the stairs. Sarah calls Jack, who tells her he can't handle their kid but doesn't want Sarah back. Sarah decides to take a night out and winds up at a bowling alley, where she meets the friendly Ken (John Roselius).

Back at Robert's house, Sarah tells Robert that what he needs is a baby, something in his life to care for other than himself. The next thing he knows, she has rounded up a virtual petting zoo full of animals: miniature horses, a goat, ducks, chickens, and a dog named Jim, a bull terrier of some sort. Robert reacts badly, unsure what to do with a yardful of animals.

Determined to set her own life right, Sarah convinces her husband and daughter to come see her. She attempts to make them laugh, but the meeting is a disaster. That night she dreams an opera in which all is reconciled with her family.

The next day, she decides to leave Robert's house. As a massive rainstorm crashes outside, Robert rounds up the animals and brings them into the house, as a way of atoning for being insensitive earlier. But Sarah is departing; she's called Ken to come and pick her up. As Robert sits with Jim the dog and contemplates losing Sarah again, the dog suddenly turns into a human and then back into a dog. (The man was played by Neal Bell, who had played the dog in the original play, both with and without a dog suit.)

Sarah greets Ken, then leaves with him. As Sarah looks back, she can see Robert standing in the living room, holding his rainhat in his hand. He waves it very slowly as the scene fades out.

It wasn't until they saw the finished film that journalist Michael Ventura turned to Gena Rowlands and said, "You know, when John waves out the window? I think he was saying good-bye to us."

"Oh shit," Rowlands muttered.

What Cassavetes had made was a film that dealt with messy, sprawling lives, spinning out of control. The brother and sister have always provided each other with balance, as a safe haven from the rest of the world—and so they require this brief recharging of being together to steady themselves enough to go on. It is a film with an elegiac feel to it, a sense of looking back at life, rather than confronting the moment, that was not usually a part of Cassavetes' sensibility.

For Cassavetes, the chance to make the film was incredibly gratifying, particularly because he knew that, unlike the multiplex fodder that was filling screens across America, he was making a movie not so very unlike the ones he'd made on his own in the late 1960s and early 1970s.

"In 1983, we started making a film that was so psychologically dangerous, lonely, terrifying and so uncommercial that Ted Allan, the two producers and I looked at one another and pretended that we had a comedy," Cassavetes wrote about the film in the *New York Times*.

While the original play of *Love Streams* had been set in London, Cassavetes easily converted the locale to Los Angeles for the film, the better to use his own house as the setting for Robert Harmon's beehive of a home, which seemed to be perpetually buzzing with the activities of women.

Though they hadn't worked together in several years, Cassavetes asked Al Ruban to produce *Love Streams*. The director of photography,

David Gurfinkel, was a Cannon regular and brought with him an Israeli crew. Randy Carter, who was first assistant director on the film, referred to them as "very talented indentured servants for Cannon," who were making $500 a week flat rates for unlimited hours. Despite the bargain, Cassavetes rebelled.

Granted, the first two days of dailies looked good. Cassavetes was even loudly complimentary of the footage while watching the dailies: "That was a danger signal to me," Ruban said. "When he goes on too effusively, something is lurking."

On the third day, Cassavetes turned to Ruban and said, "I hate this guy's work—I can't work with him."

By the fourth day, it was Gurfinkel saying to Ruban, "I can't work with him. I'm leaving. I can't stand him." Though Ruban tried to talk him out of it, Gurfinkel quit.

"There was not a lot of symbiosis with John," Carter, the assistant director, recalled. "They were there to work hard, but John was there to explore the text. They had no idea what that was about. They had to get on to their next five pictures for Cannon."

As soon as he heard about Gurfinkel's resignation, Cassavetes said to Ruban, "Good, he left. I want you to shoot it."

"But, John, I'm already doing all this other shit," Ruban said, indicating the rest of the production office, from which the film moved forward.

"No, you've got to," Cassavetes said, then picked up a phone and, on the spot, called Menahem Golan in Israel: "Al won't shoot my picture," he barked at Golan. "You talk to him."

Cassavetes handed the phone to Ruban, who tried to sound ameliorating as he explained to Golan how much he already had on his plate: "But he appealed to my ego and my vanity," Ruban recalled. "He said, 'You must do this.' So now I'm shooting it, I'm producing it and I'm the production manager. So now it's a seven-day, twenty-four-hour job—which I kind of thrive on."

Ruban hired Alan Caso, one of what was then an extremely small group of camera operators trained on the Steadicam. First used in *Bound for Glory* and *Rocky* in 1976, the Steadicam was a gyroscopically balanced handheld-camera rig that allowed for extreme camera mobility, minus the jittery, bouncy image most handheld camerawork tended toward.

"He had used handheld cameras all the time, so to him, the Steadicam was just a means to an end," Caso recalled. Yet, Cassavetes was ultimately thrilled when Caso, after just two rehearsals, was able to navigate three flights of stairs—backward—while keeping Cassavetes in the center of a well-composed frame, take after take, for a shot that ultimately didn't make it into the film.

Michael Ventura was a film critic and journalist who had won favor with Cassavetes for some of the things he'd written about his earlier films in the *L.A. Weekly.* When *Love Streams* got the green light, Cassavetes tracked Ventura down—the writer had married and moved to Austin, Texas—and asked him if he wanted to come and watch production on the film and write a production diary, which Cassavetes would help to get published. The diary itself ultimately never found a publisher (though Ventura wrote an abbreviated version for the *L.A. Weekly*), but Ventura was a daily presence on the set.

"It was clear to me that what John really wanted was someone to talk to about the film who he trusted to keep their mouth shut and who was not involved in the film itself," Ventura said. "He just wanted to hear something thought out, out loud. He would drive the crew nuts because he'd call me aside and say, 'Mike, I'm gonna do this and this and this.' He was just spreading it out for himself. I was like his human storyboard. He could sketch things on me."

Cassavetes had a new secretary, Helen Caldwell, who took shorthand at 250 words a minute. She'd met him through Ted Allan, for whom she used to work, and went to work for Cassavetes as his secretary while he and Allan were working on the *Love Streams* screenplay. "John would think of a story idea and he'd call me and say, 'Let's write.' He could write a first draft in a week," Caldwell said. "He'd talk and tell me the story and I'd take it down and type it. Then he'd make changes on the draft."

When it came time to shoot *Love Streams*, Cassavetes announced to Caldwell that, like Elaine Kagan before her, she was going to become a script supervisor.

"But I've never even been on a movie set," she protested.

"You're smart," Cassavetes said. "I'll teach you."

Cassavetes got a veteran script supervisor to tutor her before production started and had her meet with George Villasenor, the film's editor, who would be relying on her notes as he assembled the scenes.

"When John started shooting, he taught me how to be a script supervisor," Caldwell said. "He took me under his wing. I was not just his secretary. We would work until two or three in the morning and then he'd say, 'See you at nine.'"

As in *Gloria*, Cassavetes set himself the task of working with a child actor, who would play Albie, Robert's son he has never met. Cassavetes cast Sam Shaw's grandson, Jakob (whose father, Larry, was the film's still photographer).

"I remember saying to John one time when I was little, 'Can you put me in a movie?' and he said yes," Jakob Shaw recalled. "I think I had a two-second scene in *Gloria* when I was seven or eight. He came through with a part a few years later with *Love Streams*. As a kid, I thought he was this crazy, funny guy."

The script called for Robert to return from a night on the town to find a tearful Albie, who wants to go home and see his mother.

"He made me cry for that scene," Shaw recalled. "I was shocked. Time and again, he would tell me how horrible I was. He said, 'I'm going to replace you, I'll get another kid.' I didn't know he already had too much of me on film to do that. But the scene came out pretty good. I had no experience so I had on-the-job-training with John. I don't remember any directions except 'Don't be afraid to make a fool of yourself.'"

Cassavetes would later bemoan the fact that he only had two days to film that scene, when he could have really made it sing if he'd had five: "Then I could really get out of that kid all that the kid has to give," he said.

The director is the focal point of all questions on a movie set. He is bombarded with queries and requests from before first call to after the nightly wrap and screening of dailies. It is exhausting and demanding, yet Cassavetes found time during breaks and meals to chat with a crew that was clearly in awe of him.

Steadicam operator Alan Caso recalled, "During lunch, I'd quiz him about his movies, why he did this or that. He was very open and willing to share his experience. He treated me like a fellow filmmaker. I was clearly green, with this avid, toothy grin. I was just a kid who was thrilled to be there. But he could talk to you without talking down to you."

For the most part, Golan and Globus left Cassavetes alone to make the movie his way. He might have been deemed past his prime by Hollywood, but Europe still regarded Cassavetes as a major American film artist. Cannon Films hoped some of that glory would be reflected on them if they produced a Cassavetes film.

"Menahem Golan let this crazy artist make this film—he even gave him final cut," marveled Julie Allan. "Whatever you say about Menahem Golan, he gave John the money and never interfered with one second of filming."

During one set visit, Golan started chattering to Cassavetes that he wanted to make not just *Love Streams*, but a companion documentary about Cassavetes. He told Cassavetes that he had an Israeli documentary crew on its way to Los Angeles to film him. Without missing a beat, Cassavetes swung around, pointed at writer Michael Ventura, who was sitting in the office, and said, "Let him do it."

"Good, you do it," Golan said. "Shoot lots of film. I don't want a 'Making of' film. I want Cassavetes."

When he left, Cassavetes turned to the writer with that impish grin and said, "Kid, you're a director."

Ventura was given a camera operator and sound man and began to document the production, talking to Cassavetes whenever the director had time. Cassavetes' comments became the film's soundtrack. Ventura was given an editing room for three months, to complete his film, which he called *I'm Almost Not Crazy: John Cassavetes—The Man and His Work.* Cannon ultimately sent the film to several festivals and released it on video.

At one point, during a break while a shot was being set up, Cassavetes turned to Ventura, gave him the subversive smile, and said, "This picture, this picture—I don't give a fuck what anybody says. If you don't have time to see it, don't. If you don't like it, don't. If it doesn't give you an answer, fuck you. I didn't make it for you anyway."

To film one of Diahnne Abbott's scenes, Cassavetes enlisted Peter Bogdanovich as stand-in director, insisting to Bogdanovich that he needed him to shoot a scene from *Love Streams* in which Cassavetes himself appeared.

Bogdanovich had been a recluse since the murder a couple of years earlier of his lover, *Playboy* playmate Dorothy Stratten, who'd been brutally shotgunned by her ex-husband. But Cassavetes was adamant: He simply couldn't handle acting and directing at the same time.

"John, you've directed yourself before," Bogdanovich said, trying to beg off.

"Are you telling me you're not going to help me?" Cassavetes demanded. "Are we friends or not? I'm telling you I need you."

Cassavetes was so relentless that Bogdanovich finally had to agree: "So I shot this scene with Diahnne Abbott and him," Bogdanovich said. "She brings him a flower and my only contribution to the scene was the flower, except to line it up. It was shot in a pretty conventional way. And he did it to help get me out of the house."

Cassavetes' acting in the film flowed easily, effortlessly. First a.d. Randy Carter recalled, "John was loose as a goose as far as acting. He took it seriously, but that's where his innate charm worked—as an actor. That was his fallback. Whether it's Burt Reynolds or Clint Eastwood, they all have their bag of tricks that they lean on. John's was his innate charm."

Cassavetes understood how some people could hear echoes of Mabel Longhetti in Sarah Lawson: Sarah, too, had been institutionalized and suffered because she loved her family too much. But Cassavetes was upset when people questioned Sarah's mental stability. "I resent it when people say Sarah is crazy," he said. "She'd love to be something special; that's not crazy, it's just hard."

Still, her behavior was decidedly eccentric. At one point, Sarah, deciding Robert needs something to nurture, brings home an entire menagerie of animals, including fowl, a goat, and a pair of miniature horses. They're driven up to the Cassavetes house in a pair of taxi cabs, and Cassavetes assumed that, once Gena had unloaded them from the taxis, she would lead them around the side of the house to the pens in the backyard.

"Instead, I went in the front door with the parade of animals," she recalled. "We marched right through the house. Those miniature horses may be miniature, but they're still horses—and by the time we got through the house, we had a lot of poop in the place. We had to recarpet the entire house after the film was over."

As production neared its conclusion, Cassavetes reworked a scene at the end of the film in which Robert communes with the dog that Sarah has brought; it turned into one of the film's most enigmatic moments.

It is raining and Sarah is getting ready to leave. Robert sits in the living room with Jim, the dog. What the audience sees is Robert in profile at the side of the frame, suddenly doing a double-take and then bursting into laughter. The camera cuts to a bearded, silent, naked man sitting where the dog had been seated, as Robert says, "Who the fuck are you?" The man smiles mysteriously; the camera cuts back to Robert, then back to the man—who then becomes the dog, once again sitting there instead of the man. The implication seems to be that the dog has a human side or can transform itself.

"The ending stumped John," Ventura recalled. "He had a dog and he didn't know what he wanted it to do. In the script, Robert's supposed to go see Diahnne Abbott, but John didn't think that worked."

"What the fuck do I do? My movie's over," Cassavetes asked Ventura, then added, "Well, if it was easy, anyone could do it."

As Cassavetes rewrote the scene, the dog turned into a man and back into a dog. But he didn't tell the crew that's what he had in mind. All the crew could see was that the camera was on a medium shot of Cassavetes sitting by himself in the living room, doing a double-take.

He called, "Action," then just sat there for a moment. A surprised look crossed his face and, after a moment, he started laughing uproariously.

But when he started laughing, the assistant director called, "Cut!" because he thought the shot was over.

"John was furious," Ventura recalled. They did the shot again, and this time the camera continued rolling as John laughed at the blank space where, after the scene was edited, the dog/man would appear to be sitting. Then Cassavetes called, "Cut!" and walked over to where Ventura was watching.

Leaning into Ventura, he said with conspiratorial glee, "They hate it. They've been working their asses off all summer for *this*?" and started laughing. "They're thinking, '*This* is the end of the movie?'"

When Elmer Bernstein had to drop out as the film's composer, Cassavetes turned to Bo Harwood. Cassavetes had an idea of how to end the film: a vision by Sarah in which she and her family reconcile while singing about their feelings to each other operatically.

"Bo, could you write an operetta?" Cassavetes asked him.

As Harwood recalled, "I didn't know what that was. But I had two weeks to do it. John spent an evening in the music room after I had a rough melody. He started blurting out lyrics and after four hours it was done."

Otherwise, it was life as usual at the Cassavetes household: Life went on, despite the presence of a film crew and equipment all over the house.

One night Planco was in the bar at Cassavetes' house, while scenes were being shot in another part of the house. As shooting wrapped, Cassavetes asked Planco if he wanted to spend the night, rather than negotiate the various canyon roads and traffic to get him back to his hotel. But Planco found that being Cassavetes' guest was a mixed blessing, one that didn't involve a good night's sleep.

"John would come in your room in the middle of the night when you were asleep, talking like he was in the middle of a conversation," Planco recalled. "He'd wake you up as he was telling you something and you'd sit there, bleary-eyed, and listen and nod or grunt. And eventually he'd wander out. He was restless at night."

Cassavetes' health had already suffered a serious deterioration, yet he plowed ahead with *Love Streams*. Larry Shaw remembered, "I was amazed he could do it. He was drinking more than a bottle of vodka a day. I was so worried about him that I called Ted Allan. Ted didn't believe me. But I was having lunch privately with John every day and saw what he was doing.

"He wouldn't stop drinking. He wouldn't take care of himself. I called my father and told him he had to get out here because John was out of control. But he didn't believe me—because John was able to do the work."

Robert Fieldsteel said, "He would drink and promise people things and get up the next day like the millionaire in Charlie Chaplin's *City Lights*, not remembering any of it. He even called it 'City Lights Syndrome.'"

Bo Harwood recalled that, while he was living with Cassavetes, during the *Three Plays* period of intense work, "Gena reamed me out one morning because John and I were out until 4 A.M. 'If John didn't have anyone to stay up with, he wouldn't stay up,' she said. 'He drinks, he smokes—he's prone to a heart attack!'"

On the set in Las Vegas, Cassavetes came as close as he ever did to acknowledging his condition: "Oh God, the last thing I need to see is my stomach in the mirror," he complained to Robert Fieldsteel, while shooting a bathtub scene in a hotel bathroom.

Seymour Cassel remembered walking down the street with Cassavetes and noticed the way his belly was straining at the front of his shirt. "What's with your stomach?" asked Cassel, who would kid Cassavetes about being out of shape.

"Oh, I've been eating too much," was all Cassavetes said, clearly uncomfortable with the topic.

When Ben Gazzara brought up the odd weight gain, Cassavetes passed it off as a hernia. He had been wrestling with his son, Nick, who had grown to be 6-foot-4, and had played too rough, he said.

Ventura, writing about being on the set in an excerpt from his unpublished diary that ran in the *L.A. Weekly*, wrote, "Physically, he has changed again. The face is more drawn, the skin more wan and he's gained weight in the oddest way I've seen any man gain weight. His face, arms, legs and butt are skinny, but his stomach has ballooned. He looks almost pregnant."

Which didn't stop him from indulging in the vices that had always held him.

"He smoked like a fiend," Diahnne Abbott recalled. "He was always sending someone to get a carton of Marlboros. He drank a lot, but I never saw him drunk. But his skin didn't look good, and he had a pot belly."

Randy Carter, his assistant director, said the precarious nature of Cassavetes' health as he directed *Love Streams* "was very apparent and very troubling. But he never carried that into the public arena," Carter said. "You never got the feeling that he was worried or consumed. That kind of distance only made me worry a little more. I'd have been more comfortable seeing more anxiety."

Robert Fieldsteel remembered Cassavetes making references to his days being numbered as early as 1979 or 1980: "Then you'd see him," Fieldsteel said, "working twenty hours a day—and you'd think he was invincible. As he would wear everybody else out, the last thing you'd think is that he would be seriously ill."

"For being sick, the energy he had was amazing," Matthew Cassel said. "I'd show up at 6:30 in the morning at the house and he'd be in the kitchen having coffee. He never let on that he was sick. You could tell from his appearance, not by the way he acted."

But Cassavetes may have sensed the end of something was at hand. At one point during the production, Cassavetes turned to Ventura and said, "This is a sweet film. If I die, this is a sweet last film."

In late 1983, having finished shooting *Love Streams*, Cassavetes rounded up all the footage and took it with him to New York. There, he planned to edit *Love Streams* at his suite at the Wyndham Hotel, even as he began rehearsals for a new play he was directing.

The play, called *Thornhill*, had been written by Meade Roberts, a playwright Cassavetes had known since his earliest days as an actor, when he met him through Sam Shaw. Roberts had been a writer with the Actors Studio, then had become a mainstay of the early days of live television, working for shows like *Suspense*, *The Kate Smith Evening Hour*, and *The Schlitz Playhouse*, even writing a well-regarded TV adaptation of Henry James' *The Wings of the Dove*. Like writers such as Reginald Rose, Paddy Chayefsky, and Rod Serling, Roberts' name on a TV script was the mark of quality.

Balding, pear-shaped, and dyspeptic—and flamboyantly gay long before it was fashionable—Roberts had been selected to adapt two of Tennessee Williams' plays, *Orpheus Descending* and *Summer and Smoke*, from stage to screen. The assignments brought him to Hollywood, where he signed a studio contract.

Still, he complained about Williams' behavior when they worked together: "He treated me abominably during rehearsals for *The Fugitive Kind*," Roberts recalled of the retitled *Orpheus Descending*. "He didn't want to share the spotlight with anyone, including the writer he chose to work with."

Not that his collaboration was an entirely negative experience: "From Williams, I learned to write freely," Roberts said. "His motto was, 'Let it all hang out.' From John Houseman, I learned discipline: how to structure, cut and weight every word. Elia Kazan taught me how to blend the two— to trust your intuition and use your brains."

But things turned sour, according to Johnnie Planco, because, though Roberts had signed a studio contract, "he fell in love with a young studio executive and started stalking him. And that was the end of his studio career."

Roberts spent the decades before his death writing and teaching, landing berths at the New School for Social Research, Brooklyn College, New York University, and the London Film School. He continued to write, trying to attract interest to his subsequent plays.

Cassavetes, who had cast Roberts as Mr. Sophistication in *The Killing of a Chinese Bookie* and as a grieving father in *Opening Night,* even gave him free office space for years. Roberts was an entertaining guy to have around, someone with outrageous opinions and a happy willingness to express them.

That included a sense of self-dramatization, which often took the form of suicide threats.

"Meade would threaten suicide all the time," John Roselius recalled, noting Roberts' continual threats to leap out a window. But as Mike Ferris observed, "It would take a lot of nerve to kill yourself, so there was no chance Meade would do it."

John Finnegan recalled a day when he was in the office Cassavetes had overlooking the Wilshire Theater, where *Opening Night* had just opened. Roberts, perpetually at the end of his rope about something, announced that he was going to jump out the window and end it all.

"Don't jump, you fuck," Finnegan snapped. "There are eighteen people in line for the movie and you might land on them."

"Meade Roberts was like a Hollywood ghost story," Jeff Lipsky recalled. "He was a brilliant mind, a real writer. But his scripts were about subjects that wouldn't interest you. But John was dedicated to him beyond belief."

In the late 1970s, Roberts had brought Cassavetes the 400-page script for a film based on his play *The Garden of Allah.* Cassavetes read it and announced that it should be a mini-series; when Robert insisted that it had to be a film, Cassavetes decided that a reading would help them see just what it was they had.

He called Peter Bogdanovich to see whether he would participate, then said, "Actually, it's got a lot of characters, so I'd like to do it at your place." Before he knew what was happening, Bogdanovich was hosting a group that ran from Tatum and Ryan O'Neal to John and Gena to Ben Gazzara and Buck Henry.

Jeff Lipsky, whom Cassavetes had grabbed from the office to read a part as well, recalled it as "this fascinating and ridiculously long screenplay. But everyone was there because of John's dedication to Meade."

Roberts had based *Thornhill* on the life of Eugene O'Neill. It was a long psychological drama about an aging playwright who has ill-treated both his young mistress and his unhappy wife because of his dedication to his un-yielding muse.

Cassavetes read and liked the play and held some readings of it, before the money for *Love Streams* fell into his lap. He convinced Ben Gazzara to sit in for one reading, but Gazzara was unimpressed.

"We were dealing with a writer much like Eugene O'Neill, for whom writing is the paramount thing in his life," Gazzara recalled. "A play about an artist is always a difficult sell. That's how I saw it."

But Cassavetes took him aside after the reading to tell him that he thought the play had fantastic potential and that then-fledgling Broadway producers Fran and Barry Weissler wanted to produce it, after first doing a workshop to cut the play to a manageable length.

Gazzara turned him down, then relented a few weeks later when, after Cassavetes' mother's funeral (at the same Port Washington cemetery where they'd shot *Husbands*), Cassavetes came at him again: "So you're really not going to do the play?" he asked over lunch after the funeral.

"How could I say no?" Gazzara said later. "He was my friend and his mother just died."

Rehearsals began in the fall of 1983, after shooting finished on *Love Streams*. The Weisslers at first wanted to workshop the play in a college set-ting, then talked about putting it on its feet at Lucille Lortel's White Barn Theater in Westport, Connecticut, before bringing it to New York.

Eventually, the workshop was convened at the Westbeth Theater Center on West Seventeenth Street, just north of Greenwich Village. Cassavetes put together a cast led by Gazzara, with Patti LuPone as Thornhill's wife and Carol Kane as his young lover.

"The cast is making $175 a week in the workshop and that's what I call dedication," Fran Weissler told the *New York Times* in an October story, which said the workshop would be followed by an out-of-town tryout and then an opening in New York. There would be a cast of fourteen, and the show would be capitalized at $900,000.

"It's going to be hard to make money if we don't do capacity busi-ness," Fran Weissler admitted.

Patti LuPone observed, "It was a terrible play. I never understood why John agreed to do it. It was a long boring play about Carlotta and Eugene O'Neill. I'd fall asleep between cues under the prop table."

But LuPone had taken the role for the chance to work with Cassavetes and wasn't disappointed by the experience: "I loved being directed by him," she said. "He said, 'Make mistakes, stop being careful.' It was no holds barred."

Everyone knew the play was long; that was the focal point of all discussions between the Weisslers, Roberts, and Cassavetes. The goal of the workshop production was to trim it to a reasonable length.

So they worked daily on the play: "John had more energy than anybody I'd ever met," Carol Kane said. "He could go and go and go. I never wanted to go home in case I missed something."

Kane recalls that, despite the fact that the workshop was virtually unpaid, she would meet Cassavetes and Gazzara each morning for breakfast at the Plaza Hotel's Oak Room. Then they'd share a cab downtown: "We'd start our day in this magical way," Kane said, still sounding slightly awed by the memory twenty years after the fact.

After four weeks of rehearsal, the Weisslers came to see what had been accomplished—and found that Cassavetes, despite assurances that cuts were already in the works, had not shortened the play at all.

"In spite of the play's excessive length, John hadn't cut a line," Ben Gazzara recalled of the first workshop performance. "He liked the play as it was. He thought that when the Weisslers saw what we'd done, they'd be happy. Boy, was he wrong."

"Was the play long?" Barry Weissler said. "It went on for two days. I became angered by the way in which John said one thing to our faces and did something else behind our backs."

The Weisslers immediately pulled the plug on the workshop. Cassavetes put up his own money to finish out the last three workshop performances. But *Thornhill* was, for all practical purposes, dead.

"Meade was out in the hall, beating his head against the wall," Johnnie Planco remembered. "We called 911 and got an ambulance."

The performances caused a sensation. There was an extremely limited seating capacity, and it had been publicized as John Cassavetes directing Ben Gazzara and Patti LuPone (who had recently won a Tony Award for *Evita*). Gazzara recalled, "I arrived for the first performance and there was a line snaking its way down the block and around the corner. People were standing against the walls and sitting on the floor. Some people told us they liked it, some said they hadn't, but nobody walked out. But to go to Broadway, the play would have to have been cut in half."

Actor Bob Balaban saw one of the performances, which he remembered as "a five-hour play," he said. "It was like an off-off-off-Broadway theater and it was like a butterfly, this small, delicate thing that he lavished attention on. It was very typical of John; he was only doing it for the thing itself, for the experience, because he believed in it."

* * *

Love Streams opened in August 1984: "This is a very different picture for us," Cassavetes said, "a very crazy film. I don't know how to compare it to anything we've done before."

Asked whether he still considered himself outside the mainstream, he said, "God, I hope I'm a Hollywood outsider, though it's hard to say after twenty-five years of doing this stuff. I fear I'm becoming more establishment than I'd like to be."

He sounded an optimistic note about his relationship with Cannon. He and Ted Allan had been working on a screenplay for *The Third Day Comes,* and had even had discussions with Golan about producing it, though they'd been honest and told him the drama was probably too serious to have any real commercial potential. And, Cassavetes noted, "I won't make it unless it can be three hours long. It has to be and I won't do it shorter to fit commercial demands."

"Why would I want to make a picture that's not going to make any money?" Golan asked him. "We're not in the business of throwing away money."

But when Cassavetes told him the story, Golan started becoming emotional about the plot—of two children clinging to each other in the face of a tyrannical father—and said, "No, it won't make money but we must do it."

That, however, was early on, when *Love Streams* had just won the Golden Bear at the Berlin Film Festival in February 1984, before Cannon began scrambling for its financial life, thanks to Golan and Globus' overreaching.

In April MGM, which provided distribution for Cannon, refused to allow the film to be shown at the San Francisco Film Festival, which was staging a tribute to Cassavetes. The distributor had a deal in which the film would complete its European run before it opened in the U.S. But its London opening produced only lukewarm reviews, cooling Cannon's belief in its prospects in the U.S. When *Love Streams* did receive its abortive American release, the reviews were respectful, mildly so, carrying a "Hey, I remember him," vibe.

"There's no other American director who can do what John Cassavetes does on the screen," Janet Maslin said, adding, "There may not be many who would want to." She gave him the benefit of the doubt saying, "Once again, he is able to galvanize a long, rambling, quirky psychodrama through sheer force of personality."

Richard Schickel sang Rowlands' praises effusively, saying her performance was the film's salvation: "You can never tell when Rowlands is going to do something astonishing," he wrote. "It is the unpredictable grace and goofiness of her behavior, the subtle complexity of emotions she generates that finally overcome all obstacles to enthrallment."

David Sterritt noted, "It's a film based on extravagant risks by director and actors alike . . . For all its goofiness, *Love Streams* has more passion, imagination and courage than most directors dream of."

Forty-eight

Big Trouble

Perhaps it is simply courting disaster to call a movie *Big Trouble*.

In 2001 director Barry Sonnenfeld made a dark comedy, based on a best-selling Dave Barry novel of that name. It featured a climax in which a terrorist carries a nuclear device onto an airline flight.

It was slated for release in the fall of 2001—a plan that was quickly scuttled after the attacks of September 11, 2001. It opened almost a year later and disappeared almost instantly, the victim more of its own weak script than of history—seemingly jinxed nonetheless by a name that invited "big trouble."

Sonnenfeld could have taken a lesson from the previous filmmakers to use the title: Andrew Bergman and John Cassavetes, as odd a cinematic pairing as you could imagine. "It's aptly named, that project," Bergman said. "There's karma to that name."

Bergman had written *Big Trouble* as a sequel of sorts to a previous hit he had written: 1979's *The In-Laws*, which starred Peter Falk and Alan Arkin and was directed by Arthur Hiller. Strictly speaking, the new film wasn't a sequel; it wasn't about the same characters and didn't continue (or, as is more often the case, repeat) the story from the first film. Rather, like the "Road" pictures of Bob Hope and Bing Crosby, in which they played recognizable types but didn't repeat characters, *Big Trouble* was meant to capitalize on the reunion of the two actors in a comedy: Arkin playing the meek, nervous one, and Falk playing the bluff, explosive one.

Where *In-Laws* had made comedy out of the conventions of a spy film, *Big Trouble* was meant as a spoof of *Double Indemnity*, the sexy, hard-bitten James M. Cain noir that Billy Wilder had turned into a classic in 1944. In this version, Arkin was the insurance salesman, who finds himself pulled into a plot by a client (Beverly D'Angelo) to murder her husband (Falk) and collect the insurance. His motive, however, was not lust for the prospective widow but a desperate need for money to send his triplet sons to an Ivy League college.

Bergman had written the film as a project for himself to direct. But after only a couple of weeks of shooting, it was obvious that the film wasn't working. So Bergman walked away from the film, and Guy McElwaine, who was running Columbia Pictures, turned to John Cassavetes.

For Bergman, the problems began with the script itself: He had never figured out the ending. The third act degenerated into violent silliness about terrorists and bank robbers that came out of left field. And Bergman could never solve the problem.

"We went into shooting without a third act, which is never a good way to open production," Bergman recalled. Even as he struggled on the set, he was dealing with the incipient birth of his second child and the fact that his pregnant wife was in New York while Bergman was shooting in Los Angeles. Bergman was also going through contractor hell with serious cost overruns on the remodeling of a home in the Berkshires.

The combination of those pressures and the clear fact that the movie was not funny finally pushed Bergman over the brink. He went to see McElwaine on a Saturday and told him it would be better for the film if he quit.

McElwaine called Falk and they put their heads together: "What about John?" McElwaine said, knowing his former client had been unable to get another film off the ground since *Love Streams*. Falk and McElwaine both liked the idea and ran it by Arkin, who seemed sanguine about it. So McElwaine called Cassavetes and got him the script. The next day, Sunday, Cassavetes called and agreed to do it. He was on the soundstage that Monday.

But *Big Trouble* was a mess and all Cassavetes could do was try to shepherd the organized chaos to the finish line.

Yet it was also a major studio picture, at a time when studios spent an average of $16 million per film. So Cassavetes faced the irony of directing a picture that obviously didn't work while having what was, for him, virtually an unlimited budget. The studio provided him with a car to the set each day and a trailer of his own, as well as props and technical equipment that Cassavetes wasn't used to.

"At one point, he needed a fire truck for a scene and they let him have three fire trucks," Jeff Lipsky recalled. "He was cracking up. He couldn't believe it. And with a crew of seventy-five, it really did direct itself."

Fieldsteel recalled visiting him on the soundstage: "It was not that John couldn't direct a more conventional movie," he said. "But it was sort of: What's wrong with this picture? Some days he had fun, some days were frustrating."

On his first day, he called a meeting in his trailer with all of the cast principals. He asked each person what his or her character's desire was, in terms of the caper that was being pulled off in the film. It was a basic acting exercise: What's your intention?

Actor Richard Libertini, who played a crooked police pathologist in the film, said, "Obviously, I'm in it for the money."

Cassavetes nailed him with a stare and said, "That's no reason. That's worse than pornography."

As Libertini later said, "He made me reconsider my motives, to work on something a little deeper. Not that there were deep psychological problems here. It was a farce-thriller. But if we took it too lightly, he'd really get pissed. He said, 'You do comedy the same way you do everything else: You've got to approach it seriously.'"

Alan Arkin was unhappy with Cassavetes. He found him manipulative and feared that he was giving all the laughs to Falk (though, in fact, Arkin has the film's funniest extended moment—and what may be the world's longest cinematic spit-take—in a scene where he is forced to sample sardine liqueur).

"Alan Arkin was a pain in the ass on that film," Seymour Cassel recalled. "It was not John's kind of a film."

Helen Caldwell, who was still working as Cassavetes' secretary, recalled, "Alan considered himself a talented actor who didn't need to be tricked or goaded into exuding what was required. The tensions ran deep, rather than surface bickering and fighting."

Yet at one particular moment, Cassavetes was able to say just the right thing to Arkin. It was a scene in a bathroom, with Falk explaining something to the nervous Arkin, who is in a stall. They had done three or four takes before Cassavetes leaned in and whispered something to Arkin. The next take was distinctly better. Helen Caldwell turned to Cassavetes and said, "What did you say to him?"

"I told him to hold his breath," Cassavetes replied.

Cassavetes knew what he had in *Big Trouble*—and it wasn't much. The film was a comedy of so much noticeable effort—to so little obvious effect—that it could be painful to watch. Cassavetes had been a hired hand, doing a favor for friends. The script had been underwritten to start with. He had made as much sense as he could of what he had to work with, but he knew it wasn't enough.

Still, he was able to put together a cut he liked. He invited John Roselius to a screening because he trusted Roselius' laugh: "It was hysterical," Roselius said of that version. "Then the film came out and I took my dad. And I didn't know what film I was watching."

One day, Fieldsteel said, Cassavetes walked into the office and said, "Well, Columbia just fired me from *Big Trouble*." To which Fieldsteel said, "Congratulations."

"Working on that movie sapped his energy," Fieldsteel recalled. "The editing was a nightmare. It dragged on and on. They did reshoots and there was a lot of blaming going on. Still, I wonder if he knew, as miserable as it was, that he was not too likely to get another movie."

John Finnegan recalled asking McElwaine about *Big Trouble* after it finally snuck into theaters virtually unnoticed in May 1986. "Finn, I only produce them—I don't see them," McElwaine replied.

It barely registered with critics that Cassavetes had directed a new film. Richard Schickel, always a supporter, had to admit that "in a frantic search for a funny ending, it blows its cool." But he added, "The movie is rich in strong comic acting and mad little inventions."

Vincent Canby, so hard on Cassavetes over the years, wrote, "It's great seeing Mr. Cassavetes direct a heedless comedy that appears to be a result of special friendships, rather than (like *Husbands*) an exhausting analysis of them."

Bergman said that, in the end, a film with two directors means a film with no director. There were some of Bergman's scenes in the finished film—including the sardine liqueur—along with the footage Cassavetes shot: "Texturally, it was very different," Bergman said. "It wound up as kind of a hybrid picture, partly my sensibility, partly his, ultimately nobody's. With me and Peter, it's like a car accident we don't talk about."

As he watched the film limp into theaters after sitting on the shelf for several months, Cassavetes was thinking of his legacy. "God, I don't want this to be my last picture so I'll be known for this piece of shit," Cassavetes said to Al Ruban. "Promise me you'll never show it."

Forty-nine

Valedictory

John Cassavetes had been living on borrowed time since 1983, when cirrhosis of the liver was diagnosed.

"I became aware of his illness in 1981, when his belly started swelling up," recalled Bo Harwood, who had worked with him for a decade at that point. "When he was first diagnosed, in '83, they thought he had a year. He changed his diet, ate steamed vegetables and quit smoking."

Until the actual diagnosis—indeed, until he stopped drinking in 1984—Cassavetes had denied his illness for as long as he could, to himself and to those around him.

Cassavetes celebrated the symbiosis of writing and drinking in *East West Game (Mood Indigo)*, having the jaded secretary Schwartz tell the idealistic young writer, "Writers drink so that they can relax. So that they can forget the money and remember how to smile. When you're drunk, you dream on your feet. Magical things happen. It's dangerous for a writer to see things clearly."

Critic Jay Cocks, who saw Cassavetes whenever either man was on the other's coast, recalled, "I was astonished when he took sick. He'd never been on any *Husbands*-like binges that I knew of. It's not like he was Richard Yates or F. Scott Fitzgerald, falling on the floor."

It wasn't just the drinking that did him in, however.

"He'd done so much to drain himself," Julie Allan recalled of Cassavetes during the *Three Plays* period. "He was smoking, drinking—he was too busy. He was directing three plays around the clock and not eating or sleeping."

He seemed capable of pushing himself that way forever. Some things, however, simply couldn't be denied.

Ben Gazzara recalled a Sunday he and Cassavetes had off during rehearsals for *Thornhill*. They had gotten together with a mutual friend, gameshow producer Chuck Barris, who also had a suite at the Wyndham, to watch a Knicks game on TV.

"It was an action-packed contest but, sometime during the first quarter, John fell asleep," Gazzara said. "I remember saying to Chuck that, in all the years I'd known him, I'd never seen John Cassavetes close his eyes. He slept through the entire game. That worried me."

John Finnegan remembered helping Cassavetes empty out his mother's house after her death in 1983. "I've got about this much liver left," Cassavetes observed, holding thumb and index finger an inch apart.

His secretary, Helen Caldwell, said that the close quarters in which she and Cassavetes worked also gave her a more intimate insight: "When I went into the bathroom, I noticed he had blood in his urine," she said. "I said, 'You've got to go to a doctor.'"

When he took his physical at Columbia for insurance to cover him during the completion of *Big Trouble*, he had stripped down for the insurance doctor. The doctor took one look at Cassavetes' emaciated arms and torso and his basketball-size stomach and lost his professional composure, wailing, "Oh no, not you! John, not you!"

Cassavetes could only chortle his wheezy, huffing laugh as he recounted to Peter Bogdanovich the physician's anguish at information Cassavetes had already processed and tried to come to terms with. "To him, that was funny," Bogdanovich recalled. "I was horrified: 'John, that's not funny,' but he had me laughing at the way he told it."

The facts were much scarier. Between thirty-plus years of hard drinking and his 1968 bout with hepatitis A, Cassavetes' cirrhosis had damaged his liver so severely that the outlook was dire.

While the human liver is able to regenerate and replace damaged or diseased tissue, cirrhosis causes scar tissue to grow around the new cells, impeding blood flow. The scar tissue collects into nodules that further block the flow of blood and keep the liver from regenerating itself. Eventually that leads to a loss of liver function. The liver, which serves as a filter for both the nutrients and the toxins in the blood, becomes blocked and those toxins remain in the blood.

The blockages also cause high blood pressure. The pressure forces liquid through the walls of the blood vessels by osmosis, leading to edema, or a build-up of fluids, in the abdomen, which causes the painful distension that Cassavetes suffered. By its end stages, cirrhosis is poisoning the sufferer with his own toxins, which can no longer be filtered and eliminated. It robs the sufferer of appetite, strength, energy, and, eventually, mental acuity.

Yet the diagnosis surprised most of his friends. They all knew that John drank; they'd all been drinking with him for years. But the fact that he never seemed to register the effects overtly made them think there was no problem: How could John be an alcoholic when he always seemed to be on top of his game? Drinking was just part of who he was; it didn't seem to control him or alter him for the worse.

Said Seymour Cassel, "You never knew if John was drinking or not. He was a great drinker."

Al Ruban recalled, "John couldn't talk unless he had a cigarette and a full glass of whatever he was drinking. It added to his freedom."

"John didn't get drunk," Guy McElwaine said. "Alcohol was a tool. I never saw him drinking when he shouldn't be. But he did it for so long that it caught up with him."

Peter Bogdanovich remembered meetings for *Dancing in the Dark*, a film the two of them had tried to make shortly before *Gloria*, about two sailors on the town in Las Vegas with two showgirls. Cassavetes and Falk would play the sailors; Cybill Shepherd and Raquel Welch would play the showgirls. And Bogdanovich would direct. But nothing ever came of it.

"It was during a long script conference that I noticed John finish off, by himself, a fifth of whiskey," Bogdanovich recalled. "Never having been a drinker, I had no idea what this indicated, but the key thing I remember is that John never even slightly slurred his words as the evening progressed into the small hours, nor in any other way seemed inebriated. He would tell me a few years later that this was one of his biggest problems with booze—he couldn't get drunk, which is why he drank too much."

Diagnosed in 1983 with cirrhosis and given less than a year to live, he managed to stop drinking for the last five years of his life. As he told *People* magazine in 1984, while chain-smoking and drinking black coffee, "I've had a lot to drink in my life and my liver just went bananas. I haven't had a drink in four months. I'm trying to be a good boy and learn to like tomato juice. Those days are gone."

"He quit smoking cold turkey and went on a health kick," Helen Caldwell said. "When he quit drinking, I didn't notice withdrawal or emotional misgivings. It was, 'It was fun while we did it but now I can't so I'm not going to.' After he quit, he just quit."

"He was very tough—never a complaint," Bogdanovich said.

Still, the reactions he got from his friends and fans wore on him as well. One evening, while with Ruban at a Chinese restaurant in the San Fernando Valley, John stopped to pay the check on the way out. A woman coming into the restaurant stopped in her tracks and said out loud, "Is that John Cassavetes?" Then she gasped and put her hands to her face.

In 1987 Cassavetes wrote and directed one more play, *A Woman of Mystery*, with Gena, Carol Kane, and Charles Durning. Staged in the sixty-six-seat Court Theater in Los Angeles, it was the story of a homeless woman who moves in with a younger woman who may or may not be her daughter. Cassavetes used real street people as background characters for the play.

Richard Kaye, one of Cassavetes' assistants, was living in New York, and Cassavetes convinced him to come to Los Angeles to work on the play, giving him the title of producer.

"He didn't look well," Kaye recalled. "Over the course of a year or two, he had changed dramatically. He was in physical discomfort. I saw him leap off the stage and then wince and say, 'I used to be so athletic.' He put on a game face. But one night I was going out to my car and I looked back and saw him by his own car. But he wasn't getting in. I asked him if he was OK and he wasn't. He said, 'I just need a moment.' He was in pain. But he directed this thing anyway."

Carol Kane began rehearsals hating her role in the play and was having problems connecting with the character. Cassavetes adjusted the relationship between her character and Gena's, which was supposed to be that of an estranged mother and daughter—with rewrites in the midst of previews. They put the changes in with only a day's rehearsal.

"And we got to another level," Kane said. "For me, it was like he made a shoe fit. When I'd been having problems, he said, 'If I don't make it something you're in love with, you have my word, you can leave on opening day.' He made big promises creatively—but he came through on everything he promised, always."

As sick as he was, his enthusiasm was unquenchable, Kane said: "There was no such thing for John as just OK," she said. "He'd go crazy and make sure it got much, much, much better or much, much, much worse. He was not interested in mediocrity. Sometimes he'd just explode things and start over."

Lelia Goldoni, who had moved back to Los Angeles after a decade in London, went to see the play at Seymour Cassel's invitation and ran into Cassavetes for the first time in several years. Goldoni had always thought of

Cassavetes as a troubled man who felt he had something to hide, which he masked with his energy and voluble demeanor. But in his weakened state, she said, it was almost as if he had been distilled to his essence.

"I always thought he was hiding or lying," she said. "But when I saw him before the end of his life, that thing was gone and his soul was so close to the surface. I was right. There had been this mask that he'd put up. And now the mask was gone. There was just this extraordinarily pure entity."

As they chatted, Goldoni couldn't resist asking, "Do you still like *Shadows?*"

"I love it," Cassavetes replied. Asked why, he said, "Because we were all so innocent."

A Woman of Mystery was barely reviewed at the time. A number of years later, critic Jonathan Rosenbaum wrote, "With the exception of Judith Malina's production with the Living Theater of Jack Gelber's *The Connection,* which I saw several times in New York in the early '60s, *A Woman of Mystery* is the greatest American stage production I've ever seen . . . Why there has apparently been no move on the part of Cassavetes' family to publish this play is beyond my comprehension, so I can only voice my conviction that if and when this happens, the public's sense of the size and meaning of Cassavetes' work will expand."

Cassavetes continued writing with Caldwell: "I think he always hoped to do another film," Caldwell said. "When we got a draft we thought was good, we'd send it out. There were a lot that didn't get made."

Cassavetes had rewritten "She's De-Lovely" and held readings of it. He gave the script to Sean Penn, who had come over for a reading of another play: "He said he had a script for me to read," Penn recalled. "It was this one and I liked it a lot."

Penn, who was acknowledged as the most dynamic young actor to emerge from the group that followed the Hoffman-Pacino-De Niro-Hackman generation of the 1970s, seemed a natural fit with Cassavetes' actor-based approach. Penn was interested enough in playing the luckless central character, Eddie Quinn, that he attached himself to the project, which gave Cassavetes the leverage to shop it around as a package: Penn acting, Cassavetes directing.

But Cassavetes knew that his health would make it impossible for anyone to insure him for the film. The deal could only be put together if he had a back-up, someone who would sign on to step in and finish the picture, should Cassavetes be unable to.

He called Bogdanovich, who quickly agreed to be Cassavetes' second, though Cassavetes assured him he wouldn't be needed. To seal the deal,

John arranged a meeting with himself, Bogdanovich, and Penn. Bogdanovich recalled, "Sean Penn acted a bit suspicious of me and was less than communicative. John did most of the talking."

Cassavetes began a round of meetings to find a production company willing to stake him to a budget for a Sean Penn film; he even had some nibbles from Norman Lear's company. But it all fell apart when Penn suddenly announced that he had signed to shoot *Casualties of War* in Thailand with Brian De Palma for a larger payday than Cassavetes could ever offer.

That put an end to Cassavetes' plans for "She's De-Lovely." Cassavetes could tell that, by the time Penn finished the picture and returned from Thailand, his own health would no longer be strong enough to direct a film. To Bogdanovich, Cassavetes expressed annoyance and disappointment at Penn's choice.

It was only after Cassavetes' death that Bogdanovich learned the truth: Penn had told Cassavetes that he didn't want Bogdanovich as Cassavetes' back-up. Incensed, Cassavetes had told Penn it was Bogdanovich or no one. Enter *Casualties of War* and exit Sean Penn.

(Penn ultimately did wind up playing Eddie Quinn in the film, which was retitled *She's So Lovely* because the Cole Porter estate wanted an exorbitant fee for the use of the word "De-Lovely." Penn won a best-actor award at the Cannes Film Festival in the 1997 film, which was directed by Nick Cassavetes.)

Still, Cassavetes tried to keep his hand in. At one point, John Finnegan put together a one-man show, *Unsung Heroes,* in which he played an Irish undertaker telling a generational story. The show was a hit in Los Angeles, and Finnegan was invited to take it to New York, to the Lamb's Theater. When he got back to L.A., Cassavetes, who had seen the show, called him and said, "Get your shit together. I've got a theater." He arranged a venue for a day and shot the entire program with three cameras.

"Nobody wanted it," Finnegan recalled, "until he died. And after he died, then they came calling, wanting 'John Cassavetes' last film.'" To which Finnegan said, "No sale."

Cassavetes spent the last couple of years of his life mostly staying at home in the house on Woodrow Wilson Drive. His son, Nick, was married with children and visited often. Daughter Xan, who had moved out at the age of fifteen, moved back home. Daughter Zoe was finishing high school. The family coalesced around him, not to mourn but to enjoy the time that was left.

He continued, however, to work with Helen Caldwell as often as possible on new scripts. "At a certain point after *Big Trouble,* he got more and more ill," Caldwell recalled. "He wouldn't see Peter or Ben. He said, 'You're my only contact with the outside world.' He was driven to write. He had a passion."

He also joked to her, "I don't mind dying. At least then, I don't have to have lunch with anybody."

But Caldwell wasn't always available when Cassavetes wanted her. He'd done his job too well, launching her into a career as script supervisor. So, at one point, in 1987, as he began to rework "She's De-Lovely," he called her to come up to the house.

Caldwell, just back from working on another film, went to see Cassavetes, who promptly handed her a check for $5,000 and said, "I want to buy your time for a month." She agreed and went home, only to get a call that night, offering her the job of script supervisor on *The Dead*, the adaptation of a James Joyce story that proved to be director John Huston's last film. Huston was extremely ill, in the final stages of emphysema, and needed an oxygen tank at all times. But Caldwell couldn't resist the lure of working with the legendary filmmaker.

But when she called Cassavetes, he responded with silence, then hissed, "You fucking bitch. If you go, I swear I'll never talk to you again." Caldwell turned down Huston and showed up the next day at Cassavetes' house, more than a little disgruntled.

"I know you're pissed," he told her. "That will probably be his last film. But this will be mine, too."

"Nick told me after John died, 'You were one of the last people he let come around,'" Caldwell recalled. "In the end, he ran everybody off."

When he let her go, he brought in feisty Carole Smith, Falk's former assistant who had run the production office for him on *Love Streams*.

"As he got sicker, he wouldn't let me see him," Elaine Kagan recalled. "He would talk to me on the phone but he wouldn't let me see him. I think he thought I would fall apart, and he didn't want to see that. Carole was tough."

As he grew weaker, he would speak to friends on the phone and see the occasional visitor, but only a select few. One person he spoke with regularly, until her death in 1988, was Anne Shaw, Sam Shaw's wife, who was battling cancer in New York. They would have elaborate conversations about life, about their children, about their spouses. Cassavetes would encourage her, even as he minimized his own infirmity.

"John never talked about it," Edie Shaw recalled. "He was always laughing, even when he was ill. He called my mother daily and they had these long talks."

Most of his friends felt he was avoiding them because he didn't want to have to deal with the look on their faces when they saw him as he had become: gray, paradoxically emaciated and bloated, with an abdomen more massive than ever.

"He made himself scarce at the end," Bo Harwood said. "He looked horrible and he knew he did. So he closed himself off and did his writing."

Matthew Cassel visited John with Seymour toward the end and remembered Cassavetes joking about the size of his stomach: "Ahh, this goddam shit is kicking my ass," Cassavetes said.

Noted Richard Dreyfuss, "He was like a Giacometti sculpture when he was desperately ill: He was translucent, his hands, his face."

Robert Fieldsteel remembered a photograph Cassavetes treasured, of himself with both Akira Kurosawa and Federico Fellini: "He was excited about that," Fieldsteel said. "He felt he deserved to be in the picture, but he was also tickled by it, too."

Yet Cassavetes admitted he had avoided the opportunity to meet Kurosawa, one of his cinematic heroes, for a long time. Kurosawa had once written Cassavetes a letter, in which he talked about how much he admired *Shadows* and how it had inspired him to make a film about the street life of Japan. Cassavetes' use of locations in *Shadows*, Kurosawa wrote, had been thrilling to him as a filmmaker.

"How could I tell him that we hardly used locations?" Cassavetes said. "I mean, we did a lot of shooting in the street, if you want to call that a location, but we had this one little room, and we made it look like anything we needed it to look like. I felt like such an asshole when I got the letter. I could never face the man. I avoided meeting him for years."

As sick as he was, he didn't seem to lose his spark, his sense of humor—or at least he seemed capable of summoning it for his friends.

As Peter Falk observed in an interview more than a decade later, "If I ever face death, I'll have an advantage—because I will have seen how John did it. I can't imagine anyone doing it better."

The Woodrow Wilson Drive house had a steep, winding driveway—seen from the backseat of Robert Harmon's car as he races after the runaway Albie in *Love Streams*—and Cassavetes would try to walk down it each day to get the newspaper. One day, Cassavetes told Falk, his aging German shepherd followed him down the hill, as he always did, followed him back up, then wandered to the back of the property, threw up, and died.

"Peter, do you think they're trying to tell me something?" Cassavetes said with a phlegmy laugh.

Seymour Cassel would attend AA meetings, then go visit Cassavetes, who would complain when Cassel would light a cigarette: "I quit drinking—one thing at a time," Cassel told him.

Gazzara recalled a reading at Cassavetes' house of "Begin the Beguine," about two aging men who rent an apartment and engage hookers—not for sex but to talk about life and love. Gazzara arrived to find Cassavetes in the kitchen, poking at several massive artichokes in a kettle of boiling water.

"I hadn't seen him for a year but I wasn't prepared for what had happened," Gazzara wrote in his memoir. "His thin, lean body had been massacred. His stomach was distended, blown up, ballooned. His shoulders had become bony. I could see that beneath his clothes, his arms and legs were much too thin. But his face, though gaunt and having suffered, was more handsome than I'd ever seen it."

Cassavetes looked up at him from beneath his shock of gray hair and said, "Would you like an artichoke? They're supposed to be good for your liver. It's probably too late for mine, but maybe it'll do yours some good."

At that point, the doctors had told Cassavetes, there was no way to treat the damage to the liver. They could tap the stomach to drain the fluid, but that was only palliative and cosmetic. The changes in diet and health regimen (such as giving up smoking and alcohol) could potentially reverse the damage he'd done to the organ. But that was unlikely.

"John," Gazzara began, "you do know that there've been quite a few successful liver transplants done in this country."

"Not for me," Cassavetes replied, "no thanks."

Seymour Cassel recalled, "He wouldn't have a liver transplant because he didn't trust doctors. He said, 'If I go to the hospital, I'll never come out.' So he lied and said it didn't hurt: just some mild discomfort. But how could it not hurt, with his stomach as big as it was?"

At one point, during a reading of "Begin the Beguine" with Falk, Gazzara looked up to see the bathrobed Cassavetes's with an 8mm camera to his eye, filming the two actors as they read, zooming and panning.

"I knew right away that he was already thinking of turning it into a movie," Gazzara recalled. "But how? A movie takes far more energy than a play and even holding that small camera for a short length of time seemed to tire him."

Cassavetes kept writing with Carole Smith, who worked with him three days a week from September 1988 to mid-January 1989. She had been working with Elaine May, and Cassavetes had her come over and work on a script with him.

He dictated a script for "Gloria 2": It is years later, and Gloria is married to a physician in Portland, Oregon. She's a mother and a member of the social set—until a squad of mob hitmen pull up in limos and spray her tea party with machine guns. She then must track down Phil, now grown, to tell him he's in real danger.

Despite the healthy diet Cassavetes was following, the size of his stomach seemed only to increase. It obviously pained him and finally Smith asked, "Why don't you just go to the hospital and get it drained?"

Cassavetes eyed her warily and said, "When I go to the hospital, I will not come out."

Gazzara had dinner with an obviously weakened Cassavetes less than a month before his death. As the two embraced in the parking lot, Gazzara said throatily, "Keep battling."

"I'm not worried, Ben," Cassavetes told him with a smile. "I know you'll come to my funeral."

"John, if you die, I ain't gonna speak to you again," Gazzara said, attempting a gruff joke.

"OK, then, I won't," Cassavetes said, giving his friend's arm a squeeze.

A couple of weeks before he died, he said to John Roselius, "I haven't had a drink in five years. My writing has gotten better because I'm sober. Just the smell of alcohol makes me sick now."

Al Ruban remembered getting a call from Cassavetes in the same time frame: "He was so nice to me that I knew it was over," Ruban said. "He thanked me very much and asked me not to get involved with people doing biographies. I said, 'Yeah,' but I had no intention of doing that. But he said that, if people wanted to know him, they should see his films because his work was his life."

In January 1989 Cassavetes was given a retrospective at the U.S. Film Festival in Park City, Utah—what would later be renamed the Sundance Film Festival. It was only appropriate: The festival had been created to showcase independent films. At the time of the retrospective, it had been thirty years since *Shadows* and twenty years since *Husbands* and *Faces*.

Too sick to do anything other than give his blessing, Cassavetes pointed the festival representatives to Michael Ventura, who he believed would provide the right kind of critical perspective on his work as curator for the festival's purposes.

Cassavetes was in bed as he talked to Ventura: "I look at my films, all of them, good and bad, they're like soldiers going over the hill." Still, some films could be allowed to go AWOL. Just to be sure, Ventura asked,

"Not *Big Trouble,* right?" And Cassavetes shook his head in mock horror and said, "No."

Ventura called John afterward to report on the success of the films at the festival: "People who'd only heard of his films were packing the place," Ventura said. "And they had better prints and sound than John ever had on *Shadows.*"

Ventura had watched *Husbands* at the festival and told Cassavetes that he'd understood it better than when he'd seen it as a teen: "I hadn't become a man when I first saw it," he said.

Cassavetes, with a wheezy laugh, said, "I love men. We're so stupid."

As sick as he was, Cassavetes wasn't quitting: "I don't know what He's waiting for," he said to Ventura. "I'm not going to do it for Him."

After its triumphant showing at the New York Film Festival in October 1988, *Opening Night* was invited to open the Rotterdam Film Festival in Holland, scheduled for early February 1989. The festival offered to cover all of John and Gena's expenses to attend the first showing, but Cassavetes was far too ill, and Rowlands wouldn't leave his side.

So Cassavetes asked Peter Bogdanovich whether he would serve as Cassavetes' stand-in at the festival. Bogdanovich agreed and flew to Holland to introduce the screening and offer John's appreciation and salutation.

Watching the film—and listening as the audience reacted positively to the moment when Myrtle Gordon does battle with the ghost of the dead girl—Bogdanovich was transported back to an early screening of the film. Cassavetes had asked him afterward what he thought and, as Bogdanovich tried to carefully select his words, Cassavetes said abruptly, "You think I should cut the ghost scene?"

"Well, that might be a good idea," Bogdanovich said. "It might make things simpler for people."

"No," Cassavetes said after a moment's consideration, "I'm going to keep it in," and Bogdanovich instantly felt he'd failed some small test.

Now, listening to the audience's approval of the film, he was eager to tell Cassavetes about the screening and that John had been right about the ghost scene after all.

But as the screening wrapped up and the audience for the post-screening discussion filed out, a festival director took Bogdanovich aside and broke the news: John Cassavetes had died a few hours earlier. It was February 3, 1989. He was not quite sixty years old.

Already in considerable pain, Cassavetes had been taken to Cedars Sinai suffering severe shortness of breath. The build-up of poisons in his system because of his liver failure ultimately caused all systems to crash in a cascading series of failures that proved fatal.

The funeral was held at Westwood Village Memorial Park, with more than 200 people on hand. As cameraman Mike Ferris approached Gena Rowlands, she threw her arms around him and said, "Big Mike, you'll never know how proud John was of you."

Afterward Ferris couldn't quite believe it: "I'd never heard that even from a blood relative," Ferris said.

Matthew Cassel remembers how devastated Seymour was: "I felt so bad for my dad, he was so upset. It was horrible."

The crowd then retired to the Cassavetes/Rowlands house on Woodrow Wilson Drive. "When we got back to the house, everybody was there at the bar," John Finnegan recalled. "Thank God, Benny came. Benny made it a party. He kept it going. We'd say, 'Tell 'em about the time . . .'"

Elaine Kagan said, "Everybody was there, telling stories. They had so many friends and everybody came."

But even recounting tales of the good times in Cassavetes' life could only take them so far. "That was a sad fucking day, man," Finnegan said.

The memorial service for John Cassavetes was held at the old Directors Guild of America building on Sunset Boulevard in April 1989. It was organized by Jeremy Kagan and Peter Bogdanovich, who put together a series of film clips that showcased Cassavetes' work as both actor and director. They also arranged a speakers' list that included everyone from agent Martin Baum and journalist Michael Ventura to Seymour Cassel, Ted Allan, and Peter Falk.

"There weren't enough chairs to go around at the memorial," John Finnegan recalled. Added Elaine Kagan, "The place was packed and they had speakers set up in the parking lot for the overflow."

Most shed tears as they spoke, but also provoked laughs with stories of Cassavetes and his eccentricities.

Cassel told the story about the time he and Cassavetes were accosted by a very nervous mugger with a gun who asked them for their money. After a brief back-and-forth in which Cassavetes refused to surrender his cash, Cassavetes turned things around on the would-be robber: "How about if I give you a job?" he said. "I'll give you a job. You'll work on a film and get paid for it." And he did.

"And I think he went on in the business," Cassel added.

Falk recalled a Lakers game at which Cassavetes got into an argument with the guy sitting next to him. Pushed to his limit, the stranger looked at Cassavetes and said, "Fuck you!"

Cassavetes dared him, "Stand up and say that." So the stranger rose to his full height—a solid 6-foot-3. Cassavetes gave him the once-over and said, "Now sit down and say that."

Ted Allan talked about an evening, while working on *Love Streams*, when he and Cassavetes decided to write each other's obituaries.

"I'll say you were the greatest playwright who ever lived," Cassavetes offered.

"Better than Shakespeare?" Allan asked.

"Yeah."

"How about Tennessee Williams?"

"OK, the greatest living playwright," Cassavetes amended.

"John—greater than Harold Pinter?"

"Oh, yeah."

"Greater than Arthur Miller?"

"Of course."

"Well," Allan said, "what does that make you? Because you change 50 percent of everything I write."

"I guess," Cassavetes said with a smile that was as much sheep as wolf, "that makes me greater than you."

"I was a zombie there for a couple of years," Rowlands said of her reaction to Cassavetes' death. "I don't even remember them very well. I was just sort of slugging. Doctors are always saying, 'Now you must prepare yourself.' Yeah, how do you do that? Is there a school where you can go to learn to prepare yourself?"

Rowlands remembered a conversation with Cassavetes on a day when the pain was bad and the end seemed more possible.

"Well, I made three pictures I would live or die for," he allowed, sounding at peace with the idea.

Rowlands said later, "Now wouldn't you think that I would say, 'Which pictures were those, John?' But I felt I knew. Now I don't know and I can't say for certain, because I don't want to speak for John."

Rowlands remains an acting icon, still the first lady of independent film. She has acted in almost three dozen films since Cassavetes' death, working for directors as diverse as Jim Jarmusch, Terence Davies, Lasse Hallstrom, and Mira Nair, as well as acting in three films directed by her son, Nick.

"All kinds of actors now owe more to Gena than anyone else in terms of timing," said Michael Ventura. "It was the jazz equivalent of Lester Young. Off the beat, behind the beat. People like Jennifer Jason Leigh. Before Gena, there were no actors like that."

All three Cassavetes offspring have gone into the film industry as well. Nick started as an actor and writer, then became a director of such films as

The Notebook, *Unhook the Stars* (which he wrote), and *John Q.*, as well as his father's script *She's So Lovely*. John had left the script to Nick when he died, and Nick had optioned it to Sean Penn, who couldn't put a production together. When Nick got the rights back, he decided to make it himself and offered the role to Penn.

Since it had been written almost a decade earlier, Nick rewrote parts of it: "I have to admit that sometimes John wrote things that I didn't understand," Nick said. "But he understood them. Since the job of any filmmaker is to understand your material, I made the sorts of minor adjustments any director would make on a script.

"I remember one day on the set I was sitting there and things were going well and we were on schedule and the performances were great. The notion came to me, Gosh, this is going to be my favorite film I ever do. Here it is. I'm in it. I'm experiencing it. My mother's in the film, along with three wonderful actors and a script of my dad's. It doesn't get a whole lot better than that."

Zoe has been a music video director and music producer. Xan, too, has become a director, creating the well-reviewed documentary *Z Channel: A Magnificent Obsession* and making preparations for her first feature.

None of which surprises Rowlands, except perhaps son Nick's move into directing.

"Nick and John were very close and had written a couple of scripts together while John was ill," she recalled. "And that gave Nick a chance to talk about a lot of things with John. Since writing came so naturally to Nick, I was a little surprised when he decided he wanted to direct."

The Cassavetes legacy continues. An award named for John Cassavetes has been given annually since 2002 by the Independent Film Project at its annual IFP Independent Spirit Awards, presented to the best film of the year made for less than $500,000.

The Cassavetes films go on as well: "After John died, Gena said, 'What do you want to do with the pictures?'" Al Ruban said. "I said, 'Here's what I think. They should go on and let people see them.' And that was really the beginning."

In 1990 the Walker Art Center in Minneapolis organized a retrospective that toured to more than a dozen cities over thirteen months, with new prints of the films struck for the exhibition. Cassavetes' retrospectives have been organized at film festivals around the world in the intervening years.

In 2004 the Criterion Collection released *Five Films by John Cassavetes*, a boxed set that includes *Shadows*, *Faces*, *A Woman Under the Influence*, *The*

Killing of a Chinese Bookie, and *Opening Night.* It included both the long and short version of *Chinese Bookie,* as well as several audio interviews with Cassavetes and the documentary *A Constant Forge.*

Within a month after Cassavetes' death, Rowlands received a letter from George Cuttingham, the president of the American Academy of Dramatic Arts in New York, expressing condolences and enclosing an anonymous poem, hand-written, that had been taped to the portrait of John in the framed picture of Cassavetes' AADA class:

> "I drank a toast
> To John today, I
> Heard that he had died.
> I raised my glass and shed
> A tear, there are
> Reasons why I cried.
>
> For John, my friends,
> Was one of us,
> A rogue, a vagabond,
> We shared a common bond.
>
> You did good work, John.
> You did good work.
> That's all I've got to say.

The American Academy of Dramatic Arts mourns the passing of John Cassavetes, grad of 49–50."

Looking back while talking about *Tempest,* a film about an artist taking stock of his life, Cassavetes told a reporter, "If I had my artistic life to do over again, I don't think that I would be as lucky as I have been. Certainly, I can look upon my life as not being wasted. People say to me, 'You're an iconoclastic kind of guy who just does this kind of thing. You're a maverick, an angry young man.' I'm not a young man, number one. I'm not angry at anyone, number two.

"And I'm not a maverick. I just like to make movies."

Filmography

Shadows (1959)

CAST: Ben Carruthers, Lelia Goldoni, Hugh Hurd, Anthony Ray, Dennis Sallas, Tom Allen, David Pokitillow, Rupert Crosse, Davey Jones, Pir Marini, Victoria Vargas, Jack Ackerman, Jacqueline Walcott, Cliff Carnell, Jay Crecco, Ronald Maccone, Bob Reeh, Joyce Miles, Nancy Deale, Gigi Brooks, Lynn Hamelton, Marilyn Clark, Joanne Sages, Jed McGarvey, Greta Thysen.

Directed by John Cassavetes. Produced by Maurice McEndree. Associate producer: Seymour Cassel. Presented by Jean Shepherd's Night People. Lighting: David Simon. Assistant to lighting: Cliff Carnell. Sound: Jay Crecco. Supervising film editor: Len Appelson. Editor: Maurice McEndree. Cameraman: Erich Kollmar. Assistant to camera: Al Ruban. Sets by Randy Liles, Bob Reeh. Assistant director: Al Giglio. Production manager: Wray Bevins. Production staff: Maxine Arnolds, Ellen Paulos, Anne Draper, Leslie Reed, Mary Anne Ehle, Judy Kaufman. Saxophone solos: Shafi Hadi. Additional music: Charles Mingus.

Too Late Blues (1961)

CAST: John "Ghost" Wakefield: Bobby Darin. Jess Polanski: Stella Stevens. Benny Flowers: Everett Chambers. Nick: Nick Dennis. Tommy: Vince Edwards. Frielobe: Val Avery. Countess: Marilyn Clark. Reno: James Joyce. Baby Jackson: Rupert Crosse. Charlie: Cliff Carnell. Pete: Richard Chambers. Red: Seymour Cassel. Shelley: Dan Stafford.

Produced and directed by John Cassavetes. Written by John Cassavetes and Richard Carr. Director of photography: Lionel Lindon. Art direction: Hal Pereira, Tambi Larsen. Editor: Frank Bracht. Special photographic effects: John P. Fulton. Set decoration: Sam Comer, James Payne. Assistant director: Arthur Jacobson. Costumes: Edith Head. Makeup supervision: Wally Westmore. Hair style supervision: Nellie Manley. Sound recording: Gene Merrit, John Wilkinson. Music by David Raksin.

A Child Is Waiting (1962)

CAST: Dr. Matthew Clark: Burt Lancaster. Jean Hansen: Judy Garland. Sophie Widdicombe Benham: Gena Rowlands. Ted Widdicombe: Steven Hill. Reuben Widdicombe: Bruce Ritchey. Douglas Benham: Lawrence Tierney. Goodman: Paul Stewart. Holland: John Marley. Miss Fogarty: Elizabeth Wilson.

Directed by John Cassavetes. Produced by Stanley Kramer. Written by Abby Mann. Associate producer: Phillip Langner. Production design: Rudolph Sternad. Director of photography: Joseph La Shelle. Film editors: Gene Fowler Jr., Robert C. Jones. Assistant directors: Douglas Green, Lindsley Parsons Jr. Camera operator: Charles Wheeler. Production manager: Nate Edwards. Sound engineer: James Speak. Sound editor: Walter Elliott. Set decoration: Joseph Kish. Music editor: Art Dunham. Company grip: Morris Rosen. Script supervisor: Marshall Schlom. Property master: Jack Kirston. Costumer: Joe King. Assistant company grip: Sam van Zenten. Hair stylist: Al Paul. Makeup: George Lane. Chief gaffer: Don L. Carstensen. Miss Garland's wardrobe: Howard Shoup. Music: Ernest Gold.

Faces (1968)

CAST: Richard Forst: John Marley. Jeannie Rapp: Gena Rowlands. Maria Forst: Lynn Carlin. Freddie: Fred Draper. Chet: Seymour Cassel. Jim McCarthy: Val Avery. Florence: Dorothy Gulliver. And: Joanne Moore Jordan, Darlene Conley, Gene Darfler, Elizabeth Deering, Anne Shirley, Anita White, Edwin Sirianni, George Dunne, David Rowlands, Jim Bridges, Don Kraatz, John Hale, Midge Ware, Dave Mazzie, Julie Gambol, Liz Satriano, Jerry Howard, Carolyn Fleming, Kay Michaels, Laurie Mock, Christina Crawford, George Sims.

Written and directed by John Cassavetes. Producer: Maurice McEndree. Associate producer: Al Ruban. Director of photography: Al Ruban. Camera operator: George Sims. Sound: Don Pike. Editors: Al Ruban, Maurice McEndree. Stage manager, gaffer, and key grip: Charles Akins. Production manager: James Joyce. Assistant to the producer: Carolyn Fleming. Script supervisor: Pat Smith. First assistant director: George O'Halloran. Assistant directors: John Nastu, James Victor, Jerry Howard. Dialogue director: Bud Cherry. Art director: Phedon Papamichael. Set decorations: Phedon Papamichael. Production secretaries: Liz Satriana, Bianca Chambers, Pat Buckley. Pre-production: Dick Balduzzi. Post-production: James Auker, Jack Woods. Musical director: Jack Ackerman. Assistant to musical director: Richard Grand. Miss Carlin's hair: Harold Chaleff.

Husbands (1970)

CAST: Archie: Peter Falk. Harry: Ben Gazzara. Gus: John Cassavetes. Mary Tynan: Jenny Runacre. Pearl Billingham: Jenny Lee Wright. Julie: Noelle Kao. Annie: Meta Shaw. Leola: Leola Harlow. The Countess: Delores Delmar. Mrs. Hines: Eleanor Zee. Stuart Jackson: David Rowlands. Grandmother: Judith Lowry. Red: John Red Kullers.

Written and directed by John Cassavetes. Produced by Al Ruban and Sam Shaw. Cinematography: Victor Kemper. Editors: Tom Cornwell, Peter Tanner, Jack Woods. Art direction: Rene D'Auriac. Costume design: Lewis Brown. Makeup: Robert Laden, Tommie Manderson. Assistant directors: Edward Folger, Alan Hopkins, Simon Hinkly. Camera operator: Michael Chapman. Gaffer: Len Crowe. Musical director: Stanley Wilson.

Minnie and Moskowitz (1971)

CAST: Minnie Moore: Gena Rowlands. Seymour Moskowitz: Seymour Cassel. Zelmo Swift: Val Avery. Morgan Morgan: Tim Carey. Sheba Moskowitz: Katherine Cassavetes. Girl: Elizabeth Deering. Florence: Elsie Ames. Georgia Moore: Lady Rowlands. Irish: Holly Near. Wife: Judith Roberts. Dick Henderson: Jack Danskin. Mrs. Grass: Eleanor Zee. Ned: Sean Joyce. Minister: David Rowlands. Jim: John Cassavetes (uncredited).

Written and directed by John Cassavetes. Produced by Al Ruban. Associate producer: Paul Donnelly. Assistant directors: Kevin Donnelly, Lou Stroller. Cinematography: Michael Margulies. Editing: Fred Knudtson. Sound: M. M. Metcalfe. Senior Script supervisor: Dalonne Jackson. Prop master: Victor Petrotta Sr. Costume designer: Helen Colvig. Musical supervisor: Bo Harwood. Camera operators: Thomas O. Laughridge, Don Thorin, Lou Barlia. Gaffers: Norman Neil Cassaday, Vince DeLaney. First assistant cameramen: Charles J. Correll, Lou Farkas. Costumer: Jules M. Melillo. Assistants to producer: James Joyce, Elaine Goren.

A Woman Under the Influence (1974)

CAST: Mabel Longhetti: Gena Rowlands. Nick Longhetti: Peter Falk. George Mortenson: Fred Draper. Martha Mortenson: Lady Rowlands. Mama Longhetti: Katherine Cassavetes. Angelo Longhetti: Matthew Laborteaux. Tony Longhetti: Matthew Cassel. Maria Longhetti. Christina Grisanti. Garson Cross: O. G. Dunn. Dr. Zepp: Eddie Shaw. Eddie: Charles Horvath. Vito Grimaldi: Angelo Grisanti. Bowman: James Joyce. Clancy: John Finnegan. Gino: Vince Barbi. Aldo: Cliff Carnell. Adolph: Frank Richards. Willie Johnson: Hugh Hurd. Billy Tidrow: Leon Wagner. Dominique Jensen: Dominique Davalos. Adrienne Jensen: Xan Cassavetes. John Jensen: Pancho Meisenheimer. Aldo: Sonny Aprile. Nancy: Ellen Davalos. Angela: Elizabeth Deering. Tina: Jackie Peters. Principal: Elsie Ames. Adolph: N. J. Cassavetes.

Written and directed by John Cassavetes. Produced by Sam Shaw. In charge of lighting: Mitchell Breit. Lighting crew: Chris Taylor, Bo Taylor, Merv Dayan. Gaffer: David Lester. Camera operators: Mike Ferris, David Nowell. Additional camera: Gary Graver. Additional photography: Caleb Deschanel. Camera assistants: Tony Palmieri, Fred Elmes, Leslie Otis, Larry Silver. Key grip: Cliff Carnell. Supervising editor: Tom Cornwell. Editors: David Armstrong, Sheila Viseltear, Beth Bergeron. In charge of post-production: Robert Heffernan. Music: Bo Harwood. Sound: Bo Harwood. Boom: Nick Spalding. Mix: Henry Michael Denecke. First assistant director: Jack Corrick. Second assistant director: Roger Slager. Art director: Phedon Papamichael. Production secretary/wardrobe: Carole Smith. Script continuity: Elaine Goren. Props: Kevin Joyce. Graphics: Steve Hitter.

The Killing of a Chinese Bookie (1976)

CAST: Cosmo Vittelli: Ben Gazzara. Flo: Timothy Carey. Mort Weil: Seymour Cassel. Phil: Robert Phillips. The Boss (John): Morgan Woodward. The Accountant: John Red Kullers. Marty Reitz: Al Ruban. Rachel: Azizi Johari. Mama: Virginia Carrington. Mr. Sophistication: Meade Roberts. Sherry: Alice Friedland. Margo Donner: Donna Marie Gordon. The Entertainers: Haji, Carol Warren, Derna Wong Davis, Kathalina Veniero, Yvette Morris, Jack Ackerman. And: David Rowlands, Trisha Pelham, Eddie Ike

Shaw; Salvatore Aprile, Gene Darcy, Benny Marino, Arlene Allison, Vince Barbi, Val Avery, Elizabeth Deering, Soto Joe Hugh, Catherine Wong, John Finnegan, Miles Ciletti, Mike Skloot, Frank Buchanan, Jason Kincaid, Frank Thomas, Jack Krupnick.

Written and directed by John Cassavetes. Producer: Al Ruban. Associate producer: Phil Burton. Production manager: Art Levinson. Camera operators: Fred Elmes, Michael Ferris. In charge of lighting: Mitchell Breit. Lighting crew: Donald Robinson, Chris Taylor, Bruce Knee. Cinemobile operator: Steve Brooks. Camera assistants: Mike Stringer, Catherine Coulson, M. Todd Henry, Robert Hahn. Sound/music: Bo Harwood. Sound mixer: Buzz Knudson. Music conductor/arranger: Anthony Harris. Supervising editor: Tom Cornwell. Assistant editors: Terri Messina, Fran Morgenstern, Neal Meisenheimer. Art director: Phedon Papamichael. Production design: Sam Shaw. Graphics/stills: Richard Upper. In charge of post-production: Robert Heffernan. Post-production consultant: Jack Woods. Production secretary: Teresa Stokovic. Second assistant director: Nate Haggard. Script supervisor: Sandra King. Director's secretary: Lanie Heffernan. Assistant art director: Bryan Ryman. Wardrobe: Mary Herne. Props: Miles Ciletti. Set construction: Verna Bagby, Robert Vehon, Bruce Hartman.

Opening Night (1977)

CAST: Myrtle Gordon: Gena Rowlands. Maurice Aarons: John Cassavetes. Manny Victor: Ben Gazzara. Sarah Goode: Joan Blondell. David Samuels: Paul Stewart. Dorothy Victor: Zohra Lampert. Nancy Stein: Laura Johnson. Gus Simmons: John Tuell. Jimmy: Ray Powers. Prop man: John Finnegan. Kelly: Louise Fitch. Leo: Fred Draper. Vivian: Katherine Cassavetes. Melva Drake: Lady Rowlands. Carla: Carol Warren: Lena: Briana Carver. Charlie Spikes: Angelo Grisanti. Eddie Stein: Meade Roberts. Sylvia Stein: Eleanor Zee. Doorman: David Rowlands.

Written and directed by John Cassavetes. Produced by Al Ruban. Executive producer: Sam Shaw. Editor: Tom Cornwell. Assistant editors: Kent Beyda, Nancy Golden, Hal Bowers. Sound editor: Joe G. Woo, Jr. Director of photography: Al Ruban. Camera operators: Frederick Elmes, Michael Ferris. Camera assistants: Catherine Coulson, Jed Skillman. Gaffers: Donne Daniels, Joseph L. Rezwin, Donald Robinson, Richard Ross. Graphics/still photographer: Richard Upper. Sound: Bo Harwood. Boom operator: Crew Chamberlin. Sound assistant: Joanne T. Harwood. Sound mixer: Bill Varney. Art director: Brian Ryman. Composed music: Bo Harwood. Arranged/conducted: Booker T. Jones. Musical consultant:

Lee Housekeeper. Associate producer: Michael Lally. Production managers: Foster H. Phinney, Ed Ledding. Second assistant director: Lisa Hallas. Production co-ordinator: Teresa Stokovic. Chief set construction: Verna Bagby. Assistant set construction: Abraham Zwick. Props: Robert Vehon. Costumes: Alexandra Corwin-Hankin. Wardrobe masters: Miles Ciletti. Charles Akins. Location supervisor: Jack Krupnick. Script supervisors: Joanne T. Harwood, Tom Cornwell. Stunt drivers: Victor Paul, Charles Picerni. Stunt double: Donna Garrett. Post production: Kathleen Barker. Assistant to the producer: Sharon van Ivan. Production assistants: Carol Roux, Robert Bogdanoff, Raymond Vellucci. Secretaries: Arlene Harris, Michelle Hart. Accounting: Susan Howell.

Gloria (1980)

CAST: Gloria Swanson: Gena Rowlands. Phil: John Adames. Jeri Dawn: Julie Carmen. Jack Dawn: Buck Henry. First man/gangster: Tony Knesich. Second man/gangster: Tom Noonan. Third man/gangster: Ronald Maccone. Heavyset man: George Yudzevich. Kid in elevator: Gregory Cleghorne. Margarita Vargas: Lupe Garnica. Joan Dawn: Jessica Castillo. Irish cop: Gary Klar. TV newscaster: William E. Rice. Riverside Drive men: Frank Belgiorno, J. C. Quinn, Alex Stevens, Sonny Landham, Harry Madsen. Car flip cabbie: Shanton Granger. Bank teller: John Pavelko. Assistant bank manager: Raymond Baker. Ron/vault: Ross Charap. Clerk/Adams Hotel: Irvin Graham. Uncle Joe: Michael Proscia. Desk clerk/Star Hotel: T. S. Rosenbaum. N.Y. cemetery cabbie: Santos Morales. Hostess: Meta Shaw. Waitress: Marilyn Putnam. Frank: John Finnegan. Mister: Gaetano Lisi. Penn Station hoods: Richard M. Kaye, Steve Lefkowitz, George Poidomani. Broadway bartender: Lawrence Tierney. Sill: Val Avery. Tony Tanzini: Basilio Franchina.

Written and directed by John Cassavetes. Produced by Sam Shaw. Editor: George C. Villasenor. Music: Bill Conti. Casting: Vic Ramos. Ms. Rowlands' clothes: Emanuel Ungaro. Costume designer: Peggy Farrell. Art director: Rene D'Auriac. Director of photography: Fred Schuler. Production manager/associate producer: Steve Kesten. First assistant director: Mike Haley. Second assistant director: Tom Fritz. Assistant editor: Lori Bloustein. Music editor: Clifford C. Kohlweck. Camera operator: Lou Barlia. First assistant cameraman: Sandy Brooke. Second assistant cameraman: Ricki-Ellen Brooke. Sound mixers: Dennis Maitland Sr., Jack S. Jacobsen. Rerecording mixers: Wayne Artman, Tom Beckert, Michael Jiron. Boom: Tod Maitland. Sound recordists: Danny Rosenblum, James Perdue. Script supervisor: Nancy Hopton. Property master: Wally Stocklin. Special effects:

Connie Brink, Al Griswald, Ron Ottesen. Set decorator: John Godfrey. Wardrobe: Marilyn Putnam. Hairstylist: Verne Caruso. Makeup: Vince Callahan. Second unit director: Gaetano Lisi. Location managers: Tom Lisi, Jim Foote. Still photographers: Jessica Burstein, Adger Cowan. Production assistants: Harvey Portee, Chip Cronkite, Liz Gazzara, Jed Weaver, Mark Sitley, John Thomas. Production office coordinator: Eileen Eichenstein. Assistants to producer: Larry Shaw, Robert Fieldsteel. Assistant to the director: Kate Barker. Aerial photography: Peter Gabarini. Dialogue coach: Richard Kaye. Title design: Sam Shaw. Title paintings: Romare Bearden.

Love Streams (1984)

CAST: Sarah Lawson: Gena Rowlands. Robert Harmon: John Cassavetes. Susan: Diahnne Abbott. Jack Lawson: Seymour Cassel. Margarita: Margaret Abbott. Albie Swanson: Jakob Shaw. Agnes Swanson: Michele Conway. Stepfather: Eddy Donno. Judge Dunbar: Joan Foley. Milton Kravitz: Al Ruban. Sam the lawyer: Tom Badal. Debbie Lawson: Risa Martha Blewitt. Psychiatrist: David Rowlands. Dr. Williams: Robert Fieldsteel. Ken: John Roselius. Taxi driver (animals): John Finnegan. Mrs. Kiner: Doe Avedon. Back-up singer: Alexandra Cassavetes. Charlene: Julie Allan.

Directed by John Cassavetes. Written by John Cassavetes and Ted Allan. Based on a play by Ted Allan. Produced by Menahem Golan and Yoram Globus. Executive producer: Al Ruban. Consultant: Sam Shaw. Director of photography: Al Ruban. First assistant camera: Sam Gart, Ronny Dana. Second assistant camera: Michael Pinegar, Diane Schneier. Second camera operator: George Sims. Steadicam operators: Alan Caso, Stephen St. John. First assistant directors: Randy Carter, Frank Beetson. Second assistant director: Michael Lally. Dialogue coach: Robert Fieldsteel. Production office supervisor: Carole Smith. Unit production managers: Al Ruban, Chris Pearce. Art director: Phedon Papamichael. Music: Bo Harwood. Editor: George C. Villasenor. Assistant editor: Dan Sackheim. Apprentice editor: Elizabeth Gazzara. Supervising sound editor: Leslie Troy Gauylin. Sound effects editor: Effi Reuven. Assistant sound effects: Michael Pappas. Production sound mixers: Bo Harwood, Richard Lightstone, Mike Denecke. Boom men: Ken Brocious, Kevin Patterson. Dialogue editor: Dessie Markovsky. Costume designer: Jennifer Smith-Ashley. Prop master: Tommy Estridge. Stunt coordinator: Eddy Donno. Stunts: Mike Washlake. Script supervisor: Helen Caldwell. Post-production supervisor: Karen Hoenig. Makeup: Michael Stein. Hairdresser: DeAnn Power. Wardrobe: Lydia Manderson, Emily Draper. Assistant set decorators: Edward Call, Eva

Giera. Production assistants: Charlie Ruban, Darrell Ruban, Matt Cassel, Laurie Cohen. Post-production assistant: Nick Cassavetes.

Big Trouble (1986)

CAST: Steve Rickey: Peter Falk. Leonard Hoffman: Alan Arkin. Blanche Rickey: Beverly D'Angelo. O'Mara: Charles Durning. Noozel: Paul Dooley. Winslow: Robert Stack. Arlene Hoffman: Valerie Curtin. Dr. Lopez: Richard Libertini. Peter Hoffman: Steve Alterman. Michael Hoffman: Jerry Pavlon. Joshua Hoffman: Paul La Greca. Det. Murphy: John Finnegan. Police captain: Karl Lukas. Gail: Maryedith Burrell. Doris: Edith Fields. Chief terrorist: Jaime Sanchez. Gaetano Lopez: Gaetano Lisi.

Directed by John Cassavetes. Written by Warren Bogle. Music: Bill Conti. Costume designer: Joe I. Tompkins. Editors: Donn Cambern, Ralph Winters. Production designer: Gene Callahan. Director of photography: Bill Butler. Unit production manager: Howard Pine. First assistant director: Duncan Henderson. Second assistant director: Chris Ryan. Camera operator: Jim Connell. First assistant cameraman: John Walker. Second assistant cameraman: Walt Fraser. Set decorator: Lee Poll. Script supervisor: Julie Pitkanen. Production sound mixer: Martin Bolger. Boom man: Dennis Jones. Assistant editors: William Meshover, Kevin Stitt. Apprentice editor: Robert Hyams. Supervising sound editor: Tom McCarthy Jr. Sound editors: Gordon Davidson, Jerry Rosenthal, David Spence. ADR editor: Jay Engel. Assistant ADR editor: Maria Stinnett-Busby. Art director: Peter Smith. Set designer: Joseph Hubbard. Prop master: Sammy Gordon. Men's costumer: Bruce Ericksen. Women's costumer: Pam Wise. Hair stylist: Cheri Ruff. Makeup artist: Monty Westmore. Stunt coordinator: Gray Johnson. Chief lighting technician: John Brumshagen. Key grip: George Hill. Production coordinator: Jeannie Jeha. Construction coordinator: Mike Muscarella. Assistant to the producer: Elyse A. Mayberry. Assistant to the director: Helen Caldwell. Title design: Sam Shaw. Production assistants: Michael Myers, Greg Long.

Notes

Introduction

(p. ix) "It's not so important . . .": "John Cassavetes: I Really Like What I Do," by Nicholas Pasquariello; *Weekly Californian*, 4/18–25/75.

(p. ix–x) "Independent film is film . . .": "A Conversation with Seymour Cassel," by Michael Lee; indieWire.com, 8/4/97.

(p. x) Guy McElwaine quote: From author interview.

Chapter 1

(p. 3) Mark Rydell story: From author interview.

(p. 4) Stuart Poller story: From author interview.

(p. 5) Burton Lane story: Burton Lane interviewed by Jack Mathews, 2/02.

(p. 5) "I'm a New York street kid . . .": "A Talk with John Cassavetes," by Russell AuWerter; *Action*, Jan./Feb. 1970.

Chapter 2

(p. 9) "He studied at . . .": *The Night Holds Terror* studio biography; Columbia Pictures, 1955.

(p. 9) "John Cassavetes has been preparing . . .": "Cassavetes Prepared Long for Break," by Jack O'Brian; *New York Journal American*, 11/9/55.

(p. 10) "The field of fiction . . .": *Crime in the Streets* studio biography; Allied Artists, 1956.

(p. 10) "An olive-skinned black-haired man . . .": "John Cassavetes, Delinquent," by Don Ross; *New York Herald Tribune*, 1/20/57.

(p. 10) "chose to become an actor . . .": *Virgin Island* studio biography; British Lion Film, 1958.

(p. 10) "He majored in English . . .": "Cassavetes: Why Do Marriages Go Sour?" by Patricia Bosworth; *New York Times*, 12/1/68.

(p. 10) "Mr. Cassavetes majored in English . . .": "John Cassavetes, Major Director in U.S. Cinema Verité, Dies at 59," by Albin Krebs; *New York Times*, 2/4/89.

(pp. 11–14) Nicholas Cassavetes story, including quote "Every time he'd run into money difficulties . . .": "The Playboy Interview: John Cassavetes," by Lawrence Linderman; *Playboy*, 7/71.

(p. 12) "In the middle of his schooling . . .": "Take It from Gena—It's a Man's World," by Hedda Hopper; *Los Angeles Times*, 9/23/62.

(p. 13) Elaine Kagan quotes: From author interview.

(p. 13) Seymour Cassel quotes: From author interview.

(p. 13) "John's father was . . .": "Michael Ferris Shooting *Faces* for Cassavetes," by Mike Plante; *Cinemad*, no. 6.

(p.13) "I'm told that at school . . .": "An Interview with John Cassavetes," by Michel Ciment and Michael Henry; *Positif*, no. 180, 4/76.

(p. 13) "My brother and I . . .": "This TV Deception Draws No Gripes," by Roland Lindbloom; *Newark Evening News*, 11/8/59.

(p. 14) "I used to size up . . .": "Cassavetes' Personal Rebellion," by Dan Knapp; *Los Angeles Times*, 11/9/69.

(p. 14) "We never knew . . .": "John Cassavetes Gets His Reward," by Dolores Barclay; Associated Press, 7/8/80.

(p. 14) "At one point during the Depression . . .": *Cassavetes on Cassavetes*, edited by Ray Carney; Faber and Faber, 2001.

(p. 14) "I have had every . . .": "John Cassavetes, Delinquent," by Don Ross; *New York Herald Tribune*, 1/20/57.

(p. 14) "my childhood idol, the guy most . . .": "The Playboy Interview: John Cassavetes," by Lawrence Linderman; *Playboy*, 7/71.

(p. 15) "One of my favorite movies . . .": "John Cassavetes: Film's Bad Boy," by James Stevenson; *Film Comment*, 1–2/1980.

(p. 15) "my family was a wild . . .": "The New Hollywood Is the Old Hollywood," *Time*, 12/7/70.

(p. 15) "I was a totally uninterested . . .": "The Playboy Interview: John Cassavetes," by Lawrence Linderman; *Playboy*, 7/71.

(p. 15) "'Cassy' is always . . .": 1947 Port Washington High School yearbook.

(p. 15) "When I was fourteen years old, . . .": "The Playboy Interview: John Cassavetes," by Lawrence Linderman; *Playboy*, 7/71.

(p. 16) "It was important to my family . . .": "The Playboy Interview: John Cassavetes," by Lawrence Linderman; *Playboy*, 7/71.

(p. 16) Quotes from Carl Goldberg, Stuart Poller, and Nick Petras: From author interviews.

(p. 17) "At college all we did . . .": From "Husbands," an unpublished novel by John Cassavetes; used by permission.

Chapter 3

(p. 19) "At least it's something . . .": "The Playboy Interview: John Cassavetes," by Lawrence Linderman; *Playboy*, 7/71.

(p. 19) "I went to the Academy to escape . . .": From John Cassavetes/Gena Rowlands appearance at AADA, April 1970.

(p. 19) "Up until then, all I'd ever . . .": "The Playboy Interview: John Cassavetes," by Lawrence Linderman; *Playboy*, 7/71.

(p. 20) "I loved it because . . .": "The Playboy Interview: John Cassavetes," by Lawrence Linderman; *Playboy*, 7/71.

(p. 20) Harry Mastrogeorge quotes and anecdotes: From author interview.

(p. 20) "They told me they couldn't . . .": "Tintypes: John Cassavetes," by Sidney Skolsky; *New York Post*, 7/29/67.

(p. 21) Erich Kollmar quotes: From author interview.

(p. 22) "He was the greatest . . .": From John Cassavetes/Gena Rowlands appearance at AADA, April 1970.

(p. 22) Renee Taylor quote: From author interview.

(p. 22) "If you must sneeze . . .": "Wisdom for Budding Actors," by Ed Wallace; *New York World-Telegram and Sun* feature magazine section, 2/18/61.

(p. 22) Jehlinger aphorisms, from "Charles Jehlinger in Rehearsal," as transcribed by Eleanor Cody Gould; reprinted 1958 by AADA.

(p. 24) "Screw you . . .": Burton Lane interviewed by Jack Mathews, 2/02.

Chapter 4

(p. 25) "I spotted this doll . . .": "Cassavetes in New York," by Frank Quinn; *New York Mirror*, 3/16/58.

(p. 25) "That's the girl . . .": "The Playboy Interview: John Cassavetes," by Lawrence Linderman; *Playboy*, 7/71.

(p. 25) "I was a woman with a plan . . .": *John Cassavetes: To Risk Everything to Express It All*; Kultur Films, Inc., 1994.

(p. 26) "I brushed him off . . .": "Cassavetes Prepared Long for Break," by Jack O'Brian; *New York Journal American*, 11/9/55.

(p. 26) "My dad never forbade . . .": "A Woman Out from Under the Influence," by Sandra Shevey; *New Times*, 3/7/75.

(pp. 26–27) "My mother is an artist . . .": "Gena Rowlands: Portrait of a Happy Actress," by Marni Butterfield; *Show*, 2/71.

(p. 27) "I was brought up . . .": "John/Gena/Peter Interview," by Dick Adler; *Viva*, 12/74.

(p. 27) "Everything I know . . .": "Gena Rowlands, the Reluctant Superstar," by Robert Osborne; *Flightime*, 11/76.

(p. 27) "I did a little in drama . . .": "Gena Rowlands Makes Film Debut in Comedy," by Hedda Hopper; *Los Angeles Times*, 12/1/57

(p. 27) "So I quit college . . .": "Cassavetes Prepared Long for Break," by Jack O'Brian; *New York Journal American*, 11/9/55.

(p. 27) "an understanding man" and "Dear, do anything . . .": "Broadway Love Story," by Jack Hamilton; *Look*, 6/11/57.

(p. 27) "Golden Age of Greece . . .": "Grande Dame," by Jack Matthews; *Newsday,* 11/3/96.

(p. 27) "I had no sense of humor . . .": From John Cassavetes/Gena Rowlands appearance at AADA, April 1974.

(p. 28) Erich Kollmar quote: From author's interview.

(p. 28) "It's funny . . .": "Film Scouts Interviews," by Henri Behar; www.film scouts.com, 10/30/96.

Chapter 5

(p. 30) Army reserve unit anecdote: From *John Cassavetes: Lifeworks,* by Tom Charity; Omnibus Press, 2001.

(p. 30) "I was a young guy . . .": "Marriage Drama Yields Performance of Decade," by David Sterritt; *Christian Science Monitor,* 3/25/75.

(p. 31) "Nobody would cast me . . .": "Cassavetes: Why Do Marriages Go Sour?" by Patricia Bosworth; *New York Times,* 12/1/68.

(pp. 31–32) Erich Kollmar quotes: From author interview.

(p. 32) "John hates subways . . .": "A Recollection of Cassavetes," by Meade Roberts; *Hollywood,* 12/90–1/91.

(p. 32) "I was young . . .": "Cassavetes: Show Me the Magic," by Michael Ventura; *L.A. Weekly,* 8/20–26/82.

(p. 32) Harry Mastrogeorge quotes and anecdotes: From author interview.

(p. 32) "I thought I was brilliant . . .": "The Playboy Interview: John Cassavetes," by Lawrence Linderman; *Playboy,* 7/71.

(p. 33) "with a bunch of guys": "No Torn Shirts for Him"; *TV Guide,* 10/10/57.

(p. 33) "Film was unknown . . .": From John Cassavetes/Gena Rowlands appearance at AADA, April 1970.

(pp. 33–34) "the really good writers were working fast . . .": "A Mr. and Mrs. on the Way Up!" by John Fink; *Chicago Daily Tribune TV Week,* 5/17/58.

(p. 34) "I couldn't even wind . . .": "Broadway Love Story," by Jack Hamilton; *Look,* 6/11/57.

(p. 34) "I don't sing at all . . .": "Gena Rowlands: Portrait of a Happy Actress," by Marni Butterfield; *Show,* 2/71

(p. 34) Max Wilk quotes, anecdotes: From author interview.

(p. 35) "Before TV was unionized . . .": From John Cassavetes/Gena Rowlands appearance at AADA, April 1974.

(p. 35) Paul Mazursky anecdote, quotes: From author interview.

(p. 35) "We would laugh . . .": From John Cassavetes/Gena Rowlands appearance at AADA, April 1974.

(p. 36) "The day that I am crazy": "His'n and Her'n," by Jesse Zunser; *Cue,* 6/7/58.

(p. 36) "After working with Ratoff . . .": "Cassavetes Prepared Long for Break," by Jack O'Brian; *New York Journal American,* 11/9/55.

(p. 36) "the Greek": "John Cassavetes Wants Wife to Star," by Frank Quinn; *Sunday Mirror,* 4/29/56.

(p. 36) "There was a fellow backstage . . .": From John Cassavetes/Gena Rowlands appearance at AADA, April 1970.

Chapter 6
(p. 37) "He came up to me and . . .": "An Evening at Columbia College"; Columbia College Press, Chicago, 3/5/75.

(p. 37) Quotes from Edie Shaw Marcus, Larry Shaw, Meta Shaw Stevens: From author interviews.

(p. 39) "You have to give Marilyn credit . . .": "Sam Shaw, 87, Film Producer and Photographer"; *New York Times*, 4/9/99.

(p. 40) Quotes from Al Ruban: From author interview.

(p. 40) "I know a great writer . . ." and the rest of the Edward McSorley anecdote: "An Evening at Columbia College"; Columbia College Press, Chicago, 3/5/75.

Chapter 7
(p. 42) Harry Mastrogeorge quotes and anecdotes: From author interview.

(p. 43) "If you can't have fun . . .": "People to be Seen on Video This Week," by J. P. Shanley; *New York Times*, 4/12/56.

(pp. 43–44) Budd Schulberg quotes: From author interview.

(p. 44) Daniel Petrie quotes: From author interview.

(p. 44) "And this is the way . . .": From John Cassavetes/Gena Rowlands appearance at AADA, April 1970.

(p. 44) "I didn't know what the hell . . .": "Competitive Cassavetes," by David Galligan; *Hollywood Dramalogue*, 10/7–13/82.

(p. 45) Kim Stanley quotes: "Competitive Cassavetes," by David Galligan; *Hollywood Dramalogue*, 10/7–13/82.

(pp. 45–46) Dialogue from "Paso Doble," by Budd Schulberg; *Omnibus*, NBC, 2/14/54.

(p. 46) "The day after the show . . .": "The Playboy Interview: John Cassavetes," by Lawrence Linderman; *Playboy*, 7/71.

(p. 46) "I suggested John Cassavetes . . .": "Take It from Gena—It's a Man's World," by Hedda Hopper; *Los Angeles Times*, 9/23/62.

(p. 46) Seymour Cassel quote: From author interview.

(p. 46) "If he gets Twentieth Fox's . . .": "Making Book on Cassavetes as Find of the Year"; *Variety*, 2/24/54.

(p. 47) "He decided the role . . .": MGM studio biography, 6/11/57.

Chapter 8
(p. 48) Joyce van Patten quotes: From author interview.

(p. 48) Everett Chambers quotes: From author interview.

(p. 49) "I did thirty-nine live shows . . .": "Cassavetes' Personal Rebellion," by Dan Knapp, *Los Angeles Times*, 11/9/69.

(p. 49) "He was getting famous . . .": Burton Lane interviewed by Jack Mathews, 2/02

(p. 49) Daniel Petrie quotes: From author interview.

(p. 49) John Finnegan quotes: From author interview.

(p. 49) "We feel we're very lucky . . .": "Cassavetes Prepared Long for Break," by Jack O'Brian; *New York Journal American*, 11/9/55.

(p. 49) "He's a firecracker . . .": "No Torn Shirts for Him"; *TV Guide*, 10/10/57.

(pp. 49–50) "John Cassavetes, one of the most important . . .": "Dostoyevsky Great on TV," by Jack O'Brian; *New York Journal American*, 8/10/56.

(p. 50) "He has that rare animal . . .": "John Cassavetes Wants Wife to Star," by Frank Quinn; *Sunday Mirror*, 4/29/56.

(p. 50) "Those who have seen him . . .": "No Torn Shirts for Him"; *TV Guide*, 10/10/57.

(p. 50) "I was playing . . . :" "How Three of Its Principals See New Hit Play, *Middle of the Night*," by Wayne Robinson; *Philadelphia Bulletin*, 1/29/56.

(p. 51) Martin Baum anecdote, quotes: From author interview.

(p. 52) Anne Jackson quotes: From author interview.

(pp. 52–53) "Gena Rowlands makes a . . .": "The City Around Us," by Henry Hewes; *Saturday Review*, 2/25/56.

(p. 53) "Gena Rowlands is especially . . .": "Theater: Edward G. Robinson Back on Broadway," by Brooks Atkinson; *New York Times*, 2/9/56.

(p. 53) "I'm not sure whether its chief . . .": "The Triumph of Edward G. Robinson," by Richard Watts Jr.; *New York Post*, 2/19/56.

Chapter 9

(p. 54) "John Cassavetes . . . turns out to be . . .": "John Cassavetes: Biography," Columbia Pictures, 1955.

(p. 54) "When you start out . . .": "John Cassavetes: A Change of Heart," by Bob Salmaggi; *New York Herald Tribune*, 8/2/59.

(p. 54) Peter Bogdanovich quote: From author interview.

(p. 56) Peter Bogdanovich quote: From author interview.

(p. 56) "May well cut . . .": *Time*, 8/1/55.

(p. 56) "while offering nothing . . .": Brog, *Variety*, 7/12/55.

(p. 56) "The slender . . .": *Newsweek*, 7/25/55.

(p. 57) "delivers the artistic shock . . .": *Newsweek*, 5/28/56.

(p. 57) "a fairly serious . . ."; "Marlon Sinatra"; *Time*, 5/28/56.

(p. 57) "plays the bitter . . .": By Paul V. Beckley; *New York Herald Tribune*, 5/24/56.

(p. 57) Budd Schulberg quote: From author interview.

(p. 57) "I've been looking . . .": "People to be Seen on Video This Week," by J. P. Shanley; *New York Times*, 1956.

(p. 57) "I'm not a torn-shirt . . ."; "John has set very high . . .": "No Torn Shirts for Him"; *TV Guide*, 10/10/57.

(p. 58) Martin Baum quotes, anecdotes: From author interview.

(p. 58) Sidney Poitier quotes: From author interview.

(p. 59) "John Cassavetes gives an . . .": By Dorothy Masters; *New York Daily News*, 1/30/57.

(p. 59) "Sense of personal . . .": By Archer Winsten; *New York Post*, 1/30/57.

(p. 60) "a worthy attempt . . .": By Brendan Gill, *New Yorker*, 2/9/57.

(p. 60) "There have been few . . .": By Bosley Crowther; *New York Times*, 2/3/57.

Chapter 10

(p. 62) David Susskind, Robert Alan Aurthur quotes: From "David Susskind's Open End," 11/11/58.

(p. 62) "Maybe I could get a couple of tons . . .": "His'n and Her'n," by Jesse Zunser; *Cue*, 6/7/58.

(p. 63) Burton Lane quotes: Burton Lane interviewed by Jack Mathews, 2/02.

(p. 63) "just didn't come off . . .": "Temperament Normal in Film Team," by Irene Thirer; *New York Daily News*, 10/26/57.

(p. 64) Richard Erdman quotes: From author interview.

(p. 64) "Nobody can kill . . .": "Cassavetes in New York," by Frank Quinn; *New York Mirror*, 3/16/58.

(p. 64) "One of the distinctions . . .": By Cook; *New York World-Telegram and Sun*, 3/20/58.

(p. 65) "excellent performance . . .": by Paul V. Beckley; *New York Herald Tribune*, 3/21/58.

(p. 65) "Cassavetes, who talks and looks . . .": *Newsweek*, 3/24/58.

(p. 65) "a Stanislavsky-type . . .": *Time*, 3/24/58.

(p. 65) "A happy go lucky pick . . .": *Variety*, 10/30/58.

(p. 65) "It had the added . . .": *I'd Hate Myself in the Morning*, by Ring Lardner Jr.; Nation Books, 2000.

(p. 65) Ruby Dee quotes: From author interview.

Chapter 11

(p. 67) "Cameras do not make film . . .": "Amateur Versus Professional," by Maya Deren; *Film Culture* no. 39, winter 1965.

(p. 67) "The underground film is . . .": *An Introduction to the American Underground Film*, by Sheldon Renan; E. P. Dutton, 1967.

(p. 67) "I'm a great believer . . .": "The Playboy Interview: John Cassavetes," by Lawrence Linderman; *Playboy*, 7/71.

(p. 69) "I was working all . . .": Documentary by Georg Alexander, WDR (German television), 1979.

(p. 71) "We spent thirty weekends . . .": "The Playboy Interview: John Cassavetes," by Lawrence Linderman; *Playboy*, 7/71.

(p. 71) Burton Lane quotes: Burton Lane interviewed by Jack Mathews, 2/02.

(p. 71) "the heroics of acting . . .": "Broadway Love Story," by Jack Hamilton; *Look,* 6/11/57.

(pp. 71–72) Meta Shaw Stevens quotes: From author interview.

(p. 72) Lelia Goldoni quotes: From author interviews.

Chapter 12

Seymour Cassel quotes and anecdotes: From author interviews, except:

(p. 75) "From the minute I started . . ."; "We talked for a while . . .": "Suddenly Seymour," by Kristine McKenna; *Los Angeles Times,* 11/8/92.

(p. 78) Erich Kollmar quotes and anecdotes: From author interview.

(pp. 78–79) "I dreamed up some . . .": "The Playboy Interview: John Cassavetes," by Lawrence Linderman; *Playboy,* 7/71.

(p. 79) "a feature-film project . . .": "Cooperative"; *New York Times,* 1/20/57.

(p. 80) "Jean Shepherd's people . . .": From author interview with Lelia Goldoni.

(p. 80) "We didn't know . . .": From John Cassavetes/Gena Rowlands appearance at AADA, April 1970.

Chapter 13

(p. 88) Martin Scorsese quote: From author interview.

Chapter 14

(p. 89) "I chose a basic . . .": "Shadows," by John Cassavetes; *London Weekend Review,* 10/14/60.

(p. 89) "The scenes were predicated . . .": "Masks and Faces," by David Austen; *Films and Filming,* 9/68.

(p. 90) "*Shadows* is the story . . .": From "*Shadows* synopsis," by John Cassavetes; 1957; used by permission.

(p. 90) "I gave them neighborhoods . . .": "Direct It: John Cassavetes," by Christopher Paul Denis; *Video Review,* 11/85.

(pp. 90–91) "First we improvised . . .": "Mr. John Cassavetes on the Actor and Improvisation"; *Times* of London, 8/11/60.

(p. 91) "The actor is expected . . .": "And the Pursuit of Happiness," by John Cassavetes (in a recorded interview); *Films and Filming,* 2/61.

(p. 91) "I didn't pick and choose . . .": "And the Pursuit of Happiness," by John Cassavetes (in a recorded interview); *Films and Filming,* 2/61.

(p. 91) Erich Kollmar quotes and anecdotes: From author interviews.

(pp. 91–92) "The cameraman had . . .": "And the Pursuit of Happiness," by John Cassavetes (in a recorded interview); *Films and Filming,* 2/61.

(p. 92) "actor John Cassavetes . . .": "Actor Shooting Off B'way Film," by William Peper; *New York World-Telegram Sun,* 2/10/57.

(pp. 92–93) Seymour Cassel quotes: From author interview.

(p. 93) "I think we made all . . .": "Direct It: John Cassavetes," by Christopher Paul Denis; *Video Review,* 11/85.

(p. 93) "Not having a script girl . . .": "Out of the Shadows"; *Newsweek*, 11/7/60.

(p. 93) "We filmed it with a 16mm . . .": "I Welcome the New Johnny Staccato," by David Nathan; *London Daily Herald*, 10/10/60.

(p. 93) "The sound department . . .": "Shadows," by John Cassavetes; *London Weekend Review*, 10/14/60.

(p. 94) "There seemed nothing else in . . .": "Zen and the Art of John Cassavetes," by Michael Ventura; *L.A. Weekly*, 9/21–27/84.

(p. 94) "I loved the relationship . . .": "And the Pursuit of Happiness," by John Cassavetes (in a recorded interview); *Films and Filming*, 2/61.

(p. 95) "We began shooting . . .": "A Way of Life; An Interview with John Cassavetes," by Andre S. Labarthe; *Evergreen Review*, 1/71.

(p. 95) "What a way to tell . . .": "Actor Directs No-Script Film," by Cecil Smith; *Los Angeles Times*, 1/31/60.

(p. 95) David Pokitillow anecdote: "American Film Institute Dialogue on Film: John Cassavetes and Peter Falk," 1/71.

Chapter 15

(p. 97) "The editing took two . . .": "John Cassavetes, New Boy Genius?" by Rick Du Brow; *Citizen News*.

(p. 99) Al Ruban quote: From author interview.

(p. 99) "One friend of mine patted . . . :" "The Playboy Interview: John Cassavetes," by Lawrence Linderman; *Playboy*, 7/71.

(p. 99) "He ran up . . .": Burton Lane interviewed by Jack Mathews, 2/02.

(p. 99) could not be shown commercially: "Actor Shooting Off B'way Film," by William Peper; *New York World-Telegram Sun*, 2/10/57; "A Most Independent Film," by Joe Hyams, *New York Herald Tribune*, 5/19/58.

(p. 100) "When we made *Shadows* . . .": "And the Pursuit of Happiness," by John Cassavetes (in a recorded interview); *Films and Filming*, 2/61.

(p. 100) "Nobody knows who . . .": "His'n and Her'n," by Jesse Zunser; *Cue*, 6/7/58.

(p. 100) Henry Jaglom quote: From author interview.

(p. 100) "Everyone left . . .": "Cineastes de Notre Temps," directed by Hubert Knapp and Andre S. Labarthe; from *Five Films by John Cassavetes*; Criterion Collection, 2004.

(p. 100) Jonas Mekas quotes: From author interview.

Chapter 16

(p. 102) "The motion picture . . .": "Morning for the Experimental Film," by Lewis Jacobs; *Film Culture*, no. 19, 1/59.

(p. 103) I wanted films that . . .": "An Interview with Amos Vogel": From *Cinema 16: Documents toward a History of the Film Society*, by Scott McDonald; Temple University Press, 2002.

(p. 103) Formation of Filmmakers Cooperative: "All Pockets Open," by Calvin Tomkins; *New Yorker*, 1/6/73.

(p. 104) "We know Cassavetes as an actor . . ."; "My opinion concerning . . .": "New York Letter: Toward a Spontaneous Cinema," by Jonas Mekas; *Sight and Sound*, summer/autumn 1959.

(p. 104) "The screening of John Cassavetes' *Shadows* . . .": "Movie Journal," by Jonas Mekas; *Village Voice*, 12/23/71.

(p. 104) ". . . to point out original . . .": "The Independent Film Award," *Film Culture*, no. 19, 1/59.

(pp. 104–105) "Cassavetes in *Shadows* . . .": "The Independent Film Award," *Film Culture*, no. 19, 1/59.

(p. 105) "Basically, they all: Mistrust . . ."; ". . . clearly point up a new spirit.": "A Call for a New Generation of Film Makers," by Jonas Mekas; *Film Culture*, no. 19, 1/59.

(p. 105) "To tell the truth, I don't know . . :" "A Way of Life; An Interview with John Cassavetes," by Andre S. Labarthe; *Evergreen Review*, 1/71.

(p. 106) "Hollywood is not failing . . .": "What's Wrong with Hollywood," by John Cassavetes; *Film Culture*, no. 19, 1/59.

(p. 106) "I think the old filmmakers . . .": "And the Pursuit of Happiness," by John Cassavetes (in a recorded interview); *Films and Filming*, 2/61.

(p. 106) Jonas Mekas quotes: From author interview.

(p. 107) "Like all failures . . .": "Cineastes de Notre Temps," directed by Hubert Knapp and Andre S. Labarthe; from *Five Films by John Cassavetes*; Criterion Collection, 2004.

(p. 107) "The first time he showed *Shadows* . . .": "Gena Rowlands Talks to Gary Oldman About Life with John Cassavetes from the Beginning: Part II," by Gary Oldman; *Venice*, 10/01.

(p. 108) Erich Kollmar quotes: From author interview.

(p. 109) Seymour Cassel anecdote: From author interview.

(p. 109) "At this fateful night . . .": *To Free the Cinema: Jonas Mekas and the New York Underground*, David E. James, editor; Princeton University Press, 1992.

(pp. 109–110) "In a recent edition of *The Voice* . . .": Letter to the editor by John Cassavetes; *Village Voice*, 12/16/59.

(p. 110) "I have been praising . . .": "Movie Journal," by Jonas Mekas; *Village Voice*, 1/27/60.

(p. 110) "This is very insulting . . .": "John Cassavetes," *Film Quarterly*, Spring 1961.

Chapter 17

(pp. 112–113) "Since the investors . . .": "The Playboy Interview: John Cassavetes," by Lawrence Linderman; *Playboy*, 7/71.

(p. 113) *Johnny Staccato* offer anecdote: "The Playboy Interview: John Cassavetes," by Lawrence Linderman; *Playboy*, 7/71.

(p. 113) "What baby?" anecdote: "Movie Nonconformists"; *Saturday Evening Post*, 4/7/62.

(p. 114) "We never had a written . . .": Burton Lane interviewed by Jack Mathews, 2/02.

(p. 114) Everett Chambers anecdote and quotes: From author interview.

(p. 115) "I'm fighting to make . . .": "*Staccato* is out of *Peter Gunn*," by Hal Humphrey; *Mirror News*, 9/10/59.

(p. 115) "Don't get any big . . .": "I Welcome the New Johnny Staccato," by David Nathan: *London Daily Herald*, 10/10/60.

(p. 115) "First of all, I don't . . .": "A Change of Heart," by Bob Salmaggi; *New York Herald Tribune*, 8/2/59.

(p. 115) Hal Humphrey quotes: "*Staccato* is out of *Peter Gunn*," by Hal Humphrey; *Mirror News*, 9/10/59.

(p. 116) Hollis Alpert quotes: From author interview.

(p. 116) "I tried to do each one . . .": "The Playboy Interview: John Cassavetes," by Lawrence Linderman; *Playboy*, 7/71.

(p. 118) "It is virtually impossible . . .": "Staccato Blast Fired at Timidity of Sponsors," by Maria Torre; *New York Herald Tribune*, 12/8/59.

(p. 119) Albert Johnson review of *Shadows: Film Quarterly*, spring 1960.

(p. 119) Anecdote about *Shadows* print and BFI: From author interview with Seymour Cassel.

(p. 119) "It is a landmark . . .": "Substance in the Shadows," by Derek Prouse; *London Sunday Times*, 7/17/60.

(p. 119) "To an art half-strangled . . .": "This Film Called *Shadows*," by Nigel Gosling; *The Observer*, 8/7/60.

(p. 119) "Listen, John, *Shadows* was . . .": "The Playboy Interview: John Cassavetes," by Lawrence Linderman; *Playboy*, 7/71.

(p. 120) "I like this film . . .": "At the films: Improvisation," by C. A. Lejeune; *The Observer*, 10/16/60.

(p. 120) "As a work of art . . .": "Out of the Shadows"; *Newsweek*, 11/7/60.

(p. 120) "case where an . . .": By Mosk; *Variety*, 8/31/60.

(p. 121) "He never paid . . .": Burton Lane interviewed by Jack Mathews, 2/02.

(p. 121) Lawsuit information: "4 Principals in Prize Film Sue for Profit," by Charles Gruenberg; *New York Post*, 4/16/61.

(pp. 121–122) Marvin Lichtner quotes: From author interview.

(p. 122) "There is much that . . .": "At the Movies," by Paul V. Beckley; *New York Herald Tribune*, 3/22/61.

(p. 122) "*Shadows* is an unfinished . . .": "Ad-Lib *Shadows*," by Bosley Crowther; *New York Times*, 3/22/61.

(p. 122) "The technical quality . . .": Tube; *Variety*, 2/15/61.

(p. 123) Martin Scorsese quotes: From author interview.

(p. 123) "When we opened *Shadows* . . .": "I'm Almost Not Crazy: John Cassavetes—the Man and His Work," directed by Michael Ventura; Cannon Films, 1984.

(p. 123) Burton Lane quotes: From interview with Jack Mathews.

(p. 123) "All that tremendous hoopla . . .": "The Playboy Interview: John Cassavetes," by Lawrence Linderman; *Playboy*, 7/71.

(p. 124) "All this was terribly exciting . . .": "John Cassavetes"; *Film Quarterly*, spring 1961.

Chapter 18

(p. 125) "Actually, there are two . . .": "And the Pursuit of Happiness, by John Cassavetes (in a recorded interview); *Films and Filming*, 2/61.

(p. 126) "Given that the 1957–58 . . .": "A personal statement by Ray Carney," "The John Cassavetes Pages," http://people.bu.edu/rcarney.

(p. 126) "What made the *Shadows* story . . .": "Chasing Shadows," by Ray Carney; "The John Cassavetes Pages," http://people.bu.edu/rcarney.

(p. 126) Ray Carney quotes: From author interview.

(p. 127) Al Ruban quotes: From author interview.

(p. 127) "Please note that the version . . .": From the website, http://www.filmfestivalrotterdam.com.

(p. 128) "looking at the sketchbooks . . .": "A personal statement by Ray Carney," "The John Cassavetes Pages," http://www.people.bu.edu/rcarney.

(p. 128) "Her goal was not merely . . .": "Chasing Shadows: A postscript," by Ray Carney; "The John Cassavetes Pages," http://people.bu.edu/rcarney.

Chapter 19

(p. 129) "I'll never make a film . . .": "How *Shadows* Was Born," by Patrick Gibbs; *Daily Telegraph*, 10/15/60.

(p. 130) "a jazz or blues type . . .": "By Way of Report," by A. H. Weiler; *New York Times*, 9/28/60.

(p. 130) "It's about time . . .": "Cassavetes Strives for New Concept and Paramount Completely Sympatico"; *Variety*, 2/8/61.

(p. 130) "The fact that a major . . .": "John Cassavetes: The Actor Who Taught Hollywood How to Make Films," by Alexander Ross; *Macleans*, 5/69.

(p. 131) "The one picture I made . . .": "Cassavetes Striven for New Concept and Paramount Completely Sympatico"; *Variety*, 2/8/61.

(pp. 131–132) "I believe in my players . . .": "Does Flood of Improvisations Mean New Wave in Films," by Philip K. Scheuer; *Los Angeles Times*, 5/21/61.

(p. 132) Larry Shaw quote; From author interview.

(p. 134) "except hope . . .": "Nothing Is Film's Synopsis," by Erskine Johnson; *Los Angeles Mirror*, 3/8/61.

(p. 134) "The studio people liked . . .": "A Way of Life: An Interview with John Cassavetes," by Andre S. Labarthe; *Evergreen Review*, 1/71.

(p. 134) "It's a system based . . .": *The Film Director as Superstar*, by Joseph Gelmis; Doubleday, 1970.

(p. 135) "I intend to make it . . .": "John Cassavetes"; *Film Quarterly*, spring 1961.

(p. 135) "There is no such thing as . . .": *The Film Director as Superstar*, by Joseph Gelmis; Doubleday, 1970.

(p. 135) "People were thinking . . .": "Cineastes de Notre Temps," directed by Hubert Knapp and Andre S. Labarthe, French TV, 1968; from *John Cassavetes: Five Films*, Criterion Collection, 2004.

(p. 135) "nobody sees it . . .": "Cassavetes' *Blues* Invading Europe Before U.S. Dates; *Variety*, 9/19/61.

(p. 136) *"Too Late Blues* is what happens . . .": Review by Philip Oakes; *Sight and Sound*, winter 61/62.

(p. 136) "The finished picture . . .": Review by Philip Hartung; *Commonweal*, 1/26/62.

(p. 136) "one of the most fascinating . . .": Review in *Newsweek*, 2/5/62.

(p. 136) "The dark-eyed darling . . .": Review in *Time*, 2/2/62.

(p. 136) *"Too Late Blues*, John Cassavetes' first . . .": "Movie Journal," by Jonas Mekas; *Village Voice*, 3/8/62.

Chapter 20

(p. 137) "When *Too Late Blues* was over . . .": *The Film Director as Superstar*, by Joseph Gelmis; Doubleday, 1970.

(p. 138) "I wasn't going to play . . ."; "He began going . . .": "The Playboy Interview: John Cassavetes," by Lawrence Linderman; Playboy, 7/71.

(p. 138) "Mr. Cassavetes said he . . ."; "Low Cost Series of Films Shelved," by Murray Schumach; *New York Times*, 3/29/62.

(p. 141) "That boy doesn't . . ."; "I'm going to kill him": *Get Happy: The Life of Judy Garland*, by Gerald Clarke; Diane Publishing, 2000.

(p. 141) Mark Rydell quotes: From author interview.

(p. 141) "overwhelmed her; sometimes . . .": *Judy*, by Gerold Frank; Harper-Collins, 1975.

(p. 141) "Did Burt improvise . . ."; "Is walking . . .": "He's not a bad guy . . .": "Zen and the Art of John Cassavetes," by Michael Ventura; *L.A. Weekly*, 9/21–27/84.

(p. 142) "Cassavetes really wanted me . . ." and Lancaster-Kramer anecdote: *Take 22: Moviemakers on Moviemaking*, by Judith Crist; Viking Penguin, 1984.

(p. 143) "I found the kids funny and human . . .": "The Playboy Interview: John Cassavetes," by Lawrence Linderman; Playboy, 7/71.

(p. 144) "Kramer had one kind . . .": *Los Angeles Times*, 1/9/66.

(p. 144) "When you attempt a subject . . .": *A Mad, Mad, Mad, Mad World: A Life in Hollywood*, by Stanley Kramer; Harcourt Brace, 1977.

(p. 144) "I knew that it would cost me . . .": "The Playboy Interview: John Cassavetes," by Lawrence Linderman; Playboy, 7/71.

(p. 144) "I didn't make a film for six . . .": 'Acting Independently," by Bob Lardine; *New York Sunday News*, 9/21/69.

(p. 144) "The phone didn't . . .": Why Do Marriages Go Sour?", by Patricia Bosworth; *New York Times*, 12/1/68.

(p. 144) "I'm blackballed, baby": "A Recollection of Cassavetes," by Meade Roberts; *Hollywood*, 12/90–1/91.

Chapter 21

(p. 145) Mark Rydell quote: From author interview.

(p. 145) "After *A Child Is Waiting,* I was relegated . . .": "Masks and Faces," by David Austen; *Films and Filming,* 9/68.

(p. 145) "When I get sore . . .": "Mavericks John Cassavetes and Gena Rowlands Make Movies the Hard Way—With Their Own Money," by Jim Calio; *People,* 10/8/84.

(p. 145) "Gena became the breadwinner . . .": "The Playboy Interview: John Cassavetes," by Lawrence Linderman; *Playboy,* 7/71.

(p. 146) "I'll never forget a scene . . .": "They're a Team, Mostly," by Ann Guarino; *New York Daily News,* 8/11/82.

(p. 147) "I don't have to read . . ."; "You don't read the script . . .": *A Siegel Film: An Autobiography,* by Don Siegel; Faber & Faber, 1993.

(p. 147) *Crime without Passion* anecdote: *A Siegel Film: An Autobiography,* by Don Siegel; Faber & Faber, 1993.

(pp. 148–149) Robert Altman quotes: From author interview.

(p. 149) "Mo remembered a ten-page . . .": "The Playboy Interview: John Cassavetes," by Lawrence Linderman; *Playboy,* 7/71.

(p. 149) "I had to pay for it myself . . .": "The Playboy Interview: John Cassavetes," by Lawrence Linderman; *Playboy,* 7/71.

(p. 150) "My wife and I have . . .": From John Cassavetes/Gena Rowlands appearance at AADA, April 1970.

Chapter 23

(p. 156) Al Ruban quotes and anecdotes: From author interview.

(p. 158) "It is a picture about the middle . . .": "*Faces,* a New Film by John Cassavetes"; *Cinema,* spring 1968.

(p. 158) "Gee, what a heck . . .": "Masks and Faces," by David Austen; *Film and Filming,* 9/68.

(p. 159) "The first part of the script . . .": *The Film Director as Superstar,* by Joseph Gelmis; Doubleday, 1970.

(p. 159) John Finnegan quote: From author interview.

(p. 159) "I was happy because . . .": "Faces: Actor Seymour Cassel Reflects on His Collaboration with Cassavetes and Peckinpah," by Peter Henne; *Village View,* 11/6–12/92.

(p. 160) "Could you help us . . .": From author interview with Lynn Carlin.

(p. 160) Seymour Cassel quotes: From author interview.

(p. 161) "That way of making a film . . .": "A Conversation with Seymour Cassel," by Michael Lee; indieWire.com, 8/4/97.

(p. 161) "We were using different . . .": "Masks and Faces," by David Austen; *Film and Filming,* 9/68.

(p. 162) Haskell Wexler anecdote: From author interview.

(p. 162) "The first Communist film shot in America": "Seymour Cassel Finds His Home on Sunset Strip," by Kevin Thomas; *Los Angeles Times,* 4/30/69.

(p. 163) "The rehearsal is not just for the actors . . .": "Cassavetes' Working Methods: Interviews with Al Ruban and Seymour Cassel," by Martin Viera; *Post Script*, 3/88.

(p. 163) "In *Faces*, Al Ruban did . . .": *The Film Director as Superstar*, by Joseph Gelmis; Doubleday, 1970.

(p. 164) Val Avery quotes: From author interview.

(p. 165) "Things didn't start out . . .": "Keep Your Eye on Gena Rowlands," by William Wolf; *Harper's Bazaar*, 9/82.

(p. 165) "My idea of the future . . .": "Why would anyone want to see a movie about a crazy, middle-aged dame?" by Duncan Campbell; *The Guardian*, 3/2/01.

(p. 165) "That was just not seen . . .": "Why would anyone want to see a movie about a crazy, middle-aged dame?" by Duncan Campbell; *The Guardian*, 3/2/01.

(p. 165) Val Avery suit story: From author interview with Val Avery.

(p. 166) "*Faces* became more than . . .": "A Way of Life: An Interview with John Cassavetes," by Andre S. Labarthe; *Evergreen Review*, 7/71.

(p. 166) "I think all these problems . . .": "Laughable: One Man's View of Marriage," by Sue Freeman; *Daily Express*, 12/17/68.

(p. 167) "Marley was standing there . . .": "John Cassavetes: *A Woman Under the Influence*," by Larry Gross; *Millimeter*, 3/75.

(p. 167) Anecdote about rooftop shot: From author interview with Seymour Cassel.

Chapter 24

(p. 168) "We've shot 250,000 . . .": "Cineastes de Notre Temps," directed by Hubert Knapp and Andre S. Labarthe, 1968; from *John Cassavetes: Five Films*, Criterion Collection, 2004.

(p. 169) *Devil's Angels* review by Robe; *Variety*, 5/3/67.

(p. 169) "I don't watch my acting . . .": "Acting independently," by Bob Lardine; *New York Daily News*, 9/21/69.

(p. 169) "At one point, they threatened . . .": "Cassavetes: The Actor Who Taught Hollywood How to Make Films," by Alexander Ross; *Macleans*, 5/69.

(p. 170) "When *Faces* was done . . .": "Cineastes de Notre Temps," directed by Hubert Knapp and Andre S. Labarthe, 1968; from *John Cassavetes: Five Films*, Criterion Collection, 2004.

(p. 170) "Bob Aldrich treats . . .": "Cassavetes: Why Do Marriages Go Sour?" by Patricia Bosworth; *New York Times*, 12/1/68.

(p. 171) "When I want a moon . . .": "A Recollection of Cassavetes," by Meade Roberts; *Hollywood*, 12/90–1/91.

(p. 171) *Dirty Dozen* review by Bosley Crowther; *New York Times*, 6/16/67.

(p. 171) *Dirty Dozen* review by Paul D. Zimmerman; *Newsweek*, 7/3/67.

(p. 171) *Dirty Dozen* review by Richard Schickel; *Life*, 7/21/67.

(p. 172) *Rosemary's Baby* casting anecdote: *Polanski: The Filmmaker as Voyeur*, by Barbara Leaming; Simon & Schuster, 1981.

(pp. 172–173) "John's approach could not . . .": *What Falls Away: A Memoir*, by Mia Farrow; Nan Talese Books, 1997.

(p. 173) "He isn't a director . . .": *Polanski: The Filmmaker as Voyeur*, by Barbara Leaming, Simon & Schuster, 1981.

(p. 173) *Rosemary's Baby* review; *Time*, 6/21/68.

(p. 173) *Rosemary's Baby* review by Murf.; *Variety*, 5/29/68.

(p. 173) *Rosemary's Baby* review by Penelope Gilliatt; *The New Yorker*, 6/15/68.

(p. 173) *Rosemary's Baby* review by Stanley Kauffman; *New Republic*, 6/15/68.

(p. 173) "I've always thought John . . .": "Ira Levin," by F. Paul Driscoll; *Opera News*, 10/1/97.

(p. 173) "You could see . . .": "An Evening at Columbia College with John Cassavetes"; *Columbia College Press*, Chicago, 3/5/75.

(p. 174) "It just wasn't necessary to explain . . .": *The Film Director as Superstar*, by Joseph Gelmis; Doubleday, 1970.

(p. 175) "The McCarthy scene . . .": "Masks and Faces," by David Austen; *Films and Filming*, 9/68.

(p. 175) "We started with $10,000 . . .": "Cineastes de Notre Temps," directed by Hubert Knapp and Andre S. Labarthe, 1968; from *John Cassavetes: Five Films*, Criterion Collection, 2004.

(p. 175) "I'm the sole financier . . .": "Masks and Faces," by David Austen; *Film and Filming*, 9/68.

(p. 175) "*Faces* has got to be . . .": "Cassavetes: Why Do Marriages Go Sour?" by Patricia Bosworth; *New York Times*, 12/1/68.

(p. 175) "The wonderful thing about *Faces* . . .": From John Cassavetes/Gena Rowlands appearance at AADA, April 1970.

Chapter 25

(p. 176) "the picture bombed" and *Faces* screening anecdote: "The Playboy Interview: John Cassavetes," by Lawrence Linderman; *Playboy*, 7/71.

(p. 177) New York Film Festival anecdote: From author interviews with Andrew Sarris, Al Ruban.

(p. 177) Andrew Sarris quote: From author interview.

(pp. 177–178) Martin Scorsese quotes: From author interview.

(p. 178) Jay Cocks quote: From author interview.

(p. 178) *Faces* review by Robe; *Variety*, 6/28/68.

(p. 178) *Faces* review by Renata Adler; *New York Times*, 9/28/68.

(p. 178) *Faces* review by Jonas Mekas; *Village Voice*, 9/26/68.

(p. 179) Al Ruban quotes: From author interview.

(p. 179) *Faces* review by Frances Herridge; *New York Post*, 11/25/68.

(p. 179) *Faces* review by Judith Crist; *New York*, 12/2/68.

(p. 179) *Faces* review by Richard Schickel; *Life*, 1/17/69.

(p. 179) *Faces* review by Andrew Sarris; *Confessions of a Cultist*, by Andrew Sarris; Simon & Schuster, 1970.

(p. 179) *Faces* review by Claire Clouzot; *Film Quarterly,* spring 69.

(p. 179) "Trash, Art and the Movies," by Pauline Kael; *Harpers,* 2/69.

(p. 180) *Faces* review by Pauline Kael; *New Yorker,* 12/7/68.

(p. 180) "I call the box office every night . . .": "After *Faces,* a Film to Keep the Man-child Alive," by Ann Guerin; *Life,* 5/9/69.

(p. 180) "How long have we been . . .": *The Film Director as Superstar,* by Joseph Gelmis; Doubleday, 1970.

(p. 181) "John grew intent . . . if you try": "Interview Becomes Confrontation," by Phyllis Funke; *Suffolk Sunday,* 12/5/68.

(p. 181) "I didn't find *Faces* boring . . .": *The Film Director as Superstar,* by Joseph Gelmis; Doubleday, 1970.

(p. 181) "Surprise of surprises . . .": "The Playboy Interview: John Cassavetes," by Lawrence Linderman; *Playboy,* 7/71.

(p. 181) "You know, I think I'm crazy . . .": "After *Faces,* a Film to Keep the Man-child Alive," by Ann Guerin; *Life,* 5/9/69.

(p. 182) "This is union heresy . . .": *In the Arena: An Autobiography,* by Charlton Heston; Simon & Schuster, 1995.

(p. 182) "I'd been an actor . . .": "The Case on Cassavetes," by Harry Haun; *New York Daily News,* 4/30/91.

(p. 182) Seymour Cassel anecdote: From author interview.

(p. 183) "We always try to think . . ." "The Playboy Interview: John Cassavetes," by Lawrence Linderman; *Playboy,* 7/71.

Chapter 26

(pp. 187–188) Stella Stevens quote: From author interview.

(p. 188) Everett Chambers quote: From author interview.

(p. 188) Seymour Cassel quotes: From author interview.

(p. 188) Al Ruban quotes and anecdotes: From author interview.

(p. 189) Larry Shaw quotes: From author interview.

(p. 189) John Finnegan quotes: From author interview.

(p. 189) "It's not autobiographical . . .": "Three Husbands Hold Court," by Molly Haskell; *Show,* 9/69.

(p. 190) "My brother taught . . .": "Husbands," an unpublished novel by John Cassavetes; used by permission.

(p. 190) "His older brother, Nicholas . . .": "John Cassavetes: Bio," MGM, 6/11/57.

(p. 190) "I am so happy he was . . .": "Temperament Normal in Film Team," by Irene Thirer; *New York Daily News,* 10/26/57.

(p. 190) "We found a subject . . .": "Masks and Faces," by David Austen; *Films and Filming,* 9/68.

(p. 190) "*Husbands* has to do . . .": *The Film Director as Superstar,* by Joseph Gelmis; Doubleday, 1970.

(p. 191) "You could say it's about three . . .": "Cassavetes' Personal Rebellion," by Dan Knapp; *Los Angeles Times,* 11/9/69.

(p. 191) "Falk, Gazzara and myself started . . .": "American Film Institute Dialogue on Film: John Cassavetes and Peter Falk," 1/71.

(p. 191) "There are phases . . .": "After *Faces*, a Film to Keep the Man-child Alive," by Ann Guerin; *Life*, 5/9/69.

(p. 191) "At a certain age . . .": "A Talk with Ben Gazzara," by Beverly Solochek; *New York Post*, 12/26/70.

(p. 191) "It's the first time . . .": "For the Love of Pete," by Earl Wilson; *New York Post*, 12/12/70.

(p. 192) Val Avery quote: From author interview.

(p. 192) "For one thing . . .": "The Faces of Husbands"; *New Yorker*, 3/15/69.

(p. 192) "Louis B. Mayer . . .": "A Talk with Ben Gazzara," by Beverly Solochek; *New York Post*, 12/26/70.

(p. 192) "It's like having flat feet . . .": "I'd Rather Sketch a Nude than Do Most Anything," by Bob Lardine; *New York Daily News*, 12/17/72.

(p. 192) "There's a time when . . .": "Talk with Falk," by Arthur Marx; *Cigar Aficionado*, 11–12/97.

(p. 193) "In Ossining, when I was . . .": "Talk with Falk," by Arthur Marx; *Cigar Aficionado*, 11–12/97.

(p. 193) "You're going to paint . . .": From author interview with Peter Falk.

(p. 193) "Jesus Christ, I'm 26 . . .": "Talk with Falk," by Arthur Marx; *Cigar Aficionado*, 11–12/97.

(p. 193) "a man of long indecisions . . . I inch": "Peter Falk Says Goodbye to Columbo and to Marriage for One Last Shot at Movie Stardom," by Lois Armstrong; *People*, 8/9/76.

(p. 194) Eva Le Gallienne anecdote: "Talk with Falk," by Arthur Marx; *Cigar Aficionado*, 11–12/97.

(p. 194) "You know, son . . .": "Talk with Falk," by Arthur Marx; *Cigar Aficionado*, 11–12/97.

(p. 194) "What the hell are . . .": "Talk with Falk," by Arthur Marx; *Cigar Aficionado*, 11–12/97.

(p. 194) "That play established . . .": "I'd Rather Sketch a Nude than Do Most Anything," by Bob Lardine; *New York Daily News*, 12/17/72.

(p. 195) "For the same money . . .": "Peter Falk," www.imdb.com.

(p. 195) "I was proud of . . .": "I'd Rather Sketch a Nude than Do Most Anything," by Bob Lardine; *New York Daily News*, 12/17/72.

(p. 196) "What I really . . .": "After *Faces*, a Film to Keep the Man-child Alive," by Ann Guerin; *Life*, 5/9/69.

(p. 196) "I've heard that bull . . .": "After *Faces*, a Film to Keep the Man-child Alive," by Ann Guerin; *Life*, 5/9/69.

(p. 196) "Did Marty call . . .": *In the Moment: My Life as an Actor*, by Ben Gazzara; Carroll & Graf, 2004.

(p. 196) "Coming to know him . . .": *The Player: The Profile of an Art*, by Lillian Ross and Helen Ross; Simon & Schuster, 1961.

(p. 197) "Even then, Ben was . . .": "Ben Gazzara," by Maurice Condon; *TV Guide*, 1/7/67.

(p. 197) "stunned by the theatricality . . .": *The Player: The Profile of an Art*, by Lillian Ross and Helen Ross; Simon & Schuster, 1961.

(p. 197) "got me terribly wrought . . .": *The Player: The Profile of an Art*, by Lillian Ross and Helen Ross; Simon & Schuster, 1961.

(p. 197) Anne Jackson quote: From author interview.

(p. 197) "At the Actors Studio . . .": "Fun with Ben and John," by Gavin Smith; *Film Comment*, 5–6/89.

(p. 198) Peter Bogdanovich quote: From author interview.

(p. 198) "At that time, if I wasn't . . .": *The Player: The Profile of an Art*, by Lillian Ross and Helen Ross; Simon & Schuster, 1961.

(p. 198) "I thought those wonderful . . .": "They're acting married," by May Okon; *New York Daily News*, 6/19/66.

(p. 198) "I never took advantage . . .": From author interview with Ben Gazzara.

(p. 199) "I was made a star . . .": "New Look Actor," by Emory Lewis; *Cue*, 3/19/55.

(p. 199) "I had a rude . . .": "Irreverence Is a Word He Digs," by Judy Stone; *New York Times*, 12/19/65.

(p. 199) "I'm not satisfied . . .": "On the Air," by Bob Williams; *New York Post*, 12/6/63.

(p. 199) "I want to tell you the story . . ." and Hamburger Hamlet conversation: *In the Moment: My Life as an Actor*, by Ben Gazzara; Carroll & Graf, 2004.

(p. 200) "Did you get the offer . . ." and dialogue from Falk/Cassavetes phone conversation: "After *Faces*, a Film to Keep the Man-child Alive," by Ann Guerin; *Life*, 5/9/69.

(p. 201) "I thought it was silly . . .": "Cassavetes' Personal Rebellion," by Dan Knapp; *Los Angeles Times*, 11/9/69.

(p. 201) "What happens if Ben . . .": "Three Husbands Hold Court," by Molly Haskell; *Show*, 9/69.

(p. 201) "Ben, don't get killed . . ." and anecdote about Prague Spring: *In the Moment: My Life as an Actor*, by Ben Gazzara; Carroll & Graf, 2004.

(p. 201) Leonard Maltin quote: From author interview.

Chapter 28

(p. 207) "The reason no one . . .": "Cassavetes' Personal Rebellion," by Dan Knapp; *Los Angeles Times*, 11/9/69.

(p. 208) "I'm involved in . . .": "Cassavetes: Why Do Marriages Go Sour?" by Patricia Bosworth; *New York Times*, 12/1/68.

(p. 208) "The script we first read . . .": *In the Moment: My Life as an Actor*, by Ben Gazzara; Carroll & Graf, 2004.

(p. 209) "We didn't know . . .": "Competitive Cassavetes," by David Galligan; *Hollywood Dramalogue*, 10/7–13/82.

(p. 209) "Look, since we have to . . ." and character-naming conversation: "The Playboy Interview: John Cassavetes," by Lawrence Linderman; *Playboy*, 7/71.

(p. 209) "The only Jewish boy . . .": *In the Moment: My Life as an Actor,* by Ben Gazzara; Carroll & Graf, 2004.

(p. 209) "By the end of . . .": "The Playboy Interview: John Cassavetes," by Lawrence Linderman; *Playboy,* 7/71.

(p. 210) "Is my eye straight?" and glass eye. *In the Moment: My Life as an Actor,* by Ben Gazzara: Carroll & Graf, 2004.

(p. 210) "If that picture succeeded . . .": *In the Moment: My Life as an Actor,* by Ben Gazzara; Carroll & Graf, 2004.

(p. 210) "In *Husbands,* Gazzara's character . . .": "The Playboy Interview: John Cassavetes," by Lawrence Linderman; *Playboy,* 7/71.

(p. 210) "I didn't think it was . . .": "Cassavetes, Rowlands and Falk," by Dick Adler; *Viva,* 12/74.

(p. 211) "Once we began to read . . .": *In the Moment: My Life as an Actor,* by Ben Gazzara; Carroll & Graf, 2004.

(p. 211) "There was a whole script . . .": "Competitive Cassavetes," by David Galligan; *Hollywood Dramalogue,* 10/7–13/82.

(p. 211) Street-repair crew anecdote: Documentary by Georg Alexander, WDR (German television), 1979.

(p. 211) Tristram Powell quotes: From author interview.

(p. 212) "By John's behavior . . .": *In the Moment: My Life as an Actor,* by Ben Gazzara; Carroll & Graf, 2004.

(p. 212) "There was a lot of pacing . . .": *In the Moment: My Life as an Actor,* by Ben Gazzara; Carroll & Graf, 2004.

(p. 212) "We're gambling . . .": "The Faces of *Husbands*"; *New Yorker,* 3/15/69.

(p. 212) "I worked for nothing . . .": "Hollywood Mavericks," by Hollis Alpert; *Saturday Review,* 11/16/74.

(p. 213) Victor Kemper quotes and anecdotes: From author interview.

(p. 214) "When I saw Vic's first work . . .": "American Film Institute Dialogue on Film: John Cassavetes and Peter Falk," 1/71.

(p. 215) "This is the worst piece of shit" and surrounding anecdote: *In the Moment: My Life as an Actor,* by Ben Gazzara; Carroll & Graf, 2004.

(p. 215) Charles Champlin quote: From author interview.

(p. 216) "I thought we were making . . .": "Gazzara: Rewards for the Regular (and Riled) Guy," by Gene Siskel; *Chicago Tribune,* 4/28/74.

(p. 216) "The characters weren't vomiting . . .": "The Playboy Interview: John Cassavetes," by Lawrence Linderman; *Playboy,* 7/71.

(p. 216) "It's not really interesting to me . . .": "American Film Institute Dialogue on Film: John Cassavetes and Peter Falk," 1/71.

(p. 216) "I liked the camera low . . .": "American Film Institute Dialogue on Film: John Cassavetes and Peter Falk," 1/71.

(p. 217) "We knew that people . . .": "American Film Institute Dialogue on Film: John Cassavetes and Peter Falk," 1/71.

(p. 218) "John is more interested . . .": "Ben Gazzara: The Best Is Yet to Come," by Lewis Archibald; *The Aquarian,* 3/9/83.

(p. 218) "Peter was upset . . .": "Three Husbands Hold Court," by Molly Haskell; *Show,* 9/69.

(p. 218) "Peter was a little hesitant . . .": "Why would anyone want to see a movie about a crazy, middle-aged dame?" by Duncan Campbell; *The Guardian,* 3/2/01.

(p. 218) "With Peter, on take 32 . . .": From John Cassavetes/Gena Rowlands appearance at AADA, April 1970.

(p. 218) "On *Husbands,* he'd run . . .": *A Constant Forge,* directed by Charles Kiselyak; from *John Cassavetes: Five Films,* Criterion Collection, 2004.

(p. 218) "When you write something for Ben . . .": "American Film Institute Dialogue on Film: John Cassavetes and Peter Falk," 1/71.

(p. 218) "Don't rush, Pete . . .": "Cassavetes: The Actor Who Taught Hollywood How to Make Films," by Alexander Ross; *Macleans,* 5/69.

(p. 218) "Do you understand . . .": *In the Moment: My Life as an Actor,* by Ben Gazzara; Carroll & Graf, 2004.

(p. 218) "In some ways . . .": From the documentary, *John Cassavetes: To Risk Everything to Express It All;* Kultur Films, Inc., 1999.

(p. 219) "Peter couldn't take . . .": "American Film Institute Dialogue on Film: John Cassavetes and Peter Falk," 1/71.

(p. 219) "As director, I went under . . .": "American Film Institute Dialogue on Film: John Cassavetes and Peter Falk," 1/71.

(p. 219) "It's very hard to just . . .": "American Film Institute Dialogue on Film: John Cassavetes and Peter Falk," 1/71.

(p. 220) "The money ran out . . .": *In the Moment: My Life as an Actor,* by Ben Gazzara; Carroll & Graf, 2004.

(p. 220) Round House, Sportsman's Club anecdotes: From author interview with Al Ruban.

(pp. 220–221) "John had no intention . . ." *In the Moment: My Life as an Actor,* by Ben Gazzara; Carroll & Graf, 2004.

(p. 221) Simon Hinkly quotes: From author interview.

(pp. 222–223) *Husbands* casting anecdote: Jenny Runacre, interviewed by Tom Charity, 1999.

(p. 222) "The *Omnibus* thing was . . .": Jenny Runacre, interviewed by Tom Charity, 1999.

(p. 223) "I thought they were all mad . . .": Jenny Runacre, interviewed by Tom Charity, 1999.

(p. 223) "Go all the way all the time . . .": "The Making of *Husbands*" documentary, directed by Tristram Powell; *Omnibus,* BBC, 1970.

(p. 223) "That neurosis—he wanted it . . .": Jenny Runacre, interviewed by Tom Charity, 1999.

(p. 224) "I was terrific . . .": "Three Husbands Hold Court," by Molly Haskell; *Show,* 9/69.

(p. 224) "It was right in the middle . . .": "Three Husbands Hold Court," by Molly Haskell; *Show,* 9/69.

Chapter 29

(p. 226) Don Siegel anecdote: From author interview with John Badham.

(p. 226) "Al, I never want . . .": From author interview with Al Ruban.

(p. 227) "I began to understand . . .": "Editing the Personal Feature—John Cassavetes' *Husbands,*" by Russ AuWerter; *The Cinemeditor,* Fall 1969.

(p. 227) *"Husbands* at its best:": *In the Moment: My Life as an Actor,* by Ben Gazzara; Carroll & Graf, 2004.

(pp. 227–228) Al Ruban quotes: From author interview.

(p. 228) "I'm not here to please . . .": From author interview with Al Ruban.

(p. 228) Edie Shaw Marcus quotes: From author interview.

(p. 228) "Of course, she likes . . .": From author interview with Carole Smith.

(p. 228) Elaine Kagan quotes: From author interview.

(pp. 228–229) "Ben, it's all gonna . . ." and Gazzara tantrum anecdote: *In the Moment: My Life as an Actor,* by Ben Gazzara; Carroll & Graf, 2004.

(pp. 230–231) Character quotes: From "Husbands," an unpublished novel by John Cassavetes; used by permission.

(p. 231) "They were booing . . ." and San Francisco Film Festival dialogue ending with ". . . Seymour would say, 'Bullshit'": "An Evening at Columbia College with John Cassavetes"; Columbia College Press, Chicago, 3/5/75.

(p. 231) "I thought the whole . . ."; "Will you talk . . .": "Don't you think . . .": "Cassavetes Retrospective Perks Up San Francisco Film Festival," by Rick Setlowe; *Variety,* 10/28/70.

(p. 232) The epithet "Middle class!" . . .": "John Cassavetes: I Really Like What I Do," by Nicholas Pasquariello; *Weekly Californian,* 4/18–25/75.

(p. 232) *Husbands* review by Rick Setlowe; *Variety,* 10/20/70.

(p. 233) "The studio says . . .": "American Film Institute Dialogue on Film: John Cassavetes and Peter Falk," 1/71.

(p. 233) "I love that . . ." and East Side screening anecdote: "The New Hollywood Is the Old Hollywood," *Time,* 12/7/70.

(p. 234) *Husbands* review by Jay Cocks; *Time,* 12/7/70.

(p. 234) *Husbands* review by Archer Winsten; *New York Post,* 12/9/70.

(p. 234) *Husbands* review by Hollis Alpert; *Saturday Review,* 12/12/70.

(p. 234) *Husbands* review by Richard Schickel; *Life,* 2/5/71.

(p. 234) *Husbands* review by Gene Shalit; *Look,* 2/7/71.

(p. 234) *Husbands* review by Andrew Sarris; *Village Voice,* 12/10/70.

(p. 234) *Husbands* review by Vincent Canby; *New York Times,* 12/9/70.

(p. 235) *Husbands* review by Rex Reed; *New York Daily News,* 12/13/70.

(p. 235) *Husbands* review by Judith Crist; *New York,* 12/31/70.

(p. 235) *Husbands* review by Pauline Kael; *New Yorker,* 1/2/71.

(p. 235) Seymour Cassel quote: From author interview.

(p. 235) Kael ban from screening: "Mavericks John Cassavetes and Gena Rowlands Make Movies the Hard Way—With Their Own Money," by Jim Calio; *People*, 10/8/84.

(p. 236) "It was a personal thing . . .": "For Gena Rowlands, Acting Is Still Tied to the Home," by Margy Rochlin; *New York Times*, 11/3/96.

(p. 236) "The way I figure . . .": From author interview with Frederick Elmes.

(p. 236) Jay Cocks quotes: From author interview.

(p. 236) Harvey Weinstein quote: From author interview.

(p. 236) "*Husbands* zeroes in on . . .": Column by Betty Friedan; *New York Times*, 1/31/71.

(p. 236) "If I wrote it down . . .": "The Making of *Husbands*" documentary, directed by Tristram Powell; *Omnibus*, BBC, 1970.

(p. 237) "Many people walked out . . .": "The Playboy Interview: John Cassavetes," by Lawrence Linderman; *Playboy*, 7/71.

(p. 237) "I was watching television . . .": "John Cassavetes: I Really Like What I Do," by Nicholas Pasquariello; *The Weekly Californian*, 4/18–25/75.

(p. 237) "I don't edit what I say . . ." and "No head of any major studio . . .": "The Playboy Interview: John Cassavetes," by Lawrence Linderman; *Playboy*, 7/71.

(p. 237) "The question was asked . . .": "Maybe There Really Wasn't An America—Maybe It Was Only Frank Capra," by John Cassavetes; *Variety*, 10/27/70.

(p. 238) "It's a film about male love . . .": "Ben Gazzara: Still Running, but Not for His Life," by Peace Sterling; Associated Press, 5/3/71.

(p. 238) "I had people tell me . . .": "Gazzara: Rewards for the Regular (and Riled) Guy," by Gene Siskel; *Chicago Tribune*, 4/28/74.

(p. 238) "People are more interested . . .": "*Husbands* Proves Actors' Commune; Even Extends to Ballyhoo on Playoff," by Rick Setlowe; *Variety*, 12/30/70.

(p. 238) "My next three guests . . .": From author interview with Leonard Maltin.

(p. 238) *David Frost Show* quotes: *The David Frost Show*, syndicated, 10/70.

(p. 239) *Dick Cavett Show* quotes: *The Dick Cavett Show*, ABC, 9/21/70.

(p. 239) "Let's not say anything . . .": From author interview with Ben Gazzara.

(p. 240) Ben Gazzara quote: From author interview.

(p. 240) "I got a wire . . .": "American Film Institute Dialogue on Film: John Cassavetes and Peter Falk," 1/71.

(p. 241) "This is absolutely a man's . . .": "After *Faces*, a Film to Keep the Man-child Alive," by Ann Guerin; *Life*, 5/9/69.

(p. 241) "I think the three men . . .": "Three Husbands Hold Court," by Molly Haskell; *Show*, 9/69.

(p. 241) "They absolutely loathed . . .": "John Cassavetes: I Really Like What I Do," by Nicholas Pasquariello; *The Weekly Californian*, 4/18–25/75.

(p. 241) "I have a great idea . . .": "John Cassavetes Talks It Up for the Star System," by Sue Cameron; *Hollywood Reporter*, 12/24/70.

(p. 241) "Let's go to Brazil" and check anecdote: From author interview with Seymour Cassel.

Chapter 30

(pp. 243–244) Jay Cocks quotes and anecdotes: From author interview.
(p. 244) Martin Scorsese quotes and anecdotes: From author interview.
(p. 244) "It's great . . .": From author interview with Jay Cocks.
(p. 245) Jeremy Kagan quote: From author interview.
(p. 245) Henry Jaglom anecdotes and quotes: From author interview.
(p. 245) Peter Bogdanovich anecdotes and quotes: From author interview.
(p. 246) Gordon Parks anecdotes and quotes: From author interview.
(p. 247) Bo Harwood anecdotes and quotes: From author interview.
(p. 248) "I'm sure John thought . . ." and "Most Dangerous Game" anecdote: "OK, now, does everyone know who John Cassavetes is?" by Bill Kelley; *Sarasota Herald-Tribune,* 4/6/01.
(p. 248) Alexandre Rockwell quotes and anecdotes: From author interview.
(p. 249) Tom Noonan quotes and anecdotes: From author interview.
(p. 249) Tamar Simon Hoffs quotes and *The Haircut* anecdotes: From author interview.
(p. 250) "Moskowitz was the last hippie": Documentary by Georg Alexander, WDR (German television), 1979.
(p. 250) "I'm kind of weird . . .": "Seymour on Seymour," by Richard Cuskelly; *Los Angeles Herald Examiner,* 3/26/72.
(p. 251) Matthew Cassel quote: From author interview.
(p. 251) "I like the mystery of the way . . .": "Seymour Cassel: A Street-Smart Actor," by Joseph Gelmis; *Los Angeles Times,* 2/13/72.
(p. 251) Al Ruban quotes: From author interview.
(pp. 251–252) "Coincides with my own . . .": "Seymour Cassel: A Street-Smart Actor," by Joseph Gelmis; *Los Angeles Times,* 2/13/72.

Chapter 31

(p. 253) "*Husbands* is the last time . . .": "John Cassavetes Talks It Up for the Star System," by Sue Cameron; *Hollywood Reporter,* 12/24/70.
(p. 253) Al Ruban quotes: From author interview.
(p. 254) "because the idea had been around . . .": "The Playboy Interview: John Cassavetes," by Lawrence Linderman; *Playboy,* 7/71.
(p. 254) "The initiative . . .": "The New Movies"; *Newsweek,* 12/7/70.

Chapter 32

(p. 263) "I've been fired . . .": "Rebels with a Cause," by Ara Corbett; *Filmfax,* 5–6/96.
(p. 263) "Make this a good one . . .": "Rebels with a Cause," by Ara Corbett; *Filmfax,* 5–6/96.
(p. 263) "I was tired of seeing movies . . .": "Rebels with a Cause," by Ara Corbett; *Filmfax,* 5–6/96.
(p. 263) "an apparent waste . . .": "World's Greatest Sinner" review; *Hollywood Reporter,* 1962.

(p. 263) "It has the brilliance . . .": "Cracked Actor," by Grover Lewis; *Film Comment*, 1–2/04.

(p. 264) Richard Kaye quotes and anecdote: From author interview.

(p. 264) "It's amazing how people . . .": "Cracked Actor," by Grover Lewis; *Film Comment*, 1–2/04.

(p. 265) "You made the film, Tim": "Rebels with a Cause," by Ara Corbett; *Filmfax*, 5–6/96.

(p. 265) Ned Tanen anecdote: From author interview with Al Ruban.

(p. 265) Elaine Kagan quote: From author interview.

(p. 266) Michael Margulies quotes: From author interview.

(p. 267) "The secret is that the . . .": *Take 22: Moviemakers on Moviemaking*, by Judith Crist; Viking Penguin, 1984.

(p. 267) "Gena didn't get up . . .": "John Cassavetes' Family Shtick," by Bridget Byrne; *Los Angeles Herald-Examiner*, 2/13/72.

(p. 268) "If we ever get . . .": "John Cassavetes/Gena Rowlands/Peter Falk," by Dick Adler; *Viva*, 12/74.

(p. 268) "I learned to keep . . .": "Seeing," by Judith Thurman; *Ms.*, 11/80.

(p. 268) "Don't do anything . . ." and anecdote: "New Hero for Hollywood," by Todd Mason; Pensacola *News-Journal*, 2/27/72.

(p. 268) John Finnegan quotes: From author interview.

(p. 269) Martin Scorsese quotes and anecdotes: From author interview.

(p. 270) *I Escaped from Devil's Island* remake: From author interview with Jay Cocks.

(p. 272) "If I never made another . . .": "Seymour on Seymour," by Richard Cuskelly; *Los Angeles Herald-Examiner*, 3/26/72.

(p. 272) "*Faces, Husbands* and *Minnie* . . .": "Movie Journal," by Jonas Mekas; *Village Voice*, 12/23/71.

(p. 272) *Minnie and Moskowitz* review by Jay Cocks: *Time*, 12/27/71.

(p. 272) *Minnie and Moskowitz* review by Wanda Hale: *New York Daily News*, 12/23/71.

(p. 272) *Minnie and Moskowitz* review by Stanley Kauffman: *New Republic*, 1/22/72.

(p. 272) *Minnie and Moskowitz* review by Murf: *Variety*, 12/22/71.

(p. 272) *Minnie and Moskowitz* review by Vincent Canby: *New York Times*, 12/23/71.

(pp. 272–273) "Before I met Gena . . .": "Eye View," by Kathleen Brady; *Women's Wear Daily*, 12/27/71.

(p. 273) "marriageable age," Gena Rowlands anecdote and quotes: *Take 22: Moviemakers on Moviemaking*, by Judith Crist; Viking Penguin, 1984.

(p. 273) Utopia Theater, Paris, anecdote and Seymour Cassel quotes: "Cassel's in the Sky," by Heidi Sigmund; *Venice*, 11/92.

Chapter 33

(p. 274) "You can do well in Hollywood . . .": "The Playboy Interview: John Cassavetes," by Lawrence Linderman; *Playboy*, 7/71.

(p. 275) "I don't want it . . .": "Peter Falk Back as the Raincoat," by Cecil Smith, *Los Angeles Times*, 7/7/72.

(p. 275) "I would like to do . . .": "American Film Institute Dialogue on Film: John Cassavetes and Peter Falk," 1/71.

(p. 275) "She's a good woman . . .": "An Evening at Columbia College with John Cassavetes"; Columbia College Press, Chicago, 1975.

(p. 275) "One of the reasons I made . . .": "John Cassavetes: I Really Like What I Do," by Nicholas Pasquariello; *Weekly Californian*, 4/18–24/75.

(p. 280) "People have said . . .": "John Cassavetes/Gena Rowlands/Peter Falk," by Dick Adler; *Viva*, 12/74.

Chapter 34

(p. 281) "Am I anti-Hollywood? . . .": Documentary by Georg Alexander, *WDR* (German television), 1972.

(pp. 281–282) Martin Baum, David Wolper quotes: "Hollywood—Broke and Getting Rich," by Fletcher Knebel; *Look*, 11/3/70.

(p. 282) "What you're seeing now . . .": "The New Hollywood"; *Newsweek*, 12/7/70.

(p. 282) "The New Hollywood is the New . . .": "The New Hollywood," by Charles Michener; *Newsweek*, 11/25/74.

(p. 282) "It's hard to explain what independence . . .": "An Evening at Columbia College with John Cassavetes"; Columbia College Press, Chicago, 1975.

(p. 282) "The main thing with Hollywood . . .": "Hollywood Mavericks," by Hollis Alpert; *Saturday Review*, 11/16/74.

(pp. 282–283) Al Ruban quote: From author interview.

(p. 283) "Everyone is not going . . .": "John Cassavetes: I Really Like What I Do," by Nicholas Pasquariello; *Weekly Californian*, 4/18–24/75.

(p. 283) "I don't say I've been a saint . . .": "*A Woman Under the Influence*: An Interview with John Cassavetes," by Judith McNally; *Filmmakers Newsletter*, 1/75.

(p. 283) "I only knew one thing . . .": "Cassavetes: Show Me the Magic," by Michael Ventura; *L.A. Weekly*, 8/20–26/82.

(pp. 283–284) "I couldn't believe John wrote . . .": *Take 22: Moviemakers on Moviemaking*, by Judith Crist; Viking Penguin 1984.

(p. 284) "You can spend . . .": "Even Crazy People Retain Their Individuality," by Bridget Byrne; *Los Angeles Herald-Examiner*, 12/8/74.

(p. 284) "It was hard to cut down . . .": "*A Woman Under the Influence*: An Interview with John Cassavetes," by Judith McNally; *Filmmakers Newsletter*, 1/75.

Chapter 35

(p. 285) "Nobody wants to see . . .": *Take 22: Moviemakers on Moviemaking*, by Judith Crist; Viking Penguin, 1984.

(p. 285) "Working in television . . .": "John Cassavetes Talks It Up for the Star System," by Sue Cameron; *Hollywood Reporter*, 12/24/70.

(p. 285) "There isn't too much respect . . .": From John Cassavetes/Gena Rowlands appearance at AADA, April 1974.

(p. 285) "We didn't have the money . . .": *Take 22: Moviemakers on Moviemaking,* by Judith Crist; Viking Penguin, 1984.

(pp. 285–286) "I laughed out loud . . .": "John/Gena/Peter Interview," by Dick Adler; *Viva,* 12/74.

(p. 286) *Day of the Dolphin* anecdote and quotes: "An Evening at Columbia College with John Cassavetes"; Columbia College Press, Chicago, 1975.

(p. 286) Elaine Kagan quotes and anecdotes: From author interview.

(p. 286) Paul Mazursky quote: From author interview.

(p. 286) "My filmmaking is an expensive . . .": "Hollywood Mavericks," by Hollis Alpert; *Saturday Review,* 11/16/74.

(p. 286) Seymour Cassel quote: From author interview.

(pp. 286–287) Bo Harwood quotes: From author interview.

(p. 287) "I've been very lucky . . .": "Gena Rowlands, the Reluctant Superstar," by Robert Osborne; *Flightime,* 11/76.

(p. 287) "one way of controlling . . .": *The Tomorrow Show with Tom Snyder,* NBC, 12/9/77.

(p. 287) "With John's scripts, it's like . . .": "John/Gena/Peter," by Dick Adler; *Viva,* 12/74.

(p. 287) "I got a lot of people together . . .": "An Evening at Columbia College with John Cassavetes"; Columbia College Press, Chicago, 1975.

(p. 287) "In *Woman,* the crew worked . . .": "An Interview with John Cassavetes," by Michel Ciment and Michael Henry; *Positif,* 4/76.

(p. 288) Elaine Kagan quotes and anecdotes: From author interview.

(pp. 288–289) Quotes from AFI press release: "AFI Press Release: Cassavetes First Filmmaker in Residence at AFI's Center for Advanced Film Studies," 10/20/72.

(p. 289) Caleb Deschanel quotes: From author interview.

(p. 289) "What kind of nut . . ." and Haskell Wexler anecdote, quotes: From author interview with Haskell Wexler.

(pp. 289–290) "I feel there is no such thing . . .": "*A Woman Under the Influence:* An Interview with John Cassavetes," by Judith McNally; *Filmmakers Newsletter,* 1/75.

(p. 290) Michael Ferris quotes: From author interview.

(p. 290) "We looked at maybe 150 houses . . .": "*A Woman Under the Influence:* An Interview with John Cassavetes," by Judith McNally; *Filmmakers Newsletter,* 1/75.

(pp. 290–291) "I knew what I was . . .": "An Interview with John Cassavetes," by Michel Ciment and Michael Henry; *Positif,* 4/76.

(p. 292) "I really believe almost anyone . . .": "*A Woman Under the Influence:* An Interview with John Cassavetes," by Judith McNally; *Filmmakers Newsletter,* 1/75.

(p. 292) Matthew Cassel quotes and anecdotes: From author interview.

(p. 292) "Whatever plan I had . . .": "Interview with Peter Falk and Gena Rowlands," from *John Cassavetes: Five Films,* Criterion Collection, 2004.

(pp. 292–293) "The emotional strain was so . . .": "The Family That Films Together May Win Oscars Together," by Charles Higham; *New York Times*, 4/6/75.

(p. 293) "It's mainly Gena . . .": "An Evening at Columbia College with John Cassavetes"; Columbia College Press, Chicago, 1975.

(p. 293) "If you have a good actor . . .": "An Interview with John Cassavetes," by Michel Ciment and Michael Henry; *Positif*, 4/76.

(p. 293) John Finnegan quotes: From author interview.

(p. 293) "You change your energy . . .": *A Constant Forge*, directed by Charles Kiselyak; from *John Cassavetes: Five Films*, Criterion Collection, 2004.

(p. 294) "All I know is . . .": *Take 22: Moviemakers on Moviemaking*, by Judith Crist; Viking Penguin, 1984.

(p. 294) "Gena put so much . . .": "John Cassavetes: *A Woman Under the Influence*," by Larry Gross; *Millimeter*, 3/75.

(p. 294) "Almost made me as wacko . . .": "Gena Rowlands, the Reluctant Superstar," by Robert Osborne; *Flightime*, 11/76.

(p. 294) "I find it difficult . . .": "John Cassavetes: *A Woman Under the Influence*," by Larry Gross; *Millimeter*, 3/75.

(p. 294) "I remember going there . . .": "Grande Dame," by Jack Matthews; *Newsday*, 11/3/96.

(p. 295) "I have to get a take . . .": "*A Woman Under the Influence*: An Interview with John Cassavetes," by Judith McNally; *Filmmakers Newsletter*, 1/75.

(p. 295) "The focus puller . . .": "Gena on John," by Matthew Hays; *Montreal Mirror*, 2/7/02.

(p. 295) "That, in my opinion, is . . .": "A Woman Out From Under the Influence," by Sandra Shevey; *New Times*, 3/7/75.

(pp. 295–296) "It's a very difficult thing . . .": "An Evening at Columbia College with John Cassavetes"; Columbia College Press, Chicago, 1975.

(p. 296) "John told me to go all . . .": "The Family That Films Together May Win Oscars Together," by Charles Higham; *New York Times*, 4/6/75.

Chapter 36

(p. 297) "Everyone who makes a movie . . .": "*A Woman Under the Influence*: An Interview with John Cassavetes," by Judith McNally; *Filmmakers Newsletter*, 1/75.

(p. 298) Jeff Lipsky quotes: From author interview.

(p. 298) Al Ruban quotes: From author interview.

(p. 298) Peter Bogdanovich quotes: From author interview.

(p. 298) "When we finished *Woman* . . .": "Rowlands Shoots for Stardom as Gun Moll Gloria," by Tom Burke; *Chicago Tribune*, 10/12/80.

(p. 298) "There is a belief . . .": "An Interview with John Cassavetes," by Michel Ciment and Michael Henry; *Positif*, 4/76.

(p. 299) "When someone walks . . .": From author interview with David Sterritt.

(p. 299) "A lot of guys looked at me . . .": *A Constant Forge,*" directed by Charles Kiselyak; from *John Cassavetes: Five Films,* Criterion Collection, 2004.

(p. 299) New York Film Festival anecdote: "Interview with Peter Falk and Gena Rowlands," from *John Cassavetes: Five Films,* Criterion Collection, 2004.

(p. 299) "To hear 1,800 people . . .": "A Woman Out from Under the Influence," by Sandra Shevey; *New Times,* 3/7/75.

(p. 299) "We were fully prepared . . .": "Interview with Peter Falk and Gena Rowlands," from *John Cassavetes: Five Films,* Criterion Collection, 2004.

(p. 299) *A Woman Under the Influence* review by Joseph Gelmis; *Newsday,* 10/27/74.

(p. 299) *A Woman Under the Influence* review by Verr. *Variety,* 10/16/74.

(p. 299) *A Woman Under the Influence* review by Nora Sayre; *New York Times,* 10/14/74.

(p. 299) "John, how are we. . . .": "Interview with Peter Falk and Gena Rowlands," from *John Cassavetes: Five Films,* Criterion Collection, 2004.

(p. 300) Moe Rothman anecdote, Al Ruban quotes: From author interview with Al Ruban.

(p. 300) *A Woman Under the Influence* review by Kathleen Carroll; *New York Daily News,* 11/18/74.

(p. 300) *A Woman Under the Influence* review by Rex Reed; *New York Daily News,* 11/29/74.

(p. 300) *A Woman Under the Influence* review by David Sterritt; *Christian Science Monitor,* 11/27/74.

(pp. 300–301) *A Woman Under the Influence* review by Paul D. Zimmerman; *Newsweek,* 12/9/74.

(p. 301) *A Woman Under the Influence* review by Stanley Kauffmann; *New Republic,* 12/28/74.

(p. 301) *A Woman Under the Influence* review by Pauline Kael; *New Yorker,* 12/9/74.

(p. 301) "I'm John Cassavetes. Jay Cocks . . .": From author interview with Jay Cocks.

(p. 301) "You know a lot of . . .": and box office anecdote: "Woman Still Under the Influence," by Dorothy Manners: *Los Angeles Herald-Examiner,* 3/2/75.

(p. 302) "The new art of American life . . .": "John Cassavetes: I Really Like What I Do," by Nicholas Pasquariello; *Weekly Californian,* 4/18–24/75.

(p. 302) "Cassavetes was 'a little amazed' . . .": "Cassavetes Goes It Alone Against Closed Distribution," *Variety,* 2/12/75.

(p. 302) Jonas Mekas quotes: From author interview.

(p. 302) Martin Scorsese quote: From author interview.

(p. 305) "At a certain point . . .": *Take 22: Moviemakers on Moviemaking,* by Judith Crist; Viking Penguin, 1984.

(p. 305) "Inevitably, several people . . .": "Gena Rowlands Talks to Gary Oldman About Life with John Cassavetes from the Beginning, Part 1," by Gary Oldman; *Venice,* 9/01.

(p. 305) Richard Dreyfuss quotes and *Mike Douglas Show* anecdote: From author interview with Richard Dreyfuss.

(p. 306) John Finnegan quotes and Tim Carey anecdote: From author interview with John Finnegan.

(p. 306) Carole Smith quote: From author interview.

(pp. 306–307) Molly Haskell quote: From author interview.

(p. 307) "There are vast areas . . .": "A Woman Out from Under the Influence," by Sandra Shevey; *New Times*, 3/7/75.

(p. 307) "I don't think I could ever . . .": *"A Woman Under the Influence:* An Interview with John Cassavetes," by Judith McNally; *Filmmakers Newsletter*, 1/75.

(p. 307) "I'm an artist . . .": "A Recollection of John Cassavetes," by Meade Roberts; *Hollywood*, 12/90–1/91.

Chapter 37

(p. 308) Paul Mazursky quote: From author interview.

(p. 308) Guy McElwaine quote: From author interview

(p. 308) "I've always thought of my whole life . . .": "Gena Rowlands, the Reluctant Superstar," by Robert Osborne; *Flightime*, 11/76.

(p. 309) "There's so much . . .": "Cassavetes—Filming 'Em Where They Live," by Kathleen Carroll; *New York Daily News*, 11/3/74.

(p. 309) "I do think that I can . . .": "John/Gena/Peter Interview," by Dick Adler; *Viva*, 12/74.

(p. 309) "Gena and I have a normal . . .": "Marriage Drama Yields Performance of Decade," by David Sterritt; *Christian Science Monitor*, 3/25/75.

(pp. 309–310) "It's easy to be in love . . .": "Inside the Eye of the Storm," by Francesca Simon; *Los Angeles Herald-Examiner*, 8/27/82.

(p. 310) "It makes for unhappiness . . .": "John Cassavetes: What's a Good Marriage without a Good Fight?"; *Coronet*, 11/69.

(p. 310) "For years, I claimed the artist's . . .": "Cassavetes Recalled," by Brent Lewis; *Films and Filming*, 4/89.

(p. 310) "The greatest love affair . . .": "The Case on Cassavetes," by Harry Haun; *New York Daily News*, 4/30/91.

(p. 310) "When Gena and I are home . . .": Documentary by Georg Alexander, WDR (German television), 1979.

(p. 310) Jack Cocks quote: From author interview.

(p. 311) Gena Rowlands piano anecdote: "Cassavetes Left His Imprint on a Generation of Film Makers," by Sheila Benson; *Los Angeles Times*, 2/6/89.

(p. 311) "Unlike Mabel, I know how . . .": "A Woman Out from Under the Influence," by Sandra Shevey; *New Times*, 3/7/75.

(p. 311) "A lot of problems are built into . . .": A Woman Out from Under the Influence," by Sandra Shevey; *New Times*, 3/7/75.

(p. 311) "We talk about scripts . . .": *Take 22: Moviemakers on Moviemaking*, by Judith Crist; Viking Penguin 1984.

(p. 311) "There are many times . . .": "Gena Rowlands, the Reluctant Super-star," by Robert Osborne; *Flightime*, 11/76.

(pp. 311–312) "How can you be married to the . . .": "Seeing," by Judith Thurman; *Ms.*, 11/80.

(p. 312) "So much of our . . .": "Weekend at Gena's," by Charlie Huisking; *Sarasota Herald-Tribune*, 1/9/00.

(p. 312) "I think of John as my husband . . .": "Gena Rowlands and Ted Al-lan," *On Stage*, 7/78.

(p. 312) "I consider that gossip . . .": "Gena Rowlands and Ted Allan," *On Stage*, 7/78.

(p. 312) "I've always made a rule . . .": "Gena Rowlands, the Reluctant Super-star," by Robert Osborne; *Flightime*, 11/76.

(pp. 312–313) "John believes in the superstition . . ." and separation rumor: "Show Business in the News," by Marilyn Beck; 8/27/75.

(p. 313) "I just can't understand . . .": "Rumors of Our Separation Are Greatly Exaggerated," by Marty Gunther; *Faces and Places*, 10/5/75.

Chapter 38

(pp. 314–315) "In the course of one night . . .": "Peter Falk," by D. D. Ryan; *Interview*, 11/76.

(p. 315) "He explained that . . .": "Hollywood Mavericks," by Hollis Alpert; *Saturday Review*, 11/16/74.

(p. 316) Frank Yablans quotes: From author interview.

(p. 316) Al Ruban quotes: From author interview.

(p. 316) Michael Hausman quotes and anecdotes: From author interview.

(p. 317) Hitting Joyce van Patten anecdote: From author interview with Joyce van Patten.

(p. 317) Ned Beatty quotes: From author interview.

(p. 317) Jay Cocks quote: From author interview.

(p. 318) Stolen film reels anecdote: *The Compass: The Improvisational Theater Company That Revolutionized American Comedy*, by Janet Coleman; Alfred A. Knopf, 1990.

(p. 318) Julian Schlossberg quotes: From author interview.

(p. 318) *Mikey & Nicky* review by Stanley Kauffmann; *The Nation*, 1/1–8/77.

(p. 318) *Mikey & Nicky* review by Judith Crist; *Saturday Review*, 1/22/77.

(p. 318) *Mikey & Nicky* review by Frank Rich; *New York Post*, 12/22/76.

Chapter 39

(p. 319) "I can't take the fight . . .": "Cassavetes—Filming 'Em Where They Live," by Kathleen Carroll; *New York Daily News*, 11/3/74.

(p. 319) "So I got everybody . . .": John Cassavetes interviewed by Michel Ciment and Michael Wilson, 1976; from *John Cassavetes: Five Films*, Criterion Collection, 2004.

(p. 320) Jeff Lipsky quotes and anecdotes: From author interview.

(p. 320) "It was then that I understood . . ." and *Bookie* filming anecdote: *In the Moment: My Life as an Actor,* by Ben Gazzara; Carroll & Graf, 2004.

Chapter 40

(pp. 329–330) *Mean Streets* anecdote and Martin Scorsese quotes: From author interview. Synopsis: From "I.O.U. (I've Got a Yen for You)," a treatment by John Cassavetes, 1972. From the files of Martin Scorsese; used by permission.

(p. 330) Al Ruban quotes: From author interview.

(p. 330) "We did *Bookie* just as . . .": "Cassavetes on Cassavetes"; *Monthly Film Bulletin,* 6/78.

(p. 330) "He told me he did . . .": John Cassavetes interviewed by Michel Ciment and Michael Wilson, late 1970s; from *John Cassavetes: Five Films,* Criterion Collection, 2004.

(p. 331) "John is going to start . . .": "A Recollection of John Cassavetes," by Meade Roberts; *Hollywood,* 12/90–1/91.

(p. 331) "I figured he was just . . .": *In the Moment: My Life as an Actor,* by Ben Gazzara; Carroll & Graf, 2004.

(p. 331) Jeremy Kagan quotes: From author interview.

(p. 331) Bo Harwood quotes: From author interview.

(p. 331) Seymour Cassel quotes: From author interview.

(p. 332) "Well, hit him over the head . . ." and Cassel–Carey anecdote: From author interview with Romeo Carey.

(p. 332) "Do you think we . . .", anecdote and dialogue about killing the bookie: *In the Moment: My Life as an Actor,* by Ben Gazzara; Carroll & Graf, 2004.

(p. 332) "It's the only film I've ever made . . .": "What Are They Doing to This Man's Baby?" by Mary Murphy; *Los Angeles Times,* 3/7/76.

(p. 333) "Cassavetes is obviously hoping . . .": "Recent Instances of On-Own Trend," by Addison Verrill; *Variety,* 2/18/76.

(p. 333) Westwood screening and "Was it really . . .": "What Are They Doing to This Man's Baby?" by Mary Murphy; *Los Angeles Times,* 3/7/76.

(p. 333) "People went en masse . . .": John Cassavetes interviewed by Michel Ciment and Michael Wilson, late 1970s; from *John Cassavetes: Five Films,* Criterion Collection, 2004.

(p. 333) "I think it became a sad . . .": "Cassavetes on Cassavetes"; *Monthly Film Bulletin,* 6/78.

(p. 333) *The Killing of a Chinese Bookie* review by Vincent Canby; *New York Times,* 2/16/76.

(p. 333) *The Killing of a Chinese Bookie* review by Frank Rich; *New York Post,* 2/16/76.

(pp. 333–334) *The Killing of a Chinese Bookie* review by John Simon; *New York,* 3/1/76.

(p. 334) *The Killing of a Chinese Bookie* review by Jack Kroll; *Newsweek,* 3/15/76.

(p. 334) *The Killing of a Chinese Bookie* review by David Sterritt; *Christian Science Monitor,* 3/5/76.

(p. 334) *The Killing of a Chinese Bookie* review by Jay Cocks; *Time,* 3/8/76.

(p. 335) "We offered to play . . ." and Minneapolis anecdote: "*Chinese Bookie* to Film Society, After $15K Advance Is Nixed"; *Variety,* 4/14/76.

(p. 335) "I'd like to make that film . . .": "Cassavetes on Cassavetes"; *Monthly Film Bulletin,* 6/78.

Chapter 41

(p. 336) Al Ruban quote: From author interview.

(p. 336) Guy McElwaine quote: From author interview.

(p. 337) John Finnegan quote: From author interview.

(p. 337) Joseph Bologna quote: From author interview.

(p. 337) "Gena and I are going . . .": "Cassavetes: Why Do Marriages Go Sour?" by Patricia Bosworth; *New York Times,* 12/1/68.

Chapter 42

(p. 345) "Filmmaking is a craft . . .": "What Are They Doing to This Man's Baby?" by Mary Murphy; *Los Angeles Times,* 3/7/76.

(pp. 346–347) Laura Johnson quotes and anecdotes: From author interview.

(p. 347) "I hope he doesn't follow . . .": *In the Moment: My Life as an Actor,* by Ben Gazzara; Carroll & Graf, 2004.

(p. 347) IATSE anger over nonunion camera crew: "Camera Union: We'll Picket Cassavetes"; *Variety,* 1/26/77.

(p. 347) "Thirty years from now . . .": *A Constant Forge,* directed by Charles Kiselyak; from *John Cassavetes: Five Films,* Criterion Collection, 2004.

(p. 347) Al Ruban quotes: From author interview.

(p. 348) "But we were doing this . . .": *Take 22: Moviemakers on Moviemaking,* by Judith Crist; Viking Penguin, 1984.

(p. 348) Bo Harwood quotes: From author interview.

(p. 348) Cassavetes blows up at Harwood anecdote: From author interview with Bo Hardwood.

(pp. 348–349) "I saw a version . . .": *I'm Almost Not Crazy: John Cassavetes—the Man and His Work,* a documentary directed by Michael Ventura; Cannon Films, 1984.

(p. 349) "After it first played . . .": "*Streams* Withheld from Frisco Fest; Cassavetes Blames Distrib," by Herb Michelson; *Variety,* 4/25/84.

(p. 349) "Now there are people who . . .": *Take 22: Moviemakers on Moviemaking,* by Judith Crist; Viking Penguin, 1984.

(p. 349) "It's just been a terrible experience . . .": "Cassavetes on Cassavetes"; *Monthly Film Bulletin,* 6/78.

(p. 349) Jeff Lipsky quotes: From author interview.

(p. 349) "I've sold it in England . . .": "Filmcues," by William Wolf; *Cue,* 4/15/78.

(p. 350) "Those fucking distributors . . .": From author interview with David Sterritt.

(p. 350) *Opening Night* review by William Wolf; *Cue,* 6/30/80.

(p. 350) *Opening Night* review by Judith Thurman: *Ms.,* 11/80.

(p. 350) "which I resented . . .": "The Past but Not the Last," by Ann Guarino; *New York Daily News,* 7/1/80.

(p. 350) New York Film Festival anecdotes: From author interview with David Sterritt.

Chapter 43

(p. 352) "This is a good part . . .": "Filmcues," by William Wolf; *Cue,* 4/15/78.

(p. 352) Robert Fieldsteel quote: From author interview.

(p. 352) Cassavetes' *Brass Target* salary: From author interview with Jeff Lipsky.

(pp. 352–353) Bruce Davison quotes and anecdotes: From author interview.

(p. 353) "not just the mythical star . . .": "Filmcues," by William Wolf; *Cue,* 4/15/78.

(p. 353) John Hough quotes: From author interview.

(p. 354) "It was great . . .": From author interview with Richard Kaye.

(p. 354) *Brass Target* review by David Ansen; *Newsweek,* 1/15/79.

(p. 354) John Roselius quotes and anecdotes: From author interview.

(p. 355) *Flesh & Blood* review: *Cue,* 10/26/79.

(p. 355) "*Star Wars* made 200 million dollars . . .": East West Game (Mood Indigo), by John Cassavetes, copyright 1978 (revised 7/14/80); used by permission.

(p. 356) *Knives* anecdote and quotes: From author interview with Robert Fieldsteel.

(p. 356) John Finnegan quotes and anecdote: From author interview.

Chapter 44

(p. 357) "The truth of the matter . . .": "Cassavetes Returns to Director's Chair in Cannon Production of *Love Streams,*" by Gary Linehan; *On Location,* 1/84.

(p. 359) John Finnegan quotes and anecdotes: From author interview.

(pp. 359–360) "The film is an accident...": and Ricky Schroder anecdote: "John Cassavetes: Film's Bad Boy," by James Stevenson; *Film Comment,* 1–2/1980.

(p. 360) "Streisand said she didn't . . .": "Gena on John," by Matthew Hays; *Montreal Mirror,* 2/7/02.

(p. 360) "I've got good news . . .": "John Cassavetes: Film's Bad Boy," by James Stevenson; *Film Comment,* 1–2/1980.

(p. 360) "Columbia insisted I direct it . . .": "A Perfect Couple," by Geoff Andrews and Chris Peachment; *Time Out London,* 3/8/84.

(p. 360) Guy McElwaine quotes: From author interview.

(p. 361) "I never thought anybody . . .": "John Cassavetes: Film's Bad Boy," by James Stevenson; *Film Comment,* 1–2/1980.

(p. 361) "It's confusing to go and . . .": "Cassavetes Pleased with Museum Exhibit," by Tom Topor; *New York Post,* 6/20/80.

(p. 361) "Sam kept pushing it . . .": "John Cassavetes: Film's Bad Boy," by James Stevenson; *Film Comment*, 1–2/1980.

(p. 361) "I have a way of taking . . .": "John Cassavetes: Film's Bad Boy," by James Stevenson; *Film Comment*, 1–2/1980.

(p. 362) "There was originally a line . . .": *Take 22: Moviemakers on Moviemaking*, by Judith Crist; Viking Penguin, 1984.

(p. 366) Fred Schuler quotes and hiring anecdote: From author interview with Fred Schuler.

(p. 367) "ten trillion kids" and Juan Adames casting anecdote: *Take 22: Moviemakers on Moviemaking*, by Judith Crist; Viking Penguin 1984.

(p. 367) Mike Haley quotes and anecdotes: From author interview.

(p. 368) Buck Henry quotes: From author interview.

(p. 368) "John's agent is Buck's agent . . .": *Take 22: Moviemakers on Moviemaking*, by Judith Crist; Viking Penguin 1984.

(p. 368) "There were Gloria's ideal clothes . . .": "Rowlands Shoots for Stardom as Gun Moll Gloria," by Tom Burke; *Chicago Tribune*, 10/12/80.

(p. 368) "I tried very hard not . . .": *Take 22: Moviemakers on Moviemaking*, by Judith Crist; Viking Penguin 1984.

(p. 369) "When I read the script . . .": "Gena/Gloria/Gena/Gloria," by David Galligan; Hollywood Dramalogue, 11/6–12/80.

(p. 369) "There must have been 6,000 cats . . .": "John Cassavetes: Film's Bad Boy," by James Stevenson; *Film Comment*, 1–2/1980.

(p. 369) John Finnegan quotes: From author interview.

(p. 369) "I've lived in New York . . .": "Gena Rowlands Leads 2 Lives," by Sibyl Farson; *Sunday Telegram*, 10/5/80.

(p. 370) "I don't know how to describe what . . .": *Take 22: Moviemakers on Moviemaking*, by Judith Crist; Viking Penguin 1984.

(p. 370) "At first the gun was . . .": "Movies," by David Denby; *New York*, 9/22/80.

(p. 370) "You'll just go over . . ." and Adames rehearsal anecdote and quotes: *Take 22: Moviemakers on Moviemaking*, by Judith Crist; Viking Penguin 1984.

(p. 370) "He's neither sympathetic . . .": "John Cassavetes Gets His Reward," by Dolores Barclay; Associated Press, 7/8/80.

(p. 372) "Mainly, he complained . . .": *Who the Hell's in It*, by Peter Bogdanovich; Alfred A. Knopf, 2004.

(p. 372) "You're a spy . . ." From author interview with Fred Schuler.

(p. 372) "I wish they would fire . . .": From author interview with Fred Schuler.

(p. 373) "Playing a fearless . . .": "Movies," by David Denby; *New York*, 9/22/80.

(p. 373) *Gloria* review by Richard Corliss; *Time*, 10/6/80.

(p. 373) *Gloria* review by David Ansen; *Newsweek*, 10/6/80.

(p. 373) "If I've emerged as an . . .": "In Defense of Mom and Pop Moviemaking," by Rex Reed; *New York Daily News*, 10/5/80.

(p. 373) "There are lots of actresses . . .": "Movies," by David Denby; *New York*, 9/22/80.
(p. 374) "If you watch . . .": "Cassavetes: Making of a Movie Maker," by Charles Schreger; *Los Angeles Times*, 9/16/80.

Chapter 45

(p. 375) "In my later life . . .": "John Cassavetes: Film's Bad Boy," by James Stevenson; *Film Comment*, 1–2/1980.
(p. 375) "By the age of fifty . . .": "John Cassavetes Gets His Reward," by Dolores Barclay; Associated Press, 7/8/80.
(p. 376) "I think it's his method . . .": "Cassavetes and Filmex: Party Off?" by Charles Schreger; *Los Angeles Times*, 3/11/80.
(p. 376) "I'm so honored because . . .": "John Cassavetes Gets His Reward," by Dolores Barclay; Associated Press, 7/8/80.
(p. 376) "Ordinarily, I don't care . . .": "Cassavetes Pleased with Museum Exhibit," by Tom Topor; *New York Post*, 6/20/80.
(p. 376) Robert Fieldsteel quotes: From author interview.
(p. 376) "I'm interested in shaking . . .": "Up from Underground," by William Wolf; *New York*, 6/30/80.
(p. 376) "The types of film we do . . .": "John Cassavetes Gets His Reward," by Dolores Barclay; Associated Press, 7/8/80.
(p. 376) "The next picture we make . . .": "The Past but Not the Last," by Ann Guarino; *New York Daily News*, 7/1/80.
(p. 377) "I take some roles because I'm broke . . .": "Cassavetes: Sunshine amid a Midlife Tempest," by Dale Pollack; *Los Angeles Times*, 8/12/82.
(p. 377) John Hough quotes: From author interview.
(p. 377) "I'm so pleased . . ." and *Incubus* quotes, anecdotes: From author interview with John Hough.
(p. 377) *The Incubus* review by Vincent Canby; *New York Times*, 9/4/82.
(pp. 377–378) John Badham quotes: From author interview.
(p. 378) "Why do I have to say . . ." and *Whose Life* anecdotes, quotes: From author interview with John Badham.
(p. 380) Paul Mazursky quotes, *Tempest* anecdotes: From author interview with Paul Mazursky.
(p. 380) "I didn't fully understand . . .": "Pitch & Roll on Tempest Set," by Diana Maychick; *New York Post*, 8/12/82.
(p. 381) Molly Ringwald quotes, anecdotes: From author interview with Molly Ringwald.
(p. 381) Bob and Adele Ringwald quotes, anecdotes: From author interview with Bob and Adele Ringwald.
(pp. 382–383) *Tempest* review by Jack Kroll; *Newsweek*, 8/16/82.
(p. 383) *Tempest* review by Vincent Canby; *New York Times*, 8/13/82.
(p. 383) *Tempest* review by Penelope Gilliatt; *New Yorker*, 9/20/82.
(p. 383) "wonderfully imperfect": "Cassavetes: Sunshine Amid a Midlife Tempest," by Dale Pollock; *Los Angeles Times*, 8/12/82.

(p. 383) "I think, from my standpoint . . .": "Cassavetes: Show Me the Magic," by Michael Ventura; *L.A. Weekly*, 8/20–26/82.

Chapter 46

(p. 384) Richard Dreyfuss quotes and anecdotes: From author interview.

(pp. 386–387) "If I had to spend my life . . .": "Competitive Cassavetes," by David Galligan; *Hollywood Dramalogue*, 10/7–13/82.

(p. 387) Al Ruban quotes: From author interview.

(p. 387) Robert Fieldsteel quotes and anecdotes: From author interview.

(p. 387) Bo Harwood quotes: From author interview.

(p. 387) Carole Smith quotes: From author interview.

(p. 388) "I had never directed a play before . . .": "Competitive Cassavetes," by David Galligan; *Hollywood Dramalogue*, 10/7–13/82.

(p. 388) Richard Kaye quotes and anecdotes: From author interview.

(p. 389) John Finnegan quotes: From author interview.

(p. 390) "I went back and I heard . . .": *A Constant Forge*, directed by Charles Kiselyak; from *John Cassavetes: Five Films*, Criterion Collection, 2004.

(p. 390) "Cassavetes has taken over . . .": *Knives* review, by Dan Sullivan; *Los Angeles Times*, 5/13/81.

(p. 391) "If that's the case . . .": "Cassavetes Moves to Little Theatre in Big Way," by Bill Edwards; *Variety*, 5/15/81.

(p. 391) *The Third Day Comes* review by Jack Viertel; *Los Angeles Herald-Examiner*, 5/11/81.

(p. 391) *The Third Day Comes* review by Lawrence Christon; *Los Angeles Times*, 5/14/81.

(p. 391) *Knives* review by Dan Sullivan; *Los Angeles Times*, 5/13/81.

(p. 391) *Love Streams* review by Sylvie Drake; *Los Angeles Times*, 5/12/81.

(p. 392) Johnnie Planco quotes and anecdotes: From author interview.

(p. 394) Wanda Dell quotes and anecdotes: From author interview.

(p. 395) Carol Kane quotes and anecdotes: From author interview.

Chapter 47

(p. 397) Johnnie Planco quotes and anecdotes: From author interview.

(p. 398) "I've already played this role . . .": From author interview with Robert Fieldsteel.

(p. 398) "I was so angry with Jon . . .": "Retracing the Stream of Love," by Richard Combs; *Monthly Film Bulletin*, 4/84.

(p. 398) "John said, 'Oh, hell' . . .": "Why would anyone want to see a movie about a crazy, middle-aged dame?" by Duncan Campbell; *The Guardian*, 3/2/01.

(pp. 398–399) "It was perfectly all right . . .": "How Love and Life Mingle on Film," by John Cassavetes; *New York Times*, 8/19/84.

(p. 399) "Look, Seymour had . . ." and John Roselius quotes, anecdotes: From author interview with John Roselius.

(p. 399) Seymour Cassel quotes, anecdotes: From author interview, excerpt:

(p. 400) Matthew Cassel quotes, anecdotes: From author interview.

(p. 400) Larry Shaw quotes and anecdotes: From author interview.

(p. 402) "In 1983, we started making a . . .": "How Love and Life Mingle on Film," by John Cassavetes; *New York Times*, 8/19/84.

(p. 403) Al Ruban quotes and anecdotes: From author interview.

(p. 403) Randy Carter quotes and anecdotes: From author interview.

(p. 403) Alan Caso quotes: From author interview.

(p. 405) Jakob Shaw quotes and anecdotes: From author interview.

(p. 405) "Then I could really get . . .": "Zen and the Art of John Cassavetes," by Michael Ventura; *L.A. Weekly*, 9/21/-27/84.

(p. 406) "This picture, this picture . . .": "State of Grace," by Michael Ventura; *Sight and Sound*, 4/89.

(p. 406) Peter Bogdanovich quotes and anecdotes: From author interview.

(p. 407) Michael Ventura quotes and anecdotes: From author interview.

(p. 407) "I resent it when people say . . .": "Still a Maverick Movie Maker," by Charles Champlin; *Los Angeles Times*, 8/27/84.

(p. 407) "Instead, I went in the front . . .": "Gena on John," by Matthew Hays; *Montreal Mirror*, 2/7/02.

(p. 408) "John was furious . . .": "John Cassavetes' Last Scene," by Michael Ventura; *Austin Chronicle*, 3/8/02; and from author interview with Michael Ventura.

(p. 408) Bo Harwood quotes and anecdotes: From author interview.

(p. 409) "Physically, he has changed . . .": "Zen and the Art of John Cassavetes," by Michael Ventura; *L.A. Weekly*, 9/21/-27/84.

(p. 409) Diahnne Abbott quotes and anecdotes: From author interview.

(p. 410) "This is a sweet film . . .": "John Cassavetes' Last Scene," by Michael Ventura; *Austin Chronicle*, 3/8/02.

(p. 410) "He treated me abominably . . .": "Meade Roberts, Playwright," by Michael Puller; *The Advocate*, 10/23/90.

(p. 410) "From Williams, I learned . . .": "Meade Roberts, Playwright," by Michael Puller; *The Advocate*, 10/23/90.

(p. 411) Meade Roberts biographical facts: "Meade Roberts, Writer, 61, dies; Tennessee Williams Collaborator," by William Honan; *New York Times*, 2/15/92.

(p. 411) John Finnegan quote, anecdote: From author interview.

(p. 411) Jeff Lipsky quote: From author interview.

(p. 412) "We were dealing with a writer . . .": *In the Moment: My Life as an Actor*, by Ben Gazzara; Carroll & Graf, 2004.

(p. 412) "So you're really . . .": *In the Moment: My Life as an Actor*, by Ben Gazzara; Carroll & Graf, 2004.

(p. 412) "The cast is making $175 . . .": "On Stage," by Carol Lawson; *New York Times*, 10/28/83.

(p. 413) Carol Kane quotes and anecdotes: From author interview.

(p. 413) "In spite of the play's excessive . . .": *In the Moment: My Life as an Actor*, by Ben Gazzara; Carroll & Graf, 2004.

(p. 413) "I arrived for the first performance . . .": *In the Moment: My Life as an Actor*, by Ben Gazzara; Carroll & Graf, 2004.

(p. 413) Bob Balaban quote: From author interview.

(p. 414) "This is a very different . . .": "Streams Withheld from Frisco Fest; Cassavetes Blames Distrib," by Herb Michaelson; *Variety*, 4/25/84.

(p. 414) "God, I hope I'm a Hollywood outsider . . .": "A Perfect Couple," by Geoff Andrews and Chris Peachment; *Time Out London*, 3/8/84.

(p. 414) "I won't make it . . .": "Still a Maverick Movie Maker," by Charles Champlin; *Los Angeles Times*, 8/27/84.

(p. 414) "Why would I want to . . .": "Retracing the Stream of Love," by Richard Combs; *Monthly Film Bulletin*, 4/84.

(p. 414) *Love Streams* review by Janet Maslin; *New York Times*, 8/24/84.

(p. 414) *Love Streams* review by Richard Schickel; *Time*, 9/17/84.

(p. 415) *Love Streams* review by David Sterritt; *Christian Science Monitor*, 10/1/84.

Chapter 48

(p. 416) Andrew Bergman quotes and anecdotes: From author interview.

(p. 417) Guy McElwaine quotes and anecdotes: From author interview.

(p. 417) "an average of $16 million per film": From Boxofficemojo.com.

(p. 418) Jeff Lipsky quotes and anecdotes: From author interview.

(p. 418) Richard Libertini quotes and anecdotes: From author interview.

(p. 418) Seymour Cassel quotes: From author interview.

(p. 418) Helen Caldwell quotes: From author interview.

(p. 419) John Roselius quotes: From author interview.

(p. 419) *Big Trouble* review by Richard Schickel; *Time*, 6/30/86.

(p. 419) *Big Trouble* review by Vincent Canby; *New York Times*, 5/30/86.

(p. 419) Al Ruban anecdote: From author interview.

Chapter 49

(p. 420) Bo Harwood quotes and anecdotes: From author interview

(p. 420) "Writers drink so that . . .": From *East West Game (Mood Indigo)*, by John Cassavetes; copyright 1978; used by permission.

(p. 420) Jay Cocks quotes: From author interview.

(pp. 420–421) Julie Allan quotes: From author interview.

(p. 421) "It was an action-packed contest . . .": *In the Moment: My Life as an Actor*, by Ben Gazzara; Carroll & Graf, 2004.

(p. 421) John Finnegan quotes: From author interview.

(p. 421) Helen Caldwell quotes and anecdotes: From author interview.

(p. 421) Peter Bogdanovich quotes and anecdotes: From author interview.

(p. 422) Seymour Cassel quotes: From author interview.

(p. 422) Al Ruban quotes and anecdotes: From author interview.

(p. 422) Guy McElwaine quotes: From author interview.

(p. 422) "It was during a long script conference . . .": *Who the Hell's in It*, by Peter Bogdanovich; Alfred A. Knopf, 2004.

(p. 422) "I've had a lot to drink . . .": "Mavericks John Cassavetes and Gena Rowlands Make Movies the Hard Way—With Their Own Money," by Jim Calio; *People*, 10/8/84.

(p. 423) Richard Kaye quotes: From author interview.

(p. 423) Carol Kane quotes and anecdote: From author interview:

(pp. 423–424) Lelia Goldoni quotes, anecdote: From author interview.

(p. 424) "With the exception . . .": Book review, by Jonathan Rosenbaum; *Cineaste*, 12/01.

(p. 424) "He said he had a script . . .": "The Lovely Couple Take Their Work Home," by Joshua Mooney; *Entertainment News Wire*, 8/29/97.

(p. 425) "Sean Penn acted . . ." and "She's De-Lovely" anecdotes: *Who the Hell's in It*, by Peter Bogdanovich; Alfred A. Knopf, 2004.

(p. 425) Finnegan quote: From author interview.

(p. 426) Elaine Kagan quotes: From author interview.

(p. 427) "Ahh, this goddam shit . . .": From author interview with Matthew Cassel.

(p. 427) Richard Dreyfuss quotes: From author interview.

(p. 427) Robert Fieldsteel quotes and anecdotes: From author interview.

(p. 427) Peter Falk quote and dog anecdote: From author interview.

(p. 428) "I hadn't seen him for a year" and dialogue with Cassavetes: *In the Moment: My Life as an Actor*, by Ben Gazzara; Carroll & Graf, 2004.

(p. 428) "I knew right away that he . . .": *In the Moment: My Life as an Actor*, by Ben Gazzara; Carroll & Graf, 2004.

(p. 428) Carole Smith quotes and anecdotes: From author interview.

(p. 429) "Gloria 2" plot: "Penn in Hand," by Leonard Klady; *Los Angeles Times*, 10/9/88.

(p. 429) "Keep battling . . ." and dialogue with Cassavetes: *In the Moment: My Life as an Actor*, by Ben Gazzara; Carroll & Graf, 2004.

(p. 430) Michael Ventura quotes and Sundance anecdote: From author interview.

(p. 430) "You think I should cut . . ." and Rotterdam Film Festival anecdote: *Who the Hell's in It*, by Peter Bogdanovich; Alfred A. Knopf, 2004.

(p. 431) Seymour Cassel, Peter Falk, and Ted Allan quotes from Cassavetes memorial: From a videotape provided by Tom Charity.

(p. 432) "I was a zombie for . . .": "Grande Dame," by Jack Mathews; *Newsday*, 11/3/96.

(p. 432) "Well, I made three . . ."; and "Now wouldn't you think . . .": "Why would anyone want to see a movie about a crazy, middle-aged dame?" by Duncan Campbell; *The Guardian*, 3/2/01.

(p. 433) "I have to admit that sometimes . . .": "An Interview with Nick Cassavetes of *She's So Lovely*," by Tom Cunha; indieWire.com, 8/29/97.

(p. 433) "Nick and John were very close . . .": "A Ghost Rules This Film," by Duane Dudek; *Milwaukee Journal Sentinel*, 9/2/97.

(p. 434) AADA poem: Courtesy, American Academy of Dramatic Arts, New York, N.Y.

(p. 434) "If I had my artistic life . . .": "Cassavetes: Making of a Movie Maker," by Charles Schreger; *Los Angeles Times*, 9/16/80.